Wriothesley's Roses

In Shakespeare's Sonnets, Poems and Plays

Wriothesley's Roses

In Shakespeare's Sonnets, Poems and Plays

Martin Green

Clevedon Books
Baltimore, Maryland

1993

Jacket Design by John Yanson
Manufactured in the United States of America

Dedicated to the memory

of my parents,

Harry and Sadie Green

PREFACE

I end this book, after nine years of research and writing, not because I have exhausted the subject, but because the subject has exhausted me. I believe that in this book I conclusively identify at least two of the persons about or to whom the Sonnets were written, and that, by establishing Shakespeare as an intimate friend of the third Earl of Southampton, through whom he had access to the learned and travelled persons in the service of the Earl of Essex, I have explained the appearance in Shakespeare's poems and plays of ideas, plots and facts otherwise difficult to account for, and have opened the way for many discoveries with respect to the sources of Shakespeare's knowledge and concepts. A few such sources I discuss; there are many more which I think I detect, and would like to trace, but the work involved would unreasonably delay the publication of this book and the opportunity, already too long deferred, and in some cases gone forever, to acknowledge my indebtedness and gratitude to persons who have helped me to acquire essential information and material, or have in other ways aided or encouraged my work. So now I thank:

The Duke of Buccleuch and Queensberry, K.T., for permission to reproduce the portrait, at Boughton House, Kettering, of Henry Wriothesley, third Earl of Southampton;

Lord Montagu of Beaulieu, for permission to reproduce the portrait, at Palace House, Beaulieu, of Thomas Wriothesley, first Earl of Southampton;

Mrs Ann Matthews, Secretary of the Archives at Palace House, Beaulieu, for information relating to, and copies of, various documents in the Muniment Room at Beaulieu;

Michael J. Hare, M.A., F.S.A., for his translation of the bond of Garret Johnson for the construction of the Wriothesley tomb, together with other materials relating to Titchfield and the Wriothesley Monument in the Titchfield Church; and

Mr D. M. Archer, of the Department of Ceramics of the Victoria and Albert Museum, London, and Linda Fraser of the Stained Glass Conservation section of the Burrell Collection, Glasgow, for information relating to the Radford collection of stained glass.

I also thank the institutions whose collections of books and documents I was privileged to use: the British Library, the Public Record Office (in London), the Hampshire Record Office, the Southampton City Record Office, the Folger Shakespeare Library, the Library of Congress, the New York Public Library, The Newberry Library in Chicago, the Milton S. Eisenhower Library at the Johns Hopkins University in Baltimore, and the Walters Art Gallery, also in Baltimore.

To the authors, editors, collectors and curators of those books and documents I am, of course, profoundly indebted, as my text and notes, I hope, make clear.

Readers of this book will understand how much I owe to Joseph A. M. Sonderkamp, the "friend from Berlin," and Philip Buckley, the "resident of Southampton," whose observations and comments that day in Southampton were the lightning bolt which fused a thousand grains of sand into a solid, and, I would like to think, crystalline, whole.

And finally, I gratefully acknowledge the support and assistance, beyond itemization, of my brother, Edward Green, and my sister, Florence Packer.

                                                    Martin Green
                                                    30 October 1992

Contents

Plates
(following page 50)

Figures

Genealogical Tables

A Note on Dates and Names

From an early time, and until 31 December 1751, when "An Act for regulating the commencement of the Year, and for correcting the Calendar now in Use" went into effect, the legal year in England commenced on 25 March; that is, until 1751, a date such as 25 February 1600 was a date which *followed*, rather than *preceded*, December 1600. The practice since 1752 in writing dates falling between 1 January and 25 March of any year prior thereto has been to write both the year as it had been originally designated, and also as it would be designated under the 1751 statute: e.g., 25 February 1600/1601. (The 1751 statute also "corrected" the calendar by adopting the Gregorian Calendar, which had been adopted throughout most of Europe in or about 1582, with the result that from 1582 until 1752 dates written on the Continent were 10 or 11 days ahead of dates written on the same day in England. The dates in this book are not adjusted to show this ten-day difference, but are reported as I found them in my sources.)

In Elizabethan times, names, like all other words of the language, were spelled as each writer saw fit — and even then, not uniformly by the same writer. Consequently, there are variations in the spelling of even the simplest names, as for example Cuf, Cuff, Cuffe, or Smith, Smyth, Smythe, and almost infinite variety in the spelling of names like Burleigh, Merrick and Wriothesley (to say nothing of Shakespeare). I have tried to be consistent in my spelling of names, but to the extent that I have failed in this, I have been true to the spirit of Elizabethan England.

Wriothesley's Roses

In Shakespeare's Sonnets, Poems and Plays

CHAPTER I

"If only we could be sure. . . . "

"The *Sonnets* tell us so much of our greatest writer — if only we
could be sure what all of it is!"

Charlton Ogburn[1]

Almost all of the factual information we possess about the life of William
Shakespeare is derived from brief entries in a variety of official registers, a
few documents prepared in connection with real estate conveyances and law-
suits, and a will. The little that these entries and documents tell us was
summarized by George Steevens over two hundred years ago: *"he was born
at Stratford-upon-Avon, — married, and had children there, — went to
London where he commenced actor, and wrote poems and plays, — returned
to Stratford, made his will, died, and was buried. . . . "*[2] Of the private life
of a man whose writings are universally acclaimed to be the greatest literary
monuments of the English language, we know practically nothing: no letters
remain, nor were any memoirs of him written by his contemporaries. We do
not know who were his friends, whom he loved (probably not his wife, who
was three months' pregnant when he married her,[3] and who seems to have
remained in Stratford during the 15 or 20 years that Shakespeare lived chiefly
in London), what his relations were with his fellow actors and playwrights,
what his views were on the religious and political issues which racked his
times, with what traits his character was imbued, or by what idiosyncrasies
his behaviour may have been marked.

It is not surprising, therefore, that Shakespeare's Sonnets have been
seized upon as a possible source of information about the life of their author.
Although the Sonnets were published by Thomas Thorpe in 1609, knowledge
of their existence seems not at that time to have been widespread. Indeed,
when the Sonnets were reprinted by John Benson in 1640 in a somewhat
altered version (the sonnets being rearranged, some deleted, and the sex of the
person addressed editorially obscured), Benson's craftily worded preface
strongly suggested that the poems were then being presented to the readers'
view for the first time, the poems not having had "the fortune by reason of
their Infancie in . . . [Shakespeare's] death, to have the due accomodation of
proportionable glory, with the rest of his everliving Workes. . . ."[4] The
blatant falseness of Benson's implication that the Sonnets had not previously
been published has led a number of persons to conclude that the 1609 edition
of the Sonnets may have been suppressed, or for some reason removed from
general sale, else the publisher of the 1640 edition would not have essayed so
flagrant a deception.[5] In any event, the 1640 edition of the Sonnets made no

1

greater impression upon the public than had the 1609 edition. The Sonnets are not even mentioned in the first biography of Shakespeare ever written — that of Nicholas Rowe, published in 1709 — except in the last paragraph, where Rowe stated that he had "but very lately seen" a book of poems published in 1640 under the name of William Shakespeare, and "won't pretend to determine whether it be his or no."[6]

However, by the last third of the eighteenth century, as a result of the editions of the 1609 text published by George Steevens in 1766 and Edmond Malone in 1780 and 1790,[7] the existence and general tenor of the Sonnets became well known. Many who now for the first time had access to the text of the Sonnets perceived that the poems could be autobiographical,[8] and that, if studied carefully, "something of Shakespeare's life might be revealed, or, at any rate, be illustrated by them."[9] An exciting prospect, to learn from the poet himself the otherwise unknown details of his life!

In the ensuing two hundred years, however, the expectation that the 154 poems which comprise the Sonnets might disclose something about Shakespeare has been made a mockery of, as almost every person who has examined the poems upon the premise of their being autobiographical (and it must be noted that a number of critics reject this premise[10]) has come up with a different conclusion as to what they reveal of the life and character of their author. To be sure, among most critics, both those who believe the poems to be autobiographical, and those who believe them to be merely literary exercises, a consensus has developed as to the general outlines of the story of the Sonnets. The first 126 sonnets, to the extent that they are addressed to anyone at all, are addressed to a beautiful youth, whom the author loves. Sonnets 1 through 17 each urge the youth to perpetuate his beauty through procreation, but the eighteenth and many subsequent sonnets[11] assure the youth that his beauty will be immortalized by the author's verse. Other sonnets addressed to the youth, or Fair Friend (as he is called in Sonnet 104), praise his character,[12] or his beauty,[13] express or reflect love,[14] devotion,[15] fear of losing him,[16] sorrow over separation,[17] recriminations,[18] and reconciliations.[19] These are, of course, such sentiments as are generally elicited by love, but some poems, especially those of recrimination and reconciliation, seem to refer to two occasions when the youth was, or appeared to be, receptive to the amorous advances of others.

The first such occasion is the subject of Sonnets 41 and 42. In Sonnet 41, we are told, somewhat obliquely, that a woman pursues the youth:

> Gentle thou art, and therefore to be wonne,
> Beautious thou art, therefore to be assailed.

And when a woman woes, what womans sonne,
Will sourely leave her till he have prevailed.

And from Sonnet 42, we learn that she caught him:

That thou hast her is not all my griefe,
And yet it may be said I lov'd her deerely,
That she hath thee is of my wayling cheefe,
A losse in love that touches me more neerely.

The second occasion is the subject of or alluded to in Sonnets 78 through 80, and 82 through 86, which give their author's reaction to the campaign of a "Rival Poet" for the youth's favours. The Sonnets reflect the heartache this caused — Sonnet 80 declares

O how I faint when I of you do write,
Knowing a better spirit doth use your name —

but do not indicate whether or not the campaign was ultimately successful.

Following the 126 sonnets addressed to the youth is a series of 26 sonnets addressed to a woman whose beauty, eyes, hair, deeds and personality are, in some of those sonnets,[20] described as "black." This is the so-called Dark Lady of the Sonnets, who is probably the same woman mentioned in Sonnets 41 and 42, and whose affairs with both the author and the youth are mentioned again in Sonnets 133, 134 and 144.[21] Sonnet 144, in fact, seems to recapitulate a major part of the tale of the Sonnets:

Two loves I have of comfort and dispaire,
Which like two spirits do sugiest me still,
The better angell is a man right faire:
The worser spirit a woman coulour'd il.
To win me soone to hell my femall evill,
Tempteth my better angel from my side,
And would corrupt my saint to be a divel:
Wooing his purity with her fowle pride.
And whether that my angel be turn'de finde [fiend],
Suspect I may, yet not directly tell,
But being both from me both to each friend,
I gesse one angel in an others hel.
    Yet this shal I nere know but live in doubt,
    Till my bad angel fire my good one out.

3

Most critics interpret the last three lines of this poem to mean: "I suspect one angel is intimate with the other, yet this shall I never know, but live in doubt, until my bad angel — the 'woman colour'd il,' — infects my good angel — the 'man right faire' — with venereal disease."[22] Since we already know from Sonnet 42 that "thou hast her" and "she hath thee," we may suppose that Sonnet 144, which merely expresses doubt over the Friend's fidelity, is earlier than Sonnet 42, which reveals certainty about the Friend's infidelity.

Following the 26 sonnets relating to the Dark Lady and ending the entire sequence are two sonnets, 153 and 154, which appear to be exercises in translating into English a Greek epigram describing how a hot bath was created by nymphs who, thinking thereby to end the pain to mankind caused by Cupid, took his torch while he lay sleeping, and plunged it into a cool well, only to find that the water did not extinguish the fire, but was instead itself heated. These two sonnets have no discernible connection with the story of the preceding 152 sonnets, and most critics have ignored them.[23]

Although the story of the poet, his Fair Friend, the Dark Lady and the Rival Poet is not uninteresting, it is not particularly enlightening, and never will be, until the identities of the parties involved in the story are discovered. But on this, there is no consensus at all. Disputatious scholars contend that the Fair Youth of the Sonnets is Willie Hughes, William Herbert, Henry Wriothesley, or any one of half a dozen others; that the Rival Poet is Christopher Marlowe, George Chapman, Samuel Daniel, Thomas Nashe, or any one of half a dozen others, and that the Dark Lady is Luce Morgan, Emily Lanier, Mary Fitton, or any one of half a dozen others. The *New Variorum Edition of the Sonnets*, edited by Hyder Edward Rollins, devotes 161 pages merely to *summarizing* the various theories which up to 1944 had been advanced with respect to the autobiographical nature of the Sonnets, and the identities of the Fair Friend, the Dark Woman and the Rival Poet.[24] But none of these theories, nor any of the scores of new ones advanced since 1944, has yet satisfactorily established the claim of any specific historical personage to have been a player in the Sonnets. The sheer number of theories, and the patent daffiness of some of them, have made it fashionable among the more recent writers on the Sonnets to congratulate themselves for not addressing their possible autobiographical implications.[25] But if the chief interest of the Sonnets is their beauty and intensity, then an interest of almost equal importance must be the occasions and persons which gave rise to them; to avoid the subject is to miss the point of the Sonnets.

The clues upon which are based the disparate conclusions as to the identities of the personages in the Sonnets are few and, obviously, far from definite. The poems are prefaced by an enigmatic dedication, which was written not by Shakespeare, but probably by the publisher, Thomas Thorpe, whose initials are affixed to it. As printed in the 1609 edition of the Sonnets, the dedication reads:

TO. THE. ONLIE. BEGETTER. OF.
THESE. INSVING. SONNETS.
M#r#. W.H. ALL. HAPPINESSE.
AND. THAT. ETERNITIE.
PROMISED.
BY.
OVR. EVER-LIVING. POET.
WISHETH.
THE. WELL-WISHING.
ADVENTVRER. IN.
SETTING.
FORTH.

T.T.

Some persons, interpreting this to be a greeting by the publisher to the Fair Friend to whom the Sonnets promise eternal life in verse, conclude that the Fair Friend must have been a "M#r#. W. H." It was on this premise that in the eighteenth century one William Hews, or Hughes, was the first candidate ever put forward for the distinction of being the Fair Friend. The supposed existence of this otherwise unknown man was inferred in two stages. First, Thomas Tyrwhitt conjectured that a capitalized and italicized word in Sonnet 20, describing the Fair Friend as

A man in hew all *Hews* in his controwling,

indicated that a man named Hews was the person in question. Second, Edmond Malone further conjectured that if Hews or Hughes was the last name of the Friend, then (assuming this Hughes to be the "M#r#. W. H." in the publisher's dedication), the initial of his first name should be "W." From this, the first name of "William" was by some scholars bestowed upon Mr Hughes, probably because it seemed to them that the punning use of the word "Will" in Sonnets 135 and 136 indicates that the man with whom Will Shakespeare was reluctantly obliged to share the Dark Lady was also named Will.[26]

5

A hundred years later, Oscar Wilde, in a work put forward as nothing more than a fictional story[27] (in which respect he was, perhaps, more honest than many "scholars"), postulated the existence of a boy actor named Willie Hughes who was the "W. H." beloved of Shakespeare. At about the same time, Samuel Butler, reviewing the *State Papers* for people named William Hughes, opined that a cook of that name in the Royal Navy, who died a month or two prior to March 1636/7, might well have been the W.H. of the Sonnets.[28]

The suggestion that the W.H. of the Sonnets was an actor or cook named William Hughes has been accepted by few scholars, and other W.H.'s have been put forward as the Fair Friend. Among these are William Harbert who in 1629 became the first Lord Powys,[29] William Houghton, a Lancashire gentleman,[30] William Hathaway, Shakespeare's brother-in-law,[31] and William Hall, a printer.[32] A relatively recent addition to this club is the candidate proposed by Leslie Hotson: one William Hatcliffe, who was designated Prince of Purpoole for the Christmas revels at Gray's Inn in 1587/8.[33] And it cannot be doubted that any Elizabethan with the initials W.H. who was a young man between 1588 and 1598, if he has not already been nominated for the honour, is likely, in the fullness of time, one day to be.

The most distinguished of the W.H.'s thought to be the Fair Friend of the Sonnets is William Herbert, third Earl of Pembroke. He was pricked out for this post by James Boaden in 1832,[34] and his cause was championed subsequently by Keats' friend, Charles Armitage Brown,[35] by Thomas Tyler,[36] and even, although not ardently, by E. K. Chambers.[37] The best evidence for him is that his initials are W.H., and that John Heminges and Henry Condell, the editors of the First Folio of Shakespeare's plays published in 1623, dedicated that work to him (and to his brother Philip, the Earl of Montgomery). The dedication's observation that the two earls "haue beene pleas'd to thinke these trifles something, heeretofore; and haue prosequuted both them and their Authour liuing, with . . . much fauour" suggests more than a merely formal relationship between the poet and the earls. Also, most readers see in the Fair Friend of the Sonnets a young man of good birth, and this seems a better description of William Herbert than of any of the Willie Hughes' so far discovered. In addition, there was an event in Herbert's youth which some persons think may explain the first seventeen sonnets urging the young man to procreate: when William Herbert was only 15, an attempt was made to effect his marriage to the daughter of Sir George Carey; later, when William Herbert was 17, negotiations were under way for his marriage to Bridget Vere, daughter of the Earl of Oxford. Both times, the young man resisted giving up his state of single bliss. Either of these incidents could, some suggest, have been the occasion for the composition of those poems urging the youth to do his duty by the world and — after first marrying, of course — to have children.[38] The only internal inconsistency in this limited body of evidence on behalf of William Herbert is Thomas Thorpe's designation of the W.H. to whom he dedicated the Sonnets as a "M^r." — the abbreviation in Tudor times for "Master." Generations of critics have insisted that no publisher (or anyone else) in 1609 would have presumed to address an earl merely as a "M^r.," and that the M^r. W.H. of the Sonnets, therefore, could not have been the third Earl of Pembroke, or any other earl.[39]

This brings us, then, to those critics who deem the "M^r. W. H." of the dedication to be the "begetter" of the Sonnets not in the sense that he *inspired* them, but in the sense that he somehow *obtained*, *procured* or otherwise physically *acquired* copies of them, and passed them on to the fortunate publisher, who in the dedication expressed his thanks. By this interpretation, "M^r. W.H.," the publisher's benefactor, is a person entirely separate from the Fair Friend, the poet's beloved. Consequently, the person addressed in the Sonnets, not being either a "M^r." or a "W.H.," could be a youth of any rank and any name. Espousing this view are most of the persons who contend that not a "W.H." but an "H.W." — Henry Wriothesley, third Earl of Southampton — was the Fair Friend of the Sonnets[40] (although some Southamptonians claim that Henry Wriothesley *is* M^r. W.H., the initials having been reversed either through error or to disguise his identity[41]). The evidence for Southampton is that Shakespeare dedicated to him the poems *Venus and Adonis*, published in 1593, and *The Rape of Lucrece*, published in 1594. These dedications are the only non-literary writings of Shakespeare we possess (other than, perhaps, his will[42]). The dedication of *Venus and Adonis* is:

TO THE RIGHT HONORABLE
Henrie Wriothesley, Earle of Southampton,
and Baron of Titchfield.

Right Honourable, I know not how I shall offend in dedicating my unpolisht lines to your Lordship, nor how the worlde will censure mee for choosing so strong a proppe to support so weake a burthen, onelye if your Honour seeme but pleased, I account my selfe highly praised, and uowe to take advantage of all idle houres, till I have honoured you with some grauer labour. But if the first heire of my invention prove deformed, I shall be sorie it had so noble a god-father: and never after eare so barren a land, for feare it yeeld me still so bad a haruest, I leave it to your Honourable suruey, and your Honor to your hearts content, which I wish may alwaies answere your owne wish, and the worlds hopefull expectation.

Your Honors in all dutie,

William Shakespeare.

The dedication of *The Rape of Lucrece* is:

TO THE RIGHT
HONOURABLE, HENRY
Wriothesley, Earle of Southhampton,
and Baron of Titchfield

The loue I dedicate to your Lordship is without end: wherof this Pamphlet without beginning is but a superfluous Moity. The warrant I haue of your Honourable disposition, not the worth of my vntutord Lines makes it assured of acceptance. What I haue done is yours, what I haue to doe is yours, being part in all I haue, deuoted yours. Were my worth greater, my duety would shew greater, meane time, as it is, it is bound to your Lordship; To whom I wish long life still lengthned with all happinesse.

Your Lordships in all duety.

William Shakespeare.

Southamptonians contend that the warm tone of these dedications, especially the second, suggests an intimacy and love such as that revealed by the Sonnets, and points to Henry Wriothesley as the Fair Friend.[43] The contention has also been made that Sonnet 26 is so similar to the dedication of *The Rape of Lucrece* as to suggest the same occasion, and the same addressee.[44]

And if there is any validity to the notion that the Fair Friend's disinclination to marry caused the composition of the first seventeen sonnets, then there is an incident in Southampton's life which puts his qualifications to be the Fair Friend on the same footing as Pembroke's, for when Southampton was 16, and the ward of Lord Burghley (Southampton having been only eight years old when his father died), an attempt was made by Burghley to betroth the young man to his granddaughter, Elizabeth Vere — sister of that Bridget Vere whom Pembroke declined to marry. Southampton was reluctant, and Lord Burghley gave him a year to think about it, during which time it is supposed that, perhaps at the request of Southampton's mother, the first seventeen sonnets were written, urging procreation (and, by implication, as a condition precedent thereto, marriage).[45] If this is so, they were unsuccessful, for Southampton did not marry Elizabeth Vere, and reportedly ended up paying to Burghley an immense sum of money — £5000 — for his failure so to do.[46]

Those who believe that Henry Wriothesley was the Fair Friend of the Sonnets, and that "M^r. W.H." was someone else who procured for Thorpe the manuscript of the Sonnets, suggest as possible procurers either Sir William Harvey, third husband of Southampton's mother, who may have gathered the Sonnets addressed to his step-son and made them available for publication,[47] or William Hall, the same printer nominated by some to be the fair youth himself, who may somehow have obtained copies of the Sonnets, and passed them on to his friend and fellow-printer, Thomas Thorpe.[48]

Such, substantially (aside from my own previous writing on the subject), is the evidence for Southampton. The partisans of Pembroke respond to the case for Southampton by attaching great weight to the fact that although Southampton was still alive in 1623, it was not to him, but to William Herbert and his brother, that the First Folio was dedicated.[49] Advocates of Southampton[50] reply that some of the first seventeen sonnets suggest that the father of the youth to whom they were addressed was dead ("You had a Father, let your Son say so" (Sonnet 13)), thus eliminating William Herbert from consideration, for his father was alive during Herbert's minority, while Wriothesley's father died when the lad was only 8 years old. And the advocates of each earl contend that the other earl was not handsome enough to have been the youth described in the Sonnets.[51]

The task of uncovering the true identity of the youth of the Sonnets would be considerably easier if we knew when the Sonnets were written — or more precisely, if we knew when the first seventeen sonnets, the "procreation sonnets," manifestly addressed to a young man, were written. William Herbert was born in 1580, became the Earl of Pembroke upon his father's death in 1601, and died in 1630; Henry Wriothesley was born in 1573, became the Earl of Southampton upon his father's death in 1581, and died in 1624.[52] If we knew that the procreation sonnets had been written, say, between 1595 and 1600, then the more likely recipient, as between the two earls, would have been William Herbert, who in those years was between his fifteenth and twentieth years (while Wriothesley was between 22 and 27 years old); if we knew that the procreation Sonnets had been written between 1588 and 1593, then the more likely recipient would have been Henry Wriothesley, who was then between his fifteenth and twentieth years (while Herbert was between 8 and 13 years of age). (Presumably, an adolescent named Willie

Hughes can be found for *any* dates assigned to the Sonnets.) But we have no clues as to the date of composition of these first seventeen sonnets.

Nor do we have any real clues as to the dates of the composition of any of the other sonnets, save that, of course, since they were all published in 1609, they must all have been written some time before that. But when? The Sonnets themselves do not refer to any specific date, or to any specific historical event whose date can be fixed. Outside of the four corners of the Sonnets, two items of evidence exist which are helpful, but not dispositive. These are the reference by Francis Meres in *Palladis Tamia*, a book published in 1598, to Shakespeare's "sugred Sonnets among his private friends," and the publication in 1599, in a volume of verse entitled *The Passionate Pilgrim*, of two sonnets substantially the same as those numbered 138 and 144 in the 1609 edition.[53] While these two items of evidence show that some of the sonnets were in existence as much as eleven years before they were all published in 1609, the evidence is silent as to the date of composition of the crucial procreation sonnets. Merely knowing that they might have been in existence by 1598 or 1599 does not help, for these dates, like the date of publication, are so late as to permit the procreation sonnets to have been written to either earl, or to any number of other persons. However, the publication in 1599 of Sonnet 144 (the encapsulation of that portion of the Sonnet story involving the affair between the Fair Friend and Shakespeare's Dark Lady), necessarily gives us the latest date by which the three legs of that triangle had been joined.

Despite the failure of the Sonnets to refer to identifiable historical events which can be dated, those who favour a particular candidate have been astute to divine in the Sonnets allusions to events occurring at a time consistent with the candidacy they advocate (although the pretense is usually that it is the other way around). This is illustrated by the interpretations which have been made of Sonnet 107, this being the one sonnet which seems most clearly to refer to some contemporary happening. The sonnet reads:

> Not mine owne feares, nor the prophetick soule,
> Of the wide world, dreaming on things to come,
> Can yet the lease of my true love controule,
> Supposde as forfeit to a confin'd doome.
> The mortall Moone hath her eclipse indur'de,
> And the sad Augurs mock their own presage,
> Incertenties now crowne them-selves assur'de,
> And peace proclaimes Olives of endlesse age.

> Now with the drops of this most balmie time,
> My love lookes fresh, and death to me subscribes,
> Since spight of him Ile live in this poore rime,
> While he insults ore dull and speachlesse tribes.
>> And thou in this shalt finde thy monument,
>> When tyrants crests and tombs of brasse are spent.

Attention has focussed on the first 8 lines of this sonnet: who or what was "Supposde as forfeit to a confin'd doome"; who or what is the "mortall Moone" who "hath her eclipse indur'de"; what "incertenties now crowne them-selves assur'de"; which "peace proclaimes Olives of endlesse age"?

Leslie Hotson states that the "mortall Moone" is the Spanish Armada in battle position, and that Sonnet 107 dates from 1588;[54] Samuel Butler had earlier proposed the same date for Sonnet 107,[55] although this might be a little early for *his* William Hughes, who was still a navy cook when he died in 1636, by which time, one would imagine, he should have been super-annuated; Thomas Tyler, a William Herbert exponent, thinks the "mortall Moone" is Queen Elizabeth, and that the reference is to the Earl of Essex's uprising against the Queen which began and ended on 8 February 1601, and resulted in Essex's conviction for treason and execution;[56] E. K. Chambers who also, albeit lukewarmly, supports William Herbert, suggests that the reference is to the illness of Queen Elizabeth in 1599, and the fears in England during that year and the next of a possible Spanish invasion;[57] A.L. Rowse, a Southamptonian, finds "no real difficulty here" — the reference is to the peace following the submission of Henri IV to the Roman church in 1593 and to Queen Elizabeth's surviving, in 1594, the supposed attempt of her personal physician, Dr. Lopez, to poison her;[58] Sir Sidney Lee, also a Southamptonian, sees in the sonnet a reference to the death of Queen Elizabeth in 1603 ("mortall Moone her eclipse hath endured"), the coming to the throne of James I ("Olives of endlesse age"), and the release from the Tower of London of the Earl of Southampton ("my true love . . . Supposed as forfeit to a confin'd doome").[59] (For Henry Wriothesley had joined Essex in his uprising in 1601 against the Queen, and was, like him, convicted of treason and sentenced to death, but, unlike Essex, had his sentence commuted to imprisonment in the Tower; one of the first official acts of James I after succeeding to the throne in 1603 was to order the release of Wriothesley from the Tower.) This last interpretation has won wide favour. A problem it presents, however, is that it requires Shakespeare still to be writing sonnets to a friend first loved as a Fair Youth at a time when that Youth (if he is Henry Wriothesley) is almost 30 years old. But this is not an insuperable

11

problem, for love often ripens into friendship, and may have done so in this case. We know from Sonnet 104 that the relationship between the author and the Fair Friend lasted for at least three years:

> To me faire friend you never can be old,
> For as you were when first your eye I eyde,
> Such seemes your beautie still: Three Winters colde,
> Have from the forrests shook three summers pride,
> Three beautious springs to yellow *Autumne* turned,
> In processe of the seasons have I seene,
> Three Aprill perfumes in three hot Junes burn'd,
> Since first I saw you fresh which yet are greene.

No reason exists why this relationship might not, perhaps on a less passionate plane, have lasted for much longer than three years.

But however long the relationship lasted, the Sonnets give us no hint as to when it began. And thus the hope of acquiring some clue to the identity of the Fair Friend by ascertaining the date of the composition of the procreation sonnets, like all the other approaches which have so far been followed, proves futile.

Similarly, the identity of the Rival Poet, who is the subject of Sonnets 78 through 80, and Sonnets 82 through 86, remains a mystery, in spite of the clues which Sonnet 86 seems to offer:

> Was it the proud full saile of his great verse,
> Bound for the prize of (all to precious) you,
> That did my ripe thoughts in my braine inhearce,
> Making their tombe the wombe wherein they grew?
> Was it his spirit, by spirits taught to write,
> Above a mortall pitch, that struck me dead?
> No, neither he, nor his compiers by night
> Giving him ayde, my verse astonished.
> He nor that affable familiar ghost
> Which nightly gulls him with intelligence,
> As victors of my silence cannot boast,
> I was not sick of any feare from thence.
> > But when your countinance fild up his line,
> > Then lackt I matter, that infeebled mine.

A. L. Rowse, who believes that Sonnet 86 was composed in 1593, writes: "There is only one possible rival who could be described in terms such as Shakespeare describes him, and that is Marlowe." This, according to Rowse, is because only Marlowe's poetry has the majesty to answer to the description, "proud full sail of . . . great verse," and also because "that affable familiar ghost/ Which nightly gulls him with intelligence" "would seem fairly certainly to refer to Mephistophilis" in Marlowe's *Doctor Faustus*.[60] For Southamptonians, Marlowe's death in 1593 is no chronological obstacle to this identification, since Southampton would have been almost 20 years old by that time, and could have been the object of Marlowe's affections. But William Herbert would then have been only 13 years old, and those who champion Herbert as the Fair Friend must find their Rival Poet elsewhere. This, of course, is not hard to do. For instance, exactly the same phrases in Sonnet 86 which Rowse believes could only describe Marlow are found by William Minto to apply "with almost too literal exactness to the Alexandrines of Chapman's Homer," and also to be allusive to a statement in Chapman's dedicatory epistle to *Shadow of Night* that the true poet cannot succeed "but with invocation, fasting, watching; yea, not without having drops of their souls like an heavily familiar."[61] The Chapman identification has also been made by a number of Southamptonians, notably Professor Akrigg.[62] But as E. K. Chambers points out, "Chapman . . . dedicated nothing Elizabethan to Herbert, or to Southampton, or to a 'Mr. W.H.'."[63] Other poets surmised to have been the Rival Poet include Samuel Daniel (who was Herbert's tutor at Wilton, his childhood home, and who in 1603 dedicated to him a book entitled *Defence of Rhyme*), Michael Drayton, Barnabe Barnes, Gervase Markham, Thomas Watson and Thomas Nashe.[64]

The Dark Lady is the most difficult of the characters to attempt to identify, for the Sonnets tell us nothing about her, except that she is "black" and not chaste. Thomas Tyler, who put William Herbert forward as the Fair Friend, thought that the Dark Lady might be Queen Elizabeth's maid of honour Mary Fitton, who in about 1601 bore Herbert a son, who died. Herbert refused to marry her, and for this was sent to prison, where he remained for several months.[65] Portraits of Mary Fitton, examined after Tyler published his thesis, show her to be fair, rather than dark,[66] and Tyler's theory today has few subscribers. Luce Morgan, a prostitute referred to in the *Gesta Grayorum* of 1594 as Lucy Negro, has been nominated by G. B. Harrison and seconded by Leslie Hotson.[67] Also in the running are Lady Penelope Rich, the sister of the Earl of Essex and thought by some to be the "Stella" of Sir Philip Sidney's sonnets, and Mrs. Jane Davenant, mother of Sir William Davenant, who is reputed to have fostered the impression that Shakespeare was his father.[68] A. L. Rowse, believing that a manuscript he examined stated that she had been "very brown in youth,"[69] found and advocated as the Dark Lady an Emilia Lanier, the daughter of Baptista Bassano, one of the Queen's Italian musicians. It later turned out that Emilia had been described, in that often difficult-to-read script of Elizabethan times, as very *brave* rather than very *brown*.[70] Nevertheless, Rowse continues to maintain that she is the Dark Lady,[71] and although the claim on her behalf is nothing more than an inference based upon an admitted misreading of a document having no discernible connection with Shakespeare, it is at least as good as any other woman's claim, for she is a documentable person of easy virtue who seems to have moved in theatrical circles (she was until 1592 the mistress of Henry Carey, the Lord Chamberlain Hunsdon, who from about 1594 until his death in 1596 was the patron of the company of actors to which Shakespeare belonged) and thus could have known Shakespeare.

This review of the little evidence and many theories as to the identities of the personages in the Sonnets, brief as it is, is sufficient to establish two points: first, not one word or phrase has so far been found *within* the Sonnets which incontrovertibly identifies any specific person as the individual to whom or about whom the poems were written, and second, not one piece of contemporary writing (including Thomas Thorpe's dedication of the Sonnets) or other evidence has so far been found *outside* the Sonnets which incontrovertibly identifies a specific person as the individual to whom or about whom the poems were written.

In light of this, the reader will understand with what excitement — and trepidation — I begin now to show that, on the basis of clues provided by words *within* the Sonnets, I have found *outside* the Sonnets evidence which I believe *does* incontrovertibly identify two of the players in the Sonnets: the Fair Friend and the Rival Poet. The certain identification of the Fair Friend places Shakespeare squarely amidst a group of poets, playwrights, scholars and statesmen from whose reservoir of knowledge Shakespeare surely drew in writing his poems and plays, thus explaining otherwise inexplicable allusions, information and sources in Shakespeare's writings.

Although I have found no similarly conclusive evidence as to the identity of the Dark Lady, I have found within the Sonnets clues which I believe point to her name, and which, because they are of the same nature as the clues which have led to the hard evidence solving the Fair Friend and Rival Poet mysteries, bring us, I venture to suggest, as close to a solution of this riddle as we are likely ever to get.

CHAPTER II

A Single Fact

> ". . . many modern maniacs have written on Shakespeare, but not one of them has produced a single fact."
>
> Leslie Hotson[1]

This book is about a single fact — or more precisely, an artifact — I have found which solves most of the mysteries of the Sonnets, and ultimately most of the mysteries of Shakespeare's life, learning, and associations. The clue which led me to the artifact has long been noticed, although many have thought it of no consequence, and no one has hitherto gone very far down the road to which it pointed. The clue is the word, "Rose." In the text of the Sonnets as published in 1609, the word "Rose," which is used 13 times (counting the plural as well as the singular), is always capitalized. The first time it is used, in the first two lines of the first sonnet, it is italicized as well as capitalized:

> From fairest creatures we desire increase,
> That thereby beauties *Rose* might never die.

Not only is the word always capitalized, but also, consistently throughout the first 126 sonnets, it is used as a symbolic representation of the fair friend:[2] as the Rose is or does, so are or do you, or so should you be and do. Thus, in these first two lines, which epitomize the theme of the initial seventeen sonnets — that the young man to whom the poems are addressed should preserve his beauty through issue — the Fair Friend is implicitly equated to a Rose whose beauty the world wishes to see perpetuated. And so in all the other Rose sonnets — 35, 54, 67, 95, 99 and 109 — the young man and the Rose are one, and what is true of the Rose is true of the youth. Sonnet 35 states:

> No more be greev'd at that which thou hast done
> Roses have thorns, and silver fountaines mud,
> Cloudes and eclipses staine both Moone and Sunne,
> And loathsome canker lives in sweetest bud.

That is, do not grieve over your (unspecified) defect, for even the beautiful Rose which (by necessary implication) you resemble, is less than perfect, because it has thorns. To be sure, the youth is likewise in this sonnet compared to a silver fountain soiled with mud, to the moon and the sun

15

spotted by clouds and eclipses, and to a "sweetest bud" infected by a worm (caterpillar, or insect larva, being one of the meanings for "canker" shown in the Oxford English Dictionary), but that the youth is compared to several beautiful things with inherent flaws does not vitiate the Rose = youth comparison, which in subsequent sonnets emerges as the primary and most significant of Shakespeare's metaphors for the youth.

Sonnet 54 is devoted entirely to Roses, true and false, floral and human:

> Oh how much more doth beautie beautious seeme,
> By that sweet ornament which truth doth give,
> The Rose lookes faire, but fairer we it deeme
> For that sweet odor, which doth in it live:
> The Canker bloomes have full as deepe a die,
> As the perfumed tincture of the Roses,
> Hang on such thornes, and play as wantonly,
> When sommers breath their masked buds discloses:
> But for their virtue only is their show,
> They live unwoo'd, and unrespected fade,
> Die to themselves. Sweet Roses doe not so,
> Of their sweet deathes, are sweetest odours made:
>   And so of you, beautious and lovely youth,
>   When that shall vade [fade], by [my?] verse distils your truth.

The point of this disquisition on Roses is that you are not a false rose, like a canker bloom (another of the definitions of canker in the Oxford English Dictionary is "an inferior kind of rose"), but a *true* Rose, whose sweet odour, after your death, will through the distillation effected by my verse, endure.

Sonnet 67 pursues this idea:

> Why should false painting immitate his cheeke
> And steale dead seeing of his living hew?
> Why should poore beautie indirectly seeke,
> Roses of shadow, since his Rose is true?

A difficult four lines, but the essential Rose meaning is that the Fair Friend is a true Rose, and either cannot be improved by cosmetics (false painting)[3] or cannot be accurately represented by painters (false painting).[4]

Sonnet 95 returns to the "loathesome canker in sweetest bud" theme broached in Sonnet 35:

> How sweet and lovely dost thou make the shame,
> Which like a canker in the fragrant Rose,
> Doth spot the beautie of thy budding name?

That is, as the exterior form of the Rose beautifies the worm within it, so do you make lovely the shame (whatever that may be[5]) which spots your "budding name."

Finally, the equation of the Friend with the Rose, implicit in and the premise of the foregoing sonnets, is made explosively explicit in Sonnet 109:

> Never beleeve though in my nature raign'd,
> All frailties that besiege all kindes of blood,
> That it could so preposterouslie be stain'd,
> To leave for nothing all thy summe of good:
>   For nothing this wide Universe I call,
>   Save thou my Rose, in it thou art my all.

The concluding lines are remarkable for their piercing intensity: you, my Rose, are my everything; without you, the Universe is nothing. This, the last use of the word Rose in the first 126 Sonnets, identifies the Fair Friend with a Rose too immediately, too unequivocally, too passionately, for anyone to doubt that the Friend is a Rose — a Rose not in a casual, lightly flattering way, but in some profound, meaningful way.

Two sonnets are omitted from the foregoing catalogue of Rose sonnets addressed to the Fair Friend; these are Sonnets 98 and 99, which I shall discuss in the next chapter. Roses appear in one (and only one) of the sonnets addressed to the Dark Lady — Sonnet 130 — but there they are introduced merely to be withdrawn:

> I have seen Roses damaskt, red and white,
> But no such Roses see I in her cheekes. . . .

In the Sonnets, Roses — and specifically, "Roses damaskt, red and white" — are the emblem of one person only, the Fair Friend; once we know who bears that emblem, we know who the Friend is.

I am not, of course, the first person to assume that Shakespeare's denomination of his friend as a Rose necessarily has a special meaning; a number of scholars have thought that Shakespeare's substantively significant and typographically arresting use of the word "Rose" must in some way allude to an objective fact which, if discovered, would reveal the identity of the youth to whom the Sonnets are addressed. In 1918, Martha Hale Shackford wrote:

That Shakespeare should have characterized his friend only tritely and sentimentally is incredible; the "rose" is not an epithet thoughtlessly employed in a series of unsurpassed sonnets, but a word of some hidden meaning.[6]

Professor Shackford's surmise as to the hidden meaning of the Roses in the Sonnets was that Wriothesely, the family name of the third Earl of Southampton, was pronounced "Rōse-ly," and that the Rose of the Sonnets, consequently, was Henry Wriothesley, the young man to whom Shakespeare had dedicated both *Venus and Adonis* and *The Rape of Lucrece*. This conclusion has been reached independently by others, both before and after Professor Shackford: G. H. Skipwith in 1916, and Charlton Hinman in 1937, each wrote letters to the *Times Literary Supplement* suggesting the same pronunciation,[7] and Arthur Acheson, in a book published in 1933,[8] takes it for granted that Wriothesley was pronounced Rōse-ly.

This supposed pronunciation of Wriothesely, however, has not been generally accepted, even by persons who advocate the Earl of Southampton as the Fair Friend of the Sonnets. G.P.V. Akrigg, a Southamptonian, believes that the name was "probably pronounced Rye-ose-ley but usually elided to Rise-ly," with a few persons possibly saying "Rosely."[9] Akrigg notes that other writers have put forward other pronunciations: "Wresley" was suggested by C. C. Stopes, "Wreesley" by E. I. Fripp, and "Wrisley" by A. F. Pollard.[10] A. L. Rowse, who vigorously maintains that Southampton is the Fair Friend of the Sonnets, asserts that the name "is pronounced Wrisley, and may be rhymed with grisly. . . ."[11]

It is not surprising, therefore, that Professor Shackford's identification of Wriothesley as the Rose of the Sonnets, based solely on the surmise that Wriothesley was pronounced Rosely, has met with so little attention. In addition to refusing to hear a Rose in Wriothesley, the mainstream of Shakespearean scholarship, believing, perhaps, that the rose is too conventional a literary image to have been infused by Shakespeare with any special or personal meaning, has declined to impute any significance to the Rose typography and imagery in the Sonnets: the typography is dismissed as "probably a typesetter's whim,"[12] and the imagery is either ignored,[13] or glossed as embodying esoteric Platonic or medieval concepts of ideal beauty,[14] having no relationship to the identity of the Fair Friend.

Furthermore, the proponents of candidates other than Henry Wriothesley for the honour of being the fair youth of the Sonnets have not been at a loss to explain how "Rose" could be a reference to their nominee: the partisans of William Herbert, third Earl of Pembroke, point out that since one of his titles was Lord Ros of Kendal, he must be the Ros(e) of the Sonnets; another contends that Rose means Ro. Es., i.e., Robert Essex (Robert Devereux, the Earl of Essex, executed in 1601 for his uprising against the Queen), while others, perhaps reluctant to acknowledge that the Rose addressed in the Sonnets is a young man, have surmised that Rose is Shakespeare's mistress, or that Rose is Shakespeare's own soul "materialized."[15]

Here I must "declare my interest," and acknowledge that over twenty years ago, in the course of writing a book on the Sonnets ultimately published in 1974, I became convinced (for the reasons stated in that book and summarized in Chapter V of this book) that the "Rose" of the Sonnets is Henry Wriothesley, third Earl of Southampton.[16] Although my 1974 conclusion was not based upon the Rosely/Wriothesley wordplay, I was aware of, and found support in, the conjecture of Shackford and others that Wriothesley was pronounced "Rosely." Such a pronunciation is not as unlikely as the orthography of the name might suggest, since it is not unknown, in English, for a "th" to be unpronounced before an "s." The most obvious example of this is "clothes," generally pronounced today as "klōz," and doubtless also so pronounced in Shakespeare's time, as we may infer from the rhyme in *Hamlet* (IV,v,52), "Then up he rose and donn'd his clothes." Another example of the disappearance of the "th" before an "s" is the Duke of Alencon's statement, in *I Henry VI* (I,ii,33), that the English soldiers fighting the French were all "Samsons and Goliases." Also, the statement in Sonnet 67 that "his Rose is true," seemed to me to mean that the Fair Friend is *genuinely* a Rose, because that is his name, and the phrase in Sonnet 54, "thy budding name," in my opinion, was another allusion to a name which is like a flower.[17]

So for a while I sought some evidence which might support the existence of a Rosely/Wriothesley pun, and thus buttress a conclusion reached on other grounds. One track I pursued led me to the coat of arms of the Earls of Southampton, where I hoped to find a visual pun, or rebus, which might give some indication of the pronunciation of the family name. As Anthony R. Wagner has written, "the commonest explanation of heraldic design lies in the medieval fondness for a canting coat, punning on the owner's name."[18] Such canting or punning arms, or *armes parlantes*,[19] were not confined only to medieval times, but are "highly characteristic of Heraldry at all dates."[20] Typical examples of punning arms are "Or, three ravens [i.e., corbeaux] sable" of Corbett, "Argent, three falcons gules in chief, as many pellets," of Faukenor, "Gules, a boar argent armed or," of Bore, and "Sable, two wolves passant or" of Wolfe.[21] The arms of Shakespeare himself — a falcon shaking

Figure 1. Arms of Wriothesley.

a spear gripped in its talon — are an example of punning heraldry.[22] I thought it possible that if the members of the Wriothesely family actually had pronounced their name "Rose-ly," then their coat of arms might reflect visually the pun to which the Wriothesley name naturally lent itself. But in the book I consulted[23] the Wriothesley arms were blazoned as "Azure a cross or between four falcons close argent." This translates into: on an azure field, a golden cross dividing the field into four quarters, on each quarter of which is a silver (or white) falcon, with its wings closed (i.e., by its side, rather than *éployés* — spread out or elevated). These arms are depicted in Figure 1, taken from a book published in 1610,[24] during the lifetime of the third Earl. No roses here, and thus, apparently, no heraldic support for the identification of Wriothesley as the Rose of the Sonnets. And there, for a long time, the matter rested.

In October, 1983, I visited Southampton, England, and toured some of the old buildings which are open to the public. I was, I think, in the Bargate (the North Gate through the medieval walls surrounding Southampton) when a friend from Berlin who was with me noticed and called to my attention a rosette carved upon the wall. Another friend, a resident of Southampton who was showing us his city, informed us that the rose appears on the coat of arms of the town of Southampton, and is thought of locally as the symbol of that city.

This information elec-
trified me, for immediately
came to mind the possibility
that if roses were on the
Southampton coat of arms,
then the Earls of South-
ampton, during their lifetimes, might have associated
themselves with the roses on
the coat of arms of the town
from which they derived
their honour,[25] thus establishing a Wriothesley/Rose-ly
connection of the type I had
hoped, but failed, to find in
the Wriothesley arms pro-
per. Upon my return to the
United States, I ascertained
that the coat of arms of the
town of Southampton was
indeed "per fesse argent and
gules, three roses counterchanged."[26] This succinct
but esoteric blazon translates
into verbose but plain English as: a shield divided
horizontally through the middle into a white (or silver) field on top and a red
field on the bottom, upon which two fields are placed alternately three roses,
the two roses falling in the white (top) field being red, and the rose falling in
the red (bottom) field being white. This coat is depicted in Figure 2.

Figure 2. Arms of Southampton.

It is sometimes stated that these arms, along with a crest and supporters,[27] were granted to the town of Southampton by patent of 4 August
1575.[28] This would suggest, to the unwary, that the arms had no existence,
and could not have been used, prior to that date. But the fact is that the
patent, which is available for inspection in the City Record Office in
Southampton, and which is reproduced in Plate I, commences by reciting that
the town had borne arms since its incorporation by Henry VI (which incorporation occurred in 1445[29]) and ends by declaring that Robert Cooke,
Esquire, alias Clarencieux, at the request of the Mayor, Bailiffs and burgesses
of Southampton has "assigned, deviced and granted to them their said

auncient armes" (emphasis supplied). By its very terms, therefore, the patent, although it is a grant of supporters and crest, is not a grant in 1575 of new arms, but a confirmation or ratification in 1575 of arms which by that time had been borne by the town for at least 130 years.[30]

Or perhaps even longer: a brochure published by that City states that

No one knows . . . when the three roses on their contrasting backgrounds were first granted or adopted, although the simplicity of the design points to a fairly early date — thirteenth or fourteenth century. The opinion of Miss Thomson, the City Archivist, is that the most likely period for their adoption is the second half of the fourteenth century, a period when many military expeditions of the Hundred Years War sailed wholly or in part from Southampton and the Solent, including those led by Henry, Duke of Lancaster and his son-in-law John of Gaunt, also Duke of Lancaster. John's younger brother, the Duke of York, also had similar connections with the Port, and it seems to be a reasonable guess that the red and white rose badges of the Dukes of Lancaster and York should have been used as a compliment to these important royal princes. However, it must be stressed that this is only a guess, no proof of it survives.[31]

Also pointing to a very early origin for the use of the rose as the symbol of Southampton are the observations of C. Wilfrid Scott-Giles that "roses appear, with other emblems, on a fourteenth-century staple seal of South-ampton", and that "according to tradition, the red rose was granted to the *County* [emphasis supplied] by John of Gaunt, Duke of Lancaster."[32] The County of Southampton (by which style was officially known until 1959 what is now called "the County of Hampshire"[33]) itself has no arms,[34] but a red rose appears upon the device or badge of the Hampshire County Council[35] and upon the devices or coats of arms of many towns and institutions within the County.[36] Moreover, and of importance to what follows, the arms of the *town* of Southampton are frequently quoted and used as those of the *county*, "often with the colours reversed."[37]

Having confirmed that, as my friend had said, Southampton bore roses, and that these arms were of great antiquity, I turned next to attempting to determine whether the Wriothesleys associated themselves with that coat of arms, perhaps by displaying it in their dwelling along with (or even instead of) their own coat of arms.

To ascertain this, I went to my then local library (the incomparable Library of Congress), to discover what I could about Place House, some-times called also either Palace House or Titchfield House, in Titchfield, Hampshire, this having been the chief residence of the Wriothesley family.[38]

Before becoming the Wriothesley residence, Place House had been Titchfield Abbey, a Premonstratensian monastery. In 1537, upon the suppression of the monasteries, the Abbey was granted by Henry VIII to Thomas Wriothesley who in 1547 became the first Earl of Southampton (of the Wriothesley line). In the course of converting it into his manor house, Wriothesley made extensive changes in the old Abbey.[39]

Place House is today a ruin, for the building was largely demolished late in the 18th century by the Delmé family, which then owned it. The property is now administered by the Ancient Monuments and Historic Buildings Section of the Department of the Environment. The Department of the Environment's *Official Handbook* for Titchfield Abbey describes the Abbey as it had been prior to its suppression, and notes the changes afterwards effected by Thomas Wriothesely. With respect to the eastern range of Place House, the *Handbook* states:

> The Tudor alterations to the range include two mullioned and transomed windows, flanking a projecting doorway, with a four-centered head and shields and foliage in the spandrels. One shield is plain; *the other bears two roses on a chief* [emphasis supplied]. . . .[40]

My conjecture was correct: the Wriothesleys *had* decorated their home with heraldic roses!

In June of 1984, I returned to Southampton. My friend who lived there met me at the train station whence we walked two blocks to the bus station, and boarded the bus to Titchfield. It was a hot day, and after we arrived in Titchfield, we stopped first at the Bugle Hotel[41] (which featured "lasagne," and "chilli con carne," as well as more traditional dishes), to refresh ourselves. Then we walked the half mile from the center of Titchfield, past the Titchfield Abbey Fruit Farm, Ltd., to the one pile of stone which is the ruins both of Titchfield Abbey and of Place House.

Plate II-A shows the still impressive south front of the building. Plate II-B is a photograph taken from the west wall of Place House, and looks across what had been the inner courtyard of the Wriothesley manor to the east wall of Place House facing this inner courtyard. Almost all that remains of the east wall are the "two mullioned and transomed windows, flanking a projecting doorway," which are the Tudor alterations described in the *Official Handbook* for Titchfield Abbey. (The wooden structure over the doorway,

23

and the curtain in the doorway, were put up in connection with the use of the Place House site for plays which were being presented during the summer of 1984.) On this projecting stone doorway in the wall of what had been the Wriothesley residence, I found the Roses I sought.

The stone doorway, shown in Plate III-A, is in the form of a gothic, or pointed arch. On either side of the doorway, in the spandrel (triangular area above the curve of the arch), is an heraldic shield. The heraldic shield on the viewer's right, shown in Plate III-B, bears upon its surface, in high relief, carvings of two roses. The spandrel and shield are shown in greater detail in Plate V. An ordinary heraldic rose would consist of five petals of equal size, with seeds in the center of the flower.[42]   But the roses on this doorway clearly consist of two ranges of petals surrounding the center area of seeds, and are thus Tudor roses, which consist of a five-petaled flower (representing the white rose of York) superimposed   upon another five-petaled flower (representing the red rose of Lancaster).[43] A Tudor example of a Tudor rose is shown in Plate IV-A; this is the Tudor rose painted upon a large round wooden table popularly thought to have been the Round Table of King Arthur and his knights. The rose was painted in 1522, at the direction of Henry VIII, upon the occasion of the visit of Charles V to Winchester.[44] The table now is affixed to the west wall of the Great Hall of Winchester Castle, in Hampshire.

Under the two roses on the shield at Titchfield, a horizontal line has been incised, and the plane of the shield below that line is almost a half-inch lower than the plane of the shield above that line. As can be seen on Plates III-B and V-B, the area below the horizontal line appears to have been chiseled away.

The heraldic shield on the left of the doorway is completely blank, as is shown in Plate IV-B. The surface of the shield is rough, and in its entirety projects from its stone background only about as far as the surface of the lower portion of the shield on the right projects from its stone background. This suggests that the shield on the left once bore a heraldic device in as high relief as the roses on the shield on the right, but that this device was chiseled away completely — probably at the same time that the shield on the right, with the heraldic roses, was only partially defaced.

Although the shield on the right is only partially intact, that part which is intact is completely consistent with the Town of Southampton's coat of arms, and the probability is that the shield was at one time fully emblazoned with Southampton's arms. The only two references I have ever found to this shield (aside from the reference in the *Official Handbook* for Titchfield Abbey) expressly describe it as blazoned with the arms of the Town of Southampton. An article on "Titchfield Abbey and Place House" by the Reverend

G. W. Minns, published in 1898, contains a floor plan of the building, reproduced on page 26 as Figure 3.

On this plan, features of the old Abbey are identified by upper case roman letters, and features of the building after it was transformed into Place House are identified by lower case italicised letters. In describing the east side of the ruins of that building, the article states that "Beyond [the *armarium*, or library] we come to the Sacristy, F., which now has a Tudor door-way *f.* with the arms of the *town of Southampton* [emphasis supplied] in the spandril,viz., 'Per fesse, argent and gules, three roses counter-changed of the field.'"[45] The *Victoria History of Hampshire and the Isle of Wight*, published ten years later, in its description of the ruins of Titchfield Abbey, written by Miss A.M. Hendy, also refers to "a doorway with the arms of *Southampton* in the head, masking the western entrance to the inner parlour. . . [emphasis supplied]."[46] Conceivably, of course, the Reverend G. W. Minns and Miss Hendy, writing at the turn of the century, may have seen the shield in a more complete state than that in which it now exists (which would only confirm that it bore the coat of arms of the Town of Southampton). More likely is it, however, that these two persons saw the shield in its present state, and merely assumed, as I do, that before its defacement, the shield depicted the arms known to everyone in the area: those of the Town of Southampton (or of the County of Southampton, depending upon whether the shield was argent on top and gules on the bottom, or *vice versa*).

On one level, the reason for the Southampton arms on the Wriothesley home is obvious: the arms signal the identification of the family with the area, even as functionaries all over the world tend to display in their offices and homes the arms or badges of the political entity over which they have jurisdiction, or in which they live. But on another level, the Roses of Southampton, I believe, had an intense personal and dynastic meaning for the man who placed them in his home.

This man, Thomas Wriothesley, had been born into a family but recently emerged from obscurity. Thomas' grandfather, John Wrythe (also frequently spelled as Writh or Writhe), had attained distinction as a herald. He is said to have been Antelope and Rouge Croix Poursuivant in the time of Henry V.[47] He was designated Falcon Herald in about 1473, Norroy Herald in 1477, and Garter King of Arms in 1478.[48] As Garter King of Arms, he became *ex officio* the principal officer of the College of Arms upon its incorporation in 1483/4 by Richard III.[49] He died in 1504,[50] by which time he must have been a very old man, if indeed he had been a poursuivant during the reign of Henry V (who died in 1422).

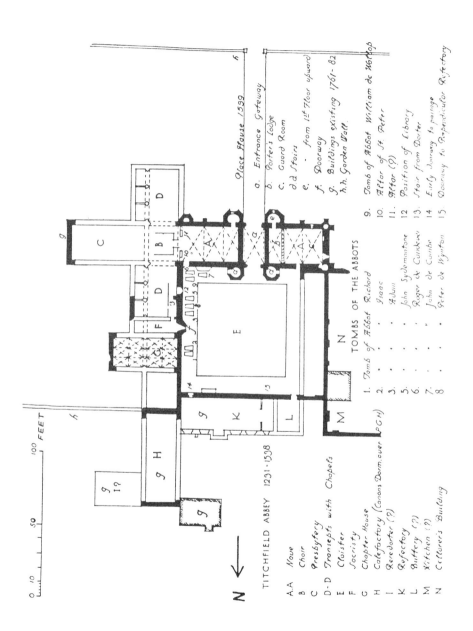

N ↓

0 10   50   100 FEET

TITCHFIELD ABBEY 1231-1538

A.A Nave
B   Choir
C   Presbytery
D-D Transepts with Chapels
E   Cloister
F   Sacristy
G   Chapter House
H   Calefactory (Canons Dormr. over PGH)
I   Reredorter (?)
K   Refectory
L   Buttery (?)
M   Kitchen (?)
N   Cellarer's Building

TOMBS OF THE ABBOTS

1. Tomb of Abbot Richard
2.   "   "   "   Isaac
3.   "   "   "   Adam
5.   "   "   "   John Sydemantone
6.   "   "   "   Roger de Cumbur
7.   "   "   "   John de Cumbe
8.   "   "   "   Peter de Wynton
9. Tomb of Abbot William de Wottop
10. Altar of St. Peter
11. Altar (?)
12. Position of Library
13. Stair from Dorter
14. Early stairway to passage
15. Doorway to Perpendicular Refectory

Place House 1599

a. Entrance Gateway
b. Porter's Lodge
c. Guard Room
d d Stairs
e.   " from 1st floor upward
f. Doorway
g. Buildings existing 1761-82
h.h. Garden Wall.

Figure 3. Plan of Titchfield Abbey and Place House.

Over his long life, John Wrythe was married three times (see genealogical Tables I and II, on pages 28 and 29). Thomas and William, his sons by his first marriage, followed their father into "the like plagiary profession."[51] Thomas, the older son (the uncle of the Thomas with whom we are primarily concerned), was "first an Herauld by the Title of Walingford" in about 1489.[52] In 1505 he succeeded his father as Garter King of Arms, and held this position until his death in 1534.[53] Thus Thomas makes an appearance in one of Shakespeare's plays, for he is the Garter King of Arms who participates in the coronation of Anne Bullen (as the name is spelled in the play) in Act IV, scene 4 of *Henry VIII*, and who in Act V, scene 5, at the christening of the issue of Anne and Henry, says, "Heaven, from thy endless goodness send prosperous life, long, and ever happy, to the high and mighty Princess of England, Elizabeth!"

This Thomas' greatest claim to our attention, however, is that he changed the family name from Wrythe to Wriothesley. No doubt this man, who as Garter King of Arms spent much of his time investigating the pedigrees of persons claiming the right to bear arms, and confirming or rejecting — and sometimes, it can be supposed, collusively fabricating[54] — those rights, was finally tempted to manufacture for himself an aristocratic pedigree which included *nunc pro tunc* a bevy of forebears with the regal-looking but newly made-up name of Wriothesley. In 1724, John Anstis, who was himself Garter King of Arms from 1719 until his death in 1744,[55] wrote about his predecessor:

. . . though this Officer [Thomas Wrythe] was adanced to this Employment [i.e., Garter King of Arms] by the Monosyllable Surname that his Father used, yet he disliked the shortness of it, either with regard to the Explication of the Ancient Proverb, *Omnis herus servo Monosyllabus*, or some other whimsical Humour, and therefore augmented it with the high Sound of three Syllables, which added nothing to the Smoothness in pronunciation, and after some variations in the spelling, he at last settled upon *Wriothesley*, wherein his Brother *William York* Herald concurred, and their Descendants followed this precedent; and, which is somewhat particular, in order to countenance this Affectation, he attributed the new coined Appellation to all his paternal ancestors in the Draughts he made of his own Pedigree; and therein he deduces himself by his Mother from the *Walters* of *Dunstanvil*, ancient Lords of *Castlecomb* in *Wiltshire*: He was so very fond of this new Surname thus devised by him, that when the Salary granted by Hen VII was determined by his Demise, he took a new one from his Successor, wherein he procured his Father to be stiled "*John Wriothesley* alias *Writhe* late *Garter*," at which Time the Reflection that Judge Catalin once made upon an *Alias* might be out of his Memory.[56]

27

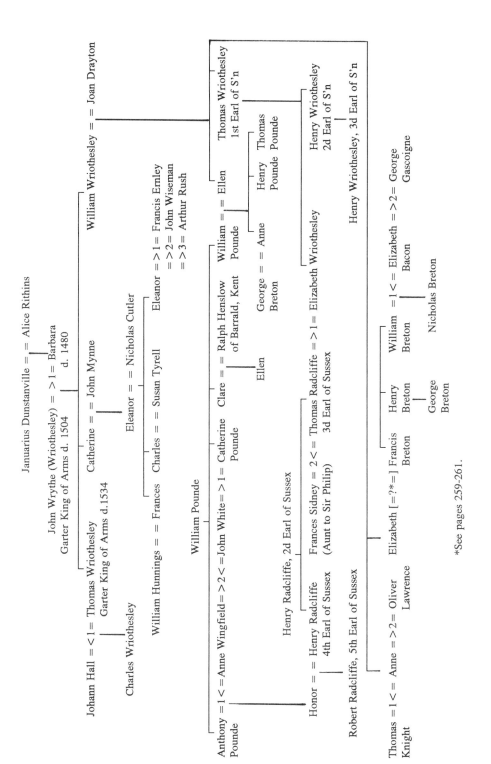

TABLE I - John Wrythe and his first wife; Pounde, Radcliffe

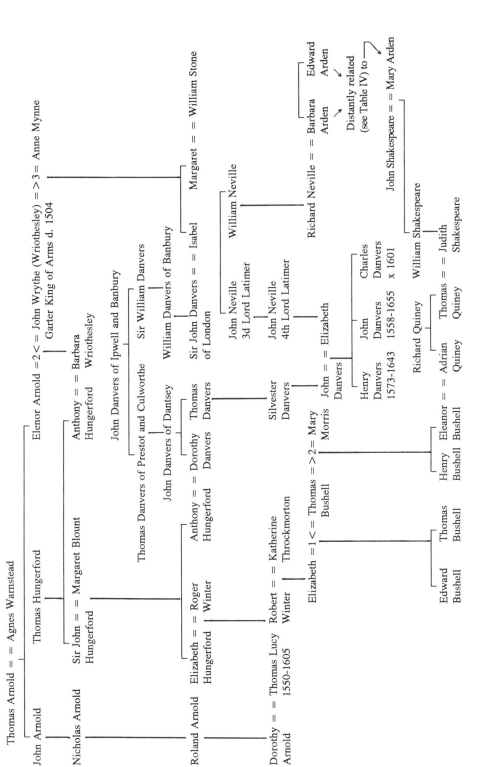

TABLE II - JOHN WRYTHE AND HIS SECOND AND THIRD WIVES; HUNGERFORD, DANVERS

Thus at least by 1509 (the year of the death of Henry VII), the Wrythe brothers, Thomas and William, had become the Wriothesleys.

The change in the family name did not, of course, change the family coat of arms, which, in any event, was itself not of very great antiquity: the Wriothesleys, as T.C. Banks wrote, "do not appear to have been derived from any very ancient or noble house, but to have acquired more honour from their office, than from their blood."[57] John Wrythe, the first of his family to achieve any distinction, had no paternal arms,[58] and experimented with a couple of blazons. Anstis writes:

In the Ordinary of Arms made by Thomas Wall Wyndesor in 1530 (who was afterwards himself Garter) "*Wryth Garter* beryth Asur three doves silver membry geules in a double tressoir florette contre-florette Gold — *Wryothesly* beryth Gold a bend ingrayed Geuls; but at length his Descendants bore a plain Cross Or betwixt four Doves closed Argent." If these were Doves (wherein several MSS. agree) the same might be orginally taken in Correspondene [sic] to the practice of former Herals, who upon their Creations frequently took Doves; but Sir *William Dugdale* [in *The Baronage of England*, II, 384] blazons them *Faucons*, (as many others have done) and conjectures they might be in Allusion to his Title of *Faucon* Herald: *Ballard March* King of Arms his Contemporary, calls them only Birds, without describing the Species; there hath been also another Coat of Arms ascribed to him, and a variety also of Crests, whereof one in particularly said to belong to him as *Garter*. A late Author [identified by Anstis in a footnote as "Buc in his Universities of England at the end of Stow's Survey"] writes, That the College of Arms it self borrowed its Coat from a Gentleman of the most signal Name and Family that had ever been of it, by which he doubtless means this *Wrythe*; but it is more probable that those Officers might discontinue their old Seal, and assume Doves in conformity to the practice mentioned by *Upton*, wherein by chance they have likewise followed the Directions of a Learned Father of the Primitive Church.[59]

The "Learned Father of the Primitive Church" to whom Anstis refers is probably Isidore of Seville (Isidorus Hispalensis), the seventh century bishop and encyclopædist; according to Gerard Legh, "Of the natural properties of the dove Isidore writeth, that the Dove is the messenger of peace, which he brought between God and man, into the Arke of Noah, as plainly appeareth in Genesis."[60]

The coat of arms of the College of Arms, depicted in Figure 4, is *Argent a cross gules in each quarter a dove azure with one wing open and the other close beaked and legged gules.*[61] The resemblance between this coat of arms, and the Wriothesley coat of arms shown in Figure 1, is apparent. However, the authors of *The College of Arms*, published in 1963, agree with Anstis that

30

it is more likely that John Wrythe based his coat on that of the College of Arms than *vice versa*.[62] Whichever coat came first, it is reasonable to assume that the birds on both coats are intended to be the same. Therefore, since the College of Arms birds are definitely doves, the Wriothesley birds are probably doves, rather than falcons. Certainly, in those sixteenth and early seventeenth century representations of the Wriothesley arms which I have seen, the charges definitely look more like doves than like

Figure 4. Arms of College of Arms.

falcons: I have particularly in mind the arms on the Wriothesley tomb constructed in the 1590's, shown in Plate VI-A (to the right of the figure of the third Earl of Southampton as a boy), the arms on the book in the painting, probably of 1603, of the third Earl in the Tower of London, a photograph of which is reproduced in Plate VI-B, and the arms depicted in a book published in 1610, as shown in Figure 1. Also, as Anstis noted, early blazons of the arms of Thomas Wriothesley, Garter King of Arms, describe the birds as doves.[63]

Thomas Wriothesley's son Charles, born in 1508, was also a herald, being appointed Rouge Croix poursuivant in 1524 and Windsor Herald in 1535.[64] He is best remembered as the author of the *Wriothesley Chronicle*, an important source of information about Tudor England. Charles died in 1562, without issue.[65]

Thomas' brother William, the younger son of John Wrythe, was appointed Rouge Croix poursuivant in 1505, and York Herald in 1509.[66] He appears to have died prior to 26 April 1513, by which date Thomas Tonge had succeeded to the position of York Herald.[67] William's son Thomas, who was born in 1505, is the Thomas upon whom we wish to focus: he is the Thomas who acquired Titchfield Abbey, became the Lord High Chancellor of England and first Earl of Southampton, and was the grandfather of the Henry Wriothesley to whom Shakespeare dedicated *Venus and Adonis* and *The Rape of Lucrece*.

If it was Thomas Wriothesley, the herald, who acquired for his family an aristocratic-looking name, it was his nephew, Thomas Wriothesley, the bureaucrat, who attained for his family the station, estates and titles which in fact made them aristocrats. His worldly success seems to have been compounded of almost equal measures of intelligence, charm, good looks, luck, ability, ruthlessness and greed, some of which qualities are suggested in the portrait reproduced in Plate VII.[68] No full length biography of him has ever been written. But his life should be of interest to students of Shakespeare, not only because he was the grandfather of Shakespeare's patron, but equally significantly, because a knowledge of the extensive family he founded, and that family's connections by blood and marriage to other families, furnishes valuable insights and clues to the circumstances which may have brought together the playwright and the peer. For this reason, I have assembled in Appendix I some information and surmises about Thomas Wriothesley's life and character. Although he was in many respects an attractive person, no assessment of his life can ignore the fact that from 1526 on, his was the hand which unquestioningly executed the tyrannous will of that monstrous despot, Henry VIII, securing or helping to secure on his behalf the fall of Wolsey, the divorce from Catherine of Aragon, the execution of Anne Boleyn, the fall and execution of Cromwell, the divorce from Anne of Cleves, the torture and execution of Anne Askew, the execution of Catherine Howard, the execution of the Earl of Surrey, the almost-execution of the Duke of Norfolk, and the attempted disgrace of Catherine Parr.

Suffice it at this point to note that these services were well rewarded. On 28 December 1537, Thomas Wriothesley was granted Titchfield Abbey, in the County of Southampton on the east side of the Southampton Water.[69] A description and history of Titchfield House are set forth in Appendix II, and show that the conversion of the Abbey into a residence began immediately upon its acquisition and was largely completed by about 1542 or 1543, although portions of the house and various details may have been constructed or added in subsequent years, and as late as 1550, the year of Wriothesley's death. So it may have been as early as 1538, and certainly no later than 1550, that Wriothesley's "projecting doorway" on which is incised the heraldic shield bearing the coat of arms of the Town (or County) of Southampton was constructed.

I earlier stated that the Southampton arms had an intense personal and dynastic meaning for Thomas Wriothesley. Some of these meanings are now evident. First: the arms commemorate Wriothesley's close connection with Southampton. Even before Henry VIII so amply rewarded him with estates and honours in the county of Southampton, Wriothesley owned property in Titchfield; in a draft lease dated 27 Henry VIII (i.e., 1535-1536), he styles himself "Thomas Wriothesley of Tychefeld."[70] Subsequently, as is recounted in Appendix I, Wriothesley acquired immense estates in the County of

Southampton, was admitted a free burgess of the Town of Southampton, was a member of Parliament for Southampton County, and was designated Constable of Southampton Castle. So the arms over the door, if not properly the arms of his county seat (because not the arms of his family), were at least frequently employed as the arms of the county in which he had his seat.

Second: (if, as I hope, none will now doubt that the hypothesis leading me to the spandrel at Titchfield has been proven, and that the family name of the Earls of Southampton was, indeed, pronounced "Rōse-ly") the Southampton coat of arms, in addition to reflecting Wriothesley's distinction in and associations with the town and county of Southampton, also, because it bears Roses, cantingly depicts his name. The coming together of residence and name in this one coat was doubtless a coincidence (for the family took the name long before it had any connection with Southampton), but one can easily imagine with what relish Thomas Wriothesley seized upon this fortuitous combination of signs and sounds to claim for himself so apt a symbol.

And third, of course, the arms on the doorway are the arms of the locale whence he derived his honour (i.e., his title). Whether it is of the Town or of the County of Southampton that Wriothesley was Earl is far from clear, for no documents relating to his title which might clarify this seem to exist.[71] In the very earliest times, the area of which an Earl (the English equivalent of Count[72]) had the government was a County.[73] As J. H. Round has written, in his important discussion of comital titles in 12th century England, "each earl is the earl of a county. . . . an earl without a county was a conception that had not yet entered into the minds of men."[74] But, Round goes on to say, an earl did not automatically take his title from the name of the county of which he was earl: that was only one of four possible sources for his comital title, the other three sources being the capital town of the county, the earl's chief residence, or the earl's family name. Round continues:

The result of this system, or rather want of system, was, as we might expect, in the case of earls, that no fixed principle guided the adoption of their styles. It was indeed a matter of haphazard which of their *cognomina* prevailed, and survived to form the style by which their descendants were known. Thus, the Earls of Herts and of Surrey, of Derby and of Bucks, were usually spoken of by their family names of Clare and of Warenne, of Ferrers and of Giffard; on the other hand the Earls of Norfolk and of Essex, of Devon and of Cornwall, were more usually styled by those of their counties. *Where the name of the county was formed from that of its chief town, the latter, rather than the county itself, was adopted for the earl's style.* [Emphasis supplied.] Familiar instances are found in the earldoms of Chester, Gloucester, and Hereford, of Lincoln, of Leicester, and of Warwick.[75]

In view of this practice described by Round, it would appear to have been not only possible, but probable, that the place name in Southampton's title was the eponymous Town, rather than the eponymous County.

But which eponymous county? For complicating this matter — and perhaps rendering this whole discussion moot — is the fact that the Town of Southampton, which had been incorporated by a charter granted by Henry VI in 1445,[76] was, only two years later, itself designated a county. Henry VI's charter of 1447 declares that

> our said town [of Southampton], with the port and precincts of the same, and the port of Portsmouth, which is now called the town of Southampton, and the precincts of the same town, shall be one entire county incorporate in word and deed, distinct and separate from the county of Southampton for ever, and that the same county so incorporate, distinct and separate from the county of Southampton shall always be entitled, named and called the county of our town of Southampton. . . .[77]

This style for the town of Southampton continued until 24 February 1964, when by the Charter of that date of Elizabeth II, the town became a city, and its style was changed to "The City and County of the City of Southampton"[78] Thus, even if the Southampton comital title necessarily alludes to a county, that county could be the "county of our town of Southampton," rather than, as is sometimes assumed, the "county of Southampton."[79]

But the more tenable conclusion, I think, is that the Southampton of Wriothesley's title is the town and not the county, and this I base on the fact that William Fitzwilliam, Wriothesley's friend and neighbor, who in 1537 was created the first Earl of Southampton since the eleventh century,[80] was frequently referred to as the Earl of *Hampton*, and his house in London was called Hampton House.[81] Ham*pton* is the usual designation in Tudor times for the *Town* of Southampton,[82] and is a name never applied to Hamp*shire*, the *County* of Southampton. Fitzwilliam died in 1542, leaving no male heirs, as a consequence of which the title became extinct, until revived in 1547 and conferred upon Wriothesley. I think it probable that Wriothesley took the title thinking of it, as his predecessor had, as being derived from the town of Hampton, rather than from the shire of Southampton. Others supposed as much: a foreign ambassador writes in March, 1547 that Wriothesley was raised to the rank of Earl of Southampton, "near which *town* [emphasis supplied] he owns much property",[83] (rather than "in which *county* he owns much property"), and at least one reference to Wriothesley from Elizabethan times gives him the title of *Comes in Hampton*.[84]

I am not suggesting that the territorial designation in Thomas Wriothesley's title was necessarily understood by all of his contemporaries to be of the town of Southampton; to the contrary, I believe that most people of his time — and certainly most people of his grandson's time — if they thought about it at all, took it for granted that the honour was of the county of Southampton — i.e., Hampshire. What I am suggesting is that Thomas Wriothesley, who was more than casually acquainted with heraldic principles and facts, and who without doubt selected his own comital title, *knew* that he was the Earl of the *Town* of Southampton, and also knew that the Town's arms, with the colours reversed, served as the arms of the County in which he lived, and that this knowledge explains why he proclaimed and celebrated his associations with Southampton by causing to be chiseled on a doorway of his family residence the arms which blazon the family's honour (the town of Southampton), the family's residence (Southampton County), and the family's name (Rōse-ly).

But this does not exhaust the symbolism in the Titchfield arms: the roses with which they are charged are not merely the alternately red and white roses of the town or county of Southampton but are in addition the simultaneously red and white roses of the Tudors, thus overlaying all the other symbolism of the shield with this recognition of and hommage to the fount of Wriothesley's offices, properties and titles, Henry VIII.

Why the shield on the left spandrel at Titchfield is completely defaced, and why the shield on the right is only partially defaced are puzzling questions, but not beyond all profitable conjecture. A reasonable initial assumption is that the blazon on the now completely defaced left shield was the Wriothesley arms, and that it and the shield on the right, bearing the arms of the Town of Southampton, were displayed on either side of the doorway in the same manner as a person having arms of office might display both his own and his *ex officio* arms on two separate shields.[85]

However, the arms of the Town of Southampton were not the *ex officio* arms of the the Earl of Southampton. What little authority on the subject exists indicates that in the sixteenth century an Earl would not have had the right, by virtue of his title alone, to display as arms of office the arms of the locality whence he derived his honour. To be sure, in the nineteenth century, the Duke of Westminster displayed on a chief on his escutcheon the arms of the City of Westminster — but this was by virtue of an express grant made to Robert Grosvenor, who was created Marquis of Westminster at the coronation of William IV on 13 September 1831: "On this occasion the arms of the city of Westminster, a portcullis, with chains pendent, were granted to him as a coat of augmentation."[86]

Nor may any citizen of a town display its arms merely by virtue of his citizenship. While it is true that in 1954, the High Court of Chivalry (sitting for the first time in over 200 years), refused, upon application by the City of Manchester, to require a theatre to remove the city's arms displayed above the main curtain in the auditorium (one reason being that such a holding might make illegal the sale to American tourists of ash trays and similar objects unauthorizedly decorated with the coats of arms of Universities, Colleges, etc.), the court at the same time recognized that a decision 250 years earlier might have been different.[87] The fact is that a decision in the 16th century certainly would have been different, for, at least from 1530 on, Heralds regularly visited private homes and churches, to make sure that no person displayed on any "scochens squares or lozengis" any "cote of armes not havyng auctorite so to doo," which "false armorye," when found, the Heralds would "deface & take away wheresoever they besett . . . whether it be in stone wyndowes plate or any other maner of wyse sett. . . . "[88] The account of Thomas Hawley, then Carlisle Herald, of his visitation in 1530 to various churches in London, shows how ruthless were the heralds as, in the discharge of their duties, they examined the tombs and monuments of the dead, and again and again "defaced and tooke away dyverse Scochyns of Armes unlawfulley borne; and dyverse Scochynse wth markes and tokinse in them agen the Lauce of oner [against the laws of honour]."[89]

But we cannot be correct if we suppose that a scourging visit of the Heralds to Titchfield is the explanation for the defacement of the shields, because the shield which remains (albeit only partially) is the probably *improperly* displayed shield — the shield of the Town of Southampton — and it is this shield, rather than the (as I suppose) *properly* displayed shield of the Wriothesley family, which the heralds should have defaced.

Nor is it likely that the shields were defaced in the eighteenth century when Place House came into the possession of the Delmés, for if this family, on the ground that it had no right to display the Southampton (Earl) or the Southampton (Town) arms, had sought to effect their removal, then *both* shields would have been completely erased.

The most plausible explanation for the present condition of these two shields is that they were defaced when Place House, as well as all the rest of the property of the third Earl of Southampton, was forfeited to the crown as a consequence of the attainder automatically attendant upon Henry Wriothesley's conviction for High Treason in February 1600/01.[90] "[A] man forfeited his arms entirely by attainder. They were torn down from his banner of knighthood; they were erased in the records of the College of Arms. . . ."[91] It would be no surprise, therefore, if they were also chiseled off the wall. But the only arms which might properly thus be removed are those of the individual attainted. This, I believe, accounts for the survival of the one shield, and not the other: I surmise that the mason who had scraped the Wriothesley arms off the first shield automatically commenced to remove the arms from the second shield, but was arrested in this action by someone who realized that the shield with the Roses displayed the arms of the Town of Southampton, and therefore did not come within the ambit of the requirement of destruction by virtue of attainder.

At the end of the day, whether my conjectures as to the reasons for the existence, design and present condition of the shields in the spandrels at Titchfield be right or wrong, the fact is that carved in stone in the home of Henry Wriothesley is a coat of arms bearing roses which, before the paint wore off, were both red and white, on backgrounds which were alternately white and red.[92] This coat of arms, like all coats of arms, is the symbol by which its bearer is to be known, and its presence in the Wriothesley manor enables us to decipher the rose imagery of the Sonnets. The spandrel at Titchfield with its carved glyph is literally a Rosetta stone, which by its juxtaposition of rebus and situs — the Rōse-ly cartouche in the Wriothesley home — reveals the identity of "thou, my Rose." Henry Wriothesley: he whose name sounded of roses, he whose honour was of a town which had roses in its coat of arms, he who lived in and was identified with a county having a rose for its badge, he whose principal home displayed roses in heraldic shields, he of the "budding name" whose dearness to Shakespeare is expressly proclaimed in the dedications of *Venus and Adonis* and *Lucrece* — in fine, he whose Rose was true: Henry Wriothesley is the Rose of the Sonnets.

CHAPTER III

The Rose of the World

Thou rose of the world!
Thou rose of all the roses!

Tennyson[1]

Having shown in the preceding chapter that Henry Wriothesley is the Fair Friend — the Rose — of the Sonnets, I shall in this chapter show that Henry Wriothesly is more than the Rose merely of the Sonnets, and that Rose imagery inspired by, and laudatory of, this youth permeates Shakespeare's early poems and plays.

At the outset, however, a brief consideration of exactly what kind of rose is here involved might be appropriate. The Tudor rose, which was created to symbolize the union in 1485 of the red rose of Lancaster with the white rose of York, and which appears in the shield at Titchfield, is a heraldic rose, existing on escutcheons, but not in nature; the only roses actually growing in England in the fifteenth century (and available to be plucked in the Temple Garden) were either all red or all white. (Pliny wrote that the Romans named England Albion because of the white roses they found there.[2]) In France at some time in the middle ages appeared a variegated red and white rose, upon which was bestowed the name Rosa mundi — Rose of the world — "because it united the rose colours of the world, i.e., red and white, given that white meant anything from pure white to pale pink or gold, in its striped petals."[3] But this rose seems not to have been well known even in France, and was not in general cultivation until the 16th century.[4]

At about the same time, another variegated red and white rose, called the Damask rose because of its supposed provenance, was introduced into England, reputedly by Thomas Linacre, the renowned classical scholar and physician to Henry VII and Henry VIII.[5] This rose differs from the Rosa mundi, according to modern authorities, in that "it is not so much striped as white with an occasional blush-pink blotch."[6] The purchase by the Royal Household, in 1546 (for six shillings eight pence) of one thousand slips of Damask roses,[7] convincingly shows that the Damask rose, with its discrete white and red elements intermingled, was officially deemed in 16th century England to be the closest approximation in nature to the heraldic Tudor Rose. And Shakespeare's references to the "mingled damask" (*As You Like It*, III, v, 123) and "Roses damaskt, red and white" (Sonnet 130), indicate that to Shakespeare, too, the Damask rose consisted of mingled, but discrete, red and white colours,[8] and thus was the Rose in nature nearest to the *sub rosa* Wriothesley emblem.

Henry Wriothesley's beauty, as emblematized by this heraldic Rose, is the model of the beauty of the protagonists of *Venus and Adonis* and *The Rape of Lucrece*, the two poems expressly dedicated by Shakespeare to Henry Wriothesley: for unmistakably stamped upon the faces and bodies of Adonis, Venus and Lucrece are the Roses which, like the Roses above Wriothesley's door, are of mingled or alternating red and white.

In *Venus and Adonis*, no sooner has the first stanza set forth the plot — that Venus loves Adonis, but Adonis prefers venery (hunting) to venery (lovemaking) — than does the second stanza, where Venus 'gins to woo "Rose cheekt Adonis," establish that Adonis and Wriothesley are one: for Venus' description of Adonis' beauty is nothing more than a blazoning of the Wriothesley emblem:

> Thrise fairer than myself, (thus she began)
> The fields chiefe flower, sweet above compare,
> Staine to all Nimphs, more lovely than a man,
> More white, and red, than doves, or roses, are:
> > Nature that made thee with her selfe at strife,
> > Saith that the world hath ending with thy life.
>
> [Lines 7-12.]

"The fields chiefe flower, . . . more white, and red, than doves, or roses, are": no substantial difference exists between the arms of Southampton and the person of Adonis. "Field" is more than a green meadow: it is also "the surface of an escutcheon or shield on which the 'charge' is displayed".[9] The "charge," in turn, is the "figure or figures disposed upon the field which together with that make up the coat of arms."[10] The "charge" displayed on this field is its "chiefe flower," that being the term used both by poets and heralds to describe the rose. In verses composed for Anne Boleyn's coronation in 1533, Nicholas Udall had praised "the Rose, chiefe flour that euer was,"[11] and Gerard Legh, in *The Accedence of Armorie*, first published in 1562, and reprinted in 1568, 1576, 1591, 1597 and 1612, says of the rose that

This flower of al others is the beautifullest to beeholde, and of most comfortable smell. Plinie writeth that amongst all flowers of the world, the Rose is chiefest, and beareth the prise.[12]

So, to decribe Adonis as "the field's chief flower," was really to blazon him as a rose — or, more accurately, as *the* Rose. The colour of the rose is expressly stated: white and red — "more *white*, and *red*, than *doves*, or *roses*, are" — an unmistakable reference not only to Wriothesley's arrogated Town of Southampton coat of arms, with its white and red roses, but also to the rightful coat of arms of the Wriothesley family, undoubtedly understood by the Wriothesleys and by Shakespeare to depict four doves, in allusion to the profession of the founder of the family.

The red and white theme so prominently introduced at the beginning of *Venus and Adonis* appears, with variation, throughout the poem: Venus will smother Adonis with kisses, making his lips "red, and pale, with fresh varietie" (line 21); shortly thereafter, she is

> red, and hot, as coles of glowing fier,
> He red for shame, but frostie in desier.
>
> [Lines 35-36.]

Later, still she entreats, but

> Still is he sullein, still he lowres and frets,
> Twixt crimson shame, and anger ashie pale,
> Being red she loves him best, and being white,
> Her best is betterd with a more delight.
>
> [Lines 75-78.]

She perseveres:

> O what a sight it was wistly to view,
> How she came stealing to the wayward boy,
> To note the fighting conflict of her hew,
> How white and red, ech other did destroy:
> But now her cheeke was pale, and by and by
> It flasht forth fire, as lightning from the skie.
>
> [Lines 343-348.]

She faints:

> The sillie boy beleeving she is dead,
> Claps her pale cheeke, till clapping makes it red.
>
> [Lines 467-468.]

Adonis tells Venus of his plan to hunt the boar,

> whereat a suddain pale,
> Like lawne being spread upon the blushing rose,
> Usurps her cheeke, she trembles at his tale.

[Lines 588-590.]

The boar comes on the scene,

> Whose frothie mouth bepainted all with red,
> Like milke, & blood, being mingled both togither,
> A second feare through all her sinews spred.

[Lines 900-902.]

The boar wounds Adonis; Venus sees

> the wide wound, that the boare had trencht
> In his soft flanke, whose wonted lillie white
> With purple tears that his wound wept, had drēcht.

[Lines 1052-1054.]

Many of these "red and white" images stress the alternation of colour between red and white; this is exemplified by lines 345 and 346 which describe the "conflict of her hew, /How white and red, ech other did destroy. . . ." It is not surprising, in view of the number and variety of "red and white" images in *Venus and Adonis*, that the first known reference to this poem, found by Leslie Hotson, describes it as having "much ado wth red & whyte. . . ."[13] This description appears in a letter by one William Reynolds to Queen Elizabeth; the top of the letter is endorsed "A Submission & Supplication to yᵉ Queen, of one Reynolds a distracted person."[14] If Reynolds was, as Hotson calls him, "an Elizabethan madman," he was at least a perceptive madman, and had the acumen to draw attention to a Shakespearean obsession with red and white which most readers do on some level notice, but think unworthy of comment.

The most striking of the poem's red and white images occurs near the end: after the fair youth dies, his body

> Was melted like a vapour from her sight,
> And in his blood that on the ground laie spild,
> A purple floure sproong up, checkred with white,

> Resembling well his pale cheekes, and the blood,
> Which in round drops, upon their whitenesse stood.
>
> [Lines 1165-1170.]

The youth who at the beginning of the poem was figuratively a rose ("the fields chiefe flower"), "more white, and red, than doves, or roses, are," at the end of the poem becomes literally a white and red flower. The reason for this is obvious: the symbol of the real live youth of this poem, carved in stone over a doorway of his manor, is white and red roses.

This doorway with its two coats of arms may be more profoundly connected with *Venus and Adonis* than I have so far suggested. One coat of arms, as we know, bears the roses of Southampton; the other coat of arms is now blank, but, for the reasons stated in the preceding chapter, can confidently be assumed to have at one time borne the four doves of the Wriothesleys. This brings us to a curious circumstance: roses, the most prominent feature of the Southampton coat of arms, and doves, the most prominent feature of the Wriothesley coat of arms, are, as every Renaissance poet knew, peculiarly associated with, and dedicated to, Venus. Many prose statements and poetic examples of the association of Venus with doves and roses could be cited, but the best and clearest of both are in this poem by Thomas Watson, from his *Hekatompathia*, published in 1582:

The chiefe grounde and matter of this Sonnet standeth uppon the rehearsall of such thinges as by reporte of the Poets, are dedicated unto Venus, whereof the Authour sometime wrote these three Latine verses.

> *Mons Erycinus, Acidalius sons, alba columba,*
> *Hesperus, ora Pathos, Rosa, Myrtus, et insula Cyprus,*
> *Idaliumque nemus; Veneri haec sunt omnia sacra.*

And *Forcatulus* the French Poet wrote upon the same particulars, but more at large, he beginneth thus,

> *Est arbor Veneri Myrtus gratissima, flores*
> *Tam Rosa, quam volucres alba columba praeit.*
> *Igniferum coeli prae cunctis diligit astris*
> *Hesperon, Idalium saepe adit una nemus, etc.*

> Sweete *Venus* if as nowe thou stand my friende,
> As once thou didst unto Kinge *Priams* sonne,
> My ioyfull muse shall never make an end
> Of praising thee, and all that thou hast done:
>   Nor this my penne shall ever cease to write
>   Of ought, wherein sweete *Venus* takes delite.

> My temples hedged in with *Myrtle* bowes
> Shall set aside *Apolloes Lawrell* tree,
> As did *Anchises* sonne, when both his browes
> With *Myrtle* hee beset, to honour thee:
>> Then will I say, the *Rose* of flowers is best.
>> And silver *Dooves* for birdes excell the rest.
> I'll praise no starre but Hesperus alone,
> Nor any hill but *Erycinus* mounte,
> Nor any woodde but *Idaly* alone,
> Nor any spring but *Acidalian* founte,
>> Nor any land but onely *Cyprus* shoare,
>> Nor Gods but Love, and what would *Venus* more?[15]

Thus by an astonishing coincidence, the roses and doves which from antiquity were associated with Venus were also from a more recent era and for entirely unrelated reasons associated with Henry Wriothesley. Shakespeare could not be the person his writings show him to be, if the confluence of the symbols and signs of Venus with those of Henry Wriothesley had not a powerful impact upon his imagination. Inevitably, after meeting and being smitten by Henry Wriothesley, Shakespeare would have written *some* poem in his honour; it seems to me likely to the point of certainty that the territorial markings of Venus on either side of the doorway at Titchfield not merely inspired, but *demanded*, the particular poem which in due course was written, equating the beautiful youth who lived there and whom he loved with the beautiful youth whom Venus had loved.[16] And just as Venus made of the dead Adonis she loved a flower, to be remembered "whyle the world doth last,"[17] so Shakespeare made of the mortal Wriothesley he loved a flower who

>> hence immortall life shall have. . . .
> And toungs to be, your beeing shall rehearse,
> When all the breathers of this world are dead,
>> You still shall live (such vertue hath my Pen)
>> Where breath most breaths, even in the mouths of men.
>> [Sonnet 81.]

The red and white flower which was Wriothesley, and which is blazoned throughout *Venus and Adonis*, is even more in evidence in *The Rape of Lucrece*. In *Lucrece*, as in *Venus and Adonis*, red and white are early established as the colours of the protagonist's beautiful complexion. In the second stanza of *The Rape of Lucrece*, the heroine's boastful husband

43

unwisely did not let,
To praise the cleare unmatched red and white,
Which triumpht in that skie of his delight. . . .

[Lines 10-12.]

This praise causes Sextus Tarquinius to become "enflamed with Lucrece beauty"; post haste, and with the basest of intentions, he hies him to her house, where he is made welcome by the unsuspecting noblewoman:

When at Colatium this false lord arived,
Well was he welcom'd by the Romaine dame,
Within whose face Beautie and Vertue strived,
Which of them both should underprop her fame.
When Vertue brag'd, Beautie wold blush for shame,
When Beautie bosted blushes, in despight
Vertue would staine that ore with silver white.

But Beautie in that white entituled,
From Venus doves doth challenge that faire field,
Then Vertue claimes from Beautie Beauties red,
Which Vertue gave the golden age, to guild
Their silver cheekes, and cald it then their shield,
Teaching them thus to use it in the fight,
When shame assaild, the red should fence the white.

This Herauldry in LUCRECE face was seen,
Argued by Beauties red and Vertue's white,
Of eithers colour was the other Queene:
Proving from worlds minority their right,
Yet their ambition makes them still to fight:
The soveraignty of either being so great,
That oft they interchange ech others seat.

This silent warre of Lillies and of Roses,
Which TARQUIN view'd in her fair faces field,
In their pure rankes his traytor eye encloses,
Where least betweene them both it shoud be kild.
The coward captive vanquished, doth yeeld
To those two Armies that would let him goe,
Rather then triumph in so false a foe.

[Lines 50-77.]

The description of the face of Adonis in the earlier poem becomes the description of the face of Lucrece in the later poem: his beautiful face was more white, and red, than doves, or roses are; her face displayed beauty's red and virtue's white, with a few additional splashes of white added by Venus' doves. Her face is called both a field and a shield — a shield where red and white again alternate with each other, even as they did in *Venus and Adonis*. The alternation of "Beauties red and Vertues white," the "silent warre of Lillies and of Roses": these constitute the "Herauldry in LUCRECE face." This curious coat of arms, in which the red and white colors were of equal dignity, and thus capable of changing places,

> The soveraignty of either being so great,
> That oft they interchange ech others seat,

is obviously in concept and reification identical to the one coat of arms shared by the Town of Southampton and the County of Southampton, the only difference between the two Southampton coats being that the red and white colours of the one are the reverse of the white and red colours of the other:

> The soveraignty of either being so great,
> That oft they interchange ech others seat [!]

These two lines, otherwise incomprehensible, are crystal clear when read in the light of the Southampton arms: the face of Lucrece, like the person of Adonis, blazons the badge of Wriothesley.

Indeed, all of the allusions in *Venus and Adonis* and *The Rape of Lucrece* to fields, shields and heraldry, to doves and roses, and to red and white intermingled and alternating, become meaningful only when illuminated by the Wriothesley name and the blazons of both the proper and appropriated coats of arms of the Wriothesleys,[18] which name and blazons explain not only why Shakespeare's principal metaphor for his patron, as for Adonis and Lucrece, who are surrogate Wriothesleys, was a Rose, but also why that Rose, when a colour is ascribed to it, is always a Rose both red and white.[19]

Just as the Rose's patronymic (both cantingly and as heraldically depicted on the family's Rose badges) is the inspiration for the metaphor which is his peculiar designation in the Sonnets and poems, so, there can be little doubt, is the Rose's matronymic the inspiration for the magnificent play in which he is actually represented. For Henry Wriothesley's mother, Mary Browne, was a Montagu: she was the daughter of Anthony Browne, the first Viscount Montagu. This Anthony Browne, a loyal adherent to the old religion during the perilous reigns of Henry VIII and Edward VI, had for his steadfastness been rewarded by Philip and Mary who, at a ceremony held at Hampton Court on 2 September 1554, conferred upon him the title of Viscount Montagu[20] — a title allusive to the fact that, as shown on the facing page in genealogical Table III, his grandmother, Lady Lucy Neville, was the daughter of John Neville, Marquess of Montagu. On the west side of the Wriothesley tomb, near the head of the sculptured effigy of the third Earl of South-ampton's father, are three coats of arms. The coat on the viewer's right is that of the first Earl of Southampton, showing 6 quarterings; in the middle is the achievement of the second Earl, showing the Wriothesley arms (this time with eight quarterings), crest, supporters and family motto, "*Une par tout.*" Both of these coats are shown in Plate VIII. The third coat, and the one of most significance, is again that of the second Earl, this time showing Wriothesley impaled by Montagu. Unfortunately, because of a stolen camera (something one does not expect in England), I do not have a good photograph of this coat of arms; however, reproduced as Figure 5, on page 48, is a useful sketch[21] of this coat, identifying each of its many quarterings. The third Earl's being, on his mother's side, a Montagu, is the reagent which combined with Shake-speare's genius to precipitate *Romeo and Juliet.*

The story of the ill-fated love of Romeo and Juliet is not, of course, Shakespeare's invention; it had been well known in England ever since the publication of poetic versions of the story, based upon Italian and French sources, by Arthur Brooke in 1562 (*The Tragicall Historye of Romeus and Juliet*) and William Painter in 1567 (*The Palace of Pleasure*).[22] Nor is even the identification of the Montagus of Italy with those of England an invention of Shakespeare, for George Gascoigne had already expressly made this equation in the mask he wrote for the marriage in 1572 of two of Viscount Montagu's children, Anthony and Elizabeth (the brother and half-sister of Henry Wriothesley's mother[23]) to Mary and Robert, children of Sir William Dormer.

In his introductory comments to the mask, Gascoigne explains the reason for his devising an intimate (and, needless to say, completely fictional) connection between the English and Italian Montagus: he was requested to prepare the mask by eight gentlemen, "all of blood or alliaunce to the sayd L. Mountacute," who planned to present at the Montagu–Dormer wedding an entertainment while wearing some elaborate Venetian style clothing which they had had made for themselves. But after thinking about it a bit, the eight gentlemen concluded that "it would seeme somewhat obscure to have Vene-tians presented" rather than Englishmen:

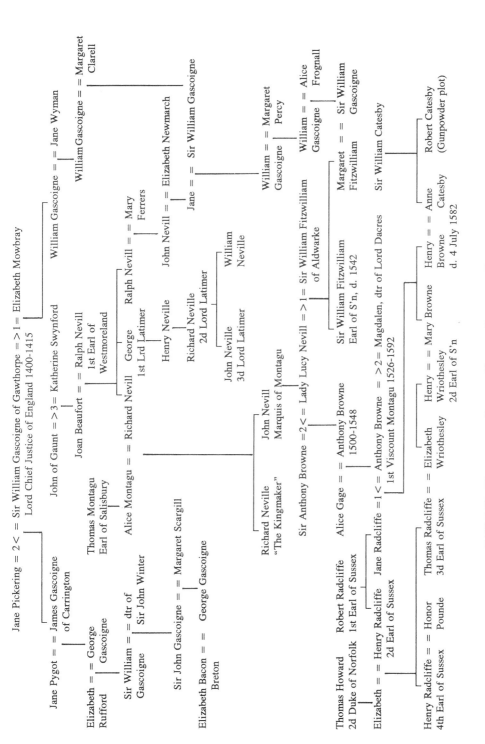

TABLE III - WRIOTHESLEY, BROWNE, NEVILLE, RADCLIFFE, GASCOIGNE

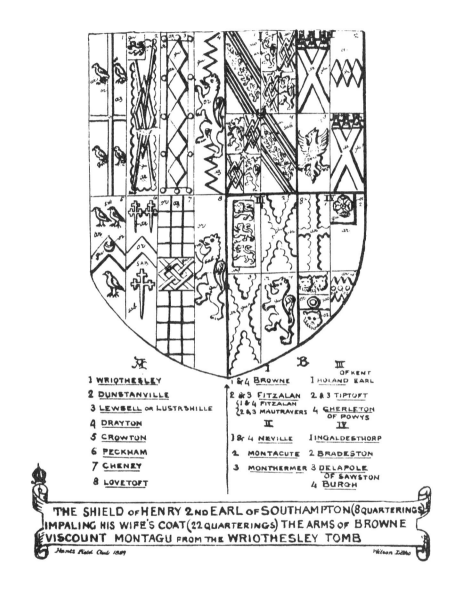

THE SHIELD of HENRY 2ND EARL of SOUTHAMPTON(8 QUARTERINGS) IMPALING HIS WIFE'S COAT(22 QUARTERINGS) THE ARMS of BROWNE VISCOUNT MONTAGU FROM THE WRIOTHESLEY TOMB

Figure 5. Arms of Wriothesley impaled by those of Montagu.

48

Whereupon they entreated the Aucthour to devise some verses to bee uttered by an Actor wherein might be some discourse to render a good cause of the Venetians presence. The Aucthour calling to minde that there is a noble house of the Mountacutes in Italie, and therwithall that the L. Mountacute here doth quarter the coate of an auncient English Gentleman called Mounthermer, and hath the inheritaunce of the sayde house, dyd threupon devise to bring in a Boye of the age of twelve or .xiii. yeeres, who should faine that he was a Mounthermer by the fathers side, and a Mountacute by the mothers side, and that his father being slaine at the last warres against the Turke, and he there taken, hee was recovered by the Venetians in their last victorie, and with them sayling towardes Venice, they were driven by tempest upon these coastes, and so came to the marriage. . . .[24]

It is likely (assuming Gascoigne's explanation to be true) that the friends of Viscount Montagu who asked Gascoigne to write an entertainment with a Venetian setting were aware that this might be especially gratifying to the Viscount because of his pleasant memories of a visit to Venice eighteen years earlier. In February, 1555, Viscount Montagu, along with Thomas Thirlby and Edward Carne, had been sent by Queen Mary as an ambassador to Rome to "make her obedience to the Pope," who was then Julius III.[25] During the ambassadors' journey to Rome, Pope Julius died, and was succeeded by Pope Marcellus, who shortly thereafter also died. Browne and the other ambassadors, with a train of 140 horse of their own attendants, arrived in Rome on 23 May 1555, on which day Paul IV succeeded to the papacy. Procedural and diplomatic problems delayed the audience with the new Pope until 23 June.[26] At this audience, Pope Paul demanded among other things that the monasteries and other Church lands acquired by Henry VIII be returned to Church ownership, a demand which Viscount Montagu found difficult to support, for, Catholic although he was, much of his estate consisted of abbey lands acquired by his father upon the dissolution of the monasteries.[27] A few days after this ultimately nonproductive meeting with the Pope, Viscount Montagu was in Venice, where on 28 June 1555 the Venetian Council of Ten accorded him the honour of viewing its armoury halls, and the jewels of its Sanctuary.[28] He probably left Venice before 21 July 1555, on which date Sir John Masone in Brussels transmitted to London "a letter from the English Ambassador at Venice, which will probably declare at good length the great honour and courtesy shown by that state to Lord Montacute."[29] Perhaps some of the Venetian clothing used by the players in Gascoigne's mask had actually been purchased in Venice by Viscount Montagu himself.[30]

The mask begins with the storm-tossed "Boye," apparelled in his glittering golden Venetian clothes, justifying his presence as the chief presenter:

What wõder you my Lords? why gaze you gentlemen?
And wherefore marvaile you *Mez Dames*, I praye you tell mee
then?
Is it so rare a sight, or yet so straunge a toye,
Amongst so many nooble peeres, to see one *Pouer Boye*?
Why? boyes have been allowed in everye kind of age,
As *Ganymede* that pretye boye, in Heaven is *Jove* his page.
Cupid that mighty God although his force be fearse,
Yet is he but a naked Boye, as Poets doe rehearse.
And many a preetye boye a mightye man hath proved,
And served his Prince at all assayes deserving to bee loved.[31]

The boy tells us who he is:

Fyrst then you must perstande, I am no straunger I,
But English boye, in England borne, and bred but even hereby.
My father was a Knight, *Mount Hermer* was his name,
My mother of the *Mountacutes*, a house of worthy fame.[32]

The boy then narrates the story summarized by Gascoigne in his prefatory remarks. Captured by the Turks, he is eventually liberated by some Venetians, to whom he tells his father's name,

and howe I dyd descende,
From *Mountacutes* by Mothers side. . . .
This grave *Venetian* who heard the famous name,
Of *Montacutes* rehersed there, which long had bene of fame
In *Italy*, and he of selfe same worthy race,
Gan straight with many curteous words, in arms me to imbrace.
Any kyssed me on cheeke, and bad me make good cheere,
And thank the mighty hand of God, for that which hapned there,
Confessing that he was him selfe a *Montacute*,
And bare the selfe same armes that I dyd quarter in my scute:
And for a further proofe, he shewed in his hat,
This token which the *Mountacutes* dyd beare alwaies, for that
They covet to be knowne from *Capels* where they passe,
For auncient grutch which lõg ago, twene these two houses was.[33]

The young English Montagu is by his Italian relatives richly apparelled in Venetian dress, including the distinctive Montagu token in his cap, because, as a marginal note takes pains to explain again, "the Montacutes and capels in Italye do were [wear] tokens in their cappes to be knowen one from

50

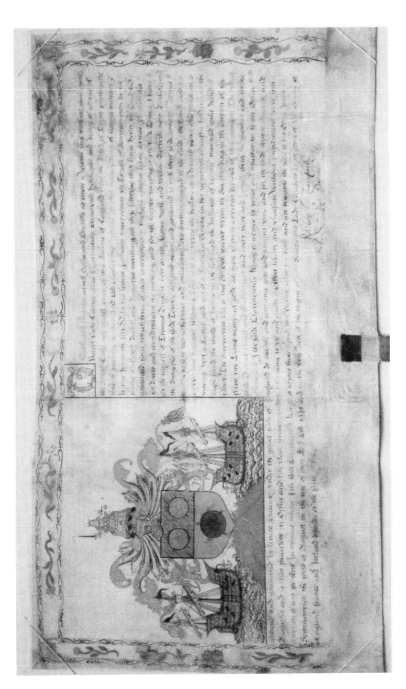

Grant of Crest and Supporters to the Town of Southampton,
4 August 1575 (Southampton Record Office).

Plate I

A. Place House, Main Entrance (South front).

B. Interior of Place House, looking toward East Wall.

Plate II

B. Detail of shield with roses on stone doorway, Place House (viewer's right).

Plate III

A. Stone doorway in East Wall, Place House.

← A. Tudor Rose on Round Table, Winchester Castle

B. Blank shield on stone doorway (viewer's left).
↓

Plate IV

A. Spandrel on stone doorway (viewer's right).

B. Another detail of shield with roses, Place House (viewer's right).

Plate V

B. Henry Wriothesley in Tower of London
(In the collection of The Duke of Buccleuch and
Queensberry, K.T., at Boughton House,
Kettering, England).

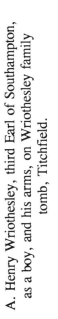

A. Henry Wriothesley, third Earl of Southampton,
as a boy, and his arms, on Wriothesley family
tomb, Titchfield.

Plate VI

Thomas Wriothesley, first Earl of Southampton
(In the Collection of Lord Montagu
at Palace House, Beaulieu, Brockenhurst, England).

Plate VII

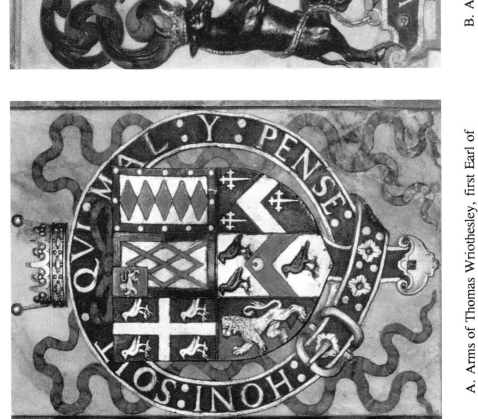

A. Arms of Thomas Wriothesley, first Earl of Southampton, Wriothesley family tomb, Titchfield.

B. Achievement of Henry Wriothesley, second Earl of Southampton, Wriothesley family tomb, Titchfield.

Plate VIII

another."[34] Blown off their course on their way back to Venice from Turkey, the boy and his Venetian relatives land in England (a most remarkable storm), just in time to appear at the wedding and present their mask.

The Venetian presence being thus explained, the boy actor takes by the hand Master Thomas Browne, another one of Viscount Montagu's children, and brings him to the Venetians, with these words:

> *Guardate Signori* my lovely Lords behold,
> This is another *Mountacute*, hereof you may bee bold.
> Of such our patrone here, *The viscont Mountacute*,
> Hath many comely sequences, well sorted all in sute.
> But as I spied him [i.e., Thomas] first, I could not let him passe,
> I took the carde that likt me best, in order as it was.
> And here to you my lords, I do present the same,
> Make much of him, I pray you then, *for he is of your name*
> > [empasis in last line supplied].[35]

The Venetians embrace their English cousin, this young Master Thomas Browne thus presented to them as being of their name, Montacute (and consequently, like them, necessarily an enemy of the Capels), and whisper into his ear their good wishes for the bridegrooms and brides, which young Thomas, in the short speech which closes the mask, conveys to his brother and sister, and all the assembled guests.

This mask was published in 1573 and again in 1575 as one of Gascoigne's *A hundreth sundrie Flowers*. This book was known to Shakespeare: Gascoigne's *The Supposes*, printed in both the 1573 and 1575 editions, is a major source for *The Taming of the Shrew*.[36] So in Gascoigne's mask, known to Shakespeare, we have a compelling precedent for associating the Montagus of England generally with the Montagus of Italy; from this to associating one specific English Montagu, the grandson of the first Viscount Montagu, with the most famous of all the Italian Montagus ("One Romeus, who was of race a Montague"[37]), was for Shakespeare but a small, and logical, step.

That *Romeo and Juliet* was the product of the same passionate impulse which produced the Sonnets, *Venus and Adonis*, and *The Rape of Lucrece*, and that it was written at the same time as these works, most critics agree.[38] This is indicated not only by the general spirit of the play, but also by the frequent use of the sonnet form in *Romeo and Juliet*.[39] A date frequently assigned to the play is 1591, on the basis of the Nurse's allusion to an earthquake eleven years earlier, there having been an earthquake in England in 1580.[40] This would seem to be not too firm a basis upon which to date the play, but there is a circumstance which lends credence to this date. From 15 August to 21 August 1591, Queen Elizabeth on one of her royal progresses was at the residence of Viscount Montagu at Cowdray, in Sussex, and on 2 and 3 September, she was at the residence of Lord Montagu's daughter and grandson at Titchfield, in Southamptonshire. We have a fairly complete account of the entertainments arranged for her at Cowdray;[41] no plays were among them. We have no record of the entertainments offered the Queen at Titchfield, but it is not inconceivable that *Romeo and Juliet*, celebrating the Earl of Southampton and (by the poetic license first exercised by George Gascoigne) his maternal ancestors from whose seat at Cowdray the Queen had just arrived, was written especially for the Queen's visit, and received its first presentation before her in the Earl's home at Titchfield, in September, 1591. Nor is it inconceivable that Henry Wriothesley, who was then seventeen years old, himself played the part of Romeo, for his paternal grandfather, also at about the age of seventeen, had played, as a student at Cambridge, at least one long and difficult part,[42] and the talent could have been inherited. Henry's maternal grandfather, the first Viscount Montagu, might well have accompanied the Queen on her progress from Cowdray to Titchfield, and there seen this play, the ultimate and improbable fruit of his long-ago visit to Italy.

Again, I emphasize that the literary relationship between the Italian and English Montagu families is not something conjectural, or which need be hypothesized, but is a relationship which was firmly established by Gascoigne who, as is shown on Table III on page 47, was distantly related by marriage to the Viscount Montagu (and may also have been the brother-in-law of the first Earl of Southampton, and thus an uncle by marriage to the second Earl of Southampton[43]). Gascoigne's poem repeatedly stresses that the Montagus of England and the Montagus of Italy are of the same family, those of Venice bearing "the selfe same arms that I dyd quarter in my scute." The poem also stresses that the boy's kinship to the reknowned Montagu family of Italy is through his mother: a politic observation, for the Brownes, too, derived their connection to the Montagus through Lady Lucille Nevill, the daughter of John Nevill, Marquess of Montagu. Lady Nevill's second husband was Sir Anthony Browne, the grandfather of the first Viscount Montagu.

Now, if Thomas Browne, the son of the first Viscount Montagu, is, as the boy in the mask states, "another Montacute," then so is his sister Mary — and this relationship the masker expressly affirms, for after identifying Thomas Browne as "another Montacute," he notes that "The viscont Montacute, Hath many comely sequences, well sorted all in sute." And, if the boy in the mask can be a Montagu "by Mothers side," then Mary's son, Henry Wriothesley, the third Earl of Southampton, can also be (as indeed he was) a Montagu "by mothers side." Without doubt, all who knew that Southampton was a Montagu (which included at least every one at court) knew also that the play was a tribute to him.

But even in this play, born of the fact that Wriothesley happens to be a Montagu, the fact that above all he is a Rose is not forgotten; it vivifies one of the most famous scenes that Shakespeare wrote, and is the occasion for some of the best-known lines in world literature. This is, of course, the balcony scene, where Juliet bemoans the fact that she loves a man whose name makes him the enemy of her family:

> O Romeo, Romeo! wherefore art thou Romeo?
> Deny thy father and refuse thy name;
> Or if thou wilt not, be but sworn my love,
> And I'll no longer be a Capulet. . . .
> 'Tis but thy name that is my enemy;
> Thou art thyself, though not a Montague.
> What's Montague? It is not hand, nor foot,
> Nor arm, nor face, nor any other part
> Belonging to a man. O, be some other name!
> What's in a name? That which we call a Rose
> By any other word would smell as sweet;
> So Romeo would, were he not Romeo call'd,
> Retain that dear perfection which he owes
> Without that title.
>
> [II,ii,33–36; 38–47.]

The assertion, "That which we call a Rose/ By any other word would smell as sweet," is, I am confident, a loving and not too cryptic message to the Rose of the Sonnets, represented here not as a Wriothesley but as a Montagu, telling him something like "Even if your name really were Montagu, or anything else instead of Wriothesley, you would still have all the rose-like qualities which I have ascribed to you on the basis of the accident of your name's sounding like a Rose." (In the modern edition from which the above quotation is taken, the word "Rose" is not capitalized; however, it is capitalized in the first quarto and in the First Folio, and so, the better to make my point — and, I hope I may truly say, Shakespeare's point — I have capitalized it here.) Exactly what this line may mean, vis-à-vis Southampton, is not too important; what is significant is that in the great love declaration in this play, addressed to a Montagu who is also a Wriothesley, the comparison of him to a Rose irresistibly, inevitably, appears.

Although I have stated that the reference to Romeo as a Rose was a not too cryptic affirmation of Shakespeare's love and admiration for Henry Wriothesley, it was from the point of view of Romeo/Wriothesley (and his friends) that I was gauging the degree of obscurity in that particular line. To "the general," the message probably was not all that clear. For whatever may have been the practice of the first Earl of Southampton, the third Earl of Southampton does not appear ever to have identified himself in public with the arms of the town of Southampton, nor, so far as I can discover, was either Earl's display in his home of the town's arms a matter of public knowledge or comment. Thus, only a person who had actually been in the family home and there seen the heraldic shield with the arms of the town of Southampton upon it would associate the third Earl with the red and white roses of the town of Southampton. For this reason, I think we may safely deduce, in light of the clear allusions to the arms of Southampton in *Venus and Adonis* and *The Rape of Lucrece*, that Shakespeare at some time prior to writing those poems had been in Place House, had seen the Southampton arms, and had come to associate the red and white roses of those arms with the beautiful youth who lived there.[44]

I think we may also infer that a number of the Sonnets were written before Shakespeare composed *Venus and Adonis*. In Sonnet 53, Shakespeare states,

> Describe *Adonis* and the counterfet,
> Is poorely immitated after you. . . .

Under any circumstances, this, of course, is a compliment. But the observation that Adonis is only a pale imitation of Henry Wriothesley is not one likely to have been made by someone who had composed a poem extravagantly extolling Adonis' beauty, and who, by endowing Adonis with all of Henry Wriothesley's heraldic attributes, implicitly also attributed to him Henry Wriothesley's personal qualities. For this reason, I believe that Sonnet 53 (and doubtless many other Sonnets, including the procreation series) preceded the composition of *Venus and Adonis*.

But after the composition of *Venus and Adonis*, something happened, and Shakespeare, who had previously employed "red and white" only to represent beauty and virtue, now detected other qualities in those hues. An early example of this occurs near the end of *The Rape of Lucrece*, where Lucrece looks at a painting of "perjur'd Sinon," who was depicted as having

> Cheeks neither red nor pale, but mingled so
> That blushing red no guilty instance gave,
> Nor ashy pale the fears that false hearts have.
>
> [Lines 1510-1512.]

Here, the red and white complexion praised throughout *Venus and Adonis* and at the beginning of *Lucrece*, is suddenly and unexpectedly depicted as a mask for deceit: the red disguises the guilty blushes that might otherwise betray duplicity; the white disguises the pallor of fear that might otherwise betray iniquity.

Obviously, there is, if not an inconsistency, at least a tension, between "red and white" as an insignia of beauty, on the one hand, and a facade for treachery, on the other. When Armado, in *Love's Labour's Lost* (generally considered to have been written at about the same time as *Lucrece*[45]) praises his beloved's red and white beauty, Moth brings to his attention the possibility of his beloved's red and white duplicity:

Armado. My love is most immaculate white and red.
Moth.   Most maculate thoughts, master, are mask'd under such colours.
Armado. Define, define, well-educated infant.
Moth.   My father's wit and my mother's tongue, assist me!
Armado. Sweet invocation of a child; most pretty and pathetical.
Moth.   If she be made of white and red,
         Her faults will ne'er be known,
         For blushing cheeks by faults are bred
         And fears by pale white shown.
         Then if she fear, or be to blame,
         By this you shall not know
         For still her cheeks possess the same
         Which native she doth owe.
         A dangerous rhyme, master, against the reason of white and red.

[I,ii,89–105.]

The *reason* of white and red is beauty; the dangerous rhyme against it is the suggestion that white and red may conceal faults, fears, and blame, or, more to the point, infidelity. Why does Shakespeare now entertain this possibility, and impute dissimulation to those very features which earlier had seemed to him to be the quintessence of truth and beauty?

Sonnets 98 and 99 tell us what happened, if we understand that the story there related about Roses is really about The Rose:

Sonnet 98

From you have I beene absent in the spring,
When proud pide Aprill (drest in all his trim)
Hath put a spirit of youth in every thing:
That heavie *Saturne* laught and leapt with him.
Yet nor the laies of birds, nor the sweet smell
Of different flowers in odor and hew,
Could make me any summers story tell:
Or from their proud lap pluck them where they grew:
Nor did I wonder at the Lillies white,
Nor praise the deepe vermillion in the Rose,
They weare but sweet, but figures of delight:
Drawne after you, you patterne of all those.
    Yet seem'd it Winter still, and you away,
    As with your shaddow I with these did play.

Sonnet 99

The forward violet thus did I chide,
Sweet theefe whence did thou steale thy sweet that smels
If not from my loves breath, the purple pride,
Which on thy soft cheeke for complexion dwells?
In my loves veines thou hast too grosely died,
The Lillie I condemned for thy hand,
And buds of marjerom had stolne thy haire,
The Roses fearefully on thornes did stand,
One blushing shame, an other white dispaire:
A third nor red, nor white, had stolne of both,
And to his robbry had annext thy breath,
But for his theft in pride of all his growth
A vengful canker eate him up to death.
    More flowers I noted, yet I none could see,
    But sweet, or culler it had stolne from thee.

Sonnet 98 sets the stage for Sonnet 99 by explaining that once in a spring made joyless by the absence of the Friend, the poet addressed the burgeoning flowers, which, after all, were modelled after the Friend (who was the pattern for the "Lillies white" and the "deepe vermillion in the Rose"), as though they actually were the Friend: "As with your shaddow I with these did play." (Shakespeare not infrequently uses the word "shadow" to designate the symbolic representation of a thing, as in "'Tis but the shadow of a wife you see,/ The name and not the thing." [*All's Well That Ends Well*, V,iii,308].)

Then begins Sonnet 99, which is unique among the Sonnets not only in having fifteen, rather than fourteen lines, but also in the low esteem in which it is held. Critics have dismissed it as "rubbish," "the poorest [Sonnet] in the entire collection," and a "mechanical and tiresome piece of ingenuity."[46] Whatever its literary merit, however, it is one of the most significant of all the poems. The first seven lines, to be sure, seem to justify the criticism: Shakespeare addresses a violet, a lily, and "buds of marjerom," calling them thieves for having stolen their perfume, complexion and hair from the beloved friend. But in response to these seemingly playful accusations of theft,

> The Roses fearefully on thornes did stand,
> One blushing shame, an other white dispaire.

The changes, both in complexion and in tone, are ominous. Moth has already explained to us the significance of the change in complexion:

> . . . blushing cheeks by faults are bred
> And fears by pale white shown.

So we know the reason for the changes in tone and complexion: the Roses stand fearfully on thorns because they are apprehensive that the seemingly casual and complimentary allegory about the flowers' thefts of beauty and graces may reveal the poet's awareness of the theft of virtue. "Theft" or "robbery" were words used by Shakespeare to signify the sexual taking of someone who "belongs" to someone else; in Sonnet 40, after he knows that the Fair Youth and the Dark Woman have each deceived him with the other, he writes to the youth:

> I doe forgive thy robb'rie gentle theef
> Although thou steale thee all my poverty. . . .

The Rose blushing shame — a red Rose, obviously, which by its blushing reveals its "fault" — is undoubtedly the Dark Lady, and the other Rose, the Rose of white despair, is the floral equivalent of the poet himself, the fear which his pale white discloses being that the other roses, in reacting to his casual compliments, have betrayed their infidelity to him. Of the identity of the third Rose, a Rose "nor red nor white, [who] had stolne of both," and whose breath was that of the Fair Friend, there can be no doubt: he is the

Fair Friend himself. That the third Rose is neither red nor white does not mean that it is altogether some other colour; rather it means that the Rose was not all red, nor all white, but a commixture of the two — exactly like the heraldry in Lucrece's face, exactly like the purple flower, checkered with white, which grew from Adonis' blood, exactly like the coat of arms chiseled over the door in the Wriothesley manor at Titchfield.

The statement in the next two lines — that for this theft, "a vengful canker eate him up to death" — means, as I have elsewhere shown,[47] that the fair friend contracted a venereal disease from this encounter. In short, Sonnet 99 tells in terms of flowers the same story told in Sonnet 144 in terms of people, except that Sonnet 144, after expressing the author's fear that the Fair Friend and the Dark Lady may be deceiving him, concludes by stating that

> Yet this shall I nere know but live in doubt,
> Till my bad angel fire my good one out

(that is, unless and until the Fair Friend contracts a venereal disease), while in Sonnet 99, what was formerly in doubt is now known:

> But for his theft in pride of all his growth
> A vengful canker eate him up to death

(for he has contracted a venereal disease as a consequence of his "theft").

After the grisly reference to the vengeful canker, Sonnet 99 concludes by returning to the complimentary figure with which it began, thereby softening and dissipating somewhat the grim insights in the body of the poem. The roses, who were standing fearfully on tenterhooks as the poem proceeded, may now, perhaps, relax a bit, but only because the poet, in the interest of amity (or sarcasm), chooses not to make directly the accusation for which he knows he has grounds.

Some writers[48] have perceived in Sonnet 99 a similarity to lines 477 through 483 of *The Rape of Lucrece*, where Tarquin responds to Lucrece's demand to know "Under what colour he commits this ill" (i.e., her rape):

> Thus he replies, the colour in thy face,
> That euen for anger makes the Lilly pale,
> And the red rose blush at her owne disgrace,
> Shall plead for me and tell my louing tale.
> Vnder that colour am I come to scale

Thy neuer conquered Fort, the fault is thine,
For those thine eyes betray thee vnto mine.

On the basis of this similarity, these writers conclude that Sonnets 98 and 99 were written at about the same time as the stanza in *The Rape of Lucrece*, which would have been, of course, no later than 1594, the date of the publication of *Lucrece*, and probably a or two year earlier. If this conclusion is correct, it not only gives us the *terminus ad quem* for the Fair Friend's liaison with the Dark Lady (which, as I hope I have demonstrated, is what Sonnet 99 is all about), but also provides yet another piece of evidence that the Sonnets were written at too early a date to have been addressed to William Herbert, who was only 14 in 1594.

So, for a time at least, "immaculate red and white" — the character and complexion of Lucrece, Adonis and Henry Wriothesley — had become "maculate" red and white, the character and complexion of a deceiver, disfigured by a flaw which spotted the beauty of a "budding name." If Sonnets 98 and 99 were, as I believe, written before 1594, and if Sonnet 107, as I and many others believe, was written in 1603, then we can assume that the strain in the relationship between Shakespeare and Wriothesley was more or less healed by the latter date, and probably well before, although, as is often the case in this type of situation, some scar may have remained. Certain it is that there is far less red and white imagery in those plays written after 1594 than in those plays written before.

CHAPTER IV

The Reason of White and Red

Here I must pause to address what I am confident will be the chief objections to my conclusion that the Rose and red and white imagery in Shakespeare's Sonnets, poems and plays is due to Henry Wriothesley's name, title, and appropriated heraldic badge: those objections being, first, that the rose is so conventional, so common a poetical symbol of a loved person, that Shakespeare's designation of his beloved as a Rose (whatever the colour) cannot possibly have a special, private meaning, and second, that the use of red and white imagery in 16th century English poetry is so common, that no special significance can be imputed to its appearance in Shakespeare's poetry.

The analytical reader will immediately realize that these objections have no basis either in logic or in human experience: every one of us (to proffer an example in which a commonly-used symbol, image or expression might most readily be conceded to be devoid of any significant personal meaning) has at least once sent to a friend a commercial greeting card whose message, although pre-printed and mass produced, nevertheless possessed a special and unusually apposite private application, because of experiences or knowledge shared by the sender and the recipient. Thus there can be and as a matter of fact very often are situations where those phrases and metaphors which are the common currency of the day may yet apply with especial acuteness to specific persons and private occasions.

A good literary example of this is afforded by those poems of Tennyson addressed to or rhapsodizing upon roses, poems such as "The Gardener's Daughter," "The Rosebud," "Roses on the Terrace," and the exquisite Canto XXII of "Maud." The uninformed reader might see nothing particularly significant in Tennyson's apparently conventional use of rose imagery, and dismiss it as summarily as some are ready to dismiss Shakespeare's rose imagery. But as Ralph Wilson Rader has shown in his important and excellent book, *Tennyson's Maud: The Biographical Genesis*, the rose imagery of these and other poems, ranging from Tennyson's early sonnets and unpublished poems through the "Idylls of the King" to some of his last works, alludes to, and was inspired by, a real Rose: Rosa Baring, for whom Tennyson had a youthful infatuation which haunted him all his life.[1] Tennyson knew and loved Shakespeare's Sonnets,[2] but no responsible critic would, or indeed, could argue that Tennyson's rose imagery is merely a literary convention, in light of the demonstrated fact that there really was a Rose in Tennyson's life; similarly, the demonstration in the preceding chapters that there really was a Rose in Shakespeare's life in and of itself refutes the objection that the Rose imagery in Shakespeare's writings must be merely a convention and cannot possibly have its source in the circumstances of Shakespeare's life.

Moreover, if we look behind the objection to the premise for the objection, we find that the designation of a person as a rose is not so common a metaphor as might be supposed. To be sure, in the translation reputedly by Chaucer of the *Roman de la Rose*, first published in 1532, the poet says that she for whom the book is written

> So worthy is biloved to be,
> That she wel ought, of pris and ryght,
> Be cleped Rose of every wight.
>
> [Lines 46-48.]

But thereafter she is hardly so cleped at all, and John Vyvyan, who believes that *The Romaunt of the Rose* had some influence upon Shakespeare's philosophy and writing, states that

we may wonder whether it is she herself, or her love, that is really the Rose. There is some ambiguity about this. . . . the Rose may be both; but it is less often the person than the quality, and in general we must picture it as the lady's love. It is that, and not her person only, that must be won.[3]

In the version of the *Song of Songs* most familiar to Elizabethans occurs the statement, "I am the rose of the field, and the Lilie of the valleys,"[4] but repetitions of this idea by 16th century poets are infrequent. A not too exhaustive search of Elizabethan poetry reveals, outside of Shakespeare's poetry, only one other example of the equation of a person with a rose — a poem by Thomas Lodge, published in 1593:

> When I admire the rose
> That nature makes repose
> In you the best of many,
> More fair and blessed than any,
> And see how curious art
> Hath decked every part,
>   I think, with doubtful view,
> Whether you be the rose, or the rose is you.[5]

And even this example is not quite on point. There may, of course, be better examples, and it is possible that a body of religious verse exists addressing either Christ or his mother as a Rose. But in the mainstream of secular English literature, Shakespeare's impassioned cry to "thou, my Rose," if not unique, is far from commonplace. Nor can we ignore the fact that the person designated a Rose by Shakespeare is a male — a fact unusual enough in itself to reveal rather convincingly that we do not have here the idle repetition of a hackneyed image.[6] So the contention that the rose appellation used in the Sonnets is so common in Elizabethan or Renaissance or English literature as to permit no inferences to be drawn from it, is based upon a premise which is incorrect.

Even more basic and encompassing a refutation of the notion that the Rose in the Sonnets must be a meaningless symbol because it is so common a symbol is provided by Barbara Seward's study of *The Symbolic Rose*. Seward's book is primarily concerned with rose symbolism in the works of William Butler Yeats, James Joyce, T. S. Eliot and other twentieth century writers, but she precedes her discussion of their use of rose symbolism by a review of rose symbolism in ancient, medieval, renaissance and nineteenth century literature. Although her review is not extensive (Dante is the only writer upon whom she dwells more than a little; she barely mentions Shakespeare and does not mention Tennyson), it is adequate for her limited purpose, which is to establish that the Rose by the beginning of the twentieth century had been used by a host of authors, ancient and modern, as a symbol for a host of things and concepts, secular and religious, thus providing a foundation for her observation that the "simple but versatile" Rose is a remarkably "flexible vehicle" for the expression and representation of "private experience," "personal meanings," "subjective vision" and "personal ideals."[7] Having made this point, Seward then proceeds to examine the ways in which Yeats, Joyce, Eliot and other modern writers "applied symbols from public sources [and Seward, of course, focusses upon the rose] to contemporary social or personal problems," and finds numerous instances where her authors have vested the rose with "a particular meaning for our war-shattered times," "a personal creed," "a symbol suited to . . . private needs" or "a symbol of his own idea of fulfillment."[8] Seward's demonstration of the nontraditional peculiarly personal symbolic uses to which the rose has been put in this century alone completely deflates any suggestion that Shakespeare, who was at least as imaginative as the writers studied by Seward, was incapable of vesting the rose with a particular meaning peculiarly applicable to his personal situation.

And with the conclusion just stated, I doubtless would be wise to let the matter rest, except that there exists in the body of western literature one so striking a precedent not only for the designation of a youth as a rose, but also for the writing of amorous compositions to persons of both sexes, that I believe I would be remiss not to discuss this work, which is the $E\pi\iota\sigma\tau o\lambda\alpha\iota$ $E\rho\omega\tau\iota\kappa\alpha\iota$, or *Love Letters*, of Philostratus.

The vexed question of exactly who was the Philostratus who wrote these letters need not detain us. He (or, as appears to be more accurate, the several men named Philostratus who wrote at about the same time, and were probably related to each other) lived in about the second or third century C.E. The principal writings of the Philostrati, in addition to the *Love Letters*, are *Lives of the Sophists*, *In Honour of Appollonius of Tyana*, and a work designated either as *Eikones* from its Greek title or as *Imagines* from its title in Latin translations. The *editio princeps* of the *Letters*, edited by Marcus Musurus, was published in Venice by Aldus Manutius in 1499, as part of a collection of the letters of a number of Greek authors.[9] Some of Philostratus' letters may have been included in anthologies published in Paris in the mid and late 1500's,[10] but I have not had the opportunity to examine these anthologies to confirm this. The *Letters* were reprinted in an edition of the complete works of Philostratus published in Geneva in 1606, and again in Paris in 1608. Both of these editions contain also Latin translations by Antonio Bonfini.[11] I have examined the 1499 and 1608 editions, and find that all of the letters in the 1499 edition are reprinted in the 1608 edition, and in the same order. Because the 1608 edition is paginated, my citations to the *Letters* are to that edition.

There are 63 letters in the *editio princeps*. Sixteen are written to named persons, 23 are written to unnamed boys, and 24 are written to unnamed women. The letters written to named persons are not love letters (some, such as a letter to "Chariton", express contempt) but most (although not all) of the letters written to unnamed women and boys *are* love letters.

The feature of these letters of immediate interest — the designation of roses as boys, or boys as roses — is illustrated by the following excerpts (the translations are from the *Love Letters* of Philostratus by Allen Rogers Benner and Francis H. Fobes printed in the Loeb Classical Library edition; the first number in the brackets after each excerpt is the number of the letter as given in the Loeb Classical Library edition, and the second number, separated from the first by a comma, is the page of the 1608 Paris edition on which the letter can be found, all of these letters also being, of course, in the 1499 edition):

The roses, borne on their leaves as on wings, have made haste to come to you. Receive them kindly, either as mementos of Adonis or as tinct of Aphroditê or the eyes of earth. Yes, a wreath of wild olives becomes an athlete, a tiara worn upright the Great King, and a helmet crest a soldier; but roses become a beautiful boy, both because of affinity of fragrance and because of their distinctive hue. You will not wear the roses: they will wear you. [1, 894.]

. . . Now a larkspur suits a boy who has a light complexion, a narcissus a boy who is dark; but a rose suits all, inasmuch as it has long existed both as a boy [i.e., Adonis, from whose blood roses sprang] and as a flower. . . . [3, 893.]

What possessed the roses? Before they came to you they were beautiful and were truly roses — for I should not have sent them to you to begin with if they had not had some quality worth having — but when they arrived they straightway withered and expired. The cause is not altogether clear to me, for they would not tell me anything. But it is easy to guess that they could not bear to be surpassed in reknown nor could they endure the rivalry with you; no, as soon as they touched a more fragrant skin they perished. . . . [9, 895.]

Both beauty and the rose have their spring; and he who enjoys not what is to hand is foolish; for he delays among delights that do not brook delay, and in the face of fleeting joy he loiters. Time indeed is grudging and effaces the bloom on the flower and carries away the heyday of beauty. Do not delay at all, O rose with voice of man, but while you may and while you live, share with me what you have.[12] [17, 896.]

You have done well to use the roses for a bed also. . . . If you wish to do a favour for a lover, send back what is left of them, since they now breathe a fragrance, not of roses only, but also of you. [46, 894.][13]

Roses and rose imagery appear also in some of the letters addressed to women (e.g., 2, 894; 20, 895; 21, 897; 54, 894; 55, 896; 63, 896), and in one of them Philostratus tells a woman who asks for roses that "your nature and theirs is the same" (21, 897), but I think it fair to say that in the rest of these letters, roses are *associated* with women, rather than *identified* with them — and, indeed, in at least three of the letters addressed to women, roses, when mentioned, are equated with males:

. . . I for my part think that the petals of of roses that have fallen to pieces resemble dying men and nothing else . . . . [21, 897.]

Though you shun me, yet do at least accept the roses in my place. . . . I have told the roses to kiss your throat and to cling to your breasts and to play the part of a man, if you will permit; and I know that they will obey. O happy roses! [54, 894.]

Truly roses are Love's [i.e., Eros', or Cupid's] flowers, for they are young like him, and lithe like Love himself, and both have golden locks, and they resemble one another in their other traits as well: roses have thorns for shafts, red blushes for torches, and they have petals for feathers, and neither Love nor yet roses know length of time, for this god [Time] is hostile both to beauty's autumn and to roses' lingering stay. [55, 896.]

So here we have a literary work, written twelve or thirteen centuries before the time of Shakespeare, which resembles Shakespeare's Sonnets in two important respects: first, it contains much rose imagery, which imagery for the most part describes the persons or attributes of young men, and second, it consists of a series of declarations of love (or perhaps, just desire) directed to both males and females.

I mention Philostratus' letters primarily to make a "when you see it, you shall know it" argument: had it really been a convention of the poetry of Shakespeare's time and place[14] to address persons, male or female, as roses, in the clear and straightforward manner of Philostratus, then that convention would long since have been identified, published and cited by scholars as accounting for Shakespeare's imagery (and the personal significance of the imagery no doubt discounted to the extent that it was conventional; improperly so, as I shall endeavor to show in my discussion of red and white imagery). In fact there was no such convention, and the presence of the unusual rose = youth imagery in the Sonnets is an element contributing to their distinctiveness.

But having brought up Philostratus' letters, and their rose imagery so markedly similar to that of the Sonnets, I cannot leave them without addressing the possibility of Shakespeare's familiarity with them: a possibility which indeed verges on certainty, in light of the late 15th and early 16th-century *explosion* of interest in Greek texts which characterizes — nay, defines — the Renaissance. Aldus Manutius (1450-1515), the publisher in 1499 of the first edition of Philostratus' *Letters,* was only one — although the foremost — of a number of scholars and publishers who collected, edited and disseminated Greek texts. An accomplished Greek scholar, he gathered around him a host of dispossessed Greek scholars and compositors, including Constantine Lascaris (d. ca. 1500) who wrote the first book published by Aldus, a Greek grammar called *Erotemata*, Joannes Lascaris (ca. 1445-1535), who was probably Constantine's brother, and Joannes' pupil Marcus Musurus (ca. 1470-1517). Aldus called his group of co-workers the Neacadamia, or New Academy. Its constitution was written in Greek, and its members, while engaged in official business, were permitted to speak only Greek. Scholars other than refugees from Byzantium were members of the New Academy: English humanist and physician, Thomas Linacre, famed in his time for his mastery of Greek, was for a while a member, and translated into Latin a work by Proclus entitled Σφαῖρα (*De sphaera*), which was published by Aldus (along with the Greek original) in 1499 as part of a collection of the works of ancient astronomers;[15] and Erasmus, too, was a member. Like a volcano, the Aldine press spewed into the skies of Europe carefully edited and beautifully printed editions of the works (some of which but for Aldus would probably have been lost) of Greek[16] philosophers, dramatists, poets and historians — Theocritus, Aristotle, Aristophanes, Lucian, Sophocles, Herodotus, Euripedes, Demosthenes, Homer, Plato, and dozens more — which many tomes in the European atmosphere diffracted into unprecedentedly varied and brilliant spectra the light which for the next one hundred years fell upon that part of the earth.

As a consequence of this, some degree of familiarity with Greek literature on the part of every sixteenth century European who was himself a writer is virtually certain, and, indeed, scholars over the years have found in the works of Shakespeare evidences of varying degrees of acquaintance with, borrowings from and indebtedness to, all of the Greek writers named in the preceding paragraph, as well as numerous others.[17] It can tax no one's credulity to suppose that Philostratus should be added to this list. In support of this suggestion I shall now attempt to show first, that Shakespeare was generally familiar, either directly or through translations, with Greek works of the epoch in which Philostratus' letters were written, especially Greek romances and the Greek Anthology, and second, that the Sonnets seem to echo and even consciously duplicate specific language and themes found in Philostratus' letters, over and above those associating boys with roses.

A. Greek Romances and the Greek Anthology.

At the outset, we find a general recognition that the works of Shakespeare and his contemporaries contain many elements derived from the Greek romances. The Greek romances are fanciful, sensual, and by professed Christian standards often amoral or immoral tales dating from the early centuries of the Christian era, the same period in which lived the Philostrati. The best-known of these tales are *Apollonius of Tyre*, whose author is unknown, *Clitophon and Leucippe*, by Achilles Tatius, *Chaereas and Callirhoe*, by Chariton of Aphrodisia (who some scholars believe is the same "Chariton" to whom Philostratus addressed a contemptuous letter[18]), *Daphnis and Chloe*, by Longus, the *Aethiopica* by Heliodorus of Emesa, the *Ephesiaca* by Xenophon of Ephesus, and the *Babylonica* of Iamblichus. The extent to which these tales were known in Shakespeare's time has been the subject of studies by Samuel Lee Wolff and Carol Gesner, whose conclusions I shall briefly summarize. Wolff, who limited his study to the influence of Greek romances upon the chief Elizabethan writers of prose fiction (except that he does examine at some length the influence, by way of Robert Greene's *Pandosta*, of *Daphnis and Chloe* upon *The Winter's Tale*), finds that the romances had no impact upon the works of Thomas Nashe or Thomas Lodge, some influence upon the works of Lyly and Greene (although Wolff perversely declines to impute Lyly's euphuistic style to the Greek romances[19]), and, as is obvious, a pervasive and important impact upon Sidney, as seen in his *Arcadia*, and, consequently, upon all those writers who were influenced by the *Arcadia*.[20]

Gesner's study, more to our point, is of the influence of the Greek romances, directly and indirectly, upon the writings of Shakespeare. She finds suggestions of *Clitiphon and Leucippe* in *Comedy of Errors* and *Twelfth Night*, of *Chaereas and Callirhoe* in *Much Ado About Nothing*, of the *Aethiopica* in *Othello*, and of *Daphnis and Chloe* in *As You Like It*, but in each case she believes the resemblances are not close enough to warrant the conclusion that the Greek romances had a direct influence upon these plays.[21] On the other hand, she finds a discernible influence of *Apollonius of Tyre* in *Pericles, Prince of Tyre*; of *Chaereas and Callirhoe*, *Daphnis and Chloe*, *Clitiphon and Leucippe* and the *Ephesiaca* in *Cymbeline*; of *Daphnis and Chloe* and the *Aethiopica* in *The Winter's Tale*; and *Daphnis and Chloe* in *The Tempest*.[22] Gesner's conclusions with respect to the plays by Shakespeare deemed influenced by Greek romances, along with the probable dates of composition of those plays and the possible sources of Shakespeare's knowledge of the romances (in terms of published editions of those romances), are summarized in the table on the next page.

Both Gesner and Wolff are quite conservative in claiming Greek romances as significant sources for the writings of Shakespeare and his contemporaries, doubtless for the reason so well stated by Barbara A. Mowat: "the history of Greek Romance and its influence on medieval saints' legends and on miracle plays based on saints' legends makes the problem of proving direct influence almost impossible; any unsympathetic critic can simply point to intermediate medieval sources or to Renaissance forms influenced by Greek Romance: romantic epics, Italian novella, Elizabethan prose romances, the *Arcadia*, or the *Faerie Queene* — and say, justly, that one cannot prove direct influence on Shakespeare's Romances by Achilles Tatius or Heliodorus."[23] Nevertheless, that the Greek romances were well known to the Elizabethans generally, and to Shakespeare in particular, is a point tellingly made by S. Gaselee, in his observation that "Shakespeare's casual reference to 'the Egyptian thief' who 'at point of Death Killed what he loved' [slightly misquoted from *Twelfth Night*, V,i,121] should indicate that a knowledge of the *Aethiopica* was common property of the ordinary well-read man among his hearers."[24]

Greek Romances	Editions (From Wolff, pp. 8-10 and Gesner, pp. 154–162. Not all editions listed by Wolff and Gesner are included here.)	Play Influenced and Approximate Date of Composition
Clitiphon and Leucippe by Achilles Tatius	1544, Latin (Books V-VIII), tr. Annibale Cruceio 1545, French, tr. Colet 1546, Italian (Books V-VIII), tr. Dolce 1550, Italian (Books I-VIII), tr. Coccio 1551, Latin (Books I-VIII), tr. Annibale Cruceio 1556, French, tr. de Rochemaure 1568, French, tr. Comingeois 1597, English, tr. W [illiam] B [urton] 1601, Greek and Latin, ed. Juda and Nicolaus Bonnuitius	*Cymbeline* ca 1610
Apollonius of Tyre	(The Greek original of this work is lost.) 1470(?), Latin 1471, German, tr. Steinhöwel 1483, English (in Book VIII of Gower's *Confessio Amantis*) 1510, English, tr. R. Copland 1576, English, tr. L. Twyne	*Pericles* 1608
Chaereas and Callirhoe by Chariton of Aphrodisia	1750, Greek and Latin 1764, English, tr. anonymous	*Cymbeline*, ca 1610
Aethiopica by Heliodorus of Emesa	1534, Greek 1547, French, tr. Amyot 1567, English, Jas. Sanford 1569 (?), English, tr. Underdowne 1591, English, Abraham Fraunce	*The Winter's Tale* ca 1610-1611
Daphnis and Chloe by Longus	1559, French, tr. Amyot 1587, English, tr. Angell Daye 1598, Greek, ed. Raphaelis Columbanius 1601, Greek and Latin, ed. Juda and Nicolaus Bonnuitius	*Cymbeline* ca 1610 *The Winter's Tale* ca 1610-1611 *The Tempest* ca 1611
Ephesiaca by Xenophon of Ephesus	1489, Latin (fragment of Book I) 1726, Greek and Latin 1727, English, tr. "Mr. Rooke"	*Cymbeline* ca 1610

This does not necessarily indicate that the ordinary well-read Elizabethan man knew Greek, for the *Aethiopica* had been translated into English in 1567 by James Sanford in a small volume with the long title *Amorous and Tragicall Tales of Plutarch, Whereunto is annexed the History of Cariclea & Theagenes* [this being the *Aethiopica*] *and the sayings of the Greek Philosophers*, as well as by Thomas Underdowne in about 1569, and (the beginning only) by Abraham Fraunce in 1591, in *The Countesse of Pembrokes Yvychurch*. Also, most of the other Greek romances which Gesner finds influenced Shakespeare's work were accessible to Shakespeare in English translations, but two of them, *Chaereas and Callirhoe* and the *Ephesiaca*, were not. As to these two romances, Gesner points out that the sole source of their texts is a 13th century codex well-known during the Renaissance,[25] but she offers no theory as to how knowledge of these romances, not printed in any language until the eighteenth century, might have reached Shakespeare. Francis Douce, who in 1807 was the first to notice a similarity between incidents in the *Ephesiaca* and in *Romeo and Juliet* and *Cymbeline*, suggested that "some novel, imitated from the *Ephesiacs*, was existing in the time of Shakespeare, though now unknown."[26]

With respect to the Greek romances, then, the studies of Wolff and Gesner show that this literature of the same period as Philostratus' letters was known to, and exercised an influence upon, the writings of Shakespeare and his contemporaries, and that while most of these elements can be traced to printed sources in Latin or English, a few at least cannot be so explained. These studies also suggest either that Shakespeare's "less Greek" was at least adequate to read the romances, or that Shakespeare had access to this literature independently of printed sources which have survived, probably by way of conversations with Greek-speaking friends and associates.

Shakespeare was familiar also with the Greek Anthology, which is not surprising, since the Greek Anthology was, in the sixteenth century, one of the most frequently published and best known of all Greek works. The *editio princeps*, edited by Joannes Lascaris, who later edited texts for Aldus Manutius, was printed in Florence in 1494. In 1503, Aldus published his own edition, and his successors at the Aldine Press put out editions again in 1521 and 1550-51. Other complete editions of the Greek Anthology were published in 1519 by Juntine in Florence, in 1531 by Badius Ascensius in Paris, in 1549 by Jean Brodeau in Basel, in 1550 by Nicolini in Venice, in 1566 by Henricus Stephanus in Paris, and in 1600 by Wechel in Frankfurt.[27] Lascaris, in a lecture given the year prior to the publication of his edition of the Greek Anthology, described its approximately 2,650 epigrams[28] written over a period of 1,000 years as possessing "exquisite judgments on almost everything that falls within the realm of human action, together with such brevity and elegance, such grace and charm, that you might think the genius and judgment of all the wisest of men, rivaling and vying with one another, had been brought together into this single volume," and he urged "Let each one, therefore, translate these pieces, delight in them, imitate them; among them let him practice, who wishes, besides other advantages, to attempt any like poem and to succeed."[29] Practicing what he preached, Lascaris translated many of the epigrams into Latin, as did over the next one hundred years innumerable other persons. Many books of selections from the Anthology, almost always in Latin translation, were published in the 1500's: Professor James Hutton, from whose works on the Greek Anthology most of the foregoing information is obtained, lists as the best-known of such selections the *Epigrammata Graeca* of Joannes Soter, with editions in 1525, 1528 and 1542, the *Selecta epigrammata Graeca* of Janus Cornarius in 1529, and the *Epigrammata Graeca* of Henricus Stephanus, or Henri Estienne, published in 1570.[30] Most of the translations in Stephanus' edition (all into Latin) were the work either of Stephanus himself, or of his friend, Paul Schede, the German humanist who signed his writings with the name Melissus. Many of the Stephanus and Melissus translations, together with additional translations (also into Latin) by John Stockwood, were published in London in 1597 by Adam Islip in a work entitled *Progymnasma Scholasticum, hoc est, Epigrammatum Graecorum, ex Anthologia Selectorum ab HE. Stephano*, and dedicated by Stockwood to Robert Devereux, Earl of Essex. The first translation of the entire Greek Anthology into Latin was that of Eilhardus Lubinus, published in Heidelberg in 1603.

Shakespeare's familiarity with the Greek Anthology is revealed in the Sonnets. It has been known at least since 1849 that the first six lines of Sonnet 153 and the first eleven lines of Sonnet 154 — those last two sonnets which seem to have no connection to the story unfolded by the preceding 152 sonnets — are derived from an epigram by Marianus Scholasticus, who lived in the same general period as the Philostrati, but is otherwise unknown to fame.

Marianus' epigram as translated by W. R. Paton in the Loeb Classical Library edition of the Anthology is as follows:

Here under the plane-trees tired Love lay softly sleeping, having entrusted his torch to the Nymphs. Said the Nymphs among themselves: "Why not do it at once? Would that together with this we could put out the fire in men's hearts." But it was the torch that set fire to the water, and henceforth the Love-Nymphs pour forth here hot water for men to bathe in.[31]

Shakespeare's versions are as follows:

Sonnet 153

Cupid laid by his brand and fell a sleepe,
A maide of *Dyans* this advantage found,
And his love-kindling fire did quickly steepe
In a could vallie-fountaine of that ground:
Which borrowd from this holie fire of love,
A dateless lively heat still to indure,
And grew a seething bath which yet men prove,
Against strang malladies a soveraigne cure:
But at my mistres eie loves brand new fired,
The boy for triall needes would touch my brest,
I sick withall the helpe of bath desired,
And thither hied a sad distemperd guest.
  But found no cure, the bath for my help lies,
  Where *Cupid* got new fire; my mistres eye.

Sonnet 154

The little Love-God lying once a sleepe,
Laid by his side his heart inflaming brand,
Whilst many Nymphes that vou'd chast life to keep,
Came tripping by, but in her maiden hand,
The fayrest votary took up that fire,
Which many Legions of true hearts had warm'd,
And so the Generall of hot desire,
Was sleeping by a Virgin hand disarm'd.
This brand she quenched in a coole Well by,
Which from loves fire took heat perpetuall,
Growing a bath and healthful remedy,
For men diseasd, but I my Mistrisse thrall,
  Came there for cure and this by that I prove,
  Loves fire heates water, water cooles not love.

The initial question — are Shakespeare's sonnets based directly upon the Marianus epigram, or upon some translation or imitation of that epigram? — was addressed fifty years ago by Professor Hutton, who looked for translations or imitations of the Marianus epigram in books which could have been available to Shakespeare.[32] He found only one literal translation of the epigram, that into Latin by Fausto Sabeo in his *Epigrammata*, published in

Rome in 1556,[33] but he found also a number of Latin, French and Italian epigrams and poems bearing a general resemblance to the Marianus epigram although differing from it in the details of the action, and also in the venue, having their setting at Baiae, an ancient city in Italy famous for its warm sulphur springs. As an aid to determining the genealogy and interrelationship of all these epigrams and poems, Professor Hutton isolated seven "elements" in the Marianus epigram which he used as "tracers" for ascertaining whether or not Shakespeare's poems are derived directly from the Greek poem, or indirectly through imitations which do not retain all of the elements of Marianus' poem, and may even add a few new ones. The table on the facing page shows the application to these poems of Professor Hutton's "elements": in column I is the English translation of the entire text of the poem by Marianus, each clause (in its correct order) being printed on a separate row. In column II are the specific "elements" identified by Professor Hutton, each element being based on the substance of a clause in the Greek poem. In column III is the text of those lines of Sonnet 153 which correspond with the same element in the Greek poem, and in column IV is the text of those parts of Sonnet 154 which correspond with the same element in the Greek poem.

That five of Hutton's seven elements are present in Shakespeare's poems, and that there are no extraneous elements from other poems, seems to me a striking enough agreement of content to warrant the conclusion that Shakespeare translated either directly from the Greek poem, or from Fausto Sabeo's Latin translation of it. Hutton's own conclusions with respect to this are confused — or at least confusing. He wrote at the beginning of the article in which he makes this analysis that "there is little, or rather no, likelihood that he [Shakespeare] lifted it [the epigram] directly out of the Anthology,"[34] and later, after making the "elements" analysis which, in my opinion, shows Shakespeare's direct recourse to the original text of the epigram, or a literal translation thereof, concluded that Shakespeare's "management of the theme suggests that he did not draw immediately on the epigram [by Marianus]," and even that "there is little likelihood, therefore, that the [Latin] translations by Sabeo [1556] or Lubinus [1603] were known to Shakespeare."[35] But five years later Hutton wrote that "Shakespeare's two sonnets, however derived, seem to attach definitely to this Greek original [i.e., Marianus' epigram]."[36] Although this latter statement is not necessarily inconsistent with the earlier statements, it seems to be a recognition, upon mature consideration, of the direct, rather than the mediated, connection between the epigram and the sonnets.

I	II	III	IV
Marianus Scholasticus	**Hutton's Elements**	**Sonnet 153**	**Sonnet 154**
Here under the plane-trees	1. plane trees		
tired Love lay softly sleeping	2. Love asleep	*Cupid* . . . fell a sleepe [line 1]	The little Love-God lying once a sleepe [line 1]
having entrusted his torch to the nymphs.	3. his torch entrusted to the Nymphs	[*Cupid*] laid by his brand. . . . [line 1] A maide of *Dyans* this advantage found [line 2]	Laid by his side his heart inflaming brand,/ Whilst many Nymphes . . . came tripping by, but in her maiden hand, the fayrest votary took up that fire [lines 2-5]
Said the Nymphs among themselves, "Why not do it at once?	4. their conspiracy		
Would that together with this we could put out the fire in men's hearts."	5. the "reflective" phrase		Which many Legions of true hearts had warm'd,/ And so the Generall of hot desire,/ Was sleeping by a Virgin hand disarm'd [lines 6-8]
But it was the torch that set fire to the water,	6. the heating of the waters	And his love-kindling fire did quickly steepe/ In a could vallie-fountaine of that ground: / Which borrowd from this holie fire of love,/ A dateless lively heat still to indure, [lines 3 - 5]	This brand she quenched in a coole Well by,/ Which from loves fire tooke heat perpetuall [lines 9-10]
and henceforth the Love-Nymphs pour forth here hot water for men to bathe in.	7. the subsequent existence of the hot bath of "Eros"	And grew a seething bath . . . [line 6]	Growing a bath [line 11]

In view of the existence in some of Shakespeare's plays and in at least two sonnets of influences unmistakably derived from Greek literature of the early centuries of this era, the possibility of the existence in Shakespeare's writings of influences derived from the *Epistolae Philostrati* of the same period cannot be dismissed out of hand. That there may be no translations of Philostratus' letters from Greek into Latin or modern European languages earlier than the Greek/Latin edition published in Geneva in 1606 does not undermine this possibility, since, as we have seen, other Greek influences perceived in the works of Shakespeare similarly are not based on any non-Greek written sources so far found.

B. Writings of Philostratus.

More directly in support of the possibility of Shakespeare's being familiar with the Letters of Philostratus is the appearance in the Sonnets of a number of passages (in addition to those utilizing boy/rose imagery) which strikingly echo passages in Philostratus' letters. These passages are here set forth in parallel columns:

Philostratus' Letters	Shakespeare's Sonnets
How many times, do you think, have I unclosed my eyes to release you, even as hunters open their nets to give their quarry a chance to escape? And you sit fast . . . Lo, once more, as so often in the past, I raise my eyelids; now at long last, I pray you, fly away, and raise the siege, and become a guest of other eyes . . . . [11, 905]	Is it thy wil, thy Image should keepe open My heavy eielids to the weary night? Dost thou desire my slumbers should be broken, While shadowes like to thee do mocke my sight? [61]
. . . take time by the forelock — time which alone ends the rule of handsome boys even as the populace overthrows that of princes. . . . So before your springtime quite departs and winter comes upon you, grant springtime's gifts in the name of Love . . . . [13, 911]	O thou my lovely Boy who in thy power, Doest hould times fickle glasse, his sickle, hower: Who has by wayning growne, and therein shou'st, Thy lovers withering, as thy sweet selfe grow'st. . . . Yet feare her [Nature, or Time] O thou minnion of her pleasure, She may detaine, but not still keepe her tresure! Her *Audite* (though delayd) answer'd must be, And her *Quietus* is to render thee. [126]
For I fear — yes, I will speak out my thoughts — lest while you linger and hesitate, your beard may make its advent and may obscure the loveliness of your face, even as the concourse of clouds is wont to hide the sun! [13, 911]	Even so my Sunne one early morne did shine, With all triumphant splendor on my brow, But out, alack, he was but one hour mine, The region cloude hath mask'd him from me now. [33]
. . . it is not becoming to the sun, either, to shield his face with a cloud [24, 908]	Full many a glorious morning have I seen . . . Anon permit the basest cloudes to ride, With ougly rack on his celestiall face. . . .[33]

Philostratus' Letters	Shakespeare's Sonnets
Eyes underlined with kohl, false hair, painted cheeks, tinted lips, all the enhancements known to the beautifier's art, and all the deceptive bloom achieved by rouge have been invented for the correction of defects; the unadorned is the truly beautiful. [22, 899]	
	Why should false painting immitate his cheeke, And steale dead seeing of his living hew? Why should poore beautie indirectly seeke Roses of shaddow, since his Rose is true? [67]
For self-adornment is a courtesan's trick, and beauty achieved by paint deserves intense disgust — it suggests knavery; pure and honest and guileless beauty is a trait peculiar to those on whom the very essence of beauty has been bestowed [27, 898]	

To the foregoing examples of the possible appearance in the Sonnets of imagery derived from Philostratus' letters, we must in conclusion add two more, both to be found, appropriately enough, in the "Greek Sonnets," that is, Sonnets 153 and 154. The table on page 73 shows that while each of these two sonnets tracks closely the form and substance of the entire epigram by Marianus, the portion of Sonnet 153 which constitutes the translation of the epigram is completed by line 6 and the translation portion of Sonnet 154 is completed by line 11. So in each case, lines had to be added, not only to fill out the 14 line sonnet stanza, but more pertinently, as Professor James Hutton has noted, "to invent for it a pointed ending. . . ."[37] For although both sonnets are almost literal translations of the Greek epigram, they omit the one part of the epigram which gives it its point: its title. As printed both in Greek editions and in the Latin translation by Fausto Sabeo, the poem is entitled "On a bath called Love [Eros]": by recounting the creation of a hot spring or bath from Eros' (i.e., Cupid's) torch, the poem explains the reason for the name of the bath. But Shakespeare's translations do not tell us the name of the bath created by Marianus' Nymphs, and consequently explaining how the bath got its name is not the point of Sonnets 153 and 154.

The "pointed ending" devised by Shakespeare for his sonnets is that the bath created by Cupid's torch, although reputedly medicinal, in fact does not cure the wounds caused by Cupid's darts, from which circumstance a moral is drawn. The manner in which this idea is developed in Sonnets 153 and 154 is illustrated by the table on the following page:

Additional elements in Sonnets 153 and 154	Sonnet 153	Sonnet 154
1. The bath is medicinal.	a seething bath which yet men prove,/ Against strang malladies a soveraigne cure: [lines 7-8]	Growing a bath and healthfull remedy,/ For men diseasd, [lines 11-12]
2. The poet is stricken by love.	But at my mistres eie loves brand new fired,/ The boy [Cupid] for triall needes would touch my brest, [lines 9-10]	but I my Mistrisse thrall [line 12]
3. And goes to the bath for cure,	I sick withall the helpe of bath desired,/ And thither hied a sad distempred guest. [lines 11-12]	Came there for cure [line 13]
4. but finds no cure,	But found no cure [line 13]	and this by that I prove, [line 13]
5. and states a moral:	the bath for my helpe lies,/ Where *Cupid* got new fire; my mistres eye. [lines 13-14]	Loves fire heates water, water cooles not love. [line 14]

Although the first four additional elements of the story are, in each of the sonnets, substantially the same, the fifth element of each, the moral, is different. The moral Shakespeare came up with in Sonnet 154 is that men who resort to the bath in the hope of finding a cure for love will find only that

Love's fire heates water, water cooles not love.

This is similar to, and I believe has its source in, the conceit at the end of Philostratus' letter to the boy whose image has taken possession of Philostratus' eyes, and refuses to leave:

You are not listening, not you! You are pressing ever further on, into my very soul! And what is this new fiery heat? In my perilous plight I cry for water; but no one assuages the heat, for the means of quenching this flame is very hard to find, whether one bring water from a spring or from a stream; yes, for *love's fire sets even the water ablaze*. [11, 905; emphasis supplied.]

As a "pointed ending" for Sonnet 154, this is not very good, because lines 9 and 10 of the sonnet have already told us that the waters in a cool well took heat perpetual from love's fire, and the "punchline" is merely a restatement of the same fact. It is not artistic for the moral of a story to be the same as something already expressly set forth in the story. Whether for this or some other reason,[38] Shakespeare wrote another version of the translation of

76

the Greek epigram. In Sonnet 153, the number of lines required to express the original epigram is reduced to six (as compared to eleven in Sonnet 154), thereby leaving eight lines for the development of a more trenchant ending. This time, Shakespeare supposes that although the quenching of Cupid's brand in the spring (which thereupon became the seething bath) extinguished Cupid's love-kindling fire, Cupid was able to reignite his brand at "my mistres eie," and with his brand once again as potent as ever, infected the poet with love's always painful symptoms, for the relief of which he went to the bath

> But found no cure, the bath for my helpe lies,
> Where *Cupid* got new fire; my mistres eye.

The image of burning eyes appears in at least two of Philostratus' letters; the first, addressed to a boy, states that

beauty, just like fire, kindles them [i.e., eyes], and it is inevitable that beauty should blaze and that eyes should immediately burn [8, 902]

and the second, addressed to a woman, declaims

From what vantage point did you seize upon my soul? Is it not plain that it was from the eyes, by which alone beauty finds entrance? For even as tyrants seize on citadels, kings on strongholds, and gods on high places, so too love seizes on the citadel of the eyes. . . . The eyes, as soon as they become aware of beauty, take fire therefrom in earnest; a god, I think, has willed for them one and the same path of delight at seeing and of occasion for pain. Why, I beg of you, *O base torches of love* [emphasis suppied] and all too curious witnesses of corporeal charm, were you the first to signal the image of beauty to us, and the first to teach our soul to remember impressions from without, and the first to force it to abandon the sun and extol an alien flame? [12, 906]

Shakespeare's conceit of Cupid's getting new fire from "my mistres eye" seems to me to be similar enough to Philostratus' designation of the eyes as being on fire, and as "torches of love," to suggest that he found his ending to Sonnet 153, like his ending to Sonnet 154, in Philostratus' letters. There is a difference, of course: in Philostratus, it is the beauty of the loved person which creates fire in the eyes of the beholder, while in Shakespeare it is fire in the eyes of the loved person which ignites love's ardor in others. But in either case, the eyes burn, and this is the element which, *mutatis mutandis*, makes the point both of Shakespeare's Sonnet 153 and of Philostratus' letters. Nor can it surprise us that Shakespeare, having undertaken to translate a

Greek epigram, should look to the same great body of literature which provided him with the initial text for appropriate material to give that text a point.

In addition to these instances of the possible influence of Philostratus' letters upon the Sonnets of Shakespeare, the possible influence of another work of Philostratus upon another work of Shakespeare should be noted. In *The Rape of Lucrece*, Lucrece "cals to mind where hangs a peece/ Of Skilfull painting" in which are depicted a number of scenes showing the siege of Troy. The extended description of the painting which follows (lines 1366 to 1568) has been thought by some writers[39] not only to imitate a technique (*ecphrasis*) characteristic of Greek literature in general, but also, in one short passage, to imitate a passage from a description of a painting in Philostratus' *Eikones* or *Imagines*. The passage in *Lucrece* is

> For much imaginarie work was there,
> Conceipt deceitfull, so compact so kinde,
> That for ACHILLES image stood his speare
> Grip't in an Armed hand, himselfe behind
> Was left unseene, save to the eye of mind,
> A hand, a foote, a face, a leg, a head
> Stood for the whole to be imagined.

[Lines 1422-1428.]

The similar passage in Philostratus is:

Some are seen in full figure, others with the legs hidden, others from the waist up, then only the busts of some, heads only, helmets only, and finally just spear-points. This, my boy, is perspective; since the problem is to deceive the eyes as they travel back along with the proper receding planes of the picture.[40]

"Even in translation," writes S. Clark Hulse, "the parallel strikes me as sufficiently full and detailed to be an actual borrowing."[41]

Whether this parallel in *Lucrece*, together with the other parallels between the Letters of Philostratus and the Sonnets which I have listed, as well as the inferences to be drawn from Shakespeare's obvious knowledge of Greek romances and the Greek Anthology, are "sufficiently full and detailed" to demonstrate conclusively the influence of the letters of Philostratus upon the Sonnets of Shakespeare, is something each reader must decide for himself; in my own opinion, the similarities between Philostratus' letters and Shakespeare's Sonnets are close enough, and numerous enough, to warrant the inference that the former work was known to Shakespeare, and was a source of some of the ideas and imagery embodied in the Sonnets, even though the means of transmission cannot be ascertained. To be sure, the ideas and imagery derived from Philostratus, if they are so derived, undergo *in tone* a sea-change in the hands of Shakespeare, who uses them in aid of what seem truly to be poems expressive of love at the highest as well as the lowest level, whereas the letters of Philostratus (pragmatically, perhaps), operate exclusively on lower levels, dwelling upon physical beauty and devoted to persuading various boys and women to "share with me what you have."

Having stated this, I must stress that whether or not Philostratus is in fact the *source* for some of the Rose imagery in the Sonnets is a matter of no consequence to the main thesis of this chapter, which is that the *reason* for the Rose imagery in the Sonnets, plays and poems is that Henry Wriothesley, because of the Roseli-ness of his name and the roses in the arms of the Town whose honour he bore, was a Rose; the letters of Philostratus, if an influence at all, at most merely suggested images involving young men and roses which Shakespeare, because of the already-existing Rose/Wriothesley association, found useful to appropriate to his own purposes.

Nevertheless, this review of the influences, some certain, some possible, of Greek authors upon the writings of Shakespeare is not without point, for it demonstrates in the work of our author a knowledge of a body of Greek literature depicting nonjudgmentally relationships involving that for which the Elizabethans had no name other than sodomy or pederasty, and illustrates the point upon which I shall dwell in Chapter VI, that a consequence of the knowledge of this body of Greek literature by educated and powerful persons of the Elizabethan era was the development among them of an attitude permitting the discreet expression of love by one man for another, thus encouraging the composition and making possible the circulation of the Sonnets and other works of a similar tenor among groups of "private friends."

But here, lest my digressions have too much obscured it, I return to the main point in this chapter so far: that the poetic designation of a person as a rose is not a common device, let alone so common a device that its utilization in the Sonnets can be dismissed as unmeaningful.

Even if representing a person as a rose were a common literary device, we could not for that reason conclude that its utilization by Shakespeare is without personal significance; Barbara Seward's study of *The Symbolic Rose* demonstrates how unwarranted would be such a conclusion. By the same token, the fact that the other category of imagery upon which I have placed

79

great weight — the various red and white skin-colour images which Shakespeare uses to a remarkable extent and which I contend are employed primarily because they glorify Henry Wriothesley — *is* common in Elizabethan poetry does not deprive that imagery of the significance which I claim for it.

The extraordinarily frequent utilization of red and white complexion imagery by Elizabethan authors is a surprising discovery resulting from the same non-exhaustive review of sixteenth century English poems, plays and books which dis-Lodged the one poem referred to earlier designating a person in her entirety as a rose. Examples of the red and white images thus found, which surely can represent only the tip of the iceberg, are assembled in Appendix III. These excerpts are listed chronologically in five categories, depending on the nature of the image.

The first category — Category A — contains twenty images extolling the beauty of white and red complexions. The first eight excerpts were published before 1593 (the date of the publication of *Venus and Adonis*) and the remaining twelve were published in or after 1593. Here, as in each of the other categories, it is quite possible, and indeed likely, that the poems published after *Venus and Adonis* and *The Rape of Lucrece* utilize red and white and rose imagery in imitation of Shakespeare's poems, and this is a factor which must be considered in deciding to what extent Shakespeare really was emulating others. But enough examples exist of these images written prior to the publication of Shakespeare's poems to indicate that he was utilizing (taking advantage of, I would assert) already well-known poetical conventions.

The excerpts in Category A disclose the surprising and helpful fact that in Tudor times, the phrase "red and white" was used as a synonym for "beauty."[42] Excerpt 9 goes so far as to declare that white alone is "far from fair, where white doth want his red." "Red and white" is certainly used by Shakespeare to mean "beauty" in the description of Adonis as "More white, and red, than doves or roses are," and in the reference to Lucrece's "unmatched red and white." The poems by Campion, Donne, Herbert and Marvell (Numbers 14, 16, 17 and 20, respectively) show how well understood this usage must have been by the first half of the 17th century, for they depend on this meaning of "red and white" to make their point (the poem by Herbert, addressed to Christ, in an arresting way), while the poem by Suckling (Number 18), rejecting the idea that *only* red and white can be beautiful, makes clear how widespread that notion previously had been.

Category B contains phrases employing the colours red and white, as embodied in various flowers, to denote beauty or to describe beautiful complexions. Twenty-six items are listed (Numbers 21 through 46), thirteen of which were published prior to 1593 and thirteen subsequent thereto. The flowers almost always invoked for this purpose are either the red rose and the white rose or lily, or the Damask Rose, which is itself both red and white.

Category C contains figures (Numbers 47 through 54) dwelling on the especial beauty of those complexions in which white and red alternate with each other, either physically (e.g., both colours simultaneously on the cheeks), or temporally (e.g., one colour succeeding another). Hence this image too, which I claim Shakespeare uses in allusion to the Southampton badge at Titchfield, with its alternating white and red fields and roses, is a common image of the period. The excerpt by Michael Drayton (Number 52) is of interest because it sets forth the supposed physiological reasons (derived from Galen, and based upon the interaction of the humours) for this alternation of the colour of the skin between red and white.[43]

Category D contains those figures (Numbers 55 through 60) which, startlingly at odds with the attributes of red and white developed in the first three categories, dispraise red and white complexions either for the way in which they betray their owners' fears and shames (by turning white for fear and red for shame), or for the way in which they enable their owners to conceal fears and shames (because their naturally red and white colours camouflage the blushings and blanchings caused by sudden emotions). These poems are essentially the same as that poem in *Love's Labour's Lost* which Moth called "a dangerous rhyme . . . against the reason of white and red." So here again, a red and white image to which I attach biographical significance in the exposition of the story of the Sonnets appears to be but a convention of the time.

The two excerpts in Category E (Numbers 61 and 62) are an interesting variation of this theme: they praise black, because it, unlike red and white, is "always one" (61) and "cannot blush for shame, look pale for fear" (62). This, surprisingly, is not a theme used in the Sonnets (where it might have been expected were the Dark Lady literally dark), but the idea does appear in *Titus Andronicus*, where Aaron, who, like Othello, is a Moor, says

> Coal-black is better than another hue,
> In that it scorns to bear another hue . . .

and, to one who blushes,

> Why, there's the privilege your beauty bears.
> Fie, treacherous hue, that will betray with blushing
> The close enacts and counsels of thy heart!
>
> [IV,ii,99-100; 116-118].

The excerpts in Appendix III seem to show that the entire corpus of the red and white imagery in Shakespeare's poems and plays, in which I find allusions and tributes to Henry Wriothesley, is but a commonplace of Elizabethan literature. The same is true, however, for almost every figure and theme Shakespeare ever used;[44] does this compel us to conclude that the figures and images used by Shakespeare in his Sonnets and poems, because they are so common, have no personal meaning? The universal recognition of Shakespeare's genius requires this notion, founded upon Shakespeare's being nothing more than a mechanical imitator of other people's poetic stock in trade, to be rejected out of hand.

This leaves us, then, with the only other possible critical approach to Shakespeare's language and imagery — and by default, perhaps, with a canon which must be the foundation for Shakespeare studies: that Shakespeare was preternaturally inventive, incisive and discriminating in his use of language and images, and that, even where (as is so often the case) his language and imagery are conventional, or traceable to a specific source, they convey, in ways which may not be obvious, sensibilities, ideas and thoughts peculiarly his own.

Caroline F. E. Spurgeon, who studied Shakespeare's imagery on the premise that it revealed something about Shakespeare (she called her book *Shakespeare's Imagery and What it Tells Us*), did not waste much time agonizing over the fact that his contemporaries used many of the same images that he did, but merely asserted that "a poet's imagery reveals his own idiosyncrasies, and not only the usages of his period."[45] She was perhaps right to dismiss the topic so summarily; nevertheless, the analysis of John Vyvyan, in discussing Shakespeare's borrowings from Brooke's poem about *Romeus and Juliet*, and in arriving at the same conclusion as Dr. Spurgeon, is enlightening in its discussion of what would be the consequences of a contrary conclusion:

Are Shakespeare's borrowings to be discounted from the point of view of parable and plot? Are we to say, "he took this detail from so-and-so, and therefore he must not be given credit for the thought"? Or, on the other hand, should we maintain that Shakespeare was selective in his appropriations; that he took from his sources only what would fit into his own pattern; and that because this new context gives a new, or enhanced significance to the old ideas, they must therefore be accounted Shakespearean?

Fine critics could be cited in support of either contention. But if we were to press the first to logical finality, substracting from Shakespeare every phrase and

conception for which we could find a source, the outcome would be near disinte-
gration. The plays would begin to look like rag-mats, stitched together out of
innumerable pieces of ancient material. We are compelled to revolt against this
grotesque conclusion. . . . By selecting [a detail] . . .with deliberation, he makes it,
from our standpoint, his own. Details that are used with allegorical consistency from
play to play must, it seems to me, be treated as Shakespeare's, whatever their
source.[46]

So, the only reasonable conclusion, the only rational basis for literary
criticism and scholarship, is to treat a writer's imagery, however derivative,
as his own, and personally meaningful.

We have already seen how productive was this principle when applied to
Tennyson's poems about roses, to say nothing about the poems and works
examined by Barbara Seward. Some of the poems in Appendix III also illustrate the validity of this common-sense principle. For instance, excerpt 23
from a poem by Spenser refers to "the Redde rose medled with the White
yfere [together]," and excerpt 46 from a poem by Fulke Greville states that
"Under a throne I saw a virgin sit,/ The red and white rose quartered in her
face. . . ." Since "red and white roses in the face" is a very common image,
are we to conclude that finding a reference in these poems to Queen Elizabeth
would be fanciful? Obviously not: we are familiar with Queen Elizabeth's
badge, and we immediately grasp the import of the lines. (And, in the case
of the Spenser poem, the gloss by E.K. expressly tells us that this is a
reference to Queen Elizabeth.) Similarly, can we assume that Spenser's praise
of a red and white complexion, in excerpt 38, from his *Epithalamion*, is
meaningless because it is common, or because he had previously applied the
image to Queen Elizabeth, or may we to the contrary assume that he was
sincerely praising the beauty of the woman he was about to marry?

In Shakespeare too, we must treat his images, however conventional, as
his own, and attempt to find, if we can, the reason he used them. Shakespeare's designation of his friend as a Rose invites, rather than precludes, the
conclusion that the designation has its source in facts peculiarly apposite to the
friend. And once we start looking specifically for the reason for Shakespeare's
abundant use of seemingly trite red and white imagery, we are led back to the
main theme of this book and the only reason for Shakespeare's addiction to
white and red that anyone has ever suggested:[47] the spandrel at Titchfield,
and the convergence in the red and white roses in the shield on that spandrel
of the arms, name, title and beauty of Shakespeare's Friend. In the light of
that shield, what seemed banal and conventional becomes fresh and novel —
and above all, to Shakespeare and his Friend, personally meaningful.

Some indication of just how meaningful this red and white Southampton badge was to Shakespeare can be gleaned from instances where Shakespeare takes a *non* red and white image available to him and then paints it over with the red and white Wriothesley tinctures.

An example of this can be found in *Venus and Adonis*. Commentators have noted certain discrepancies between this story as Shakespeare wrote it and the story as written by Ovid, who was Shakespeare's source. J.A.K. Thomson pinpoints the problems:

But what is most remarkable is the freedom with which he [Shakespeare] has treated his source. If he kept a Latin Ovid open before him, he troubled very little to consult it. Thus in the original story Adonis upon his death changes into a red flower, 'all one colour with the blood,' says Golding. But what Shakespeare says is:

> A purple flower sprung up, chequer'd with white,
> Resembling well his pale cheeks and the blood
> Which in round drops upon their whiteness stood.

Thomson then quotes Golding's account of the demise of *Narcissus*, with a description of "his lively hue of white and red," and concludes:

It looks as if Shakespeare had got mixed up in his recollection — at least he could not have been looking at the Latin here. Nor could he, when he says at the end that Venus

> yokes her silver doves: by whose swift aid
> Their mistress mounted through the empty skies
> In her light chariot quickly is convey'd;

for in Ovid the chariot is drawn not by doves but by swans. He was trusting to his memory, which told him that the sacred bird of Venus was the dove. And in fact her chariot is drawn by doves in *Metamorphoses*, xiv. 597.[48]

Shakespeare's confused memory *may* be the reason for the red and white flower and silver doves, but I suggest that Adonis became a red and white flower instead of a red flower because of the roses argent and gules on the Southampton coat of arms, and that Venus was transported by white doves, instead of swans, partly because her sacred bird was a dove, but mostly because Shakespeare's sacred friend bore doves argent on his coat of arms.

Another and a most striking instance of Shakespeare's adapting conventional images to honour and commemorate his friend's name, insignia,

84

badges and emblems is in Scene iv of Act 2 of *Henry VI, Part I* — the so-called Temple Garden Scene. Although the authorship of much of the play is in doubt, this scene is universally conceded to be the work of Shakespeare.[49] The scene depicts the event which resulted in the white rose becoming the badge of the house of York, and the red rose the badge of the house of Lancaster; the remarkable thing about this scene is that the event depicted therein is not founded on historical fact, and there is no known source from which Shakespeare might have drawn the incidents set forth.[50] The imagery of this fictional event is on its face the same conventional red and white rose imagery which fills Appendix III:

[The Earls of Somerset, Suffolk and Warwick, Richard Plantagenet, Vernon and a lawyer are in the garden adjacent to the "Temple Hall". An argument has developed between Plantagenet and Somerset over a matter — never disclosed by Shakespeare — on which the others seem reluctant to express their views:]

Plantagenet.   Since you are tongue-tied and so loath to speak,
             In dumb significants proclaim your thoughts.
             Let him that is a true-born gentleman
             And stands upon the honour of his birth,
             If he suppose that I have pleaded truth,
             From off this brier pluck a white rose with me.
Somerset.   Let him that is no coward nor no flatterer,
             But dare maintain the party of the truth,
             Pluck a red rose from off this thorn with me.
Warwick.   I love no colours, and without all colour
             Of base insinuating flattery
             I pluck this white rose with Plantagenet.
Suffolk.   I pluck this red rose with young Somerset,
             And say withal I think he held the right. . . .
Vernon.   Then for the truth and plainness of the case,
             I pluck this pale and maiden blossom here,
             Giving my verdict on the white rose side.
Somerset.   Prick not your finger as you pluck it off,
             Lest bleeding you do paint the white rose red
             And fall on my side so, against your will. . . .
Plantagenet.   Now, Somerset, where is your argument?
Somerset.   Here in my scabbard, meditating that
             Shall dye your white rose in a bloody red.
Plantagenet.   Meantime your cheeks do counterfeit our roses;
             For pale they look with fear, as witnessing
             The truth on our side.

Somerset.   No, Plantagenet,
              Tis not for fear, but anger, that thy cheeks
              Blush for pure shame to counterfeit our roses,
              And yet thy tongue will not confess thy error.
Plantagenet. Hath not thy rose a canker, Somerset?
Somerset.   Hath not thy rose a thorn, Plantagenet?
Plantagenet. Ay, sharp and piercing, to maintain his truth;
              Whiles thy consuming canker eats his falsehood.

                                    [Lines 24-38; 46-51; 59-71.]

And so on. Some might say that this scene is nothing more than the appropriation of the red and white imagery so popular at the time to a dramatic use, but more likely an explanation, I believe, is that it is another example of the appropriation of conventional red and white and rose imagery to the service and glory of Henry Wriothesley, focussing this time on the historical aspects of the arms over the door of his family home. Like most of the Tudor peerage (to say nothing of the Tudor monarchs), Henry Wriothesley had ancestors who had fought for both York and Lancaster. The ones we know about were on his mother's side: John Nevill, Marquis of Montagu, the great, great grand-father of Wriothesley's mother, was the brother of "the king-maker," Richard Nevill, initially Earl of Warwick, and later Earl of Salisbury. These two brothers, who figure prominently in *Henry VI, Parts II* and *III*, had at various times fought for (or perhaps *against* would be more accurate; at all times what they were really fighting *for* was their own property and power) both the York and Lancaster factions.[51] John and Richard Nevill were killed on Easter Sunday in 1472, fighting at the battle of Barnet against Edward IV, who had their bodies displayed at St. Paul's Cathedral as proof of the demise of his then chief enemies (who in earlier times had been instrumental in his accession to the throne). By the time of Shakespeare, a family's allegiance during the War of the Roses was not a social or political liability, for the promise made at the end of *Richard III* by the founder of the Tudor line, "We will unite the white rose and the red" (V,v,19), had been fulfilled. Shakespeare's injection into the history of the war between the houses of Lancaster and York of a profusion of nonhistorical red and white rose imagery was calculated, I believe, to compliment his Rose on his high descent (red rose of Lancaster and white rose of York), title (red and white roses of Southampton) and beauty ("red and white").

Others will say, but what could be more natural or obvious, in a play about the War of the Roses, than the use of red and white rose imagery? And they will reject the idea that the imagery has anything to do with Henry

Wriothesley. The short answer to this objection is that "The War of the Roses" was not the contemporary name given to this fifteenth century conflict (in which the opposing sides did not in fact make any marked use of red and white roses to identify themselves), but a name applied to it at least a hundred years later,[52] doubtless primarily because of the red and white rose imagery employed in fictional scenes in Shakespeare's plays on the subject. In other words, for reasons associated more with Henry Wriothesley than with the Houses of York and Lancaster, or of Tudor, red and white roses, as they appeared on the shield of Titchfield, inspired the language and imagery which retroactively gave to the War of the Roses its name and symbols.

Elizabethan writers, in anagrams, puns and acrostics, frequently insinuated into their poems the names of their beloveds; Shakespeare, by the extensive use of red and white and rose imagery — tritely conventional to the general, apocalyptically illuminating to the initiate — infused throughout his verse, and in some of his early plays, the name and symbol of his beloved.

CHAPTER V

The Swelling Verse

Why, thy verse swells with stuff so fine and smooth
That thou art even natural in thine art.

Timon of Athens, V,i,87–88.

In Chapter II, I stated that before the discovery of the heraldic Roses at Titchfield, and for reasons not dependent upon any supposed Rōse-ly/ Wriothesley pun, I had concluded that Henry Wriothesley is the Rose of the Sonnets. The bases for that conclusion, along with the other and intimately connected conclusion that Thomas Nashe is the poet whose interest in the Fair Friend is the subject of the so-called "Rival Poet" sonnets, were set forth in a book published in 1974. The discovery of the roses at Titchfield confirms my identification of Henry Wriothesley as the Rose of the Sonnets; what I propose here to do is recapitulate my 1974 conclusions,[1] and show that those relating to Nashe, too, are confirmed by the same evidence.

My conclusions with respect to Henry Wriothesley and Thomas Nash were the product of a chain of reasoning consisting of five links. The first link is the fact that, whoever the Fair Friend of the Sonnets may have been — Henry Wriothesley, William Herbert, William Hughes or anyone else — Shakespeare uses the word "Rose" as a metaphor for that friend. The instances of this have already been given in Chapter II of this book, and establish beyond peradventure of doubt that "Rose" is Shakespeare's symbol for his friend.

The second link is not a fact, but a conclusion based upon my interpretation of one of the "Rival Poet" sonnets, Sonnet 86:

Was it the proud full saile of his great verse,
Bound for the prize of (all to precious) you,
That did my ripe thoughts in my braine inhearce,
Making their tombe the wombe wherein they grew?
Was it his spirit, by spirits taught to write,
Above a mortall pitch, that struck me dead?
No, neither he, nor his compiers by night
Giving him ayde, my verse astonished.
He nor that affable familiar ghost
Which nightly gulls him with intelligence,
As victors of my silence cannot boast,
I was not sick of any feare from thence.
  But when your countinance fild up his line,
  Then lackt I matter, that infeebled mine.

My conclusion was that in this sonnet, the rival poet's "great verse,/ Bound for the prize of (all to precious) you" was a phallic poem written to the young man of the Sonnets. The route to that improbable conclusion was this: my analyses of Shakespeare's writings revealed that the puns in Shakespeare's poems and plays are unrelentingly sexual, and intensely phallic.[2] The abundance in Shakespeare's writings of readily apparent plays upon phallic words led to the suspicion that many passages in Shakespeare's writings might acquire an acuity otherwise lacking if words not on their surface phallic were read as references to the male member. Among the many words whose phallic potential seemed particularly to add wit[3] to the passages in which they are found are *verse* and *boat* (or other words meaning "boat," such as *barge, bark, ship* or *pinnace*). This suspicion was easily confirmed, for with respect to these words (and many others, too) Shakespeare left clues revealing how "they that dally with words may quickly make them wanton" (*Twelfth Night*, III,i,16) and in various *loci*, almost as if to make sure that we will understand his jokes, he explicitly associates these not-too-apparently phallic words with obviously phallic words. Thus we are told in a passage in *Love's Labour's Lost* that a *verse* is a "staff" (IV,ii,101–107) — a staff, in the sense of "stick," "pole" or "rod," being an obvious phallic metaphor — and in *King Lear* we learn that a *boat* is a "cock" (IV,vi,17–20), that is, a cockboat.[4] The verse = staff or penis pun proved to be the key to the unravelling of Sonnet 86 and the identification of the Rival Poet, and the boat = cock or penis pun confirms in a different way the conclusion reached by the verse/penis pun.

To demonstrate, before proceeding to the third link in my chain of reasoning, that the penis/verse equation which constitutes the second link really does exist, I ask those readers who may think that I, like Falstaff, am mistaking my erection, and building upon a false premise, to consider the two lines from *Timon of Athens* at the beginning of this chapter. These lines provide a clear and relatively unambiguous (*relatively*, because a pun, by definition, *must* be ambiguous) example of the penis/verse pun so critical to my argument. The pun reveals itself through the peculiar cluster of words accompanying "verse" — i.e., "swells," "stuff," and "natural" — words having meanings which describe attributes of a penis as well as (if not better than) those of a verse. "Swells" needs no explication; "stuff" means "semen" (Partridge, s.v. *stuff*); and "Nature," in Shakespeare's time, among other things meant, to quote from the definition of the Italian word *natura* in John Florio's *New World of Words*, "the quaint of a woman, or priuie parts of any man or beast." Farmer and Henley define "nature" as "the generative organs: male or female; and (2) the semen." See also OED, s.v. nature, (II, 7 and 8) and Rubinstein, s.v. nature. "Natural," of course, is the adjectival form of the word. So the statement that an object distended and filled with semen is "natural" is tantamount to an explicit identification of that object. Indeed, what gives the lines from *Timon of Athens* their point is the penis in them, for their surface meaning, that someone's verse is packed with such *fine stuff* that it is *natural*, is rather oxymoronic, whereas the subsurface meaning, that someone's swelling penis, distended by much good seminal matter, is observable even in his writing, is not only amusing, but is also, as it happens, a just description of a characteristic of Shakespeare's own writing.

On the basis, then, of the perception that in some contexts a "verse" can be a penis,[5] I concluded that the word used by Shakespeare to designate the object whose "proud full saile" was in Sonnet 86 pointing in the youth's direction could, as a matter of semantics, signify a penis as well as a verse, and was undoubtedly intended to signify both (for in a good pun, all possible meanings of the pun-word are operative).

Even as I reached the conclusion that the first line of Sonnet 86 was a reference to "the proud distention of a great penis/verse" (literally, a "verse that swells"), I fully appreciated the ridicule which this conclusion invited, and would have suppressed it, had it not yielded so rich a result.

For — and now we come to the third link — there had been written in Elizabethan times a poem which fits remarkably well the description of a penis/verse: the *Dildo* of Thomas Nashe.

Nashe, his Dildo, or *Nashe's Dildo*, was the name by which was commonly known a poem more properly called *The Choise of Valentines*.[6] The poem is about a young man who visits his girl friend, recently retired to a brothel. In their amorous foreplay, he has a premature ejaculation, much to the annoyance of the young woman who, however, by rubbing and chafing, restores the "silly worm" to life. But this second life is brief; the silly worm again expires ("Why shouldst thou fade, that are but newelie borne?" she mournfully asks), and so the girl turns from this "faint-hearted instrument of lust" to "my little dildo,"

> That bendeth not, nor fouldeth anie deale,
> But stands as stiff, as he were made of steele.[7]

The poem then ends with a detailed description of the dildo.

Nashes's poem is referred to by name by Gabriel Harvey in *The Trimming of Thomas Nashe*, published in 1597: "Your Dildoe & such subjects are fit matter for you, for of those you cannot speak amisse."[8] But the poem must have been written at least four or five years prior to 1597, for

Harvey, in his *Pierce's Supererogation*, the text of which was completed on 27 April 1593, and published later in the same year, refers clearly to the same poem, in his excoriation of Nashe:

I will not here decipher the unprinted packet of bawdy and filthy rhymes, in the nastiest kind; there is a fitter place for the discovery of that foulest shame, and the whole ruffianism of thy brothel Muse, if she still prostitute her obscene ballads, and will needs be a young courtezan of old knavery.[9]

So it is certain that Nashe's poem was written before the end of 1593, and it is more than probable that the poem was written a year or two prior to 1593.

The fourth link is that one of the manuscripts of Nashe's *Dildo* which has come down to us bears the dedication, "To the right Honorable the Lord S". In this manuscript, one dedicatory sonnet precedes the *Dildo*, and another dedicatory sonnet follows it. This is the first of the two dedicatory sonnets:

> Pardon sweete flower of matchless Poetrie,
>   And fairest bud the red rose euer bare;
>   Although my Muse deuor'st from deeper care
>   Presents thee with a wanton Elegie.
> Ne blame my verse of loose unchastitie
>   For painting forth the things that hidden are,
>   Since all men acte what I in speache declare,
>   Onelie induced by varietie.
> Complaints and praises euerie one can write,
>   And passion-out their pangu's in statelie rimes,
>   But of loues pleasure's none did euer write
>   That hath succeeded in theis latter times.
> Accept of it Dear Lord in gentle gree,
>   And better lynes ere long shall honor thee.[10]

The significant thing in this sonnet is the first two lines, in which "the Lord S" is addressed first as a flower — not only a flower, but a flower of matchless poetry — and then specifically as a rose.

On the basis of these four interlinked observations — (1) that the friend in the Sonnets is denominated a Rose, (2) that (by my interpretation of Sonnet 86) a rival poet had written a phallic poem to that Rose, (3) that a phallic poem had in fact been written by Thomas Nashe, and (4) that Nashe's phallic poem is dedicated to a Lord S, who is described in the prefatory Sonnet as a "sweet flower of matchless Poetrie" and the "fairest bud the red rose euer bare," — I arrived at the conclusion that the "matchless" poetrie of which Lord S was the flower was the Sonnets, and that the Fair Friend of the Sonnets and Lord S of the *Dildo* are one and the same.

I then turned to consider who this Lord S might be. Only two persons have been seriously advanced as candidates for the honour of being the patron of the *Dildo*: Ferdinando Stanley, Lord Strange, who was born in 1559, became the Earl of Derby in September, 1593, and died in April, 1594,[11] and Henry Wriothesley, Earl of Southampton, who was born in 1573, and succeeded to the earldom in 1581. While the writers on this subject who favour Lord Southampton are in the majority,[12] no one has offered any hard evidence for his conclusions. Those who, like E. K. Chambers, think that Lord S could not be Lord Southampton, dwell on the point that "Southampton had no claim to be addressed as the 'fairest bud the red rose euer bare,'"[13] in supposed contrast to Lord Strange who was descended from Henry VII, the Lancastrian king whose badge was a red rose. Lord Strange's connection with the red rose, a recent biographer of Nashe has written, "rules out the only plausible competitor, the Earl of Southampton,"[14] and establishes Strange as the dedicatee of the *Dildo*.

But if my analysis equating Lord S of the *Dildo* with the Rose of the Sonnets is correct, then the Lord S of the *Dildo*, if he could be only either Lord Southampton or Lord Strange, must be Lord Southampton. This is because (and this is the fifth and last fact or link in my chain of reasoning) Lord Strange was five years older than Shakespeare, and thus unlikely to be referred to by Shakespeare as a "beautious and lovely youth," whereas Southampton was nine years younger than Shakespeare, and was only 20 in 1593 when Shakespeare, who had probably by then known him for some time, dedicated to him *Venus and Adonis*.

In this wise, determining on the basis of internal evidence in each poem that the dedicatee of Nashe's poem and the Fair Friend of Shakespeare's Sonnets are one and the same, and then making inferences about the dedicatee of Nashe's poem from what we know of the Friend in Shakespeare's poems, and *vice versa*, I arrived at my conclusions that the Fair Friend of the Sonnets was Henry Wriothesley, and the poet who was Shakespeare's rival for his favours was Thomas Nashe.

These conclusions were not based upon any assumption that the Fair Friend used a *Rose* as a badge or a rebus, but upon the indisputable fact that Shakespeare used the Rose as a poetic metaphor for the young man of the Sonnets. The subsequent discovery of the shield at Titchfield which discloses that the Roses of Southampton were in fact employed by the Wriothesley family both as their badge and as a rebus for their name, instantly provides a compelling explanation for Shakespeare's use of that metaphor, and not only confirms that Henry Wriothesley is the Rose of Shakespeare's Sonnets, but also establishes that he is at least as qualified as Lord Strange to be the Lord S of Nashe's *Dildo*: for although the red rose is a Lancastrian badge, and may thus have been associated with Lord Strange, it is also, as we have seen, the ancient badge of the County of Southampton, whence most people during the lifetime of the third Earl of Southampton assumed he derived his honour. Thus if a discernible connection with a red rose is required of "Lord S," then handsome young Henry Wriothesley of the Rose badge and Rose name has a claim as good as (and, in my opinion, patently better than) Lord Strange — who was 34 years old in 1593, and not famous for his beauty — to be called the "fairest bud the red rose euer bare."

A validating consequence of the identification of the Nashe's bawdy *Dildo* as the "great verse" by which the Rival Poet hoped to win the patronage of the Earl of Southampton is that it solves a number of mysteries. What, for instance, is the significance of the quotation from Ovid's *Amores* on the title page of Shakespeare's *Venus and Adonis*? That quotation,

> *Vilia miretur vulgus: mihi flavus Apollo*
> *Pocula Castalia plena ministret aqua*

translates as "Let the base vulgar admire trash; to me golden-haired Apollo shall serve goblets filled from the Castalian spring."[15] (The Castalian spring, on Mount Parnassus, was sacred to Apollo and the Muses, and the source of inspiration.)

The answer to this is readily supplied by the valedictory Sonnet which follows Nashe's *Dildo*:

> Thus hath my penne presum'd to please my friend;
>> Oh mightst thow lykewise please Apolo's eye.
>> No: Honor brooke's no such impietie;
>> Yett Ouids wanton Muse did not offend.
> He is the fountaine whence my streames do flow.
>> Forgiue me if I speake as I was taught,
>> A lyke to women, utter all I knowe,
>> As longing to unlade so bad a fraught.
> My mynde once purg'd of such lasciuious witt,
>> With purifide word's and hallowed verse
>> Thy praises in large volumes shall rehearce,
>> That better maie thy grauer view befitt.

> Meanewhile yett rests, yow smile at what I write,
> Or for attempting, banish me your sight.
>
> Thomas Nashe[16]

Obviously, the epigraph to *Venus and Adonis*, quoting Ovid's disdain for the vulgar, is Shakespeare's rejoinder to the claim in Nashe's sonnet to Lord S that his *Dildo* is in the spirit of Ovid, and is an invitation to Southampton to compare the elegant eroticism of Shakespeare's poem with the coarse lewdness of Nashe's, and to decide which of the two poets truly continues the tradition of the Master they both invoke.

Another mystery solved by Nashe's being the Rival Poet and the Dildo's being the "great verse" bound for the Fair Friend is the identity of the person referred to by Spenser in three stanzas of the "Lament of Thalia" in *The Teares of the Muses*, published in 1591:

> And he the man, whome Nature Selfe had made
> To mock her selfe, and Truth to imitate,
> With kindly counter under Mimick shade,
> Our pleasant *Willy*, ah is dead of late:
> With whom all ioy and iolly merriment
> Is also deaded, and in dolour drent.
>
> In stead thereof scoffing Scurrilitie
> And scornfull Follie with Comtempt is crept,
> Rolling in rymes of shameles ribaudrie
> Without regard, or due Decorum kept,
> Each idle wit at will presumes to make,
> And doth the Learneds taske upon him take.
>
> But that same gentle Spirit, from whose pen
> Large streames of honnie and sweete Nectar flowe,
> Scorning the boldnes of such base-born men,
> Which dare their follies forth so rashlie throwe;
> Doth rather choose to sit in idle Cell,
> Than so himselfe to mockerie to sell.[17]

Sonnet 86, it will be remembered, describes its author as one whose ripe thoughts were in his brain inhearced, and who was "struck . . . dead" by the Fair Friend's favourable reception of the Rival's "great verse." Spenser's account of a poet named Willy, a "gentle Spirit, from whose pen/ Large streams of honnie and sweet Nectar flowe," and who is "dead of late" and "sit[s] in idle Cell" silenced by "rymes of shameles ribaudrie," is so remarkably similar to the story I have inferred from the language of Sonnet 86, as to compel the conclusion that both poems describe the same event.[18]

Another curious Nashe–Spenser connection with Sonnet 86 exists. At the conclusion of *Pierce Penilese*, published in 1592, Nashe complains that although at the end of that portion of the *Faerie Queen* published in 1590 Spenser had addressed poems to an "honourable catalogue of our English Heroes" (English nobles such as Lord Burghley, the Earl of Oxford, the Earl of Northumberland, the Earl of Essex, and others), he had let pass one "special piller of Nobilitie." Of this pillar, Nashe wrote:

The verie thought of his far deriued discent, & extraordinarie parts, wherewith he astonieth the world, and drawes all harts to his loue, would haue inspired the forewearied Muse with new furie to proceede to the next triumphs of thy statelie Goddesse: but as I, in fauour of so rare a scholler, suppose, with this consell he refrained his mention in this first part, that he might with *full saile* [emphasis supplied] proceed to his due commendations in the second. Of this occasion long since I happened to frame a sonnet, which, being wholie intended to the reuerence of this renoumed Lord (to whom I owe all the vtmoste powers of my loue and dutie), I meante heere for variety of stile to insert.

> Perusing yesternight, with idle eyes,
>   The Fairy Singers stately tuned verse,
> And viewing after Chap-mens wonted guise,
>   What strange contents the title did rehearse;
> I streight leapt ouer to the latter end,
>   Where like the queint Comœdians of our time,
> That when their Play is doone do fal to ryme,
>   I found short lines, to sundry Nobles pend;
> Whom he as speciall Mirrours singled fourth,
>   To be the patrons of his Poetry:
> I read them all, and reuerenc't their worth,
> Yet wondred he left out thy memory.
>   But therefore gest I he supprest thy name,
>   Because few words might not cōprise thy fame.[19]

Who this "special piller of Nobilitie" is, Nashe doesn't say. Some have suggested that he is Southampton,[20] and this I believe to be the case: the audacious suggestion, that since Spenser had not proceeded "full saile" to honour this special pillar of nobility, Nashe would remedy the omission by his own sonnet, undoubtedly accounts for part of Shakespeare's mocking phrase, "the proud full saile of his great verse."

But the passage of hitherto unnoticed significance in the writings of Nashe which seems primarily to have inspired the nautical metaphors in the Rival Poet Sonnets is Nashe's preface to the first and evidently unauthorized edition of Sir Philip Sidney's *Astrophel and Stella*, published in 1591. Toward the end of the preface, Nashe writes:

Indeed, to say the truth, my style is somewhat heavy-gaited, and cannot dance and trip so lively; with "Oh my love," "Ah my love," "all my loves gone," as other Shepherds that have been fools in the Morris time out of mind: nor hath my prose any skill to imitate the "Almond leape verse," or sit tabering five years together nothing but "to be," "to he," on a paper drum. Only I can keep pace with Gravesend barge, and care not if I have water enough to land my ship of fools with the Term (the tide I should say). Now every man is not of that mind, for some, to go the lighter away, will take in their freight of spangled feathers, golden pebbles, straw, reeds, bulrushes, or any thing, and then they bear out their sails as proudly as if they were ballasted with Bulbiefe [bullbeef?]. Others are so hardly bested for loading that they are fain to retail the cinders of Troy, and the shivers of broken trunchions, to fill up their boat that else should go empty: and if they have but a pound weight of good merchandise, it shall be placed at the poop, or plucked in a thousand pieces to credit their carriage.[21]

Here Nashe, using ships and their contents as metaphors for poets and their writings, compares himself to a heavily loaded Gravesend barge (Gravesend is a bustling area of wharves and docks near the mouth of the Thames): his content is weighty; whether water enough exists to land his ship is something which doesn't concern him. He speaks disparagingly of those poets who carry a lighter freight — feathers, pebbles, straws, reeds or bulrushes — and then "bear out their sails as proudly" as if they were loaded with a more substantial cargo.

One of the poets accused by Nashe of being desperate for matters of substance to put in his verse is clearly Nicholas Breton, for "Oh my love, ah my love, all my love gone" is a line from *Amoris Lachrimae*, Breton's poem on the death of Sir Philip Sidney, printed in *Brittons Bowre* in 1591.[22] Another such matterless poet is probably William Shakespeare: the "tabering . . . on a paper drum" (which would appear to mean "pounding out on a piece of paper the same words or themes, again and again") of "to he" is explicable as a reference to the many sonnets addressed to the Fair Friend, and the "to be" seems to be a reference to the soliloquy from *Hamlet*.[23]

That Shakespeare was the target of Nashe's gibes at those who fill up "their boat that else should go empty" with worthless cargo and then "bear out their sails as proudly as if they were ballasted" with weightier cargo, although not all that clear to us, seems to have been clear enough to Shakespeare, for his Sonnets 80 and 86 respond, with remarkably apposite boat imagery of their own, to Nashe's accusations. In Sonnet 86, as we have seen, Shakespeare jeeringly points out that the "great verse," or weighty cargo, borne out by Nashe's "proud full saile" is his obscene *Dildo!*; so much for Nashe's pretensions. Sonnet 80 deals at greater length with Nashe's mockery; addressing the Fair Friend, Shakespeare says:

> O how I faint when I of you do write,
> Knowing a better spirit doth use your name,
> And in the praise thereof spends all his might,
> To make me toung-tide speaking of your fame.
> But since your worth (wide as the Ocean is)
> The humble as the proudest saile doth beare,
> My sawsie barke (inferior farre to his)
> On your broad maine doth willfully appeare.
> Your shallowest helpe will hold me up a floate,
> Whilst he upon your soundlesse deepe doth ride,
> Or (being wrackt) I am a worthlesse bote,
> He of tall building, and of goodly pride.
> > Then if he thrive and I be cast away,
> > The worst was this, my love was my decay.

Cheerfully, and with relish for its phallic potential, Shakespeare here adopts Nashe's boat imagery, which makes of Nashe a heavily loaded barge who cares not if he has enough water to land his ship, and of Shakespeare a lightly loaded boat — a "sawsie barke (inferior farre to his)": but then, in compliment to the young man to whom he writes the poem, Shakespeare asserts that these differences between the two poets are inconsequential, the only significant thing being whether the youth favours one or the other, for the youth is like the ocean who "the humble as the proudest saile doth beare," and his "shallowest helpe" — which I take to be the "slightest indication of favour" — will keep Shakespeare up, whereas if Shakespeare is "wrackt" — put down, or denied favour — then, and for that reason alone, he will be a "worthlesse bote," while if his rival obtains favour, then, and for that reason alone, the rival will be "of tall building, and of goodly pride."

But Nashe did not thrive; in this rivalry of poets, it was Shakespeare, and not Nashe, who carried the field, as I believe is evident from the publishing history of Nashe's book, *The Unfortunate Traveller*, which was entered in the Stationers' Register on 17 September 1593.[24] As published some time in 1594 (presumably early), the book bears a dedication "to the right Honorable Lord Henrie Wriothsley, Earle of South-hampton and Baron of Tichfeeld," which reads in part as follows:

Long haue I desired to approoue my wit vnto you. My reuerent duetifull thoughts (euen from their infancie) haue been retayners to your glorie. . . . Incomprehensible is the heigth of your spirit both in heroical resolution and matters of conceit. Vnrepriueably perisheth that booke whatsoeuer to wast paper, which on the diamond rocke of your iudgement disasterly chanceth to be ship-wrackt. A dere louer and cherisher you are, as well of the louers of Poets, as of Poets themselues. Amongst their sacred number I dare not ascribe my selfe, though now and then I speake English: that smal braine I haue to no further vse I conuert, saue to be kinde to my frends and fatall to my enemies. A new brain, a new wit, a new stile, a new soule will I get mee, to canonize your name to posterities, if in this my first attempt I be not taxed of presumption. . . .Your Lordship is the large spreading branch of renown, from whence these my idle leaues seeke to derive their whole nourishing: it resteth you either scornfully shake them off, as worm-eaten & worthles, or in pity preserue them and cherish them, for some litle summer frute you hope to finde amongst them.[25]

This dedication to the then 20-year old earl so far exceeds all norms of Elizabethan hyperbole that I believe it to be a mocking parody of Shakespeare's dedication to Southampton of *Venus and Adonis*. Whether a serious request for favour, or a bitter satirization of the perceived sycophancy of a rival seeker of favour, the dedication is absent from a second edition of Nashe's work, also published in 1594 (presumably late).[26] An obvious suspicion is that the second edition was required so soon because the first edition with its objectionable dedication was, at Southampton's insistence, suppressed. In sharp contrast to this evident denial of favour to Nashe is the extension of favour to Shakespeare so clearly revealed in Shakespeare's dedication to *The Rape of Lucrece*, a work entered in the Stationer's Register on 9 May 1594, and published in the same year; secure in the knowledge that "your Honourable disposition . . . makes it assured of acceptance," Shakespeare dedicated not merely his poem to Henry Wriothesley, but also his love, "whereof this Pamphlet without beginning is but a superfluous Moity," and himself: "What I haue done is yours, what I haue to doe is yours, being part in all I haue, deuoted yours." Shakespeare had prevailed over his rival.

CHAPTER VI

Scholars, Statesmen, Soldiers, Spies, Sodomites and Sources

I have no doubt that Shakespeare's love for the Fair Friend was sexual as well as spiritual. This is, of course, a conclusion based upon a subjective evaluation of the language and tenor of the Sonnets, and a conclusion not too long ago generally rejected by influential critics who (on the basis primarily of their own subjective evaluations) wrote things such as "homosexuality had no place in Elizabethan social life,"[1] "Shakespeare alludes to homosexuality very seldom and most cursorily,"[2] and "Shakespeare's love for the young man . . . was not homosexual."[3]

Recently, however, the pendulum has swung the other way. The close reading of the poems and plays, and the application thereto of lexicological and linguistic knowledge and skills, as well as pure common sense and understanding of the human condition, have revealed in Shakespeare's writings situations, characters and expressions inexplicable except as depictions of the whole gamut of human sexual passions and desires, not excluding those between persons of the same sex. And it has become increasingly realized that when the author of the Sonnets, and male characters in *The Merchant of Venice*, *Twelfth Night*, and *Troilus and Cressida*, speak and act in such a way as to permit the inference that they are in love with other males, their words and actions, far from being aberrant, faithfully reflect a behaviour not uncommon among the educated people of the time.[4]

This behaviour is exemplified by the private life of the man who was King of England when the Sonnets were published. James I married, when he was 24, Anne of Denmark, who was then 14, and by her had seven children. At the same time, James loved — more dearly than anyone else, he would frequently tell them — a number of beautiful young men who during his lifetime came within his orbit, and most particularly Robert Carr and George Villiers, of both of whom may be said what Lord Clarendon said of the latter, "that his first introduction into favour was purely from the the handsomeness of his person."[5] No one ever saw (or at least let posterity know that he saw) the King *in flagrante delicto* with any of his minions, but then neither did anyone ever doubt the basic nature of the relationships.[6] And it was with the King's blessing, and not in any way disruptive of the King's relationship with them, that Robert Carr and George Villiers, initially of undistinguished families but by the King's grace transformed into the Earl of Somerset and the Duke of Buckingham, respectively, followed the example of the King himself in marrying, and having issue.[7]

The sexual proclivities and activities of the King and his favourites are instances at the highest level of what was not an unusual feature of upper-class life generally in 16th and early 17th century England. The King, to be sure, was from Scotland, but he found when he came to England a court which offered no objection, and indeed was receptive, to the overt expression of romantic interest by a male in persons of either sex.

The reason for that receptiveness was, I believe, the familiarity of the English aristocracy with the mores of antiquity, as reported and illustrated in Greek and Latin literature, and the licence to emulate those mores (contrary though they may have been to the teachings of the Christian Church) which those who were predisposed so to do felt was conferred by the authority and example of universally admired great men of antiquity. The seed from which sprouted and eventually flourished this sexually tolerant atmosphere had been planted in England more than a hundred years before James' accession to the throne, by the introduction there of humanism, the movement — whether the child or the parent of the Renaissance is hard to say — dedicated to the recovery and study of non-Christian Greek and Latin texts.

Although Henry VII's court was graced by a number of illustrious Italian humanists, the denization of humanism was accomplished by native Englishmen such as William Grocyn, William Latimer, Thomas Linacre, Thomas More and John Colet, whose labours were praised, sanctioned and sealed by the foremost northern European humanist of his day, Erasmus Desiderius, who from time to time worked among them. It was at the invitation of one of his students, William Blount, Lord Mountjoy, that Erasmus went to England for the first time in 1499 ("Where, indeed, would I not follow a young man so enlightened, so kindly and so amiable? I would follow him, as God loves me, even to the lower world itself"[8]). John Colet and Erasmus became good friends, and it may be that Erasmus' greatest contribution to the humanist movement while in England was convincing Colet, either by argument or example, of the importance to a Christian of the reading and study of pre-Christian authors.[9] For in about 1507, having inherited a large amount of money from his father, Colet (who did not know Greek) took by far the most significant step of anyone of his time toward institutionalizing and spreading the study of pagan literature by founding St Paul's School, in London, for the purpose of teaching 153 boys "good litterature both Laten and Greke."[10] His ultimate objective was "to incresse knowledge and worshipping of God and oure lorde Crist Jesu and good Cristen lyff and maners in the children."[11]

Other schools were founded on the model of St Paul's (one of the most famous was the Merchant Taylor's School, established in London in 1561 —

this was the school attended by Edmund Spenser; another was the Grammar School at Shrewsbury, founded in 1553 — Philip Sidney attended this school), and by this means a knowledge of Greek and Latin spread among the children of the upper classes. One widely-used technique of teaching languages at these schools was the production by the boys (only boys went to these schools) of Greek and Latin plays, the female characters being portrayed by boys in women's clothing.[12] The teaching of Greek was introduced in Cambridge, and, not without some opposition, in Oxford. By the winter of 1542/3, Roger Ascham could write to a friend that

Aristotle and Plato are now read by the boys in the original language, but that has been done among us at St. John's for the last five years. Sophocles and Euripedes are now more familiar to us than Plautus was when you were here. Herodotus, Thucydides, and Xenophon are more read now than Livy was then. They talk now as much of Demosthenes, as they did of Cicero at that time. There are more copies of Isocrates to be met with now than there were of Terence then. Yet we do not treat the Latin writers with contempt, but we cherish the best of them who flourished in the golden age of their literature.[13]

Unfortunately, not all of the boys who learned "Laten and Greke" necessarily confined their readings in those languages to books which advanced "good Cristen lyff and maners." Juan Luis Vives complained of "Ovid's books of Love, which we read and carry them in our hands, and learn them by heart, yea, and some schoolmasters teach them to their scholars, and some make expositions and expound the vices,"[14] and suggested that these writings, like those denounced by Plato, be banished from the Commonwealth.

But they weren't, and indeed it seems that no restrictions were ever imposed either by the State or the Universities on what the boys of England could read, so long as they read it in Greek and Latin. Thus the great body of Greek and Latin literature published by Aldus Manutius and his fellow scholar-printers in Italy, France and Germany was read in the mid-sixteenth century by the young persons who became the statesmen, philosophers, poets and playwrights of the late sixteenth-century. Inevitably, some of the lads (perhaps, as Vives charges, guided by their schoolmasters) must have encountered texts in which, in startling contrast to the sermons they heard at church, the love of men for other men was presented without pejorative comment in as matter-of-fact a way as was the love of men for women. An example of this which at an early date found its way into English translation is from Plutarch's *Morals*, which constituted the *Amorous and Tragicall Tales* part of James Sandford's translation, in 1567, of *Amorous and Tragicall Tales of Plutarch, Whereunto is annexed the History of Cariclea & Theagenes and the sayings of the Greek Philosophers*. The first amorous tale in Sandford's book is of Strato the Horchomenian and Callisthenes the Aliartian, both of whom were in love with a beautiful maiden, Aristoclea. She chose Callisthenes. Strato attempted to take her by force. Partisans of both sides pulled and tugged at her, as a consequence of which the maid was "rent in pieces and deprived of her life." The second tale in the book is of Acteon, son of Melissus, who excelled all other lads "both in beautie and modestie. . . . Very many loved hym, but most fervently of al, Archias. . . . When he had tempted the yong man, but all in vaine, he sought by force to obtaine his desire." Archias physically seized Acteon at a party given by Melissus; Melissus also grabbed hold of the youth. Acteon was rent in pieces. The second tale is told as naturally and straightforwardly as the first: that men might fight with each other for the love of a youth was no more worthy of comment than that men might fight with each other for the love of a maiden.

This little tale of the love of a man for a youth gave to an English-speaking audience of the sixteenth century but a tiny glimpse of the theme we have already examined in the *Love Letters* of Philostratus, which theme is prominent also in the Greek Anthology and in Greek romances, and, indeed, permeates Greek literature. The theme is conspicuous also in Latin literature — in, for example, the many poems in which Horace, Catullus and Tibullus express their love for various young men,[15] and most notoriously in Virgil's Second Eclogue, where the account of one shepherd's unrequited love for another —

Formosum pastor Corydon ardebat Alexin —

appears without comment, excuse, or perceptible embarrassment among nine other Eclogues by the ancient poet most loved by the humanists (which Eclogues also treat of the love of swains for maids — and one of which, the Fourth, was thought by some to foretell the birth of Christ). The existence, details and range of this theme were a part of the basic education of the students at Cambridge and Oxford, and inevitably had some effect upon their attitudes and actions.

To demonstrate the relationship, not causal, perhaps, but certainly dispensating, between classical literature and the expression of homosexual impulses in Elizabethan literature and life, I shall first review the extensive knowledge of Greek and Latin literature possessed by a specific group of statesmen and writers of the later Elizabethan era, and then show the presence in the lives and writings of some of this group of the same homoerotic elements so prevalent in Greek and Latin literature; after which, on the basis of the existence and nature of this group, and upon the premise of Shakespeare's easy access to the members of the group, I shall draw certain conclusions which put the eroticism of the Sonnets into a proper context and also, unexpectedly but gratifyingly, illuminate and demystify problems relating to Shakespeare's unlikely (if, as most people suppose, he had no more formal education than that provided by the local grammar school) but seemingly comprehensive knowledge of classical and contemporary European literatures.

1. A group of persons familiar with classical literature.

The specific group of persons upon whom I shall focus are those who were associated with, in the employ of, related to, or friends of Robert Dudley, Earl of Leicester, or his friend, Sir Francis Walsingham, and who subsequently, after the deaths of Leicester and Walsingham, became associated with, in the employ of, related to or friends of Robert Devereux, second Earl of Essex.

A. Leicester House.

As is well known, Robert Dudley had a curious hold upon the affections of Queen Elizabeth. On 11 January 1559, four days before her coronation, she granted him the office of Master of the Horse.[16] He was appointed a member of the Privy Council on 23 April 1559, and installed as a Knight of the Garter on 3 June 1559.[17] She bestowed upon him generous grants of revenues and lands (including Kenilworth Castle) "for the queen's great favour whereof she has declared him worthy above the rest of men on account of his many excellent virtues and gifts of mind."[18] On 29 September 1564, she created him Earl of Leicester, and on 31 December 1564 he was appointed Chancellor of Oxford University.[19]

At some not readily ascertainable time early in his career, but by 1569 at the latest, he acquired as his London residence a great house built orginally in the 14th century to serve as the Inn or lodging of the Bishops of Exeter. In 1548, this house, at the direction of the crown, had been conveyed by the Bishop of Exeter to William Paget,[20] for many years the friend and associate of Thomas Wriothesley (see Appendix I). It was then called Paget House, "because *William* Lord *Paget* enlarged and possessed it." After Paget died in

1563, title to the house passed, in a way that is not clear, ultimately to Robert Dudley, Earl of Leicester, during whose lifetime the house was called Leicester House, "because *Robert Dudley* Earle of Leycester of late new builded there. . . ." Leicester House was located between the Strand and the Thames, and was described by John Stow as being "first amongst other buildinges memorable for greatnes on the riuer of Thames. . . ."[21]

From Leicester House, Robert Dudley dispensed the patronage for which he was famous. Arthur Golding (1536?-1605?) dedicated to him, in 1565 and 1567, his translations of Ovid's *Metamorphosis*; James Sandford, whose 1567 translation of *Amorous Tales* by Plutarch has already been noted, dedicated to Leicester in 1573 his translation of Ludovico Guicciardini's *Detti, et Fatti*, a collection of anecdotes and sentences, some derived from the Greek Anthology,[22] published under the title of *The Garden of Pleasure*, and in 1583 his translation, under the title of *The Reuelation of S. Iohn reveled*, of a work by Giacopo Brocardo; and Richard Grafton (1512-1572) in 1563, Raphael Holinshed (1529-1580?) in 1577, and John Stow (1525-1605) in 1580, dedicated to him their various *Chronicles of England*.[23]

Leicester was able not only to give monetary gifts and positions in his household to those whom he favoured, but also, by virtue of being Chancellor of Oxford University, he could exercise his influence there to secure appointments and other benefits for his protégés.[24] Among those so helped by Leicester were a number of Italian Protestants resident in England: it was upon the recommendation of Leicester that Alberico Gentili (1552-1608), subsequently famed as one of the founders of international law, was enabled to teach at Oxford;[25] also attributable to Leicester appears to be the presence at Oxford in the late 1570's of John Florio (1553-1625) who there taught Italian to the scholars and translated accounts of the first two voyages of Jacques Cartier for Richard Hakluyt.[26] Fortuitously, perhaps, but more likely through their mutual connections with Leicester, Gentili and Florio met each other at Oxford, and each dedicated to Leicester an early work: Florio, in 1578, *His firste Fruites*, and Gentili, in 1582, his *De Iuris Interpretibus Dialogi Sex*.[27] Florio and Gentili were friends of Giordano Bruno, who lived at the home of the French ambassador in London from 1583 to 1585, during most of which time Florio was almost daily at the house, in his capacity of interpreter and tutor to the ambasador's daughter. It was with Florio and Florio's Welsh friend Matthew Gwynn, a physician, scholar, poet and author, that on 14 February 1584 Bruno attended the famous *Cena de le ceneri* at Fulke Greville's residence.[28] Four or five years later, these three friends,

Florio, Gwynn and Greville, worked together in preparing for the press Sidney's *Arcadia*.[29]

Leicester was also the patron, from 1559 until the time of his death, of a distinguished company of actors, including James Burbage and William Kempe, the latter of whom (rather than Shakespeare) is generally supposed to be "Will, my lord of Lester's jesting plaier" who with others of the troupe accompanied Leicester on his military expedition to the Low Countries in 1586, and presented pageants and other entertainments for him and his retinue.[30]

But the focus of Leicester's working life was politics, domestic and foreign, in aid of which he employed at Leicester House an extraordinarily accomplished staff of learned secretaries who wrote and dispatched letters to political and literary figures throughout England and the Continent, and translated for their master the extensive incoming correspondence from abroad. Before mentioning the best known of these secretaries and their accomplishments, I shall turn to the remarkable person who was the friend of the secretaries and who, after 1575, more even than its eponymous earl, brought fame to Leicester House as a centre for the conception and nurturing of the arts: this was Philip Sidney, the nephew of the Earl of Leicester.

Philip Sidney was born in 1554, the eldest child of Henry Sidney and of Leicester's sister, Mary Dudley. A sister Mary was born in 1561, a brother Robert in 1563, and a brother Thomas in 1569. Mary, in 1577, married Henry Herbert, second Earl of Pembroke, and was the mother of William and Philip Herbert, the third and fourth Earls of Pembroke. Aubrey writes that Sidney was "not only of an excellent witt, but extremely beautiful," although "not masculine enough; yett he was a person of great courage." Sidney much resembled his sister, who was "a beautifull Ladie." (Aubrey reports that "there was so great a Love between him and his faire sister that I have heard old gentlemen say that they lay together, and it was thought that the first Philip earle of Pembroke was begot by him, but he inherited not the witt of either brother or sister."[31])

Sidney also was extraordinarily charming, and captivated everyone who met him. He was enrolled at Shrewsbury Grammar School on 17 October 1564, on the same day as Fulke Greville, who then was, or soon thereafter became, one of Sidney's two closest friends, and who devoted his life to perpetuating Sidney's memory. Greville (created Lord Brook in 1620) never married, and for his epitaph wrote these words: "Fulke Greville, servant to Queen Elizabeth, Councillor to King James, and friend to Sir Philip Sidney, Trophaeum Peccati."[32] Sir Edward Dyer, who doubtless met the young Sidney (eleven years Dyer's junior) as a consequence of being in attendance upon the Earl of Leicester (as Dyer was as early as 1571), became, after Sidney's return from the Continent in 1575, the other of Sidney's two closest friends.[33] Like Greville, Dyer never married. Sidney bequeathed his books to Dyer and Greville, and both were pallbearers at his funeral.

At Christ Church, Oxford, where Sidney studied from 1568 to 1571, "the circle of his admirers grew"; chief among them were Richard Hakluyt, "an omniverous reader of accounts of voyages in Greek, Latin, Italian, Spanish, Portuguese and French," and William Camden, the antiquarian-to-be.[34] In May 1572, Sidney embarked upon his famous three years' excursion through Europe, going first to Paris in the train of Edward Fiennes de Clinton, the newly created Earl of Lincoln, who was sent to France by the Queen to sign the Treaty of Blois (a pact whereby France and England each agreed not to assist Spain in an attack upon the other).[35] Sidney was accompanied by then 27 year old Lodowick Bryskett, who had been a member of the Sidney household since about 1571. Bryskett was the son of Antonio Bruschetto, an Italian merchant from Genoa who had settled in England in 1535.[36] Bryskett's sister Lucrece (or Lucrezia) in 1558 married Vincent (or Vincenzo) Guicciardini, another Italian merchant (from Florence) living in England.[37] This Vincent was the nephew of the famous historian, Franceso Guicciardini, and the brother of the Ludovico Guicciardini whose *Detti, et Fatti* had been translated by James Sandford and dedicated to Leicester.[38]

Sidney carried with him to Paris a letter written by Leicester to the English ambassador there, commending the seventeen year old youth to the ambassador's care and counsel.[39] The ambassador was Francis Walsingham, who is a pivotal figure in connecting to each other many of the persons in the groups under consideration. Born in about 1530, and brought up as a Protestant, Walsingham left England in 1553 upon the accession of Queen Mary to the throne, and lived on the Continent until the accession of Elizabeth in 1558. By the end of the following decade he was engaged in intelligence-collecting activities for the English government, his knowledge of European languages and his network of friends on the Continent giving him particularly good qualifications for the task.

Walsingham served as English ambassador to France from the autumn of 1571 to the spring of 1573, and it was he who, along with Sir Thomas Smith, the statesman and famous Greek scholar,[40] and Henry Killigrew, negotiated with the French the treaty which the Earl of Lincoln was sent to Paris to sign. After his return to England in 1573, Walsingham was appointed secretary of state jointly with Sir Thomas Smith (who died in August, 1577), and retained this position for the rest of his life. He was knighted on 1 December 1577 and died on 6 April 1590.

One of Walsingham's chief interests as secretary of state was in organizing and improving the intelligence service, on which endeavor he spent a substantial amount of his personal fortune, at one time having in his pay fifty-three agents in foreign courts, and eighteen spies "who performed functions that could not be officially defined."[41] Among the persons supplying information to Walsingham, either gratuitously or as paid agents, were Christopher Marlowe (1564-1593), the playwright and poet;[42] Anthony Bacon (1558-1601) who from 1579 to 1591 resided on the Continent, for a while in Geneva where he stayed with Théodore Beza, but otherwise in France, where he met and enjoyed the friendship of Henri of Navarre, Philippe du Plessis Mornay, and Michel de Montaigne;[43] Anthony Standen, at one time in the service of Mary Queen of Scots but subsequently an agent for Walsingham in Italy and Spain, and from 1591 on, a friend of Anthony Bacon who, while living in France, had managed to secure Standen's release from a prison in Bordeaux, where he was being held under suspicion of being an agent for the King of Spain;[44] Richard Hakluyt (1552?-1616), the author of books on voyages of discovery;[45] Edward Dyer (1543-1607), the diplomat and poet, and intimate friend of Philip Sidney;[46] Anthony Munday (1553-1633), the translator and writer of plays and pageants, who was in Rome in 1578-1579, and who is deemed by some to be the "Palinode" whose visit to Rome is referred to by Spenser in the æglogue for July in *The Shepheardes Calendar*,[47] and Henry Constable (1562-1613), the poet.[48] John Florio, employed at the French embassy in London for several years from 1583 on, is thought to have been one of Walsingham's spies.[49] Working for Francis Walsingham as a courier and probably as a spy was his young cousin, Thomas Walsingham (1563-1630).[50] It seems likely, on the basis of *noscitur a sociis*, that the poet Thomas Watson (1557?-1592) also worked for Francis Walsingham as a spy — in any event, Watson became a friend and protégé of Francis Walsingham when the two met in Paris, and became especially a friend to Francis Walsingham's cousin, Thomas Walsingham, who in turn was the friend and patron of his fellow-spy Christopher Marlowe.[51] Watson, too, knew Christopher Marlowe, and the two were together on 18 September 1589 when a feud between factions consisting of Watson and his brother-in-law Hugh Swift on the one hand, and a William Bradley and a George Orrell on the other hand, resulted in an encounter in which Thomas Watson, after being suddenly accosted by William Bradley, slew him. Marlowe and Watson were arrested, but Marlowe was detained for only a few days and Watson, after several months in jail, was pardoned.[52]

Having come to this act of violence, I must for one (long) paragraph depart from my declared intention to treat of "A group of persons familiar with classical literature" to mention a few who probably were not. Their shortcomings in this respect were not necessarily handicaps, for these were "men of action" — the agents who did the dirty work for Walsingham: men such as Robert Poley, the undercover agent who pretended to be working with Anthony Babington and others conspiring to deliver the Queen of the Scots from her imprisonment and kill Queen Elizabeth, but all the while was betraying their activities to Walsingham who had gone to the extent even of placing Poley in the household of Sir Philip Sidney where, Mary and her agents thought, Poley was spying on *their* behalf;[53] Poley's confederates, Nicholas Skeres, Michael Moody, and a man (or men) named John, James or Thomas Tipping, who were involved in the Babington matter and other espionage activities;[54] and Richard Baines and Richard Cholmley.[55] Robert Poley and Nicholas Skeres have won for themselves immortality by having, along with Ingram Frizer (probably also a spy for Walsingham[56]), passed 30 May 1593 in the company of Christopher Marlowe, and having been present on the evening of that day when, after supper, Marlowe was fatally stabbed by Frizer in a dispute over *le recknynge*.[57] Baines and Cholmley also are remembered for their associations with Marlowe. In January 1591/2, Richard Baines, then in Flushing as the "chamber fellow" of "Christofer Marly, by his profession a scholer, and the other Gifford Gilbert a goldsmith," reported to Sir Robert Sidney, the governor of Flushing, that these two had underfoot a project to counterfeit Dutch shillings. Marlowe and Gilbert were questioned, and, along with Richard Baines, sent under guard to London to be tried. What may have come of this is unknown. Robert Sidney, in his letter reporting the matter to Burghley, states that the men, examined apart, "never denied anything, onely protesting that what was done was onely to se[e] the Goldsmiths conning: and truly I ame of opinion that the poor man was onely browght in under that couler, what ever intent the other twoe had at that time." Of especial interest to us are Sidney's further statements that Marlowe and Baines "do one accuse the other to have bin the inducers of him [the goldsmith], and to have yntended to practice yt heereafter," and "do also accuse one another of intent to goe to the Ennemy or to Rome, both as they say of malice one to another."[58] The fact that Baines and Marlowe at one time shared a chamber, and that an occasion arose which created ill-will between them, to a certain extent explains, and gives considerable credibility to, the famous note "Containing the opinion of on[e] Christopher Marley Concerning his Damnable Judgement of Religion, and scorn of gods word" delivered by Baines to the Privy Council shortly before Marlowe's death. Some of the "damnable judgments" set forth in the note were "That St John the Evangelist was bedfellow to [Christ] and leaned alwaies in his bosome, that he used him as the sinners of Sodoma," "that all they that loue not Tobacco & Boies were fooles," "that he had as good Right to Coine as the Queene of England, and that he was acquainted wth one poole a prisoner in newgate who hath great Skill in mixture of mettals and hauing learned some thinges of hime he ment through help of a Cuninge stamp maker to Coin ffrench Crownes pistolets and English shillinges," and "that on[e] Ric Cholmley hath Confessed that he was perswaded by Marloe's Reasons to become an Atheist."[59] In another note from another source, this "Ric Cholmley" is quoted as saying that he "verely beleveth that one Marlowe is able to showe more sounde reasons for Atheisme then any devine in Englande is able to geve to prove devinities & that Marloe told him that hee hath read the Atheist lecture to S^r walter Raliegh & others."[60] The significance to our story of this group of men will later become clear.

As English ambasador, Walsingham, when Sidney first met him in Paris, was frequently in contact with French Protestants, many of whom were personal friends from the days of his "Marian exile". These included the philosopher Pierre de la Rameé, commonly known as Petrus Ramus; the Huguenot diplomat, Hubert Languet; the jurist Jean Lobbet, who latinized his name as Lobetius or Lubetius, and the scholarly friend and advisor of Henry of Navarre, Philippe du Plessis Mornay[61]: with all of whom Sidney also became acquainted. Sidney could have known Ramus but briefly, for Ramus was sought out and killed during the course of the St. Batholomew's day massacre, which occurred on 26 August 1572 while Sidney was in Paris; Languet remained Sidney's devoted friend until his (Languet's) death in 1581, and Lobbet and Du Plessis Mornay maintained friendly personal contact with Sidney until the late 1570's or early 1580's. In 1578, Du Plessis Mornay designated Sidney as the godfather of his daughter; Sidney, in turn, so much admired Mornay's book, *De Veritata Christiana*, published in 1581, that he undertook to translate it, but after completing only a few chapters, he turned the task over to his uncle's protégé Arthur Golding, who published the completed translation in 1587 under the title *A Woorke concerning the trewnesse of the Christian Religion*, dedicated, at Sidney's request, to the Earl of Leicester.[62]

From Paris, Sidney traveled throughout central Europe, accompanied now by one of Walsingham's aides, Edward Wotton (1548–1626), who had lived in Europe for a number of years, and was described by a contemporary as "a man of great learning and knowledge of languages," speaking proficiently French, Spanish and Italian.[63] During the course of his travels, Sidney met and won the admiration and devotion of innumerable persons, among the most captivated of whom were the renowned scholar and publisher

Henri Estienne (1528–1598) — the same Henricus Stephanus so famed for his editions of Greek works, and whose publication in 1566 of the Greek Anthology we have already had occasion to notice — and Théophile de Banos (1519–1605), a pupil of and former secretary to Ramus. Estienne dedicated two books to Sidney: his New Testament in Greek, published in 1576, and *Herodiani Historiarum Libri VIII*, published in 1581. In the dedication to the New Testament, Estienne states that he had met Sidney first at Heidelberg, then at Strasburg, and later at Vienna, and that

at Strasburg the love which I had felt for you at Heidelberg greatly increased, and at Vienna the love I felt for you at Strasburg grew still more. Not that it is at all surprizing that my love for you should have grown in this way, since your gifts of mind, which aroused it, seemed also to have grown.[64]

De Banos edited and dedicated to Sidney Ramus' *Commentariorum de Religione Christiana Libri Quatuor*, published in Frankfurt in 1576, and in his letters wrote to Sidney such things as "I well remember the first time I saw you, when I contemplated with wonder your unusual endowments of mind and body; and I thought of [Pope] Gregory's words that the *Angli* or English whom one saw in Rome [in the slave markets] were really *Angeli* or angels."[65]

Sidney returned from the Continent in May, 1575, just in time to accompany his parents and brother and sister on Queen Elizabeth's famous progress of that year to Warwicksire,[66] where at Kenilworth Castle Leicester provided for her, during her nineteen day stay, the entertainment "of which the splendour far exceeded what had any where else been given, that the Earl of Leicester exerted his whole munificence in a manner so splendid, as to claim a remembrance even in the Annals of our country. . . ."[67] Many of the speeches, poems and masks prepared for the Queen's entertainment were written by George Gascoigne,[68] who but recently had performed various missions as an agent of Walsingham (and was to perform a few more in the following year)[69] and was now enjoying the patronage of the Earl of Leicester. Gascoigne personally participated in the presentation of his works,[70] and it is most unlikely that Sidney and Gascoigne did not meet during the Queen's progress, and exchange some talk on literary subjects. Unfortunately, Gascoigne died only two years later, but the influence of his productions at Kenilworth upon a few early poems of Sidney has been noted.[71]

In February 1577 Sidney again went abroad, this time ostensibly as a special ambassador to convey Elizabeth's condolences to Rudolph II, in

Prague, upon the death of his father, Maximilian (to whom Sidney had been presented in 1575), and to the Counts Palatine, Ludwig and Casimir, in Heidelberg, upon the death of their father, Frederick. But the true purpose of this visit was to explore "the ways by which a league between the English and Protestant Germans [against Spain and France] may be arranged to protect the safety of our religion."[72] Accompanying Sidney on this trip were his friends, Edward Dyer and Fulke Greville.[73]

It is stated by one scholar, but questioned by another, that also accompanying Sidney in the early stages of this mission was Daniel Rogers, the English diplomat and neo-Latin poet.[74] Whether this detail of their association is correct or not, the two in fact at about this time had numerous contacts with each other. Rogers was born in Wittenberg. He was the son of John Rogers, an English priest who while serving as chaplain to the Merchant Venturers Company at Antwerp became a zealous adherent of the new religion, and "knowing . . . that unlawful vows may lawfully be broken,"[75] married a first cousin of the great geographer, Abraham Ortelius.[76] John Rogers moved out of the frying pan of the low countries to the England of Edward VI which, upon becoming the England of Mary, burned him at the stake on 4 February 1555, his wife and eleven children looking on.[77] Daniel, then probably about seventeen, thereafter for a while lived on the Continent, returning to England upon Elizabeth's accession. He took an Arts degree at Oxford in 1561, and then went to France where he entered the household of the then English ambassador, Sir Henry Norris. Rogers was still in Paris in 1571 when Walsingham became the English ambassador and his "especial frende and patrone,"[78] but he apparently was in Ireland during the brief period of time in 1572 that Sidney was Walsingham's charge in Paris,[79] and thus may not have met Sidney at so early a date. But by 1575 he had written the first of a number of Latin poems in praise of Sidney, and thereafter moved into his family of intimate friends, his writings during the following five years[80] revealing a close acquaintance not only with Sidney, but also with Edmund Spenser, Gabriel Harvey, Fulke Greville and Edward Dyer.[81] Rogers was "one that was especially beloved by the famous antiquary and historian W[illiam] Cambden,"[82] and was also a close friend to Hubert Languet;[83] these friendships, formed apparently independently of Sidney, may have helped to bring together Sidney and Rogers.

Earlier, Rogers' classical leanings and love of letters had given him the reason, and his residence on the Continent had given him the opportunity, to meet and become friends with French humanists and poets Jean-Antoine de Baïf and Pierre Ronsard, and other stars of the famous *Pléiade*; Rogers' subsequent intimate association with Sidney and his circle establishes him as a "link between the French Renaissance and a number of English writers[,] . . . . a clearly visible tie between the Continent and England."[84] Other persons whom Rogers knew well from his early days in France included the Dutch humanist, poet and statesman Janus Dousa (then young, but eventually required to be designated the Elder, to distinguish him from his accomplished son), Dousa's friend, the Huguenot scholar and jurist, François Hotman, the Flemish scholar Justus Lipsius, and the German poet Paul Schede (or Paulus Melissus, as he generally signed himself) who had been associated with the *Pléiade*, and was the poet-laureate of the Emperor Maximilian whose death was the occasion for Sidney's mission to Prague.[85] One of Rogers' closest friends was the Scottish humanist and neo-Latin poet George Buchanan (1506-1582), who lived on the Continent for many years. Buchanan for a while taught at the Collège de Guyenne in Bordeaux, where Montaigne was one of his pupils. Among Buchanan's friends and associates were Henricus Stephanus, Philip Duplessis Mornay, Theodore Beza, Justus Lipsius, Jan Douza and Hubert Languet.[86] Except for Buchanan, who was by this time back in Scotland, Sidney on his 1577 mission met all of these friends of Daniel Rogers, and whatever he may have felt about them, they were delighted with him, as their poems to him and letters to each other show.[87] Although Sidney may never have personally met Buchanan, the two corresponded with each other,[88] and Buchanan's constant communication with members of the Leicester House group has led one scholar to describe him as a member *in absentia* of that group.[89]

Sidney returned in June 1577 to an England whose sovereign seemed unwilling to recognize or reward this person in whom the rulers and scholars of the Continent saw so much to admire. He settled down to a quiet life, centered around literary pursuits.

When he was in London, Sidney lodged almost always at Leicester House, his uncle's home on the Strand. Here he mingled with the Elizabethan intellectual élite, and now, many persons who might have dedicated books to his uncle, dedicated them to Sidney (more out of admiration and friendship, I suspect, than hope for immediate advantage, for Sidney himself had little fortune and no position): Hakluyt in 1582 dedicated his *Divers Voyages* to Sidney; Timothy Bright in 1584 his *In physiciam G. A. Scribonii animad-uersiones* (in which dedication he recalls being sheltered along with Sidney and "others of our nation — as long as they were free from Papist superstition" in Walsingham's house during the St. Batholomew's day massacre); Alberico Gentili in 1585 his *De Legationibus Libri Tres*; and

Giordano Bruno in 1584 his *La cena de le ceneri* and *Spaccio de la besta trionfante* and in 1585 his *De gli eroici furori*.

And it was at Leicester House that Sidney met (and, as usual, was loved by) the remarkable group of people who composed his uncle's staff of secretaries and aides. Edmund Spenser, who was proficient in both Greek and Latin, was Leicester's secretary from 1578 to 1580;[90] Spenser and Sidney quickly became friends and along with Sidney's friends Edward Dyer and Fulke Greville, and Spenser's friend Gabriel Harvey, established (probably not formally, and perhaps never seriously) a literary club they called "Areopagus," dedicated to developing a way of writing English verse in classical meters.[91] In 1580 Spenser obtained a position as private secretary to Arthur, Lord Grey of Wilton, who had just been appointed Lord Deputy of Ireland, and with Grey went to Ireland, where he lived for most of the rest of his life. Succeeding Spenser as Leicester's secretary was Gabriel Harvey, who held this position only briefly,[92] and by about September 1580 was succeeded by Arthur Atey, a scholar of repute having many associations with Merton College, Oxford.[93] Joining Atey in 1581 or 1582 was Jean Hotman. Both Atey and Hotman remained in Leicester's service until Leicester's death in 1588.[94]

Jean Hotman (1552-1636) was the son of the famous Huguenot François Hotman (1524-1590) who had met many English Protestants during their "Marian exile" on the Continent, and whose admiration for the English resulted in his sending his son Jean to Oxford.[95] The elder Hotman knew Francis Walsingham and Daniel Rogers, as well as Hubert Languet,[96] and thus it could have been through any of these persons, or doubtless many others, that Sidney and François Hotman met, as Sidney says they did in a letter sent early in 1581 to Jean Hotman at Oxford. In this letter, written before Sidney actually met the younger Hotman, Sidney promised to be helpful to him, and after they met and became friends, Sidney used his influence with his uncle to secure for Jean Hotman a position as secretary to Leicester.[97] Before arriving in England, Hotman undoubtedly knew, because they were friends of his father,[98] many of the great humanists Sidney had met on his stay in Europe — among them, Henri Estienne (Henricus Stephanus), Estienne's friend Paul Schede (Melissus), and Jean Lobbet (Lubetius); and after arriving in England, Hotman came to know, by virtue of his enrollment at Oxford, many distinguished English scholars and humanists: men such as the antiquarian and Greek scholar, William Camden (whom Sidney, of course, had met at Oxford), Thomas Savile, a Latin and Greek scholar, and proctor of Merton College, who died young (in 1592); Thomas' brother Henry Savile, also a Greek scholar and the warden of

Merton College, who translated into English the works of Tacitus, and collected and published in Greek an eight volume edition of the works of St. Johannis Chrysostomi, and Henry Cuffe, another accomplished Greek scholar who was an intimate friend of William Camden and both Thomas and Henry Savile, and who in 1590 was elected to the Greek professorship at Oxford.[99] When Jean Hotman returned to France in 1592, he became, like his father before him (to whose title, Sieur de Villiers St. Paul, he had by then succeeded), a trusted advisor to Henry of Navarre, now Henry IV of France, and after Henry's death, to Louis XIII; during the last 20 years of his life he was a friend of Hugo Grotius (1583-1645), the classical scholar, theologian, and writer on principles of international law.[100] From the number and variety of his friends and associates, we can infer that Jean Hotman, like Sidney, had a remarkably charismatic personality, and it is certain that one consequence of his knowing almost all of the leading French, English and northern European poets, philosophers, humanists and statesmen of his time, and providing them with a fecundating access to each other, was to enrich the fabric of Elizabethan literature in more ways, and more profoundly, than has hitherto been recognized.

Henry Savile knew Sidney,[101] as did probably also his brother Thomas, so it is likely that Henry Cuffe, through his friendships with Hotman, Camden and the Savile brothers[102] also had access to Sidney: all brought together, perhaps, by their interest in Greek literature, for Sidney too knew Greek — perhaps even well enough to justify Estienne's statement, in his dedication to Sidney of the Latin translation of Herodian's works published in 1581, that Sidney was so learned in reading Greek that translations were superfluous for him.[103]

In January, 1583, Philip Sidney was knighted, and on 20 September 1583, at the age of 28, he married Frances Walsingham, the then fourteen or fifteen year old daughter of Sir Francis Walsingham. Like his uncle, Sidney was a proponent of aid to the Protestant princes of the Low Lands in their struggles against Philip II of Spain (for whom Philip Sidney had been named[104]), and when that policy won favour with the Queen, and Leicester in 1585 was sent to the Netherlands in command of a British army to aid the Dutch, Sidney went with him, and was appointed Governor of Flushing. Sidney engaged as his secretary William Temple (1555–1627), a philosopher active in championing in England the views of Ramus with respect to logic and philosophy. Temple had in February, 1584 dedicated to Sidney his annotated edition of Ramus' *Dialectics*, published under the title *P. Rami Dialecticae libri duo scholiis G. Tempelli Cantabrigiensis Illustrati*, and apparently Sidney offered Temple the position in appreciation of this dedication.[105] Sidney was wounded in an encounter with the Spanish near Zutphen on 22 September 1586, and it was in Temple's arms that he died, on 17 October 1586. In a codicil to his will signed on the day of his death, Sidney bequeathed to Temple "the yearly Annuity of thirty Pounds by Year . . . during his Life natural."[106]

And, in the same codicil, Sidney gave "to my beloved and much honoured Lord, the Earl of *Essex*, my best sword."

B. Essex House.

Robert Devereux, the son of Walter Devereux, first Earl of Essex and Lettice Knollys, was born on 19 November 1566. He had two elder sisters, Penelope and Dorothy; his brother Walter was born in 1569. The first Earl, who knew and admired Sir Philip Sidney, died on 22 September 1576, whereupon the 10 year old Robert succeeded to his father's title. His guardian during his minority was Lord Burleigh, at whose home he from time to time resided. The young Earl of Essex studied at Cambridge and was created M.A. in 1581, after which he lived for several years quietly in the country.

The most significant event of Essex' minority was the marriage of his mother, on 21 September 1578, to the Earl of Leicester. As a consequence of this connection, Essex was not only brought into intimate contact with the Leicester House circle, and thus with Sir Philip Sidney, but also became a person of some importance at court, where Leicester in 1584 presented him to Queen Elizabeth, who doted upon his handsome person, and eventually commenced with him a relationship which brought pain to her and death to him.

In December 1585, Essex accompanied the Earl of Leicester on his military expedition to the Low Countries, where for the next nine months he was constantly in the company of his step-father and his step-father's nephew, Sir Philip Sidney. At an encounter with the Spanish at Zutphen on 22 September 1586, the 19 year old Essex fought boldly and bravely, and was for his valour created a knight banneret by his step-father. But in the same battle, Sir Philip Sidney suffered the wound from which 25 days later he died, bequeathing on the day of his death his best sword to his "beloved" Essex.

Sidney's uncle, the Earl of Leicester, died in 1588, and Sidney's father-in-law, Sir Francis Walsingham, died in 1590. After Leicester's death, Essex succeeded Leicester not only as Master of the Horse but also as master of his House,[107] and after Walsingham's death, Essex succeeded Sidney as the husband of Walsingham's daughter, Frances. Thus Leicester House became Essex House, and Lady Sidney became the Countess of Essex. Although

115

Sidney's bequest of his sword to Essex was an act doubtless having for both Sidney and Essex only very personal implications, it was viewed by many persons, and probably eventually by Essex himself, as symbolizing Essex' succession to Sidney's famed knightly qualities; certainly, Essex' subsequent occupation of Leicester's house and his marriage to Walsingham's daughter appear to have been acts deliberately designed by Essex to promote himself as the successor, not only to Sidney's knightly valour, but also to the statesmanship and patronage of the arts that had been associated with Sidney, Walsingham and Leicester.

While Essex' marriage to Lady Sidney for a while angered the Queen, it did not permanently disrupt the relationship between them, which endured to encounter and weather other storms, until its final shipwreck.

In the summer of 1591, Henry IV, through an emissary to the Queen and a letter to Essex, pleaded for English assistance in fighting the Catholic league. Essex urged Elizabeth to send a force to aid Henry, and also strenuously sought for himself command of that force. Against her better judgment, Elizabeth agreed to both requests. Essex landed at Dieppe in August, 1591. Shortly thereafter, leaving his main force, he traveled with only a few troops through enemy country to Noyon, to meet with Henry and Marshal Biron, who had just captured the town. After three days, he returned to where his troops were, and proceeded, as had been requested by Henry and Marshal Biron, to assist in the siege of Gournay, which fell on 27 September 1591. Henry and Essex then put Rouen under siege, but that well-provisioned city showed no signs of succumbing, while the English forces were noticeably decreasing in numbers, through sickness, death and desertion. Essex was recalled to England on 8 January 1591/2, having demonstrated on a number of occasions during the expedition great personal courage, but otherwise having little good to show, and a painful loss to grieve, for his brother Walter had been killed during the campaign.[108]

In September, 1592, Essex was one of the 60 or so nobles who accompanied Queen Elizabeth to Oxford, whither she went at the invitation of its new Chancellor, Thomas Sackville, Lord Buckhurst. Her only previous visit to Oxford had been in 1566, at the time of the inauguration of Leicester as Chancellor. When Leicester died in 1588, Essex had expected to succeed him as Chancellor, as did also the University (which, supposedly in anticipation of his appointment, incorporated him M. A. on 11 April 1588[109]) but the Chancellorship was conferred upon Christopher Hatton. When Hatton died in 1591, Essex again expected to be named Chancellor, the authorities at the University having stated this to be their wish. But while Essex was in the trenches before Rouen, the Queen instead chose Buckhurst. The bitter disappointment which Essex originally felt[110] had probably somewhat abated by the time of this trip to Oxford; the mere fact that he was of the company indicates that he was once again inching into the Queen's good graces.

The Queen and her company were in Oxford for seven days. When her procession entered the City of Oxford on Friday, 22 September 1592, it stopped at Carfax, where Henry Cuffe, professor of Greek at the University, welcomed her with an oration in Greek, for which she, in Greek, thanked him. Thomas and Henry Savile and Matthew Gwynn participated in the programs presented to her on Saturday. Sunday was devoted to a sermon in the morning and a play in the evening. On Monday, after dining with Sir Henry Savile (who had once been her tutor in Greek), the Queen and the nobles and others in her company were entertained by a disputation, in Latin, on the question whether differences of opinion among citizens are beneficial to the state. Henry Cuffe argued in the affirmative, and four colleagues upheld the negative; the moderator was Thomas Savile. The disputation received great applause, and was deemed to reflect creditably upon Merton College, and the disputants. After a few more days of such delights, the Queen departed Oxford on Thursday, 28 September.[111]

Five months later, on 25 February 1593, Essex, then only 26, was advanced by the Queen to the Privy Council.[112] This was his opportunity to establish himself as a dominant force in the Government. Aware now that Sidney's sword, Leicester's house and Walsingham's daughter gave him only the trappings of Sidney, Leicester and Walsingham, Essex as Privy Councillor began to emulate substantively those whose successor he would be by organizing in the manner of Walsingham a great network of international intelligence, by conducting in the manner of Leicester a correspondence with the rulers and leading citizens of the continent, and by encouraging and patronizing in the manner of both Leicester and Sidney the production of literary works.

For the conduct of these activities, Essex augmented his previously small household staff, consisting of his steward, Gelly Merrick, and his secretary, Edward Reynolds,[113] by installing in Essex House as secretaries and aides many of the same individuals who had been so intimately associated with Walsingham, Leicester and Sidney. Anthony Bacon, an intelligencer for Walsingham, was engaged to establish and supervise a program of intelligence gathering activities;[114] William Temple, Sidney's secretary, and in whose arms Sidney had died, and Henry Wotton, the half-brother of Edward Wotton, Sidney's friend and traveling companion in Europe, handled correspondence in French, Italian and Latin, as well as English; and Henry

Cuffe, the Greek scholar from Oxford and friend to Jean Hotman, handled miscellaneous and apparently more sensitive or private matters.

Jean Hotman left England in 1592, and thus was never a formal member of Essex' staff. But he performed, prior to his departure, at least one secret mission for Essex. This was in October 1589, when Hotman carried to James VI of Scotland letters from Essex and his sister Lady Rich, and in "many secret conferences with the King," assured James of Essex' service, fidelity and love.[115] With Hotman on this mission was Henry Constable, a friend of Sir Philip Sidney and a former agent for Walsingham. Hotman and Constable either then were, or at that time became, friends; after his return to London, Hotman sent to one of the persons he had met in Scotland a "book" of Constable's poems (this must have been in manuscript, because none of Constable's poems are known to have been published before 1592).[116] In 1591, Constable was one of the contingent of "romantic young gentlemen"[117] who accompanied Essex to France to help the protestant Henri of Navarre quell the forces of the rebelling Catholic League. His motives in going are not clear, for not long after arriving in France, Constable became a Catholic, left the English forces, and, sustained by a pension from Henry IV, remained in France, not returning to England until the accession to the throne of James I in 1603.[118] However, during the 1590's he remained in contact with Essex and Essex House, supplying information from time to time for Essex as he had for Walsingham,[119] and, it would seem, arranging through his contacts at Essex House for the publication in England of *Diana*, editions of which appeared in 1592 and 1594.

Anthony Standen, ever since 1591 the close friend to Anthony Bacon (who in that year had delivered him from prison in France), at Bacon's behest entered upon the service of Essex at the same time as Bacon, and, becoming very close to Essex, remained in that service until the end,[120] although — whether through luck or wisdom is not clear — he does not seem to have participated in the fatal "rebellion" of 8 February 1601.

Also of the Essex House group was Henry Savile, the intimate friend both of Leicester's secretary Jean Hotman and of Essex' secretary Henry Cuffe. Savile, who had been tutor in Greek to Queen Elizabeth, and from 1585 on Warden of Merton College, was warmly supported by Essex in his ultimately successful bid to secure the provotship of Eton College (at the same time retaining the wardenship at Merton).[121] Savile published in 1591 a translation of Tacitus for which Essex is reputed to have written the preface,[122] and his intimacy with Essex and Cuffe was the cause of his arrest for complicity in the Essex uprising of February 1601.[123]

Sidney's two closest friends, Edward Dyer and Fulke Greville, had significant associations with Essex House: Dyer, who had long known Leicester's step-son, and was devoted to the youth, engaged in various secret missions for Essex in 1598, and perhaps at other times as well;[124] Greville, also a long-time friend of Essex (and incorporated M.A. at Oxford with him on 11 April 1588[125]), was the beneficiary of his patronage in the mid-1590's, and actually lived in Essex House from September of 1596 until March of 1600, when he and all the others then living at Essex House were ordered by the government to vacate the premises so that Essex, in disgrace because of his flight from his command in Ireland, might be isolated there under house arrest.[126]

Others in the Essex House circle who had been connected with Leicester House were Sir Henry Killigrew (ca 1525-1603), who was knighted by Essex during the French campaign in 1591, and his brother William Killigrew (d. 1622), Groom of the Privy Chamber from 1573 until his death, both of whom had been friends and associates of Francis Walsingham, and were, through Henry Killigrew's marriage with Catherine Cooke, brothers-in-law to Lord Burleigh (who had married Catherine's sister Mildred), to Thomas Hoby (who had married Catherine's sister Elizabeth), and to Nicholas Bacon (who had married Catherine's sister Ann), and thus uncles to Robert Cecil on the one hand, Thomas Posthumous Hoby on the other hand and Anthony and Francis Bacon on the (literarily permissible) third hand.[127]

Francis Bacon's relationship to Essex, unlike that of his brother Anthony, was not that of a paid retainer, but rather that of a friend and counsellor. Essex' high regard for Bacon, his persistent but unsuccessful attempts to secure for Bacon the positions of Attorney General and of Solicitor General, and his gift to Bacon of his own property as compensation for his inability to secure for Bacon the preferment which Essex thought he merited, constitute an oft-told and well-known story,[128] and make even more incomprehensible and unforgivable the active role played by Bacon in the prosecution of Essex for treason, when it might be thought that other lawyers, not obligated to Essex, could have been available to take on that task.[129]

The most intimate of Essex' friends seems to have been the young Earl of Southampton, Henry Wriothesley. Essex and Southampton probably first met in the home of Lord Burleigh. Southampton, like Essex, had succeeded to the title at a young age (Southampton's father died on 4 October 1581) and, like Essex, was the ward of Lord Burleigh during his minority. (A practice based on feudal notions, but maintained through Tudor times because of its lucrative consequences, gave the Crown the wardship of certain minor heirs; the Crown, through its Master of the Wards, granted the wardships to favoured persons. Burleigh, who was Master of the Wards from 1561 to 1598, conferred upon himself a few select wardships, including those of Essex and Southampton.[130]) Essex, who became Burleigh's ward in 1576, attained his majority in 1588, and Southampton, who became Burleigh's ward in 1581, attained his majority in 1594. They undoubtedly were bedfellows at Lord Burleigh's house more than once during the seven years that Southampton's wardship overlapped Essex' wardship — perhaps after dining together with their joint guardian, or perhaps while staying with him for a few days' visit during a break from studies. But these encounters could not have been frequent, for neither Essex nor Southampton seems to have spent any protracted period of time with Burleigh. Essex, as we have seen, after taking his M.A. from Cambridge at the age of 15 (in 1581), lived a quiet life removed from London until, at the age of 19 (late in 1585), he went with Leicester and Sidney to fight the Spanish in the Low Countries, after which, for the next three or four years, he divided his time between flirting with the Queen at Court and fighting for her in Portugal and France. Southampton entered St. John's College at Cambridge in 1585, took his M.A. in 1589, and seems from there to have gone on to Gray's Inn, to which he had been admitted on 29 February 1587/8. The few things known about Southampton's activities between 1588 and 1592 (the years during which, in my opinion, most of the Sonnets were written) are that he refused to marry Burleigh's granddaughter, Elizabeth Vere,[131] that one of Burleigh's secretaries, John Clapham, in 1591 published the first work dedicated to Southampton, a Latin poem entitled *Narcissus*,[132] and that also in 1591 Southampton, then 18, returned to Cambridge briefly to visit his friend, Roger Manners,[133] the 15 year old Earl of Rutland.

Wriothesley and Roger Manners may have met at Cambridge as early as 1587, when both were students there.[134] Manners was only 12 years old when, upon his father's death in 1588, he became the fifth Earl of Rutland, and a ward of the Crown. His wardship, like those of Essex and Southampton, was assigned by the Master of the Wards (Lord Burleigh) to the Lord Treasurer of England (Lord Burleigh).[135] That Southampton and Rutland were both wards of the same guardian probably drew these noble scholars closer together than might otherwise have been the case. Rutland's friendship with Southampton inevitably brought him within the ambit of the Essex House circle. When Rutland left England in 1596 for a two years' tour of the Continent, a manual of "Profitable Instructions" was prepared for him either by Essex, or by Francis Bacon.[136] Rutland travelled through the Low Countries, Germany, Switzerland, Italy and France; while in France, he saw Henry Constable, and gave him 40 crowns,[137] a fact reflective not so much of the good-will toward each other of these friends of Essex as of the relationship between the two: for Henry Constable's grandmother, Katherine, was the sister of the young Earl of Rutland's great-grandfather, Thomas Manners, first Earl of Rutland.[138]

Another young earl whose being a ward of Burleigh brought him into early contact with Southampton, and hence with Rutland and Essex, was Edward Russell who, in 1585 at the age of 13, succeeded his grandfather as Earl of Bedford.[139] We may assume that Southampton, Bedford and Rutland, when in each other's company, were high-spirited and somewhat affected, for Rutland's sister, Bridget Manners, who must have seen these young earls often, in 1594 declined to consider marriage with either Southampton or Bedford, because "they be so yonge and fantastycall and woulde be so caryed awaye."[140]

Like Southampton and Rutland, Bedford was devoted to Essex, but he cannot be considered a member of the Essex House circle, for he avoided the Court and London as much as possible, his one notable appearance there being, as we shall see, a disaster. On the other hand, his wife, Lucy Harington (whom he married in December, 1594), was often in London, and is remembered today as the Countess of Bedford who was the patron of, and seems to have been genuinely admired by, Ben Jonson, John Donne, John Davies of Hereford, Samuel Daniel and George Chapman.

Other friends of Southampton's youth were Sir Charles and Sir Henry Danvers, brothers to whom he was distantly related (Isabel, a half-sister of Henry Wriothesley's grandfather, Thomas Wriothesley, had married into a branch of the Danvers family, as shown on Table II). On 4 October 1594, the two brothers attacked and killed their distant cousin, Henry Long (the fatal shot being fired by Henry Danvers). Charles and Henry fled to Titchfield, where Henry Wriothesley, who was then there (probably for a celebration of his 21st birthday, which was on 6 October 1594), harboured them, and helped them escape to France, where they entered the service of Henry IV.[141]

From 1592 on, Southampton and Essex were often together. Southampton, as well as Essex, was one of the nobles who accompanied Queen Elizabeth to Oxford in September 1592. A poem written to commemorate the event praises Essex, not too long returned from the unsuccessful siege of Rouen, for his valour, and Southampton, who was then not quite 19 years old, for his beauty.[142] On 3 January 1594/5, Essex and Southampton were among the "great and noble personages" who, together with "a great number of knights, ladies, and very worshipful personages," attended the festivities at Gray's Inn (where ten or so days before a presentation of Shakespeare's *Comedy of Errors* had been given).[143] Two of the other "noble personages"

121

in attendance were Essex's brother-in-law, Lord Rich, and Southampton's new step-father, Thomas Heneage, Treasurer of the Chamber, who had married Southampton's widowed mother on 2 May 1594. Heneage had been a friend to Sir Philip Sidney (Sidney, in his will, gave to "my singular good Friend, Sir *Thomas Heneage*," a jewel of twenty pounds value, "in token of my great Love unto him"[144]), and after Walsingham's death, he seems, along with Burleigh, to have taken over management of the government's intelligence system.[145] Heneage died in October 1595, at the age of about 63, and his personal influence upon either Essex or Southampton could not have been great.

One writer has speculated that also attending the Gray's Inn revels of January 1594/5 as a guest of the Earl of Essex was Antonio Pérez[146] (1540-1611), one of the most interesting persons of the sixteenth century. The illegitimate son of Gonzalo Pérez, an ecclesiastic probably of Jewish descent who was Secretary of State to Charles V, Antonio at the age of 26 was appointed Secretary of State to Philip II, and for thirteen years was a great power in Spain. But in 1579 he was arrested, not so much because he had at the king's behest arranged for the murder of Juan de Escobedo, as because, to the king's embarrassment, he had failed to effect the murder without leaving any trace of its royal inspiration. For eleven years, Pérez was held in prison, and occasionally tortured in unsuccessful attempts to wring from him a "confession" that the murder was committed without the connivance of the king. It seems certain, in light of Philip's obsession with securing from Pérez a statement exculpating the King from responsibility for the murder, that Pérez' refusal to make such a statement was the only thing that kept him alive during these years. In 1590, Pérez escaped from prison, making his way to Aragon, which at that time had a degree of autonomy. But while Aragon might have been beyond the political jurisdiction of Philip II, it was not beyond his ecclesiastical jurisdiction, through tribunals of the Inquisition, which in Spain were controlled by the monarch. And so even in Aragon Pérez was kept in custody, while the Inquisition leveled against him the charges of being a heretic, a Jew, and a sodomite. Aided by popular uprisings protesting this exercise in Aragon of power by the King of Spain, Pérez in November 1591 escaped to France, where he was well received by the Princess of Béarn, Catherine of Navarre, who presented him to her brother, Henry IV. On 29 March 1593, Henry IV wrote to Queen Elizabeth that although he had decided to retain Pérez in his service, he thought that because the information possessed by Pérez would be of service to the Queen, he was sending Pérez to England to be of such use as she might judge proper, after which Pérez was to return to France.[147] It is generally supposed that "Perez's secret mission from the French King [was], with the aid of Essex, to exacerbate English feeling against Spain nationally, and to pledge Elizabeth to help him against the common enemy, independently of the question of religion."[148] (The last phrase is important, because although Henry IV became a Roman Catholic in July, 1593, thereby ending domestic dissension, his conversion did nothing to lessen the enmity between France and Spain, or Henry's continued need for whatever assistance against Spain England could provide.)

Pérez arrived in England on about 20 April 1593 and remained (on this his first visit) until 9 August 1595. He was indifferently received by Elizabeth,[149] but warmly received by Essex, at whose house he lodged during much of his stay in England. Living in Essex House, Pérez had frequent and intimate contact with the Earls of Essex and Southampton, Lady Rich, Anthony Bacon, Anthony Standen, Henry Wotton, Henry Cuffe, Henry Saville,[150] and doubtless with the scores, if not hundreds, of other persons who frequented that establishment. His dramatic personal history, witty conversation, extravagant manners, and calculating obsequiousness, fascinated and amused his English acquaintances; as Martin Hume has written, "Perez was the pet for a time of the greatest literary set in England, that which sat under the shade of Essex and the Bacons, and his affected wit and preciosity, as well as his sententious philosophy, set its mark upon most of the English writing of the end of the sixteenth century. . . ."[151] While in England, Pérez published an enlarged version of his work, *Un pedazo de Historia*, first published in France in 1591. This edition was dedicated to the Earl of Essex, for whom an English translation was prepared (but never published) by Leicester's old secretary, Arthur Atey, who seems to have been engaged from time to time by Essex more or less as a "consultant." But Atey did not live at Essex House, or even in London, and in the letter by which he transmitted to Anthony Bacon his translation of Pérez' book, he signs himself, "Yo' muche devoted, though vnacquaynted, Arth. Aty,"[152] thus revealing that, luckily for him, he was not physically a part of the Essex House circle.

When Pérez in August 1595 finally acceded to Henry IV's repeated requests, and returned to France, he was given a farewell banquet by his English friends, and was accompanied by Essex as far as Greenwich.[153] His mission to England had been a success for him, personally, but seems not to have accomplished the objectives sought by Henry IV.

Eight months later, the Spanish siege of Calais impelled Henry IV to send Pérez back to England, along with the Duc de Bouillon, to attempt once more to secure English aid in the war with Spain. This time the English were not only disposed to do something, but also were prepared, for Essex, beginning in April, had been assembling an army to come to the aid of Calais

123

— but too late, for Calais fell on 15 April 1596, the very day that Essex' force was ready to sail, and the very day (albeit designated on the Continent as 25 April) on which Pérez and the Duc de Bouillon sailed for England.[154] Essex was at Folkestone, near Dover, when the Duc de Bouillon and Pérez landed there on the following day; it is recorded that Essex at that time conferred with de Bouillon, and it is most likely that Pérez participated in the conference.[155] Later on the same day, the Duke and Pérez rode towards the Court.

The decision was made to pit against Spain elsewhere the ships and soldiers assembled for the relief of Calais. On 1 June 1596, Essex' small army of gentlemen volunteers and impressed soldiers, aboard ships commanded by Sir Walter Raleigh, set forth to disrupt Spanish shipping and wreak havoc on the Spanish mainland, on what has come to be called the Cadiz expedition.[156]

On or about the same day, Pérez returned to France, after having been in England for a little more than a month, during which time he had seen Essex only on the day of his arrival at Folkestone. Many writers have suggested that the Cadiz expedition was the brainchild of Pérez, but it is likely that Pérez had nothing to do with the conception or execution of this operation, and indeed Gustav Ungerer argues that Pérez at first disapproved of what was planned, and attempted to persuade Elizabeth to send to Spain not a few harrassing ships, but an invading army.[157]

Southampton participated with Essex and his advisors in planning the Cadiz expedition,[158] and doubtless hoped to accompany them into battle. But the Queen had earlier expressly forbidden Southampton to sail with Essex to Calais, and Essex, in the absence of overriding instructions, deemed this prohibition to extend also to the Cadiz operation, and sailed for Spain without Southampton.[159] The reason for the Queen's order is unknown; it could not have been Southampton's age, for Southampton's cousin, Robert Radcliffe, fifth Earl of Sussex, who was born in the same year as Southampton, was "Colonel of a Regiment of Foot" on this campaign.[160] On 20 June 1596, the English defeated the Spanish fleet near Cadiz, after which they landed with 3,000 men, and captured the town. On 27 June, in the cathedral of Cadiz, Essex created 53 new knights, among them his steward, now Sir Gelly Merrick, and Robert Radcliffe, Earl of Sussex. The English left Cadiz on 5 July, destroyed some more shipping, sacked Faro, seizing the library of Jerome Osorio (or Osorius), Bishop of Algarve, and returned to Plymouth with a substantial amount of booty.[161] Essex was hailed as a hero.

Memorably so by Edmund Spenser. Spenser, whose various positions with the government kept him in Ireland during most of the five or six years that Essex House flourished, happened to be in London in the autumn of 1596, during which time he stayed at Essex House.[162] In his *Prothalamion*, written for the marriage at Essex House on 8 November 1596 of two daughters of the Earl of Worcester, Spenser mentions the house, his connections with it and its owners, and the military exploits of the noble peer who now lived there: by the Thames, he writes, next to where the Templar Knights used to abide and where the studious lawyers now have their bowers,

> there standes a stately place,
> Where oft I gayned great giftes and goodly grace
> Of that great Lord, which therein wont to dwell,
> Whose want too well now feeles my frendles case. . . .
> Yet therein now doth lodge a noble Peer,
> Great *Englands* glory and the Worlds wide wonder,
> Whose dreadful name, late through all *Spaine* did thunder,
> And *Hercules* two pillors standing neere,
> Did make to quake and feare:
> Faire branch of Honor, flower of Cheualrie,
> That fillest *England* with thy triumphs fame,
> Ioy haue thou of thy noble victorie,
> And endless happiness of thine owne name [i.e., *ever heureux*]
> That promiseth the same:
> That through thy prowesse and victorious armes,
> Thy country may be freed from forraine harmes;
> And great *Elisaes* glorious name may ring
> Through al the world, fil'd with thy wode Alarmes,
> Which some braue muse may sing
> To ages following. . . .
>
> [Lines 137-140, 145-160.]

Essex attempted in the following year to repeat his military success with a voyage of pillage to the Azores. This time Southampton, and the Earl of Rutland, too, who was now back from his travels on the Continent, accompanied him.[163] Southampton was given the command of a ship called *Garland*, and acquitted himself well, although the expedition as a whole — called the Islands Voyage — was not very successful in terms of victories and booty, and added no lustre to Essex' reputation.

In the next year, 1598, Southampton married Essex' first cousin Elizabeth Vernon, one of the Queen's Maids of Honour, to whom he had been paying court as early as 1595.[164] Evidently, at the beginning of 1598, he had had no intention of doing this, for in January he disposed of some of

125

his property in order to raise money to travel on the Continent, and on 12 February 1597/8 he was granted a license "to travel beyond seas and remain two years, with ten servants, six horses and 200 l in money."[165] But his plans caused Elizabeth Vernon almost to weep out her eyes,[166] and it was at about this time, we may infer from subsequent events, that her Love Melancholy was abated by what Robert Burton has called the "last refuge and surest remedy."[167] Mistress Vernon thus temporarily assuaged, Southampton commenced his Grand Tour, as Sidney had before him, by accompanying a government official on a mission to France, the official this time being Robert Cecil, sent to dissuade Henry IV from making peace with Spain. It was probably at some resting point en route that Southampton wrote to Essex a letter declaring his devotion to his friend:

> Though I have nothing to write worth your reading, yet can I not let pass this messenger without a letter be it only to continue the profession of service which I have heretofore verbally made unto your lordship; which, howsoever in itself it is of small value, my hope is, seeing it wholly proceeds from a true respect borne to your own worth and from one who hath no better present to make you than the offer of himself to be disposed of by your commandment, your Lordship will be pleased in good part to accept it, and ever afford me your good opinion and favour, of which I shall be exceeding proud, endeavouring myself always with the best means I can think of to deserve it. As I shall have opportunity to send into England, I will be bold to trouble your lordship with my letter; in the mean time, wishing your fortune may ever prove answerable to the greatness of your own mind, I take my leave.[168]

In March, Southampton was presented to Henry IV, who "very favourably embraced and welcomed" him,[169] the King doubtless already having had some report of the young man not only from the Earl of Essex and from Anthony Bacon, but also from those in his own service — Jean Hotman, Henry Constable, Charles and Henry Danvers and Antonio Pérez — who knew well so many of the people at the English Court in general, and at Essex House in particular.

Cecil, unsuccessful in his mission, returned to England in April, leaving Southampton in Paris. Such delights and pleasures as he no doubt encountered there were brought to an end by the news, conveyed to him probably by some agent of Essex, that Elizabeth Vernon was pregnant. In August, Southampton slipped over secretly to England, and married the girl, returning immediately to Paris, where his gambling — he lost 3000 crowns to Marshal Biron[170] in only a few days — and self-destructive behaviour, were on 22 September reported to Essex by one of his agents, who urged that Southampton be recalled to England, before he ruined himself in France.[171] Southampton by this time had in fact already been ordered by the Queen to return to England, and his attempt to acquire some money by gambling was probably directly related to that order, for as, also on 22 September, he wrote to Essex, "when I am returned, I protest unto your Lordship I scarce know what course to take to live, having at my departure let to farm that poor estate I had left for the satisfying my creditors and payment of those debts which I came to owe by following her court. . . ."[172] In November he finally returned to England to face the music. He was confined in the Fleet prison, in the "sweetest and best appointed lodging" of which the Queen had already immured his wife,[173] and where on or about 8 November was born his daughter, named Penelope in honour of Essex' sister (and the first cousin of the child's mother), the Lady Rich. By the end of November, the entire young Wriothesley family was out of prison.[174]

At about the same time, Sir Charles and Sir Henry Danvers, having received pardons for the murder of Henry Long, returned to England,[175] where, not surprisingly in view of their friendship with Henry Wriothesley, they became associated with the Essex House circle. But Southampton was not their only contact with this group, for Henry Danvers, who in his youth had been a page to Sir Philip Sidney, and may have been present at the battle of Zutphen in 1586, had been knighted by Essex at the siege of Rouen in 1591,[176] while Charles Danvers, as early as 1584, when he was a student in Paris, was corresponding with Anthony Bacon, then in Bordeaux, and may have met Essex in the Low Countries, where in 1588 Charles was knighted by Peregrine Bertie, Lord Willoughby de Eresby, who had succeeded Leicester as commander of the English forces.[177]

Spenser, who had returned to Ireland in 1597, was forced to flee the following year, when the castle of Kilcolman, where he was living, was burned to the ground by Irish rebels. Spenser was back in London in December, 1598, but died the following month. He was buried in Westminster Abbey, the Earl of Essex, in a fine gesture, paying the costs of the funeral.[178]

Forced at the same time and for the same reason as Spenser to flee from his sinecure in Ireland was Lodowick Bryskett, Sidney's traveling companion of yore. Although Bryskett's nephew James Guicciardini for a number of years supplied Essex with intelligence from Italy,[179] Bryskett himself seems not to have been associated with the Essex House group. However, at least two of the Anglo-Italians so prominent in Leicester House were: one was Alberico Gentili, who having dedicated works to Leicester and Sidney (and Francis Walsingham[180]), in 1598 dedicated to Essex his *De Iure Belli*

Commentationes duae; the other was Gentili's friend John Florio, who in 1594 had been a tutor to the Earl of Southampton and in 1598 dedicated his *Worlde of Wordes* to Henry Wriothesley, Earl of Southampton, Roger Manners, Earl of Rutland, and, not the dull, never-in-London Earl, but the vivacious, frequently-in-London Countess, of Bedford.[181]

In the spring of 1599, Essex was able to persuade a dubious Elizabeth that he was the general who could reclaim Ireland from the hands of the rebels, chief of whom was Hugh O'Neill, Earl of Tyrone. With Southampton at his side, Essex arrived in Dublin on 14 April 1599, and on the following day, in defiance of the express wishes of the Queen (who, perhaps because of her continued pique over Southampton's marriage of Elizabeth Vernon without her permission did not wish to see him advanced to a command position), appointed Southampton Lord General of the Horse in Ireland.[182] Also with Essex in Ireland was his new step-son-in-law, the Earl of Rutland: for Rutland, following Southampton's example, had allied himself by marriage to the family of his much-admired friend and mentor, the woman in his case being Essex' 14 year old step-daughter, Elizabeth Sidney, the daughter of the great Sir Philip Sidney.[183] Rutland was not in Ireland long, for the Queen, who had expressly prohibited Rutland from going to Ireland, expressly ordered his return.[184] Rutland, who perhaps thought that ignoring the first order and going into battle might be excused because of the zeal it showed on the Queen's behalf, could not ignore the second order, and was back in England in June — not however, before being knighted, as he was by Essex on 30 May 1599.[185]

On 10 June 1599, upon orders from the Queen, the Privy Council directed Essex to remove Southampton from his position as General of the Horse.[186] It was at this time, stung by the Queen's rebuke and frustrated by military defeats on the field, that Essex seems first to have entertained the idea, as Professor Akrigg has put it, of "invading England instead of Ulster,"[187] an idea he then put aside. In a command position or not, Southampton was in Essex' company during the whole of the brief and disastrous Irish campaign, which ended when Essex, after a private conversation with Tyrone, negotiated a truce leaving the rebellious earl not only in possession of the lands he held, but also as free as he had ever been (except now upon fourteen days' notice) to resume his forays against the English. The Queen expressed her amazement and concern over this unsatisfactory issue of the Irish campaign; Essex' response was to gather around him a small group of captains and friends, including Southampton, and, unauthorizedly turning over command of the army to someone else, to return to England (in September 1599) to see the queen. He saw and talked to the Queen, but she had him put under house arrest, and he never saw her again. He was confined at York House until 20 March 1599/1600, at which time he was permitted to return to Essex House, but still under house arrest, pending some decision as to the action to be taken for his unauthorizedly leaving his command. The persons then lodging at Essex House — Fulke Greville, Lord and Lady Southampton, Anthony Bacon, Lady Leicester (i.e., Essex' mother), and all the others, except for a few servants — were required to vacate the premises.[188]

Essex' followers, deprived of access to their leader, were at a loss what to do with themselves. Southampton and Rutland, in the months after Essex' arrest, "came not to the Court; the one [Southampton?] doth but very seldome; they pass away the Tyme in *London* merely in going to Plaies every Day."[189] Eventually tiring of this, they went off to the wars. In the spring of 1600, Southampton led a small force of men to Ireland, and remained there until July, leaving in disappointment after the Queen rejected the recommendation of Lord Mountjoy, the Lord Deputy for Ireland, that Southampton be appointed Governor of Connaught.[190] Perhaps a more basic reason for Southampton's disappointment was Mountjoy's refusal to agree to Essex' plan, proposed in letters secretly delivered by Southampton, to move four or five thousand troops from Ireland to Wales to compel (exactly how is not clear) an official declaration that James would succeed Elizabeth to the throne.[191] From Ireland, Southampton went directly to the low countries, where Rutland already was.[192] Again, his ostensible purpose was to fight for the Queen, but again, his real purpose may have been something else, for it is possible, although not certain, that while in Holland he fought a prearranged duel with Thomas, Lord Grey of Wilton.[193]

In the meantime, Essex on 5 June 1600 had been charged with various crimes of malfeasance and misfeasance, convicted, and sentenced to be removed from all offices of state, and to remain a prisoner in Essex House at the Queen's pleasure. This restraint on his movement was lifted on 26 August 1600.[194] The following month, in response to a request from Essex, Southampton returned to England,[195] and, during the next few and fatal months, was one of the persons constantly in attendance upon Essex and active in planning with him a means whereby Essex could gain access to the royal presence, and have the opportunity to persuade the Queen to restore him to favour.

Before their ill-laid plans destroy their Arcadia, let us consider some so-far unmentioned persons associated with Essex House.

John Harington (1560-1612), the author of *The Metamorphosis of Ajax* and the translator of *Orlando Furioso* was a friend of Essex;[196] Harington was a captain of horse under Essex in Ireland and was knighted by Essex on

30 July 1599. Harington was also a friend to the Earl of Southampton, and it was in the company of Southampton, his sister Mary, her husband Thomas Arundell and Southampton's friend Sir Henry Danvers, that Harington, in about 1594, conceived the useful fixture which is the subject of his best known work.[197]

Barnabe Barnes (1569–1609), another of the "romantic young gentlemen" who went to France with Essex in 1591, and who in 1593 included in his *Parthenophil and Parthenophe* sonnets addressed to Essex, Southampton, Rutland's sister Bridget Manners, and the Countess of Pembroke, was a friend to Gabriel Harvey and John Florio,[198] and undoubtedly moved within the Essex House circle. The same is true for George Chapman (1559?-1634), a friend to Christopher Marlowe and expressly charged by Marlowe, so Chapman seems to say,[199] to complete *Hero and Leander*. The poem, as completed, was published in 1598. The first two sestiads, the work of Marlowe, were dedicated by the printer, Edward Blount, to Marlowe's friend, Thomas Walsingham; the remaining four sestiads, written by Chapman, were dedicated by Chapman to Thomas Walsingham's wife. Also in 1598, Chapman published his translations of Homer's Iliad and Odyssey, and by his dedication of these works to Essex clearly established his presence in the Essex House circle.

Michael Drayton (1563-1631) also must have had connections with Essex House. He was a friend to William Camden,[200] and therefore probably also to Jean Hotman, Henry Savile and Henry Cuffe. Francis Mere's praise of Drayton's honest life, upright conversation and virtuous disposition[201] suggests that Meres knew Drayton personally; if this is so, then Drayton probably knew Mere's friend, Richard Barnfield,[202] who mentioned Drayton (under the pastoral name of "Rowland" which Drayton had adopted for himself[203]), in *The Affectionate Shepheard*, and praised him in "A Remembrance of some English Poets" as one

> whose wel-written Tragedies,
> And sweete Epistles, soare thy fame to skies.

Many of Drayton's plays were written in collaboration with Anthony Munday, who after being an intelligencer for Leicester and Walsingham, went on to make his living as a translator and composer of romances, plays and masks. As early as 1588, Munday dedicated his translation of *The famous, pleasant and variable Historie of Palladino of England* to the Earl of Essex. This, together with his collaboration with Drayton, and his friendship with

John Stow the antiquarian (who in turn was the friend of Camden and Henry Savile[204]), indicates Munday's presence in the Essex House circle.[205]

In the same poem in which Barnfield praised Drayton, he also praised Samuel Daniel (1562–1619)

> for thy sweet-chast Verse:
> Whose fame is grav'd on *Rosamonds* black Herse.[206]

Daniel was, like Drayton, a friend to William Camden, and also to Fulke Greville, John Florio and Matthew Gwinn,[207] and is sometimes said, probably incorrectly, to have married Florio's sister.[208] In *Colin Clouts come home againe*, Daniel was hailed by Spenser as

> a new shepheard late vp sprong,
> The which doth all afore him far surpasse.

> [Lines 416-417.]

On the basis of these associations, plus Daniel's dedication to the Earl of Essex of the first two books of his *Civile Wars between the two Houses of Lancaster and Yorke*, published in 1595, and the evident sympathy for Essex revealed in *The Tragedy of Philotas*, published in 1605, Daniel's connection with Essex House can also be assumed.[209] To be sure, in the early 1590's, Daniel enjoyed the patronage of Sidney's sister, the Countess of Pembroke, and was the tutor at Wilton to her son, the future third Earl of Pembroke, but this is not, of course, in any way inconsistent with his having been deeply involved with the Essex House circle, for although Sidney's sister was, after Sidney's death, a person about whom the remnants of Leicester House circle (and newcomers who wished to accrete to that circle) had for a while assembled, it was eventually in Essex House that the followers of Sidney, Walsingham and Leicester, and those who became the friends and disciples of these followers, found their home.[210]

These persons were not only friends or dependents, first of Leicester and later of Essex, but also friends and supporters of each other: William Camden wrote commendatory verses for Hakluyt's *English Voyages* and Thomas Watson's translation of Sophocles' *Antigone*; Henry Cuffe wrote Greek and Latin verses commending Camden's *Britannia*; John Florio dedicated his manuscript of *Giardino di Recreatione* to Edward Dyer, as did also Gabriel Harvey his manuscript of a projected, but never completed, volume of his verse and prose, and Richard Hakluyt in his preface to *English Voyages* described Dyer as "that man whose only name doth carry with it sufficient estimation and love"; Anthony Munday wrote dedicatory verses in 1598 for John Stow's *Survey of London* and in 1599 for Hakluyt's *English Voyages*; Barbabe Barnes wrote commendatory verses for the 1598 edition of Florio's *World of Wordes*, and Alberico Gentili and Samuel Daniel wrote verses in praise of Florio for the 1611 edition of that work; Samuel Daniel and Matthew Gwinn wrote prefatory poems for Florio's translation of Montaigne's *Essays*; Samuel Daniel dedicated his *Musophilis* to Fulke Greville: Francis Bacon dedicated his first book of essays to his brother Anthony — and these are only such dedications and complimentary poems I have made note of as, unsought for, they came to my attention, and can represent only a few of the total number of mutually helpful and congratulatory notices addressed to each other by the members of this large but closely-knit and intellectually incestuous group.

Finally we come to those persons who had worked as spies and cutthroats for Walsingham, and are now similarly employed by Essex. As early as 1591, Michael Moody, working out of Antwerp, was supplying Essex with intelligence (and also, at Essex' request, looking for tapestries to hang in Essex House).[211] At the same time, Moody was working for Burleigh, too,[212] and his complicated situation seems to have led to his arrest in Antwerp in 1595, and his death soon thereafter.[213] Nicholas Skeres was in Essex' service in March 1594/5,[214] and was in prison on 31 July 1601,[215] for a reason I cannot discover, but which may have been connected with the Essex uprising. Thomas Tipping also was in Essex' service, for he was among the followers of Essex imprisoned immediately after Essex' "rebellion".[216] Also in Essex' retinue at the time of the uprising were George Orrell[217] (a friend of the William Bradley killed by Thomas Watson), and a Richard Cholmley,[218] who I believe must have been the same Richard Cholmley who had known Marlowe and accused him of being an atheist: for if Skeres, Moody, Tipping and Orrell, disreputable characters who had been associated with Marlowe in the early 1590's, all subsequently ended up together in the service of the Earl of Essex, how can we doubt that the Richard Cholmley who was of their company in the early 1590's was the Richard Cholmley who was subsequently with them in the service of Essex?[219]

These unsavoury persons perform a service for us, too: the fact that they, as well as their reflective and scholarly superiors, are now to be found at Essex House, demonstrates at the lowest level the point which I wish to make of Essex House at all levels: that Essex House was not the *successor* to Leicester House but in fact the *resumption* and *continuation* of Leicester House, providing almost until 1601 a home and focus for the very same people who had known and worked with Walsingham and Leicester — and,

132

more importantly from our perspective, with Golding, Gascoigne, Sidney, Spenser and Marlowe. Thus those who had not been a part of Leicester House in the 1580's and who somehow thereafter became associated with Essex House, had access not only to persons familiar with the whole body of literature, philosophy, history and science then known to the Western world, but also to persons who had been the friends, and at first hand knew the principles, writings, techniques, theories, quirks and secrets, of the very founders of the Elizabethan literary tradition.

2. "Greek" elements in the writings and lives of this group.

In 1579 Leicester's secretary, Edmund Spenser, published and dedicated to Sir Philip Sidney his first important work, *The Shepheardes Calender*, described on the title page as "Conteyning twelve AEglogues proportionable to the twelve months." An unusual feature of this book was that each eclogue was glossed by one E.K., who may have been a real person (Spenser's friend Edward Kirke is a candidate for this honour[220]), but who many persons think was either Gabriel Harvey, to whom E.K. addresses the introductory letter at the beginning of the book, or Spenser himself. E.K., whoever he was, makes sure that no one misses any of the fine points of the poem, or their grounding in classical literature.

In "January," the first eclogue, Colin Cloute "complaineth him of his unfortunate love" for Rosalind. But first he tells us whom he does *not* love:

> It is not *Hobbinol*, wherefore I plaine,
> Albee my love he seeke with dayly suit:
> His clownish gifts and curtsies I disdaine,
> His kiddes, his cracknelles, and his early fruit.
> Ah foolish *Hobbinol*, thy gifts be vaine:
> Colin them gives to *Rosalind* againe.[221]

The phrase, "his clownish gyfts," E.K. explains, "imitateth Virgil's verse, Rusticus es Corydon, nec munera curat Alexis."

On the basis of this explanation, few educated sixteenth-century readers of *The Shepheardes Calendar* were likely to misunderstand the nature of Hobbinol's interest in Colin Cloute, an interest which is not returned, but perhaps only because Colin loves someone else — Rosalind. Nevertheless, lest the point of the reference to Virgil's verse about Corydon pass over the heads of those readers unfamiliar with the classics, E.K., in his note on the name "Hobbinol," explains everything: "Hobbinol," he writes, is a fained country name, whereby, it being so commune and usuall, seemeth to be hidden the person of some his very speciall and most familiar freend, whom he entirely and extraordinarily beloved, as peradventure shall be more largely declared heafter. In thys place seemeth to be some savour of disorderly love, which the learned call paederastice: but it is gathered beside his meaning. For who that hath red Plato his dialogue called Alcybiades, Xenophon and Maximus Tyrius of Socrates opinions, may easily perceive, that such love is muche to be alowed and liked of, specially so meant, as Socrates used it: who sayth, that in deede he loved Alcybiades extremely, yet not Alcybiades person, but his soule, which is Alcybiades owne selfe. And so is paederastice much to be preferred before gynerastice, that is the love which inflameth men with lust toward woman kind. But yet let no man thinke, that herein I stand with Lucian or hys develish disciple Unico Aretino, in defence of execrable and horrible sinnes of forbidden and unlawful fleshlinesse. Whose abominable errour is fully confuted of Perionius, and others.[222]

It is difficult to know what to make of this gloss, which goes so far out of its way to find in Spenser's poem an allusion to the "paederastice" of Plato and Socrates, and then disclaims any intention to defend those horrible sins which but for the gloss might never have been imputed to the author in the first place. (One writer calls this "a gloss of curious pruriency."[223]) If E.K.'s comments were intended to put to rest anticipated objections based upon the unseemliness of the theme, they were not successful, for seven years later the same objections were again being responded to, this time by William Webbe. In his *Discourse of English Poetrie*, published in 1586, Webbe praised the author of *The Shepheardes Calendar* as "ye best of all English Poets that I have seen or hearde," and of the poem itself observed that he "never hearde as yet any that hath reade it, which hath not with much admiration commended it." *But*:

One only thing therein have I hearde some curious heades call in question: viz: the motion of some unsavery love, such as in the sixt [*sic*] Eglogue he seemeth to deale withal (which say they) is skant allowable to English Eares, and might well have been left for the Italian defenders of loathsome beastlines, of whom perhappes he learned it: to thys objection I have often answered and (I thinke truely) that theyr nice opinion over shooteth the Poets meaning, who though hee in that as in other thinges, immitateth the auncient Poets, yet doth not meane, no more did they before hym, any disordered love, or the filthy lust of the devilish Pederastice taken in the worse sence, but rather to shewe how the dissolute life of young men intangled in love of women, doo neglect the freendshyp and league with their old freendes and familiers. Why (say they) yet he shold gyve no occasion of suspition, nor offer to the viewe of Christians, any token of such filthinesse, how good soever hys meaning were: whereunto I oppose the simple conceyte they have of matters which concerne learning or wytt, wylling them to gyve Poets leave to use theyr vayne as they see good: it is their foolysh construction, not hys wryting that is blameable. Wee must prescrybe to no wryters, (much lesse to Poets) in what sorte they should utter theyr conceyts.[224]

And then, at the end of his book, ostensibly to illustrate the good use of Latin meters in English (the members of the "Aeropagus Society," it will be remembered, advocated the use of Greek and Latin meters in English poetry), but perhaps also to demonstrate that Spenser was writing in a noble tradition, Webbe prints his own translation of Virgil's Second Eclogue,

> That Sheepheard Corydon did burne in love with Alexis,
> All his masters deare: and nought had he whereby to hope for

which is the first translation into English of that poem. (Accompanying this is also Webbe's translation of Virgil's First Eclogue.)

E. K.'s gloss is remarkable not only in pointing out the pederastic content of *The Shephearde's Calendar*, but also in telling us explicitly what might in any event perhaps have been guessed, that it is a *poème à clef*, that "Colin Cloute" is Spenser himself, and that Gabriel Harvey, the friend of Sidney and Spenser, and with them a member of "Areopagus," was "Hobbinoll," who "with dayly suit" sought Colin's — that is, Spenser's — love, even as Corydon had sought Alexis'. If Thomas Nashe (who hated Harvey) is to be believed, Harvey had also at one time been a suitor for Sidney's love: in *Have with you to Saffron-walden, or, Gabriell Harveys Hunt is up*, published in 1596, Nashe claims that

I have perused vearses of his, written under his owne hand to *Sir Philip Sidney*, wherein he courted him as he were another *Cyparissus* or *Ganimede*; the last Gordian true loves knot or knitting up of them is this:

> *Sum iecur ex quo te primum Sydnee vidi,*
> *Os oculosque regit, cogit amare iecur.*
>
> *All liver am I, Sidney, since I saw thee;*
> *My mouth, eyes, rules it, and to love doth draw mee.*[225]

The tenor of Spenser's poem, and the contemporary identification of Harvey with Hobbinol is by itself, I believe, sufficient to demonstrate that the courting — and perhaps sometimes the capture — of the affections of one man by another, far from being a practice abhorred and almost unknown in the sixteenth century, was a casually noted and not reproved social phenomenon: not reproved, for mark well, whether Spenser reciprocated Harvey's love or no, Harvey always was Spenser's "especiall good freend."[226] And the friend, too, of the other persons of that circle, who obviously found in Harvey's Corydon-like pursuit of Alexis and Ganymede no reason to shun him. Even Nashe's statement about Harvey seems to be more a criticism of Harvey's poetic talents than of Harvey's attraction to men.

If Harvey was indeed smitten by Philip Sidney, he was not the first man to be so afflicted; as we have seen, a good many of the people Sidney met in his youth, and in his teen-age travels in Europe, spoke to him and of him in the language of love. Chief among these was his boyhood friend, Fulke Greville, who literally worshipped Sidney, and whose love for Sidney we may assume was not unmixed with sexual desire, Greville having been one of the few persons of his time whose lifestyle recognisably "approximate[s] to what would now be called homosexual."[227] Another admirer was the eminent Huguenot diplomat and statesman, Hubert Languet, who, as James M. Osborn writes, "developed a deep love for Sidney, almost amounting to adoration."[228] Languet wrote many letters to Sidney, who, to his credit, seems always to have treated the older man (Languet, born in 1518, was 37 years older than Sidney) with respect and genuine affection.

One series of letters between them is amusing and suggestive. In a letter written to Sidney in December, 1577, Languet ("who loves you better than himself") refers to the possibility of Sidney's getting married, and says "for my part I should be glad if you were caught, that so you might give to your country sons like yourself."[229] But this argument had no greater weight with Sidney than it was later to have with Southampton, for Sidney did not then get married. In a letter written in March, 1578, Languet, suggesting that Sidney had decided to stay single in emulation of Queen Elizabeth, told Sidney to "consider how great is their happiness to whom, as they returne home, (in the words of the Poet) 'Sweet children run to be the first to kiss, /And fill the breast with joy too deep for words.'"[230] Responding to "my very dear Hubert" (these letters were all written in Latin, in which language phrases such as "very dear," "most dear," etc., seem to be less remarkable, and perhaps less meaningful, than their English equivalents), Sidney expressed his wonder "that when I have not as yet done any thing worthy of me, you would have me bound in the chains of matrimony; and yet without pointing out any individual lady, but rather seeming to extol the state, itself, which however you have not as yet sanctioned by your own example." Then Sidney continues with this mysterious passage:

to speak candidly. I am in some measure doubting whether some one, more suspicious than wise, has not whispered to you something unfavourable concerning me, which although you did not give entire credit to it, you nevertheless prudently, and as a friend, thought right to suggest for my consideration. Should this have been the case, I entreat you to state the matter to me in plain terms, that I may be able to acquit myself before you, and of whose good opinion I am most desirous: and should it only prove to have been a joke, or a piece of friendly advice, I pray you nevertheless to let me know; since every thing from you will always be no less acceptable to me, than the things that I hold most dear.[231]

Unless Languet wrote another answer which is lost, his rejoinder to Sidney's query was that he was only joking: "I jested about marriage in general, and the thought was suggested to me by the conversation of Beale, who often used to launch out into the praises of matrimony when he was with us."[232]

And so the matter was passed over, leaving us to speculate about what it was that Sidney feared someone might have whispered to Languet. Pertinent to that speculation, perhaps, is Katherine Duncan-Jones' observation that "Sidney's marked lack of enthusiasm for marriage, combined with the fact that his two closest friends, Dyer and Greville, were both among that 'tiny handful' of Elizabethan aristocrats who never married, provokes the suspicion that male friendship was in some ways more congenial to him than hetero-sexual union."[233] But male friendship, and especially the friendship of Dyer and Greville, was more than merely congenial to Sidney; it was essential. This is revealed in two poems by Sidney published in 1602 (sixteen years after his death) in Francis Davison's *A Poetical Rhapsody*. The first poem, entitled (evidently by Davison, since Dyer was not knighted until 1596) *Vpon his meeting with his two worthy Friends and fellow-Poets, Sir Edward Dier, and Maister Fulke Greuill*, is in part as follows:

> My two and I be met,
> A happy blessed Trinitie;
> As three most ioyntly set,
> In firmest band of Vnitie.
> > *Ioyne hearts and hands, so let it be,*
> > *Make but one Minde in Bodies three.*

> Welcome my two to me,   E.D. F.G. P.*S.*
> The number best beloued,
> Within my heart you be
> In friendship unremoued.
> > *Ioyne hands, &c. . . .*

137

Like Louers do their Loue,
So ioy I, in you seeing;
Let nothing mee remoue
From always with you beeing.
        Ioyne hands, &c.[234]

The second poem, *Disprayse of a Courtly life*, represents Sidney as a person

Once to Shepheards God retayning,
Now in seruile Court remayning,

and who, wishing ardently to return to the simple and guileless life of a shepherd, addresses this prayer to Pan:

Therefore *Pan*, if thou mayst be
Made to listen vnto me,
Grant, I say (if seely man
May make treaty to god *Pan*)
That I, without thy denying,
May be still to thee relying.

Only for my two loues sake, *Sir Ed.D. and M.F.G.*
In whose loue I pleasure take,
Only two do me delight
With their euer-pleasing sight,
Of all men to thee retaining,
Grant me with those two remaining,

So shall I to thee always,
With my reedes, sound mighty praise;
And first Lambe that shall befall,
Yearely decke thine Altar shall;
If it please thee be reflected,
And I from thee not reiected.[235]

In thus expressing his love for his friends, Sidney in his own life is not unlike the characters in his *Arcadia*, a work written in the early 1580's and, as we have seen, much influenced by the Greek romances. In the opinion of Isaac D'Israeli, the friendship of Sidney's two young Greek knights, Musidorus and Pyrocles, who frequently kiss and embrace each other, and vie with each other in expressing their mutual love, "resembles the love which is felt for the beautiful sex, if we were to decide by their impassioned conduct and the tenderness of their language."[236] Whether or not of "the beautiful sex," the young knights, as Sidney describes them, are beautiful, Pyrocles so much so that when he dons female attire as a means of getting near his beloved Philoclea (the daughter of Duke Basilius), Musidorus, who helps him dress, "could not satisy himself with looking upon him, so did he find his excellent beauty set out with this new change like a diamond set in a more advantageous sort . . ."[237] Needless to say, Philoclea falls in love with "Cleophila" (Pyrocles in female dress) thus apparently fulfilling the Delphic Oracle's prophecy that Duke Basilius' younger daughter "shall with nature's bliss embrace/ An uncouth love, which nature hateth most."[238]

Sidney's *Arcadia*, although circulated in manuscript and widely known among the Leicester House group, was not published until 1590, and then in a version edited by Sidney's sister with the help of Fulke Greville, John Florio and Matthew Gwinn, who are doubtless responsible for muting somewhat the homoerotic touches of the earlier draft. By 1590, of course, not only Sidney, but also his uncle the Earl of Leicester, were dead (Leicester having died on 4 September 1588).

With the death of its founder, the Leicester House group had no centre about which to revolve. Although Essex was immediately perceived to be the successor to Sidney's knightly virtues — George Peele writes of Essex appearing at a tournament clad all in black,

> As if he mourn'd to think of him he miss'd,
> Sweet Sidney, fairest shepherd of our green,
> Well letter'd warrior, whose successor he
> In love and arms, had ever vow'd to be . . .[239] —

he was not at first recognized as necessarily the successor to Leicester's position as Patron of the Arts, for it was not until late 1593 or early 1594 that Essex consciously decided to reassemble Leicester House in Essex House. During this interregnum, those who would have dedicated their works to Leicester or Sidney now looked to a number of others for patronage — chiefly to those whose close relationship to Leicester and Sidney cast upon them a reflected glory. Thus when Abraham Fraunce, the cost of whose education at St. John's College, Cambridge had been borne by Sidney,[240] published in 1588 a book containing a translation of Virgil's Second Eclogue,

> Seelly shepheard *Corydon* lou'd hartily faire lad *Alexis*,
> His maisters dearling, but saw no matter of hoping,

it was to Sidney's brother-in-law, the Earl of Pembroke, that he dedicated the book (entitled *The Lawiers Logike, exemplifying the praecepts of Logike by the practice of the common Lawe*), and when, two years later, Fraunce published the same translation in another book, it was to Sidney's sister that the book — the *Countesse of Pembróke's Ivychurch* — was dedicated. And all of Fraunce's subsequent published works were dedicated either to Sidney's sister, Mary, or his brother, Robert.[241]

Sidney's father-in-law, Sir Francis Walsingham, was also an obvious person to be the patron of the relicts of Leicester House, he having provided so many of them with gainful, if somewhat sordid, employment. But he died in April 1590, too soon after the death of Leicester (and too impoverished by the staggering cost of Sir Philip Sidney's funeral) to become established as Leicester's successor in this respect. However, one book dedicated to Walsingham before his death is of especial interest from our point of view: this is the eulogistic *Life of Sir Philip Sidney*, published in 1586. Our interest lies in its author, Angel Day, who in the following year (1587) published a translation, not from the original Greek (which was not generally accessible until its publication in Florence in 1598) but from the French of Jacques Amyot, of Longus' romance *Daphnis and Chloe*, thus evidencing yet once more the existence within the Leicester House group of a knowledge of and interest in Greek romances.

When Sir Francis Walsingham died, his friend, Thomas Watson, wrote a Latin elegy entitled *Meliboeus Thomae Watsoni sive, Ecloga in Obitum Honoratissimi Viri, Domini Francisci Walsinghami*, which he dedicated to his friend and fellow secret-service agent, Francis Walsingham's nephew, Thomas Walsingham; Watson also translated the poem into English under the title of *An eglogue upon the death of the Right Honorable Sir Francis Walsingham*, and dedicated the translation to Francis Walsingham's daughter Frances, Lady Sidney,[242] she evidently not yet having become the Countess of Essex. In the same year (1590), Watson published a book of madrigals, dedicated to Essex.[243]

Watson himself was dead within two years. In 1592, a pastoral poem in Latin by Watson, *Amintæ Gaudia*, was posthumously published by William Ponsonby (who had also published Sidney's *Arcadia)*; prefacing the work was a dedication to Sidney's sister, the Countess of Pembroke, written in Latin by a writer signing himself *C.M.*, who can have been none other than Watson's friend Christopher Marlowe.[244]

With Marlowe, we pick up more pronouncedly the thread we have been following, and which immediately after the death of Sidney was but weakly manifested in Fraunce's translation of Virgil's *Alexis* Eclogue. If Marlowe indeed was of the opinion, as Baines alleged, that "all they that loue not Tobacco & Boies were fooles," then it cannot surprise that passages in his works reflect this taste. One of the best known such passages is the scene with which *The Tragedie of Dido Queene of Carthage* opens, showing Jupiter dandling on his knee the handsome young Ganymede, who has presence of mind enough to request "a iewell for mine eare,/ and a fine brouch to put in my hat" as the consideration for which "Ile hugge with you an hundred tymes." "And [these you] shall haue *Ganimed,*" replies Jupiter, "if thou wilt be my loue." But here Venus enters and upbraids Jupiter for playing with "that female wanton boy," after which attention-getting commencement both Jupiter and Ganymede leave the scene (never to return) and the play gets down to business.

A richer passage of this ilk is found near the beginning of *Hero and Leander*, in the description of youth whose beauty captivated both women and men.

> Amorous *Leander*, beautifull and yoong,
> (Whose tragedie diuine *Musaeus* soong)
> Dwelt at *Abidus*: since him dwelt there none,
> For whom succeeding times make greater mone.
> His dangling tresses that were neuer shorne,
> Had they beene cut, and vnto *Colchos* borne,
> Would haue allur'd the vent'rous youth of *Greece*
> To hazard more than for the golden fleece.
> Faire *Cinthia* wisht his armes might be her spheare,
> Greefe makes her pale, because she mooues not there.
> His bodie was as straight as *Circes* wand,
> *Ioue* might haue sipt out *Nectar* from his hand.
> Even as delicious meat is to the tast,
> So was his necke in touching, and surpast
> The white of *Pelops* shoulder. I could tell ye
> How smooth his brest was, & how white his bellie,
> And whose immortall fingars did imprint
> That heauenly path, with many a curious dint,
> That runs along his backe, but my rude pen
> Can hardly blazon foorth the loues of men,
> Much lesse of powerfull gods: let it suffise
> That my slacke muse sings of *Leanders* eies,
> Those orient cheekes and lippes, exceeding his
> That leapt into the water for a kis

> Of his owne shadow, and despising many,
> Died ere he could enjoy the loue of any.
> Had wilde *Hippolitus Leander* seene,
> Enamoured of his beauty had he beene,
> His presence made the rudest paisant melt,
> That in the vast vplandish countrie dwelt,
> The barbarous *Thratian* soldier moou'd with nought,
> Was moou'd with him, and for his fauour sought.
> Some swore he was a maid in mans attire,
> For in his lookes were all that men desire,
> A pleasant smiling cheeke, a speaking eye,
> A brow for loue to banquet roiallye,
> And such as knew he was a man would say,
> *Leander*, thou art made for amorous play:
> Why art thou not in loue, and lou'd of all?
> Though thou be faire, yet be not thine owne thrall.

[Lines 51–90.]

Marlowe's *Edward II*, a play where the love of one man for another is presented "in casual, occasionally elevated, frequently moving, and always human terms . . .",[245] differs from all the works I have to this point discussed in that for the first time the "Greek love" theme is presented in an English context, being based upon events narrated in Holinshed's Chronicle. But in the play (which at its very beginning has a reference to Leander) — just as I believe to have been the case in the lives of Marlowe and his contemporaries — it is the classical precedent that makes such love, if not respectable, at least tolerable: the elder Mortimer advises his nephew that since Edward so dotes on Gaveston,

> Let him without controulement haue his will.
> The mightiest kings haue had their minions,
> Great *Alexander* loude *Ephestion*,
> The conquering *Hercules* for *Hilas* wept,
> And for *Patroclus* sterne *Achillis* droopt;
> And not kings onelie, but the wisest men:
> The Romaine *Tullie* loued *Octavis*,
> Graue *Socrates*, wilde *Alcibiades*:[246]
> Then let his grace, whose youth is flexible,
> And promiseth as much as we can wish,
> Freely enjoy that vaine light-headed earle,
> For riper yeares will weane him from such toyes.

[*Edward II*, lines 686– 698.]

142

Marlowe died in 1593, the same year in which Shakespeare's *Venus and Adonis* was published. Shakespeare's poem, to the extent that it contained passages dwelling on the beauty of its hero, was very much in the spirit of Marlowe's *Hero and Leander*, with the additional element (as I believe, for the reasons set forth in Chapter III) that Adonis' beauty was described in terms peculiarly applicable to Henry Wriothesley. At the same time, Shakespeare was writing his Sonnets which, more clearly even than *Venus and Adonis*, continued this vein of poetry. But the Sonnets, although circulated in manuscript among the Essex House group (of which group Francis Meres, who refers to the circulation of the poems among Shakespeare's private friends, was doubtless a member), were not published until 1609, and so the writer who in the mid-1590's most visibly carried on the Marlovian tradition was Richard Barnfield. According to Harry Morris, Barnfield "was clearly on terms of intimate friendship with two important members of the Sidney circle: Watson and Fraunce; he admired greatly Spenser and Sidney [and] . . . must have known also . . . Marlowe."[247] It was doubtless because of Barnfield's perception that Essex House was a continuation in personnel and in spirit of Leicester House that in 1594, at the dawn of the Essex House era, when he was only 20 years old, he dedicated a remarkable book of poems to Essex' sister, Lady Penelope Rich. This book, *The Affectionate Shepheard*, published anonymously, consisted of four poems: "The Complaint of Daphnis for the Love of Ganimede," "The Shepheard's Content," "The Complaint of Chastitie," and "Hellens Rape." Daphnis was Barnfield's pastoral name for himself, and was the name over which appeared the dedication to Lady Rich. In the first poem, Daphnis indites,

> If it be sinne to love a sweet-fac'd Boy,
> (Whose amber locks trust up in golden tramels
> Dangle adowne his lovely cheekes with joy,
> When pearle and flowers his faire haire enamels)
>> If it be sinne to love a lovely Lad;
>> Oh then sinne I, for whom my soule is sad.
>
> His Iuory-white and Alabaster skin
> Is staind throughout with rare Vermillion red,
> Whose twinckling starrie lights do neuer blin
> to shine on louely *Venus* (Beauties bed:)
>> But as the Lillie and the blushing Rose,
>> So white and red on him in order growes.[248]

And on Daphnis goes, through many stanzas. In 1595, another book of poems by Barnfield was published, this time signed by the author. In the preface to this book, entitled *Cynthia, with Certain Sonnets, and the Legend of Cassandra* (which was dedicated to William Stanley, Earl of Darby), Barnfield acknowledges that he was the author of *The Affectionate Shepheard*, and while he expresses satisfaction over the "friendly fauor" accorded his "Country Content," addresses other comments which had been made about his book:

Some there were, that did interpret *The affectionate Shepheard*, otherwise then (in truth) I meant, touching the subiect thereof, to wit, the love of a Shepheard to a boy; a fault, the which I will not excuse, because I never made. Onely this, I will unshaddow my conceit: being nothing else, but an imitation of *Virgill*, in the second Eglogue of *Alexis*.[249]

But Harry Morris is dubious, and observes that the appearance in the "Certain Sonnets" published in *Cynthia* "of an aberrant love more extreme than any in *The Affectionate Shepheard* discounts completely the poet's defense."[250] A subdued example of this is Sonnet XI:

> Sighing, and sadly sitting by my loue,
>> He ask't the cause of my hearts sorrowing,
>> Coniuring me by heavens eternall King
> To tell the cause which me so much did moue.
> Compell'd: (quoth I) to thee will I confesse,
>> Loue is the cause; and only loue it is
>> That doth depriue me of my heavenly blisse.
> Loue is the paine that doth my heart oppresse.
> And what is she (quoth he) whom thou dos't loue?
>> Looke in this glasse (quoth I) there shalt thou see
>> The perfect forme of my fælicitie.
> When, thinking that it would strange Magique proue,
>> He open'd it: and taking off the couer,
>> He straight perceau'd himselfe to be my Louer.[251]

In 1598, Barnfield published his last book, containing *The Encomion of Lady Pecunia* ("the famous Queene of rich *America*") and a number of other poems, including, at the end, a series of *Poems: In diuers humors*, among which are "If Musique and sweet Poetrie agree," and "As it fell upon a day," both for a long time erroneously ascribed to Shakespeare. Another poem in this series, "A Remembrance of some English Poets," commends the works of Spenser, Daniel, and Drayton, and concludes with a tribute to Shakespeare, with whom Barnfield very likely was acquainted:

> And *Shakespeare* thou whose hony-flowing Vaine,
> (Pleasing the World) thy Praises doth obtaine.
> Whose *Venus*, and whose *Lucrece* (sweete, and chaste)
> Thy Name in fames immortall Booke haue plac't.
> Liue euer you, at least in Fame liue euer:
> Well may the Bodye dye, but Fame dies neuer.[252]

With this, his work having been praised by his friend Francis Meres,[253] Barnfield seems to have left London and poetic pursuits. He died in Dorlestone, in Staffordshire, on 20 March 1626/1627, leaving a son Robert and a granddaughter Jane.[254]

The last work of this nature to be associated with the Essex House group is one which neatly ties together some the the threads I have been tracing in the literature and lives of the members of this group, for it is an English translation of a Greek romance, it contains a striking defence of "Greek love," and it was dedicated by its translator to Henry Wriothesley, third Earl of Southampton. The work is *The Most Delectable and Pleasaunt History of Clitiphon and Leucippe*, by Achilles Tatius (sometimes written "Statius"), who is thought to have lived in the second century after Christ.[255] The English translation, published in 1597, and signed only "W. B.," was the work of William Burton, the brother of the Robert Burton who wrote *The Anatomy of Melancholy*.[256] After publishing the translation, William Burton retired to his country estate in Leicestershire, married, had a son, and wrote only one more book, *The Description of Leicestershire*, published in 1622 and dedicated to George Villiers, the favourite of James I, and at that time Marquess and Earl of Buckingham. (Villiers had been made Earl of Buckingham on 6 January 1616, and Marquess of Buckingham on 1 January 1617. He was created Duke of Buckingham on 18 May 1623.)

William Burton's association with Essex House is hinted at by his statement, in his book on Leicestershire, that "that ingenious Poet *Michael Drayton* Esquire" was "my neere Countriman and olde acquaintance."[257] Other bits of information scattered here and there provide further evidence of the connection between the Essex House group and the Burtons.

We shall start with John Florio and his friend, Matthew Gwinne, both incontestably very much a part of Essex House. We have already encountered Matthew Gwinne (1558?-1627), a physician of Welsh descent, as one who in 1584 accompanied Florio and Giordano Bruno to the famous *Cena de le ceneri* at Fulke Greville's home, who later may have assisted Florio and Greville in preparing Sidney's *Arcadia* for publication, and who was a junior Proctor at Oxford at the time of Queen Elizabeth's visit in 1592, and, like Cuffe and the Saville brothers, participated in the academic disputations staged for the Queen's entertainment.[258]

Florio and Gwinne were friends too of William Vaughan (1577-1641), also of Welsh descent, and also closely connected with the Leicester/Essex House crowd.[259] William Vaughan at some point in his career was an intelligencer for the crown,[260] and must have known other intelligencers and spies, and something of their unsavoury world: his book, *The Golden Grove*, first published in 1600, correctly identified the murderer of Christopher Marlowe as a man named Ingram[261] (that this was the first name only of the person may indicate that these persons either were on intimate terms with each other, or did not trust each other enough to reveal their family names), a fact which became obscured and forgotten until understood and confirmed by the brilliant discoveries of Leslie Hotson in 1925.[262] *The Golden Grove*, which at its conclusion contains a poem in Latin by Matthew Gwinne, was dedicated to William's brother, John Vaughan, of Golden Grove. William Vaughan wrote a number of other books; among a series of Latin works published in 1598 were *Speculum humane condicionis*, dedicated to Essex' secretary, Gelly Merrick, to whom Vaughan says he is bound by ties both of consanguinity and love, and *Poematum Libellus*, containing, among other poems, an "Encomium illustrissimi Herois, D. Roberti Comitis Essexi."

William's brother John Vaughan (1572-1634) had equally strong connections of his own with the Essex group: he had served in Ireland under Essex, and had "there receive[d] the Honour of Knighthood, at the hands of *Robert* Earl of Essex, then Lord Lieutenant of that Kingdom."[263] Even more, John Vaughan's wife, Margaret, was the daughter of Sir Gelly Merrick — and Merrick's wife Elizabeth (or Margaret) was the widow of one John Gwyn (who was probably a brother, or not too distant a relative, of Matthew Gwinne), by whom she had had two sons, David and William Gwyn.[264] After Gelly Merrick was arrested for his participation in the Essex uprising, "the greatest part of the goodes and plate of Sir Gellie Mericke were conveyed" to the house of Sir John Vaughan,[265] in an apparent attempt to circumvent the orders sent out by the Privy Council that all of Merrick's lands, goods and chattles should be seized[266] (confiscation of property being one of the consequences of conviction for treason). John Vaughan was sought for questioning with respect to "what ends the same were brought thether and how farr he had by the said Sir Gelly bin in any way made acquainted with the purposes of the late Earle of Essex."[267] But Vaughan voluntarily presented himself to the Privy Council, which found "no certaine matter to charge him with,"[268] and Vaughan emerged from this matter with no loss, except of a father-in-law, Merrick being executed, along with Henry Cuffe, at Tyburn on 13 March 1600/1601.

In 1626, William Vaughan published a book entitled *The Golden Fleece*, having as its ultimate aim publicizing and promoting his attempt to colonize Newfoundland. In its circuitous peregrination to that end, a number of imaginary and sometimes anachronistic conversations among various human beings and several deities are related. In one of these conversations William Vaughan, "whom his Maiestie graced with the title of *Orpheus Junior*," Robert Burton, "*Democritus Junior*, which published *the Anatomie of Melancholie*," and John Florio, "a learned Italian,"[269] plan and, after securing a warrant from Florio's "friend" Walsingham, accomplish the arrest of a Jesuit.[270] Vaughan's reference to Robert Burton in *The Golden Fleece* is reciprocated by Burton's reference in *The Anatomy of Melancholy* to "that noble Gentleman Mr. Vaughan, or Orpheus Junior" and to his book, *The Golden Fleece*.[271] Also, Robert Burton undoubtedly knew Matthew Gwynne, one of whose works he refers to in the prefatory material to his play, *Philosophaster*.[272] And if he personally knew Sir Henry Saville, for whom he wrote an elegaic verse in 1622,[273] then he may also have known some of Saville's friends and protégés, including William Camden and Henry Cuffe, the latter of whom he could also have met through Gwynne.

This does not tell us directly anything about Robert Burton's brother William, or his connections with Essex House, but from the facts that Robert mentions William several times in his book,[274] and that William (who was the executor of Robert's will) erected the monument to Robert, with a bust in colour, in Christ Church Cathedral,[275] we may assume that the two were on good terms with each other, and knew each other's friends.[276] Since we know that Robert Burton, the bookworm and recluse who spent his life from 1599 until his death in 1640 living at "Christ Church College, reading mathematics, divinity, astrology, magic, medicine and the classics,"[277] was the friend of William and John Vaughan, John Florio and Matthew Gwinn, all of whom were, and had close connections with, persons at the very heart of the Essex House group, we cannot doubt that his brother William, who was a friend to Michael Drayton and who dedicated his translation of *Clitiphon and Leucippe* to one of the most illustrious of Essex' followers, was, if not himself a member of that group, at least as acquainted and involved as his recluse brother with those who were.[278] In fine, William Burton was not an outsider seeking preferment by his dedication, but an

147

insider whose dedication may have been based upon his personal knowledge of the interests of the Earl of Southampton.

Clitophon and Leucippe is the story of the unsmooth path of the love of Clitiphon, a Phoenician youth, for Leucippe, a beautiful maiden. Clitiphon's best friend is his kinsman Clinias: "he was two yeares elder then I, and was in love with a yong boy" named Charicles. Clitiphon used to mock Clinias, not that he loved a boy, but that he should waste his time in love for anyone, but now: "O Clinias, do I suffer punishment for the reproches which I bestowed on thee: for now I my self am taken in love also. . . ."[279] Clinias proceeds to give Clitiphon a lot of knowledgeable advice on how to win the affection, and more, of the beautiful Leucippe. But while they talk, news comes that Charicles is killed by a fall from a horse, and Clinias is grief-stricken. Later, Clitiphon, Leucippe and Clinias are on a ship, sailing to Alexandria. Leucippe retires, and Clitiphon and Clinias strike up a conversation with a stranger, who tells them that he is Menelaus, an Egyptian, returning to Egypt after having been banished for three years for allegedly causing the death in a hunting accident of his beloved friend, who, in truth, fell off his horse in spite of, rather than because of, Menelaus' actions. Clinias weeps, because of the memories this brings back. In order to divert Clinias' mind from his loss, Clitiphon starts a conversation on a subject Clinias always likes to talk about, and asks Menelaus, "what is the cause why so many are in love with boyes?" Menelaus answers that "boyes are more perfect than women, and their beautie is of more force to delight ye senses with pleasure." After all, the Gods, "incensed with bewtie of this Boy," took Ganymede to heaven, and "never was there woman for bewtie brought up to heaven, although Jupiter loved women well." Clitiphon responds that woman kinde seems to him to be most heavenly. And what if Ganymede is Jupiter's cup-bearer; it is Juno who is lying in bed next to Jupiter. A woman's body is tender to embrace, her lips soft for to kiss, "in touching of her tender breasts, what great delight there is," while the kisses of boyes are rude, "their imbracings unapt, and unnatural: whose delight doth languish, and is voyd of all true pleasure indeed." To this Menelaus responds that

the bewtie of boyes is not besmeared with the counterfeyt of painting, neither spunged up with borrowed perfumes: the very sweate of the browes of a boy, doth excell all the sweete savours of Muske and Civet about a woman: and a man may openly talke and play with them and never bee ashamed:[280] neither is there any tendernesse of flesh which is like to them: their kisses do not savour of womens curiositie: neither beguile with a foolish error: the kisses of them are sweete and delightfull, not proceeding of art, but of nature: and the very image and picture of their kisses are so sweete and pleasant, that you might very wel thinke, that heavenly Nectar to bee betweene your lippes.[281]

In this work also, the love of a man for a boy is deemed no more remarkable than that of a man for a maid. The shipboard discussion relates to what is preferred, not what is allowed.[282]

Burton's dedication of his translation "To the Right Honourable Henry Wriothesley, Earle of Southampton, and Baron of Titchfield," to whom "W.B. wisheth continuance of health with prosperous estate and felicitie," suggests (to those who have "inquiring minds") that Burton may have had reason to know that this story of the love of men for both women and other men would be well received by the Earl of Southampton because of his like proclivities. There is at least one contemporary report of the Earl's physical expression of affection for another man: the ubiquitous William Reynolds[283] whom we have earlier had occasion to quote with respect to the "much ado wth red & whyte" in *Venus and Adonis*, wrote to Robert Cecil, after Southampton's arrest for participation in the Essex "rebellion," that Piers Edmonds, who was "corporall generall of the horse in Ierland under the earle of Sowthamton [in 1599], he eate and drancke at his table and lay in his tente, the earle of Sowthampton gave him a horse, which edmonds refused a 100 markes for him, the earle sowthamton would cole and huge [embrace and hug] him in his armes and play wantonly with him."[284] Although Leslie Hotson characterizes Reynolds as a "madman," he nevertheless demonstrates that Reynolds' mental condition "did not prevent him from observing closely and reporting accurately."[285] So Reynolds' story, if true, reveals a sexuality on the part of the third Earl completely consistent with that of the Fair Friend of the Sonnets, who loved both the Dark Lady and our Poet, and seemed for a while seriously interested in a Rival Poet; and Butler's dedication to Southampton of his translation of a Greek romance may reveal an awareness both of the Earl's taste, and of the precedent and sanction for that taste in the literatures of Greece and Rome.

What then of Essex himself, he who built Arcadia in England's green and pleasant land, and assembled in his house the remarkable group of men whose non-Christian sexual preferences, covertly practiced and obliquely referred to as they were, can nevertheless be descried at a remove of 400 years? Given the economic and social exigencies of the time, little can be inferred from the fact that he was married and had children, although something perhaps may be inferred from the fact that he had at least one child out of wedlock.[286] Balancing such inferences to be made from these physical proofs of his having had heterosexual impulses are the inferences arising from his associations over

149

a twenty year period with persons whose equivocal sexuality we have touched upon: Philip Sidney, Fulke Greville, Edward Dyer, Spenser, and Gabriel Harvey, all of whom Essex knew, and Marlowe, Barnfield and William Burton, whom Essex probably knew as a consequence of their close contacts with persons whom Essex certainly knew. Essex cannot have been ignorant of what his friends wrote and how they lived, and the fact that he found their persons and presumably their writings congenial suggests that their attitudes and inclinations were not unlike his own.

Indeed, of the basically homosexual orientation of the men who appear to have been Essex' closest friends and associates — Anthony and Francis Bacon, and Henry Wriothesley — there can be no doubt. Anthony Bacon, as has been discovered by Daphne du Maurier, was arrested for sodomy in 1586, while he was living in France (he was accused of "abusing" his pages and then bribing them to keep silent), but was spared the application of the full rigours of the law by the intervention on his behalf of his friend, Henry of Navarre.[287] Anthony's brother Francis was a παιδεραστης, writes Aubrey, and Sir Simonds D'Ewes, in his autobiography, charges Francis Bacon with an "abominable and darling sin" with specifics in language which the nineteenth century editor of the D'Ewes autobiography found "too gross for publication,"[288] but whose general tenor was understood by a clergyman early in our century to indicate that Bacon was "an ardent lover of pure and beautiful youths."[289]

And perhaps not altogether immune from the charms of some older men; of a possible liaison with at least one, some hints remain. The older man was Antonio Pérez, the Spaniard who lived at Essex House during most of his first stay in England, and who so captivated Essex, Francis and Anthony Bacon and Lady Rich, as well as many others. It turns out that Pérez was in fact the sodomite that the Inquisition claimed he was. One biographer, Gregorio Marañon, supplies details of Pérez' sexual encounters with young men in Spain, and later, after his escape from prison, with young men in France,[290] and another biographer, Gustav Ungerer, provides information (and speculation) with respect to the young men in England with whom Pérez got involved.[291] Pérez' predilections were known to Essex and others: a contemporary Spanish account of the sacking of Cadiz relates a conversation concerning Pérez in which one Mateo Márquez Gaitán, a Spaniard then taken prisoner, was told by Essex, Christopher Blount and Anthony Standen that "lo han hallado algunas veces envuelto con muchachos, y ha cometido el pecado nefando . . .",[292] translated by Gustav Ungerer as "he [Pérez] has sometimes been found involved with young men and has committed sodomy"[293] ("pecado nefando" being literally the familiar "sin not-to-be-named").

So it is not surprising that, perhaps because of their mutual interests in young men, or perhaps because of their interest in each other, Pérez and Francis Bacon became especially close friends during Pérez' first sojourn in England. Bruit of their association was loud enough to reach the ears of Francis' mother, Lady Anne Bacon, who in April 1594 wrote to her son Anthony: "though I pity your brother [Francis]; yet so long as he pities not himself, but keepeth that Bloody Perez, as I told him then, yea as a coach companion, & Bed companion, a proud, profane, costly fellow, whose being about him I verily fear the Lord God doth mislike, & doth less bless your Brother in credit & otherwise in his health, surely I am utterly discouraged & make a conscience [i.e., scruple?] further to undo myself to maintain such wretches as he is that once never loved your Brother in deed but for his own credit, living upon your Brother. . . ."[294] Lady Bacon also complained of Anthony's association with Sir Anthony Standen and of the behaviour of Francis' Welsh servants;[295] if these complaints had the same basis as her complaint about Pérez, Essex House must have been an interesting place. Nor did it cease to be interesting when in 1595 Pérez left England, for, at Essex' invitation, Anthony Bacon, heedless of the objections of his mother, moved to the very apartment vacated by Pérez,[296] and lived there for five years, until Essex was placed under house arrest, and all his live-in relatives and retainers at Essex House, except for a few servants, required by the Government to leave.

As to Essex' other close friend, Southampton (who was also living at Essex House when the order came to vacate it): that he was sexually attracted to males as well as to females is a principal argument of this and my previous book, and the reader by now is either persuaded or not. Interestingly, the one item of evidence I have been able to find tending to show that Essex shared Southampton's taste in this respect is a specific one, for the very same Captain Piers Edmonds whom Southampton is said to have embraced and hugged and played wantonly with, is also reported to have been by the Earl of Essex "so favoured as he often rode in a coach with him, and was wholly of his charges maintained, being a man of base birth in St. Clement's parish."[297] The imputation which so clearly informs Lady Bacon's complaint about her son's riding in a coach with Antonio Pérez most likely informs also the report of Essex' riding in a coach with Piers Edmonds; that the imputation is true is more probable than not, and is given some support by the account of Dr. Godfrey Goodman, Bishop of Gloucester, of Essex' role in securing the conviction and execution for treason of the Queen's Jewish Portuguese physician, Dr. Roderigo (or Ruy) Lopez.

Lopez, who settled in London in about 1559, and was probably in his 70's at the time of his execution, had enjoyed a successful medical career in England, becoming in 1569 a member of the College of Physicians, in 1571 physician to Francis Walsingham, in 1576 or 1577 chief physician in the household of the Earl of Leicester (where Essex might first have met him), and in 1586 chief physician to Queen Elizabeth.[298] As is well known, Essex charged Dr. Lopez with a plot to poison the Queen, and ultimately, through the use of torture, secured the Doctor's confession (although when not subject to torture, and prior to his execution in 1594, Lopez always maintained his innocence). Dr. Goodman was a contemporary of Essex, and states that he obtained his information concerning the Earl's role in the Lopez matter from Sir Henry Savile, who, of course, knew Essex well. Goodman relates that one reason for Essex' animus against Lopez was that once, while vacationing at Windsor, where then resided Dom Antonio de Crato, the exiled half-Jewish claimant to the throne of Portugal, and "the King of Spain's secretary, who had fled out of Spain" — Antonio Pérez, of course — Dr. Lopez, "making merry with them, . . . began bitterly to inveigh against the Earl of Essex, telling some secrecies, how he had cured him, and of what diseases, with some other things that did disparage his honour. But as soon as Lopez was gone, they went instantly to the Earl of Essex, and, to ingratiate themselves in his favour, did acquaint him with all the several passages. Here the earl was so much incensed, that he resolved to be revenged on him; and now he began to possess the Queen that Lopez was a very villain . . . and did intend to poison the Queen. . . ."[299] Pérez' modern biographer Gregorio Marañon, in relating this incident, states that "the doctor broke his professional secrecy and spoke to the two émigrés of some shameful anomaly of the instincts which, according to him, the Earl of Essex suffered from."[300] If Marañon has no source for his statement other than Bishop Goodman, he can be accused of giving an unwarrantedly specific interpretation to the Bishop's rather vague language, but the interpretation is insightful, for a disclosure merely that the Earl had, say, syphilis (i.e., the pox, which was common enough at the time), would seem not by itself sufficient to explain the vigour and ferocity with which Essex pursued Lopez to an unjust conviction and cruel death. But quite another thing would have been a disclosure, say, that this warrior-earl and seducer of women had at some time (perhaps even when a young man in Leicester House) required treatment because of the effects of a pathic's penchant.

One other person who probably shared the sexual interests of Southampton and Essex, although of this I concede there is no hard proof, was Roger Manners, the fifth Earl of Rutland. Like them, he knew Captain

Edmonds, to whom, on 2 March 1601/2, he gave 40 pounds,[301] which is not of itself, perhaps, a basis for any conclusion. But a curious fact is that in his own time, Rutland was famed in song and story for never having consummated his marriage with his wife, Elizabeth Sidney, whom he married when he was 23 and she 14.

This omission on Rutland's part is alluded to by Ben Jonson, in an epigram universally recognized as having been addressed to the Countess of Rutland.[302] The epigram begins:

> The Wisdome, Madam, of your private Life,
>   Wherewith this while *you live a widow'd wife*,
> And the right wayes you take unto the right,
>   To conquer rumour, and triumph on spight;
> Not only shunning, by your act, to doe
>   Ought that is ill, but the suspition, too,
> Is of so brave example, as he were
>   No friend to vertue, could be silent here. [Emphasis supplied.] [303]

In an Elegy written upon the death of the Countess of Rutland (she died in August, 1612, a few weeks after her husband), Francis Beaumont wrote:

> As soon as thou couldst apprehend a grief,
> There were enough to meet thee; and the chief
> Blessing of women, *marriage, was to thee
> Nought but a sacrament of misery;
> For whom thou hadst, if we may trust to fame,
> Could nothing change about thee but thy name*;
> A name which who (that were again to do't)
> Would change without a thousand joys to boot?
> *In all things else thou rather led'st a life
> Like a betrothèd virgin than a wife.*[Emphasis supplied.] [304]

The message of these poems is that "the Earl was impotent, if not at the time of the marriage, at any rate shortly after it."[305] There are many reasons for impotency, and it is possible that one of Ben Jonson's remarks to William Drummond — that "Beamont wrot that Elegie on the death of the Countess of Rutland, and jn effect her husband wanted the half of his. jn his travells"[306] — can be construed as a statement that Rutland, as a consequence of some accident or disease (Rutland had several times been very ill during his tour of the Continent) had injured his sexual organs, rendering him incapable of normal sexual intercourse. But I do not think that Essex, who certainly would know had his friend suffered so grave a misfortune, would have permitted his step-daughter, were this the case, to proceed with the marriage, well-disposed though he was toward Rutland. So I think it possible that Rutland's impotence was what one might call "orientation-specific," and that, instead of having the bisexual proclivities of so many of his contemporaries, he was exclusively homosexual in his orientation.

A speculation not unworthy of consideration is the extent to which the like sexual preferences of Essex and King James contributed to the *entente* between them. I can find no record of the two ever having met, but they were often in contact with each other, through letters and emissaries. As we have seen, Essex as early as 1589 dispatched Jean Hotman and Henry Constable to Scotland to assure King James of his love and support. From the statements made by Henry Cuffe after his conviction for treason, we know that Essex had been in contact with James for at least two years prior to his uprising in February, 1601, and that he (Cuffe) "often heard that Anthony Bacon was an agent between the Erle and the King of Scottes, and so he was accounted."[307] Essex strongly supported the claim of James to succeed Elizabeth to the throne, and one rationalization for his attempted coup was his belief that Cecil, Raleigh and others in authority were supporting the claim of the Infanta of Spain to succeed Elizabeth, "to the evident hazarde, and almost inevitable ruine, of the whole Iland."[308] Essex' objective was not only to regain for himself the favour of the Queen, but also to oust Cecil from his position of influence, thereby ensuring the succession of James. When the coup failed, Essex, before surrendering, burned a paper which he had been carrying in a small black bag around his neck, and which was probably a communication of some kind from King James.[309] With this paper destroyed, no evidence existed of James' participation in or even encouragement of Essex' uprising — no doubt to the relief of Cecil and Elizabeth, who suppressed all reference to Essex' contacts with the King,[310] thereby avoiding obstacles, or at least embarrassments, to James' succeeding Elizabeth, an event which in due course took place peacefully and with popular support.

At the beginning of this chapter, I wrote that King James, when he came to England, found a court which was accepting of expressions of romantic interest by males toward males. The warm winds of Greece emanating from Leicester/Essex House had played a central role in the creation of this climate, a climate which did not become too chilly during the two year overcast between the execution of Essex and the death of Elizabeth, and which became warmer than ever with the accession to the throne of James I, and the restoration or bestowal anew of honours, titles, possessions and perquisites to those who had worked with Essex to ensure the succession for

James and had survived the folly of Essex' attempt upon the court. James, the pupil of that member *in absentia* of Leicester House, George Buchanan, certainly must have been aware, during the long period of his correspondence with Essex, and his meetings with persons bearing greetings and messages from Essex, of the atmosphere in Essex House, and the people at Essex House undoubtedly were aware of the congruent sympathies of the King. I would not venture to say that these interests, rather than other interests in common, particularly an antipathy toward Rome and a desire to see James succeed to the throne, played a major part in the àlliance between Essex and James, but I think it respectable to suggest that these other interests being present, the existence of shared sexual inclinations resulted in politics, for once, making congenial bedfellows.

The foregoing review of the persons who were friends, associates and servants of the Earl of Essex, and who lived in or frequented his mansion on the Strand, is the large foundation upon which, on the premise that Shakespeare had access to Essex House, I base two by now self-evident but nonetheless important conclusions. The first conclusion is that Shakespeare's love of another male would have been very much in the spirit and tradition of that group, and that the physical (as well as the literary) expression of such a love would not, in the context of that group, have been aberrant, or even unusual, but, to the contrary, common and unexceptional. In Chapter IV, I discussed the popularity and widespread knowledge in the sixteenth century of the Greek Anthology; many of the persons mentioned in this chapter who were friends to Sidney and Spenser and the Leicester/Essex House group — Henri Estienne, Paul Schede (or Melissus), Theodore de Bèze (or Beza), Pierre de Ronsard, Antoine de Baïf, George Buchanan and Ludovico Guicciardini, among others — were well known in their time as translators (usually into Latin) of epigrams from the Anthology. I refer to the Anthology here because although the whole corpus of Greek literature, as known in the sixteenth century, shaped the atmosphere which prevailed at Essex House, one epigram from the Anthology (numbered 65 of Book V in modern editions) seems most cogently to epitomize that atmosphere. As translated by W. R. Paton the epigram reads:

Zeus came as an eagle to god-like Ganymede, as a swan came he to the fair-haired mother of Helen [i.e., to Leda]. So there is no comparison between the two things; one person likes one, another likes the other; I like both.[311]

155

Whether they knew this particular epigram or not, the Lords, soldiers, statesmen, secretaries, spies, seekers of patronage and others at Essex House, doing freely what they would in their coaches and bed chambers, indulged a taste which they knew from their readings in Greek and Latin literature at large was sanctioned not only by the lives and writings of the great statesmen and poets of antiquity, but also by the the gods themselves. Encapsulated in the epigram is the spirit of Essex House, and the premise of the Sonnets.

The second conclusion is that any or all of the remarkable group of learned and travelled men assembled at Essex House could have been the source of the immense literary, political, philosophical and topographical knowledge which informs, and the identification of which illuminates our understanding of, Shakespeare's writings. Over his familiarity with so wide a range of knowledge, students of Shakespeare have puzzled; but it is no more surprising that Shakespeare, having access to Essex House, should be familiar with anything known to any habitué of that House, than that I, or anybody else, having access to a great library, should be familiar with the contents of any volume in that library. Essex House was Shakespeare's great library.

These two conclusions can with perhaps a loss in detail but a gain in succinctness be conflated into one conclusion: that in a specific place in London during a specific period of time — that is, at Essex House from 1588 to 1600 — are to be found the friends and associates, the mores and knowledge, which nurtured and shaped the genius of Shakespeare.

Lest the premise of Shakespeare's access to Essex House seem dubious because based on the premise of Shakespeare's intimacy with Southampton, I shall adduce evidence showing that, whether through Southampton or otherwise, Shakespeare in fact had connections with Essex House.

The first bit of evidence, perhaps more interesting than convincing, is that, aside from Queen Elizabeth (in *Henry VIII*), the only one of Shakespeare's contemporaries to whom we have any direct reference in Shakespeare's plays is Essex: this is the well-known passage in *Henry V*, where Chorus at the beginning of the last act compares the greeting given by the citizens of London to Henry V upon his return from France to the greeting which those in the audience would themselves accord,

> Were now the general of our gracious empress,
> As in good time he may, from Ireland coming,
> Bringing rebellion broached on his sword. . . .

If Essex is unique in being a contemporary referred to in Shakespeare's works, he is also unusual in being a contemporary who refers to Shakespeare's works, as he did in the postscript to a letter written in February 1598 to Sir Robert Cecil:

I pray you commend me to my L. of Southampton and S' F. Caro. I wrote to them both by one Constance and had written now yf I had any tyme. I pray you commend me allso to Alex. Ratcliff and tell him for newes his sister is maryed to S' Jo. Falstaff.[312]

I grant that this proves nothing more than that Shakespeare, like most Englishmen, hoped that Essex would crush the Irish rebellion, and that Essex, like most playgoing Londoners, was familiar with *Henry IV*, but at least these mutual references are not inconsistent with mutual acquaintance and regard.

The next bit of evidence also has little probative value, but like the first, is interesting. Christopher Blount, who was a friend of Essex and who, after the death of Leicester, married Leicester's widow, thus becoming Essex' stepfather, was the first cousin of John Combe,[313] a resident of Stratford-on-Avon who knew Shakespeare well enough to leave him five pounds in his will, and to whose nephew, Thomas Combe, Shakespeare in his will left his sword.[314] If Shakespeare through his evident friendship with John Combe knew also Christopher Blount, then he would have had an influential contact indeed with Essex House.

More indicative of connections between Shakespeare and Essex House is the incident involving the arrangement made by members of the Essex House group to have the Lord Chamberlain's company, of which Shakespeare was a member, stage a performance of *Richard II* on the day before the Essex uprising. Gelly Merrick, in a statement made on 17 February 1600, states that "He can not tell who procured that play to be played at that time except yt were S' Charles Percye, but as he thyncketh yt was S' Charles Percye."[315] (Sir Charles Percy was Essex' brother-in-law, Essex' sister Dorothy having married Percy's brother, the Earl of Northumberland.) A statement made on the following day by Augustine Phillips, one of the players in the Lord Chamberlain's Company, confirm's Merrick's statement: Phillips recites that "on Fryday last was sennyght or Thursday S' Charles Percy S' Josclyne Percy and the L. Montegle with some thre more spake to some of the players in the presans of thys examinate to have the play of the deposyng and kylling of Kyng Rychard the second to be played the Saterday next promysing to get them xls more than their ordinary to play yt." Phillips protested that *Richard II* was a play "so old & so long out of use that they shold have small or no

Company at yt. But at their request this Examinate and his fellowes were Content to play yt the Saterday and had their xl*s* more than their ordinary for yt and so played yt accordingly."[316] On Saturday, Sir Charles Percy and Lord Monteagle, along with Sir Gelly Merrick, Henry Cuffe, Edward Bushell and others, dined "at one Gunters howse over against Temple Gate," and after dinner, "all assembled saving Cuffe at the Globe on the bank side," and saw the play "of the kylling of Kyng Richard the second played by the L. Chamberlen's players."[317] That persons at the centre of the Essex House group frequented the Globe theatre and negotiated with its management for special performances of plays is a circumstance powerfully supporting the conclusion that Shakespeare was well known to the Essex House group.

In the depositions from which are derived the foregoing account of the playing of *Richard II* at the behest of Essex' followers, *Charles Percy* is identified, by both Sir Gelly Merrick and Augustine Phillips, as the person who negotiated with the players for the performance. However, it was *Merrick* who at his trial was charged by Coke with having made the arrangement, which charge was repeated by Francis Bacon in his *Declaration of the Practices and Treasons . . . by Robert Late Lord of Essex*.[318] This apparent misstatement of a fact, whether intentional or not,[319] may reflect the underlying knowledge of Bacon and others that Merrick had close and frequent contacts with the Globe theatre, for a report exists of at least one occasion when plays were presented at Essex House at an entertainment arranged by Merrick. The report, in a letter dated 15 February 1597 (i.e., 1597/8) from Rowland White to Sir Robert Sidney, is that

Sir *Gilly Meiricke* made at *Essex* House yesternight a very great supper. There was at yt my Ladys *Lester, Northumberland, Bedford, Essex, Rich*; and my Lords of *Essex, Rutland, Montjoy*, and many others. They had two Plaies, which kept them up till 1 o'Clocke after Midnight.[320]

In view of the Essex House resort to the Lord Chamberlain's players in February 1601, it seems likely that the plays presented at Essex House in February 1597/8 were also performed by the Lord Chamberlain's players, and that Bacon's charging Merrick in 1601 with having arranged the *Richard II* performance, even though all the depositions state that someone other than Merrick had arranged the performance, reflects Bacon's personal knowledge of a history of contacts and transactions between Merrick and the company of players to which Shakespeare belonged.

Two persons at Essex House whom we can be certain Shakespeare knew are Michael Drayton, the poet, and Edward Bushell, a soldier. Shakespeare's friendship with Drayton is shown not so much by John Ward's story that "Shakespear, Drayton and Ben Jhonson, had a merry meeting, and itt seems drank too hard, for Shakespear died of a feavour there contracted,"[321] as by the report of John Hall, Shakespeare's son-in-law, that he had cured "Mr. Drayton, an excellent Poet, labouring of a Tertian," by giving him an emetick which "wrought very well both upwards and downwards."[322] It is unlikely that Drayton could be a patient of John Hall and not be personally known to Shakespeare; indeed, it is probably because he was in the first place a friend of Shakespeare that Drayton consulted Hall.

Shakespeare's acquaintance with Bushell is revealed by the only letter written to Shakespeare which has survived (apparently because it was never sent). The letter, dated 25 October 1598, is from Richard Quiney "To my Loveinge good ffrend & countreymann Mr. Wm. Shackspere," and gets to the point in its opening sentence: "Loveinge Contreyman, I am bolde of yowe as of a ffrende, craveing yowre helpe with xxx^{ll} vppon Mr Busshells & my securytee or Mr Myttons with me."[323] As shown on Table II (on page 29), Richard Quiney had a number of sons, one of whom, Thomas, married Shakespeare's daughter Judith, and another of whom, Adrian, married Eleanor Bushell, a daughter of Thomas Bushell of Broad Marston in Gloucestershire (d. 1615) and his second wife, Mary Morris. By his first wife, Elizabeth Winter, Bushell had had other children, including two sons, Thomas and Edward, this Edward being the same Edward Bushell who was in the service of the Earl of Essex.[324] There can be no doubt that the "Mr Bushell" mentioned in Quiney's letter is either the Thomas Bushell of Broad Marston, or one of his sons. Leslie Hotson thinks that the person designated by Quiney is Thomas Bushell junior,[325] while Mark Eccles thinks that the Bushell of the letter could be either Thomas Bushell senior or Thomas Bushell junior.[326] Nothing, except a suspicion that he was impecunious, rules out *Edward* Bushell as the person to whom Quiney was referring as one who would stand with him as security for the loan.

However, whether Edward Bushell was or was not the person referred to in the letter is not important; the significant thing is that since Edward Bushell was at the very least the son or the brother of this person, he probably knew Shakespeare as well as they — if not better, since unlike his father or brother, he lived in London, and frequented the theatre. If not at the time that Quiney's letter was written, then almost immediately thereafter, this Edward Bushell was very much a part of the military contingent of Essex House. Although it is true that Essex at his trial said of Bushell that "I was never inward with him but as my servant waiting at my table,"[327] he nevertheless must have had some dealings with the man, for Bushell was in Ireland with

159

Essex in 1599, where, after being impaled by a pike, he killed his assailant, and six others; later in the same year, he carried messages between Henry Cuffe in Ireland and Edward Reynolds in London.[328] He had opportunities to observe and talk with persons at the highest level of the Essex House group, including Southampton. As we have seen, Bushell was one of the persons who on the day before the uprising dined with Merrick, Cuffe, Lord Mounteagle and others, and attended the performance of *Richard II*, after which he returned to Essex House where he "supped and lay all night."[329] And it was Bushell who on the following day told his interrogators of the black bag which Essex wore on his person, and that of all of Essex' associates, "No man was more inward with the Earl than Mr. Cuffe."[330] Bushell is thus a link, certain and substantial, between Shakespeare and Essex house.

But at the end of the day, Shakespeare's most substantial link with Essex House, as I believe and have in this book endeavored to prove, was the Earl of Southampton, who afforded Shakespeare entrée at a privileged level to persons whose sensibilities and knowledge affected, pervade and explain his writings.

That the scholars, statesmen, soldiers, sodomites and spies at Essex House were the sources of otherwise inexplicable allusions and facts in Shakespeare's poems and plays may be a conclusion repugnant to those admirers of Shakespeare who prefer to think that Shakespeare acquired at first hand, through his own reading, study, travel and experiences, the knowledge we find embedded in his writing. But Shakespeare was a poet, not a pedant; Shakespeare's genius lies not in the facts he knew or the books he read, but in his ability to express in language which transcends its own limitations truths about the human condition which, but for him, we might either not have known, or thought to be inexpressible.

Having affirmed that Shakespeare's not being an independent scholar or researcher cannot be deemed a fault in him, and indeed is irrelevant to an assessment of his achievement, I now turn to indications that at least two of Shakespeare's contemporaries did think that Shakespeare's borrowing of materials from others was a fault in him. My purpose in so doing is not to raise the question of whether this borrowing is or is not a fault, but rather to demonstrate that Shakespeare's being a borrower was a fact well-known in his time: for having shown the existence of a great reservoir of learning and experience readily accessible to Shakespeare, and from which I contend he acquired much of his literary, historical, philosophical and topographical knowledge, I suppose it can only help my case also to show that Shakespeare's inclination to appropriate from and utilize the work of others was notorious enough to be recognized and condemned by his contemporaries.

The first seeming reference to Shakespeare's borrowing or even plagiarizing other persons' work is the famous passage in *Greene's Groats-worth of Wit*, published in 1592, where in a letter addressed "*To those Gentlemen his Quondam acquaintance, that spend their wits in making plaies. . . .*" (who are generally assumed to be Christopher Marlowe, George Peele, and either Thomas Lodge or Thomas Nashe[331]), Greene warns them that

. . . there is an vpstart Crow, beautified with our feathers, that with his *Tygers hart wrapt in a Players hyde*, supposes he is as well able to bombast out a blanke verse as the best of you: and beeing an absolute *Iohannes fac totum*, is in his owne conceit the onely Shake-scene in a countrey. O that I might intreat your rare wits to be imploied in more profitable courses: & let those Apes imitate your past excellense, and neuer more acquaint them with your admired inuentions.[332]

Obscure though this passage is, it seems clearly enough to refer to Shakespeare, and to accuse him of being an imitating ape, and such is the conclusion of most persons who have written on the subject.[333]

The second possible reference to Shakespeare as an imitating ape is Ben Jonson's epigram "On Poet-Ape" published in 1616, the year of Shakespeare's death:

> Poore POET-APE, that would be thought our chiefe,
>   Whose workes are eene the fripperie of wit,
> From brocage is become so bold a thiefe,
>   As we, the rob'd, leaue rage, and pittie it.
> At first he made low shift, would pick and gleane,
>   Buy the reuersion of old playes; now growne
> To'a little wealth, and credit in the *scene*,
>   He takes vp all, makes each mans wit his owne.
> And, told of this, he slights it. Tut, such crimes
>   The sluggish gaping auditor deuoures;
> He markes not whose 'twas first: and after times
>   May iudge it to be his, as well as ours.
> Foole, as if halfe eyes will not know a flece
>   From locks of wooll, or shreds from the whole peece?[334]

This poem, similar in imagery and message to the letter in *Greenes Groatsworth of Wit*, seems to me to be similar also in target, leveling the same charge of derivativeness against the same person: Shakespeare. At first blush it may seem unlikely that the target of Jonson's "Poet-Ape" epigram could be the person so effusively praised in Jonson's poem "To the memory of my beloved, The Author Mr. William Shakespeare and what he hath left us." The two poems, however, can be reconciled: the former being written, while Shakespeare was still alive,[335] about a professional rival whose indebtedness to others for his ideas and themes invoked disdain; the latter being written, after Shakespeare was dead, about a kindly remembered colleague whose brilliant transformation of "appropriated" material could not be gainsaid.

CHAPTER VII

Chiaroscuro

For I have sworne thee faire, and thought thee bright,
Who art as black as hell, as darke as night.

Sonnet 147

A. Dark Words.

The premise of my 1974 book, *The Labyrinth of Shakespeare's Sonnets*, was that the Sonnets are autobiographical, and that in view of Shakespeare's addiction to word play, the puns in the Sonnets may give us additional information about the story of Shakespeare and his two loves "of comfort and dispair."[1] As Muriel Bradbrook has written, Shakespeare "always found difficulty in saying only one thing at a time";[2] what I tried to do, in my examination of the Sonnets, was to discover the *other thing* that Shakespeare was saying. I recognized, of course, the difficulty of detecting puns, and even while setting forth certain tests for ascertaining the possible existence of a pun (based upon the unnatural syntax sometimes required to make the several meanings of a word operative), also noted that if one meaning of a word having multiple meanings applies particularly aptly to the syntax and sense of a sentence, it might never occur to a reader to consider whether any other meaning could also apply, and may, indeed, have been intended to apply: as a consequence of which, I observed, we may have lost some of Shakespeare's best puns.[3]

My premise with respect to the revelatory potential of puns was more valid than at the time I knew, for I have since learned that at the very heart of English Renaissance poetical theory was the notion that poems must mean more in the end than at first they appear to mean. Arthur Golding, in dedicating to the Earl of Leicester in 1564 his translation of the first four books of Ovid's *Metamorphoses*, commended the work "for the nomber of excellent devises and fyne inventions contrived in the same, purporting outwardly moste pleasant tales and delectable histories, and *fraughted inwardlye* [emphasis supplied] with most piththie instructions and wholsome examples, and conteynyng bothe wayes most exquisite connynge and deepe knowledge."[4] When in 1567 Golding published his completed translation of all fifteen books (again dedicated to the Earl of Leicester) he wrote in his preface "Too the Reader,"

As Persian kings did never go abrode with open face,
But with some lawne or silken skarf, for reverence of theyre state:

163

> Even so they [i.e., "Poëts"] folowing in their woorkes the selfsame
> trade and rate,
> Did under *covert names and termes* theyr doctrines so emplye,
> As that it is *ryght darke and hard* theyr meaning too espye.
> But beeing found it is more sweete and makes the mynd more glad,
> Than if a man of tryed gold a treasure gayned had.
> For as the body hath his joy in pleasant smelles and syghts:
> Even so in knowledge and in artes the mynd as much delights.
> Whereof aboundant hoordes and heapes in Poets packed beene
> *So hid that (saving untoo fewe) they are not too bee seene.* . . .
> For this doo lerned persons deeme, of *Ovids* present woorke:
> That in no one of all his bookes the which he wrate, doo lurke
> Mo[re] *darke and secret misteries....* [Emphasis supplied.] [5]

Golding's was merely one statement and explanation of a principle understood by all the major English poets of the time: that an intellectually and aesthetically satisfying way of communicating ideas is "by shadowes",[6] and that, indeed, some ideas are fit to be communicated only darkly, for the express purpose that they might not be discerned, save by a few. "There are many mysteries contained in poetry," wrote Sidney in the conclusion to his *Defence of Poesy*, "which of purpose were written darkly, lest by profane wits it should be abused. . . ."[7]

The exposition of ideas darkly, "by shadowes," is, of course, a description of allegory. In the *Arte of English Poesie*, published in 1589, George Puttenham[8] defined *Allegoria* as encompassing all instances "when we speake one thing and thinke another, and that our wordes and our meanings meete not." He continues:

The vse of this figure is so large, and his vertue of so great efficacie as it is supposed no man can pleasantly utter and perswade without it, but in effect is sure neuer or very seldome to thriue and prosper in the world, that cannot skilfully put in vse.... Of this figure therefore which for his duplicitie we call the figure of [*false semblant or dissimulation*] we will speake first as of the chief ringleader and captaine of all other figures, either in the Poeticall or oratorie science.

And ye shall know that we may dissemble, I meane speake otherwise then we thinke, in earnest as well as in sport, vnder couert and darke termes, and in learned and apparent speaches, in short sentences, and by long ambage and circumstance of wordes, and finally as well when we lye as when we tell truth. To be short euery speach wrested from his own naturall signification to another not altogether so naturall is a kinde of dissimulation, because the wordes bear contrary countenance to th'intent.[9]

Thus we find well established by the beginning of Shakespeare's writing career the notion that almost the very essence of poetry was the device that by another course of reasoning I had assumed would be operative in the Sonnets: the duplicitous (in the sense of "double meaning") use of words.

B. Dark meanings.

What were the doctrines which the Elizabethan poets couched in covert and dark terms, the meanings which were right dark and hard, the knowledge so hidden as to be seen but by a few? We doubtless will never know them all, for an allegory may, like a pun, be so perfect as to be undetectable.[10] Indeed, Puttenham insists that allegory, strictly speaking, is a figure which does *not* give hints as to its dark and covert meanings: for instance, of this figure —

> *The cloudes of care haue coured all my coste,*
> *The stormes of strife, do threaten to appeare:*
> *The waves of woe, wherein my ship is toste.*
> *Haue broke the banks, where lay my life so deere —*

he writes:

I call him [i.e., the figure] not a full Allegorie, but mixt, bicause he discouers [reveals] withall what the *cloud, storme, waue,* and the rest are, which in a full allegorie should not be discouered, but left at large to the readers iudgement and coniecture.[11]

To avoid the eminently unsatisfying fate of writing allegories which go forever undetected, most of the poets of the Elizabethan period wrote *mixed* allegories, by which I mean, in perhaps a slight extension of the sense in which Puttenham used the term, that the poets made clear their intention to write in dark terms before proceeding to do so. That is, the poets first reveal that they conceal, and then conceal what they reveal. A striking and illuminating example of this is *The Shepheardes Calendar* and its attendant gloss.

The Shepheardes Calendar was Spenser's first significant published poem, by which he sought to establish himself as a major poet. Spenser, thoroughly familiar with the literatures of Greece and Rome, knew from his own reading that covert names and terms, dark meanings, hidden knowledge, and dark and secret mysteries, were the hallmarks of the greatest poetry of the

165

past, and that, if he hoped to equal the accomplishments of his predecessors, he, too, must enfold dark and secret mysteries in his verse. His solution to the awkward problem of informing his readers that his conceits were dark was to append to his poem explanatory material purportedly (and perhaps actually) written by a friend, "E.K.". At the outset, this E.K., in the letter to Gabriel Harvey which precedes the poem, tells us that Spenser, in his Æglogues, "chose rather to vnfold great matter of argument couertly, then professing it," and that although "touching the generall dryft and purpose of his Æglogues, I mind not to say much, him selfe labouring to conceale it," nevertheless "as I knew many excellent and proper deuises both in wordes and matter would pass in the speedy course of reading, either as vnknowen, or as not marked, and that in this kind, as in other we might be equal to the learned of other nations, I thought good to take the paines vpon me, the rather for that by meanes of some familiar acquaintaunce I was made priuie to his counsell and secret meaning in them, as also in sundry other works of his."[12]

The majority of E.K.'s explanations are such as any competent editor, then or now, would provide: E. K. explains classical allusions and the conventions of pastoral poetry, defines obsolete English words, and gives the literal significance of the emblems appearing at the end of each of the æglogues. These are things which may not be generally known, but they are not, of course, dark meanings. The only elucidations which may be of the secret meanings to which E.K. tells us he was privy are (1) that some of the emblems have a special significance for the shepherds,[13] (2) that the "great *Pan*" of the fifth æclogue who "account of shepeherdes shall aske" is "Christ, the very God of all shepheards",[14] (3) that the shepherds represent real people — specifically, that Colin Clout is the name by which "this Poete secretly shadoweth himself,"[15] that Hobbinol is "a fained country name, whereby, it being so commune and vsuall, seemeth to be hidden the person of some his very speciall and most familiar freend, whom he entirely and extraordinarily beloued,"[16] and that "Rosalinde is also a feigned name, which being wel ordered, wil bewray the very name of hys [Colin Clout's] loue and mistresse, whom by that name he coloureth. . . . as Ouide shadoweth hys loue vnder the name of Corynna,"[17] and (4) that in Hobbinol's love for Colin, set forth in the first æclogue, "seemeth to be some sauor of disorderly loue, which the learned call pæderastice,"[18] (this being the "gloss of curious pruriency" we have already had occasion to consider).

Secret meanings (1) and (2), even by the standards of Spenser's time, are rather obvious and pedestrian. Secret meaning (3) — that the names used in the poem mask the identities of real persons — is in the tradition of those (often satiric) Greek and Roman epigrams and poems where that which is

166

written is clear enough, but of whom it is written is the interesting question — and a question to which E. K. supplies a partial answer, informing us in the notes to "January" that Colin Clout is the author of the poem (thus establishing Colin's identity as Spenser, for although the poem was published anonymously, Spenser's authorship was known to the entire Leicester House circle, and to many others beside), and informing us in the notes to "September" that Hobbinol is Gabriel Harvey. The identity of Rosalinde remains a mystery.

Secret meaning (4), to the extent that it discloses the underlying homoerotic bent of classical pastoral poetry, was no secret to those who read that poetry in the original languages, but may have been deemed by E. K. a necessary explanation for the not necessarily university-trained English speaking persons whom Spenser clearly had in mind as readers of what he intended to be, and what many have deemed to be, a poem establishing English as a medium for literary works rivaling in excellence and significance those of the Greek and Roman writers. With this explanation, that audience would understand that Hobbinol's love for Colin, so unignorably revealed by E.K., was an almost necessary convention of the *genre* in which Spenser was writing, and all readers, classically learned or not, may have relished Spenser's proof of how fully and truly he was a successor to Theocritus and Virgil by his showing that around him in 1579 were persons (as, for example, our poor Hobbinol/Harvey) who yet played Corydon to latter day shepherds. Also, whether intended or not, E.K.'s gloss had the effect of conferring respectability upon "disorderly loue," for how could these children of nature, these simple but admirable shepherds, one of whom, Hobbinol, was Spencer's "especiall good freend," be doing anything that was inherently evil? Philip Sidney, to whom Spencer dedicated *The Shepheardes Calendar*, wrote in his *Arcadia* that "of all other thinges they [Arcadian Shepeardes] did especially delighte in Eglogues, wherein, they would some tyme contend for a pryze of well singing, sometymes lament the unhappy pursuite of theyre afflictions, some tymes ageane under hidden formes, utter suche matter, as otherwyse were not fitt for theyre Delivery."[19] Some of the otherwise "not fitt" matter uttered by the shepherds under hidden forms might well have been their love for each other;[20] if so, we can extract from Sidney's observation no condemnation of the shepherds, but only commendation of their discretion. In Sidney's observation, and in *The Shepheardes Calendar*, as explained by E.K., we have significant examples of the forbearance, and even tolerance, which encouraged the production at Leicester House and Essex House of the homoerotic poetry discussed in Chapter VI.

As E.K. expressly tell us, his gloss does not disclose "the generall dryft and purpose" of Spenser's æglogues, thus leaving the bulk of their allegorical meanings to the "iudgement and coniecture" of those who read and write about the poem. I do not think it unfair to characterize the few mysteries which E.K. does explain as consisting essentially of gossip and sex, which he both reveals and conceals: he reveals that the shepherds in the poems are real people, and that "pæderastice" was an activity not unknown to them, but conceals their true identities, and their actual sexual activities *vis-à-vis* each other.[21]

So too, Spenser's *Faerie Queene*, characterized by its author as a "continued Allegory, or darke conceit,"[22] reveals/conceals on the one hand perhaps profound allegorical meanings which 400 years of scholarship have yet to exhaust, and on the other hand reveals/conceals, like *The Shepheardes Calendar*, gossip and sex. The gossip, again, involves the question of identities: who are the real persons shadowed under the names of Arthur, Artegal, Calidore and Timias, presented on one level as allegorical representations of Justice, Courtesy, Truth and the like, but behind whom we can confidently suppose lurk . . . who? Leicester, Sidney, Essex, Raleigh? As for sex: whatever arcane significance may attach to the Temple of Venus, or other sexual mysteries of the *Faerie Queen*, Spencer's "morbid . . . interest in nakedness, . . . sensuous description of nudes, . . . [and] innate voluptuousness" have not gone unnoticed.[23]

There is much more to Spenser than gossip and sex: but the fact that his great allegories, whatever else they embrace, embrace these things also, may have sanctioned the dwelling on these topics by other, and, save for Sidney and Shakespeare, lesser poets. For just as M. Jourdain was delighted to find that he could produce prose merely by talking, so, apparently, were the poets of the Elizabethan age happy with the notion that they, like the great Spenser, could produce allegoric verse merely by writing poems to and about persons addressed by other than their real names, and hinting at, without clearly revealing, their amours. Sidney, in the 1580's, wrote sonnets to Stella, as did Fulke Greville to Cælica; in the 1590's, Barnabe Barnes wrote sonnets to Parthenophe, Thomas Lodge to Phillis, Giles Fletcher to Licia, Henry Constable to Diana, Samuel Daniel to Delia, William Percy to Coelia, Michael Drayton to Idea, Bartholomew Griffin to Fidessa, Richard Linche to Diella, William Smith to Chloris and Robert Tofte to Laura. Except possibly for Stella, whose true name some people think is revealed in puns in some of Sidney's sonnets,[24] the identities of these persons (if indeed all are real) remain right dark and hard to espy: they are *all*, in other words (to the extent that they are females), dark ladies.

C. The Dark Lady.

We see from the foregoing that the enfolding of dark meanings in poetry was a common practice in Elizabethan times, and considered a necessary incident of significant poetry. Prominent among the matters shadowed in the poetry of the era were the true identities of the persons about whom, or to whom, the poems were written, and their sexual activities or inclinations. That Shakespeare followed this practice I have shown in my 1974 book, demonstrating the existence in Shakespeare's Sonnets of dark and covert meanings which, as in other poems of the period, reveal/conceal the identity of real persons, and their sexual interests or activities. In Shakespeare's case, these covert meanings were concealed in puns and were revealed through the extraction from identifiable pun words of all the meanings they could be conceived of embodying.

I described in my 1974 book my thought as to way in which a pun, once suspected, may disclose information:

. . . the pun can be a key to factual truth. Consider, for example, the remark of Dr [Samuel] Johnson . . . about a university which had a small endowment, but was generous in its distribution of degrees: "Let the university persevere in its present plan and it may become rich by degrees." Since we know the factual situation which gave rise to this statement, we immediately perceive the pun, and understand its point. If we did not know the factual situation, we might not perceive the pun, and would therefore not glean from the statement all the meaning that it contains.

But a pun, although not readily perceptible to those ignorant of the circumstances which produced it, is not, if reduced to writing, irretrievably lost, for the potential of the pun-word to convey all of its meaning remains so long as the language of the person who uttered the pun is understood by men. And so today, anyone with a reasonable knowledge of English, and of the several meanings which the word *degree* posseses, might perceive, without knowing anything of the story behind Dr Johnson's remark, that the word is used in this particular sentence in a such a way that it could have either, or both, of two meanings. Having identified this equivocation, might not a person who assumes the double meaning to be intentional and therefore purposeful, be able to imagine a factual situation in which both meanings of the pun-word are apposite, and thereby reconstruct in broad outline the incident which occasioned the remark?[25]

This approach — finding the pun and then constructing a context for it — was quite productive: from the puns in Sonnets 80 and 86 I inferred, in the manner explained in Chapter V of this book, that Thomas Nashe was the "rival poet," and that Henry Wriothesley was the fair friend to whom the

Sonnets were written; from the puns in Sonnets 33 through 36, 94, 95 and 99, I inferred that the "woman collour'd il" (as the Dark Lady is called in Sonnet 144) had "fired out" (infected with venereal disease) the "man right fair" (the fair friend of the Sonnets),[26] and that Shakespeare too, in due course, became similarly infected.

As I explained earlier, in arriving in 1974 at the conclusion that Henry Wriothesley was the youth to whom the Sonnets were written, I did not rely on the possible Rose/Wriothesley puns, urged upon the community of Shakespeare scholars by Skipwith, Shackford and Hinman, but weighed and, for some not-too clear reason, found wanting. Now, however, in light of the discovery which precipitated this book — the emblem with roses carved over the door in the Wriothesley home, which demonstrates that the Wriothesleys themselves perceived, relished and flaunted their association with roses — it is clear that the Rose language of the Sonnets was all along pointing to Henry Wriothesley: and if that language was not at an earlier time adequate by itself to establish him as the young man of the Sonnets, it certainly now is more than sufficient to confirm the conclusion required by the physical evidence, that Wriothesly, who was indeed a rose, was the Rose of the Sonnets. Thus although we were at first, with respect to the Rose/Wriothesley pun, in the position of the person who perceiving the likelihood but not knowing the circumstances of a pun, was required to construct a plausible context for it, we are now, after the discovery of the rose/Wriothesley/Southampton coat of arms, in the position of the person who knows the factual situation which gave rise to the pun, the point of which, consequently, is readily apparent.

In my 1974 book (completed in 1970, but not published until 1974), I perceived no puns pointing to the identity of the Dark Lady — which does not mean that there were none. I now think it likely that her identity has been found, quite independently of such clues as Shakespeare provided in the Sonnets, but that Shakespeare's clues, now understood, provide the essential, confirming evidence. What is intriguing is that the one clue Shakespeare provides as to the identity of the woman addressed in some of the Sonnets — that she was dark — not only tauntingly tells us what is self-evident, that her identity is concealed, but also, at the same time and in the same words, reveals her name.

In 1973, A. L. Rowse announced that one Emilia Lanier was the Dark Lady. This Emilia, the daughter of Baptista Bassano, one of the Queen's Italian musicians[27] and his "reputed wife" Margaret Johnson, was christened at St Botolph's, Bishopsgate, on 27 January 1569, no doubt within a week or two of her birth. Her father was buried on 11 May 1576 and her mother on 7 July 1587. Some time in the late 1580's she was taken up as the mistress of Henry Carey, Lord Hunsdon, who was also Lord Chamberlain and, from late 1594 or early 1595 until his death in 1596, the patron of the company of actors to which Shakespeare belonged. Having become pregnant by Lord Hunsdon,[28] Emilia was on 18 October 1592 "for colour" married off to Alphonso Lanier, a musician at the court of Queen Elizabeth. In an attempt to improve his lot by loot, Lanier laid by his lute, and accompanied Essex on the Islands voyage in 1597, and on the campaign in Ireland in 1599. While Alphonso Lanier was away on the Islands Voyage, his wife went to consult the Elizabethan astrologer and medical practitioner Simon Forman, with whom she several times spent the night, and from whose notes Rowse derived most of the foregoing information.[29]

One piece of information which Rowse thought he saw in Forman's notes was that Emilia had been "very brown" in her youth, and it was on the basis of this, plus Emilia's relationship with Henry Carey and consequent possible association with Shakespeare, that Rowse concluded, and announced, that Emilia Lanier was the the Dark Lady of the sonnets. However, other persons who looked at Forman's notes deciphered the words in question as "very brave," a reading which Rowse later conceded to be correct.[30] Even so, Rowse continues to champion Emilia as the Dark Lady, but his argument now is founded only on her being a part of the same general circle in which Shakespeare moved: she was "the recognised mistress of the Lord Chamberlain himself, who was the Queen's first cousin and, moreover, patron of Shakespeare's company. How much closer could one expect to get?"[31] And although Rowse ridicules as "the mistake of an Eng. Lit. scholar at Oxford"[32] the observation that there were a hundred other women with qualifications as good as Emilia's, the fact is that that observation is a cogent one, and Rowse "never makes a final link with Shakespeare."[33]

Emilia's husband, of course, knew Southampton; it is reasonable to suppose that they met at court in the mid-1590's, and had contacts with each other when they served together under Essex on the Islands voyage in 1597, or when they were with Essex in Ireland in 1599. As Rowse shows, they certainly knew each other by 1604, in which year a letter written by the Bishop of London to Robert Cecil on behalf of a franchise for Emilia's husband, states that "he [Lanier] was put in good hope of your favour by the Earl of Southampton."[34] Rowse asks, "Is it likely, since Southampton knew the husband, that he did not know the wife?"[35] The answer is that the question is beside the mark, for while Southampton may have known Lanier's wife, he may also have known the wives of hundreds of his other friends, acquaintances and associates, any one of whom, if Rowse's reasoning were valid, has as good a claim as Emilia Lanier to be the Dark Lady.

In short, the fatal flaw in Rowse's identification of Emilia Lanier as the Dark Lady is that, his reading that she was brown in her youth having been an error, he can point to nothing — absolutely nothing — which distinguishes the *possibility* of her association with Southampton and Shakespeare from the similar possibility of such association imputable to almost any other woman then living in London whose station was such that we have some record of her existence.

Nevertheless, as the astute reader will by this time have divined, I suspect, for reasons other than those advanced by Rowse, that Emilia Lanier is the Dark Lady of the Sonnets. When in the course of research on this book I read that among manuscripts belonging in the nineteenth century to one Evelyn Philip Shirley were "a great number of receipts in 1599 and 1600 of sums of money paid by Sir Gilly Meyrick to various persons," including not only Henry Cuffe and the "P. Edmonds" of whom both Essex and Southampton were so fond, but also Alphonse Lanier,[36] I thought that this evidence of Lanier's connection with Essex House placed him, and consequently his wife, near enough to Southampton and Shakespeare to give some support to Rowse's theory. I soon realized that Emilia's propinquity to Essex House can no more establish her as the Dark Lady than does her propinquity, through Hunsdon, to the Lord Chamberlain's players, or the court. But during the few minutes that I entertained the idea that this record of Meyrick's payment of money to Alphonse Lanier somehow established Lanier's wife as the Dark Lady, I conceived the notion, which but for this new-found enthusiasm for Emilia Lanier I never otherwise would have, of searching the Sonnets for puns which, like the Rosely/Wriothesley puns, might hint at Emilia's name. That is to say: by assuming that Emilia Lanier was the Dark Lady, and then looking for puns which would support that assumption, I put myself in the position of my posited person who knows what the factual situation is, and therefore can readily perceive the puns — if any — arising out of that situation. And immediately, I realized that certain puns I had discussed in my 1974 book strongly support the claim of Rowse's candidate to be the Dark Lady of the Sonnets.

These puns, to cut short the suspense, are on the word *base*, meaning dark or black, and the name they point to is Emilia's maiden name, *Bassano* (the name by which Shakespeare would have known her if the Sonnets were written as early as I believe), which name is derived ultimately from the same Indo-European root whence is derived the word *base*, and has the same meaning: dark or black.

172

Since the number of readers of my 1974 book was not great, I shall here repeat some of the observations I then made relating to the use of the word *base* in the Sonnets.

Base (more accurately, *basest*) is a word first encountered in Sonnet 33:

> Full many a glorious morning have I seene,
> Flatter the mountaine tops with soveraine eie,
> Kissing with golden face the meddowes greene;
> Guilding pale streames with heavenly alcumy:
> Anon permit the basest cloudes to ride,
> With ougly rack on his celestiall face,
> And from the for-lorne world his visage hide
> Stealing unseene to west with this disgace. . . .

Of this, I wrote:

Base means 'low', of course, and seems also to have meant for Shakespeare 'dark' or 'black'; in any event, most editors, on the evidence of Aaron's outraged question,

> Is black so base a hue? [*Titus Andonicus*, IV,ii,71]

so interpret the word here, and I believe they are right to assign it this meaning. I have no doubt, however, that both meanings are intended, 'low' probably being the referent [obvious contextual meaning] and 'dark' the inferent [other, punning, or *dark* meaning].[37]

I went on to point out that the inferent of "cloud" is "spots," or "discoloration," and suggested that the "dark spots" ("basest clouds") of Sonnet 33 referred to spots such as disfigured the body of someone afflicted with the "French disease." *Base clouds* appear again in Sonnet 34:

> Why didst thou promise such a beautious day,
> And make me travaile forth without my cloake,
> To let bace cloudes ore-take me in my way,
> Hiding thy brav'ry in their rotten smoke.

Here again, I explained, the inferent of *base* is dark,[38] and the base clouds so bewailed by Shakespeare were the dark body spots symptomatic of venereal disease.[39]

Base things recur in Sonnet 94:

> The sommers flowre is to the sommer sweet,
> Though to it selfe, it onely live and die,
> But if that flowre with base infection meete,
> The basest weed out-braves his dignity:
>> For sweetest things turne sowrest by their deedes,
>> Lillies that fester, smell far worse than weeds.

My explanation of this, the reader can be sure, was that Shakespeare rebukes the summer's flower — who else but the Rose of the Sonnets? — for having put himself in a situation where he contracted a base infection — a venereal disease.[40]

Detecting in the sonnets references to venereal disease is not a peculiarity of mine, for the almost universally accepted meaning of the last two lines of Sonnet 144 is that "Shakespeare will not know for certain if the Friend is sleeping with the Mistress until he displays symptoms of venereal disease."[41] What is singular in my interpretation is that I see in some of the other Sonnets — 33, 34, 54, 94, 95, 99 — not only additional references to venereal disease, but also clear, if *dark*, indications that the Friend indeed did display symptoms of the venereal disease which disclosed, to Shakespeare at least, that he had been sleeping with the Dark Lady. And — more significantly than I knew — I showed that the word *base* frequently accompanied these allusions to the Fair Friend's disease.

Let us at this point assume that the Dark Lady's name was Bassano. The name is related to the Italian word *basso*, a number of whose meanings in that language are embraced by the word *oscuro*,[42] translated by John Florio in his Italian dictionary of 1611 (*Queen Anna's New World of Words*), as "obscure, darke, dim, mirke, black, not-shining, hidden, secret, hard to finde, of base place or parentage." The OED states, s.v. *Base, a[djective]* that the Italian word *basso* is derived from the Latin *bassus*, found in classical Latin also as a family cognomen. So we have in *Bassano* an ancient family name derived from a word some of whose many meanings in Latin or Italian are represented by the English words "dark," "black," or "base."

If with the assumption in mind that the "woman collour'd il" of the Sonnets was named Bassano, we re-read the *base cloud* and *base infection* sonnets in the sequence addressed to the Fair Friend, keeping also in mind one of the plots of the Sonnets, that a "woman collour'd il" infected with venereal disease a "man right fair," then we have an immediate illumination of the reason for Shakespeare's frequent use of the word *base* in conjunction with the woman and the disease: both were a form of *Bassano*.

Even more brilliantly illuminated by the assumption that the Dark Lady was named Bassano are the four sonnets addressed to her — Sonnets 127, 131, 132 and 147 — which actually employ the words *dark* or *black*. To these words Shakespeare ascribes, in three of the sonnets, the meaning of "not fair," that is, not beautiful, which gives him the opportunity to protest that the woman he is addressing is indeed beautiful. Thus Sonnet 127 begins,

> In the ould age blacke was not counted faire,
> Or if it weare it bore not beauties name:
> But now is blacke beauties succesive heire,
> And Beautie slanderd with a bastard shame. . . .

which evidently means that although in ancient times, black bore not beauty's name, it does *now*. The lines, if read as saying no more than on their surface they seem to say, constitute a rather pedestrian observation that standards of female beauty change; but if read in light of their being addressed to a woman bearing the name of Black — or, in Italian, *Bassano* — then they acquire that piquancy and intensity of meaning so characteristic of Shakespeare's writings.

In Sonnet 131, Shakespeare concedes that the Dark Lady may not have been deemed beautiful by others:

> to my deare doting hart
> Thou art the fairest and most precious Jewell.
> Yet in good faith some say that thee behold,
> Thy face hath not the power to make love grone. . . .

but Shakespeare experiences

> A thousand groanes but thinking on thy face,

and so to him,

> Thy blacke is fairest in my judgements place.

While thus affirming her beauty, Shakespeare concludes this sonnet by returning to the fact that she is indeed "black," and defends her in this wise:

> In nothing art thou blacke save in thy deeds,
> And thence this slaunder as I thinke proceeds.

175

This couplet means, I think, that "[In spite the fact you are indeed *black* (i.e., Bassano)], you really are black in nothing (that is, you are fair, beautiful, in everything), except in your deeds," these black or dark deeds being, I would suppose, in light of the amatory (rather than accusatory) nature of the poem, nothing truly reprehensible, but only the sexual couplings referred to as "deeds of darkness" in *Pericles, Prince of Tyre* (IV,vi,32) and as "act[s] of darkness" in *King Lear* (III,iv,89-90).

Shakespeare in the next sonnet (Sonnet 132) bemoans the Dark Lady's disdain of him, and says that since her eyes "Have put on black," and mourn for him, he would wish her heart to do so, too, and "mourne for me since mourning doth thee grace." Which being done,

> Then will I sweare beauty her selfe is blacke,
> And all they foule that thy complexion lacke.

Here again, Shakespeare's willingness to "sweare beauty her selfe is blacke," may be an assertion, as in Sonnet 127, that beauty is Bassano.

These three flattering sonnets, in which black (i.e., Bassano) is praised for being fair, could only have been written at a stage in their relationship when Shakespeare was well disposed toward the Dark Lady; by the time of the composition of the fourth and last "black" sonnet, Sonnet 147, the change in Shakespeare's attitude toward her is evident, and his hatred palpable:

> For I have sworn thee faire, and thought thee bright,
> Who art as black as hell, as darke as night.

The accusation, made directly to the Dark Lady, that she is is indeed black, infernally black, brings everything together, for this revulsion against her must certainly have been the consequence of Shakespeare's discovering that his bad angel had fired his good one out, which discovery explains why, in the sonnets addressed to the good angel, his infection, having its source in *Bassano*, is described as *base*, or dark.

Shakespeare's association of the word *base* with the Dark Lady discloses the real meaning of Sonnet 100, which begins:

> Where art thou Muse that thou forgetst so long.
> To speake of that which gives thee all thy might?
> Spendst thou thy furie on some worthlesse song,
> Darkning thy powre to lend base subjects light.

While this sonnet is generally, and I believe correctly, deemed to mark the resumption of Shakespeare's writing of sonnets to the Fair Friend after a period of neglect, the reason generally given by students of the Sonnets for that neglect — that Shakespeare was writing plays[43] — is, I believe, incorrect. It is clear (to me at any rate) that the worthless songs on which Shakespeare's Muse spent her fury were the sonnets to the Dark Lady, and that the Muse was *darkening* her power because the *base* subject to which she (the Muse) lent light (swearing her fair, who was as black as hell) was the *Dark* Lady (Bassano).

Were we to look only at the sonnets addressed to the Dark Lady, with their dwelling on the word *black*, we might think that the candidate advanced by G. B. Harrison and Leslie Hotson — the Luce Morgan or Lucy Negro who was the "Abbess *de Clerkenwell*" — could qualify as well as Emilia Bassano to be the person "shadowed" by Shakespeare's language:[44] but when we take into consideration the sonnets addressed to the young man which, to the extent that they deal with his being "fired out" by the Dark Lady, stress his *base* infection, and the sonnet which characterizes poems written to someone other than the young man as "worthlesse song" in which the poet darkened his powers "to lend *base* subjects light," the base/black/Bassano implications and inferences, because their dark meanings so illuminate the poems in which they appear, become compelling.

A principle enunciated in my earlier book for penetrating Shakespeare's dark meanings is that

a word was intended to have more than one meaning wherever the context in which it appears permits it to take on more than one meaning. One of the best proofs that a pun was intended is that it can be found; as I have already stated, it is not easy to construct passages, sometimes of considerable length, in such a way that one or more words, throughout the passage, can bear two or more meanings: where I find the contrivance, I shall assume the intention.[45]

Assuming an allusion to *Bassano* in the "base infection" and "base subject" sonnets addressed to the Fair Friend and in the "black is *now* beauty's name" sonnets addressed to the Dark Lady, to such an extent infuses the words and phrases of those sonnets with a point and piquancy they otherwise would not possess, that we are justified, and indeed by common sense and the terms of a poet's license warranted, in concluding that the allusion exists: where we find the contrivance, we must assume the intention.

CHAPTER VIII

A Bunch of Keys

A little Key may open a Box where lies a bunch of Keyes.

Roger Williams[1]

The coat of arms of the Town of Southampton on the spandrel above the door of the home of the Earls of Southampton at Titchfield is the evidence which definitively solves the major mysteries of the Sonnets: the identity of the Friend, and of the Rival Poet. The sure knowledge that the Sonnets are the story of the intimate friendship of Shakespeare and the Earl of South-ampton provides a factual foundation for arriving at plausible solutions to most of the remaining mysteries about Shakespeare's life and writings. Chapter VI dealt with the persons at Essex House who were probably the source of much of the learning displayed in Shakespeare's work; this chapter is devoted to a consideration of other cruxes on which we may now be able to shed some light.

In *The Winter's Tale* (V,ii,105) appears a reference to "that rare Italian master, Julio Romano" who fashioned the "statue" of Hermione. Essential to the plot of the play is that the statue be a perfect likeness of Hermione, and this, Shakespeare assures us, was eminently within the skills of this particular artist "who, had he himself eternity and could breath into his work, would beguile Nature of her custom, so perfectly he is her ape. He so near to Hermione hath done Hermione that they say one would speak to her and stand in hope of answer." (V,ii,106-110.) Julio (or Giulio) Romano, who died in 1546, is the only pictorial artist named in all the works of Shakespeare.[2] How Shakespeare came to know of him, and why he was selected for this honour, is one of those minor mysteries which has caused the felling of many a tree.[3] Karl Elze, who believes that Shakespeare traveled to Italy, holds up as evidence of that trip Shakespeare's mention of Romano's qualities as a painter: Elze contends that art manuals could not have been the source of Shakespeare's knowledge,

nor is it likely that there existed in London any of Romano's paintings, or copies of them, accessible to Shakespeare. Whence then did he obtain his knowledge, if not by having seen Romano's paintings himself? The Palazzo del T in Mantua, built by Romano, and filled with his paintings and drawings, was one of the wonders of his age. We cannot be surprised if it was here that Shakespeare became enchanted by

178

Romano's works in all their richness and beauty, and that he here learned to form a correct judgment of the peculiar nature of his art.[4]

Now, whether or not Shakespeare ever was in Italy, that he had heard of Julio Romano and of his extraordinary skill as a painter[5] should cause no wonder, in view not only of the many people in the Essex House group who had travelled to Italy, but also of the special appeal which Romano's paintings of beautiful youths, represented as "Ganymede," "Apollo," or "Cupid,"[6] may have had for some of the members of that group.[7] Nor need we suppose that, even if Shakespeare never travelled to Italy, he never saw a Romano painting, for Elze is not necessarily correct in assuming that there was no painting or copy of a painting by Romano accessible to Shakespeare in London, or elsewhere in England. Not only is it possible that such paintings were in the long halls of some great Elizabethan houses, but especially possible is it that there were, during Shakespeare's lifetime, copies of paintings by Romano at one particular house likely to have been well known to Shakespeare: Cowdray, the manor of the first Viscount Montagu and the place where the third Earl of Southampton was born and spent much time in his youth.

We know that copies of Romano paintings were at Cowdray in 1777, in which year was published *A Catalogue of the Pictures at Cowdray House.*[8] This catalogue lists as being in the North Gallery two copies of paintings by Julio Romano, each called "Marriage of Cupid and Psyche."[9] Thomas Warton, in a book published in 1783, described a visit to Cowdray, and writes that

here are innumerable curious pictures, chiefly portraits, by Holbein, Vandyke, Dobson, &c. Among others are two pieces by Julio Romano, *Assemblies of the Gods*, in a great style.[10]

Cowdray was destroyed by fire on 24 September 1793. The fire started in the North Gallery, where carpenters and glaziers had been permitted to set up their workshops, and where family portraits and historical paintings from other parts of the mansion had been moved for temporary storage while repairs to the house were in progress.[11] Richard Gough, in a list made about a month after the fire of the many paintings lost — portraits of Richard Neville, Earl of Salisbury, of his wife Alice, daughter of Thomas Montagu, of the first Viscount Montagu, and of numerous Nevilles, Fitzwilliams and Brownes whose visages are now forever lost to us — includes, "In the North gallery . . . The Marriage of Cupid and Psyche after Raphael, and above it the council of Gods by Julio Romano."[12]

From the various titles given to these two paintings by our eighteenth century sources, we can fairly certainly conclude that they were copies of portions of the murals painted by Giulio Romano on the walls of the Sala de Psiche in the Palazzo del Te, in Mantua. (Another mural showing the Banquet of the Gods and various scenes from the story of Cupid and Psyche is in a loggia of the Farnese Palace in Rome; this was painted primarily by Romano while still a pupil of Raphael,[13] and credit for the mural is sometimes given to the one, and sometimes to the other, which might explain the attribution by Richard Gough of one of the paintings to Raphael.) The paintings in the Sala de Psiche depict scenes from Apuleius' tale, in *The Golden Ass*, of Amor and Psyche, and also from the stories of Mars and Venus, and Mars, Venus and Adonis.[14] In one of the lunettes in the Sala de Psiche is a scene showing the Assembly of the Gods; in the center of the ceiling is a depiction of the Marriage of Amor, or Cupid, and Psyche.

To the crucial question, were the Romano paintings which were at Cowdray in 1777 also there at any time when Shakespeare might have seen them, we have no answer. But they could have been. An obvious possibility is that they were purchased by the first Viscount Montagu during his visit to Italy in 1555, and brought back with him to adorn a house already notable for its italianate decor. Sir Anthony Browne, the father of the first Viscount Montagu, inherited Cowdray from his half-brother, William Fitzwilliam, Earl of Southampton, in 1542. During his lifetime, this Sir Anthony Browne engaged artists of the Bernardi family to paint murals on all four walls of two chambers within the mansion, and in the great dining room he caused to be painted on the walls scenes showing himself with Henry VIII at various important events.[15] Horace Walpole, who saw these murals in the eighteenth century, thought that they marked the first occasion when this particular style of Raphaelesque decorative painting was adopted in England.[16] This Sir Anthony Browne died in 1548, at which time Cowdray passed to his son, the Anthony Browne who became the first Viscount Montagu and was the grandfather of the third Earl of Southampton.

If, as is at least possible, these paintings were at Cowdray from 1555 on, then we have, as a result of Shakespeare's friendship with Southampton and consequent presence with him at his grandfather's house, a solution to the Giulio Romano mystery. Also, the fact that these paintings depicted pagan gods might in some fuzzy way explain Shakespeare's anachronistic reference to a 16th century artist in a play set in a time when people consulted the Oracle of Apollo at "Delphos."[17]

Some writers contend that Shakespeare and the Earl of Southampton never actually met, but that they did, I think I have conclusively shown. Others contend that Henry Wriothesley could not have been the Fair Friend of the Sonnets because, they say, there was little or no social intercourse among persons of different classes in Tudor England, thus creating insuperable obstacles to Shakespeare's having with the Earl of Southampton, or any other earl, the type of relationship which the Sonnets disclose. The truth is that very many of the nobility of the time of Elizabeth had their roots in the merchant or working class of the time of Henry VIII, Henry having assiduously endeavored to destroy the old aristocracy and to raise a new aristocracy of men who owed their fortunes and positions to him. Thomas Wriothesley, the third Earl's grandfather, whose life history is recounted in some detail in Appendix I, was such a person. He, like so many of those newly elevated to high position, maintained his connections with his lower and middle class relatives and friends, and with *their* lower and middle class relatives and friends; and they, of course, tenaciously maintained their connections with him, for it was through him that their hopes lay for preferment. Thomas Wriothesley and all the other Lords and Ladies of Tudor times were dealing constantly with persons of the lower classes: their relatives.

Thinking early in my research that perhaps it was through some family connection that Shakespeare initially had access to Henry Wriothesley, I examined such records as I could find to ascertain if in fact any consanguinity existed. Information about Shakespeare's forebears, unfortunately, is sparse, for the Heralds, whose Visitations might have supplied us with valuable pedigrees, took no note of this nonarmigerous family. (The primary interest of the Heralds, in conducting their Visitations, was to make sure that all those who claimed the right to bear arms actually possessed that right, either through grant or by inheritance. Persons who did not claim the right to bear arms were not required to appear before the Heralds.) From church and municipal ledgers and documents, we know that Shakespeare's father was John; most writers on Shakespeare state that John's father was Richard Shakespeare of Snitterfield, but no documents or records support this.[18] Shakespeare's mother was Mary Arden, the daughter of Robert Arden of Wilmcote; most authorities state that Robert Arden was allied to the ancient house of the Ardens of Park Hall, but this too is speculation rather than fact, for the Visitation pedigree of the Ardens of Park Hall shows no such connection. Nevertheless, these conjectures are plausible, and in adopting them, as I do, as a basis for attempting to connect the Shakespeare family with other families, I am merely following the generally accepted convention.[19] By accepting these conjectures, and examining the pedigrees, we find, as shown on Table II (on page 29) and Table IV (on the opposite page), that Edward Arden, who married Mary Throgmorton, and Edward's sister Barbara, who married Richard Neville (who called himself Lord Latimer after the death in 1577 without male issue of his cousin John Neville, fourth Lord Latimer), were distant cousins of William Shakespeare, and through these Ardens, William Shakespeare has a not-too-remote family relationship with the third Earl of Southampton, for (a) Edward Arden's wife Mary Throgmorton was the aunt of the Anne Catesby who married Henry Browne, the third Earl's uncle,[20] and (b) Barbara Arden's husband Richard Neville was ultimately, like the Henry Wriothesley himself on his mother's side, a descendant of Ralph Neville, first Earl of Westmoreland.

Also, there may be a family connection between Shakespeare and Henry Wriothesley through Wriothesley's father. A man named Thomas Greene who was the Town Clerk of Stratford on Avon referred to William Shakespeare, in various memoranda written by him in 1614, as his "Cosen Shakespeare." The general assumption is that he and Shakespeare were indeed related, but no one knows how it is that this came to be.[21] The pedigree for this Thomas Greene taken in the 1623 Visitation of Gloucestershire shows that he was a descendant (or at least told the Heralds that he was a descendant) of John Greene, one of three brothers of Thomas Greene of Greene's Norton in Northamptonshire. The Visitation of Buckinghamshire in 1566 (s.v. Walwine, of Aylesbury) shows that a Thomas Greene of Greene's Norton was the father of an aunt of Jane Cheney, Henry Wriothesley's paternal grandmother. Other pedigrees in the Visitations show the relationships of other persons to a Thomas Greene of Greene's Norton. Table V on page 184 is a *conjectural* construction of the relationship to each other of a number of families, including that of Shakespeare's cousin and Southampton's paternal grandmother, based on their relationship to a Thomas Greene of Greene's Norton. All of the lines of descent shown on the Table from a Thomas Greene of Greene's Norton are vouched for by the Visitations; what is likely to prove not entirely accurate is my assumption that the Thomas Greene of Greene's Norton in all of these pedigrees is one and the same person, for over the course of six generations, there were six Thomas Greene's of Greene's Norton.[22] But even if I have not attached all of the lines to the correct Thomas Greene of Greene's Norton, the probability is that in any specific case I am off only by one generation, and that the families shown on Table V as being related to each other through a Thomas Greene are in fact so re-

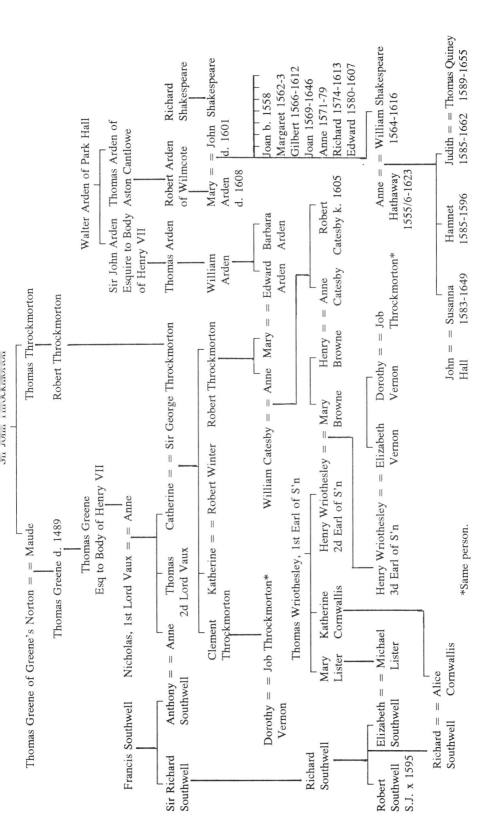

TABLE IV - SOUTHWELL, VAUX, WRIOTHESLEY, THROCKMORTON, ARDEN, SHAKESPEARE

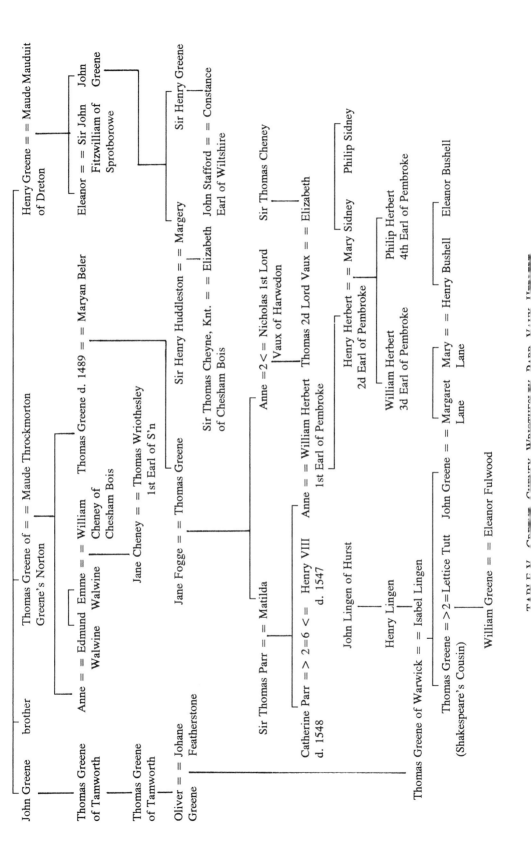

TABLE V. GREENE, CHENEY, WRIOTHESLEY, PARR, VAUX, HERBERT

lated: hence the likelihood of a familial connection, albeit remote, between the Shakespeares and the Wriothesleys, through their mutual kinship with the Greenes. (A clue to the relationship between Shakespeare and the Greenes may be provided by the fact that Sir John Arden, of the Park Hall Ardens, and Sir Thomas Greene, of the Greenes of Greene's Norton, both served as Esquires to the body of Henry VII;[23] for a marriage to have taken place between the children or relatives of fellow courtiers would not have been unusual. If this is the basis of the relationship between Greene and Shakespeare, then Shakespeare's connection with the Ardens of Park Hall would be established. In passing, it may be noted that the Thomas Greene of Greene's Norton who was an Esquire to the body of Henry VII and apparently a relative of the Thomas Greene who was Shakespeare's cousin was the grandfather of Catherine Parr, the last wife of Henry VIII: an interesting, and surprisingly illustrious, connection for the Shakespeare family. Also noteworthy is Table V's indication that even closer than Shakespeare's possible connection through the Greene family to the Earls of Southampton is his possible connection to the Earls of Pembroke.)

Another possible link between the Wriothesley and Shakespeare families is provided by the Southwell family. Sir Richard Southwell had been an associate and friend of the first Earl of Southampton, and is mentioned in the first Earl's will (see Appendix I). This Sir Richard, by his son, also Richard, had three grandchildren, two of whom married grandchildren of the first Earl of Southampton.[24] The third of Sir Richard's grandchildren was Robert Southwell — the Jesuit priest executed in 1595 (and the friend of Thomas Wriothesley's nephew Thomas Pounde; see Appendix I). Robert Southwell, and, of course, his two siblings, each of whom had married first cousins of the third Earl of Southampton, were distantly related by marriage to William Shakespeare.[25] These relationships are shown on Table VI, on the following page, and also on Table IV, on page 183. Southwell's kinship to Shakespeare is of such remoteness that one ordinarily could draw no conclusions from it; however, Southwell dedicated a book "To my worthy good cousin, Master W.S.," and he signed the dedication "Your loving cousin, R.S." A not unrespectable case can be made for the proposition that Southwell's dedication was to William Shakespeare.[26] If Southwell, who was fairly closely related to Southampton, maintained a friendship with so distant a cousin as Shakespeare, then a conjecture that Shakespeare and Southampton met each other through their mutual relative, Richard Southwell, is not implausible.

Additional examples of kinships which might explain acquaintances could be cited, but the one which to me seems most significant is founded on the alliance between the Wriothesleys and the Earls of Sussex.

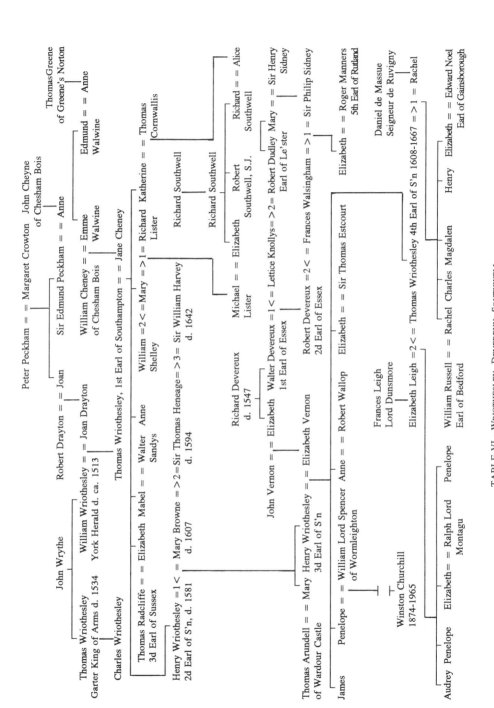

TABLE VI - WRIOTHESLEY, DEVEREUX, SOUTHWELL

Thomas Wriothesley's daughter Elizabeth in 1545 married Thomas Rad-cliffe, Lord Fitzwater (or Fitzwalter). Lord Fitzwater was the son of Henry Radcliffe, who eventually became the second Earl of Sussex (to whom Thomas Wriothesley, in his will, left a cup of the value of ten pounds). Henry Radcliffe's father, Robert, was the patron of a company of players who visited Thetford Priory at some time between 1525 and 1529.[27] When Robert was created first Earl of Sussex on 8 December 1529, his players became the Earl of Sussex's men, and between the years 1538 and 1542 played in Cambridge, Southampton, Plymouth and Bristol.[28] Robert, the first Earl of Sussex, died in 1542; Henry Radcliffe, upon becoming second Earl of Sussex, continued his patronage of the company, which played in Norwich, Plymouth, and Dover at various times between 1543 and 1556.[29] Elizabeth Wriothesley died early in 1554/5, so she was no longer alive when, upon the death of the second Earl on 17 February 1557, her husband, Thomas Radcliffe, became the third Earl of Sussex.[30] The third Earl's patronage of the company seems to have lapsed for a while; then, in 1568, the Earl of Sussex's Players appear in Nottingham, and records of their performances exist fairly continuously from 1569 to 1593.[31]

The third Earl, who was appointed Lord Chamberlain in 1572, died in 1583. His brother Henry succeeded to the title as the fourth Earl,[32] and continued his family's patronage of the Earl of Sussex's players until his death in 1593.[33]

The death of Elizabeth Wriothesley in 1554/5 does not seem to have lessened the close relationship between the families of the Earls of Southampton and the Earls of Sussex, for Thomas Wriothesley's nephew, Thomas Pounde, in 1566 wrote a mask for the marriage of the third Earl of Sussex' sister (see Appendix I). Moreover, the fourth Earl (the brother of Elizabeth's husband, the third Earl) was himself allied by marriage to the Wriothesley family, for his wife, whom he married on 6 February 1548/9, was Honor Pounde, the daughter and coheiress of Anthony Pounde,[34] and thus the niece of Thomas Wriothesley's sister "Pounde" (see Appendix I), and the first cousin of Thomas Pounde, the mask-writer. And finally, really cementing this relationship, is the fact that Jane, the wife of Anthony Browne and the mother of Mary Browne (the wife of the second Earl of Southampton and mother of the third) was the daughter of Robert Radcliffe, the first Earl of Sussex.[35] In other words, the second Earl of Southampton and his sister were each married to first cousins, both of whom were grandchildren of the first Earl of Sussex. Thus Henry Wriothesley, the third Earl of Southampton, in addition to being the grandson of the first Earl of Southampton and the first Viscount Montagu, was the great grandson of the first Earl of Sussex. These relationships, complicated in the telling, are more clearly indicated on Tables I and III.

The connections between the Wriothesleys and the Radcliffes, and the Radcliffes' patronage of the Earl of Sussex' players, present another possible link between the Wriothesley family and Shakespeare, and another possible explanation, if one is needed, of how the young actor met the young lord. To be sure, Lord Hunsdon's Company — the Lord Chamberlain's Company — is the first company with which, according to records so far found, Shakespeare was associated. The earliest known date of this association is 26 December 1594, when Shakespeare, along with William Kempe and Richard Burbage and other "servauntes to the Lord Chamberleyne," played before Queen Elizabeth at the royal palace at Greenwich, payment for which performance is recorded in an entry dated 15 March 1594/5 in the Accounts of the Treasurer of the Queen's Chamber.[36] But Lord Hunsdon's company was only formed in 1594, and it is generally supposed that Shakespeare was associated with some other company before he became a member of Lord Hunsdon's company.[37] As good a candidate as any for being the company with which Shakespeare served his apprenticeship is the Earl of Sussex' company; indeed, it is a better candidate than most, for one of Shakespeare's earliest plays, if not his earliest[38] — Titus Andronicus — as printed for the first time in 1594, bears on its title page the notation that it was played "by the Right Honourable the Earle of Darbie, Earl of Pembrooke, and Earle of Sussex their Seruants."[39] Much ink has been spilled as to how this play came to be performed by those companies, and in what order;[40] a speculation as reasonable as any that has hitherto been offered is that Shakespeare was for a period of time one of the Earl of Sussex' players, and wrote Titus Andronicus for that group, which could have been the first, rather than the last, of the companies named on the title-page to perform the play, and that as a "servant" of the fourth Earl of Sussex, he had occasion to perform before, and become acquainted with, the youth who became the fifth Earl of Sussex, and his friend and cousin, the third Earl of Southampton.

Other ties exist which, if not directly between Wriothesley and Shakespeare, are nevertheless significant because they link Wriothesley with persons in Shakespeare's circles of neighbours, friends, and business associates, thus providing a host of possible explanations for the meeting of the poet and the peer.

For example: as shown on Table II, Dorothy Arnold, a distant cousin of Henry Wriothesley, was the first wife of Thomas Lucy (1551–1605), the son of that Thomas Lucy (1532–1600) whom legend links with the young William Shakespeare.[41] The first employment of Philip Henslowe, who later became

188

the owner of a theatre where some of Shakespeare's plays were produced, was as a servant to Matthew Woodward, bailiff to Henry Wriothesley's maternal grandfather, the first Viscount Montagu;[42] it may be that Henslowe's chief qualification for this position was his being a member of that Henslowe family which, as shown on Table I, was related to the Wriothesleys.[43] Table IV shows that Henry Wriothesley's aunt by marriage, Anne Catesby, was the sister of that Robert Catesby who, along with Thomas Bushell, and other members of the Bushell, Winter, Tresham and Quiney families were neighbours and probably friends of William Shakespeare.[44]

Thus the information we have about Shakespeare and Wriothesley, incomplete as it is, shows that they had some relatives in common, as well as numerous acquaintances in common, and provides an ordinary and reasonable explanation for their becoming acquainted with each other, either through kin or kith, and entering upon a relationship as friends, although one was not the social equal of the other, nor the other the intellectual equal of the one.

In Chapter IV, I cited the Temple Garden scene in *Henry VI, Part 1* as an example of the injection by Shakespeare into his writings of imagery celebrating Henry Wriothesley. It may be, however, that attributes of Henry Wriothesley inspired not only the imagery, but also the setting, of this scene.

In the First Folio of 1623, where appears for the first time the text of *The First Part of Henry the Sixt*, the location of the scene is not specified in the stage directions. At the very beginning of the scene, however, one of the disputing characters explains that "Within the Temple-hall we were too loud; /The garden here is more convenient" (II,iv,3-4), and near the end of the scene, another disputant predicts "this brawl to-day,/Grown to this faction in the Temple-Garden,/ Shall send between the red rose and the white/ A thousand souls to death and deadly night" (II,iv,24-127). So naturally enough, editors of the works of Shakespeare have not hesitated in their emendations to this play to place this scene in London, in the Temple Garden. With all of which, I have no dispute. The question I raise is, which Temple Garden? For the interesting fact is that the *original* home of the Templars in London, and the gardens adjacent thereto, were, from about 1548 until 1652, in the possession, and for much of that time constituted the London home, of the Earls of Southampton.[45]

The Knights Templar are believed to have settled in London in about 1128, shortly after which they built their first House and their characteristic round church in the parish of St Andrew, Holborn, near the north end of what is now Chancery Lane. The Order quickly increased in wealth and numbers, and sometime between 1155 and 1162 sold its houses, chapel and gardens in Holborn to the Bishop of Lincoln, and moved to new quarters on the bank of the Thames, where it built another round church, which survives today as the famous Temple Church.[46] Thereafter, as Shakespeare's contemporary, John Stow, tells us, the Temple in Holborn was called the Old Temple, and the Temple by the river was called the New Temple. Adjoining the Old Temple was a residence called the Bishop of Lincoln's Inn, which had probably been the main House of the Templars. Stow states that the Inn was built in 1147, which would put its date of construction within the period of time that the property was owned by the Templars; Stow also states, however, that the Inn was built by the person who was Bishop of Lincoln,[47] so either the date of construction, or the supposed builder of the structure, is incorrect (it being unlikely that the Bishop of Lincoln would build the House prior to having possession of the land).

Although, strictly speaking, the Temple was the church only, and thus the term Old Temple might be thought to refer only to the round church, in common parlance the term Old Temple included all the buildings associated with it,[48] just as the term New Temple has always included all of the buildings within the area occupied by the Templars after their removal to Fleet Street. An example of the term Old Temple being used to designate the Inn of the Bishop of Lincoln is provided by an entry in the *Valor Ecclesiasticus,* compiled during the years 1535–1536 (see page 230) referring to David Griffiths, "custodian of the Inn of the Lord Bishop, called the Old Temple, in London."[49]

On August 31, 1547, the Bishop of Lincoln conveyed the House, also called Lincoln Place, together with all appurtenant gardens, to John Dudley, Earl of Warwick[50] (and brother to Robert Dudley, who later became the Earl of Leicester). Within a year or two after acquiring the property, Dudley exchanged residences with Thomas Wriothesley, first Earl of Southampton. After Wriothesley acquired Lincoln Place, it came to be called Southampton House, and it was there that Thomas Wriothesley died on July 30, 1550.[51] We know from the description of Lincoln Place in the deed of conveyance to John Dudley that included in the property were gardens, and we know from a deed of the adjacent Staple Inn executed in 1622 that the gardens were in that year still in existence, for the 1622 deed recites that the garden of Staple Inn "lies by the garden of the Earl of Southampton formerly of the Bishop of Lincoln. . . . "[52]

In view of the rather remarkable fact that the garden of the London home of him whom I deem to be the Rose of the Sonnets was a Temple garden (the

Old Temple, to be sure, but still a Temple), the possibility inevitably suggests itself that this, and not any garden on the grounds of the New Temple, was the site where, in Shakespeare's fancy, red and white roses became the symbols, first of warring factions, and then of a united nation. Nothing in the language of the scene rules out this possibility, for the Bishop of Lincoln's Inn could at one time properly have been referred to as the "Temple-Hall" mentioned at the beginning of the Rose garden scene, and the "Temple" where, in the following scene, Richard Plantagenet is said to have his chamber.

It is futile to appeal to history in support of this conjecture, for Shakespeare's English history plays treat the chronicles upon which they are based with the same freedom that Shakespeare's tragedies and comedies treat the sources upon which they are based. Thus to argue on grounds of the historical possibility of the event depicted, that Henry Wriothesley's back yard was (or, indeed, was not) the setting of the totally fictional Rose Garden scene is a meaningless exercise. Nevertheless, I offer two history-based *scintillae* in support of my conjecture.

As Peter Saccio observes,

The real York-Somerset quarrel [the beginning of which is the subject of the Rose garden scene] developed in the years covered by 2 Henry V; the Somerset of *1 Henry VI*, as I have mentioned, is historically two separate persons; and no evidence suggests that Richard of York [i.e., Richard Plantagenet] seriously contemplated a claim to the crown before the late 1450s. The modern reader of Shakespeare, as opposed to the modern historian, is more apt to be bothered by the apparent lack of motivation for their strife. Shakespeare does not bother to explain why York and Somerset start quarrelling. In the rose-plucking scene they *enter* in dispute upon a matter that is never explained, and the subsequent mention of York's dynastic pretensions merely adds fuel to a fire already raging.[53]

If we look at English history in the late 1450's, when, according to Saccio, the *real* York-Somerset quarrel had its beginning, we discover one incident when rivals such as York and Somerset might have met and had an argument like that depicted in the Temple garden scene. This was in March of 1458, at a Great Council called by King Henry VI, to the end, as Holinshed relates, "that all old grudges should be not onelie inwardlie forgotten, but also outwardlie forgiuen, which should be the cause of perpetuall loue and assured amitie." Holinshed continues:

This deuise [calling the conference] was of all men iudged for the best. Wherevpon diuerse graue persons were sent to the duke of Yorke, and all other the

191

great estates of the realme, who since the battel of saint Albons neuer met nor communed togither, commanding them for great causes to repaire to the kings court without delaie. At his commandement came to London Richard Duke of Yorke, with foure hundred men, and was lodged at Bainards castell being his owne house; and after him came the earle of Salisburie with fiue hundred men, and was likewise lodged at his owne house called the Herbour. Then came the dukes of Excester and Summerset with eight hundred men, and were lodged without Temple barre; and the earle of Northumberland, the lord Egremond, and the lord Clifford came with fifteene hundred men, and lodged without the citie. The earle of Warwike also came from Calis with six hundred men in red jackets, imbrodered with white ragged staues behind and before, and was lodged at the graie friers.

Thus were all those of the one part lodged within the citie, and those of the other without, in Holborne towards Westminster. and in other places of the suburbs, all upon wise consideration: for that the Yorke faction and the Lancastrians could not well haue beene mingled without danger of discord. After that these lords were thus come vnto London, the king and the queene shortlie followed, comming thither the seuenteenth daie of March, and lodged in the bishops palace. Bicause no riotous attempt or bickering should be begun betweene anie of the parties or their retinues, the maior and aldermen of the citie kept great watch, as well by daie as by night, riding about the citie by Holborne, and Fleetstreet, with fiue thousand men well armed and arraied, to see good order and peace on all sides kept. . . .

[An agreement was signed by all parties on 23 March.] For the open publishing of this ioifull agreement, there was (vpon our ladie daie in March) a solemne procession celebrated with the cathedrall church of saint Paule in London, at which the king was present in habit roiall, with his crowne on his head. Before him went hand in hand the duke of Summerset, the earle of Salisburie, the duke of Excester, and the earle of Warwike; and so one of the one faction, and another of the other; and behind the king the duke of York, and the queene with great familiaritie in appeerance leading hand in hand. [But what shall be said? As goodlie apples corrupted at core, (how faire coated so euer they seeme) can neuer be made to become sound againe: nor rotten walles new plastered without, can euer more staie their mooldering inward, till the putrefied matter fret through the crust laie all in the mire: so fared it on all parts in this dissembled and counterfet concord.] For after this apparant peace (but inward discord) diuerse of the nobles smallie regarding thir honors, forgot their oth, and brake their promise boldlie.[54]

The reference in this dramatic passage to Holborn as a place where noble personages lodged at a crucial time at the beginning of the War of the Roses may well have engaged the attention of Shakespeare (who drew heavily from Holinshed in the writing of his history plays), and inspired the creation of a scene set in the Rose's rose garden in Holborn — in which scene, to the delight, if nothing else, of the 16 or 17 year old master of the Old Temple, was employed for dramatic purposes all of the rose imagery which at the same time (*1 Henry VI* is generally considered to have been written in about 1590 or 1591[55]) was a prominent feature of Shakespeare's Sonnets and the slightly later narrative poems dedicated to Henry Wriothesley.

The second scintilla is the inference to be drawn from lines 86 and 87 of this scene, where Richard Plantagenet, infuriated by Somerset's accusation that he, Richard, was not of the nobility because of the attainder of his father, says threateningly:

> He bears him on the place's privilege,
> Or durst not, for his craven heart, say thus.

This raises the question, what is meant by the phrase, "the place's privilege"? Samuel Johnson explained this to mean that "The *Temple*, being a religious house, was an asylum, a place of exemption, from violence, revenge, and bloodshed,"[56] but a number of other commentators state that this explanation is historically incorrect.[57] Of course, the remarks both of Johnson and the other commentators were directed to the *New Temple*, which undoubtedly was a place of sanctuary during the 150 years after its establishment on the banks of the Thames that it served as the English headquarters for the Knights Templar. But charges against the Knight Templars of heresy and sodomy led to the seizure of their lands in England in 1308 by Edward II. When the Order was suppressed by Pope Clement V in 1312, Edward II granted the New Temple to Aymer de Valence, Earl of Pembroke, but thereafter title to the land revested, several times, in the crown, which several times again granted out the land. Although these grants by the Crown seem inconsistent with a 1324 Act of Parliament assigning to the Prior and Brethren of the Hospital of St. John in Jerusalem (the Hospitallers) the lands and appurtenant interests formerly belonging to the Order of the Templars,[58] it may be that the Act of Parliament was construed to convey to the Hospitallers only the Round Church and a few adjacent buildings. In any event, the balance of the New Temple grounds, as a result of grants or leases either from the Hospitallers or from the Crown's grantees, or their successors in interest, became, from about 1325 on, a place where lawyers lodged and congregated, their right to do so, from whatever source derived, being ultimately confirmed by a grant made by James I in 1608.[59] I assume that it is on the basis of the New Temple's having in 1308 lost its character as consecrated ground (except for the Temple Church itself), that some persons assert that Samuel Johnson's note is incorrect.

Whatever the status of the New Temple may have been, the fact is that the *Old Temple*, being from the middle of the twelfth century until 1547 the property of the Cathedral Church of St. Mary of Lincoln, *was* a place of sanctuary during the 15th century. That Southampton House had formerly been the Old Temple, and then after that the House of the Bishop of Lincoln, was well known in Shakespeare's time; John Stow, in his *Survey of London* published in 1598 wrote that

Adioyning to this old Temple, was sometime the Bishop of Lincolnes Inne, wherein he lodged when he repayred to this City. *John Russell* Bishop of Lincolne, Chauncellor of England in the raigne of *Richard* the third, was lodged there. It hath of late yeares belonged to the Earles of Southampton, and therefore called Southampton house.[60]

If Shakespeare knew Henry Wriothesley as well as in this book I try to show he did, he would certainly have known something about the history of this house. And if the garden where the Rose plucking scene takes place is the garden of the Old Temple — that is, the garden of Southampton House — then Shakespeare's knowledge that it had been a place of sanctuary from the time of its construction until at least the time of its conveyance in 1547 to the Earl of Warwick could well have been the basis for Richard Plantagenet's reference to the "place's privilege," which phrase could thus have exactly the meaning supposed by Samuel Johnson, although through a more circuitous route than ever he might have imagined.

From Southampton House in Holborne, a walk of about three long blocks south on Chancery Lane brings one to the point where Fleet Street becomes the Strand. Walking a long block west from there, past the New Temple grounds on the left, one comes to Essex Street, which marks the site of Essex House, the home, from 1588 until his execution in 1601, of Robert Devereux, second Earl of Essex.

But it is not to see the site of Essex House, important as that place is to our story, that we are walking down the Strand. We continue west two blocks to Strand Lane, where we turn left and walk about 60 feet to the entrance of a structure which might hold the solution to another of the mysteries of the Sonnets.

The mystery is this: what on earth could have been the reason for Shakespeare's composing those two Sonnets to which I have already devoted so much space: Sonnets 153 and 154, about the creation of a bath? A number of persons have suggested that these Sonnets, which in the triviality of their subject matter and tone are so unlike the other 152 Sonnets, might commemorate some occasion when the poet used a hot bath, perhaps even a bath at Bath.[61]

My proposed solution to the mystery of the reason for these Sonnets is that the poems, which describe how a bath was created, were written to mark the creation of a bath, and specifically, a bath which still exists in Strand Lane, and in front of which, in our minds, we are now standing. This bath was unknown to Stow and his eighteenth century successors (or if known, not mentioned), but by the middle of the nineteenth century Baedeker's guides to London informed their readers that on Strand Lane, the narrow passageway to the west of the Strand Theatre,

is an ancient **Roman Bath,** about 13 ft. long, 6 ft. broad, and 4½ ft. deep, one of the few relics of the Roman period in London (open to visitors on Sat., 11-12).... Close by, on the right of the passage, is another bath, said to have been built by the Earl of Essex about 1588; it is supplied by a pipe from the Roman bath.[62]

Septimus Sunderland, in a book published in London in 1915, describes the "Roman bath," and the nearby bath supposedly built by Lord Essex:

[The Roman bath] is supplied with clear water coming from springs at Hampstead, and was considered to be the overflow from St. Clement's Holy Well in the vicinity. The bath, rounded at one end and square at the other, is in the centre of a fair-sized solidly built, vaulted chamber, and lit by a little semicircular window; it is formed of thin tile-like bricks, layers of cement, and rubble-stones, all corresponding with the materials of the Roman wall of London, and now patched together with modern concrete. The walls of the chamber have recently been strengthened with modern tiles. The marble stones forming the floor of the bath were in 1893 fitted from the adjoining bath built by Lord Essex.... Adjoining the Roman Bath and deriving its water supply from it was another bath, of hectagonal shape, The Templars' Bath, used for three centuries by residents in the Temple and closed in 1893. It was built in 1588 by the Earl of Essex, whose house was near. The site is now covered by the larder of the Norfolk Hotel, erected in 1880.[63]

Some sketches of the "Roman bath" are reproduced on the following page; I can find no representations of the adjoining hexagonal bath supposedly built by the Earl of Essex.

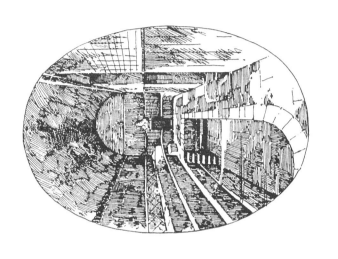

Sketch of "Old Roman Bath, Strand Lane," from *Old London's Spas, Baths and Wells*, Septimus Sunderland, facing p. 38 (London: John Bale, Sons & Danielsson, 1915).

Sketch of "Roman Bath, Strand Lane," from *London*, ed. Charles Knight, II, 165 (London, Charles Knight & Co., 1841).

Figure 6.

Recent writers on Roman London express considerable doubt over the authenticity of the "Roman bath" in Strand Lane, and Ralph Merrifield suggests that

the bath, with another that lay farther south [evidently the bath supposedly built by the Earl of Essex], was originally a reservoir used for domestic purposes in the sixteenth or seventeenth century. During this period the site was occupied by a building of unknown use in the grounds of Arundel House, the great town mansion of the Earls of Arundel, where a large supply of water would have been required. Nevertheless, the rounded end certainly makes the structure look more like a bath than a reservoir.[64]

I can find nothing certain about the history of these baths, but squaring both with the surmise of Merrifield that the baths date from the sixteenth or seventeenth centuries and the tradition, as reported by Baedeker, Sunderland and others, that one of the baths, at least, had been built by the Earl of Essex in 1588, is the fact that it was in 1588 that Essex, upon the death of Leicester, acquired his house on the Strand. Also, consonant with Sunderland's conjecture that the Earl of Essex's bath was used by residents of the Temple is the fact that on 13 October 1588 (a month before his 21st birthday) Essex was admitted to the Inner Temple[65] (whose grounds were immediately adjacent to Essex House). These two facts provide circumstantial evidence for Essex' having, in 1588, both a reason and the means to construct a bath for his now fellow, and perhaps hitherto unacceptably smelly, Templars. Of this supposed reason for their construction, however, I am wary: Sunderland's statement that the baths were used by the Templars is unsupported by any evidence, and the total absence of allusion in the 16th, 17th or 18th centuries to these baths as a place of abstergence for the law students of the Inner Temple (or for anyone else)[66] leads me to believe that access to these baths was severely restricted, and that the persons who used them were more likely to be Essex and his fellow Arcadians at Essex House than the Templars.

If we assume that both baths — the so-called Roman bath and the almost immediately adjacent Earl of Essex bath — were built by and for the Essex House group, then the mystery of the "Roman" design is solved, for the tastes of this classically-learned and much travelled group would naturally incline toward a bath with Roman or Greek touches. Many of these persons might have seen a Roman bath without even travelling, for Robert Burton, in his discussion of Roman baths, notes that "we have many ruins of such Baths found in this Island."[67] It is unlikely, however, that any of them had seen a Greek bath — hence the design of Essex' bath, by default, was Roman.

Burton also notes that in the countries circling the Mediterranean, "the richer sort have private Baths in their houses;"[68] he might have added that this was true in England, too. Aubrey mentions that in the house Francis Bacon designed for himself at Gorhambury, a house which Aubrey called "the most ingeniosely contrived little pile, that ever I saw," were "two Bathing-roomes or Stuffes, whither his Lordship retired afternoons as he sawe cause. All the tunnelles of the Chimneys were carried into the middle of the Howse, and round about them were seates."[69] This description is of great interest, not only for establishing the existence of a hot air bath in an English manor during the Shakespearean era, but also for revealing, from its mention of the *seats* that were in the room, that the bath might have been used occasionally, or even often, by several persons simultaneously: a revelation which inevitably calls to mind the age-old association of communal bathing with sexual activity.[70] Indeed, the word *bagnio*, the Italian word for *bath*, is understood in most European languages to mean brothel, and has its origin in the activities so common at the bath. Similarly, *stew*, another word commonly used in Shakespeare's time to mean brothel, is derived from the same word as is the word used by Aubrey to describe the hot-air bath in Bacon's house, i.e., *stuffe*, the "brothel" meaning having attached to the word *stew* "on account of the frequent use of the public hot-air bath-houses for immoral purposes."[71]

That the Essex bath too, installed in the basement of some building near the Strand, lent itself to such uses can hardly be doubted (however chaste the purpose of its founder may have been); probably it was with an eye to this bath, or some similar facility, that Robert Burton, in the portion of his great book he felt constrained to write in Latin (but which Floyd Dell and Paul Jordan-Smith have happily Englished), after stating that the agents of Henry VIII who inspected the monasteries in 1538 (see page 230, and note 95 to Appendix I) found among them a great number of "wenchers, gelded youths, debauchees, catamites, boy-things, pererasts, Sodomites . . . [and] Ganymedes," goes on to declaim, "If 'tis thus among monks, votaries, and such-like saintly rascals, what may we not suspect in towns, in palaces? *what among nobles, what in cellars*, how much nastiness, how much filth!" (Emphasis supplied.)[72]

Whether or not "Greek" in this respect, the "Roman" bath in Strand Lane was, I suggest, by its frequenters associated with the spirit of Greece at least to the point of requiring a suitable poem or sentence in the manner of those baths epigrammatized in the Greek Anthology, which was, in Shakespeare's time, as in ours, the only known repository of bath-house poems. If we accept what I have in the last chapter attempted to demonstrate, that

Shakespeare was intimately connected with many if not all of the persons in the Essex House group, we can well imagine either that Essex, if indeed he built and made available to his retinue a place to bathe, might have requested Shakespeare to compose some little poem or epigram appropriate for the facility, or that the idea for such a poem might have originated with Shakespeare himself, he not being deficient in imagination or wit.

My surmise that these sonnets were written either to dedicate or to celebrate the Earl of Essex' bath has the advantage of explaining not only why but also how the undistinguished epigram by Marianus Scholasticus was chosen by Shakespeare for the immortality it could not otherwise have achieved. The "why" we have just explained — the members of the Essex House group felt that their classical little bath must be embellished with a classical epigram; the "how" is this: the epigrams in the Greek Anthology are not randomly arranged, but were placed in some kind of order by one Constantinus Cephalas, who probably lived in the tenth century. In the 14th century, a monk called Maximus Planudes edited the work of Cephalas, reducing it from 15 to 7 books, but adding some things that were not in Cephalas' edition. The Planudean version of the Greek Anthology, first published in 1494 in Florence by Janus Lascaris, was reprinted, with slight variations, a number of times in the sixteenth and early seventeenth centuries, and was the only version known until the unique surviving copy of the Cephalas manuscript was discovered in the Palatine Library at Heidelberg in 1606. The Palatine manuscript was not published, however, until 1776, and so for all practical purposes was not accessible to Shakespeare during his lifetime.[73]

The order in which Cephalas had arranged the poems and epigrams of the Greek Anthology was based upon subject matter. To the extent that Planudes retained the poems in the Cephalas manuscript (one large group of poems and epigrams omitted by Planudes was Strato's *Musa Puerilis*, treating of the love of boys; this constitutes Book XII of the Palatine edition), he retained their categorizations. One category consists of epigrams and poems which purport to be inscriptions on buildings, paintings or statues. On pages 351 to 356 of Henricus Stephanus' 1566 edition of the Planudean Anthology (the title and text are in Greek, but Stephanus provided for the work a Latin subtitle, *Florilegium diversorum epigrammatum veterum, in septem libros divisum*) are 38 inscriptions supposedly found on structures associated with public or private baths, among which, on page 354, is the epigram by Marianus Scholasticus of which Shakespeare's Sonnets 153 and 154 are translations.[74]

My suspicion is that Shakespeare knew enough Greek to read the epigrams in the Anthology.[75] But if he didn't, we can have no difficulty in imagining that members of the Essex household might have directed Shakespeare to them, and acquainted him, if he was unable to read them, with their sense. The epigram by Marianius Scholasticus was probably selected by Shakespeare as the foundation of his own poems because, although it is not the best or the most interesting of all the "bath" epigrams in the Anthology, it is the one most apposite to the establishment of a new bath.

A question to consider, if only because it seems susceptible of answer, is the identity of the individual in the Essex household who may have been Shakespeare's mentor in matters Greek. One person stands out for his Greek learning — Henry Cuffe, who was Secretary to the Earl of Essex from 1594 until the Earl's execution for treason on 25 February 1601, and who was himself executed on 13 March 1601.

Cuffe was born in Somersetshire in 1563, and in 1578, at the age of fifteen, was elected a scholar of Trinity College, Oxford, where he excelled in Greek studies. He there met and came to know well Sir Henry Savile, Sir Henry's brother Thomas, who died young (on 22 January 1592/3), William Camden and Jean Hotman,[76] all of whom were Greek scholars and interested in all aspects of Greek literature. Cuffe was expelled from Trinity College because of a remark deemed disrespectful to Sir Thomas Pope, the founder of the College,[77] but Cuffe's friend Sir Henry Savile immediately offered Cuffe a tutorship at Merton College (of which Savile was Warden), and there Cuffe pursued his Greek studies, receiving his M.A. in February 1588/9. He was subsequently promoted to the Greek professorship at the University and, as already described, participated in the entertainments presented to the Queen and her entourage of nobles, including Essex and Southampton, when they visited Oxford in September, 1592.

On 10 April 1594 Cuffe was chosen Proctor of the University, but he left Oxford soon thereafter, and by the end of the year was in London employed as a secretary to the Earl of Essex, with whom Cuffe may have become acquainted as early as the mid-1580's, by virtue of his friendships with Jean Hotman, Henry Savile and William Camden.

If Shakespeare was a member of the Essex House group, as I have tried to show he was, then Shakespeare and Cuffe must have known each other. Cuffe was "a celebrated wit,"[78] and thus the kind of person to whom we can be confident Shakespeare would have been attracted. If my hypothesis with respect to the date and occasion of Shakespeare's "bath" sonnets is correct, they may have come to know each other, through their acquaintances with people associated with Leicester House, as early as 1588. Through this postulated friendship with Cuffe, Shakespeare could have acquired, from conversations and exposure to Cuffe's enthusiasms, all the knowledge about and from Greek literature with which his writings are so pungently spiced: from Cuffe he could have learned about the love letters and rose imagery of Philostratus, about the themes and images of the poems and epigrams in the Greek Anthology, and about the characters and stories in the Greek romances. For these were things that Cuffe was interested in, both as an academician and as a man of letters.

Cuffe's poems, in Greek and Latin, which constituted part of the preliminary matters in his friend Camden's *Britannia*, published in 1590, have already been mentioned. Another Greek language work with which Cuffe is associated is the first printed edition of the Greek text of *Daphnis and Chloe*. Cuffe's involvement in this seems to have been the result of a happy accident. Cuffe was in Florence from the spring or summer of 1597 until the summer of 1598,[79] on a mission for Essex. While in Florence, Cuffe had contacts with James Guicciardini,[80] who was Essex' agent there, but what the object of Cuffe's mission was, I am unable to discover.[81] Some time after he arrived occurred an event which Cuffe thought (or perhaps, pretended to think, to deflect possible criticism for wasting his time on Greek letters when he was supposed to be involved in Byzantine plots) would afford him a good "cover" for his being in Florence: in a letter dated 9 October 1597, Cuffe wrote to his fellow secretary Edward Reynolds, in London:

My little knowledge in the Greek tongue hath stood me in very good stead. For one day in a bookseller's shop by occasion of Demetrius Phalereus, which lay thereupon, I fell in talk with a gentleman of this town one Marcello Adriani, son to John Baptista Adriani [1513-1579], who wrote the story [i.e., *Istoria dei suoi tempi*, published posthumously in 1583 by his son Marcello]. What he reported to others, I know not. But the next day two of the chief of our Academia Crusca sent unto me, and I am now admitted to be a disciple of that blessed corporation; and to make up the number a friar, confessor to the Duchess, and of very great reckoning here, desired to speak with me, and in conclusion we are grown to very strict acquaintance. If I gain nothing else yet I hope by this means I shall the better conceal my principal design, which I see I am the more carefully to do, as well in regard of the Duke's jealousy, as also for the folly of some of our nation, who have in divers places reported me to be my Lord's [i.e., Essex'] secretary.[82]

The Accademia della Crusca, founded in Florence in 1582, was one of the numerous Italian literary, artistic and generally humanistic societies of the era which brought together men of learning to share their enthusiasms, and sometimes to apply their knowledge to some large joint project. The undertaking for which the Accademia della Crusca is best remembered is its compilation of a great *Vocabolario*, intended to establish a standard for the proper usage of the Tuscan tongue.[83] Evidently, Cuffe in the book store had stumbled upon a member of this Accademia,[84] and, no doubt in some way not inconsistent with a becoming modesty, had let him know of his knowledge of the Greek tongue, which encounter led to Cuffe's subsequent association with others of his own tastes and education, and ultimately to the opportunity to participate in the editing for publication of the Greek text of *Daphnis and Chloe* contained in a manuscript in the library of Louis Allemanni, a Florentine bibliophile. The work, bearing the Latin subtitle *Longi Pastoralium, de Daphnidae & Chloë, Libri Quatuor* was published in Florence in August 1598, not long after Cuffe departed the city. The editor of the work was Raphael Columbanius, who in the preface acknowledges the assistance given him by Henry Cuffe and Marcello Adriani, which assistance seems to have consisted principally of suggested readings of obscure words and difficult constructions on the basis of examples from other Greek texts. The notes to this first printed Greek text of *Daphnis and Chloe* contain references not only to the Greek text of the *Aethiopica* of Heliodorus,[85] which had been printed in 1534, but also to the Greek text of *Clitiphon and Leucippe*,[86] which was not printed until 1601 (in Heidelberg, by Juda and Nicolaus Bonnuitius). Although the exact contribution of Cuffe to this edition of *Daphnis and Chloe* is unascertainable, the mere fact that he was engaged in the project demonstrates his more than superficial interest in and knowledge of the Greek romance, and thus qualifies Cuffe as a most plausible source for Shakespeare's knowledge of the subject.

Cuffe is known to have written only one other work requiring a knowledge of the Greek language, and this is his translation, into Latin, of a work in Greek by Gelasius Cyzicenus. The translation, entitled *De Rebus Gestis in sancto concilio Nicæno*, is in manuscript, and has never been published. The likelihood that the work was transcribed by Cuffe from the original in the Vatican Library points to Cuffe's having visited Rome during his sojourn in Italy.[87]

Cuffe wrote a number of things in English. "A Book on the state of Ireland, addressed to Robert, Earl of Essex, by 'H.C.'," preserved in the Public Record Office in London,[88] is probably the work of Henry Cuffe who, after his return from Italy in 1598, accompanied Essex to Ireland in April, 1599. The work describes the activities of the rebels in Ireland from the autumn of 1597 until the spring of 1598, and is told in the form of a dialogue between "Peregryne" and "Sylvyn," which happen to have been the names of two of Edmund Spenser's sons, both of whom died young.[89] (Spenser, it should be remembered, left Leicester's service in 1580 for a position in Ireland, where he lived, except for brief visits to England, until the destruction of his home two months prior to his death.) Cuffe was with Essex in Ireland until 30 August 1599, on which day Essex dispatched him to Queen Elizabeth with a letter, probably drafted by Cuffe, in which Essex attempted to explain his dealings with Tyrone, and his decision to return to England.[90]

That many of the letters signed by Essex were actually composed by Cuffe, his secretary, is to be expected; a little surprising is that some of the poems supposedly written by the Earl of Essex were probably written by Cuffe, and perhaps other of Essex' secretaries. One poem formerly attributed to Essex which seems certainly to have been written by Henry Cuffe was printed, with a musical setting, in 1603 in Henry Dowland's *Third and Last Booke of Songs or Aires*:

> It was a time when silly Bees could speake,
> and in that time I was a sillie Bee,
> who fed on Time until my heart gan break,
> yet neuer found the time would fauour mee.
> Of all the swarme I onely did not thriue,
> Yet brought I Waxe & honey to the hiue.
>
> Then thus I buzd, when time no sap would giue,
> Why should this blessed time to me be drie,
> Sith by this Time the lazie drone doth liue,
> The waspe, the worme, the gnat, the butterflie,
> Mated with griefe, I kneeled on my knees,
> And thus complaind vnto the king of Bees.
>
> My liege, God graunt thy time may neuer end,
> And yet vouchsafe to heare my plaint of Time,
> Which fruitlesse Flies have found to haue a friend,
> And I cast downe when Atomies do clime.
> The king replied but thus, Peace, peeuish Bee,
> Th'art bound to serve the time, the time not thee.[91]

A much longer version of this poem (which length, in my opinion, dilutes its effectiveness) appears in at least two manuscripts, in one of which it is entitled "A poem made on the Earle of Essex (being in disgace with Queen Eliz): by mr henry Cuffe his Secretary,"[92] and in the other of which it is entitled "The Earl of Essex his buzze, made on his decayed estate by Mr. Henry Cuffe, his secretary."[93]

Another unpublished manuscript relating to Essex and attributed to Cuffe is "Aphorismes Political, gathered out of the Life and End of that most noble Robert Devereux, Earle of Essex, not long before his death."[94] While Cuffe may have kept a record of the Earl's aphorisms, it is unlikely, since Cuffe's death so soon followed that of Essex, that the title of the manuscript and such aphorisms in the manuscript as may relate to the "End" of that noble earl, could be the work of Cuffe.

The only work of Cuffe in English which has been published is entitled *The Differences of the Ages of Mans Life, Written by the learned Henry Cuffe, sometime Fellow of Merton College in Oxford, 1600*. The book, published posthumously in 1607, was dedicated by "R.M."[95] to Robert Lord Willough-by, Beake and Eresby. This work is of interest to our inquiry because, like Jaques' famous speech in *As You Like It*, it describes and discourses upon the "seven ages of man." After discussing (on pages 115 and 116 of the 1607 edition of this work; there were other editions in 1638 and 1640) Pythagoras' division of life into four ages, and Aristotle's division of life into three, Cuffe (on pages 120 and 121) both sums up and synthesizes their divisions:

. . . and so haue we seuen seuerall parts of our life, comprising our *Pubertatem* and *adolescentiam* under one: accordingly whereto the Astrologers haue assigned to euery of them their peculiar predominant Planet: our *Infant age* is allotted to the *Moones* milde and moist dominion, cherishing vs with her sweet influence which she hath especially upon moist bodies: *our Boy-hood*, Mercury hath charge ouer, inclining vs to *sportfulnesse, talke,* and *learning: Venus* guides ovr blossomming *lustfull age:* our youthfull *prime*, by the *Sunnes* lively operation is lifted up from base delights, to a loftier and more man-like resolution and livelinesse. *Mars* the sterne god of warre, hath the precincts of his dominion limited within compasse of our man-age, adding courage to our liuelihood, and whetting our otherwise dull spirits, vnto a more ventrous boldnesse in quarrelling combats: *Old age* from *Iupiter* receiueth grauities and staiednesse: Decrepit *crooked age*, from the angrie aspect of drie *Saturn* sucketh the poisonous infirmities of crasie sicknesse and waiward pettishnesse: and this is briefly the summarie explication of the differences of mans ages. . . .

Although not published until six years after his death, Cuffe's work was "for some time after his decease, handed about at Oxford in manuscript, and considered as a very great curiosity,"[96] and it is tempting to see in this passage by Cuffe a source for Jaques' speech (of which one scholar has written that "no convincingly precise source . . . has ever been found"[97]), but in fact this division of life into seven ages — or for Shakespeare, seven actors' parts — seems not to have been an uncommon conceit: Virgil K. Whitaker writes that during one summer's reading in Elizabethan books on the natural sciences and psychology, he found discussions of the "ages of man," ranging from five to seven, in four books published from 1565 to 1600.[98] Interestingly, one of these books, the one published in 1600, was by William Vaughan, the author of *The Golden Grove* and *The Golden Fleece*, the friend of Essex, John Florio, Matthew Gwinne, Robert Burton, and Gelly Merrick, and the person who knew the details about the murder of Christopher Marlowe. The book in which Vaughan gave his description of the ages of man is *Approved Directions for Health, both Naturall and Artificiall, Derived from the best Physitians as well moderne as auncient*; addressing the question, "Into how many ages is a mans life divided?," Vaughan writes

Mans life by the computation of Astrologers, is divided into seaven ages: over every one of which, one of the seaven planets is predominant. The first age is called infancie, which continueth the space of seaven yeares. And then the Moone raigneth, as appeareth by the moyst constitution of children agreeing well with the influences of that planet.

The second age named childhood, lasteth seven yeares more, and endeth in the fourteenth of our life. Over this age, *Mercurie* (which is the second sphere) ruleth; for then children are unconstant, tractable, and more enclined to learne.

The third age endureth eight yeares, and is termed the strippling age: It beginneth at the fourteenth yeare, and continueth until the end of the two and twentieth. During which time, governeth the planet *Venus*. For then we are prone to prodigality, gluttonie, drunkennes, lechery, & sundry kinds of vices.

The fourth age contayneth twelve yeares, till a man be foure and thirtie, and then is he named a young man. Of this age the *Sunne* is chiefe Lord. Now a man is wittie, well advised, magnanimous, and come to know himselfe.

The fift age is called mans age, and hath sixteene yeares for the continuance thereof, subiect to *Mars*, for now a man is choleric and covetous.

The sixt age hath twelve yeares, that is, from fiftie till three score and two. This age is termed (although improperly) olde age: of which *Iupiter* is master, a planet significant of equity, temperance and religion.

The seaventh and last (by order) of these ages continueth full 18. yeares, ending at four score, to which few attaine. This age, by the meanes of that planet *Saturne*, which is melancholick & most slow of all others, causeth man to be drooping, decrepit, froward, cold and melancholick.[99]

I quote this passage in its entirety to show how similar it is in substance to the passage written by Cuffe, whom Vaughan, the friend and kinsman of Sir Gelly Merrick, certainly must have known, Cuffe and Merrick having been fellow members of the staff of the Earl of Essex. The significance, if any, of these two writers' both dilating upon the seven ages of man, is not clear. Perhaps it demonstrates that the members of the closely-knit Essex House who read each others' manuscripts had no qualms about publishing as their own what their friends had written, and that in this respect Shakespeare was no different from his fellows; perhaps it suggests that Jaques' speech in *As You Like It*, a restatement of material which the people at Essex House would recognize had first been written by either Cuffe or Vaughan (Cuffe, I suspect), and then copied by the other (who, if he was Vaughan, also published it), was not intended to be the profound statement on the human condition which many people take it to be, but a satire upon the pretentiously pedestrian and superficial musings of some of the personages in the Essex House circle. In either case, whether Jaques' speech is a shameless borrowing of other peoples' work, or a parody of that work, Shakespeare's adaptation of the material — the deletion of the astrological trappings and the addition of vivid images of the human being at each of the seven stages of his life — is an example of how Shakespeare, as almost always, in the laboratory of his mind, converted lead into gold.

I cannot leave this review of Cuffe's writings without offering my speculations that Cuffe was the author of several other published works which have not hitherto been attributed to him. The first work is the anonymous translation into English of *Six Idillia* by Theocritus, dedicated to "E.D." and published at Oxford by Joseph Barnes in 1588.[100] I have no objective evidence for this attribution, which is only a hunch based upon the facts that Cuffe had the skills to translate these Greek poems into English, that he was living in Oxford at the time of their publication, and that Joseph Barnes, the first official printer of Oxford University, was a protégé of the Earl of Leicester,[101] and thus someone to whom Cuffe would have access through his friendship with the Earl's secretary, Jean Hotman. Cuffe's friendship with Hotman and doubtless other members of Leicester's household is completely consistent with the "E.D." of the dedication being, as some writers have surmised,[102] Edward Dyer, who in the 1580's was in the service of the Earl of Leicester.

One of the *Six Idillia*, the "Thirty-First Idillion,"[103] tells of the death of Adonis at the tusks of a boar, and it has been suggested[104] that the boar's statement, in this poem, that he intended not to hurt Adonis, but only to kiss his naked thigh, is the source for Venus' acknowledgement, in Shakespeare's poem, that

> If he [the boar] did see his [Adonis'] face, why then I know
> He thought to kisse him, and hath kild him so.
>
> [*Venus and Adonis*, lines 1109-1110.]

Another published work which on the basis of no evidence whatsoever I am bold to suggest may have been written by Henry Cuffe is *Piers Plainnes seauen yeres Prentiship*, published in London in 1595 by John Danter. The author is identified on the title page only by the initials "H.C." This work is remembered today primarily because of its reference to Richard Barnfield's "The Shepheards Content," one of the poems in his *The Affectionate Shepheard*: at the end of the story, after listening to Piers' explanation of his reason for wishing to live the quiet life of a shepherd, Corydon says,

Godamercie Piers . . . for thy good ende. The Euening Starre is vp, and ruddie Thetis welcommeth the Sunne. After long troubles I like thy desire of rest: for in shepheards life is both repose and recreation. I [i.e., aye] quoth Menalcas, Young Daphnis hath giuen his verdict of *The Shepheards Content:* duely praising it, as it meriteth.[105]

Because of the initials H.C., and nothing else, the work has been attributed by some persons to Henry Constable and by others to Henry Chettle;[106] thus, at the outset, my attribution of the work to Henry Cuffe rests on at least as solid a foundation as the attributions to Chettle and Constable. The only argument in support of Cuffe's authorship suggested by the work itself is that, aside from Piers, the names of all the characters in the story — Menalcas, Corydon, Lycoris, Hylenus, Celinus, Aemilius, Celydon, etc. — are Greek, and the story is very much in the style and spirit of a Greek romance, with which genre Cuffe was so familiar. But there is another consideration which, if my contention that Cuffe knew and was a preceptor to Shakespeare is correct, makes Cuffe's authorship of *Piers Plainnes seauen yeres Prentiship* an attractive and plausible hypothesis.

Whoever wrote *Piers Plainess* may be assumed to have written also the poems in it. One of these poems is sung by the contented shepherd, Piers, to his sheep, as he weaves a straw hat to protect himself from "the violence of the Sunnes beames":

> Feede on my flocke securely,
> Your shepheard watcheth surely;
> > Runne about my little Lambs,
> > Skip and wanton with your Dams:
> Your loving Heard with care will tend you.
>
> Sport on faire flock at pleasure,
> Nip Vestaes flouring treasure;
> > I myself will duely harke,
> > When my watchfull Dogg doth barke:
> From Woolfe and Foxe wee will defende yee.[107]

This poem was reprinted in 1600 in *Englands Helicon*, over the initials H.C. In addition, the author or authors of three other poems in *Englands Helicon* are identified only by the initials H.C.; these poems are "Damelus *Song to his* Diaphenia," "*A Pastorall Song betweene* Phillis *and* Amarillis, *two Nimphes, each aunswering other line for line,*" and "*The Sheepheards Song of* Venus *and* Adonis".[108] The H.C. who wrote *Piers Plainness* is no doubt the H.C. who wrote the "Feede on my flocke" poem, and this poem, consequently, has been assigned by students of the period either to Henry Chettle or Henry Constable. And, on the not unreasonable assumption that the H.C. who wrote the "Feede on my flocke" poem is the same H.C. who wrote the three other poems printed over those initials, these other poems also, on the basis only of the initials appended them, are attributed either to Henry Chettle or Henry Constable.[109]

As already pointed out, however, the claim of Henry Cuffe to the authorship of *Piers Plainness* is just as good as the claims of Henry Constable and Henry Chettle, and thus the claim of Henry Cuffe to have written the H.C. poems in *Englands Helicon* — all of them on Greek themes — is just as good as those of Constable and Chettle, and much more enlightening in its implications — for "*The Sheepherds Song of* Venus *and* Adonis," which is quite a good poem, reads like an outline of Shakespeare's *Venus and Adonis*. Most modern scholars, being unable to state for sure who wrote "*The Sheepherds Song*" or when it was written (it was *published* seven years after Shakespeare's poem), out of an abundance of caution conclude that it is an imitation of the Shakespeare poem. But the great eighteenth century Shakespearean scholar Edmond Malone thought otherwise:

I am persuaded that the Shepheard's Song of Venus and Adonis, by Henry Constable [as Malone assumed], preceded the poem before us [i.e., Shakespeare's *Venus and Adonis*]. Of this, it may be said, no proof has been produced; and certainly I am at present unfurnished with the means of establishing this fact, though I have myself no doubts upon the subject.[110]

If, as I maintain, Shakespeare and Cuffe were friends well before 1594, and Cuffe was Shakespeare's mentor in classical matters, then we can easily imagine that Cuffe, at Shakespeare's request, wrote an outline of the story of Venus and Adonis to serve as a basis for Shakespeare's poem for Henry Wriothesley: this would explain the similarity of H.C.'s "*The Sheepherds Song of* Venus *and* Adonis" to Shakespeare's *Venus and Adonis*, and vindicate Malone's insight that the former poem preceded the latter.

While no evidence exists to show that Cuffe knew Shakespeare, ample evidence exists of Cuffe's knowledge of Southampton, and probably as early as the time that Shakespeare was writing *Venus and Adonis*: for in 1592, Southampton, then 18, was one of the peers, along with Essex, who accompanied the Queen to Oxford, where Cuffe played a prominent part in the programs offered for her entertainment, and it is unlikely that the academic and social events which filled the week did not bring them into each other's company more than a few times. And the two certainly had many contacts after 1594, when Cuffe became a member of Essex' staff. They clearly were on good terms with each other, for when Cuffe in 1598 returned to England from his mysterious sojourn in Italy, he traveled by way of Paris, where he attempted to be of aid and comfort to the miserable Southampton who then also was in Paris,[111] spending his time at the gaming tables in an effort not to think about what might befall him when he returned to England to face the Queen's wrath over his seduction of her Maid of Honour. Southampton must have valued Cuffe's company, for he caused Cuffe to tarry with him in France until he (Southampton) could put off no longer his return to England.[112]

In the following year, Cuffe and Southampton accompanied Essex on the expedition to Ireland, the failure of which led to that shame and disgrace which ultimately goaded Essex to his final fatal error. Cuffe is reputed to have played a major part in urging Essex into his unwise course of action: Edward Bushell, it will be remembered, stated that "no man was more inward with the Earl than Mr. Cuffe," and the influence of Cuffe upon Essex is generally regarded as evil. Essex, too, at one time seems to have thought so and, according to one of Essex' secretaries, Sir Henry Wotton, directed Sir Gelly Merrick to discharge Cuffe from all further attendance upon or access to him, "out of a glimmering oversight that he [Cuffe] would prove the very instrument of his ruine."[113] But shortly after, through the intercession of the Earl of Southampton, Cuffe was restored to his former position.[114]

Wotton describes Henry Cuffe as "a man of secret ambitious ends of his own, and of proportionate counsels, smothered under the habit of a scholar, and flubbered over with a certain rude and clownish fashion, that had the semblance of integrity . . . [who] spun out the final destruction of his master and himself,"[115] and William Camden, Cuffe's friend of college days, wrote that Cuffe was "a man of most exquisite learning, and of a most sharp wit but turbulent and perverse."[116] We who read these comments almost four hundred years later cannot know whether they are objective assessments of Cuffe, or the smug observations of persons gloating over the fall of a colleague who for a while seemed likely to surpass them in achievement and honours.[117] To be sure, Essex himself, after his conviction for treason, confronting Cuffe, charged him to call to God for mercy, for "none hath been a greater instigator of me than yourself, to all these my disloyal courses into which I have fallen."[118] But the disgraceful fact is that Essex, after his conviction, "charged every body that had any kindness for him, as having a hand in his plot;"[119] the persons so charged included not only Cuffe, Sir Christopher Blount and Sir Charles Danvers, all of whom were convicted and executed, but also the Earl of Southampton, Sir Ferdinando Gorges, Sir John Davies, Sir Henry Nevile, and even Essex' sister Lady Rich,[120] only two of whom (Southampton and Davies) were brought to trial and none of whom was executed.

Henry Cuffe, Sir Christopher Blount, Sir Charles Danvers, Sir John Davies and Sir Gelly Merrick, were all tried for treason on 5 March 1600. After being advised of the many charges against him, Cuffe, in his defense, argued that they could all be reduced to two heads, things plotted and things acted, and maintained that while "the thing intended was going to the Court, yet the thing acted was the going into London."[121] That is, Cuffe admitted that he had counselled Essex to present himself to the Queen at court, and to have in attendance sufficient men to ensure access to her Majesty, but contended that since Essex had not done as counselled by Cuffe but had instead attempted to raise the City of London in rebellion, an act which Cuffe had never counselled and in which he played no part, he could have committed no treason: for what he counselled, if treason (and Cuffe denied that it was), was not done, and what was done, if treason, was nothing he had counselled. But even before he made his defense, Cuffe had been labeled by Attorney General Coke as "the arrantest Traitor that ever came to the Bar, . . . a Scholar and a Sophister," and to the extent that Cuffe demonstrated the latter part of Coke's statement to be true, he failed to persuade the Commissioners before whom the case was tried of the falseness of the first part. He, and all the others tried that day, were found guilty, and sentenced to the usual punishment for treason: to be hanged, drawn and quartered.[122] Charles Danvers, who denied nothing, but claimed he had acted in the matter only at the request of "my Lord of Southampton, to whom I owed my love and life itself," requested that he might be beheaded — "and one more request, I beseech you, let me make suit to see the Earl of Southampton before I die."[123] If he had a last meeting with the Earl of Southampton, no record of it exists; because he was of noble descent, his request to be beheaded was granted, and he was executed on 18 March 1601: ". . . though the flesh of his cheekes trembled, . . . [he] put off his Gowne and Doublet in most cheerful manner, rather like a Bridegrome, then a prisoner appointed for death."[124]

Cuffe, who was not of noble descent, also ventured to request that "for human respects, I desire the law may be satisfied with my life, without torturing or quartering my flesh; and the rather for favour's sake unto learning, though I have neither place nor great birth to speak for that."[125] Merrick heard his sentence "with a resolute silence, and said no more than this, Essex *hath lifted me up, and* Essex *hath throwne me downe.*"[126] Cuffe and Sir Gelly Merrick were executed at Tyburn on 13 March 1601.

"At the place of execution all writers agree, that he [Cuffe] behaved with the utmost resolution, and the most steady composure."[127] Was Cuffe granted the compassion he requested? The accounts of his execution which I have found contain no description of the means of dispatch, but instead recount Cuffe's lengthy final speech, intemperately interrupted by his auditors when he got to the part that the plot "consisted of two parts, the intention and the means to accomplish it".[128] Some documents, indeed, record that Cuffe was hanged, drawn and quartered,[129] but Camden, who attended Cuffe's trial and probably witnessed his execution, states only that he was hanged,[130] which leads me to hope that, as was sometimes the case, the sentence was not carried out in all its savagery, but instead the victim was permitted to die by hanging, the subsequent drawing and quartering, if any, being visited upon a lifeless corpse, rather than upon a sentient being.

Thus died the man who, I believe, inspired Shakespeare's interest in, and was the primary source of his knowledge about, Greek literature, the impact of which upon Shakespeare's writings is so surprisingly pervasive, and enriching.

Shakespeare has been criticized for injecting low comedy into his tragedies, but in this respect, as in so many others, he was merely holding the mirror up to nature, as is illustrated by the "rebellion" which resulted in the executions of Cuffe, Merrick, Danvers, Blount and Essex. Essex' plan to restore himself to the Queen's favour by marching with a small band of men into Court, removing Cecil as a barrier to his access to the Queen, and then, for the first time in over a year and a half, personally speaking with her, explaining his actions and demonstrating his loyalty and love, has been characterized by Lacey Baldwin Smith as "one of the most inept, ill-planned, befuddled, and addle-headed examples of treason ever to have emerged from those sirens of Tudor politics — wishful thinking, paranoia, and desperation."[131]

The plan was concocted principally by Essex, whose feeling that he had been ill-used by the Queen and deserved better of the nation ignited a smouldering resentment which, whenever it showed signs of dying, was fanned anew by Cuffe and others. Essex was assured, in whatever course of action he might undertake, of the support of his devoted friend, Southampton, and Southampton, in turn, did not hesitate to demand of those who loved him that they support him in his support of Essex. Thus Southampton told Charles Danvers that he would adventure his life for Essex, and asked Danvers how far he would engage himself for Southampton's sake. "My awnswere was," wrote Danvers not long before his execution, "that I loued him best, and did confess my self to be most behowlding to him of any man liuing. He had saued my lyfe, and that after a very noble fashion. He had suffred for me, and made me by as many means bownde vnto him, as on[e] man coulde be bownde vnto an other. The lyfe he had saued, and my estate and means whatsoeuer, he shoulde euer dispose of."[132] Similarly, Southampton took advantage of the love borne him by his friends Rutland and Bedford to conscript their support for Essex' undertaking, although Rutland, who Southampton said "they could not trust . . . with the matter above two hours before they attempted it,"[133] probably did not have a clear idea of what was being required of him. And it was undoubtedly out of friendship for his cousin Southampton that Robert Radcliffe, the fifth Earl of Sussex, agreed to support Essex in his attempt to regain power.

But when Essex finally moved, on the morning of Sunday, 8 February 1600/1, he went, not to the Court, but up and down the streets of the city, shouting that his murder had been planned, and seeking to arouse the citizenry for love of him to march to the Court and oust Sir Robert Cecil and other evil advisors to the Queen. Bedford, making one of his rare appearances in London, joined in the foray, but Southampton's cousin, the Earl of Sussex, arrived too late to be of any assistance.[134] After four or five hours of futile clamour, during which time government forces were mobilized against them, Essex, Southampton, Rutland and Bedford, finding the streets behind them blocked, fled to the river to return by water to Essex House — except that the Earl of Bedford, no doubt by now convinced of the wisdom of his policy of leaving London life to his wife, slipped quietly away in his boat.[135] Their undertaking a failure, Essex, Southampton and Rutland prepared Essex House to withstand a siege, but upon being warned by Sir Robert Sidney that "the house is to be blown up with gun-powder unless you will yield," yielded.[136]

Eleven days later, Essex and Southampton were jointly tried for treason. Government leaders, convinced that Essex fancied himself a Henry IV who would "reframe" his own time by deposing Elizabeth as Henry had deposed Richard II,[137] made much of the fact that Essex' followers paid Shakespeare's company to perform *Richard II* for their benefit on the day prior to Essex' uprising, and Queen Elizabeth herself, in a conversation with William Lambarde six months after Essex' execution, intimated that Essex had attempted to associate her in the public mind with Richard II by securing the performance of this tragedy forty times in open street and houses.[138]

If Shakespeare's *Richard II* in fact provided Essex and his followers with a rough pattern for their assault upon the court, then it may not be too whimsical to suggest that Shakespeare's *Henry IV* provided Essex and Southampton with a rationale to make peace with themselves after their débacle: for I think I detect in the statements of Essex and Southampton at their trial for treason, after their conviction, echoes of speeches of Prince Hal and Falstaff in *Henry IV, Part 1*. This play, first published in 1598, was registered in the Stationer's Office on 25 February 1597/8,[139] three years almost to the day prior to the trial of Essex and Southampton. We cannot doubt that Essex and Southampton, who knew the Henry IV of *Richard II*, knew also the Henry IV of *Henry IV*, and indeed we know from their correspondence that both Essex and Southampton were familiar with the Falstaff character,[140] and therefore certainly with the Henry IV plays.

The speeches of which I hear echoes are those of Prince Hal and Falstaff before the Battle of Shrewsbury. Falstaff is apprehensive; he tells Hal he wishes it were bedtime, and all well; the Prince replies, "Why, thou owest God a death," upon which statement Falstaff meditates:

'Tis not due yet; I would be loath to pay him before his day. What need I be so forward with him that calls not on me. Well, 'tis no matter; honour pricks me on. Yea, but how if honour can prick me off when I came on? How then? Can honour set to a leg? No. Or an arm? No. Or take away the grief of a wound? No. Honour hath no skill in surgery, then? No. What is honour? A word. What is in that word honour? What is that honour? Air; a trim reckoning! Who hath it? He that died o' Wednesday. Doth he feel it? No. Doth he hear it? No. 'Tis insensible, then? Yea, to the dead. But will it not live with the living? No. Why? Detraction will not suffer it. Therefore I'll none of it. Honour is a mere scutcheon: and so ends my catechism.

[V,i,128-144.]

The jury of peers unanimously found Essex and Southampton guilty of High Treason. One of the jurors was Southampton's cousin, the late-arriving Earl of Sussex, who had been so successful in convincing Cecil he was not a party to Essex' plans that he was called upon (a craftily sadistic punishment, perhaps?) to sit with his fellow peers in judgment on Essex and Southampton.[141] The finding being announced, the prisoners were called to the Bar, where the Clerk of the Crown asked each, "Now what can you say for yourself, that you should not have Judgment of Death?" Essex spoke first, and briefly. He admitted the offence against the Crown, and said "that since I have committed that which hath brought me within the compass of the law, I may be counted the Law's traitor in offending the law, for which I am willing to die, and will as willingly go thereto as ever did any. . . . I do not speak to save my life, for that I see were vain: *I owe God a death* [emphasis supplied], which shall be welcome, how soon soever it pleaseth her Majesty."

Southampton spoke at greater length. He said that his ignorance of the law having made him incur the dangers of the law, he submitted himself to her Majesty's mercy: "Therefore . . . I beseech you . . . to let the Queen know that I crave her mercy. I know I have offended her, yet if it please her to be merciful unto me, I may live, and by my Service deserve my Life. I have been brought up under her Majesty, I have spent the best part of my patrimony in her Majesty's service with danger of my life. . . . but since the Law hath cast me, I do submit myself to Death, and yet I will not despair of her Majesty's Mercy, for that I know she is merciful, and if she please to extend it, I shall with all humility receive it."[142]

Of Southampton's speech, John Chamberlain, who was present at the trial, wrote:

The earle of Southampton spake very well (but methought somwhat too much . . .) and as a man that wold faine live pleaded hard to acquite himself, but all in vaine for yt could not be, whereupon he descended to intreatie, and moved great commisseration, and though he were generally well liked, yet methought he was somewhat too low and submisse, and seemed to loth to die before a prowde ennemie.[143]

214

The statements of Essex and Southampton seem to me to be repetitions, in tone, and sometimes in words, of the sentiments expressed in the face of the threat of death by Prince Hal and Falstaff. Might not Essex' resigned observation, echoing Prince Hal's words, that "I owe God a death," have triggered in Southampton's mind Falstaff's pragmatic rejoinder, "'Tis not due yet. . . . Honour is a mere scutcheon," thus precipitating his humble plea for mercy, in contrast to Essex's proud acceptance of his doom?

Essex and Southampton were sentenced to death: "You must go to the place from whence you came, and there remain during her Majesty's Pleasure; from there to be drawn on a Hurdle thro' London Streets, and so to the place of Execution, where you shall be hanged, bowelled and quartered; your head and quarters to be disposed of at her Majesty's Pleasure, and so God have mercy upon your souls."[144]

Essex' sentence was commuted to beheading, which fate he suffered on Ash Wednesday, 25 February 1600/1. The executioner's first blow struck his shoulders; the second blow his head; the third severed the head from the body,[145] after which "his eyes opened but ye other parts not moved."[146]

But for Southampton, the one-time ward of Lord Burghley, there was compassion, and through the intercession of Lord Burghley's son, Sir Robert Cecil,[147] his sentence was commuted to imprisonment. Rutland and Bedford were never formally tried for their roles in the Essex matter, but threw themselves on the Queen's mercy, and escaped with substantial fines.[148]

On 24 March 1603, Queen Elizabeth died, and on 5 April, King James, from Edinburgh, ordered the release of Southampton, which order was received in London and complied with on 10 April 1603. Southampton was restored to his property and titles on 21 July 1603. Worthy of note, in this brief interval between Southampton's release from prison and the restoration of his title, is the juxtaposition of two other events: on 16 May 1603, Henry Wriothesley was given by King James a general pardon for the crimes of which he had been convicted;[149] on 17 May 1603, King James directed the keeper of the Privy Seal to cause letters patent to be issued whereby William Shakespeare and the other players constituting the Lord Chamberlain's company became henceforth "the King's men," authorized "freely to use and exercise the arte and facultie of playing comedies, tragedies, histories, enterludes, moralles, pastoralles, stage-plaies, and such other, like as they have already studied or heerafter shall use or studie, as well for the recreation of our loving subjects as for our solace and pleasure when we shall thinke good to see them, during our pleasure."[150] Can it be doubted that the King's act of 17 May was at the direct request of the person who was the beneficiary of the King's act of 16 May?

❊

Southampton lived on for another 21 years. He died on 10 November 1624, in Holland, whither he had gone with his elder son, James (named after James I) to fight with the Dutch against the Spanish. James (called Lord Wriothesley) died in Roosendaal (valley of Roses!) of a fever on 5 November 1624; Henry, accompanying the body back to England, died five days later at Bergen-op-Zoom, also of a fever.[151] They were "both in one small Bark brought to Southampton,"[152] and are buried in the Church at Titchfield, under or near the monument there erected in 1594, on one side of which is the carving of Henry Southampton as a boy.[153]

The Wriothesley monument at Titchfield brings us to one last conjecture, relating to the possible interest shown by Southampton in Shakespeare even unto the death of the latter. Among the Wriothesley Papers now deposited in the Hampshire Record Office is a document,[154] dated 6 May 1594, whereby Garret Johnson, tomb-maker of the parish of St Saviour in Southwark, and Nicholas, his son, bind themselves to Edward Gage and Ralph Hare, two of the executors of the will of the second Earl of Southampton, in the amount of three hundred pounds, to well and truly perform the covenants, grants, articles and agreements set forth in a pair of Indentures of Covenants also dated 6 May 1594. The "Indentures of Covenants" referred to cannot be found, but it seems likely that the indentures constitute the contract between the tomb-makers and the executors of the will of Henry Wriothesley, the second Earl of Southampton, for the construction, as directed by the will, of the Wriothesley monument in the church at Titchfield.[155]

Garret or Gerard Johnson was the Anglicized form of the name of Gheeraert Janssen, a native of Amsterdam, who settled in the Parish of St Thomas, Southwark, in 1567, and soon thereafter gained a considerable reputation as a tomb-maker. In 1591 he received 200 pounds for designing and erecting in the church at Bottesford, Leicestershire, the elaborate tombs of the brothers Edward and John Manners, third and fourth Earls of Rutland.[156] John Manners was the father of Southampton's boyhood friend, Roger, fifth Earl of Rutland, and it is likely that Southampton saw the tomb either when it was transported to Bottesford in 1591,[157] or shortly thereafter. Also, between 1590 and 1595, Garret Johnson executed for the family of Edward Gage (one of the Wriothesley executors to whom the bond of 6 May 1594 was made), "a whole series of monuments at West Firle in Sussex."[158] The monument to the second Earl of Southampton's father-in-law, Anthony Browne, Viscount Montagu, who died in 1592, is so similar to the Wriothesley monument as to warrant the conclusion that Garret Johnson executed that monument, also.[159]

216

Garret Johnson died in St Saviour's parish, Southwark, in August 1611, in his will dividing his estate between his widow Mary and two of his sons, Garret and Nicholas, also tomb-makers. Nicholas is generally considered to have been the better artist of the two, and it was he who in 1618-1619 designed and executed the tomb for Southampton's friend, Roger Manners, the fifth Earl of Rutland, who died on 26 June 1612 — this tomb erected, as had been the monuments to the third and fourth earls of Rutland, at the Bottesford church.[160]

Shakespeare's luck in his portrayers was bad, for it was Garret, of the two tomb-maker sons of Gheeraert the poorer artist, who, according to Sir William Dugdale,[161] designed and executed the monument to Shakespeare on the wall of the church in Stratford-upon-Avon.

Coincidence cannot, in my opinion, account for the Wriothesley tomb at Titchfield and the Shakespeare monument at Stratford-upon-Avon being designed and executed by the same family of tomb-makers. It has generally been assumed that the connection between the Johnson family and Shakespeare is a result of their common residence in Southwark, and that the Shakespeare monument constitutes "a material link between the dramatist's professional life on the Bankside and his private career at Stratford."[162] The tomb in the Stratford church of Shakespeare's friend, John Combe, who died in 1614, is also by Garret Johnson, and some have surmised that it was Shakespeare who recommended that his Southwark neighbour, Garret Johnson, make the tomb of his Stratford neighbour, John Combe, and that Shakespeare's approval of his work, thus demonstrated, explains why Johnson was chosen to erect the Shakespeare monument in Stratford.[163]

That Shakespeare knew both Garret Johnsons, I have no doubt — but I believe that the occasion for their initial acquaintance was not their being neighbours in Southwark, but their mutual association with the Earl of Southampton while the Wriothesley family tomb was in the process of construction: for, whether the Wriothesley tomb was constructed *in situ* at Titchfield, or, like the Rutland tomb, constructed in Southwark and then moved to its permanent location, Southampton must at some time or other have had some contact with Garret Johnson, if for no reason other than to pose for his effigy on the side of the tomb. Perhaps it was while reflecting on the sculptured marble image of young Henry Wriothesley, garbed in his armour, the raiment of Mars, at the base of the tomb of his grandfather, Thomas Wriothesley, Lord Chancellor of England during the closing years of the reign of the great Henry VIII, that Shakespeare, who must have seen the tomb often, was moved to write one of the finest of all the Sonnets:

Not marble, nor the gilded monument
Of Princes shall out-live this powrefull rime,
But you shall shine more bright in these contents
Then unswept stone, besmeer'd with sluttish time.
When wastefull warr shall Statues over-turne,
And broiles roote out the worke of masonry,
Nor Mars his sword, nor warres quick fire shall burne:
The living record of your memory.
Gainst death, and all oblivious enmity
Shall you pace forth, your praise shall stil finde roome,
Even in the eyes of all posterity
That weare this world out to the ending doome.
    So til the judgement that your selfe arise,
    You live in this, and dwell in lovers eies.

The sentiment in the first two lines of this sonnet may explain why Shakespeare, unlike John Combe,[164] made no provision in his will for a monument to himself. But a monument had, by 1623,[165] been erected, and this could have been, and I like to think was, erected at the direction and expense of the Earl of Southampton, who turned to the old reliable family tomb-makers for the task. When Spenser died, Southampton's idol, the Earl of Essex, paid his funeral expenses; why might not Southampton, famous for his patronage of poets, follow the example thus set by someone he so admired, and cause to be erected at Stratford a commemorative bust[166] to honour the memory of the man who had so preposterously promised him that

So long as men can breath or eyes can see,
So long lives this, and this gives life to thee.

218

CONCLUSION

No Rose But One

No rose but one — what other rose had I?

Tennyson[1]

In the end, we return to two indisputable and pivotal facts: that the youth of the Sonnets is characterized as a Rose, nor red nor white, and that over the door of the Titchfield home of Henry Wriothesley, to whom Shakespeare dedicated *Venus and Adonis* and *The Rape of Lucrece*, is a shield with red and white roses — the symbol, *de facto* if not *de jure*, of the Earls of Southampton. From these two facts, I conclude that the Rose of the Sonnets is Henry Wriothesley, whose badge was the roses of Southampton; that Henry Wriothesley, by virtue of having been thought to have the honour of Hampshire, is the "fairest bud that red rose euer bare," and thus the Lord S to whom Nashe dedicated his *Choise of Valentines*; that *The Choise of Valentines* was the Rival Poet's "great verse, /Bound for the prize of (all to precious) you," and Thomas Nashe, consequently, the Rival Poet; that Shakespeare's association of Henry Wriothesley with red and white roses accounts for the red and white and Rose imagery not only of the Sonnets, but also of *Venus and Adonis* and *The Rape of Lucrece*, and a number of the early plays; and that in Shakespeare's intercourse with Henry Wriothesley and his circle of friends, particularly Essex and his household, lies the source and explanation of much of Shakespeare's wide-ranging knowledge.

All of which little facts and small conclusions, like the downed trees in Siberia, point to one major fact and one great conclusion, of which, like the meteorite which felled those trees, no physical evidence remains, but the reality of which cannot be doubted: that once, four hundred years ago, a man, still in his twenties, somehow finding himself in the courtyard of the manor of a former Lord Chancellor of England, saw enter that courtyard through a door over which were painted red and white roses a radiant youth whose ruddy cheeks were in sharp contrast to his otherwise fair complexion, and whose beauty, grace and charm called forth from their beholder a series of poems which are among the chief glories of English literature.

APPENDIX I

Thomas Wriothesley

A. Birth to Barony

That Thomas Wriothesley has not yet been the subject of a full-length biography may be the surest evidence we have of the adroitness with which he performed his duties in the Machiavellian court of King Henry VIII. The bloody events of that cruel monarch's despotic reign are well known, but since the many heads sacrificed to his greed, lust, dynastic ambitions and theological opinions were all cut off in seeming compliance with traditional English concepts of due process of law (that is, at the direction of Commissions or juries, or by Acts of Parliament), the King, and his aides and ministers, have by many historians been absolved of personal responsibility. But like dead bodies coming to the surface of lakes into which they had been secretly thrown, Henry's deeds are emerging from the muck, and the autopsies disclose how farcical was the King's justice, as his ministers and agents, by nods and winks, by threats and lies, by perjured testimony and fabricated evidence, by intimidation and torture, perverted the institutions of justice to secure the verdicts and sentences preordained in the King's closet. One of Henry's most effective agents was Thomas Wriothesley — a minor functionary from 1526 to 1536; a major instrument of the King's will from 1536 to 1547.

As we have already noted, Thomas Wriothesley was born into a family of heralds: his father, William Wriothesley, was York Herald, and his uncle, Thomas Wriothesley, was Garter King of Arms. After becoming Garter King of Arms, Thomas Wriothesley built a fine house, called Garter House, on Red Cross Street, near the corner of Barbican, in Cripplegate;[1] and it was there that his nephew, Thomas, was born on 21 December 1505.[2] Young Thomas attended St. Paul's School, in London, where among his classmates were William Paget and John Leland.[3] Wriothesley was known to his friends as "Yorker," or "Yorkist," after his father's office. He must have been quite young when accorded this cognomen, for his father died when he was but eight years old.[4] Although "early initiated in heraldic lore, [he] was not contented with the prospect of wearing a tabard, making visitations, examining pedigrees, and marshalling processions,"[5] and sought other avenues of advancement in life.

From St. Paul's, Wriothesley, Paget and Leland, in about 1522, went on to Cambridge: Wriothesley and Paget to Trinity Hall, Leland to Christ's College.[6] At Trinity Hall, Wriothesley and Paget met Stephen Gardiner, who was about ten years older than Wriothesley.[7] Gardiner lectured in Civil Law during the college year 1521-1522, in Canon Law in 1522-1523, and in both in 1523-1524. John Leland, in his *Encomia*, praised Gardiner for his reforms in the study of law.[8]

At some time while they were all at Cambridge together, Gardiner, Paget and Wriothesley acted in Plautus' comedy, *Miles Gloriosus*, Gardiner playing Periplectomenus (an old man), Paget Milphidippa (a clever slave girl), and Wriothesley Palaestrio (a wiley slave).[9] Leland saw the play, and in his *Encomia* complimented Gardiner on his delivery and histrionic grace, and stated that he would never forget the performance.[10] Of Wriothesley, in the same poem, he wrote, "Your beauty so shone upon your brow, your head of golden hair so glistened, the light of your keen mind was so refulgent, and your winning virtue so adorned you, that one amongst many, you were seen to be a pattern for all."[11]

In 1523, Gardiner was the representative of the University on a mission to Cardinal Wolsey, who since 1515 had been Lord Chancellor of England, and, by virtue of his occupying high religious and secular offices, reflective of the trust reposed in him by Henry VIII, exercised extraordinary powers within the Government. By the autumn of 1524, Gardiner was in the service of Cardinal Wolsey.[12] Wriothesley followed his mentor and friend, leaving Cambridge in 1524 without taking his degree, and finding employment at Court[13] in emulation of Gardiner, but not necessarily through his influence, for Wriothesley had other connections as well: his uncle was Garter King of Arms, and thus well known to the King, and Sir Edmund Peckham, the King's Cofferer, was the uncle of Wriothesley's mother — although, as was the custom of the time, Peckham and Wriothesley referred to each other as "cousin".[14]

Wriothesley began his service as an assistant to and secretary for Thomas Cromwell, a member of Wolsey's staff. Wolsey had conceived the idea of founding new colleges at Ipswich, where he was born, and at Oxford. Although the colleges were no doubt intended by Wolsey to be a memorial to himself, he devised a method to have the Church pay for them. He secured from Pope Clement VII a number of bulls authorizing the suppression of English monasteries. This involved the closing down of the religious order (sometimes on the alleged ground of sexual immorality; sometimes with the consent of the head of the order), the seizing of its property, and the transferring of that property to the new colleges.[15] It was to Cromwell that Wolsey assigned the administrative tasks incident to the suppression of the monasteries, and consequently it is no surprise to see that as this project proceeded during the years 1524 to 1529, many documents relating to it are in the hand of Cromwell's clerk, Thomas Wriothesley.[16] A close personal relationship developed between Wriothesley and Cromwell; a draft exists of Cromwell's will in Wriothesley's handwriting, and Wriothesley even seems to have had a room set aside for his use at Cromwell's home in Mortlake.[17] As late as 1539, a letter from Thomas Knight to Cromwell observes that "no son is more desirous to please his father than Wriothesley is to please Cromwell."[18]

Wriothesley, in addition to being handsome, was obviously an intelligent, able, and no doubt charming young man, and advanced accordingly. We soon find that his drafts are prepared for Wolsey, as well as for Cromwell.[19] And eventually these drafts[20] pertain to a matter of greater importance than the suppression of the monasteries for Wolsey's colleges; they pertain to the King's great, and for a long time, secret, matter, his wish to divorce Catherine of Aragon, by whom he had had no male issue, and to marry Anne Boleyn, by whom he was captivated.

In this connection, Wriothesley may have accompanied Gardiner to France in 1527, whither Gardiner went with Wolsey for the meeting with King Francis I which resulted in the negotiation of a treaty of perpetual peace between France and England.[21] The treaty with France was intimately related to Henry VIII's "great matter." Catherine of Aragon, the daughter of Ferdinand and Isabella, was the aunt of Emperor Charles V, and Henry assumed that a strong English-French alliance would counteract the influence upon Pope Clement VII of the Emperor, and thereby make it easier for the Pope (or, by his authorization, a subordinate prelate, such as Wolsey) to invalidate the marriage which — because it was of a man to his deceased brother's wife — had earlier required express Papal dispensation.[22] But in the following year, when Gardiner and Edward Fox went on a mission to the Pope to persuade him to delegate to an English cleric the authority to invalidate the marriage, this mission failed, apparently because of the Pope's continued fear of the Emperor.[23]

The King tried other stratagems to persuade the Pope. In one of these, Wriothesley played a small part. Along with William Brereton and Edward Leighton, he was sent "to divers parts of England by the King's command,"[24] to secure the signatures and seals of the prelates and temporal peers upon a memorial to Clement VII requesting that he annul the king's marriage.[25] We have a vivid description of the arrival of Wriothesley and his fellow-messenger William Brereton in the middle of the night at Southwell Palace, where Wolsey, roused from his sleep, greeted the messengers in his nightclothes. They conversed apart for a while in the bay of a great window. Then the messengers took from a coffer covered with green velvet a parchment having many seals attached, to which Wolsey affixed his seal. After sealing the document, Wolsey offered the messengers food and drink, and a place to sleep for the night. But they were in a hurry to go on to secure the signature of the Earl of Shrewsbury, and accepted only some cold meat, and a cup of wine. Wolsey, having very little money at the time, gave each messenger four old sovereigns of gold, which the messengers later (but not to Wolsey) complained of. "Indeed," writes the chronicler of this story, "they were not none of his indifferent friends, which caused them to accept it so disdainously . . . .nothing is more lost or cast away than is such things which be given to such ingrate persons."[26] But it is difficult to believe that Wriothesley, whatever his other faults may have been, would have reacted thus to the attempted generosity of the man whose secretary he had been.

On 28 July 1529, Gardiner became the Principal Secretary to Henry VIII.[27] Three months later, Wolsey was removed from the office of Lord Chancellor, and, in the gallery of his house at Westminster, the Great Seal was taken from him by a deputation consisting of the Duke of Suffolk, the Duke of Norfolk (who was Anne Boleyn's uncle), William Fitzwilliam (then the Treasurer, and later to become the first, and last, Earl of Southampton of the Fitzwilliam line), and Stephen Gardiner, who locked and retained the key of the casket in which the Great Seal was placed after it was taken from Wolsey.[28]

Also taken from Wolsey were his colleges. The one at Ipswich was destroyed, and for a time, it seemed that the college at Oxford would suffer a like fate, but Wolsey pleaded for it, and in the end the King decided that it might continue to exist — under the name of King Henry VIII's College.[29] Wolsey's arms were removed from every gate and window of the College.[30]

Not long after, on 4 November 1530, Wolsey, then at his palace at Cawood, near York, was arrested for High Treason, but while being escorted back to London, fell ill, and died at the Abbey of Leicester on 29 November 1530.[31]

Not much is known about the reasons for Wolsey's removal from office. It is generally assumed that Wolsey's fall was the result of the King's displeasure over Wolsey's failure over so long a period of time to secure the Pope's assent to the divorce from Catherine of Aragon, and Ann Boleyn's anger over the consequent delay of her marriage to the King.[32] Even before the end, rumours were heard that protégés of the Cardinal were working to bring about his downfall. On 18 September 1529, the French Ambassador had written with respect to Wolsey:

I have less hope than before of his influence, from the conversation I have had with him, for I see he trusts in some of his own *protégés (aulcuns fait de sa main)*, who, I am sure, have betrayed him *(luy ont tourné la robe)*. I should never have believed that they would have been so wicked; and the worst is that he does not understand it.[33]

If there is any truth to the Ambassador's observation, then the persons most likely to have betrayed Wolsey are Gardiner and Cromwell. Nor can it be doubted that these relatively minor functionaries were acting on behalf of those higher personages whose plans Wolsey's inaction frustrated: King Henry, and Anne Boleyn, and those of her party. Wriothesley (who in 1529 was 24 years old and had been 5 years in the service of Gardiner, Cromwell and Wolsey) probably assisted Gardiner and Cromwell. Even if he was not an active participant in the fall of Wolsey, he learned well the lesson it taught: that servants of Henry VIII fail to do his bidding at their own peril.

The fall of Wolsey did not impede the rise of Wriothesley, whose name appears in 1529 and 1530 as clerk to his cousin, Edmund Peckham, Cofferer of the Household.[34] By 4 May 1530 he was designated a Joint Clerk of the Signet,[35] and on 11 August 1530 he was granted for life, in reversion after Edward Ferres, esquire, the office of bailiff of Warwick and Snitterfield.[36] That the grandfather of the third Earl of Southampton might on a possible visit to Snitterfield have had some contact with the grandfather of William Shakespeare is an intriguing thought.

At about the same time that Wriothesley was made a Clerk of the Signet, his old friend William Paget was given a position as a signet office clerk.[37] Clerks of the Signet performed the various ministerial duties of the Principal Secretary in his capacity as custodian of the royal seal, or signet.[38] It is therefore likely that both of these protégés of Stephen Gardiner were appointed to their positions shortly after, and as a consequence of, Gardiner's becoming Principal Secretary. Wriothesley further cemented his ties with Gardiner by marrying, in about 1532 or 1533, Jane Cheney of Buckinghamshire, who appears to have been either a half-sister or sister-in-law to Gardiner's nephew, Germain Gardiner.[39] The extent to which almost all of the leading figures of the Tudor era were closely allied by marriage, while on the one hand explaining perhaps otherwise mysterious advances and preferments, leaves totally inexplicable the disregard of these family ties on the numerous occasions, some of which we will encounter, when these relatives sat in judgment upon, and judicially murdered, each other.

A week after the Great Seal was taken from Wolsey, it was entrusted to Sir Thomas More, the new Lord Chancellor, who was excused by the King from actively involving himself in the King's great matter.[40] During his two and a half year tenure as Lord Chancellor, More was chiefly concerned with deciding cases in the court of Chancery and burning heretics.[41] The King's divorce was handled by Stephen Gardiner and Thomas Cromwell, with Wriothesley doing much of the ministerial work.[42] Also recruited for this work was a new man on the scene, Thomas Cranmer, who in a conversation with Gardiner in the summer of 1529 had suggested that the best way to determine whether the king was entitled to a divorce would be to let that matter be decided by the theological faculties of the universities. Gardiner brought this idea to the attention of the King, who liked it very much, and commissioned the hitherto unknown Cranmer to write a treatise in favour of the King's position.[43] Throughout Europe, other treatises and books were written on the subject, and a lengthy manuscript in Latin in Thomas Wriothesley's hand is one of the products of Cranmer's suggestion.[44] In the end, not surprisingly, nothing came of this referral of the King's great matter to the academic world. But Gardiner continued to enjoy the King's confidence and favour, and in September, 1531, he was designated by the King to be the Bishop of Winchester, the wealthiest diocese in England, and was installed in this position on 27 December 1531.[45]

Gardiner spent little time in Winchester, a small town in the County of Southampton. Instead, his permanent residence was Winchester House, in Southwark, where he was surrounded by a "great number of gentlemen's sons, knights' sons and lords' sons," among whom were his friends and protégés from Cambridge, Wriothesley, Paget and Leland. Leland, ever ready with a Latin poem to praise his friends, called it the home of eloquence and the muses.[46]

In May of 1532, King Henry demanded that the Convocation — a body of English ecclesiastical officials — abdicate the right it had long exercised to legislate autonomously on religious matters, and henceforth to submit its determinations for royal approval. Gardiner incurred the displeasure of the King by joining Thomas More in opposing this demand. For reasons which are not clear, the Convocation, on 16 May 1532, made a full submission to the crown. On the same day Sir Thomas More resigned as Lord High Chancellor.[47] This so-called Submission of the Clergy, in which some have seen the hand of Thomas Cromwell (which would point to a finger or two of Thomas Wriothesley[48]), proved ultimately to be the key to the King's divorce.

In December, 1532, Anne Boleyn became pregnant, and in the following month was married secretly to Henry VIII.[49] On 30 March 1533, Thomas Cranmer, nominated by Henry VIII and approved by Pope Clement VII, became Archbishop of Canterbury.[50] On 5 April 1533, the Convocation of English clerics held that a marriage of a man to his deceased brother's wife was forbidden by divine law which no Pope could waive.[51] The Archbishop of Canterbury convened a court in Dunstable to apply the law thus announced to the facts of the King's case (for Catherine, prior to her marriage to Henry, had been the wife of Henry's older brother Arthur, who died in 1502). Catherine refused to appear. On 23 May 1533, Archbishop Cranmer held that Henry had not been legally married to Catherine, and that no impediment existed to his marriage to Anne.[52] On 28 May, Cranmer announced that Henry's marriage to Anne (the exact date of which is unknown, but which Cranmer said was about 25 January 1533), was valid.[53] Anne was crowned Queen on 1 June 1533.[54]

On 11 July, Pope Clement declared both the divorce from Catherine and the marriage to Anne null.[55] Henry VIII appealed from this judgment to a general council. Bishop Gardiner, who accepted the doctrine of royal supremacy after it was a *fait accompli*, was called upon to argue the King's case to the Pope in Marseilles in October; in November of 1533, the Pope rejected the appeal.[56] Wriothesley had gone to the continent in December, 1532, and was in Marseilles with Gardiner in October, 1533.[57]

In April, 1534, Gardiner was removed from his position as Principal Secretary, and replaced by Cromwell.[58] In November of that year, the Parliament declared the King to be "the only Supreme Head in earth of the Church of England" (thus enacting into law the submission of the clergy).[59] All of the king's subjects were required to renounce obedience to Rome,[60] by subscribing to an oath apparently written by Wriothesley.[61] The penalty for those found guilty of not renouncing loyalty to Rome was the usual one for treason: to be hanged, drawn, quartered and beheaded.[62] On 30 April 1535, Thomas Cromwell, and several other lawyers in the service of the Privy Council, demanded of Sir Thomas More whether he acknowledged the King to be Supreme Head of the Church; on that day, and many times thereafter, More gave either no answer, or equivocal answers, but after having been tried and convicted of high treason on 1 July 1535, and before being sentenced, he stated that Parliament had no authority to abolish the authority of the Pope. He was given the usual sentence, and beheaded on 6 July 1535.[63]

Gardiner and Cranmer, on the other hand, subscribed to the doctrine of royal supremacy, and took their oaths on 10 February 1535.[64] Gardiner went further, defending the doctrine in his first book, *De Vera Obedientia Oratio*, published in 1535.[65] But Gardiner's usefulness for the moment was at an end. He was appointed Ambassador to France, where he sojourned for three years,[66] leaving his former friend and now antagonist, Thomas Cromwell, as the King's chief advisor. Cromwell, who has been described as "the chief mover of the subordination of the Church to royal authority and the appropriation of ecclesiastical revenues to royal uses,"[67] would occasionally, after the passage of the Act of Supremacy, call Gardiner before the Council, and require him to acknowledge the King's supremacy in ecclesiastical matters[68] — a game which Gardiner must have found humiliating. This, and Cromwell's policy of seeking alliances with the Protestant princes of Germany to counter a feared Papal combination of the Holy Roman Empire and France against England,[69] were at least some of the elements contributing to the enmity which developed between these two former colleagues.

Although Lord Audley had succeded Thomas More as Lord Chancellor, it was now Cromwell who, next to the King, really ran the country. He had been Principal Secretary since 1534; the year prior to that, he had been made Chancellor of the Exchequer,[70] and in 1535 he became Vicar-General in all things ecclesiastical.[71] Wriothesley, who had been admitted to Gray's Inn in 1534,[72] could have had little or no time to pursue his legal studies, for his official duties and responsibilities must have increased commensurately with those of his master. But his increased workload was not without its reward: in January 1535/6, he was granted in reversion the office of coroner and attorney in the King's Bench, from which he derived a yearly income of 40 pounds out of the petty customs of the Port of London,[73] and on 29 May 1536 he was appointed "graver of the yrons apperteyning vnto the coynage,"[74] for which his annual fee was 20 pounds.[75] It was from emoluments from offices such as these, requiring very little in the way of real service, that Wriothesley received a steady stream of money upon which to live.[76]

In 1536, Cromwell, whose rise was attributable to his success in assisting Henry to rid himself of his first wife, Catherine, was again called on by the King to render a similar service. For the King was growing tired of Anne Boleyn, and although she had presented him with a daughter, Elizabeth, she had so far failed to present a son — and, in fact, had had a miscarriage on 27 January 1536.[77] Also, the King's affections now centered on his cousin, Jane Seymour. As a first step toward getting rid of Anne Boleyn, and with a clear view of what the last step would be, the King set up a Commission, headed by Cromwell and the Duke of Norfolk, to inquire into every kind of treason, by whomsoever committed, and to try offenders at special sessions.[78] Wriothesley was one of a number of "gentlemen" who aided the Commission in its work.[79] In the discharge of its duties, the Commission was satisfied that it had uncovered evidence that the Queen had committed adultery with a number of people, including William Brereton (who a few years earlier had been a messenger with Thomas Wriothesley), and Anne's own brother, George.[80] Adultery with the King's wife, the Commission said, constituted treason.[81] The charge against Anne was concocted by Cromwell,[82] and substantiated by the torture-induced confessions of her supposed lovers,[83] one of whom, Mark Smeaton, was taken to the Tower on 1 May 1536, to be followed in the next few days by Anne and others. On 15 May, at a trial presided over by their uncle, the Duke of Norfolk, Anne and her brother were tried and found guilty.[84] George Boleyn, along with Mark Smeaton and William Brereton (the two other men found guilty of committing adultery with Anne), were beheaded on 17 May.[85] Anne was executed on 19 May, by a headsman specially brought over from Calais.[86] On the same day, Archbishop Cranmer issued a dispensation from the bar to the marriage of Henry and Jane Seymour which their affinity in the third degree presented,[87] and on 30 May 1536, they were married.[88]

Muriel St. Clare Byrne detects in the Boleyn affair a *modus operandi* bloodily repeated many times during the reign of Henry VIII: the King decided that someone must die, and his ministers dutifully worked out the methods.[89] She supposes that with respect to Anne Boleyn, the understanding between the King and Cromwell may have been tacit, rather than express: that "at some point the interaction between their two minds, in a moment of possibly unspoken understanding, must have given Cromwell the necessary assurance that, besides wishing for her [Anne's] death, Henry was prepared to will the means, to become an actively desirous and consenting party and agree to accept the legal pretexts which his minister could provide."[90] Byrne sees this as the pattern in all the butchery so characteristic of the reign of Henry VIII, from the execution of Richard Empson and Edmund Dudley, who were arrested at the King's order on the second day of his reign,[91] to the execution of the Earl of Surrey, who was beheaded 8 days before the King's death: the will to destroy was Henry's; the means to that end were his ministers' responsibilities.[92]

The significance of that conclusion to this narration is obvious, for in due course Wriothesley became the King's chief minister, and if Byrne is right, as I believe she is, and as I think the rest of this account will show, then many of the executions which occurred during his stewardship are nothing more than judicial murders, conceived by the King and implemented by Wriothesley. But here, we need only note that Wriothesley, having while still in his twenties probably aided Cromwell and Gardiner to depose Wolsey (who escaped execution only by dying from natural causes), was an indispensable lieutenant to Cromwell in securing the death of Anne Boleyn.

Even as Anne went to her death, other events were occurring destined to make of Wriothesley a rich man. Henry VIII, as always, needed money, and decided to obtain it in the same manner as Wolsey had obtained money for his colleges: he would suppress the monasteries, take their land, and sell it, or devote it to his own uses.[93] The enormous experience in suppressing monasteries which Wriothesley and Cromwell had acquired under Wolsey now stood them in good stead as they suppressed monasteries for the King. During 1535, agents of the Crown, probably supervised by Wriothesley, were at work making an inventory of the monasteries of England, and their value. Upon the completion of this *Valor Ecclesiasticus*, Parliament, in 1536, enacted a law for the suppression of the smaller monasteries.[94] "Visitors" appointed by the Crown went to various monasteries, and either persuaded the Abbot to relinquish the lands to the crown, or discovered that such immoralities and perversions were practiced within the monasteries as to require their suppression for the well-being of the country.[95] The visitors also in the name of religious purity despoiled many of the ancient shrines of England: Wriothesley, who occasionally acted as a visitor, personally destroyed the shrine of St Swithin at Winchester Cathedral at 3 in the morning, probably to avoid facing the disapproval and possible resistance of the local citizens. He confiscated the gold, silver and precious stones, but made it a point also "to sweep away all the rotten bones that be called relics; which we may not omit lest it should be thought we came more for the treasure than for avoiding of the abomination of idolatry."[96] A few days before this, he had participated in an even greater desecration, the destruction at Canterbury of the famous shrine of St Thomas Becket,[97] murdered in the cathedral in 1170 by four knights at the order of Henry II. That all the Thomas's in Tudor England — including Wolsey, Cromwell, Cranmer, More and Wriothesley — ultimately derived their name from the venerable Thomas of Canterbury,[98] helped his shrine not one whit, his relics destroyed, as he himself had been, by the willing agents of an implacable Henry.

The dissolution of the monasteries met with resistance in the north of England. In October, 1536, a series of rebellions, called the Pilgrimage of Grace, led initially by Robert Aske, broke out in Lincolnshire, Yorkshire and neighboring counties.[99] Until its suppression in May, 1537 (after which Aske and other leaders of the Pilgrimage were executed[100]), the rebellion occupied almost all of the King's attention. However, the King's pleasure, during this trying time, was to reside at Windsor, while Cromwell, his principal minister, remained in London. Consequently, Cromwell's able assistant was assigned to be the King's amanuensis at Windsor, and thus it was that at the King's side during the rebellion, writing the hundreds of letters dictated by the King to Cromwell, and to the military commanders in the field, the Dukes of Norfolk[101] and Suffolk, was Thomas Wriothesley.[102] There can be little doubt that, as he had Gardiner, Wolsey and Cromwell before, Wriothesley favourably impressed the King by his intelligence, charm, loyalty, competency and writing abilities, and that, from this time on, it was the favour of the King, rather than of the King's ministers, which accounted for Wriothesley's advancement. Clearly, it can only have been with the approval of the King that Wriothesley secured for himself vast grants from the properties of the suppressed monasteries.

To be sure, Wriothesley had prepared for the King a list of beneficial public uses to which the proceeds from the surrender of the monasteries could be applied,[103] but in the end this great wealth was dispersed in the form initially of grants and then of bargain sales to favourites of the King or of Cromwell.[104] In this way, Cromwell, and his assistant, Wriothesley, among others, acquired extensive estates. Those who received these lands, like the King who seized them, were not necessarily friends of the new Protestant heresies which were beginning to make their way into England — Wriothesley, at this time, at least, was loyal to the old religion (except, of course, that he accepted his master and benefactor, Henry VIII, as the head of the church in England) — but they were more than willing to take for themselves as much as they could of the monastic wealth, which, I suppose they thought, might as well go to believers as to heretics.

Most of the lands granted to Wriothesley were in Hampshire. This appears to be for two reasons. First, even before the suppression of the monasteries, Wriothesley had acquired a number of Hampshire interests and connections. Wriothesley had some dealings with John Capon, also known as John Salcot, the Abbot of Hyde, as early as 1533, apparently delivering to him personally a letter from Cromwell notifying him of his nomination to be Bishop of Bangor.[105] By July of 1534 Wriothesley was joint steward of Hyde Abbey, which granted him fees, annuities, and leases of the rectory of Micheldever and the manor of Northstoneham.[106] Wriothesley was living in Micheldever north of Winchester by 1534,[107] but by 1536 was styling himself "Thomas Wriothesley of Tychefeld."[108] As a resident of the County of Southampton, Wriothesley in 1536 was called upon to supply twelve men to help route the Pilgrimage of Grace.[109] On 4 January 1537/8, Wriothesley was admitted a free burgess of the Town of Southampton.[110] In addition to being a steward of Hyde Abbey, he became the chief steward of Titchfield Abbey and Southwick Abbey.[111] So it obviously comported with Wriothesley's personal interests that such lands as he might receive be in Hampshire.

And second, and perhaps more important, this may also have comported with the interests of the King. Before the dissolution of the monasteries, the largest landholder in Hampshire was Arthur Plantagenet, Lord Lisle (who from 1533 to 1540 spent most of his time at Calais, where he was Deputy).[112] Other large landholders were the Poles, the Courtenays, and the Wests (the Lords de la Warr).[113] Lord Lisle, the Poles and the Courtenays were all related to each other: Lisle was the illegitimate son of Edward IV, Margaret Pole, Countess of Salisbury, was a daughter of Edward IV's brother, the Duke of Clarence, and Henry Courtenay, Marquis of Exeter, was the son of Edward IV's youngest daughter, Katharine.[114] Because of these connections, the Poles and their allies, including the Wests,[115] were known as the party of the White Rose.[116] One member of the Pole family, Reginald, had been made a Cardinal by Pope Paul III in 1536, for the immediate purpose of representing the Catholic Church in efforts to secure aid for the rebelling Pilgrims, and for the ultimate purpose of exacting either the downfall or submission of Henry.[117] Toward these people, whose claims to the throne were at least as good as his own, the King was not well disposed, and it seems likely that Wriothesley was showered with lands in Southampton County in order to establish there as a person of primary importance someone who was completely and unquestionably loyal to Henry VIII.[118]

In all, Wriothesley acquired 27 former monastic mansions in Hampshire. About half of these were gifts in recognition for his services; for the others, he paid.[119] Titchfield Abbey, which Wriothesley acquired on 30 December 1537, and converted into his principal residence, came burdened with debts and obligations, which Wriothesley was required to assume.[120] Other important properties acquired by Wriothesley were Quarr Abbey, on the Isle of Wight, on 23 February and 6 November 1537, and Beaulieu Abbey on 29 July 1538.[121] Wriothesley retained, however, only 16 of these 27 manors; the rest he disposed of in various ways.[122] While acquiring monastic estates, Wriothesley was at the same time engaged in acquiring other lands in Hampshire: in 1538, for example, he bought from his friend[123] Sir Thomas Wyatt, the poet (whose most famous sonnet probably alludes to his love for Anne Boleyn), the manor of Bromwich in the parish of Titchfield (which manor had previously been the property of the Uvedale, or Udall, family of Titchfield, one of whose members was Nicholas Udall, the scholar and dramatist, and also a friend of Thomas Wriothesley[124]); and in 1538 and 1540 he bought from Lord Lisle a number of manors in Hampshire.[125] But "the grants of the monastic estates alone made Wriothesley a bigger land magnate in Hampshire than any other layman had been in the years immediately before the Dissolution."[126]

All the while that he was acquiring lands in Hampshire and building his home there, Wriothesley resided primarily in London, to serve the King. On 12 October 1537, Jane Seymour was delivered by a Caesarean section of a son, who three days later was christened in the chapel at Hampton Court.[127] For the event, John Leland wrote an elaborate Latin poem.[128] A week later, the Queen died. Wriothesley (some think Cromwell; the document is not clear) wrote to Bishop Gardiner and Lord William Howard, ambassadors in France: "Our Prince, our Lord be thanked, is in good health, and sucketh like a child of his puissance; which you, my lord William, can declare. Our mistress, through the fault of them that were about her, whiche suffered her to take great cold and to eat things which her fantasye in sickness called for, is departed to God."[129] Then, stating he did so at the King's request, the writer went on to ask Gardiner to report to him which of the French princesses would in his opinion be most suitable for his majesty's next wife.

It was not only to France that Henry looked for a wife. One of the persons highly recommended to him was Christina, the sixteen-year old second daughter of the deposed Christian II of Denmark and his wife Isabella, the sister of the Emperor Charles V.[130] Christina had married the Duke of Milan at the age of thirteen, and had become a widow within one year. At the King's request, Holbein painted a portrait of the young Duchess of Milan, and Henry liked what he saw.[131] In September of 1538, the King sent Wriothesley to Brussels, to attempt to arrange a marriage with the girl.

By coincidence, on his way to the port of embarkation, Wriothesley encountered Bishop Gardiner, then returning from his three years' stay in France as Ambassador. Relations between the two formerly close friends had become strained, as Gardiner rusticated in France while Wriothesley, at the King's side in London, grew in power and influence. Also, Gardiner, who was conservative in his religious views, doubtless thought of Wriothesley as someone who had gone over to the less conservative — and perhaps even secular — views of Cromwell. Their meeting was politely formal. Thomas wrote to Cromwell, "at our meeting he did off his hat, and I in like manner mine. I told him I was glad to see him in health; he told me he was glad of mine."[132]

Gardiner arrived in London the next day, and almost immediately retired to Winchester.[133] Wriothesley continued on to Brussels, but it was a while before he was able to perform his commission, partly because of an illness of the type which seems to have frequently recurred in his life. On 20 November 1538, Wriothesley wrote to Lord Lisle,

I have a quartan fever, which on my sick day torments me badly. The second day makes me so feeble that I can do nothing, and the third day I am in such fear of the day following and must observe such diet that I live like one between this world and another.[134]

Finally, toward the end of January, 1539, Wriothesley was able to see the Duchess of Milan, and woo her for the King of England.

At this point, some mention is due Wriothesley's literary style, for if Wriothesley must be condemned for his deeds, he must also, in all justice, be commended for his gifts as a writer. His cruelty has died with him, and with those who were the victims of it; his writing has the power still to charm and captivate us — and also to amaze. It has been said of Shakespeare that he taught Kings how to speak, but the letters of Wriothesley suggest that, before Shakespeare was born, Kings had secretaries who knew well enough how to speak on behalf of their masters — perhaps even truly reflecting their masters' speech, for it should not go unnoted that King Henry is reputed to have told William Petre not to brood at his drafts' being corrected by the King, "for it is I, said he, that made both Cromwell, Wriothesley, and Paget good secretaries, and so must I do to thee. The princes themselves know best their own meaning and there must be time and experience to acquaint them with their humours before a man can do any acceptable service."[135] Whether taught by the King or not, Wriothesley wrote well. Muriel St. Clare Byrne, whose magisterial edition of the Lisle Letters is beyond praise, takes special notice of "the eloquence and the style and liveliness," "the speed, the energy and intensity, the sheer vitality" of Wriothesley's writing:

The man has style, contemporary elegance. The bold, rapid, decisive drive of his unmistakable, almost aggressive handwriting, with its pronounced forward slope and its combination of regularity and individuality, matches his balancing control and intensity of expression, even as both match the slightly arrogant, challenging poise of the handsome, thrown-back head in his portraits. It should be one of his chief claims on our interest that besides being an expert drafter of royal letters in Henry's magniloquent language, he is also an admirable, individual, and lively stylist in his own right. . . .[136]

Illustrating Wriothesley's literary style as well as anything else is the long letter he wrote to Henry after his interview with the Duchess of Milan. The letter describes first his meetings with the Duchess' aunt, Mary, the Queen Regent of the Low Countries. Wriothesely is disturbed because of statements allegedly made by the Duchess that she would not even consider marrying

Henry (one of the things the Duchess is alleged to have said is that she might marry Henry if she had two heads[137]); the Queen denies that her niece ever said any such thing. Thomas sought an audience with the Duchess herself, and was allowed to meet with her at "two of the clock after dinner":

A blind man should judge no colours, but surely, Sir, after my poor entendement [understanding], for that little experience that I have, she is marvelous wise,very gentle, and as shamefast [modest or virtuous] as ever I saw so witty a woman. I think her wisdom no less than the Queen's [i.e., her aunt's], which in my poor opinion is notable for a woman. Her gentleness exceedeth. As far as I can judge or hear for this little time that I have been here, I am deceived, if she prove not a good wife, if God send her a wise husband; and somewhat the better I like her, for that I have been enformed that of all the whole stock of them, her mother was of the best opinion in religion, and shewed it so farre, that both the Emperor and all the pack of them were sore grieved with her, and seemed in the end to have her in contempt. I would hope no less of the daughter, if she might be so happy as to nestle in England. Very pure, fair of colour, she is not, but a marvellous good brownish face she hath, with fair red lips, and ruddy cheeks, and unless I be deceived in my judgment, which in all things, but specially in this kind of judgment, is very base, she was yet never so well painted, but her lively visage doth much excel her poincture [painted portrait].[138]

Wriothesley excused himself for not having come to see her earlier, and said he had two things to ask her. "She bade me heartily welcome, and thanked me for my good will, and good considerations towards her. And as touching my request, if it should please me (she used that word) to declare my purpose, she would take it in good part, and give me such answers as she trusted should be reasonable." Accordingly, Wriothesley declared his purpose. First:

Madame, I thank Your Grace very humbly that it pleaseth you so well to accept mine excuse, and to put me therewith in good hope that I shall obtain my desire, and suit at this time made unto you. I shall therefore go to the declaration of the cause of my coming. It is so, that of late I have been advertised by some that should be honest men, for they have honest men's places, that Your Grace should of late have said, that if I, and my fellows here in commission with me, do travail to frame a marriage between the King's Majesty, my master, and Your Grace, we might lose our labours, for Your Grace would not fix your heart that way. When I had heard this tale, and [probably should be "I"] began to weigh it with myself after this sort: How can this be, that a Lady of that virtue, of that gravity, soberness and discretion that the Duchess is, should pass from her mouth so unseemly a matter? Surely this is but some lewd practice [plot, or trick]. I know, that to the Duchess herself some of them here have made the most untrue and wretched reports that their cankred hearts could devise, and all to the intent to turn her heart from my master, because they would serve another purpose. It may be, and surely I think, that they would also abuse me, to this end: that I might write to my master such matter as might cool his good inclination as fast on the other side. What shall I do? Shall I be so light, lightly to write such light sayings, as may nevertheless make matters, light and easy to be achieved, cold and heavy? No! What then? Shall I put matters of such weight in silence? Nay, neither, for then should I not serve my master truly, which next God's grace, I do above all things desire. His Majesty might say justly unto me, I did put thee in trust, I made thee one of my chief instruments for the time, where thou shouldst have been in all things faithful, and given Me just advertisement of all occurrences, leaving all judgments to Me; thou hast taken upon thee to judge in mine affairs, and by thy silence to put me in some hazard of some dishonour, with great displeasure; if thou hadst written, that it was told thee that the Duchess of Milan should speak after such sort, perchance I would have withdrawn, and so neither have sustained displeasure by loss of my time, nor have taken at any of their hands that dishonour, to have been kept thus in treaty upon bare practice [negotiating with no hope of success]. Well, quoth I to myself, how shall I then use this thing to do my duty without danger of harm to the matter? Marry! I shall take this way: the Duchess is here, and noted of such courtesy as I doubt not, upon honest request, I may know the truth of her own mouth; I shall leave all writing to my master till I shall have occasion to go to the Court, and then shall I desire that I may do Her Grace reverence, and ask the question: which resolution I have observed, so that, being this day with the Queen, I opened my desire to Her, and after by means also to Your Grace, and having now obtained that access, that may in the rest quiet me, I shall right humbly beseech Your Grace even frankly to tell me, whether ever any such thing passed you, or no, and by some words or mean also to express your affection touching the matter of this alliance.[139]

The foregoing may or may not be what Wriothesley actually said, but it is what Wriothesley told the King he said. One need not be very cynical to suppose that Wriothesley's account of the duty he owed the King was more calculated to ingratiate himself with Henry than to report events in Brussels. More outrageous sycophancy is yet to come.

In response to Wriothesley's question, the Duchess, after bidding him to put on his cap, and apologizing that she had suffered him so long to be bare, said, "I assure you, neither those words that you have spoken, nor any like to them, have passed, at any time, from my mouth; and so I pray you report for me." Wriothesley expressed his pleasure with this answer, but asked for the answer to his second question, her inclination to the matter of the alliance. She answered, "You know I am the Emperor's poor servant, and must follow his pleasure." "Marry," quoth I, "then I may hope to be one of the Englishmen that shall be first acquainted with my new Mistress, for the Emperor hath instantly desired it. . . ."[140] We who read this letter today are inevitably reminded of Shakespeare's rendition of Henry V's wooing of the French princess, Katharine of Valois:

Henry.	Wilt thou have me?
Katherine.	Dat is as it shall please de *roi mon pere*.
Henry.	Nay, it will please him well, Kate; it shall please him, Kate.

[V,ii,266-269]

Wriothesley continued:

"Oh Madame," quoth I, "how happy shall you be, if it be your chance to be matched with my master. God never help me, if I shall say not the truth to you in that which I speak, which I would say (and I knew him as I do) though I were neither his subject nor his servant. If God send you that hap, you shall be matched with the most gentle Gentleman that liveth; his nature so benign and pleasant, that I think till this day no man hath heard many angry words pass his mouth. As God shall help me, if He were no King, as He is one of the most puissant and mighty Princes of Christendom, I think, and [if] you saw him, you would say that for his virtue, gentleness, wisdom, experience, goodliness of person, and all other gifts and qualities meet to be in a Prince, He were worthy before all other to be made a King. I know Your Grace to be of noble parentage, and that you have many great Princesses of your alliance; but if God send this to a good conclusion (as I hope well His goodness will), you shall be, of all the rest, the most happy."[141]

At this she smiled, as well she might. Wriothesley probably smiled as he wrote it; the King doubtless smiled as he read it. Each for different reasons.

Waiting for some response to his suit, Wriothesley stayed on in Brussels, where the time was made light by the numerous entertainments to which he was invited. At one supper, where the Queen's chapel choir sang roundelays and drinking songs, the Queen mentioned to Wriothesley that she had heard that he loved music, and she asked him to her house the following evening, when he should hear all her "diversities of Musick." Wriothesley confessed that he loved music so well that at his poor house in England he liked to have somewhat of the kind to quicken his dull spirits. And the next evening, at the Queen's palace, after supper was served, toasts drunk and lances broken, the Queen's ensemble of two lutes, a recorder, a rebeck and a "vyall" played "the fyneliest that ever I heard."[142]

Even in the midst of this festivity, Wriothesley neglected no occasion to serve the King's interests as best he could. At one point, having managed to lure into the English compound one Henry Phillips, an English student at Louvain University, who refused to acknowledge the Royal Supremacy, Wriothesley immediately wrote a jubilant letter to Cromwell,[143] telling at length and in vivid detail of the stratagems he had used to secure Phillips. But that evening, Phillips escaped. Wriothesley, apparently terrified of the consequences for himself,[144] now wrote another letter,[145] telling Cromwell of the escape in "crisp, short, sharp sentences," "'declaring' his failure, conceal[ing] nothing, confess[ing] everything." Byrne believes that this acknowledgement of error and confession of guilt was realized by Wriothesley to be a formula for pardon,[146] a formula still relied upon by unhappy persons in despotic states, where the Supreme Chief never errs, and the only way someone who has made a mistake can save himself from the State's retribution is to proclaim his error and throw himself upon the mercy of the prince.

Whether for this reason or no, Phillips' escape brought Wriothesley no punishment. The Emperor's consent to the marriage of the Duchess of Milan to King Henry never materialized. Indeed, even as Wriothesley was being feted, relations between the two countries deteriorated. A ten year truce between Charles V and Francis I signed in June 1538 afforded Reginald Pole the opportunity to attempt to induce Charles and Francis to combine their forces against "the most cruel and abominable tyrant,"[147] the King of England. The Pope sent an envoy to Scotland, to gain the support of James V against Henry. An attack from Spain, Scotland and the Low Countries was feared; England, which, according to Wriothesley, would be "but a morsel amongst these choppers"[148] was in a panic. Henry turned vengefully on the party of the White Rose. Geoffrey Pole, the Cardinal's younger brother, was arrested, and induced to "confess," as a consequence of which his brother Henry, together with Henry Courtenay, Marquis of Exeter, and Sir Edward Neville, were convicted of High Treason and beheaded on 9 December 1538.[149] The executions occurred while Wriothesley was in Brussels, still suffering from his fever. The news "that such great traitors have been punished, and their attempts frustrated," he wrote to Cromwell, so lightened his "swollen stomach" that he accounted them the chief medicines he had received.[150] And to his brother-in-law Thomas Knight,[151] who was then shuttling back and forth between London and Brussels as a messenger for Wriothesley and Cromwell, he spoke "hourly of Cromwell's zeal for the common weal of the country."[152] Wriothesley left Brussels in mid or late March, 1539, just a step ahead of soldiers of the Emperor who, fearing that his own ambassador in London was being held hostage, sought to detain the English ambassador.[153] For reasons unrelated to Henry's butchery, the threat of invasion, which had never really been serious, subsided.

After his return, Wriothesley stood for Parliament from Hampshire, and was elected. His candidacy was supported by William Fitzwilliam, the Earl of Southampton,[154] but opposed by Gardiner, who continued to view him as a satellite and agent of Cromwell.[155] Gardiner, on his part, was involved in formulating the notorious Six Articles. These were the ultimate result of the King's request to Parliament, on 8 May 1539 to eradicate all diversity of religious opinion from the realm.[156] A Committee of Bishops was appointed to achieve that result. But the Bishops represented varying points of view, and were unable to write a statement of belief with which they could all agree. Bishop Gardiner was not a member of that Commission. However, on 16 May the Duke of Norfolk moved that the matter be settled in full Parliament, and presented for consideration six articles, which became the basis for the Act of the Six Articles. It was generally assumed that since Norfolk was not learned in matters theological, but was a friend and ally of Gardiner, the articles were written by Gardiner, and the Articles were, accordingly, called "Gardiner's Gospel."

The Six Articles declared (1) that in the Sacrament of the Altar "no substance of bread or wine" remained after consecration, but only "the natural body and blood of our Saviour;" (2) that Communion in both kinds was not necessary; (3) that the marriage of priests was contrary to God's law; (4) that vows of chastity ought, by the law of God, to be observed; (5) that private Masses were agreeable to God's law and ought to be continued; (6) that auricular confession was expedient and necessary to be retained. The penalty for denying the first article was forfeiture of property and death by burning; the penalty for public advocacy of anything contrary to the other five articles was loss of goods and death as a felon. Those who privately wrote or professed opinions contrary to the other five articles were to lose their goods for their first offense, their lives for the second.[157]

By about the middle of 1539, Henry's next wife was selected, apparently upon the recommendation of Cromwell in the interests of better relations with the German States.[158] This unfortunate woman was Anne of Cleves, whom Henry contracted to marry on the basis of a painting by Holbein. At about the same time and also with a view toward creating alliances with German States, Henry decided to arrange a marriage between his daughter, the Princess Mary, and Philip, Duke of Bavaria.[159] In December, 1539, Wriothesley went to Hertford Castle, to advise Mary of the King's wishes. He also delivered on behalf of the King a message to the Lady Elizabeth, who was then six years old. Wriothesley writes that when he gave his message to Lady Elizabeth, she replied "with as great gravity as she had been 40 years old. If she be no worse educated than she appears she will be an honour to womanhood."[160]

When, on 31 December 1539, Henry finally saw Anne of Cleves in person, he lost all interest in her. But for reasons of the alliance with the German States which this marriage was supposed to cement, he went through with the ceremony on 6 January 1540, saying to Cromwell on the morning of the wedding, "My Lord, if it were not to satisfy the world and my realm, I would not do that I must do this day for none earthly thing."[161] This was for Cromwell the handwriting on the wall.

The marriage was never consummated, and the wedding no sooner performed than attempted to be nullified. Naturally, for this task, Henry turned again to Cromwell, who had found ways to extricate him from his marriages to Catherine of Aragon and Anne Boleyn. Cromwell did little or nothing. It was perhaps to stimulate him to action (or to conceal the fate which awaited him) that Henry elevated Cromwell to the peerage on 18 April 1540, conferring upon him the title of Earl of Essex, and the position of Lord Great Chamberlain of England.[162] On the same day that Cromwell was "moved upstairs," Thomas Wriothesley and Ralph Sadler were appointed to fill the position which Cromwell had held (they were designated joint Principal Secretaries to the King), were knighted, and became members of the Privy Council,[163] of which Paget, at the same time, or shortly thereafter, became a clerk.[164]

But the Lord Great Chamberlain, strangely, seemed unable or unwilling to do anything to advance the King's latest matrimonial cause. An account exists of a conversation between Cromwell and Thomas Wriothesley on 6 or 7 June 1540. Cromwell told Sir Thomas

that one thing rested in his head which troubled him, that the King liked not the Queen, nor ever did like her from the beginning, and that the marriage had not been consummated. He (Sir. T.) said he thought some way might be devised to relieve the King, to which lord Cromwell answered that it was a great matter. The next day he asked lord Cromwell to devise some way for the relief of the King, for if he remained in this grief and trouble, they should all one day smart for it. To which lord Cromwell answered that it was true, but that it was a great matter. "Marry," said Sir. T., "I grant, but let the remedy be searched for." "Well," said Lord Cromwell, and then brake off from him.[165]

Perhaps contributing to Cromwell's reluctance to end the marriage of Anne to Henry was his awareness of the fact that Henry had become enamoured of Catherine Howard, the attractive and orthodox niece of Gardiner's friend and Cromwell's enemy, the Duke of Norfolk (of whom Anne Boleyn had also been a niece). The Duke of Norfolk and Bishop Gardiner had both

been active in bringing this woman to the King's attention, and in making it possible for the two to meet privately at various places, with the intention of gaining, through her, influence with the King.[166] For in those days, as Lord Campbell has written, "the situation of Queen was considered an office at Court to be struggled for by contending factions."[167] Cromwell was understandably reluctant to clear the way for bringing to power a faction which would strive to ruin him.

Curiously enough, in March of 1540, Gardiner met with Cromwell, and the result of this meeting appeared to have been that the two were reconciled with each other, and that Wriothesley also was once again on good terms with the friend of his youth.[168] It may be, in view of what subsequently happened, that Gardiner, with the aid of Wriothesley, was merely ingratiating himself with Cromwell to set the stage for his fall, even as Gardiner and Cromwell — and probably Wriothesley — had previously arranged (so I believe) the fall of Wolsey.

Cromwell may have had some inkling of what Gardiner was up to, for soon after the "reconciliation" he attempted to destroy Gardiner's power by destroying his allies. On 19 May 1540, Gardiner's friend, Arthur Plantagenet, Viscount Lisle, Deputy of Calais, was arrested and sent to the Tower, on the charge of being involved in a plot to deliver Calais to Cardinal Pole.[169] Others of Gardiner's party were also sent to the Tower. It seemed to observers that either Cromwell's party or that of the Bishop of Winchester must succumb.[170]

On 10 June 1540, as Thomas Cromwell was about to assume his customary place at the head of the Council table, the Duke of Norfolk jumped to his feet and shouted at him, "Cromwell, do not sit there; traitors do not sit with gentlemen." At these words, a Captain of the Guard and six halbadiers entered the chamber. The Captain of the Guard informed Cromwell that it was his duty to arrest him for high treason by order of the King.[171] Norfolk and William Fitzwilliam (the Earl of Southampton), as they had Wolsey 16 years before, stripped Cromwell of his decorations, and took him to the Tower.[172] Gardiner and Wriothesley orchestrated the case against Cromwell, preparing interrogatories for Cromwell to answer,[173] which interrogatories, so far as I can see, are designed to elicit this and no more: that Cromwell knew of the King's reluctance, after he saw Anne of Cleves, to marry her, and could think of no way to prevent or invalidate the marriage.[174] Ever inventive on his own behalf, the King had conceived the idea that Anne had previously been promised in marriage to the son of the Duke of Lorraine, that this betrothal, or "pre-contract," was in words of the present tense and thus tantamount to a marriage, and that her marriage to him (the King), therefore, was invalid.[175] His staff had the task of showing this was so: Wriothesley undertook to "make search at the Earl of Essex's house" for the contract made with the Prince of Lorraine, to ascertain "whether it was *de praesenti* or *de futuro*."[176]

Cromwell, from the Tower: "Most gracious prince, I cry for mercy, mercy, mercy!"[177] On 29 June 1540, a bill of attainder, finding him guilty of treason, maladministration, heresy and abuse of power was passed by Parliament, and on 28 July 1540, Cromwell was beheaded.[178]

In the meantime, under the much-practiced hand of Wriothesley, the divorce from Anne of Cleves was accomplished. Wriothesley and Gardiner visited Anne, who willingly consented to it, and on 9 July 1540, a Convocation of the Church anulled the marriage, on the ground that it had never been consummated.[179] On the day that Cromwell was beheaded, the King married Catherine Howard.[180]

It was to be Wriothesley's task, eighteen months later, to help the King get rid of Catherine Howard. Pending that eminently foreseeable assignment, he continued with his duties as one of the King's two Principal Secretaries, and he completed the conversion of Titchfield Abbey into his main residence. He was appointed the Constable of Southampton Castle in January1540/1.[181]

Some indication exists that in the spring of 1540, Wriothesley was arrested and sent to the Tower for a day or two. The reason for this, if it actually happened, is not clear; in any event, the difficulty soon passed, and seems to have cost Wriothesley nothing from the point of view of his career at court.[182]

In the the late summer of 1541, Henry and Catherine journeyed to York, where the King hoped to meet with his nephew, James V of Scotland. While they were out of town, the Privy Council was advised by an informant of Catherine's promiscuity. The Council sent Cranmer to Henry, to advise him of what they had been told. It has been reported that he refused to believe it, but the celerity with which Henry hit upon the notion that his marriage to Catherine was invalid because she had been previously betrothed to one Francis Dereham,[183] would suggest that everything that happened with Catherine Howard was in keeping with the King's desire to terminate his latest marriage. To this end, the Council conducted further investigations; Wriothesley obtained proof of Catherine Howard's extramarital affairs in much the same way that Cromwell had found proof of Anne Boleyn's.[184] One evening on a field outside Hampton Court, Wriothesley and Norfolk met secretly with the King, who then accompanied them to an all-night meeting of the Council at Gardiner's residence in Southwark, and heard the evidence they had gathered.[185] It was probably shortly after this that Wriothesley went to the Queen's quarters and "called all the ladies and gentlewomen and her servantes into the Great Chamber, and there openlye afore them declared certeine offenses that she had done in misusing her bodye with certaine persons afore the Kinges tyme. . . ."[186]

Catherine denied all the charges, as did those accused of having been involved with her. But the fact that she had not been chaste prior to her marriage was deemed sufficient. In January 1542 a bill of attainder against the Queen was introduced into Parliament and passed, and on 11 February it received royal assent, not by the King in person, but by a commission appointed by letters patent, to spare the King from hearing once again the "wicked facts of the case."[187] On 13 February, Catherine Howard was beheaded.[188] Earlier, on 1 December, Dereham had been sentenced to be drawn through London to the gallows at Tyburn, and there hanged, cut down alive, disembowelled, and (still living), his bowels burned, he to be then beheaded and quartered. On 10 December, that sentence was executed.[189]

Indicative of the Royal appreciation for his good work in freeing the King from his latest wife was the prestige now enjoyed by Wriothesley: he was "the man who nowadays enjoys most credit with the King, and almost governs everything here."[190] On 27 August 1542 Wriothesley was authorized to retain 40 persons in his livery.[191] In the same year, Wriothesley, retaining of course his positions at Court, was again elected a member of Parliament for Southampton County.[192] On 15 October 1542 his friend, William Fitzwilliam, the Earl of Southampton, died while leading with the Duke of Norfolk an army into Scotland.[193] Fitzwilliam's half-brother, Sir Anthony Browne, continued with the expedition, winning the appreciation and admiration of the Duke of Norfolk, who wrote to Wriothesley, "Pray God put it into the King's mind to make him his Brother's heir for the names and lands of Southampton."[194] God did not put this idea into the King's mind, and neither did Wriothesley. However, someone had the idea of appointing Wriothesley to succeed Fitzwilliam as Constable of Porchester Castle, "with profits enjoyed by Wm. late earl of Southampton."[195]

Wriothesley also was the beneficiary of King Henry VIII's almost incomprehensible decision, in May of 1541, to behead the 67 year old Margaret Pole, Countess of Salisbury, who had been in prison ever since the execution in 1538 of her son Henry (the news of whose death had been such good medicine for Wriothesley, sick in Brussels). As a consequence of her attainder and execution (allegedly for having in her coffer a shield bearing the arms of England impaled with a coat associated with Princess Mary and Cardinal Pole[196]), her lands reverted to the Crown, whence Wriothesley was granted a lease to her Manor of Warblington (or Warlington), the chief stewardship of her lands in Somersetshire, Dorsetshire, Wiltshire, Hampshire, Oxfordshire, Berkshire, Bedfordshire, Devonshire, Buckinghamshire, Hertfordshire and Suffolk, and the mastership of the deer hunt in all of the Countess' lands in England.[197]

Other offices and honours accrued: Wriothesley was appointed a Commissioner to treat with the Ambassadors of Charles V in October 1542 and again in December 1543;[198] he was appointed Joint Chamberlain of the Exchequer on 29 January 1542/3.[199] On 12 July 1543, at a ceremony performed by Bishop Gardiner, Henry married his sixth and last wife, Catherine Parr.[200] Accompanied by Thomas Wriothesley, they went on their honeymoon through the southern shires,[201] and may have spent a night or two at Titchfield.

In October, 1543, Wriothesley was again ill, and repaired from London to "the good air of Hampshire."[202] He was back in London by December,[203] and soon thereafter had the satisfying experience of being created Baron Wriothesley of Titchfield.

This occurred on 1 January 1543/4 (35 Henry VIII) at Hampton Court:

The pages' chamber being well strawed with rushes, after the King came to his closet to hear high mass, the said baron came to the pages' chamber; and when mass was done he and other lords made ready and came to the King in the presence chamber, "his Highness being under cloth of estate, with his noble council, both spiritual and temporal." The said baron, in his kirtle, was led between lords Russell and St. John, with lord Par of Horton before him bearing his robe, and Garter bearing his letters patent. Garter delivered the letters to the Lord Chamberlain of England who delivered them to the King and he to Secretary Paget to read. At the reading of the word *investimus* the baron put on his robe and then the patent was read out and delivered by the King to the baron, who gave great thanks and took leave. He was then conducted to the great chamber before the Queen's lodging "in the [o]utter court on the right side, there appointed for their dining place, preceded by the trumpets (blowing) and the officers of arms. After the second course Garter proclaimed his style, "du noble chevalier Thomas Seigneur Wryothesley et seigneur de Tichefelde et une de la Estroict Councell du Roy notre souveraine ś."[204]

B. Barony to Burial

With Wriothesley's new dignity came more responsibility. From January to April, 1544, he was Treasurer of the Wars.[205] On 22 April 1544, Lord Chancellor Audley having become ill, the Great Seal was delivered to Wriothesley, who was designated "Lord Keeper during the illness of the Chancellor."[206] On 30 April, in the Court of Chancery in Westminster Hall, Wriothesley took an elaborate oath abjuring the Pope and accepting the King as "the only Supreme Head in earth, under God, of the Churche of England and Ireland, and of all other his Highnesse's dominions. . . . "[207]

This oath may have been something more than a mere formality, for shortly before had occurred an event which necessarily touched Wriothesley closely, although the extent of his involvement, if any, in that wrenching and mysterious incident is completely unknown. Bishop Gardiner, in about 1543, had come to believe that many persons in high positions were either violating the Six Articles or ignoring the violations of others, and he launched a campaign to expose and punish these persons. At Windsor he found five heretics, three of whom were burned at the stake on 28 July 1543.[208] (One who escaped immolation was John Marbeck, composer and Royal organist: Gardiner secured his pardon because he admired Marbeck's art, "wherein he has pleased me as well as any man."[209])

In any event, Gardiner's net was aimed at a bigger fish: Thomas Cranmer, Archbishop of Canterbury, was suspect, and Gardiner encouraged a number of persons, including his nephew Germain Gardiner, John Heywood, the dramatist, and John More, the son of Sir Thomas More, to collect damaging facts.[210] When all of the accusations and charges against Cranmer were assembled and written out, Gardiner presented them to the King who, "to the amazement of everyone," turned them over to Cranmer himself to investigate.[211] Cranmer's investigation exposed the plot against him, and Germain Gardiner, John Heywood, John More and others involved in making false accusations were sent to prison.[212] On the basis of facts and allegations presumably connected with this incident (no records of the charges or of the trial exist), Germain Gardiner, on 7 March 1544, was hanged, drawn and quartered for denying the King's supremacy.[213]

Germain Gardiner, as already noted, appears to have been either the half-brother or brother-in-law of Wriothesley's wife. Germain Gardiner's activities may have in some minds raised a question as to the dedication of his brother-in-law to the principle of Royal supremacy, and this may be the reason for Wriothesley's oath in the month following Germain's execution. Of Wriothesley's reaction to Germain's execution, we have no report.

The prize upon which Wriothesley doubtless had his eye when he took his oath fell almost immediately into his hands. On 3 May 1544 Lord Audley died, and Wriothesley became Lord High Chancellor of England.[214] The following month, John Heywood received a full and general pardon.[215] In the *Metamorphosis of Ajax*, published in 1596, Sir John Harington stated that Heywood "scaped hanging with his mirth, the King being graciously and (as I thinke) truely perswaded, that a man that wrate so pleasant and harmlesse verses, could not have any harmfull conceit against his proceedings, & so by the honest motion of a Gentleman of his chamber, saved him from the jerke of the six stringd whip."[216] It is conceivable that the new Lord Chancellor might have been the Gentleman of the King's chamber who interceded on Heywood's behalf.[217]

Opinions as to Wriothesley's performance as Lord Chancellor differ. David Lloyd, in a book published in 1665, wrote that he discharged the office of Chancellor "with more applause than any before him, and with as much integrity as any since him," and Lloyd relates sayings attributed to Wriothesely: that "Force awed, but Justice governed the world," and that "He loved a bishop . . . to satisfie his conscience; a lawyer, to guide his judgment; a good family, to keep up his interest; and an university, to preserve his name." Lloyd also recounts an incident which, if true, certainly reflects credit upon Wriothesley: that the Lord Chancellor, "overhearing a servant putting off a Petitioner, because his Master was not at leasure, takes him up roundly, and replies, You had as good say, I am not at Leasure to be Lord Chancellor."[218] But the reliability of David Lloyd is seriously undermined by his statement that Wriothesly died "full of years and worth,"[219] for the fact is that, even by Tudor standards, Wriothesley was young when he died, and his "worth" at the time of his death, if by that word is meant the honour and respect accorded him by his contemporaries, was almost nil.

So perhaps more credibility is to be given to Lord Campbell's assessment of Wriothesley's tenure as Lord Chancellor. In his *Lives of the Lord Chancellors*, published in 1846, Lord Campbell writes that Wriothesley knew almost nothing of the law, and was very inadequate to the discharge of his judicial duties, causing the public to complain loudly of his delays and mistakes. He tried to make up for his deficiencies, but the task was beyond him. Accordingly, with the King's consent, on 17 October 1544, he issued a commission to Sir Robert Southwell, Master of the Rolls, and several others, to hear causes in the Court of Chancery during his absence, and although he occasionally took his seat as a matter of form, he in reality relinquished his legal duties to the Commission, and during the remainder of the reign of

Henry VIII devoted his professional life entirely to matters of state and religion.[220]

One matter of state with which Wriothesley was particularly concerned, both before and after becoming Lord Chancellor, was raising the money to pay for the wars with Scotland and France. Hostilities with Scotland began in August, 1542. France, as usual, came to the aid of Scotland. In the summer of 1543 Henry, having signed a treaty of alliance with Charles V, sent a small force to fight with the Imperial army in Flanders against the French. In the summer of 1544, Henry personally led an English army in an invasion of France (designating his wife, Catherine Parr, to be Regent during his absence, and Wriothesley one of five persons to be the Queen's Council of Regency).[221] Someone has computed the total cost of this warfare to have been £2,134,784 1s. 0d.[222] Wriothesley racked his brains to find ways of raising the money to pay for the wars.

As early as 1542, Wriothesley had calculated the gains which the Crown might realize by decreasing the amount of gold and silver in English coins,[223] and in that year the amount of gold and silver in the coins was in fact decreased.[224] In 1544, and again in 1545 (in which year Wriothesley's brother-in-law Thomas Knight was appointed Under Treasurer of the Mint[225]) and 1546 (in which year Wriothesley's "cousin," Sir Edmund Peckham, was appointed High Treasurer of the Mint[226]), the pressing need for money resulted in further, and more substantial, debasement of the currency.[227] From May, 1544, to the end of his reign, the King's profits from his mints, arising from the debasement and recoinage, were £363,000.[228] It has been suggested that Wriothesley was created a Baron as a reward for his work in augmenting the King's treasury by debasing the English coinage,[229] but it is unlikely that of all the services rendered by Wriothesley for King Henry, this one alone should have won him the peerage.[230]

Moreover, the debasement of the currency did not solve the King's financial problems, which remained to vex Wriothesley during his entire tenure as Lord Chancellor. Sharing with Wriothesley the responsibility — and the vexation — for the supervision and disbursement of the government revenue was his long-time friend, William Paget.[231] The monastic lands were an obvious source of immediate income. Wriothesley was one of a number of Commissioners empowered on 1 March 1544 to sell the King's lands and the lead from the roofs of the dissolved monasteries. From this, as well as from the sale of various privileges, almost £200,000 was raised.[232] Also, contributions were exacted from the citizenry, and money was borrowed at home and abroad[233]. It is not inconceivable that some persons, including the old and very rich Countess of Salisbury, were executed for treason primarily to enable the King to seize their property.[234]

But always the treasury was short, and so, consequently, were tempers. The Privy Council writes for money to support the war, and Wriothesley replies, "good my Lordes, though you write to me styll, 'pay, pay; prepare for this, and for that,' consider it is your partes to remembre the state of things with me,"[235] and to Paget he writes, "You bid me run as though I could make money. I would I had that gift but one year for his Majesty's sake."[236] This letter, or one like it, evidently elicited a peevish response from Paget, to whom Wriothesley, on 8 November 1545, replied with affection and warmth:

. . . I shalbe alwayes towardes you and yours of most freendly disposition, be you as jelous as you woll, and descant of my doinges, as moche out of tune as you list; and this I write with al myn harte. And nowe let me knowe, whither I may sumtyme write a mery word, without suche tragedyes, or whither I must nedes work by lyne and level, thoughe you ministre the argument. And yet suerly, when I write to youe, methink I write even to meself; and that maketh me sumtyme to forget meself, if you woll so take it, when I write frankely and freendely, and call it stomake, which is as faynt in me, as in any man. I woll contynue this brawl no lengre. I wold my Lady sawe your letter, and whereuppon it is grounded. I dare saye, thoughe my gentle nature cannot chide, she wold say sumwhat for me, whom you shall never fynde but a perfit freende; havinge a perfite and most assured trust, that I have the like of you, and shal soo fynde, in worde and dede, as I am, and ever wolbe to youe accordingly. Thus the greate feld is foughte. God be thanked no hurt doon. . . .[237]

But perhaps, as subsequent events were to show, more hurt was done than Wriothesley suspected. For the moment, however, things continued to go well for him. On 23 April 1545 he was nominated to be a Knight of the Garter, and was installed as such on 17 May 1545.[238] It was probably at this time that the portrait reproduced in Plate VII was painted, showing Wriothesley seated, his coat of arms encircled with the garter over his left shoulder, and on a table beside him, the leather bag with the coat of arms of England upon it, in which was the Great Seal.

At the same time, Wriothesley's one son who survived him was born, and at a ceremony at St. Andrew's, Holborn, on 24 April, was christened Henry, after the King, who was in attendance.[239] That the ceremony was in Holborn reflects the fact that Thomas now lived in this area,[240] in a residence which in his will he called Southampton House. On 31 May 1545, the number of retainers authorized to be in Wriothesley's service was increased to 100,[241] and on 9 June 1545 he received from a king grateful for his services a grant of the boggy area near Southampton House known as Bloomsbury, as well as other properties in London and Hampshire.[242]

Somewhere along the way, Henry VIII, or Bishop Gardiner, or Thomas Wriothesley, or any one or all of them, became concerned lest Henry's new Queen was not orthodox enough in her beliefs. This seems to account for the particular interest taken by these persons in the religious views of Anne Askew (or Ayscough, as it is sometimes spelled), one of the queen's friends,[243] who was heard to declare before a large company "that in her opinion, after the consecration of the elements in the sacrament of the Lord's supper, the substance of bread and wine still remains in them."[244] Wriothesley and Gardiner interrogated her on her opinion of the sacrament, and asked her to confess the sacrament to be blood, flesh and bone, but this she refused to do. She was sent to the Tower, and further questioned if she knew any man or woman of her sect. She said she knew none. She was told that the king thought otherwise; she replied that "the king was as well deceived in that behalf as dissembled with in other matters."[245]

Then: "they did put me on the rack, because I confessed no ladies or gentlewomen to be of my opinion, and thereon they kept me a long time; and because I lay still, and did not cry, my lord chancellor [Thomas Wriothesley] and Master Rich [Richard Rich, grandfather of the Robert Rich who married Penelope Devereux] took pains to rack me with their own hands, till I was nigh dead. . . . Then the lieutenant caused me to be loosed from the rack. Incontinently I swooned, and then they recovered me again. After that I sat two long hours reasoning with my lord chancellor upon the bare floor; where he, with many flattering words, persuaded me to leave my opinion. But my Lord God (I thank his everlasting goodness) gave me the grace to persevere, and will do, I hope, to the very end."

This statement by Anne, printed by John Foxe in his *Book of Martyrs*, is supplemented by other material which tells us more about this incident. The lieutenant at the Tower, Anthony Knevet, after initially racking Anne for as much as he thought proper, had been about to take her down, when Wriothesley commanded him to strain her on the rack again, which Knevet refused to do. Wriothesley thereupon said that he would report Knevet's disobedience to the King, and he and Master Rich, "throwing off their gowns," proceeded with the racking, after which Wriothesley and Rich returned to court by horse. Knevet took a quicker route to court, and before Wriothesley and Rich returned, told the King what had happened, and asked his pardon. The King "seemed not very well to like of their so extreme handling of the woman, and also granted to the lieutenant his pardon, willing him to return and see to his charge."[246] But it cannot be doubted that Anne would never have been tortured save at the King's command.

Anne's doom was sealed. She was convicted of having violated the Six Articles, and with several others was sentenced to be burned. On 16 July 1546, as the victims were tied to the stake, Wriothesley was present with a conditional pardon, to which, with the King's consent, he had affixed the Great Seal. After Anne and the others were tied to the stake, but before the fagots were lit, he informed them that if they would but recant, they would be saved. They refused, and "continuing their devotions, calmly saw the devouring flames rise around them," while Wriothesley watched.[247]

A more fortunate target of Wriothesley's zeal in enforcing the Six Articles was George Blagge (or Blage), "one of the king's privy chamber," who, the Sunday before Anne Askew was burned, was sent for by Wriothesley to answer the charge that he had said that if a mouse were to eat the consecrated bread used in the sacrament of the Lord's supper, "then, by my consent, they should hang up the mouse." For this statement, Blagge was the following day sentenced to be burned on Wednesday. The King supposedly heard about this only by accident, and after summoning Wriothesley, directed that Blagge be pardoned. Blagge thereafter came into the King's presence:

"Ah! my pig" (saith the king to him, for so he was wont to call him). "Yea," said he [Blagge], "if your majesty had not been better to me than your bishops were, your pig had been roasted ere this time."[248]

But persons in high positions continued to be subject to the lash of the whip with six strings. Anne Askew's failure to implicate the Queen did not relieve the suspicions of Henry, Gardiner and Wriothesley that the Queen in fact might not subscribe to the Six Articles. One morning Gardiner came to Wriothesley to tell him that the King had been complaining to him of the Queen's abetting Lutheran doctrines in their private conversations, and that the King had listened favourably to Gardiner's remark "that such misconduct could not be winked at by a King anxious for preserving the orthodoxy of his subjects."[249]

Foxe's long story of what ensued has been somewhat condensed by Lord Campbell:

The Chancellor [Wriothesley] flew into the royal presence to take proper advantage of this disposition, and eagerly represented, "that the more elevated the individual was who was made amenable to the law, and the nearer to his person, the greater terror would the example strike into everyone, and the more glorious would the sacrifice appear to posterity." Henry was so much touched by these topics, that he directed articles of impeachment to be drawn up against his consort, so that she might forthwith be brought to trial and arraigned; and ordered that the following day she should be arrested by the Chancellor himself, and carried to the Tower of London. Wriothesley joyfully drew the articles, and brought them to the King for his royal signature; without which it was not deemed regular or safe to take any further step in the prosecution. Henry signed the paper without hesitation, and the execution of another Queen seemed inevitable.[250]

But that was not to be, for the Queen found out about the plan. The first thing she did, quite naturally, was to faint, but after regaining her senses, she engaged Henry in seemingly casual conversation, and (without telling him that she was aware of the plan to arrest her) convinced him that she knew nothing about religion, and merely talked about the subject for his momentary amusement. "And is it indeed so, sweetheart?" replied the King; "then we are perfect friends."

The next day Henry and Catherine were conversing in the garden, when Wriothesley came with forty poursuivants, to carry the Queen to the Tower. Catherine withdrew, to permit the Chancellor and the King to speak together. From where she stood, she could hear the king call Wriothesley "Fool, knave, and beast," and order him to depart his presence. When Wriothesley was gone, Catherine ran up to the King, ostensibly to put in a good word for the Chancellor. "Poor soul," said the King, "you little know how ill entitled this man is to your kind offices."[251]

After this incident Gardiner, as well as those conservatives associated with him, began to lose favour with the King. By the fall of 1546, persons having Protestant leanings took no pains to hide their dislike of the conservatives: the Viscount Lisle (John Dudley, the step-son of Arthur Plantagenet, the former Deputy of Calais) struck Bishop Gardiner a blow at a meeting of the Council, and the Earl of Hertford (the brother of Jane Seymour and thus the uncle of the King's son, Edward) spoke violent and injurious words to Wriothesley.[252] Also, at about this time, Gardiner refused to exchange with the King certain lands which the King wanted, thus incurring the King's displeasure.[253] In late December the King, feeling himself near death, revised his will (originally drafted by Wriothesley[254]) to remove Gardiner's name from the Council of Regency therein appointed to govern during the minority of Prince Edward. Sir Anthony Browne, the half-brother of William Fitzwilliam, the late earl of Southampton, and a friend of Gardiner and of Wriothesley, suggested that Gardiner had been inadvertently forgotten, and should be restored; the King said, "Hold your peace. I remembered him well enough, and of good purpose have left him out; for surely if he were in my testament, and one of you [i.e., one of the Council] he would cumber you all, and you should never rule him, he is of so troublesome a nature. Marry, I could use him, and rule him to all manner of purposes, as seemed good unto me, but so shall you never do."[255]

Further undermining Gardiner's position at this time was the arrest and confinement in the Tower of Gardiner's friend and ally, the Duke of Norfolk, and Norfolk's son, the Earl of Surrey, who is best remembered today for being, along with Sir Thomas Wyatt, the person to introduce the sonnet form to England. The charge against the Earl of Surrey was high treason: his quartering on his arms the coat of Edward the Confessor was alleged to be a wrongful claim of descent from that monarch, and thus by implication an assertion of a right in himself to succeed Henry as King of England.[256] The charge against his father was misprision of treason.[257] The Privy Council, presided over by Chancellor Wriothesley and the Earl of Hertford, conducted the investigations.[258] Wriothesley made use of his heraldic knowledge to draft the interrogatories propounded of Surrey with respect to his arms,[259] agreeably surprised, no doubt, that this arcane knowledge of his should prove so useful.

Eventually, the Duke of Norfolk, probably induced by the hope of clemency, confessed that he had concealed high treason in keeping secret his son's act of using the arms of Edward the Confessor in his scutcheon, "which said Arms of St. Edward appertain onely to the King of this Realm, and to none other person or persons."[260] He also confessed that he himself had borne in the first quarter of his arms, ever since the death of his father, the arms of England, with a difference of the Labels of Silver, which are the proper arms of the King's son, Edward. For all of which, Norfolk concluded, he deserved by the laws of the realm to be attainted of High Treason.[261]

On 7 January 1547, Surrey was indicted for unlawfully quartering the royal arms of Edward the Confessor upon his escutcheon. On 13 January 1547, a Commission including Wriothesley, Hertford, and Paget among others tried the case before a jury of men from Norfolk. The trial was a farce, but Surrey stoutly defended himself for eight hours — at one point calling Paget "an inquisitor worthy to be the son of a bailiff" — which Paget was.[262] The jury returned a verdict of guilty of high treason, and the usual sentence was passed upon him. On 19 January 1547, by authority of a warrant signed by Wriothesley, Surrey was beheaded on Tower Hill.[263]

A bill for the attainder of Norfolk was passed by the House of Lords on 20 January 1547, and on 27 January Wriothesley summoned the Lords in their robes to hear the King's statement (probably written by Wriothesley) that since the King was too ill to give his royal assent in person to the bill of attainder, he had directed that the assent be given by Wriothesley and the other peers. The Clerk of the Parliament pronounced the words, "*Soit fait come il est desiré*," and the arrangements were made to behead Norfolk the next morning.[264] But that night, King Henry VIII, attended by Hertford and Paget, died.[265] It is assumed that as they kept their death watch, Hertford and Paget made the plans which within a few days diverted to Hertford the principal authority for the administration of the Government which Lord Chancellor Wriothesley had probably hoped to exercise.[266]

News of the King's death was kept secret for three days, while Hertford went to Hatfield to conduct the new King back to London, and Wriothesley and others debated what to do about Norfolk. In the end, Norfolk was not executed, but was kept prisoner in the Tower.[267]

On the 31st of January, 1547, Chancellor Wriothesley formally announced the King's death to both houses: "the mournful news was so affecting to the Chancellor and all present that they could not refrain from tears."[268]

The King's will named Wriothesley and fifteen other persons[269] to be its Executors and Councillors of the Privy Council, or Council of Regency, which Council would, until Prince Edward attained the age of eighteen years, rule England. The will made specific bequests to a number of persons; the bequest to Wriothesley was of 500 pounds.[270]

After the public announcement of Henry's death, Wriothesley and the fifteen other members of the Council of Regency assembled in the Tower to commence their Government in the King's name. Henry's will was read, and at Wriothesley's suggestion, all swore to uphold it. Then, unexpectedly from Wriothesley's point of view, the Earl of Hertford, the new King's uncle, suggested that one of their number should preside over the Council; Paget, by prearrangement, nominated the Earl of Hertford for that position, on the basis of his close relationship to the King, the fact that he himself was not in the line of succession to the throne, and that he was eminent for his abilities and virtues. Wriothesley protested, arguing that this constituted an unlawful deviation from Henry's will, which intended that all of the Executors be and remain equal. But he was ignored; the Council had already made up its mind, and Hertford became the Protector of the realm.[271]

On 16 February 1547, after a funeral Mass celebrated by Bishop Gardiner, Henry was buried at Windsor Castle.[272] Ten days earlier, on 6 February, William Paget had in a solemn deposition stated that Henry, shortly before his death, reflecting upon the execution of the Earl of Surrey and the anticipated execution of the Duke of Norfolk, and the general decay of the nobility, had decided to advance a number of persons to higher places of honour. Paget listed the persons, and their honours: the Earl of Hertford was to be the Duke of Somerset, Exeter or Hertford and Treasurer and Earl Marshal of England; his brother Sir Thomas Seymour was to be Lord Seymour of Sudely and Admiral of England; Viscount Lisle was to be a Great Chamberlain and Earl of Coventrie; Thomas Wriothesley was to be the Earl of Winchester, and others were to have titles and positions, as indicated by Paget.[273]

On the day that Henry was buried, the persons thus honoured by him were invested in their titles by the new King: the Earl of Hertford chose the title of Duke of Somerset, and was with that title invested; Viscount Lisle decided to be called the Earl of Warwick instead of the Earl of Coventry, and with that title was invested, and Thomas Wriothesley chose to be called the Earl, not of Winchester, but of Southampton,[274] which title, I believe, he had long coveted, persuading the King to withhold it from others until such time as it might be conferred, as now finally it was, upon him.

Obviously, busy days lay ahead for the Lord Chancellor, now Earl of Southampton. On 18 February 1547, as he had before with the King's consent, he again, but this time of his own motion, without royal consent, issued a commission to others to hear all manner of cases during his absence from the Court of Chancery, and to give decrees, the same as he, the Lord Chancellor might, provided that they were ratified by his signature. This delegation of authority came to the attention of Somerset, who referred the matter to the judiciary for their determination of its propriety. The Judges, "anticipating his [Wriothesley's] downfall,"[275] concluded that the Chancellor's delegation was invalid, having been made without royal authority, and that the Chancellor was therefore guilty of an offence against the King, which, at common law, was punishable with loss of office, fine and imprisonment. On the basis of this advisory opinion by the Judges, the Council debated what to do about Wriothesley. William Paget, who in earlier years had addressed Wriothesley as "my most special good friend,"[276] now was of the opinion that the Great Seal could not be permitted to remain in Wriothesley's "stout and arrogant hands,"[277] and Wriothesley's colleagues generally at this stage of his career seem to have found his personality grating.[278] A motion was made to deprive him of his office, fine and imprison him. Wriothesley "spoke boldly and ably in his defence," arguing that the delegation was justified by precedent, and that in any event, if the delegation were not valid, he was prepared to perform himself all the duties of his office. The Council decided against him, and Wriothesley, fearing the possible consequences of resisting, submitted to their will. On 6 March 1547, the red velvet bag with royal arms ("*baga de velveto rubio insigniis regiis ornat*") was taken from the

Earl of Southampton by Lord Seymour of Sudeley, Sir Anthony Browne and Sir Edward North, and Wriothesley was removed from the Council.[279] But Wriothesley was not fined or sent to prison, and lived quietly, probably mostly at Titchfield. It may be during this period of time that the coat of arms of the town of Southampton was carved on the doorway of his manor.

When Somerset received the Great Seal, he is supposed to have said "I am at last Lord Protector."[280] One of the first things he did with the Great Seal (on 12 March 1547) was to affix it to letters patent formally setting aside the King's will and conferring upon himself the whole authority of the Crown, and appointing a new Council.[281] This was merely the first of many actions by which he alienated the other members of the Council, and set the stage for his eventual fall.

The Council was not particularly disturbed, however, by Somerset's continued drift toward Protestantism, evidenced by many actions, including the imprisonment of Bishop Gardiner, who refused to concede the power of the Council to make any changes in the State religion during the minority of Edward VI.[282]

By the beginning of January 1549, in some way that "has never really been explained,"[283] Wriothesley reappears as a member of the Council. Wriothesley immediately was involved in the investigation of the charges against Somerset's brother, Lord Seymour of Sudeley. The charges against Seymour (who had married Catherine Parr after Henry's death) were that he had misused his position as Lord High Admiral to wink at and work with pirates, to take bribes from them, and to circumvent justice in the admiralty courts. He was also accused of having persuaded an official to provide him with money from the Mint at Bristol. The misallocation of funds was detected in January, 1549, and Seymour's involvement was soon suspected.[284] Leading the investigation against the Lord High Admiral were Warwick, Southampton, and Richard Rich, who was Southampton's successor as Lord Chancellor.[285] The Council — with Somerset excused from participation — decided upon a bill of attainder, which was duly enacted by the Parliament. Seymour was beheaded on Tower Hill on 20 March 1549.[286]

Having disposed of the brother, Warwick and Southampton now aimed at the Protector. Before taking on Somerset, however, Warwick went to Norfolk where his suppression of a peasant rebellion led by William Ket made him a hero of the class who had profited from the activities which sparked the rebellion.[287] His prestige thus enhanced, he joined with Southampton in an assault upon the Protector. In October, 1549, the Councillors assembled in Holborn (whether at Southampton's house or Warwicks's house is not clear[288]), and, professing to act under the powers conferred upon them as

Executors of the King's Will, stated that they were assuming the functions of Government.[289] Somerset's response to this was to take the young King to Windsor where, joined by Paget and Cranmer, he called upon the people of England for support against the usurping Council.[290] But that support was not forthcoming, and on 9 October 1549, as a consequence of negotiations conducted by letter between Warwick and Southampton of the Council in London and Paget with the King in Windsor, Somerset surrendered. The next day, he was arrested, and on 14 October, was sent to the Tower.[291]

With the imprisonment of his enemy, Wriothesley now appeared to have triumphed:

Wriothesley that before was banished the court, is lodged with his wife and sonne next to the king. Every man repaireth to Wriothesley, honourable Wriothesley, sueth unto Wriothesley (as the Assirians did to Ammon [Haman]) and all thinges be done by his advise; and who but Wriothesley?[292]

Wriothesley and other members of the Council frequently visited the Tower, to examine Somerset on various charges of mismanagement of the realm. According to a contemporary account of events in the Council of Regency, Somerset steadfastly denied any wrong-doing, and insisted that everything he had done had been by the advice, consent and counsel of the Earl of Warwick. So far as Wriothesley was concerned, this defence did not exculpate Somerset, but rather indicted Warwick: "I thoughte ever we sholde fynde them traytors both; and both is worthie to dye for by my advyse," a sentiment with which the Earl of Arundel agreed.[293]

Word of this got back to Warwick, who apparently decided that his own life depended upon the preservation of Somerset's life, and the restriction of Southampton's power. At a meeting of the Counsel at Warwick's house in Holborn, Wriothesley "begaine to declaire how worthie the lord protector was to dye and for how many high treasons," at which the Earl of Warwick, to forestall a like condemnation of himself, "with a warlyke uisage and a long fachell [falchion?] by his syde, laye his hand thereof and said: my lord you seeke his bloude and he that seekethe his bloude wold haue myne also."[294] Warwick prevailed: Somerset was released from the Tower; William Paulet, the person who had warned Warwick of the designs of the Earls of Southampton and Arundel, was created Earl of Wiltshire, and Southampton and Arundel were ordered to confine themselves to their London houses.[295]

Thus Warwick, who had seemed to be a supporter of the old religion, fell into the camp of those who sought reform. Gardiner, who opposed further reform for the moment, remained in prison. Wriothesley again became ill, and after October, 1549, ceased to attend the Council.[296] Paget, now a firm supporter of Warwick, was in December, 1549 rewarded for his services in securing Somerset's submission by being created Baron Paget of Beaudesert.[297]

Wriothesley was expelled from the Council on 2 February 1550.[298] In early March he was "dangerously ill";[299] by the middle of March, he was better, but regretted it, "desiring to be under the earth rather than upon it."[300] On 30 July 1550, not having yet reached the age of 45, he died at his home, Southampton House in Holborn.[301] It has been suggested that he took poison to avoid a worse fate,[302] but this seems unlikely.

When George Blagge, the almost-roasted pig, and friend to the Earl of Surrey, learned of Wriothesley's death, he penned (but did not publish) an epitaph:

> From vile estate, of base and low degree,
>   By false deceit, by craft, and subtle ways;
> Of mischief mould, and key of cruelty
>   Was crept full high, borne up by sundry stayes.
> Picture of pride; of papist the plat:
>   In whom Treason, as in a throne did sit;
> With ireful eye, aye glearing like a cat,
>   Killing by spight whom he thought good to hit.
> This dog is dead; his soul is down to hell,
>   The carrion corpse within the ground is laid,
> Whose festred flesh above the earth did smell,
>   Plagued with pocks; so was this wretch arrayed.[303]

Wriothesley's will is dated 21 July 1550, with a few codicils added on 23 and 24 July.[304] From its provisions, we learn much about his family and household as constituted at the end of his life.

In his will, Wriothesley mentions three sisters: Laurence, Pounde and Breton.[305] These obviously are the surnames of his sisters' husbands.[306] "Laurence" was Anne, the widow of Thomas Knight; her second husband was "the king's servant",[307] Sir Oliver Laurence of Hertingfordbury.[308]

Wriothesley's sister "Pounde," whose first name appears to have been Ellen, or perhaps Eleanor, was the wife of William Pounde, one of the three children of William Pounde of Beamondes, or Beaumonds (also sometimes written as Belmont), Farlington, in Hampshire;[309] the other two children were Katharine and Anthony.[310] William and Ellen had at least two sons, Thomas Pounde, born 29 May 1539, and Henry Pounde.[311] Thomas Pounde in his earlier years cut quite a figure at court, and was a writer of masks,[312] one of which he wrote, along with an oration, for the wedding on 19 February 1565/6 of his first cousin, Henry Wriothesley, second Earl of Southampton, to Mary Browne, daughter of Anthony Browne, first Viscount Montagu.[313] The mask was "all on great horses"; the oration consisted of 87 verses, which Charlotte Carmichael Stopes, in her biography of the third Earl of Southampton, characterized as "too inferior to reproduce."[314]

A few months later (on 1 July 1566) another mask was presented by Pounde at the wedding of the sister of Thomas Radcliffe, third Earl of Sussex, to Thomas Mildmay.[315] The third Earl of Sussex, as we have seen, was connected with the Wriothesley family, the Earl's first wife having been Thomas Wriothesley's daughter, Elizabeth, who died in January 1554/5.[316] Of Pounde's verses for this mask, Chambers states that "they are of no merit."[317] Queen Elizabeth was present at both of these weddings,[318] and revenge for the imposition upon her of Pounde's lengthy and tedious compositions may be the subconscious reason for the cruel action which ended Pounde's career of courtly masking.

On an occasion in 1569, as Pounde, apparently an accomplished athlete, was dancing before Queen Elizabeth, he twice failed in attempting to execute a whirling manoeuvre; "the Queen showed her gentle manners by kicking him as he lay dazed on the ground, exclaiming, 'Arise, Sir Ox.'" This event so mortified him that he turned his attention to religious matters. He was for the rest of his life in some vague way affiliated with the Jesuits, having at times dealings with Robert Southwell and Edmund Campion, and although he suffered many imprisonments, he lived to be 76 years old, and died (on 5 March 1615) in the same room in which he had been born.[319]

Before leaving Wriothesley's sister Ellen Pounde, we return briefly to Katharine and Anthony Pound, the sister and brother of Ellen's husband William. Katharine Pounde married one John White of Hampshire,[320] with whom, as we shall see in Appendix II, Wriothesley had many contacts. Thus White, who has been referred to as Wriothesley's "mean, fawning servant"[321] was actually Wriothesley's mean, fawning brother-in-law. This probably explains Wriothesley's securing for him the grant of Southwick Abbey. Surprisingly, the relationship of White to the Wriothesleys was unknown to Muriel St. Clare Byrne, for in commenting upon White's long letter of gratitude[322] to Wriothesley for securing the grant to him of Southwick Abbey, she writes:

Who would have thought that Mr. Wriothesley, the rising and ruthless young Tudor careerist, whose hard-thrusting drive for eminence is implicit in every stroke of his pen, would have been the kind of man whom his servant would have thought to be interested in knowing what a success 'Mrs. Elyne,' Whyte's sister-in-law, had been in the neighbourhood? He took her and his 'brother' William Pound with him to Southwick when he went to take over the Priory and its goods and to settle his own family in a house provided by Wriothesley, for which he thanks him ecstatically. This is the thing he has desired all his life — 'an honest house' to which he can welcome his friends, thanks to God and Mr. Wriothesley. He then proceeds to Mrs. Elyne's achievements. . . .[323]

But that "Mrs. Elyne" was Thomas Wriothesley's sister makes clear the calculation in White's letter.

Anthony Pounde, Ellen's brother-in-law, married Anne, daughter of Lewis Wyngfield; their daughter Honor, as we have seen, married Henry Radcliffe, fourth Earl of Sussex (whose brother Thomas, the third Earl of Sussex, had married Thomas Wriothesley's daughter Elizabeth). After Anthony Pounde died, his widow Anne married John White, left a widower by the death of his wife Katharine.[324]

Exactly to whom Wriothesley's sister "Breton" (probably Elizabeth) was married is not clear. I suggest that her husband was one of the brothers of William Breton, who lived in a fine house ("my chieff capital mansion house") in Red Cross Street in Cripplegate,[325] and was thus a neighbour of Elizabeth's uncle, Thomas, whose "Garter House," it will be remembered, was also on Red Cross Street in Cripplegate. It was in his uncle Thomas' house that the Thomas of our story was born, and that he and his sisters might often have visited, or even lived, in their uncle's fine house on Red Cross Street, and that one of the girls might have married the boy next door — or the brother of the boy next door — is a reasonable surmise. William Breton himself must be ruled out as the possible spouse for Elizabeth Wriothesley because we know that he was married to Elizabeth Bacon, and by her was the father of Nicholas Breton, "one of the best of the popular Elizabethan writers of miscellaneous prose."[326] And we know that William's brother Henry was married to Anne Cowlte.[327] This leaves William's three remaining brothers, John, Francis and Thomas, as possible husbands to Wriothesley's sister "Breton."

The brother whom I believe most likely to have been Elizabeth's husband is Francis, who may have been ill or otherwise the victim of bad luck, for William in his will specifically requests his executors to be attentive to "the ayde and helpe of my poo^r brother ffraunces Breton for the mayntennce and continuance of his lyvinge." Francis Breton's situation as suggested in William Breton's will matches the evidently straitened circumstances of the

"Breton" brother-in-law of Thomas Wriothesley, who in his will makes specific provision for the educations of "Breton" and "Larke," then at Winchester and Oxford.[328] If, as seems obvious, this Breton at Winchester is the son of Wriothesley's sister, then he is the only one of Wriothesley's nephews or nieces to receive a bequest, which would seem to reflect his parents' need. (Also, the existence of this young Breton supports the conclusion that the husband of Wriothesley's sister, if he was indeed one of William Breton's brothers, was Francis, for neither John nor Thomas had issue.[329] But who is Larke; could he be a relative of the Larke who was executed along with Germain Gardiner?)

Reinforcing the likelihood of a close connection between the Wriothesley and Breton families is the discovery by Fitzgerald Flournoy that William Breton made his money by acquiring confiscated church properties and then quickly reselling them. Flournoy noted that to engage in this speculative activity, "Breton must have had political pull."[330] Who could have been in a better position to aid Breton in his acquisition of church properties than Thomas Wriothesley, who having helped his brothers-in-law White and Knight to secure such lands, would certainly find ways to help also his brother-in-law Breton?

Another indication that the "Breton" whom Wriothesley's sister had married was one of the brothers of William Breton of Red Cross Street is that, after William Breton died in 1558, his widow Anne married George Gascoigne, the playwright[331] (although she seems first to have entered into an invalid or subsequently annulled marriage with one Edward Boyes[332]). In 1572, Gascoigne wrote the "Maske for the right honourable Viscount Mountacute" which linked the Montagu's of England with the Montagu's of Italy. The occasion for the mask, it will be remembered, was the marriage of Anthony and Elizabeth Browne to Mary and Robert Dormer. Anthony was the brother and Elizabeth the half-sister of Mary Browne, the wife of the second Earl of Southampton. It may be that the eight Gentlemen ("all of blood or alliaunce to the sayd L. Mountacute") who entreated Gascoigne to write his mask on a Venetian subject knew or were able to approach him through the woman who was both the second Earl of Southampton's aunt and George Gascoigne's sister-in law. However, it must be acknowledged that since Elizabethans were related to each other in so many different ways, an approach from Montagu to Gascoigne could have been made through a number of familial channels. Margaret Fitzwilliam, for instance, the sister of William Fitzwilliam, Earl of Southampton and half-sister of Sir Anthony Browne, the first Viscount Montagu's father, married Sir William Gascoigne who was, as shown on Table III, a distant cousin of George Gascoigne. The relationship between Gascoigne and the first Viscount Montagu, either through Wriothesley's sister or Gascoigne's cousin, would explain the otherwise mysterious election of Gascoigne as a member of parliament for Midhurst,[333] the district which included Montagu's home at Cowdray.

A final scintilla of evidence pointing to Wriothesley's sister having married Francis Breton is that, as shown on Table I, Wriothesley's niece Anne, the daughter of Wriothesley's sister Ellen Pounde, married one George Breton.[334] Henry Breton, one of the brothers of Francis Breton, had a son named George.[335] I have no evidence that the George Breton whom Anne married was the son of the Henry Breton who was the brother of Francis Breton: but it was very common in Tudor times, once families became allied by one marriage, for additional marriages to take place between members of the families, and what few facts we possess are consistent with this having occurred here.

These possible links between the Breton and Wriothesley families may provide a clue to the inception of Thomas Wriothesley's contacts with and interests in Hampshire. William Breton's will makes numerous references to William Capon: Breton leaves twenty pounds to St. Bartholomew's Hospital in Smithfield on the condition that the poor and the children "do pray euy morning and euy evening unto allmightie god for Mr Willm Capon and me as benefactors of the saied hospital"; Breton leaves to be "dystributed to and amongest the poorest people in the town of Salcote in the Countie of Essex wher the foresaied Willm Capon was borne fyve pounds to praye for the saied Willm Capon"; Breton leaves money to the town of Salcote to repair the highways and bridges "for the saied Willm Capon and in the Remembrance of me"; Breton leaves five pounds to be distributed for William Capon "to and amongest the poo^r of his Late paryshe and benefyce in Southam in the countie of Southehampton" and many other bequests of varying sums of money to the poor of many other localities "to thintent that all thafforsaied poo^r people shall praye for the sayed M^r docto^r Capon."

The William Capon so frequently mentioned in Breton's will had been a chaplain to Cardinal Wolsey, and the first dean of Wolsey's short-lived college at Ipswich.[336] He was also the brother of John Capon,[337] to whom Wriothesley, in his earliest trip to Southampton County of which we have any record, had personally delivered notification of his (Capon's) nomination to be Bishop of Bangor.[338] Thus it may have been because of his connection with the Bretons that Wriothesley established himself in the County, or the Town, or the County of the Town, whose honour one day he was to bear.

Wriothesley's will mentions and makes bequests to five daughters: Elizabeth, Mary, Katherine, Mabel and Anne.[339] Elizabeth married Thomas

Radcliffe, Lord Fitzwater, afterwards Earl of Sussex, and died in 1555;[340] Mary married one Richard Lyster and, after his death, William Shelley of Michelgrove, and died in 1561;[341] Katherine was engaged to marry one Matthew Arundell, but ultimately married Thomas Cornwallis, groom-porter to Queen Elizabeth;[342] Mabel married Sir Walter Sandys,[343] and Anne was contracted to marry one Henry Wallop, which marriage did not take place, apparently because of the death either of the prospective bride or of the prospective groom.[344]

Other people who must have been close to Wriothesley are mentioned in his will: Anne, the sister of Wriothesley's wife Jane; Anthony Rush; Sir Richard Southwell, and five cousins — Cukar (Coker?), Cutler, John Hungarford (so spelled in the will), Charles Wriothesley and, tantalizingly, one "Hemminges," otherwise unidentified, to whom Wriothesley gave 10 pounds.

The children of Henry VIII were not forgotten: to "my most gratious soveraigne lorde the kinges majestie," Wriothesley left his collar of the Garter, his gilt basin and ewer, his six gilt candlesticks, and his great gilt "wreathen pottys," beseeching God "to send him his grace, with health of bodye, till he be as olde a kinge as ever anie of his noble progenitors." In addition, "for the greate benefyttes that I haue receaved at his most noble father of famouse memory, the late Kinge Henry the eight," Wriothesley assigned to the King, during the "minoritie and nonage of my sonne," the rents and proceeds from a substantial portion of his estates and manors. To Princess Mary, Wriothesley bequeathed his best gilt standing cup; to Princess Elizabeth, his second best gilt standing cup.

To his "good Lord and brother th'erle of Sussex," Wriothesley left a gilt cup of the value of 10 pounds, and to his "assured friend," Sir William Herbert, he left his Garters and Georges, insignias of his being a Knight of the Garter.

Of great interest are Wriothesley's bequests to his colleagues at court, bequests for which the story we have just traced does not prepare us: Leland, Paget and Gardiner, the friends of Wriothesley's youth, are not mentioned in the will, but to the Earl of Warwick, who seems to have been Wriothesley's worst enemy during the last nine months of his life, Wriothesley, in this will written nine days before his death, bequeathes a gilt cup of the value of 20 pounds, and to the Countess of Warwick, a gilt cup of the value of ten pounds. Identical bequests are made to the Earl of Arundel (and his wife) who, according to accounts of Wriothesley's fall, sided with Wriothesley against Warwick, and, like Wriothesley, was put under house arrest by Warwick. This suggests either that the accounts of the enmity between Warwick and Southampton were incorrect or — more likely — that in that curious period of swiftly-shifting alliances, the former adversaries were now partners. The sermon at Wriothesley's funeral was preached by Bishop Hooper, of the reforming party, and this has been interpreted[345] to indicate that, in the end, Wriothesley went along with the tide of religious reform (although it might equally indicate that the funeral arrangements were made by Warwick, who was a friend of Bishop Hooper, without reference to the persuasions of the deceased; were this so, Wriothesley's funeral would not have been the first — and certainly not the last — where the religious views of those officiating were not consonant with those of the guest of honour).

Other bequests were made to Wriothesley's servants and retainers, and to the poor people of Titchfield and Fareham, and other places where Wriothesley owned land. Generous provision was made for Wriothesley's wife. All that was left — the great bulk of Wriothesley's vast estates — would go, upon his majority, to Thomas' son, Henry.[346] Wriothesley named as his executors his wife, his cousin Sir Edmund Peckham, Sir Thomas Pope, Treasurer of the Court of Augmentations, and two others, William Samford and William Pye, to each of whom were given, "for their faithefull paines to be taken herein," forty pounds; Sir William Petre was named "overseer," and he received a basin and a ewer.

Wriothesley's will contained no specific instructions with respect to his interment. He was buried on 3 August 1550 at St. Andrew's, Holborn, whence his body was some 40 years later removed to the great monument constructed pursuant to his son's will at the church in Titchfield.[347]

Gardiner was released from the Tower in 1553, upon the accession of Mary to the throne, and was by her made Lord Chancellor, an office he occupied until his death on 12 November 1555.[348] He is buried in Winchester Cathedral. Paget, who had supported first Somerset (and was rewarded by the grant of the mansion on the Strand which after serving a term as Paget House afterwards became Leicester House and finally Essex House) and subsequently switched to Warwick (and was rewarded by being created Lord Paget of Beaudesert), later was to support first the succession to the throne of Lady Jane Grey, and then, a month later, of Mary, during whose reign he was a member of the Privy Council. Somehow in these twists and turns avoiding the axe, he died in bed on 9 June 1563.[349] Leland, by royal commission, spent many years traveling through England, cataloguing the libraries of the cathedrals, colleges and monasteries he encountered.[350] "At length his antiquarian studies overtaxed his brain and he became incurably insane."[351] He died on 18 April 1552,[352] taking to the grave the memory of a golden haired youth and his two friends, at Cambridge together, acting in a Latin comedy.

❦

This review of Thomas Wriothesley's life, altogether too long, no doubt, for the purposes of this book, is altogether too short for the purpose of arriving at a just estimate of his place in history. A. F. Pollard, in the entry for Wriothesley in the *Dictionary of National Biography*, finds in his actions a lack of principle, noting that under Cromwell, Wriothesley was an enemy to bishops, and a patron of reformers, but after Cromwell fell and Henry adopted a more conservative policy, so did Wriothesley; and also that Wriothesley both racked Anne Askew, a follower of the new faith, and assisted in the ruin of the Howards, followers of the old faith. On the basis of such seemingly inconsistent actions, Pollard concludes that "it is difficult to trace in Southampton's career any motive beyond that of self-aggrandise-ment."

Pollard, I think, was wrong. The key to the understanding of Thomas Wriothesley is not that he had convictions which he changed when it was convenient to do so, but rather that, from the time he first came into personal contact with the King until the time of the King's death, he was guided by one conviction only: that it was his duty to realize the King's will. Cromwell's fall did not change Wriothesley's views: Wriothesley agreed with Cromwell so long as the King was pleased with Cromwell; when the King ceased to be pleased with Cromwell, Wriothesley, without a second thought, set in motion the processes leading to Cromwell's death. Wriothesley did not rack Anne Askew because he was against Protestants, or bring about the fall of the Howards because he was against Catholics; he accomplished each solely because each was what the King desired. Nor did Wriothesley come to arrest Catherine Parr because he wanted to prevent the spread of the new religion; he came to arrest her because that is what, at the time he was ordered so to do, the King wanted, and Wriothesley was unhesitatingly prepared, for that reason, and that reason alone, to get rid of Catherine Parr, as he had previously, because the King so desired, gotten rid, or helped to get rid, of Catherine of Aragon, Anne Boleyn, Anne of Cleves and Catherine Howard. (And, of course, he had in Wolsey and Cromwell — of whom he had also helped to rid the King — vivid examples of what happened to those King's ministers who did not accomplish the King's wish, however whimsical or irrational that wish might be.) Wriothesley's actions do not reveal an inconstancy in his own political or religious beliefs, but rather a constancy to a more fundamental and important creed, that it was his particular duty to do the King's bidding. This creed is best expressed in a letter nominally written by the King to one of his ambassadors. The letter is in Wriothesley's hand,

and the actual wording is probably more Wriothesley's than the King's: the ambassador, the letter says, is to throw aside all timorousness and despair, of which he shows signs in his letters, and keep "as a thing contynually lyeng befor your eyes and incessantley sowned in your eares, the justice of our cause. . . ."[353] Wriothesley never doubted the justice of the King's cause, whatever it was, and no timidity or despair impeded his doing what he could to secure the King's ends.

Had devotion such as this been placed in the service of a King Arthur, Wriothesley, who had so many fine qualities, might have been a Lancelot, and his name, for his deeds, revered; unfortunately, the monarch who had the benefit of Wriothesley's single-minded devotion was one of the most monstrous persons ever to be suffered to wield a sceptre.

C. Poets and Players

An aspect of Wriothesley's life not emphasized in the foregoing account, but one of great interest from the point of view of this book, is his complete immersion in the cultural and artistic life of his time, and his friendship, or at least acquaintance, with most contemporary writers and playwrights.

As we have seen, the young Thomas went to St. Paul's School in London, where a fellow-student was John Leland, who became the friend of most of the literary figures of his day. This school was founded in 1508 or 1510 by John Colet, the great renaissance scholar and friend of Erasmus and Sir Thomas More; it was funded by money which Colet had inherited from his father, and its 153 scholars paid no tuition.[354] Not only were the works of the Latin and Greek dramatists studied at St. Paul's,[355] but they were also acted by the students in municipal halls, the residences of great lords, and at court.[356] A play by Plautus presented in the Great Chamber at Greenwich in 1519 was probably performed by the St. Paul's boys, under the direction of John Rightwise (or Ritwise), the scholarly son-in-law of the even more scholarly first High-master of St. Paul's, William Lily.[357] It is quite possible that Wriothesley, who would have been 14 at the time, acted with the St. Paul's group in this and other Latin plays.[358] The experience thus gained probably accounts for his appearance and success in the Cambridge production of *Miles Gloriosus* in about 1522, when he was seventeen.

Two years later, Wriothesley was at court, having followed thither his friend and mentor from Cambridge, Stephen Gardiner, of whose retinue of young men at Winchester House — the home of eloquence and the muses, as Leland called it — he was for a while a member. There, unless things have changed in the last 470 years, the conversation must have been not only of philosophy and religion, and the scientific discoveries which were then being made, but also of contemporary books, poetry, music and plays — and of persons who wrote or performed them.

At the court, around which his existence revolved for the next 25 years, Wriothesley had ample opportunity to enjoy the arts, and particularly to attend the frequently-presented plays, masks and interludes[359] "which were the delight of Tudor Englishmen of every class."[360] He was, moreover, a friend of those who wrote the plays, most particularly Nicholas Udall, who was from Titchfield, and who apparently lived for a while at Wriothesley's home in Titchfield, and John Heywood, who with Wriothesley's brother-in-law, Germain Gardiner, plotted against Cranmer, and only narrowly (perhaps as a consequence of Wriothesley's intervention) escaped sharing Germain Gardiner's gruesome fate. He must also have known John Bale, who was a friend not only of John Leland,[361] but also of Erasmus, Thomas Cranmer, Cromwell and William Capon.[362]

These three persons, Udall, Heywood and Bale are the best known and most important of the dramatists of the reign of Henry VIII.[363] Their plays are generally referred to as interludes, for although "they characterize the movement away from medieval drama towards that of the later Elizabethans,"[364] they are still nearer to the old style than to the new.

Udall, or Uvedale, born in the same year as Thomas Wriothesley, was of an old Hampshire family.[365] He was a good friend of John Leland and with him had written verses for the entry of Anne Boleyn into London after her marriage to Henry VIII.[366] Udall's play *Ralph Roister Doister* is the earliest known comedy written in English. This play has its source in Plautus' *Miles Gloriosus*,[367] and it is not inconceivable either that Udall had been with his friend John Leland when Leland saw Wriothesley in the Latin play, and like him had been impressed by the production, or that Leland had brought the play, and its susceptibility to treatment in English, to Udall's attention.

In March 1541, Udall, who was then a headmaster at Eton, was by the Privy Council (of which Wriothesley was a member) sent to the Marshalsea Prison. The usually-reported reason for his imprisonment is his confession, as recorded in the Privy Council register, that "he did commit buggery" with Thomas Cheney, "late scolar of Eton."[368]

Some time thereafter, Udall wrote a long "Letter of Remorse" to "right Worshipfull and My Singular Good Master," thanking him for his "travail, pains and trouble" in attempting Udall's "restitution to the room of schoolmaster in Eton."[369] It is generally thought that the person to whom this letter was addressed was Thomas Wriothesley (whose wife, Jane Cheney, might well have been a relative of the Thomas Cheney who engaged in the offense with Udall). If the letter was indeed written to Wriothesley, it would reflect a close relationship between the two, disrupted but not necessarily interrupted by the offense for which Udall was imprisoned. Although Udall was not restored to his position at Eton, his career did not suffer seriously as a result of this incident. William Edgerton, in his biography of Udall, accounts for Udall's rapid rehabilitation on the ground that it had been *burglary*, rather than *buggery*, of which Udall and Cheney had really been convicted, the latter word having been erroneously written in or deciphered from the Privy Council register.[370] This, of course, is possible, but it is equally possible that the lenient treatment accorded Udall is merely an example of the accepting humanist attitude toward sexual relations among men which is a subject of Chapter VI.

John Heywood (who married the daughter of Sir Thomas More's sister, and whose own daughter was the mother of John Donne[371]), wrote six plays: *The Pardoner and the Friar*, *The Play of Love*, *The Play of the Weather*, *Witty and Witless*, *The Four P's*, and *John, Tyb and Sir John*. Although Heywood lived until about 1578 (spending his last years on the Continent, for he left England when Elizabeth came to the throne),[372] most of his dramatic work appears to date from the 1520's and 1530's.[373] Heywood also wrote a number of poems.

John Bale has been described as "the playwright-propagandist of the Cromwellian era," whose plays were designed to further Cromwell's "campaign to separate the English church from Rome, to destroy images, and to free the church of superstitions."[374] After Cromwell's execution in 1540, Bale left England, not to return until 1547. Among his plays, written prior to 1540, are *God's Promises*, *John Baptist*, *Temptation* and *Three Laws*. His *King Johan*, which may (or may not) have been a source for Shakespeare's *King John*, was probably also written by 1540.[375]

In addition to these makers of plays, or interludes, Wriothesley knew, as we have seen, the two most illustrious poets of his day, both of whom vie for the honour of having introduced the Sonnet into English literature: Sir Thomas Wyatt, to whom Wriothesley was a friend,[376] and Henry Howard, the Earl of Surrey, whose death Wriothesley effectuated.

Wriothesley was not at a loss for theatrical entertainments during the brief periods of his life when he was at Titchfield, for he had in his manor a room set aside for the presentation of plays.[377] That plays and masks were in fact a diversion at the Wriothesley home is reflected by Anthony Rook's letter to Wriothesley, assuring him that his wife is in good health, "and every night merry as can be with Christmas plays and masks with Anthony Gedge [Gage] and other your servants."[378]

Much as Wriothesley shared the Englishman's passion for the theatre, he did not, unlike so many of his contemporaries,[379] give his patronage to a company of actors. However, as we have seen, his son and daughter were each married to members of the family of the Earls of Sussex, which family did support a group of actors, with whom, as suggested in Chapter VIII, Shakespeare may at one time have been associated.

One is tempted to look for other possible links between people in Thomas Wriothesley's circle and the glover's son who was not born until 14 years after Wriothesley's death. Could the "cossen Hemminges" who received a bequest of ten pounds in Wriothesley's will be the father, or at least a relative, of that John Hemynges (this is the spelling used in Shakespeare's will) who was a fellow actor with Shakespeare in the Lord Chamberlain's company and who, along with Henry Condell, was the compiler and editor of the First Folio edition of Shakespeare's plays? About the ancestry of John Hemynges, almost nothing is known.[380] In 1847, one William Tyson found in the archives of the municipal corporation of Bristol an entry showing a payment in 1543 of five shillings "to M^r. henings players," and surmised that this might be a misspelled reference to an actor who could have been the father of John Hemynges.[381] This same person could also have been, of course, the legatee of Thomas Wriothesley; much would be explained if the John Hemynges who had so close a professional relationship with Shakespeare was of a family which had close ties with the Wriothesleys. (A possibility which cannot be ruled out, however, is that "Hemminges" is a mistransliteration in the printed text of the will of the name of "Hunnings." William Hunnings, or Hunnynge, or Honing, was a clerk of the Signet in the reigns of Henry VIII and Edward VI, a position he may have attained as a consequence of his marriage to Wriothesley's cousin Frances Cutler (see Table I). His father was Roger Hunning, described in his epitaph as "fishmonger, sometime porueyor of seafish to our Souereigne Lord King Henry the Eight"[382] — a good example of Tudor social mobility.)

Sir Thomas Pope, Treasurer of the Court of Augmentations, and one of the Executors of Wriothesley's will, probably was not a direct ancestor of the Thomas Pope who was a fellow actor of Shakespeare's, and whose name is "enshrined in that leaf of the great First Folio which enumerates the principal actors of Shakespeare's plays during his lifetime,"[383] because Sir Thomas Pope, the founder of Trinity College, Oxford (from which Cuffe was expelled for his disrespect to the memory of the founder), is not known to have had issue.[384] Nevertheless, the fact that Thomas Pope the actor, when applying to the College of Arms for a coat of arms, claimed a right to bear the arms of Sir Thomas Pope of the Court of Augmentations,[385] suggests that there may have been some family connection between the two, even though the heralds apparently did not grant the player the arms he claimed.

Sir William Herbert, to whom Thomas Wriothesley left his Garters and Georges, and who purchased the wardship[386] of Thomas' five year old son Henry (the second Earl of Southampton), was the grandfather[387] (if we discount Aubrey's suggestion that Sir Philip Sidney was the father of one of them) of William and Philip Herbert, Earls of Pembroke and of Montgomery, respectively, the "incomparable paire of brethren" to whom John Hemynges and Henry Condell dedicated the First Folio.

Whatever the connections between the world of Thomas Wriothesley and the world of William Shakespeare might have been, the links between Wriothesley and the world of arts in general are evident. The idea that in the 16th century the people active in the arts, including the writing and performing of music and plays, were separated by a social gulf from the aristocracy is a fiction, for, as the life of Thomas Wriothesley illustrates, the sons of the bureaucrats and bourgeoisie who in the early years of the century went to schools such as St. Paul's, and were prepared for their roles in life by studying Greek and Latin literature, and singing in choirs and acting in plays, became the aristocrats of the middle and late Tudor periods, and the impetus and audience of the English literary, musical and theatrical renaissance. These people, who appreciated the arts, did not despise those who made their livelihood in the arts, but to the contrary, with their friendship and patronage cherished and aided those who, regardless of their background, demonstrated literary or musical talents. As Leicester House and Essex House prove, Tudor nobles did not consider Tudor writers unworthy of their company.

Titchfield (or Place) House

Titchfield is a small town on the Meon River, about eight miles east of Southampton, near Fareham. Hundreds of flint tools from the paleolithic period, and some axes and sickles from the neolithic period, have been found in its general area.[1] The Jutes who after the departure of the Romans settled there and elsewhere in the Meon Valley called themselves Meonware (or Meonwara).[2] They were converted to Christianity by the end of the seventh century,[3] at which time still existing portions of the Parish Church of St. Peter in Titchfield may have been built.[4] The first written reference to the town is in 982, in a Charter of King Ethelred the Unready. The next reference to it is in 1086, in the Domesday Book.[5]

In 1222, Peter des Roches, Bishop of Winchester, who had great influence with Henry III, and was active in establishing religious houses throughout England, invited a number of Premonstratensians from the Abbey of Halesowen in Shropshire to establish a colony in Titchfield. The Premonstratensian Order, an off-shoot of the Augustinian, had been founded in 1120 by St. Norbert, Archbishop of Magdeburg, to whom the Blessed Virgin Mary had appeared, showing the exact place where a convent should be established: a green field in the depths of the forest of Coucy, near Laon. The green meadow thus pointed out was the *pré montré*, or *pratum premonstratum*, which gave the Order its name. The dress of the Premonstratensian canons was entirely white, consisting of a cassock with a rochet (similar to a surplice) over it, a long cloak over all, and a cap. Because of this, the members of the Order were usually called White Canons.[6]

The Premonstratensian Abbey founded in Titchfield was called the Abbey of St. Mary. Its charter, endowing it with many properties, was confirmed by Henry III in 1231.[7] The abbey was constructed soon thereafter.[8]

The first Abbot, Richard of Halesowen, died in 1232, and is buried on the Abbey grounds near the door to what was the Chapter House. Several of his successors are also buried on the grounds of the Abbey.[9]

Little disturbed the tranquility of the Abbey during the three hundred years of its existence. Richard II and Anne of Bohemia were entertained there in 1393, Henry V may have stayed there in 1415, before departing from Southampton for his expedition against the French, and it was either there or at Southwick Abbey that Henry VI in 1445 married Margaret of Anjou.[10]

In 1536, the statute providing for the suppression of monasteries with a net income of less than £200 was enacted. Titchfield Abbey, of which Thomas Wriothesley was then Chief Steward, was not within the purview of the statute,[11] but this did not preclude the "voluntary" surrender of the monastery,[12] and on 18 December 1537, the Abbot, who had but recently assumed his position, and was probably appointed just for the purpose, surrendered the Abbey to the King's Commissioners, John Crayford (sometimes written Crawford) and Roland Lathom (sometimes written Lathum or Laythum).[13] The property was apparently from the very beginning destined for Wriothesley, for only two days after its surrender, Wriothesley's friend Paget, "wet and weary," arrived at Titchfield with two letters from Wriothesley for Crayford and Lathom. The letters dealt, we may assume, with Wriothesley's plans for converting the Abbey into a manor — a project about which Wriothesley must have been very excited, for Lathom had already received from Wriothesley two letters sent after Paget had been dispatched.[14] Upon his arrival at Titchfield, Paget "surveyed things," and then carried back to Wriothesley Crayford and Lathom's assessment of the state of the place ("the church is most naked and barren, being of such antiquity . . . the lands are very ruinous . . . "), the debts by which it was burdened ("pensions are granted to the old quondam[15] and others to the sum of 50*l* . . . the tenth to the King is 25*l* *odd*. The debts amount to 200*l* . . . the house owes the King above 200 mks. for first fruits . . ."), and the expense of alteration ("about 300 mks. at least"). "Your first entry," they warned Wriothesley, "will be expensive."[16]

On 30 December 1537, Titchfield Abbey, and the vast estates appurtenant thereto, were granted by King Henry VIII to "our trusty servant Thomas Wriothesley," in consideration of his "good, true and faithful service to us."[17]

On 2 January 1538, Crayford and Lathom sent Wriothesley their comments on his suggested alterations to the Abbey. Although Chief Steward of the Abbey, and a resident of Titchfield, Wriothesley apparently had never been in the Abbey, for Crayford and Lathom state "we allowe [agree with] yor owne writing where you say your phantasie to be sett as the blynde caste his staffe," which implies that Wriothesley was suggesting plans without having seen the building, this implication being buttressed by the rest of the sentence, "your presence here wolle see more of yor owne [i.e., by yourself, or personally] in an owre than at Mycheldever in a yere." (Micheldever, of course, was the Wriothesley residence in Hampshire before Titchfield.) The major suggestions made by Crayford and Lathom were that the church and the steeple be torn down, and a two story building erected, with a leaded and "embattled" (i.e., fortified, or crenellated) roof. Should these suggestions be followed, they wrote, "you may have wt reasonable charge an house for the Kinge grace to bate & for any baron to kepe his hospitalitie in. . . ."

The letter ends by noting that neighbours had come to look at Wriothesley's new house, and promised to return to buy the marble stone, altars, images and tables which no longer had any function to serve; the writers urge the Wriothesleys "be not meticulous ne scrupulous to make sale of such holly things. . . ."[18]

Wriothesley appears to have moved his family from Micheldever to Titchfield almost immediately. In a letter dated 26 December 1537, John White, Wriothesley's brother-in-law, rejoices to learn that Wriothesley "will see your house of Tychefeld within 10 days,"[19] and Crayford, in a second letter written on 2 January 1538, refers to the "fine beds, carpets and cushions to furnish your house of Titchfield, lately conveyed from Michildever," and looks forward to seeing "you convey a great part of the whole, children and others, to your said manor."[20]

Illness delayed a little the renovation of Titchfield Abbey: Anthony Roke[21] in late January 1538 writes to Wriothesley that the carpenter who had been ill is now well, but that nevertheless he "stayeth from his labor taking downe the Churche of the Abbey bicause we wold be loth to adventure wt hym before the change of the moon. . . . "[22]

On 1 February 1538 Roke again writes to Wriothesley, referring to a barrel with certain "skochons" of glass, which he will send to Titchfield.[23]

In March, Wriothesley sent one Loveday to Caen, in Normandy, to secure some of that region's famous stone for the construction of parts of his new house. Loveday wrote that arranging to have the stone shipped back was difficult, for

those here will not go to Hampton for fear of men of war. I intend to go tomorrow to Humflue [Honfleur?], and see if I can get any ships of Hampton there. A man of this town who has laden certain stone to Hampton, has promised me the same for you, and I have written to Mr. Huttoff to receive it and pay the party and see it conveyed to Titchfield.[24]

While the renovation of Titchfield was proceeding, Wriothesley acquired on 7 April 1538 yet another suppressed monastery, the priory of Southwick, which he immediately granted to John White who "imitated his master Wriothesley at Titchfield, and pulled down the conventual church, establishing himself and his household in the prior's lodging and adjacent parts of the building."[25] White's dismantling of the Southwick Priory provided material for Titchfield: on 12 April 1538 John Crayford writes to Wriothesley that he was "on tuysdai last til nyght at Southwik. yesterday at the same place for ij [i.e., 2] beames lakkyng for the north yle [i.e., aisle, of the monastery church

at Titchfield] the rest of that day & this day coferryng & divising wt bortyew [i.e., Mr.Bertie[26]] wyndowes & chymneys in the said north yle beneth & other places. . . ." Crayford also acquired other things at Southwick; in a footnote to the letter, he mentions that "at Southwak [Southwick] I bowght the laver [a washing basin] certeyn white glass paving stones a Few wyndowes glass yron & stone chepe ynowghe wt othr thinge as Doctor Peter [William Petre] can sho yo. . . ."

The same letter reveals that in the meantime, the stone from Caen had arrived: Crayford states that he had gone "to Hampton to speke wt Mr. hutofft what shall be payed for stone & freight which now ys comed from Cane [i.e.,Caen] of Mr. lovedayes pvision. . . ."[27]

On 17 April, Crayford, in the last letter we have from him relating to the house, says "Many do preyse yor worke some so hieghly that they sey No-man in England wtoute exception for the quantite of it shall have a stronger more bewtyfull nete & pleasaunt house altho they or he shuld spend three thowsand pounde more than you shall. . . ."[28]

The conversion of the Abbey into a residence must have taken a few years. The work was probably substantially completed by about 1542 or 1543, for it was in one or the other of those years that Wriothesley's boyhood friend, John Leland, in his travels around England to catalogue books, visited Titchfield and wrote that "Mr Wriothesley hath buildid a right stately House embatelid, and having a goodely gate, and a conducte castelid in the midle of the court of it, yn the very same place where the late monasterie of Premonstratenses stoode, caullyd Tichfelde."[29] Because it was "embatelid" — furnished with battlements, or castellations — the new residence was regarded as fortified. Evidently it had been fortified without a royal license, for "the managing Wriothesley easily obtained a pardon for this in 1542,"[30] a fact which suggests that the bulk of the renovation had been accomplished by that time.

If these letters from Crayford, Lathom and Roke do not give us much specific information about the new construction, they nevertheless clearly reveal that the additions were extensive. And, with respect to that portion of the Abbey which remains, the parts of the original Abbey are readily distin-guishable from the parts constructed by Wriothesley. The plan of the ruins published by Reverend G. W. Minns in 1898 (Figure 3 on page 26), identifies by different shadings those portions of the building which date from the 13th century (and are thus part of the original ecclesiastical structure) and those portions which date from the 16th century (and were thus added by Thomas Wriothesley). Historians who examined and excavated the property after its acquisition by the British government assign to the ruins the same dates as those indicated by G. W. Minns, and agree with Minns in identifying the "projecting doorway" (designated in Figure 3 by the letter *f*) on which is incised the heraldic shield bearing two roses as one of the features added by Wriothesley.[31]

But there is a complication: the *Official Handbook* for Titchfield Abbey, in which I first found the (to me) electrifying information of the existence there of a shield which "bears two roses on a chief," goes on to state that the arms, while not those of Wriothesley, "surprisingly, could be the arms of Southwick Priory. . . ."[32] This identification of the arms — at odds with the identifications made by Reverend Minn and Miss Hendy — cannot be correct.

The arms of Southwick Priory were "argent a chief sable with two roses argent therein."[33] This translates into something like: across the top of a silver field, a black band, upon which are two silver roses. This coat of arms is depicted in Figure 7 (the representation is modern; I have been unable to find any pre-nineteenth century depiction of the Southwick Priory arms). Now, it may at first blush seem plausible that the arms at Titchfield were those of Southwick Priory, for the grantee of South-wick Priory was Wriothesley's brother-in-law, John White, from whom, as we have seen, Crayford purchased some of the building materials salvaged from the church at Southwick for use in the conversion of Titchfield Abbey into Place House.

Figure 7. Arms of Southwick Priory.

But for four reasons, I do not think that the coat of arms at Place House is the coat of arms of Southwick Priory. The first reason is that the roses on the shield in the doorway occupy a greater portion of the shield than would be appropriate for two roses on a "chief." The authorities on heraldry unanimously define a "chief" as "the upper third of the shield cut off by a horizontal line."[34] That a chief is one-third of a shield and one-third only is a point insisted upon by the very earliest writers on the subject. In a book published in 1496, Dame Juliana Berners expounds "Of armys whyche are callyd Cheyf":

Sothly certen men wolde that thyse armes after rehercyd shold be callid armys partyd, which certenly for yt that there is no very [i.e., true] pertycon of the colours or any lyknes of divysion of colours. Certenly in armes partyd it is requyred alwaye that the partes of the colours be equall, and that is not true in this figure [reproduced in the margin of the original] for the more parte by moche is sylver. Therfore ye shall saye of him that beryth thise armes thus Latine: Portat de argento et capud scuti de asoreo cum duabis maculis perforatis de auro: Gallice sic: Il porte dargent une cheyffe dasur et deux molettes partyes dor: Anglice sic: He beeryth sylver a cheyff or a chefrayne of asure & two molettes perforatyd of golde.[35]

Dame Juliana is doubtless the source of the similar information set forth in John Bossewell's *Works of Armorie*, published in 1572:

Whosoever beareth a Cheife in hys Armes, it is placed in the hyghest place of the Escocheon, as a thing honorable to be borne, & the fielde beneth is twise so moche as the cheife, & most commonly is seene of an other colour. Therefore certaynely they do greatly erre, which call such Armes parted, althoughe they bee of two coloures: for in parted armes it is required that the coloures bee equall, & so it is not in anye Armes that is honored with a Cheife, or a cheifetaine.[36]

The Place House roses occupy a full half of the shield, thus answering to the blazon of the Town of Southampton, where the "per fesse" indicates that the shield is divided horizontally into two equal parts.[37] On the basis of the space allocated to the band of roses, which band comprises more nearly one half than one-third of the field, the Place House shield is closer to the Southampton arms than to those of Southwick Priory.

Second, if the Place House arms are those of Southwick Priory, it would be difficult to account for the heavy cut across the middle of the shield, and the difference in the level of the top and bottom portions of the shield. In other words, that the coat of arms is obviously mutilated argues against its now representing what it was originally intended to represent.

Third, the roses on the Place House shield are Tudor (i.e., double) roses. It is unimaginable that Southwick Priory would employ Tudor roses (necessarily red and white) to represent the two roses argent on its chief sable; if nothing else, they would bring an unwelcome touch of colour to an otherwise strikingly stark escutcheon.[38] It is equally unlikely that Wriothesley would *not* use Tudor roses on the red and white shield in his house, for they add yet another layer of meaning to a blazon which Wriothesley already found to be intensely significant.

A fourth reason supporting the conclusion that the shield at Titchfield was especially carved for Wriothesley to represent his family's name, title and topographical connections is the inference to be drawn from the intriguing fact that the architectural tastes of the Wriothesley Earls of Southampton were remarkably similar to the architectural tastes of their friend, neighbour, and predecessor, the Fitzwilliam Earl of Southampton, and his heirs, the Brownes — or, to use what was from 1555 on their titular name, the Montagus. The Wriothesley monument in St. Peter's Church in Titchfield is almost identical to the Montagu Monument in Easebourne Priory in Midhurst,[39] and the Wriothesley home is strikingly similar to Cowdray, the home constructed by William Fitzwilliam and subsequently the family seat of the Viscounts Montagu.[40] Cowdray, like Titchfield, became a ruin in the eighteenth century, by a fire rather than by intentional dismantling. On the eastern range of the ruins of Cowdray is a doorway, or porch, occupying the same position relative to the rest of Cowdray as our doorway on the eastern range of Titchfield House occupies with respect to the rest of Titchfield House. In the spandrels of the Cowdray doorway, positioned exactly as in the spandrels of the Titchfield doorway, are two heraldic shields. The shield on the left bears a trefoil with a barred stalk; the shield on the right bears a tiger's head razed: "both these are FitzWilliam badges."[41] The evident fact that the Wriothesley family emulated the Fitzwilliam family in the design of its tomb, the design of its home, and the style of its honour, supports the conclusion that if the one house had family symbols on a door, then the other house also was likely to have had family symbols on the corresponding door.

For these four reasons, I believe that the doorway at Place House was newly made of the stone purchased by Wriothesley in Caen, and not an old doorway purchased at Southwick, and that the roses in the spandrel of that doorway are the red and white roses of the town of Southampton (made doubly red and white by being represented as Tudor roses) on their fields of white and red, and not the white roses of Southwick Priory, on a sable chief, fortuitously decorating a doorway bought at a Priory's going-out-of-business sale.

It is unlikely that Thomas Wriothesley lived for any extended period of time at Titchfield prior to 1547, when he was removed from the Privy Council. After that, he may have spent a year or so at Titchfield before returning to Southampton House in London, to resume his seat on the Council. When he died, in 1550, his son, Henry, who was only five years old, became the second Earl of Southampton.[42] Although the second Earl, during the latter part of his short life, devoted much time and energy toward constructing a home at Dogmersfield,[43] he probably lived principally at Titchfield, which was visited by Edward VI in 1552 and Elizabeth in 1569.[44] On 19 February 1565/6, Henry married Mary, the daughter of Anthony Browne, first Viscount Montagu, who was the son of that Anthony Browne who had been the half-brother of William Fitzwilliam, the Earl of Southampton. (Henry's marriage to Mary Browne, it will be remembered, was the occasion for which Henry's cousin, Thomas Pounde, wrote the mask performed on horseback.) Their son, Henry, was born on 6 October 1573, at Cowdray.[45] The second Earl died on 4 October 1581, at the age of 36. In his will, made three months before his death, he left one thousand pounds for the erection in the Parish Church at Titchfield of two monuments, one for his father, whose body he directed be brought thither and buried, and one for himself. Ultimately, only one monument was built, and it was not until thirteen years after the death of the second Earl that the contract for the construction of the monument was entered into, and the bond for performance signed.[46] The first Viscount Montagu in the meantime (in 1592) had died, and it is assumed that the reason for the similarity of the Montagu and Wriothesley tombs is that they were made at the same time by the same craftsmen.[47] (Perhaps the negotiations for both tombs were conducted by or on behalf of Mary, the daughter of the Viscount and the widow of the Earl, who may have received — is it cynical to suggest? — a discount because of the size of the order.)

The third Earl, as a legal consequence of his conviction of treason for participation in the Essex rebellion, lost both his house and title. In April, 1601, the Queen's Solicitor General, Sir Thomas Fleming, went to Titch-field, to make an inventory of the property which by virtue of the Earl's attainder was now the property of the Crown.[48] If I am correct in supposing that Wriothesley's conviction was the reason for the scraping of his arms off the escutcheon at Titchfield, then it was probably at this time that the actual defacement occurred. Wriothesley was fortunate that it was only a defacing, and not a beheading.

Upon the accession of James I to the throne, Wriothesley's liberty, title and possesions were restored to him. When he died in 1624, the title and possessions passed to his son Thomas.[49] King Charles I and Queen Henrietta Maria visited Titchfield in 1625.[50] Twenty-two years later, when Charles fled from Parliamentary surveillance at Hampton Court, he went to Titchfield House, where he was sheltered by the Old Countess, the third Earl's widow, and eventually taken prisoner by the Governor of Carisbrooke Castle.[51] The night following Charles' execution in 1649, Thomas, the fourth Earl, kept vigil by his body, during which time a muffled figure whom Thomas took to be Cromwell entered the chamber (the banqueting hall at Whitehall) and muttered "Stern necessity."[52] Thomas died in 1667 without male issue. He had three daughters: Elizabeth and Rachel (by his first wife) and Elizabeth (by his second wife). Through the issue of these three women the blood of the Wriothesleys is to be found in a very large number of persons in England today.[53]

The fourth Earl's vast estates were divided into three approximately equal portions, and then by lot assigned to the daughters. The Titchfield lands went to Elizabeth, the eldest daughter; the Bloomsbury estate and Southampton House went to Rachel; the Beaulieu estate, Bull Hall in Southampton, and other lands in Hampshire, Southampton and London went to Elizabeth, the youngest daughter.[54]

Elizabeth, the eldest daughter, married Edward Noël, the first Earl of Gainsborough. The second daughter, Rachel, married as her second husband William, Lord Russell, second son of the first Duke of Bedford, thus bringing him the lands in the Russell Square area of London which are a chief foundation of the present-day fortune of the Dukes of Bedford.[55] The third daughter, Elizabeth, married Ralph, Lord Montagu of Boughton; their descendants still own Beaulieu, well-known today for its manor house, automobile museum and other attractions.[56]

In 1690, when the elder Elizabeth's son, Wriothesley Baptist Noël, second Earl of Gainsborough, died without male heirs, his property, including the Titchfield estates, passed into the joint possession of Henry, first Duke of Portland, the husband of Noël's elder daughter, Elizabeth, and Henry, second Duke of Beaufort, the husband of Noël's younger daughter, Rachel. In 1739, the two Dukes agreed to divide the property, and procured an Act of Parliament for the purpose. The Duke of Beaufort received the Titchfield property; the Duke of Portland received a number of other properties, and a sum of money from the Duke of Beaufort. In 1742, the Duke of Beaufort sold his portion of the estate, including Place House, to Peter Delmé.[57]

There is no record of Titchfield House having been altered in any substantial way from the time of the death of the first Earl of Southampton until the time of its sale to Peter Delmé. Thus the engraving made by J. and N. Buck in 1733[58], and reproduced in Figure 8 shows the exterior of the building very much as it looked during the lifetimes of the first and third Earls of Southampton. Also, early 18th century Wriothesley family documents now in the Hampshire Record Office, listing the 50 or so rooms in the house,[59] together with the detailed plan of its two floors made on 17 October 1737 by one John Achard,[60] confirm what would otherwise have been safely surmised, that the interior of this great house had the gallery, drawing rooms, dining rooms, chambers, kitchens, pantries, and other features so characteristic of English manors from Tudor times on.

Like many of these manors, it was a treasure house of Tudor, Elizabethan and Jacobean portraiture. An inventory made in August, 1731,[61] lists 28 portraits in the Long Gallery at Titchfield. On the east side of the Gallery, from the window to the door, were 21 paintings, including, among others,

Figure 8. Place House (Titchfield Abbey) in 1733 from Buck's *Antiquities* (London: Robert Sayer, 1774), I, 111. Reproduced by Permission of the Folger Shakespeare Library, Washington, D.C.

portraits of Henry VIII, James I, the first Earl of Southampton (undoubtedly the same picture reproduced in Plate VII), his wife Jane, their son Henry, second Earl of Southampton, his son, "Henry 3 (son of Henry ye 2 Earl of Southn). Imprison in ye Tower in ye Reign of Qu Eliz he yn consern'd wth ye Earl of Essex" (undoubtedly the same picture reproduced in Plate VI), the Earl of Essex, "favourite of Elizabeth," Henry's wife Elizabeth, Countess of Southampton and daughter of John Vernon of Hodnet, their daughter Lady Spencer, wife of Sir William Spencer, and their elder son James (who died with his father in Holland). On the west side of the Gallery, "from the great window to ye door," were 7 paintings, including Queen Elizabeth and Queen Anne, the wife of King James I. In the drawing room were three paintings: the fourth Earl of Southampton, and his two daughters Elizabeth. In the Great Dining room was a painting of King James' son, Prince Henry, and another painting showing four of the children of the fourth Earl of Southampton (i.e., the two Elizabeths, Rachel, and Lord Wriothesley, one of the two sons of the fourth Earl who died in their infancy or childhood).

Interesting as the list of portraits is, the information in the Hampshire Record Office of most significance to our story is a piece of paper[62] on which are sketches of the heraldry at Place House. These sketches, reproduced in Figures 9, 10, 11 and 12, on pages 282 through 285, seem to have been made by John Achard in 1737, at the same time that he prepared the floor plans of the building.

Although only one heraldic shield with roses on it still remains at Place House, Achard's sketches of 1737 show the existence there at one time of an abundance of red and white heraldry, much of which is from the period of Henry VIII, and therefore undoubtedly still in place during the lifetime of the third Earl, when Shakespeare could have seen it (and, as I believe his poems disclose, did see it).

On the right hand half of one side of Achard's sheet of sketches (Figure 10) are tricked the coats on 9 shields. The first, the arms of France and England quarterly, is the coat of Henry VIII.[63] On the perimeter of the coat Achard has written, "All around a festoon of red roses with green boughs and leaves." On the second shield is the coat of Catherine Parr. Achard has blazoned the first quartering of this coat as "the midle point Geules 3 white roses in pale the two other points are gold 3 roses no colour," which is close enough to possibly more professional blazons of the actual coat of augmentation conferred by Henry upon Catherine: "Argent, on a pile, gules, between six roses of the first [colour, i.e., argent] three roses of the second [colour, i.e., gules]."[64] The other quarterings on the shield are those of the Parr family: the three water bougets (resembling Chinese characters) on the quartering to the right, over the quartering of the three stags (or bucks, as Achard designates them; this is the coat of arms of the ubiquitous Greene family), remove from this identification all possible doubt. Around this coat Achard has written, "Green oak and red apples or roses." The third shield shows the portcullis which was a badge of the house of Tudor.[65] The fourth shield is the same as the first; around it Achard has written, "Red and white roses alternately green boughs and leaves." The fifth shield looks strange: why is the royal coat of arms on the right hand side of the shield? why on that coat are the quarterings of France and England reversed? The answers lie in Achard's notation that this shield is in "The Great Bow Window in the Gallery": the shield was of stained glass, which Achard had sketched *from the wrong side*. Reversed, the shield is immediately seen to bear the arms of Jane Seymour impaling those of Henry VIII.

Although Achard has correctly tricked the greater part of Jane Seymour's coat of augmentation, he appears to have confused the charges of the Seymour coat with those of the Parr coat, and he blazons this as "En pointe celle du millieu or chargé de 3 roses les deux de cote azur chargé de 3 roses con-traires," which translates into something like "the middle point or (i.e., gold) 3 roses, the two (other points on each) side azure, 3 roses counterchanged." But the correct blazon for the coat of augmentation conferred by Henry VIII upon Jane Seymour is, "Or, on a pile, gules, between six fleurs-de-lis, azure, three lions, passant, guardant, of the first."[66] However, Achard's drawing clearly shows the very distinctive wings conjoined, with their tips downward, and three roses in a bend, counterchanged, which establish that this is the coat of Jane Seymour. Around this coat, Achard notes, are "red roses & green boughs & leaves." The sixth shield bears simply a red rose on a silver field. This is a badge of Henry VIII.[67] The seventh shield has the arms of Henry VIII impaled by a coat indicated as being the same coat shown on the second shield, that is, the arms of Catherine Parr. The eighth shield is an orange coloured fleur de lis on a silver field. The ninth shield is a lemon coloured fleur de lis on an azure field. The fleur de lis, like the red and white rose, was often used as a royal badge.[68]

Along the side of these nine shields is the notation, "All in the Gallery." Written beside the first shield is the Wriothesley motto, *Ung par tout, tout par ung*, which presumably was displayed somewhere in the Gallery.

Some, and perhaps all, of these nine shields were of stained glass, and as tricked by Achard closely resemble certain 16th century stained glass windows now in the Victoria and Albert Museum in London and the Burrell Collection in Glasgow; it is not beyond the realm of possibility that these windows are originally from Titchfield.[69]

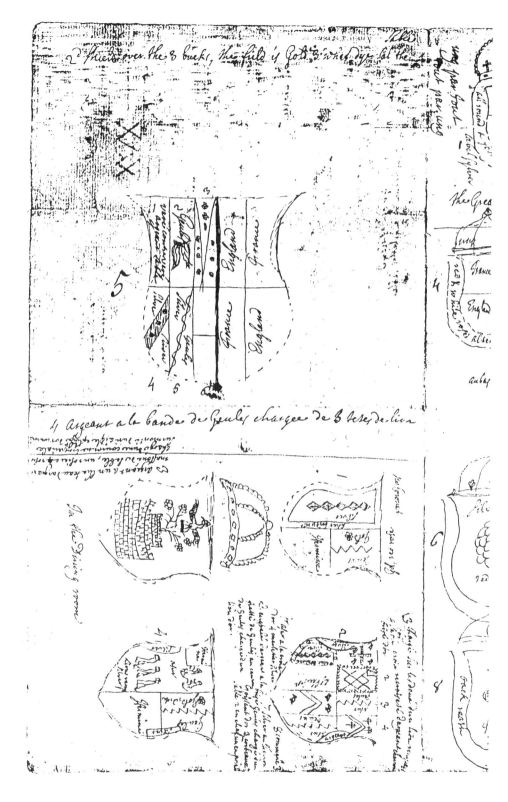

Figure 9. Trickings of heraldry at Titchfield House in 1737, left side of sheet.

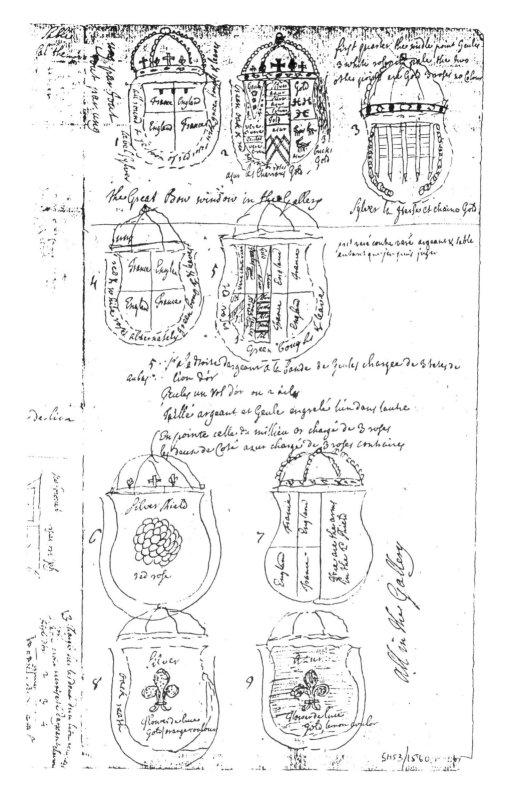

Figure 10. Trickings of heraldry at Titchfield House in 1737, right side of sheet.

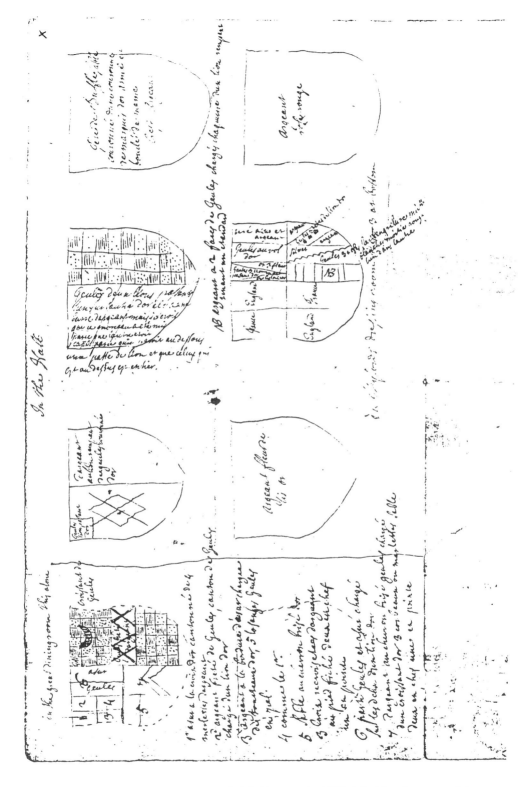

Figure 11. Trickings of heraldry at Titchfield House in 1737, left side of reverse of sheet.

Figure 12. Trickings of heraldry at Titchfield House in 1737, right side of reverse of sheet.

The significant thing about these nine shields is that each and every one of them is associated with Henry VIII, and that white and red roses figure prominently in the design of five of them.

On the top of the left hand half of this side of the piece of paper with Achard's sketches (Figure 9) is a larger tricking of the fifth shield.

Underneath that are four shields, and under them the legend, "In the Dining room." The dexter side of the first shield (the left hand side as seen by the viewer) bears the arms of the Lewsell family; the arms impaling them are probably Drayton (see Figure 5 on page 48), but I cannot be sure of this. The coat on the second shield, with its "Azur a la croix dor 4 merlettes silver" is the Wriothesley arms (*merlette* being a heraldic bird which looks very much like a dove). The third shield is arresting: Achard has blazoned it, "Argeant a un chateau dargeant [which cannot possibly be a correct blazon] massoné du sable, un rosier aux roses chargé dune couronne imperiale sur-monté dun aigle éployé dor couron." This strange device is the badge of Jane Seymour, which is by one authority described as "a curious circular castle; over the port was a hawthorne bush proper, flowered gules, and crowned; while on the green mound of the upper tower a golden crowned phoenix rose from flames of fire, a red and white rose stalked vert being on either side of the pyre."[70] The fourth coat in the dining room I cannot decipher.

On the left half of the other side of this sheet of paper (Figure 11), under the legend "in the great dining room, This alone", is a Wriothesley coat of arms (the first and fourth quarterings of the first quarter are blazoned as "azur a la croix dor cantonne de 4 merlettes dargeant"). Next to this under the caption "In the Hall" are depicted three shields. The one on the left appears to be the arms of the family of the first Earl's maternal grandfather, Januarius Dunstanville (these arms are: argent, within a bordure engrailed sable, a fret gules, over all, on a canton gules, a lion passant or[71]) impaled with a coat I cannot identify. Nor can I identify the coat on the second shield. The third shield bears not a coat of arms, but the Wriothesley crest: "Tete de Bugle sable couronné dune couronne remarquis dor armé et bouclé de meme. Crest Argeant." Under these are three shields over the legend, "In My lords Dressing room these 3 at bottom." The shield on the left is blazoned "Argeant fleur de lis or" — a badge of Henry VIII. The shield in the middle bears the arms of Henry VIII impaled with those of Jane Seymour. The shield next to it is blazoned simply, "Argeant rose rouge", that is, on a white field, a red rose: once again, a badge of Henry VIII.

And finally, on the right half of this sheet (Figure 12), without any indication as to where in Place House it might be, is a shield blazoned, "Argeant a la rose rouge chargée dune rose blanche": on a white field, a red

286

rose charged with a white rose. In other words, a Tudor rose on a silver field: the most familiar of the badges of Henry VIII, and the epitome of the heraldry at Place House.

The ubiquitousness of the red and white roses at Titchfield, as evidenced by Achard's sketches, not only removes all doubt from the conclusion that the arms on the spandrel at Titchfield are red and white roses on alternate red and white backgrounds (that is, the arms of Southampton, rather than of South-wick), but also abundantly demonstrates that red and white roses were a conspicuous decoration of the Wriothesley manor and the singular badge of the Wriothesley family. That the proper arms of the Wriothesleys are so little in evidence in these eighteenth century sketches is probably because the shields, windows, lozenges and escutcheons bearing them were destroyed at the time of the third Earl's attainder, and were not thereafter replaced.

In 1742, not long after Achard sketched the heraldry at Titchfield Place, the Duke of Beaufort sold the Titchfield estates to Peter Delmé, who soon thereafter began dismantling Titchfield Place to supply building material for the construction of Cams Hall.[72] On 19 August 1786, Thomas Warton visited Titchfield House, and wrote this description:

The Abbey of Titchfield being granted to the first Earl, Thomas, in 1538, he converted it into a family mansion, yet with many additions and alterations: we enter, to the south, through a superb tower, or Gothic portico, of stone, having four large angular turrets. Of the monastic chapel only two or three low arches remain, with the moor-stone pilasters. The greater part of what may properly be called the house, forming a quadrangle, was pulled down about forty years ago. But the refectory, or hall of the abbey, still remains complete, with its original raftered roof of good workmanship: it is embattled; and has three Gothic windows on each side, with an oreille or oriel window. It is entered by a portico which seems to have been added by the new proprietor at the dissolution; by whom also the royal arms *painted* [emphasis in original], with the portcullis and H.R. [Henricus Rex] [brackets in original], were undoubtedly placed over the high table. At the other end is a music-gallery. Underneath is the cellar of the monastery, a well-wrought crypt of chalk-built arches; the ribs and intersections in a good style. In a long cove-ceiled room, with small parallel semicircular arches, are the arms of King Charles the First on tapestry; he was protected here in his flight from Hampton-court. Two or three Gothic-shaped windows, perhaps of the abbey, in a part of the house now inhabited by a steward and other servants. In these and other windows some beautiful shields of painted glass are preserved; particularly one of Henry the Eighth impaling Lady Jane Seymour, who were married at Maxwell, twenty miles off, and who seem from thence to have paid a visit at this place to Lord Southampton.[73]

At the time of the First World War, Titchfield was bought from a descendant of the Delmés by the Ministry of Agriculture and Fisheries. The Ministry disposed of the lands in 1923, at the same time transferring the ruins of Place House to His Majesty's Office of Works, now the Department of the Environment.[74]

What would we not give to have this noble manor, with its heraldry, portraits and furnishings, its associations with Henry VIII, the Wriothesleys and Shakespeare, preserved today in the same condition as apparently it was as late as 1742? Of all that glory, only the Roses remain.

APPENDIX III

Red and White, and Rose, Imagery
1557 - 1656

Bold face or italic type in the original printed sources has been omitted; the italics appearing in the following excerpts have been added. The dates are in each case the date of first publication. Some of the texts are modernised, some are not, depending upon the sources from which I took them.

A. Red and White indicative of beauty.

1. 1567 - Arthur Golding's translation of *Ovids Metamorphosis* (from *Shakespeare's Ovid*, Book III, lines 529-531).

[Narcissus sees his reflection in a pool:]
His beardlesse chinne and yvorie necke,
    and eke the perfect grace
Of *white and red* indifferently bepainted in
    his face.
All these he woondereth to beholde....

◇

2. 1577 - John Grange: *The paynting of a Curtizan* (from Grange, *The Golden Aphroditis*, page facing sig. P.).

Yea, how, and by what meanes, they doe
    allure the youth,
To spend upon thē all they haue, whose
    beauty whettes their tooth....
With ueluet cappes, and plumes, they doe
    adorne their heddes,
*With red & white they painte their face, to
tice thē to there beddes.*

◇

3. 1578 - Anonymous: *The Lover extolleth*, etc. (from *Gorgious Gallery of gallant inventions*, p. 24).

Desire hath driven from mee my will,
Or Cupids blase hath bleard mine eyes:
Knowledge mee fayles, my sight is yll:
If kinde or cunning could devise

Nature to paynt in better plight
To set her forth with *red and white*:
Or if men had Apelles arte,
Who could her mend in any parte?

◇

4. 1580 - John Lyly: *Euphues and His England* (from Lyly, *Works*, II, 167, lines 16-21).

If there were such a Ladie in this company Surius, that should wincke with both eyes when you would have hir see your amorous lookes, or be no blabbe of hir tongue, when you would have aunswere of your questions, I can-not thinke, that eyther hir vertuous conditions, or hir *white and read* complection could move you to love.

◇

5. 1591 — Philip Sidney (d. 1587): *Astrophel and Stella*, Sonnet 9 (from Sidney Lee, *Elizabethan Sonnets*, I, 15.)

Queen virtue's court, which some call
    Stella's face,
Prepar'd by Nature's choicest furniture,
Hath his front built of alabaster pure;
Gold is the covering of that stately place.
The door by which sometimes come forth
    her grace.
Red porphir is, which lock of pearl makes
    sure,

289

Whose porches rich — which name of
  cheeks endure —
Marble, *mix'd red and white*, do interlace.

◇

6. 1587 - Abraham Fraunce's *Translation
  of Thomas Watson's Amyntas* (from
  Fraunce, *The Lamentations of
  Amyntas*, p. 27, line 25).

And cheekes *al white red, with snow and
  purple* adorned. . . .

◇

7. 1590 - Christopher Marlowe: *All Ovids
  Elegies* (from Marlowe, *Complete
  Works*, II, 371-372.

What, are there Gods? her selfe she hath
  forswore,
And yet remaines the face she had before.
How long her lockes were, ere her oath
  she tooke:
So long they be, since she her faith
  forsooke.
*Faire white with rose red was before
  commixt:*
*Now shines her lookes pure white and red
  betwixt.*

◇

8. 1591 - Anonymous: *In the praise of his
  Mistresse* (from *Brittons Bowre of
  Delights*, 1591, p. 28).

And for that *purest red*, with that most
  perfect white,
That makes those cheekes the sweetest
  chaines, of lovers high delite.

◇

9. 1593 — Giles Fletcher: *Lucian* (from
  Sidney Lee, *Elizabethan Sonnets*, II,
  65).

Your look was pale, and so his stomach
  fed:
But *far from fair, where white doth want
  his red.*

◇

10. 1596 — W. Smith: *Chloris*, Sonnet
  XVIII (from Sidney Lee, *Elizabethan Sonnets*, II, 334).

Thy *red and white*, with purest fair atones,
Matchless for beauty Nature hath thee
  framed....

◇

11. 1596 — Edmund Spenser: *An Hymne
  in Honour of Beautie* (from Spenser,
  Poetical Works, pp. 590-591).

How vainely then doe ydle wits invent,
That beautie is nought else, but mixture
  made
Of colours faire, and goodly temp'tament
Of pure complexions, that shall quickly
  fade
And passe away, like to a sommers
  shade,
Or that it is but a comely composition
Of parts well measurd, with meet dis-
  position.
Hath *white and red* in it such wondrous
  powre,
That it can pierce through th'eyes unto the
  hart,
And therein stirre such rage and restless
  stowre,
As nought but death can stint his dolours
  smart?...
But ah, beleeve me, there is more then so
That workes such wonders in the minds of
  men.
I that have often prov'd, too well it know;

And who so list the like assays to ken,
Shall find by tryall, and confesse it then,
That Beautie is not, as fond men mis-
     deeme,
An outward shew of things, that onely
     seem.
For that same goodly hew of *white and
     red*,
With which the cheekes are sprinckled,
     shal decay,
And those sweete rosy leaves so fairly
     spred
Upon the lips, shall fade and fall away
To that they were, even to corrupted clay.
That golden wyre, those sparckling stars
     so bright
Shall turne to dust, and loose their goodly
     light.

◇

12. 1598 — John Marston: *The Metamor-
    phosis of Pigmalions Image and
    Certaine Satyres* (from Marston,
    Poems, p. 11).

Her Amber-coloured, her shining haire,
Makes him protest, the Sunne hath spread
     her head
With golden beames, to make her farre
     more faire.
But when her cheeks his amorous thoughts
     have fed,
Then he exclaimes, *such redde and so
     pure white*,
Did never blesse the eye of mortall sight!

◇

13. 1600 - Sir J. Wotton: *In Praise of his
    Daphnis* (from Ault, Norman, *Eliza-
    bethan Lyrics*, p. 307).

Amidst her cheeks the *rose and lily* strive,
     Lily snow-white,
When their contend doth make their colour
     thrive,

Colour too bright
For Shepherds' eyes.

Her lips like scarlet of the finest dye,
     Scarlet blood-red;
Teeth *white as snow* which on the hills
     doth lie,
     Hills overspread
     By winter's force.

Her skin as soft as is the finest silk,
     Silk soft and fine,
Of colour like unto the *whitest milk*,
     Milk of the kine
     Of Daphnis' herd.

◇

14. 1601 - Thomas Campion: *A Book of
    Ayres*, XII (from Campion, *Works*,
    p. 12).

*Thou art not faire for all thy red and
     white*,
For all those rose ornaments in thee
Thou art not sweet, though made of meer
     delight,
Nor faire nor sweet, unlesse thou pitie
     mee.
I will not sooth thy fancies: thou shalt
     prove
That beauty is no beautie without love.

◇

15. 1630? — Philo-Balladus: *A Woman's
    Birth* (from *The Roxburghe Ballads*,
    III, Part 1, 95).

Flora bestowed upon her cheeke a hue
     Of *red and white*, to make her feature
     pleasant,
That she the easier might the heart subdue
     Of king, prince, courtier, cittizen or
     peasant;
But he that trusts her faith, it is so slacke,
Her *red and white* to wilowe turnes, and
     blacke.

◇

16. 1633 — John Donne: *The Anagram* (from Donne, *Complete Poetry*, p. 60).

If *red and white* and each good quality
Be in thy wench ne'r ask where it doth
  lye.

◇

17. 1633 — George Herbert: *Dulnesse* (from Herbert, *Works*, p. 114).

Thou art my lovelinesse, my life, my
  light,
  Beautie alone to me:
Thy bloudy death and undeserv'd, makes
  thee
  Pure red and white.

◇

18. 1646 — Suckling, Sir John: *Fragmenta Aurea* (from Suckling, *Works*, I, 47-48).

Sonnet I

Do'st see how unregarded now
  That piece of beauty passes?
There was a time when I did vow to that
  alone;
But mark the fate of faces,
That *red and white* works now no more
  on me
Than if it could not charm, or I not see.

Sonnet II

Of thee (kind boy) I ask no *red and white*
  to make up my delight;
  no odd becomming graces,
Black eyes, or little know-not-whats in
  faces;

Make me but mad enough, give me good
  store
Of Love, for her I court;
  I ask no more,
Tis love in love that makes the sport.

There's no such thing as that we beauty
  call,
  it is meer cozenage all;
  For though some long ago,
Liked certain colours mingled so and so,
That doth not tie me now from chusing
  new;
If I a fancy take
  To black and blue,
That fancy doth it beauty make.

◇

19. 1660 — William Herbert, Third Earl of Pembroke (d. 1630): *A Paradox, that Beauty lyes not in womens faces, but in their Lovers Eyes* (from *Poems Written by the Right Honorable William Earl of Pembroke*, p. 77).

Why should thy look requite so ill
  all other Eyes,
Making them Pris'ners to thy will,
Where alone thy Beauty lyes:
When men's Eyes first look't upon thee,
They bestowed thy Beauty on thee.

When thy Colours first were seen
  By judging sight,
Had men's Eyes prais'd Black or Green,
Then thy Face had not been Bright:
He that lov'd thee, then would find
Thee as little fair as kind.

If all others had been blind,
  Fair had not been;
None thy Red and White could find
Fleeting, if thou wert unseen.
To touch white Skins is not Divine:
Ethiop Lips are soft as thine.

◇

20. 1681 — Andrew Marvell (d. 1678):
   The Garden (from Marvell, *Poems
   and Letters*, I, 48).

   No white nor red was ever seen
   So am'rous as this lovely green.

B. Red and White represented by Damask Rose,
or Roses and Lilies.

21. 1557 - - Anonymous (from *Tottels
   Miscellany* (1557-1587), I, 170).

Her colour freshe and mingled with such
   sleight:
As though the *rose* sate in the *lilies* lap.

◇

22. 1575 — George Gascoigne: *In prayse
   of . . . Lady Sandes* (from Gascoigne, *Complete Works*, p. 52).

In Court who so demaundes what Dame
   doth most excell,
For my conceyt I must needes say, faire
   Bridges beares ye bell:
Upon whose lively cheeke, to proove my
   judgement true,
*The Rose and Lillie seem to strive for
   equall change of hewe.*

◇

23. 1579 — Spenser: *The Shepheardes
   Calendar* (from Spenser, *Poetical
   Works*, p. 432, lines 64-72).

   (April)

Tell me, have ye seene her angelick face,
   Like Phoebe fayre?
Her heavenly haveour, her princely grace
   can you well compare?
*The Redde rose medled with the White
   yfere* [together],
In either cheeke depeincten lively chere.

Her modest eye,
Her Maiestie,
Where have you seene the like, but there?

◇

24. 1580 — John Lyly: *Euphues and His
   England* (from Lyly, *Works*, II,
   200, lines 17-19).

There is no beautie but in Englãd. There
did I behold thẽ of *pure complexion,
exceeding the lillie, & the rose, of fauor
(wherein y̌ chiefest beautie consisteth)....*

◇

25. 1582 — Thomas Watson: *Hekatompathia*, VII (from Watson, *Poems*, p.
   43).

On either cheeke a *Rose and Lillie* lies....

◇

26. 1589 — Thomas Lodge: *Glaucus and
   Scilla* (from Lodge, *Complete
   Works*, I, 15).

Next which her cheekes appeared like
   crimson silk,
Or *ruddie rose* bespread on *whitest milk.*

◇

27. 1589 — Robert Greene: *Menaphon*, XXVIII (from Greene, *Plays and Poems*, II, 253).

Doron's Description of Samela

Her tresses gold, her eyes like glassie streanes,
Her teeth are pearle, the breasts are yvorie of faire Samela.
Her *cheekes like rose and lilly* yeeld forth gleames,
Her browes bright arches framde of ebonie:
    Thus faire Samela.

◇

28. 1589 — Robert Greene: *Tullie's Love* (from Greene, *Plays and Poems*, II, 267).

Sitting by the riuer side
Louely Phillis was descrid:
Golde hir haire, bright her eyen,
Like to Phoebus in his shine.
White hir brow, hir face was faire.
Amber breath perfumde the aire.
Rose and Lilly both did seeke,
To shew their glories on hir cheeke.

◇

29. 1590 — Robert Greene: *Greene's Mourning Garment,* XLVII (from Greene, *Plays and Poems*, II, 272).

The Description of the Shepheard and his Wife.

Faire she was as faire might be,
Like the Roses on the tree:
Buxsane, lieth, and young, I weene
Beautious, like a sommers Queene,
For *her cheekes were ruddy hued,*
As if Lillies were imbrued,
With drops of bloud to make thee white,
Please the eye with more delight....

◇

30. 1590 — Robert Greene: *Greene's Mourning Garment*, XLIX (from Greene, Robert, *Plays and Poems*, II, 274).

Hexametra Alexis in lavdem Rosamvndae

Face *Rose hued*, Cherry red, with a *silver taint like a Lilly.*

◇

31. 1590 - Edmund Spenser: *Faerie Queen*, II,iii,22 (from Spenser, *Poetical Works*, p. 83).

Her face so faire as flesh it seemed not,
But heavenly pourtraict of bright Angels hew,
Cleare as the skie, withouten blame or blot,
Through goodly mixture of complexions dew;
And in her cheekes the vermeil red did shew
Like roses in a bed of lillies shed,
The which ambrosiall odours from them threw,
And gazers sense with double pleasure fed,
Hable to heale the sicke, and to revive the ded.

◇

32. 1591 — Sir Philip Sidney (d. 1587): *Astrophel and Stella*, Sonnet 100 (from Sidney Lee, *Elizabethan Sonnets*, I, 61).

O tears! no tears, but rain from beauty's skies,
Making *those lilies and those roses* grow
Which aye most fair, now more than most fair show,
While graceful pity beauty beautifies.

◇

33. 1591 — Anonymous (from Lee, Sidney, *Elizabethan Sonnets*, I, 103).

All you that will hold watch with Love,
The Fairy Queen Proserpina
Will make you fairer than Diana's dove.
    Roses red, lilies white,
    And the clear damask hue;
    Shall on your cheeks alight.
    Love will Adorn you.

◇

34. 1593 — Barnabe Barnes, *Parthenophil and Parthenophe*, Sonnet XLVI (from Sidney Lee, *Elizabethan Sonnets*, I, 196).

Sweet *damaske rosebud*! Venus' rose of
    roses!...
Oh *damask rose*!

◇

35. 1593 — Barnabe Barnes, *Parthenophil and Parthenophe*, Ode 16 (from Sidney Lee, *Elizabethan Sonnets*, I, 298).

Where Cupid, with sweet Venus sate:
    Her *cheeks with rose, and lilies*
    decked.

◇

36. 1593 — Giles Fletcher: *Licia*, Sonnet LII (from Sidney Lee, *Elizabethan Sonnets*, II, 60).

O roses and lilies! in a field most fair,
Where modest white doth make the red
    seem pale.

◇

37. 1593 — Edward Vere, Earl of Oxford: *What Cunning Can Express*

(from Ault, Norman, *Elizabethan Lyrics*, pp. 177-178).

The lily in the field,
That glories in his white,
For pureness now must yield,
And render up his right;
    Heaven pictured in her face
    Doth promise joy and grace.

Fair Cynthia's silver light,
That beats on running streams,
Compares not with her white,
Whose hairs are all sunbeams.
    Her virtues so do shine
    As day unto mine eyne.

With this there is a red
Exceeds the damask rose,
Which in her cheeks is spread,
Whence every favour grows.
    In sky there is no star
    That she surmounts not, far.

When Phoebus from the bed
Of Thetis doth arise,
The morning blushing red
In fair carnation-wise,
    He shows it in her face
    As queen of every grace.

The pleasant lily white,
The taint of roseate red,
This Cynthia's silver light,
This sweet fair Dea spread,
    These sunbeams in mine eye,
    These beauties make me die.

(One of the minor arguments J. Thomas Looney advances [at p. 175 of his book] in support of his contention that the Earl of Oxford wrote the works of "Shakespeare" is that Oxford's description of the beauty of a woman's face in the foregoing poem is in the same spirit as "Shakespeare's" in that it "turns upon the contrast of white and red, the lily and the damask rose.")

◇

38. 1595 — Edmund Spenser: *Epithalamion* (from Spenser, *Poetical Works*, p. 582).

Behold whiles she before the altar stands
Hearing the holy priest that to her speakes
And blesseth her with his two happy hands,
How the red roses flush up in her cheekes,
And the pure snow with goodly vermill stayne,
Like crimson dyde in grayne,
That even th'Angels which continually,
About the sacred Altare do remaine,
Forget their service and about her fly,
Ofte peeping in her face that seems more fayre,
The more they on it stare.

◇

39. 1872 — Edward Vere, Earl of Oxford (d. 1604) (from *Arundell Harington Manuscript*, I, 215).

I saw a fayre yownge lady come, her secreat greefs to wayle,
Clad all in colour of a Vaer, and one her face a vayle.
Yet for the day was cleere, I might discerne her face,
as one myght see a *damaske rose* thoughe hid with Cristall glasse.

(Although not published until 1872, this poem may have circulated in manuscript; the following excerpt appears to allude to this poem.)

◇

40. 1595 — Richard Stapleton: *The Amorous contention of Phillis and Flora*. (from Chapman, *Poems*, p. 101).

Theyr soft yong cheeke-balls to the eye,
Are of the fresh vermilion Dye....
So Lillies out of Scarlet pere,
So Roses bloomde in Lady Vere....

◇

41. 1595 — Richard Barnfield: *Cynthia* (from Barnfield, Richard, *Complete Poems*, pp. 85, 86, 93).

Sonnet IX

Diana (on a time) walking the wood,
    To sporte herselfe, of her faire traine forlorne,
    Chaunc't for to pricke her foote against a thorne,
And from thence issu'd out a streame of blood.
No sooner she was vanisht out of sight,
    But loves faire Queen came there away by chance,
    And having of this hap a glym'ring glance,
She put the blood into a christall bright;
When being now comme unto mount Rhodope,
    With her faire hands she formes a shape of Snow,
    And blends in with this blood: from whence doth grow
A lovely creature, brighter than the Day.
    And being christned in faire Paphos shrine,
    She call'd him Ganymede: as all divine.

X

Thus was my love, thus was my Ganymed,
    (Heavens joy, worlds wonder, natures fairest work,
    In whose aspect Hope and Despaire doe lurke,)
Made of pure blood in whitest snow yshed....

XVII

Cherry-lipt Adonis in his snowie shape,
    Might not compare with his *pure Ivorie white*,

On whose fairefront a Poets pen may
write,
Whose *rosiate red* excels the *crimson
grape*,
His love-enticing delicate soft limbs,
Are rarely fram'd t'intrap poore gazing
eies:
His cheekes, the *Lillie and Carnation*
dies,
With lovely tincture which Apolloes dims.
His lips ripe strawberries in Nectar wet,
His mouth a Hive, his tongue a
hony-combe,
Where Muses (like Bees) make their
mansion.
His teeth *pure Pearle in blushing Correll*
set.
Oh how can such a body sinne-
procuring,
Be slow to love, and quicke to hate,
enduring?

◇

42. 1596 — R. L[inche?]: *Diella*, Sonnet
XXXI (from Sidney Lee, *Elizabethan Sonnets*, II, 317).

Fair Cheeks of *purest roses red and white*!

◇

43. 1597 — R. Tofte: *Laura*, Part II, XVI
(from Sidney Lee, *Elizabethan
Sonnets*, II, 388).

From milk of Juno, as the Poets feign,
The *Lily* had its *whiteness*, passing *white*:
And from Adonis' blood, that lovely
Swain,
The *Rose* his colour *red*, which doth
delight.
Thou, pretty Soul, hast both the colours
rare
Of these sweet flowers; which others all
exceed.
Thy breast's a bed of beauteous *Lilies fair*;
Thy dainty cheeks, pure *damask Rose*
breed.

Of fruitful garden flow'ring; where appear
The *Rose and Lily* at all times of
year!

◇

44. 1597 — R. Tofte: *Laura*, Part II,
XXXVIII (From Sidney Lee, *Elizabethan Sonnets*, II, 399).

Rich *Damask Roses* in fair cheeks do bide
Of my sweet Girl, like April in his
prime....

◇

45. 1617 — Thomas Campion: *The Fourth
Book of Ayres*, VII (Campion,
Works, p. 178).

There is a garden in her face
Where *Roses and white Lillies* grow . . .

◇

46. 1633 — Fulke Greville, Lord Brook
(d. 1628): *Caelica*, LXXXII (from
Greville, Fulke, *Caelica*, p. 147).

Under a throne I saw a virgin sit,
The *red and white rose quartered in her
face*....

◇

C. Changes in Colour between Red and White (neutral).

47. 1562 — Arthur Brooke: *Romeus and Juliet* (from Bullough, Geoffrey, *Narrative and Dramatic Sources of Shakespeare*, I, pp. 293, 297).

But she espyd straight waye, by *chaunging of his hewe*
From pale to red, from red to pale, and so from pale anewe,
That vehment love was cause, why so his tong dyd stay....
His faces *rosy hew*, I saw full oft to seeke
And straight againe it flashed foorth, and spred in eyther cheeke,
His fyxed heavenly eyne, that through me quite did perce
His thoughts unto my hart, my thoughts they seemed to rehearce.
What ment his foltring tunge, in telling of his tale,
The trembling of his joynts, and eke his cooler waxen pale?....
And whilst I talkt with him, hym self he hath exyldee,
Out of him self (as seemed me) ne was I sure begylde.
Those arguments of love, craft wrate not in his face,
But Natures hande when all deceyte was banished out of place.

◇

48. 1563 — Barnabe Googe: *Sonettes* (from Googe, *Eglogs, Epytaphes and Sonettes*, p. 95).

Thy voice when I do heare,
  then *collour comes and goes,*
Some tyme as pale as Earth I looke,
  some tyme as red as Rose.

◇

49. 1567 Arthur Golding's translation of *Ovids Metamorphosis* (from *Shakespeares Ovid,* Book IV, lines 402-409).

[Salmacis urges a beautiful young man to be her bedfellow:]
This sed, the Nymph did hold hir peace, and therewithall the boy
Waxt red: he wist not what love was: and sure it was a joy
To see how exceeding well his blushing him became.
For in his face the colour fresh appeared like the same
That is in Apples which doe hand upon the Sunnie side:
Or *Ivorie shadowed with a red*: or such as is espide
Of *white and scarlet colours mixt* appearing in the Moone
When folke in vaine with sounding brasse would ease unto hir done.

◇

50. 1590 — Edmund Spenser: *Faerie Queene*, I. ix, 16 (from Spenser, *Poetical Works*, p. 46).

Thus as he spake, *his visage wexed pale, And chaunge of hew great passion did bewray;*
  Yet still he strove to cloke his inward bale,
  And hide the smoke, that did his fire display....

◇

298

51. 1594 — Richard Barnfield: *The Affectionate Shepheard* (from Barnfield, *Complete Poems*, pp. 8, 21).

Stanza III

His *Ivory-white and Alablaster skin*
Is staind throughout with *rare Vermillion red*,
Whose twinckling starrie lights doe never blin
To shine on lovely Venus (Beauties bed):
But as the Lillie and the blushing Rose,
So white and red on him in order grows.

Stanza XVII

With Phoenix feathers shall thy Face be fand,
Cooling those Cheekes, that being cool'd wexe red,
Like Lillyes in a bed of Roses shed.

◇

52. 1594 — Michael Drayton: *Endimion and Phoebe* (from *Early Poems of Daniel and Drayton*, p. D3b).

His cheekes now pale then lovely blushing red,
Which oft increasd, and quickly vanished,
And as on him her fixed eyes were bent,
So to and fro his colour came and went;
Like to a Christall neere the fire set,
Against the brightnes rightly opposet,
Now doth reteyne the colour of the flame,
And lightly moved againe, reflects the same;
For our affection quickned by her heate,
Alayd and strengthned by a strong conceit,
The mind disturbed forth-with doth convart,
To an internal passion of the hart,
By motion of that sodaine ioy or feare,
Which we receive either by the eye or eare,

For by retraction of the spirit and blood,
From those exterior parts where first they stood,
Into the center of the body sent,
Returnes againe more strong and vehement:
And in the like extreamitie made cold,
About the same, themselves doe closely hold,
And though the cause be like in this respect,
Works by this meanes a contrary effect.

◇

53. 1595 — Richard Barnfield: *Cynthia* (from Barnfield, *Complete Poems*, p. 89).

Sonnet XIII

Speake Eccho, tell; how may I call my love?   Love.
But how his Lamps that are so christaline?   Eyne.
Oh happy starrs that make your heavens divine:
And happy Iems that admiration move.
How tearm'st his golde tresses wav'd with aire?   Haire.
Oh lovely haire of your more-lovely Maister,
Image of love, faire shape of Alablaster,
Why do'st thou drive the Lover to dispaire?
How dost thou cal the bed where beuty grows?   Rose.
Faire virgine-Rose, whose mayden blossoms cover
The milk-white Lilly, thy imbracing Lover:
Whose kisses make the oft thy red to lose.
And blushing oft for shame, when he hath kist thee,
He vades away, and thou raing'st where it list thee.

◇

299

54. 1596 — Edmund Spenser: *Faerie Queene*, V, iii, 23 (from Spenser, *Poetical Works*, p. 288).

So forth the noble Ladie was ybrought,
  Adorn'd with honor and all comely grace:

Whereto her bashful shamefastnesse ywrought
  A great increase in her fair blushing face;
  As roses did with lillies interlace.

◇

D. Changes in Colour (deceitful).

◇

55. 1557 — Earl of Surrey (d. 1547)
  (from *Tottels Miscellany*, I, 5).

And when myne eyen dyd styll pursue
The flying chace that was their quest,
Their gredy lokes dyd oft renewe
the hidden wound within my brest.
  When every loke these chekes might staine,
From deadly pale to glowing red:
By outwarde signes appeared plaine,
The woe wherein my hart was fed.
  But all to late love lerneth me,
To pinte all kinde of colours new,
To blinde thir eyes that els should see,
My specled chekes with Cupids hewe.
  And now the couert brest I claime,
That worshipt Cupid secretely:
And norished his sacred flame,
From whence no blasing sparkes doe flye.

◇

56. 1557 — Earl of Surrey (d. 1547)
  (from *Tottels Miscellany*, I, 6).

I know ... how to hide my harmes with soft dissembling chere,
When in my face the painted thoughtes would outwardly apere.
  I know how that the blood forsakes the face for dred:
And how by shame it staines again the chekes with flaming red....
  I know in harty sighes, and laughters of the splene
At once to change my state, my wyll, and eke my colours clene.

57. 1590? — Christopher Marlowe: *All Ovids Elegies* (from Marlowe, *Complete Works*, I, 24).

She blusht: red shame becomes white cheekes, but this
If feigned, doth well; if true it doth amisse.
This, and what grife inforc'd me say I say'd,
A scarlet blush her guilty face arayed.
Even such as by Aurora hath the skie,
Or maides that their betrothed husbands spie.
Such as a rose mixt with a lilly breedes,
Or when the Moone travailes with charmed steeds.

◇

58. 1590 — Edmund Spenser: *Faerie Queene*, IV,x,50 (from Spenser, *Poetical Works*, p. 265).

And next to her sate goodly Shame-fastnesse,
  Ne ever durst her eyes from ground upreare,
  Ne ever once did looke up from her desse,
  As if some blame of evill she did feare,
  That in her cheekes made roses oft appeare....

◇

300

59. 1594 — Barnfield: *The Affectionate Shepheard* (from Barnfield, *Complete Poems*, p. 24).

XXVII

Learne of the Gentlewomen of this Age,
That set their Beauties to the open view,
Making disdaine their Lord, true love their
 Page;
A custom Zeale doth hate, Desert doth
 rue:
 *Learn to looke red, anon waxe pale and
 wan,*
 Making a mocke of love, a scorn of man.

◇

60. 159? — Henry Constable: Sonet 6 (from Constable, *Poems*, p. 127).

*The whitest skinnes red blushing shame
 doth blot
And in the reddest cheekes pale envie is.*

◇

E. Poems in Praise of Black.

61. 1587 — Matthew Grove: *Pelops and Hippodemia* (from Grove, *Poems*, pp. 60-61).

The lover being demaunded wherefore he went alwaies in black attire, in comendatiō of the same, made answere to his Lady in this wise. . . .

The black and browne doe seldome
 change,
 they fixe heir lovely grace,
When other colurs light and strange,
 doe vade within short space....
*The red will change with litle payne,
 and take another hewe.*
And so the grace is shortly gone,
 their beuty soone decayes,
*But black is black, and always one,
 and serves at all assayes.*

◇

62. 1594 — Richard Barnfield: *The Affectionate Shepheard* (from Barnfield, *Complete Poems*, p. 29).

L

And last of all, in blacke there doth
 appeare
Such qualities as not in yvorie;
*Black cannot blush for shame, looke pale
 for fear,*
Scorning to wear another livorie.
Blacke is the badge of sober Modestie,
The wonted wear of ancient Gravetie.

◇

301

NOTES

Unless otherwise stated in the text, all quotations of *Shakespeare's Sonnets* are taken from the edition of that work by Martin Seymour-Smith (London: Heinemann, 1963); quotations of *Venus and Adonis* and *The Rape of Lucrece* are taken from *Shakespeare's Poems* (New Haven and London: Yale University Press, 1964), which is a facsimile of the first editions of those works; and quotations of Shakespeare's plays are from *The Complete Poems and Plays of William Shakespeare*, edited by William Allan Neilson and Charles Jarvis Hill (Cambridge [Massachusetts]: Riverside Press, 1942).

In the notes, the following abbreviations are used:

CM	*Calendar of the Manuscripts of the Marquis of Salisbury* [i.e., *Cecil Manuscripts*].
DNB	*Dictionary of National Biography.*
GEC	G. E. Cokayne, *The Complete Peerage.*
L & P	*Letters and Papers, Foreign and Domestic, of the Reign of Henry VIII.*
OED	*Oxford English Dictionary.*
PC	*Acts of the Privy Council.*
PR	*Calendar of Patent Rolls.*
SP	*State Papers, Reign of Henry VIII.*
SP Dom.	*Calendar of State Papers, Domestic.*
SP For.	*Calendar of State Papers, Foreign.*
SP Ire.	*Calendar of State Papers, Ireland.*
SP Scot.	*Calendar of State Papers, Scotland.*
SP Sp.	*Calendar of State Papers, Spain.*
VCH	*Victoria County History: Hampshire and the Isle of Wight.*
WP	*Wriothesley Papers* (5M53, on deposit in the Hampshire Record Office, Winchester, Hampshire).

Where no ambiguity will result, only the name of the author or editor (if known; otherwise the abbreviated title of the document or work) is given in the notes. All sources are completely identified in the Bibliography.

Notes to Chapter I — "If only we could be sure. . . . "

1. Ogburn, p. 346.
2. Malone, *Supplement to the Edition of Shakespeare's Plays,* I, 654.
3. A license for the marriage of William Shakespeare to Anne "Whateley" of Temple Grafton was issued on 27 November 1582, and a bond for his marriage to "Anne Hathwey" of Stratford was signed on the following day. On 26 May 1583, "Susanna daughter to William Shakespeare" was christened. Chambers, *William Shakespeare,* II, 2, 41–52.
4. Benson, pp. *2-*2ᵛ.
5. Rollins, II, 18–28.
6. Rowe, I, xl.
7. Rollins, II, 38, 39.

8. Rollins, II, 133–134.
9. Charles Armitage Brown, p. 5.
10. Rollins, II, 135–140. See also Katharine M. Wilson, p. 355.
11. Sonnets 19, 38, 54, 55, 60, 63, 65, 81, 100, 101, 104, 107.
12. Sonnets 24, 105, 124.
13. Sonnets 20, 53, 59, 67, 68, 103, 106.
14. Sonnets 21, 22, 23, 25, 26, 29, 30, 31, 32, 37, 46, 47, 72, 75, 102, 108, 114, 115, 122.
15. Sonnets 52, 56, 57, 58, 62, 66, 71, 76, 109, 110, 111, 112, 116, 123, 125.
16. Sonnets 48, 49, 73, 74, 77, 91, 92, 117, 126.
17. Sonnets 27, 28, 39, 43, 44, 45, 50, 51, 61, 64, 87, 97.
18. Sonnets 33, 34, 36, 69, 70, 88, 89, 90, 93, 94, 95, 96, 98, 99, 118.
19. Sonnets 35, 40, 113, 119, 120.
20. Sonnets 127, 130, 131, 132, 147.
21. The assumption (generally *sub silentio*) among most persons (including myself) who believe that the Sonnets are autobiographical is that the youth addressed in the first 126 sonnets is always the same person, and not a number of men, that the woman addressed in the following 26 sonnets is always the same woman, and not a number of women, that the woman referred to in some of the first 126 sonnets is the woman to or about whom the next 26 are written, that the male referred to in some of the 26 sonnets to the woman is the man to or about whom the first 126 sonnets are written, and that one person, and one person only, is the Rival Poet. See Seymour-Smith, pp. 14–24; Bush and Harbage, pp. 8–9; Acheson, *Shakespeare's Sonnet Story*, pp. 34–35; Rowse, *Shakespeare's Sonnets: The Problems Solved*, pp. xxiv–xxv; Tyler, pp. 28, 33, 44, 73; Hubler, p. 6.
22. See Rollins, I, 371: "*fire out* has its well-known meaning of 'communicate a venereal disease,'" and Martin Green, pp. 12–41.
23. See, e.g. Muir, *Shakespeare's Sonnets*, p. 87; Seymour-Smith, p. 190; Wyndham, p. 335; Bush and Harbage, p. 176. An argument is sometimes made that the baths referred to in these two sonnets are treatments for venereal disease, thus linking them to a theme prominent in the Sonnets. My own thoughts as to the contents and reasons for these poems are set forth in Chapter IV, at pages 70–78, and in Chapter VIII, at pages 195-200.
24. Rollins, II, 133–294.
25. See, e.g., Booth, pp. 546–549; Kerrigan, pp. 11–12.
26. Rollins, II, 180–181. Those who, like myself, do not believe that "Will" was the first name of the Friend, find other explanations for the puns. In my opinion, the "Will" puns are fully explained by the understanding that the word "will" signifies, in addition to the name of the poet, "genitalia" (either male or female; see Kerrigan, p. 365 and Green, p. 53). Consider:

> So thou beeing rich in *Will* adde to thy *Will*,
> One will of mine to make thy large *Will* more, [Sonnet 135]

and

> *Will* will fulfill the treasure of thy love,
> I fill it full with wils, and my will one. . . .[Sonnet 136].

27. *The Portrait of Mr. W. H.*, pp. 177–178.
28. Butler, p. 115.
29. Nisbet, pp. 42–43.
30. Pohl, pp. 121–25.
31. Rollins, II, 213.
32. Rollins, II, 216.
33. Hotson, *Mr W.H.*, p. 109. Gray's Inn is situated in the Parish of Portpool, and each year at Christmas time a "Prince of Purpoole" was chosen to preside over the students' holiday revels, called the "*Gesta Grayorum.*" A. Wigfall Green, pp. 71–74. A particularly complete account of the festivity held in 1594 survives, and is printed in Nichols, III, 262–352.
34. Rollins, II, 195.
35. Charles Armitage Brown, pp. 41–44.
36. Tyler, pp. 44-72.
37. Chambers, *William Shakespeare*, I, 567.
38. *Ibid.*; Tyler, pp. 44-48.
39. See, for example, Sidney Lee, *A Life of William Shakespeare*, p. 687; Rowse, *Shakespeare's Sonnets: The Problems Solved*, p. xliv.
40. Drake, II, 58–86; Chambrun, pp. 28–31; Rowse, *Shakespeare's Sonnets: The Problems Solved*, pp. xiii–xix.
41. Rollins, II, 187; Stopes, *Shakespeare's Sonnets*, p. xliii; Chambrun, pp. 24–25.
42. Hamilton, p. 66, argues that Shakespeare's will is in his own handwriting.
43. Rowse, *Shakespeare's Southampton*, pp. 88–89.
44. Drake, II, 63, 64.
45. Sidney Lee, *A Life of William Shakespeare*, pp. 660–661; Rowse, *Shakespeare's Southampton*, pp. 53–56.
46. Since Burghley had been granted the wardship of Southampton, he had the right to "sell" the marriage; see Hurstfield, pp. 141-142. If this money actually was paid to Burghley, it was to compensate him for the loss incurred by Southampton's unwillingness to be sold to Burghley's customer (who happened to be Burghley; the situation reminds one of Pooh-Bah's complicated transactions with himself in his many capacities).
47. Rowse, *Shakespeare's Sonnets: The Problems Solved*, p. xliv.
48. Sidney Lee, *A Life of William Shakespeare*, pp. 683-685.
49. Chambers, *William Shakespeare*, I, 567.
50. Chambrun, pp. 30–31, for example.
51. Lee, *A Life of William Shakespeare*, p. 693; Chambrun, pp. 30-31; Tyler, p. 31; Rollins, II, 191–192, 196. The many portraits of the adult Henry Wriothesley and William Pembroke do not depict strikingly handsome men, but either one, like Oscar Wilde's friend Lord Alfred Douglas, may have been much better looking in his youth than in his maturity. Is not the evanescence of beauty a common theme of poets of all times and places?
52. GEC, s.v. Pembroke (William Herbert) and Southampton (Henry Wriothesley).
53. Meres, pp. 281–282; *Shakespeare's Poems*, pp. 159, 161; Rollins, II, 53.
54. Hotson, *Shakespeare's Sonnets Dated*, p. 6, and *Mr W.H.*, p. 75.
55. Butler, pp. 103–104.

56. Tyler, pp, 23–25.
57. Chambers, *William Shakespeare*, I, 564.
58. Rowse, *William Shakespeare*, p. 182.
59. Lee, *A Life of William Shakespeare*, pp. 226–228.
60. Rowse, *William Shakespeare*, p. 175.
61. Minto, p. 223.
62. Akrigg, *Shakespeare and the Earl of Southampton*, pp. 232–233.
63. Chambers, *William Shakespeare*, I, 568.
64. Rollins, II, 286–294.
65. Tyler, pp. 55–58; 73–92.
66. Lee, *A Life of William Shakespeare*, p. 694 (note); see also Newdigate-Newdegate, pp. 32–33.
67. Harrison, *Shakespeare Under Elizabeth*, p. 310; Hotson, *Mr. W.H.*, pp. 238–245.
68. Rollins, II, 260–261, 269–271.
69. Rowse, *Shakespeare's Sonnets: The Problems Solved*, p. xxxiv.
70. For an account of the disappearance of the word which was the foundation of Rowse's Lanier theory, see *The Shakespeare Newsletter*, XXIII, pp. 1, 2 (February, 1973) and p. 24 (May, 1973); see also Schoenbaum, p. 127.
71. Rowse, *The Poems of Shakespeare's Dark Lady*, pp. 9–17.

Notes to Chapter II — A Single Fact

1. Hotson, *Shakespeare's Sonnets Dated*, p. 142.
2. This is obliquely acknowledged by a number of scholars who, while imputing some abstract meanings to Rose — beauty, or perfection — recognize that these qualities are personified in the Fair Friend. See, e.g., Tucker p. 79; H. M. Young, p. 70.
3. Wyndham, p. 298.
4. Fairchild, p. 118.
5. In *The Labyrinth of Shakespeare's Sonnets*, pp. 12–41, I suggest that the "shame" is the youth's contraction of a venereal disease.
6. Shackford, p. 122.
7. Rollins, I, 7; II, 194.
8. *Shakespeare's Sonnet Story*, p. 59.
9. Akrigg, *Shakespeare and the Earl of Southampton*, p. 3.
10. *Ibid*, n. 3.
11. Rowse, *Shakespeare's Southampton*, p. 4. He bases this conclusion on the supposed fact that "later on, we find one of the name spelling himself phonetically Risley." He does not say how much later on, or who the one was. This, of course, is no basis for a conclusion that "Risley" is a phonetic spelling of the name as it was pronounced either by the first or third Earls of Southampton. The first Earl's cousin, Charles Wriothesley (d. 1562), in his *Chronicles*, spells the family name Wriosley (I, 115), Wriothesly (I, 130), Wrothesley (I, 167) and Wrythesley (I, 183) — as well, of course, as Wriothesley (I, 187). The indices to Volumes XII, XIII, XIV, XV, XVI and XVII of the L & P, which cover the years 1537 through 1542, show the name spelled in

306

many different ways, including Writheouthley, Wrissley, Wryseley, Vrisley, Wreesley, Wysley, Voyzelay, Vrisley, Woursley, Wroysely — and yes, *Wrosley* (L & P XII, Part 2, No. 429, p. 173). Also, Oliver Lawrence, the second husband of Thomas Wriothesley's sister Anne, in his will (he died in 1558/9) spells the name Wriosley and Wrotsley, and Oliver's brother Henry, in his will (he died in 1566) spells the name Wriosley and Wrosley. *The Herald and Genealogist*, IV, 534. It is impossible to tell, of all these spellings, which is phonetic. A useful discussion is provided by Muriel St. Clare Byrne, the editor of *The Lisle Letters*, at I, 121:

> Wriothesley presents a genuine spelling/pronunciation problem. There are many variants, and as this is his [the first Earl's] own spelling one might ignore them, but for the fact that the Wrisley/Wryssley/Writhesley form, as against Husee's Wryottesley and his cousin the chronicler's Wriosley suggests that perhaps two pronunciations were current and that Thomas himself favoured the 'o' sound, so that Husee's is an effort at a genuine phonetic rendering, nearer to the modern Wrottesley than Wrisley (short *i* as in writ).

12. Booth, p. 135.
13. Rowse, *Shakespeare's Sonnets: The Problems Solved*, p. 5.
14. Wyndham, p. 261; Tucker, p. lxxxvii.
15. Rollins, II, 203; II, 223; II, 243; II, 157.
16. Martin Green, pp. 56-57, 82-84.
17. In his *Remains Concerning Britain*, William Camden, after explaining (p.182) that "Annagrammitisme" is the art of transposing the letters of a person's name so as to make a new word or phrase "making some perfect sence applyable to the person named," gives (p. 189) as an anagram for Henricus Wriothesleius, "*Heroicus, Laetus, vi virens*," which means "heroic, joyful, green (i.e.,vibrant) with strength." Carried over into this anagram is the same sense of budding or blooming which the original name suggests, and to which Sonnet 54 may allude.
18. Wagner, "Heraldry," p. 362.
19. See generally Hall, *Canting and Allusive Arms of England and Wales*; Savage, "Heraldry in Shakespeare," p. 291; Franklyn, p. 5.
20. Wagner, *Historic Heraldry of Britain*, p. 32.
21. Edmondson, s.v. raven, falcon, boar and wolf, in that portion of his work entitled *Glover's Ordinary of Arms*.
22. Tannenbaum, p. 18.
23. Burke, *The General Armory*, p. 1140. Burke's abbreviations are expanded.
24. Milles, p. 1031.
25. In ancient times, the "honorary possessions" of an Earl consisted of the castles, manors and other lands held by Knights and others whose Lord he was, and were referred to the Earl's "honour." Selden, p. 552. But by the sixteenth century the term was used merely to designate such royally-conferred dukedoms, earldoms, baronies, etc., as might bear a specific shire's or municipality's name.
26. Hope, "English Municipal Heraldry," p. 180. Figure 2 in the text is also taken from this source. The same blazon appears in a leaflet prepared by the South-

ampton City Council entitled *Coat of Arms of the City of Southampton*. Different authorities blazon the arms in slightly different ways: Speed, p. 88, writes "Per Fesse, silver and Gules, three Roses counterchanged of the Feild [sic]"; Fox-Davies, *The Book of Public Arms*, p. 738, gives "Party per fesse gules and argent, three roses counterchanged" (note that he has the colours reversed); Scott-Giles, *Civic Heraldry*, p. 154, gives "Parted fesswise argent and gules, three roses counterchanged." "Party" or "parted" means divided: "a shield divided by a horizontal central line is party per fess. . . . In blazon, the word party is often omitted." *Boutell's Heraldry*, pp. 31-32.

27. A crest is a figure placed on a helmet, or on a crest wreath, above a shield; supporters are figures or inanimate objects placed on the sides of, or behind, shields to sustain them. *Rothery*, pp. 329 and 338. Southampton's crest is: On Wreath of the Colours, Issuing out of a Castle Or, a Queen in her imperial majesty holding in the dexter hand the sword of justice and in the sinister the balance of equity all proper, Mantling Gules doubled Argent. Southampton's supporters are: On either side a Ship upon the sea proper, standing in its forepart a Lion rampant Or. *Coat of the Arms of the City of Southampton*. Fox-Davies, *A Complete Guide to Heraldry*, p. 445, calls these "the most unusual" supporters to be found in British armory. The depiction of a coat on a shield complete with its crest and supporters is called an "achievement." The simplicity and beauty of the Southampton coat of arms is in striking contrast to the complexity and gaudiness of the crest and supporters, which probably explains why the crest and supporters were for a long time ignored, and seem to have been largely forgotten. In a book first published in 1801, a local antiquarian, Henry C. Englefield, described the town's coat of arms without mentioning a crest or supporters. However, he was subsequently shown by one Arthur Hammond, Esq., a copy of the 1575 grant. In the second edition of his book, issued in 1805, Englefield writes, "It does not appear that the town ever made use of the cumbrous pomp of crest and supporters, thus added by Elizabeth, to the simple and beautiful coat of arms of the town, and they probably exist only in the Herald's Office, and in a drawing preserved in the Audit House." It may be a reflection on modern tastes that the supporters and crest are now frequently used in Southampton, and can be seen everywhere on municipal vehicles and buildings, and in official publications.

28. Fox-Davies, *The Book of Public Arms*, p. 738; Scott-Giles, *Civic Heraldry*, p. 154.

29. *The Charters of the Borough of Southampton*, I, 54.

30. Southampton City Council.

31. *Id*.

32. Scott-Giles, *Civic Heraldry*, p. 154.

33. Welch, p. 13.

34. In *The Book of Public Arms*, at p. ix, Fox-Davies writes: "In England it was held that nobody existed in a county competent to bear arms until the formation [upon the passage of the Local Government Act of 1888, 51 & 52 Vict., c. 41] of the County Councils. In most cases the arms of the County Town did duty. . . ."

35. *Hampshire County Handbook and Industrial Review*, p. 19:

> Hampshire County Council has no Coat of Arms. It has a County Badge of great antiquity, used over the centuries in slightly varying forms and said to date back to before the establishment of the College of Heralds.
>
> The essential features are a rose, surmounted by a crown, surmounted in turn by a cap, the whole surrounded by a wreath of leaves.
>
> In some forms of the badge, the rose is double, as on the centre of the Round Table [at Winchester Castle, depicted in Plate IV], with the outer petals red and the inner white. What appears to be the more ancient form has a single rose, believed to be the Lancastrian rose and therefore single red.

The present form of the County Badge was adopted in 1895. *Id*; Minns, "On the New Device of Seal of the Hants Field Club and Archaeological Society," pp. 225–228.

36. See, for example, the arms of Bournemouth, Eastleigh, Fareham, Petersfield and Southampton University, and the device of Havant and Waterloo, as described in Scott-Giles, *Civic Heraldry*, pp. 153-158, 363. In explaining the roses on the Eastleigh arms, Scott-Giles states, at page 158, "The roses are emblems of Hampshire. . . . "

37. Fox-Davies, *The Book of Public Arms*, pp. 352, 738, and *The Art of Heraldry*, p. 443.

38. Camden, *Britannia*, 1607 (Latin) p. 139; 1698 (English) column 122. Akrigg refers to the Titchfield residence as the Wriothesleys' "family seat in Hampshire" (p. 5) and "the Earl of Southampton's country seat" (p. 7). Bartlett calls it "their chief country seat" (p. 50). The importance attached to this site by the Wriothesleys is reflected by the burial of all four earls of that line, and many of their children, in the church at Titchfield.

39. See Appendix II for the history of Titchfield Abbey/Place House.

40. Graham and Rigold, pp. 14–15.

41. "Bugle" is a name having many associations with Southampton and the Wriothesleys. "Bugle" is a street in Southampton. The name is derived from the Old French word (*bugle*) for "young bull." The street has at various times in its history been called "Bull Street," "Bogle Street," etc. A residence called first "Bolehus" and eventually "Bull Hall" was erected on this street in the 11th or 12th century, was no longer there by the end of the 15th century, but was rebuilt by Henry Huttoft, merchant and Mayor during the reign of Henry VIII. In 1568, Bull Hall was purchased by the second Earl of Southampton for £600 from the heirs of John Huttoft, Bartlett, p. 55, and was listed as one of the second Earl of Southampton's properties in the *Inquisition Post Mortem* prepared after his death in 1581. Akrigg, *Shakespeare and the Earl of Southampton*, p. 21. This Bull Hall burned down in 1791, and was the next year replaced by another one, which was razed in the early 1850's. Sandell, pp. 69, 70. By what may be a coincidence, both the crest and supporters of the Wriothesley family depict a *bugle*. In a very early blazon, the crest is "A bugle's head" erased Sable, ducally crowned, ringed and guttee d'or. Metcalfe, p. 60. In later blazons, the crest and supporters

include the whole bugle. See *Cooke's Baronage*, f. 250. The crest is: a bull passant sable armed and crowned, in his nose an annulet and line or, reflecting over his back; the supporters are: dexter side, a bull rampant sable, ducally crowned, horned, hoofed, crined, muzzle-ringed and chained (the chain reflexed over the back), or; sinister side, a lion rampant or, head and mane fretty gules. Edmondson, II, s.v. Wriothesley; Greenfield, p. 78. On Plate VIII is a photograph of the splendid achievement of the second Earl of Southampton on the Wriothesley tomb, showing the Wriothesley crest and supporters.

42. Child, p. 78.
43 *Id.*
44. *Black's Guide to Hampshire*, pp. 59-60; Vesey-Fitzgerald, p. 344.
45. Minns, "Titchfield Abbey and Place House," p. 317.
46. VCH, III, 223.
47. Godfrey, Wagner and London, p. 41.
48. *Ibid.*
49. DNB, s.v. Wriothesley (more correctly Writh or Wrythe), John.
50. *Ibid.*
51. Banks, p. 671. It is surprising to discover the low esteem in which heralds were formerly held. When Essex on 8 February 1601 was urged to obey the injunctions of the heralds to lay down his arms, his response was that "a herald would do anything for 2 *s.*" SP Dom., 1598-1601, p. 547.
52. Dugdale, p. 383.
53. Godfrey, Wagner and London, pp. 43, 44. Thomas Wriothesley is credited with being the "inventor of the rectilinear pedigree." Wagner, *English Genealogy*, p. 372.
54. See, Round, *Studies in Peerage and Family History*, p. 141, and *Peerage and Pedigree*, I, 38.
55. Godfrey, Wagner and London, p. 57
56. [Anstis], I, 369-370. Anstis evidently had in mind Camden's essay on "Surnames" in *Remains Concerning Britain* as he was writing the passage here quoted. In that essay, at page 159, Camden states that "Judge Cataline took exception at one [an alias] in this respect, saying that no honest man had a double name, and came in with an Alias," to which the party to whom he addressed this comment asked "what exception his Lordship could take to Jesus Christ, alias Jesus of Nazareth?" Anstis is wrong in suggesting that when Thomas Wrythe, Garter King of Arms, took Wriothesley as an alias, Judge Cataline's remark must have been "out of his Memory," for Judge Catlin (as the name is usually spelled), who was raised to the bench in 1558 and died in 1574 (DNB, s.v. Catlin, Robert), probably was not even born when the Wrythes changed their name to Wriothesley. Judge Catlin's daughter married Sir John Spencer and was thus the grandmother of the William Spencer who married Henry Wriothesley's daughter Penelope.

Another phrase used by Anstis, *Omnis herus servo Monosyllabus* — "for a slave, every master is a monosyllable" — also occurs in the Camden essay (at page 147). Camden states that the reason every master is a monosyllable is "in respect of their short commands"; Camden also gives the opposite phrase, *Omnis*

310

servus hero Monosyllabus — "for a master, every slave is a monosyllable" — and explains that this is "in respect of the curtailing of their names, as Wil, Sim, Hodge, &c." Camden's explanations sound a bit ingenuous.

57. Banks, p. 671.
58. Godfrey, Wagner and London, p. 42.
59. [Anstis], pp. 366–367.
60. Legh, fol. 83^v.
61. Wagner, *Heralds of England*, p. 133. Figure 4 is taken from Boutell, *English Heraldry*, p. 131.
62. Godfrey, Wagner and London, p. 43.
63. For a nineteenth century example of a "dove" blazon, see Metcalfe, p. 60. The Wriothesley birds have also been blazoned as eagles (Godfrey, Wagner and London, p. 45), eaglets (*Cooke's Baronage*, f. 144), sea gulls (*The Mirrour of Maiestie*), and hawks (Robinson II, s.v. Wriothsley or Wriothesley).

Many readers will note the resemblance of the Wriothesley arms, and the arms of the College of Arms, to the the arms popularly attributed to St. Edward the Confessor. A. C. Fox-Davies, in his *A Complete Guide to Heraldry*, at page 244 observes that "there can be very little doubt that the coat of arms [of the College of Arms] itself is based upon the coat of St. Edward the Confessor. The so-called coat of St. Edward the Confessor is a cross patonce between five martlets, but it is pretty well agreed that these martlets are a corruption of the doves which figure upon his coins, and one of which surmounts the sceptre which is known as St.

Figure 13. Arms of Edward the Confessor.

Edward's staff, or 'the sceptre with the dove.'" The arms which Anstis devised for himself (see Godfrey, Wagner and London, pp. 56-57) are very similar to the arms of the Wriothesleys, Edward the Confessor and the College of Arms.

64. Godfrey, Wagner and London, p. 169.
65. DNB, s.v. Wriothesley, Charles.
66. Godfrey, Wagner and London, p. 184.
67. *Ibid*, pp. 81-82, 184.
68. The painting is based upon a drawing by Holbein, which is reproduced in *The Lisle Letters*, IV, facing page 208. Wriothesley's arms, as depicted in the painting, are as follows: the dexter top quarter (that is, the upper *left* quarter as viewed by the observer, all dexters and sinisters in heraldry being so designated from the point of view of the *bearer* of the shield) contains four cantons: the dexter top and the sinister bottom cantons display the Wriothesley arms, the sinister top canton shows the arms of Dunstanville and the dexter bottom canton shows the arms of Lewsell; the sinister top quarter bears the arms of Lovetoft, the dexter bottom quarter the arms of Peckham and the sinister bottom quarter

the arms of Crowton. the arms are encircled with a garter bearing the usual legend, *Honi soit qui mal y pense*, and under the coat is the Wriothesley motto, *Ung par tout, tour par ung*.

Unlike his grandfather, the third Earl of Southampton almost always during his lifetime used his arms in their simplest form. The earliest example of this is the carving of the young earl at the base of the Titchfield tomb (Plate VI); behind him is a shield, showing as his arms only the four silver birds on their blue backgrounds, separated by the golden cross. His arms fill half the shield only, in the obvious expectation that some day the arms of his wife's family would fill the other half; why this never happened, I don't know, for his wife's family was armigerous. See Franklin, p. 87. The tomb carving dates probably from 1594 or 1595, but representations of the third Earl's coat of arms made in 1603 and 1610 (reproduced in Plate VI and Figure 1) also show the arms without any quarterings. However, the stained glass representations of the Earl's arms in Lincoln's Inn, as illustrated in William Dugdale's *Origines Juridiciales*, pp. 238-239, bear many of the quarterings depicted in Plate VIII and Figure 5. These are in the eastern windows in the refectory and the southern windows in the chapel, under the portrait of St. Peter and next to the arms of William Herbert, Earl of Pembroke. The arms in the chapel bear the date 1623, the year before the third Earl died, and were doubtless installed during the course of the construction of the chapel, which was consecrated on Ascension Day, 1623, Dr. John Donne preaching the sermon for the occasion. *Ibid.*, pp. 235-236. The cost of constructing the chapel was raised by subscription, and it is likely that Henry Wriothesley and all the others whose arms appear in the chapel contributed substantially to the building costs. So it may be out of deference to the dignity of the chapel, rather than because of his increasing interest in his family's lustre, that the arms at Lincoln's Inn are so much more elaborate than those usually displayed by the third Earl.

69. L & P XII, part 2, no. 1311 (40), p. 473.
70. L & P IX, Appendix. No. 14, p. 407.
71. An earl did not necessarily live in the place whence he derived his honour; for example, William Fitzwilliam, Wriothesley's predecessor as Earl of Southampton, lived at Cowdray, in Midhurst, Sussex.
72. OED, s. v. Earl.
73. Francis Bacon, p. 377.
74. Round, *Geoffrey de Mandeville*, p. 273.
75. *Ibid.*, pp. 320–321. Other examples of comital titles not reflecting county names are Winchester, Arundel and Shrewsbury. GEC, s.v. Southampton.
76. *The Charters of the Borough of Southampton*, I, 54.
77. *Ibid.*, p. 74.
78. Welch, facing p. 21.
79. GEC, s.v. Southampton (William Fitzwilliam) states that the Earldom is of the "County of Southampton," but no support of any kind is offered for this conclusion.
80. There may have been Earls of "Southampton" in the ninth to eleventh centuries, of whom Bogo (or Beauvois or Bevis), a Saxon Lord defeated by the Normans

at Cardiff, in Glamorganshire, in 1070, was the last. Warner, II, 94-95. The title does not reappear until 1537, when it was granted by Henry VIII to William Fitzwilliam. GEC, s.v. Southampton (William Fitzwilliam).

81. L & P XII, Part 2, No. 921, p. 324; No. 922, p. 325; No. 1024, p. 358; No. 1153, p. 411; Kingsford, *Bath Inn or Arundel House*, p. 248. There is also a reference to Fitzwilliam's wife as "the Countess of Hamton." Machyn, p. 2.

82. See, for example, *Lisle Letters*, II, No. 132, p. 58, No. 168, p. 127, No. 281, p. 299, No. 282, p. 300, No. 435a, p. 548, No. 451, p. 589, No. 452, p. 591, No. 455, p. 595; L & P, Addenda, I, Part 1, No. 7, p. 2; No. 20, p. 6; No. 341, p. 101; No. 514, p. 172; No. 540, p. 182; No. 970, p. 340; Part 2, No. 1488, p. 507; No. 1697, p. 569; etc., etc. See also, A. T. Lloyd, p. 181.

83. SP Sp., 1547–1549, p. 48.

84. SP For., 1558–1559, no. 1303, p. 526.

85. Fox-Davies, *Heraldry*, pp. 72–73.

86. DNB, s.v. Grosvenor, Robert; Burke, *The General Armory*, s.v. Grosvenor [Duke of Westminster]; Fox-Davies, *Book of Public Arms*, p. 846.

87. *Manchester Corporation* v. *Manchester Palace of Varieties, Ltd.*, All England Reports, 1955, Vol. 1, 387, 394–395.

88. Wagner, *Heralds and Heraldry in the Middle Ages*, pp. 9-10; Fox-Davies, *The Right to Bear Arms*, p. 118.

89. Wagner, *Heralds and Heraldry in the Middle Ages*, pp. 139–146.

90. See SP Dom., 1598-1601, pp. 600-601, which is a report by Southampton's trustees of the value of the attainted earl's lands in Hampshire, and *Court Leet Records*, p. 357, note 2, which show Queen Elizabeth on the rolls of landholders in Southampton by virtue of her possession of the Earl's forfeited properties.

91. Fox-Davies, *A Complete Guide to Heraldry*, p. 73; see also Wentersdorf, pp. 216–218.

92. As is shown in Appendix II, this one heraldic shield is a lone remnant of many red and white rose decorations and badges which at one time were displayed throughout the Wriothesley home at Titchfield.

Notes to Chapter III — The Rose of the World

1. Tennyson, *Becket*, II,i,146-147. Tennyson was an admirer of the Sonnets, which he read all the time. See Tennyson, *Journal*, pp. 55, 82, 95, 129, 132, 139, 156, 363. He once said to Edward Fitzgerald, "Sometimes I think Shakespeare's Sonnets finer than his plays. . . ," a statement he immediately qualified by adding, "which is of course absurd. For it is the knowledge of the Plays that makes the Sonnets so fine." *Tennyson and his Friends*, p. 145. On another occasion, he told Benjamin Jowett that "he used to think Shakespeare greater in his sonnets than in his plays," but, in Jowett's words, "he soon returned to the thought which is indeed the thought of all the world." Rader, pp. 144–145, note 18. I nevertheless suspect that Tennyson tempered his praise of the Sonnets in order not to scandalize his friends (Jowett, for example, was perceptive enough to discern in Tennyson's love for the Sonnets "a sort of sympathy with Hellen-

ism," *ibid.*), and that he truly thought that the Sonnets were finer productions than the plays.

2. McLean, p. 165.
3. *Ibid.*, p. 167.
4. *Id.*
5. *Essays on the Life and Work of Thomas Linacre*, pp. xvii-xviii.
6. McLean, p. 167. See also Rohde, who writes, at page 108, "The Damask versicolor has an occasional red petal, and according to the leading rosarians this is the true York and Lancaster rose." However, Sir Thomas Hanmer, a 17th century botanist, distinguishes between "the VARIEGATED DAMASKE, or YORKE AND LANCASTER, which is the true Damaske, striped well with White, a fine Rose when it markes rightly," and "the Damaske [a different rose, "of a carnation color"], and no fuller of leaves, called in Latine Prenestina," both of which roses, he notes, are equally sweet. *The Garden Book of Sir Thomas Hanmer*, p. 113.
7. L & P XXI, Part 2, No. 769,ii(19), p. 402.
8. Rohde, pp. 107-108.
9. OED, s.v. "field" (def. 13a); the earliest example given by the OED dates from about 1400. For an early use of the word, see the excerpt from Bossewell, quoted in Appendix II, at p. 275.
10. Fox-Davies, *Heraldry Explained*, p. 96.
11. *Ballads from Manuscripts*, ed. Frederick J. Furnivall (London: Taylor and Co., 1868-1872, p. 389.)
12. Legh, p. 99^v. John Bossewell, in his *Works of Armorie* published in 1572, states the same, at Fo. 75^v:

> Among all flours of ye world, the Rose is the cheife, and beareth the price. And therefore ye chefe parte of man, which is the heade is ofte crowned therwith, because of hys vertues, swete smell and savoure, for by fayrenes they fede ye sight, and please the smell by odour: and accorde to medecine, both grene and drye. *Rose a specie floris nuncupata:q rutilanti colore rubeat.* Therefore our noble and most gracious Quene doth, and for euer shall use thys delectable Poesie or worde. *Rutilans Rosa sine spina.* If I were learned thereunto, I woulde speake more of thys floure. But beyng bolde of *Plinye*, the Rose shall have preheminence above all floures, and nexte to it, the floure de luce, and the thirde the violet.

13. Hotson, *Shakespeare's Sonnets Dated*, p. 143.
14. *Lord Burghley's Papers in The British Library in London*, Vol. 99, fo. 19 (Reel 36 of Microfilm edition).
15. Watson, *Poems*, p. 40.
16. And why not? Thirty years later Anthony van Dyck painted Sir George Villiers (the favourite of James I and later Duke of Buckingham) and Lady Katherine Manners, his wife, as Venus and Adonis; one suspects that Wriothesley, at 19, made a more comely Adonis than did Villiers at 29.
17. *Shakespeare's Ovid*, p. 217 (Book Ten), line 850.

18. Another example of the influence upon Shakespeare of the Wriothesley armorial bearings has already been noted by Stopes, *The Life of Henry, Third Earl of Southampton*, p. 43 and Baldwin, pp. 118, 175, 176, and this is the Wriothesley family motto, *Ung par tout, tout par ung* (see Plates VII and VIII), which may be alluded to in Sonnet 105 ("To one, of one, still such, and euer so") and in *Lucrece* ("That one for all, or all for one we gage" (line 144)).

19. People who find significance in anagrams (and the Elizabethans certainly did; see footnote 17 to Chapter II) may ponder the fact that an anagram of "Wriothesley" is "Whitely rose." "Rosely white" is more euphonious, but "rosely" is not a word used by Shakespeare, nor is the word to be found in the *Oxford English Dictionary*, whereas "whitely" appears in *Love's Labour's Lost* (III, i, 198): "A whitely wanton with a velvet brow. . . ," and is illustrated in the OED by examples going back to 1398.

20. SP Dom., 1547-1580, No. 21, p. 63.

21. The sketch is from Greenfield, facing page 77.

22. Bullough, I, 273, 274.

23. The first Viscount Montagu had two wives. His first wife was Jane, the daughter of Robert Radcliffe, the first Earl of Sussex. His children by this first marriage included Anthony Browne, who married Mary Dormer, and Mary Browne, who married the second Earl of Southampton and was the mother of the third Earl. The first Viscount Montagu's second wife was Magdalen, the daughter of William, Lord Dacres. Elizabeth, who married Robert Dormer, was one of the children of this second marriage. *Visitation of the County of Sussex*, p. 84. Some, but not all, of these relationships are shown on Table III.

24. Gascoigne, I, 75.

25. SP, Sp., 1554–1558, No. 150, p. 140.

26. Burnet, II, 482.

27. *Ibid*; see also Blore's chapter on Sir Anthony Browne (the father of the first Viscount Montagu) where he writes, at p. 4, that "no one was more liberally rewarded by his royal master out of the spoils of the religious houses than Sir Anthony Browne."

28. *Calendar of State Papers, Venice*, VI, Part 1, 1555–1556, No. 144, p. 122.

29. SP For., 1553–1558, No. 399, p. 180.

30. And this clothing may have stayed in the family for a long time, since costly clothing was often the subject of specific bequests in Tudor wills. The clothing worn by the three grandsons of the Viscount Montagu, in the famous miniature by Isaac Oliver in the Burghley House Collection, seems (to me) more Venetian than English. The clothing may, however, merely reflect the fact that the young men were traveling abroad; see note 12 to Chapter VIII.

31. Gascoigne, I, p. 76.

32. *Id.*

33. *Ibid*, pp. 82–83.

34. *Ibid*, p. 83.

35. *Ibid*, p. 85.

36. Bullough, I, 66–68.

37. *Ibid.*, I, 287, line 53 (this is a line from Arthur Brooke's poem, *The Tragicall Historye of Romeus and Juliet*).
38. See, e.g., Adams, p. 219; Chambers, *William Shakespeare*, I, 346; Neilson and Hill, p. 974.
39. Ness, p. 89; Dowden, p. xix.
40. Spenser, pp. 609-622; Chambers, *William Shakespeare*, I, 345. *Venus and Adonis* also contains a reference to an earthquake:

> a deadly grone [groan].
> Whereat ech tributarie subiect quakes,
> As when the wind imprisond in the ground,
> Struggling for passage, earths foundation shakes,
> which with cold terror, doth mens minds confound. . . .
> [Lines 1044-1048.]

41. Nichols, III, 90–96.
42. See Appendix I, p. 222.
43. See Appendix I, p. 261.
44. One occasionally encounters the unlikely hypothesis that "Shakespeare came from Stratford-on-Avon with *Venus and Adonis* in his pocket" — so described but not endorsed by Chambers, *William Shakespeare*, I, 545, or that the poem was dedicated to Southampton, in the hope of obtaining his patronage, before Shakespeare actually met him. The red and white rose imagery of the poem establishes that it was not written until after Shakespeare met Southampton.
45. Neilson and Hill, p. 53.
46. Ivor Brown, p. 210 ("rubbish"); Brooke, p. 304 ("the poorest"); Leishman, p. 195 ("tiresome").
47. Martin Green, pp. 12–41.
48. Baldwin, pp. 302–303; Schaar, pp. 89–90.

Notes to Chapter IV — The Reason of White and Red

1. Rader, pp. 22–59.
2. See note 1 to Chapter III.
3. Vyvyan, p. 79.
4. This is the language of the so-called Geneva translation of the Bible, available in many editions issued from about 1570 on. The translation of Miles Coverdale, published in 1535, and of Richard Tavener, published in 1539, render this as "I am the floure of the field, and lyly of the valleys." The Great Bible of 1540 (sometimes also called the Cromwell or the Cranmer Bible) gives this as "I am the lyly of the felde, and rose of the valleys." It was not until the publication of the King James version of the Bible in 1611 that the line achieved the form in which it is today best known: "I am the Rose of Sharon, and the lily of the valleys."
5. *Elizabethan Lyrics*, p. 172.
6. Gerald Massey, writing in 1888, maintains that certain imagery in the Sonnets "is feminine, and has been held so by all poets that ever wrote in our language; and

I consider his [Shakespeare's] instinct in such a matter to be so natural that he could not thus violate the sex of his images. . . . I doubt if there be an instance in Shakespeare of man addressing man as 'my rose,' and should as soon expect to find 'my tulip.' . . . the 'Rose' is the woman-symbol." Massey, pp. 26-28. Massey accordingly concludes that the sonnets describing the beloved as a rose were written by men to *women*: Sonnet 109, for example ("thou, my Rose") was written by Southampton to Elizabeth Vernon. *Ibid.*, p. 289. Almost 100 years later, Joseph Pequigney, while not doubting that the Rose sonnets were addressed by Shakespeare to a man, states, at page 10, that " . . . what may surprise is that the rose, a well-established female symbol, is made emblematic of a male."

7. Seward, pp. 61, 63, 76, 78.

8. *Ibid.*, pp. 119, 136, 137, 141.

9. They appear as ΕΠΙΣΤΟΛΑΙ ΦΙΛΟΣΤΡΑΤΟΥ ΑΣΠΑΣΙΑ in a collection entitled *Epistolae diuersorum philosophorum, oratorium, rhetorum sex et viginti.*

10. Benner and Fobes, on the authority of someone else, report (at p. 409) that Τῶν ἑλληνικῶν ἐπιστολῶν ἀνθολογία, published in Paris in 1583, contains selections from the *Letters* of Philostratus. A book with the same title, published in Paris in 1557 by "Guil. Morelium," i.e., Guillaume Morel, may have been an earlier edition of the same work, and may thus also include some of Philostratus' letters.

11. Benner and Fobes, pp. 409-410. The Paris edition of 1608, entitled *Philostrati Lemnii Opera Quae Exstant*, was edited by "Fed Morellus" (i.e., Fédéric Morel, who appears to have been no relation to Guillaume Morel) and published by Marcum Orry. The *Epistolae Philostrati*, as they are there styled, are on pages 884 through 914.

12. This seems to have been a common plea: another work by one of the Philostrati recounts that the Governor of Cilicia addressed to the beautiful young Apollonius of Tyana "a prayer which can only be offered to the beautiful, and which is that they may grant to others participation in their beauty and not grudge their charms." To which the young saint replied, "You are mad, you scum." Philostratus, *The Life of Apollonius of Tyana*, I, 31.

13. The reader will immediately recognize in this letter the conceit in the last eight lines of Ben Jonson's famous lyric "To Celia," beginning "Drink to me only with thine eyes. . . ." It has been known at least since 1785 that Jonson's poem is "a cento adroitly pieced together from the *Epistles* of Philostratus. . . ." A. D. Fitton Brown, p. 555; Herford and Simpson, XI, 39. The five letters from which Jonson borrowed are 33, 32, 60, 2 and 46, all, save the last, written to women. Jonson expressly acknowledges indebtedness to Philostratus' *Eikones* or *Imagines* in his notes to *The Masque of Beauty* and *Oberon* (Herford and Simpson, VII, 188, 189 and 343) and Jonson's editors have identified unacknowledged borrowings from Philostratus in *Catilene* (Epistle 13), *Pleasure Reconcild to Vertue* (*Eikones*), *The Gypsies Metamorphosed* (*Appollonius of Tyana*), and *Discoveries* (*Eikones*). Herford and Simpson, X, 135, 589, 619; XI, 257. The earliest published of the works of Johnson containing allusions to or reflecting the influence of Philostratus was *Masque of Beauty*, published in 1608; "To Celia" was first published in 1616 (in *The Forrest*), and all of the other works were

published in or after 1616. The late date of the publication of these pieces suggests that Jonson became familiar with the works of Philostratus through the Latin translations of 1606 or 1608. A. D. Fitton Brown, p. 555. For this reason, I do not think that Jonson was a source of Shakespeare's knowledge of the works of Philostratus, since the influence of Philostratus in Shakespeare's Sonnets, if it does exist, must date from a time considerably earlier than 1606.

14. I stress the words *time and place* because "one of the characteristics of Sufic poetry [which flourished in Persia, Turkey and India in the 12th, 13th and 14th centuries] was its vocabulary of love, for both women and boys, its profusion of roses, wine and intoxication, expressing in intensely sensual images the otherwise inexpressible holy mysteries." Martin, p. 206. It is unlikely that Europeans of Shakespeare's time (with the possible exception of Arabic-speaking Jews from Spain who had fled to the Netherlands and Eastern Europe) possessed any knowledge of Sufic verse. Sufic literature and philosophy was profoundly influenced by Greek literature and philosophy. The love of boys which is so prominent a feature of Sufic literature is a tradition which goes from later Greek literature into classical Arabic prose (and thence into Sufic poetry). Baldick, pp. 20–21, 66–69. Thus in Philostratus and others of his period, the Roses and youth of Shakespeare's sonnets may have the same literary ancestor as the roses and youths of Sufic poetry.

    Edward FitzGerald, the translator of the *Rubaiyat* of Omar Khayyam, seems to have been well aware of this similarity between the Sonnets and Sufic poetry: in a letter to Professor Edward Cowell which precedes his (FitzGerald's) translation of the *Salámán and Absál* of Jámí, FitzGerald states of the Persian poet Hafiz, who often in his poems celebrated handsome boys, that his "Sonnets are sometimes as close packt as Shakespeare's, which they resemble in more ways than one. . . ." FitzGerald, p. 174. FitzGerald and his friend Cowell (a student of languages who introduced FitzGerald to Persian poetry) were very much at odds over the extent to which the boys and wine in the *Rubaiyat* were to be taken literally. Cowell was eager to read drunkeness as symbolic of Divine Love, and handsome boys as representative of Absolute Beauty, but FitzGerald was of the opinion that Omar's "wine is the veritable Juice of the Grape: his Tavern, where it was to be had: his Sáki [the name of his cup bearer], the Flesh and Blood that poured it out for him: all which, and where Roses were in Bloom, was all he profess'd to want of this World or to expect of Paradise." Martin, p. 206.

15. *Astronomici Veteres, Iulii firmici libri octo, Marci Manili libri quinque . . . Procli Sphaera graece, Procli Sphaera Thoma Linacro britanno interprete.*

16. While my purpose here is to emphasize Aldus' role in spreading knowledge about Greek literature, I should also note that he published many editions of Latin authors, which contributed their share to the new illumination.

17. See John W. Velz' valuable *Shakespeare and the Classical Tradition*, and also the books by Selma Guttman and Henry Lathrop.

18. Perry, pp. 98–99.

19. Wolff, p. 256, note 3.

20. *Ibid.*, pp. 461–464.

21. Gesner, pp. 47–79.

22. *Ibid.*, pp. 80–143.
23. Mowat, pp. 2-3.
24. Gaselee, "Appendix on the Greek Novel," p. 403.
25. Gesner, pp. 151-152. This codex, Laurentianus Conv. Soppressi no. 627, is today in the Laurentian Library in Florence. In addition to containing the texts of *Chaereas.and Callirhoe* and *Ephesiaca*, for which it is the sole source, the codex contains also, but is not the sole source of, the texts of *Daphnis and Chloe* and *Clitiphon and Leucippe*. Perry, pp. 344-345; Blum, p. 160.
26. Douce, II, 199.
27. Hutton, "Analogues of Shakespeare's Sonnets," pp. 150, note 4, and 156.
28. See note 73 to Chapter VIII.
29. Hutton, *The Greek Anthology in Italy*, pp. 37-38.
30. Hutton, "Analogues of Shakespeares Sonnets," pp. 149-150, note 2.
31. *Greek Anthology*, Book IX, number 627 (Loeb Classical Library No. 84), III, 349.
32. Hutton, "Analogues of Shakespeares Sonnets," pp. 149-168.
33. Sabeo's translation, in *Epigrammata* at page 791, is as follows:

> *In Balneum Dictum Erota. E Graeco*
> Sub platano viridi apposita iam lampade Nymphis,
> > Victus erat somno nequitiosus Amor.
> Inter se haec dicunt, nitamur lampada Nymphae
> > Suffocare, hominum quae male corda cremat.
> Dumque volunt flammas extinguere, lympha calescit,
> > A Nymphis calidae sic oriuntur aquae.

Sabeo's *Epigrammata* contains Latin translations of numerous other epigrams from the Greek Anthology.
34. Hutton, "Analogues of Shakespeare's Sonnets," p. 149.
35. *Ibid.*, p. 166.
36. Hutton, *The Greek Anthology in France*, p. 431.
37. Hutton, "Analogues of Shakespeare's Sonnets," p. 165. See also Hutton's discussion of "pointed" as opposed to "naïve" epigrams on pages 51 through 55 of his *The Greek Anthology in France*.
38. Persons who translated epigrams from the Greek Anthology attempted to show their ingenuity by making numerous translations of the same epigram: "In Italy the master of multiple translation is Fausto Sabeo; in France no one surpassed Henri Estienne, who, incidentally, shows that the exercise belonged to the schools when he exhibits his skill professedly for the encouragement of the young ('ad accendendum iuvenum studium'). Sabeo never made more than thirteen versions of an epigram, most writers were content with two or three, and Estienne's *tour de force* of 106 versions of a single distich would have been a unique performance had it not been surpased by the Englishman, John Stockwood, who [in his book dedicated to the Earl of Essex in 1598] was able to write 450 translations of *A.P.* 5.224 [i.e., epigram number 224 in Book V of the Palatine Anthology]." Hutton, *The Greek Anthology in France*, pp. 29-30. So Shakespeare

may have written two versions of the Marianus epigram for no reason other than
to display his inventiveness.

39. Hulse, pp. 16–17, who cites also *Art and Illusion*, by E. H. Gombrich (New York, 1961).

40. Philostratus, *Imagines*, p. 17.

41. Hulse, p. 17.

42. Helpful, because there are some contexts in which this is not obvious. For example, in Sidney's *Arcadia*, Musidorus berates Pyrocles for loving a woman more than he loves him (i.e., Musidorus), and makes all the usual arguments for placing the love of virtue (as embodied in a male friend) above sensuous love (supposedly inextricable from the love for a woman). Pyrocles replies that "if we love vertue, in whom shal we love it but in a vertuous creature," and that is what he finds Philoclea to be, even though he admits that "enjoying" is an objective of his love. Musidorus replies, "Well, well . . . you list to abuse yourself; *it was a very white and red virtue* [emphasis supplied], which you could pick out of a painterly glosse of a visage: Confesse the truth; and ye shall finde, the utmost was but beautie; a thing, which though it be in as great excellencye in your selfe as may be in any, yet I am sure you make no further reckning of it, then of an outward fading benefite Nature bestowed upon you. And yet such is your want of a true grounded vertue, which must be like it selfe in all points, that what you account a trifle in your selfe, you fondly become a slave unto in another." Sidney, *Arcadia* (1590), pp. 80-82; see also Sidney, *Arcadia* (Original Version), p. 20.

43. Knowledge of the "theory of humours and temperaments, which formed the physiological basis of Galen's system of medicine" was transmitted to England through the publication in 1521 of Thomas Linacre's translation (into Latin) of Galen's *De Temperamentis*. Galen, p. 44. Galen's theories quickly were disseminated in English. A *Treatise of Melancolie* by Timothy Bright, published in 1586, contains (at pp. 168-169) this explanation of blushing which is probably the source for that offered by Drayton:

> These qualities of shame ioyned with anger, procureth that rednesse in the face, which we call blushing. The tincture of redde ariseth on this sorte: the heart discontented with the opennesse of the offence, maketh a retraction of bloud, and spirit at the first, as in feare and griefe; and because it feeleth no greater hurt then of laughter, or rebuke of worde, or such like touch, seeketh no farther escape, then a small withdrawing of the spirite and bloud by the first entrance of the perturbation: so that the necessitie being no more urgent, the bloud and spirit break forth again more vehemently, and fill the partes about the face more then before, and causeth the rednesse.

Galen also apparently attributed to some disorder of the humours the paleness which accompanies illness. Sidney, in Sonnet 102 of *Astrophel and Stella*, says that those who follow Galen in this are wrong: the roses in Stella's face are gone not because of illness, but because Love wishes to prepare a white surface upon which to write with beauty's reddest ink (supplied by Venus).

It is a curious coincidence that Thomas Linacre (1460–1524), a famous classical scholar, physician and humanist who was a friend of John Colet, Aldus Manutius, Erasmus, and Stephen Gardiner, introduced into England both the Damask Rose (which became in the sixteenth century one of the most common poetic metaphors for a white and red complexion) and Galen's theories about blushing and illness (which purported to explain the alternation of complexion between red and white referred to so often by Elizabethan poets).

44. It would probably be impossible to find a single image or theme employed by Shakespeare which had not previously been employed by some earlier English writer. Studies by Baldwin, Leishman, John, Schaar, Scott and Tuve of Shakespeare's indebtedness to his predecessors are listed in the bibliography. But as Harry Morris writes (*Richard Barnfield, Colin's Child*, at page 65), the seeking out of sources is ultimately a useless task:

> Scholars should stop pointing out verbal similarities between one Elizabethan work and another for the sole purpose of establishing indebtedness. The task is too exhausting, the fruits rarely worth the effort. The scholar finds always the thing he is looking for: interdependence, borrowing, paraphrase or plagiarism; but in the long run, little that is exposed contributes in any real way to an understanding or an appreciation of the poem or the poet.

45. Spurgeon, p. 43. This is Professor Spurgeon's discussion of the Shakespearean images involving change of colour in the face:

> this interest in the shifting colour of the face and the emotion it implies is one of the marked features of Shakespeare's earliest poem, and a kind of running colour symphony is there played on the shamed blushes of Adonis, or his cheeks with 'anger ashy-pale', and the flushed hue of Venus. . . . Shakespeare is so conscious of the betraying change of colour in the face, as the signal flag of various emotions, fear, anger, astonishment, pleasure, and he so vividly and constantly describes it either directly or by means of an image, that I cannot help surmising he himself, like Richard II, was fair and flushed easily, and that possibly in youth he suffered from the ease with which, under stress of feeling, he betrayed his emotions through blushing or pallor. [*Ibid.*, pp. 60-61.]

46. Vyvyan, pp. 141–142.

47. Well, *almost* the only reason: after writing this chapter, I encountered "Black and White and Red All Over: The Sonnet Mistress Amongst the Ndembu," an article by Linda Woodbridge in 40 *Renaissance Quarterly* (1987), pp. 247-297. Woodbridge points out the frequency of red and white and black imagery in Renaissance poetry generally, and in the poetry of Shakespeare in particular ("Red/white/black imagery," she writes (at page 250) "saturates Shakespeare's early poems"), and claims (on page 247) that the red-and-white scheme "is part of a semiotic code visible throughout history, worldwide, encoding seasonal fertility ritual and individual rites of passage." I do not believe that black imagery

is nearly so prevalent in the works of Shakespeare as is red and white imagery; in any event, although Woodbridge's thesis may (but probably does not) explain the ultimate source or reason for the supposed worldwide prevalence of red and white imagery, it does not explain its presence in the works of Shakespeare (unless one thinks of him as a mindless conduit of primal sexual impulses) for it ignores both the influence of literary precedents and the possibility of rational elements in Shakespeare's own experience and personality governing his choice of images. Not probative of anything, but odd, is that in the whole corpus of Ben Jonson's poetry, the word "red" appears only once. Bates and Orr, s.v. red.

48. Thomson, pp. 40–41.
49. Chambers, *William Shakespeare*, I, 291; Gaw, pp. 33–34, note 39.
50. Hart, p. 59; Neilson and Hill, pp. 747–748; Bullough, III, 35.
51. Saccio, pp. 115–155.
52. See, e.g., Kendall, p. 30; Ross, pp. 7–15 and Saccio, pp. 12-13, all of whom agree that The War of the Roses was not the contemporary name for the fifteenth century conflict, but differ as to when the conflict was first designated by this name: Kendall asserts that this was in the 16th century, Ross writes that the name was first used by David Hume in 1762, and Saccio writes that the name became current in the nineteenth century. The facts seem to be more or less as follows: Henry VII's marriage with Elizabeth of York in 1486, and his adoption of a red and white rose combined as the symbol of the unification of the two warring families caught the fancy of Tudor poets. As early as about 1504, Stephen Hawes, in *The Example of Virtue*, referred to the York and Lancaster factions by their (to a certain extent retroactively imputed) symbols, the white rose and the red, and states that the "blowen asyde" white rose was "fortyfyed and made dellycyous" when "god by grace dyd well combyne/ The rede rose and the whyte in maryage." Edwards, p. 4. Seventy-five years later, E.K., in his gloss on Hobbinol's "laye/ Of fayre *Eliza*, Queene of shepheardes all," in the "Aprill" Aeglogue of *The Shepheardes Calendar* (the lines quoted in item 23 in Appendix III) explains that "By the mingling of the Redde rose and the White, is meant the uniting of the two principall houses of Lancaster and Yorke, . . . [and the birth of] the most royal Henry the eyght aforesayde, in whom was the firste vnion of the Whyte Rose and the Redde." Spenser, p. 434. The fact that E.K. felt obliged to gloss the phrase "The Redde rose medled with the White yfere" suggests that the use of the Red and White Rose terminology to designate the two sides of the York-Lancaster conflict was not common in 1579, and needed explanation. Edward Hall's book on the war (published in 1548) was colourlessly entitled *The Union of the Two Noble and Illustre Famelies of Lancastre and Yorke*; Holinshed's *Chronicles* accord no distinctive name to the conflict, the herald Ralph Brooke's *A Discoverie of Certain Errors Published in Print in the Much Commended Britannia* (1595) calls it (at page 15) "the civill warres betwixt the families of Lancaster and Yorke," and Parts 2 and 3 of *Henry VI*, when they were published in 1594 and 1595, bore the title "the Contention betwixt the two famous Houses of Yorke and Lancaster." Similarly, Samuel Daniel's historical poem, published in 1594, bore the title "The First Fowre Bookes of the Civile Wars between the two Houses of Lancaster and Yorke," and the work, as

augmented by four more "bookes," was published in 1609 as "Civil Wars." But when Richard Barnfield in 1598 wrote a poem praising certain English poets, Daniel was commended thus:

> And *Daniell*, praised for thy sweet-chast Verse:
> Whose Fame is grav'd on *Rosamonds* blacke Herse.
> Still mayst thou liue: and still be honored,
> For that rare Worke, *The White Rose and the Red*.

And Henry Chettle in *England's Mourning Garment* (written in 1603 upon the death of Queen Elizabeth) referred to Daniel as one who

> so well could sing the fatal strife
> Between the royal Roses, white and red.

These allusions to Daniel's work on the "Civile Wars between the two Houses of Lancaster and Yorke" as "The White Rose and the Red," and as an account of a "fatal strife/ Between the royal Roses, white and red," reveal that by 1598 the York-Lancaster contention, whatever it was called by *historians*, was designated by *poets* as a battle between Roses, which designation was eventually adopted by the general public and reflects, in my opinion, the impact of Shakespeare's *Henry VI* rose imagery upon his contemporaries.

Notes to Chapter V — The Swelling Verse

1. The analyses and conclusions here summarized are set forth at length in Martin Green, pp. 42–58.
2. This view of the puns is abundantly confirmed in Frankie Rubinstein's, *A Dictionary of Shakespeare's Sexual Puns and their Significance*.
3. See Ellis, pp. 103-110, for his demonstration that one of the meanings of *wit* is *pudendum*, both masculine and feminine, a remarkable insight which illuminates many of Shakespeare's lines.
4. The passage from *Love's Labour's Lost* (IV,11,101–107) is as follows:

> *Holofernes*. Old Mantuan, old Mantuan! who understands thee not, loves thee not. *Ut, re, sol, la, mi, fa*. Under pardon, sir, what are the contents? or rather, as Horace says in his — What, my soul, verses?
> *Nathaniel*. Ay, sir, and very learned.
> *Holofernes*. Let me hear a staff, a stanze, a verse; *lege, domine*.

The passage from *King Lear* (IV,vi,17-20) is as follows:

> *Edgar*. The fishermen, that walk upon the beach,
> Appear like mice; and yond tall anchoring bark,
> Diminish'd to her cock; her cock, a buoy
> Almost too small for sight.

In my 1974 book, I attempted to deduce from the foregoing (and other) examples of unlikely words having sexual meanings a formula for the mechanism whereby Shakespeare infuses sexual meanings into words, which formula is basically this: If a word [A] has a sexual meaning [B], then any word which is a synonym or homonym of [A] (such word being designated as C) can also have the same meaning. That is:

If A (a word) = B (sexual meaning),

and C (a word which is a synonym or homonym of A) = A,

then C (the homonym or synonym of A, as well as other words which are synonyms or homonyms of C) = B (the sexual meaning of A).

Here are a few applications of this formula, beginning with an obvious one, and moving on to others less obvious:

A.   Yard [A] = penis (see OED) [B];

ell (a unit of measurement) [C] = yard (a unit of measurement)[A];

∴ ell [C] = penis [B]. (See *Love's Labour's Lost,* IV,ii, 58–64; Martin Green, pp. 4–10).

B.   Yard [A] = penis [B];

inch (a unit of measurement) [C] = yard [A];

∴ inch [C] = penis [B] (see Rubinstein, s.v. inch).

C.   Stake [A] = penis (see Partridge, s.v. stake) [B];

sowel [C], staff [C], post [C] = stake [A];

∴ sowel [C] (and its homonym *soul*) = penis [B] (see Martin Green, pp. 66-72);

staff [C] (and its synonym *verse*) = penis [B] (see text, pp. 90-91, and note 5, which follows);

post [C] (and its homonym *post* i.e., messenger) = penis [B] (see Rubinstein, s.v. post).

5.   Supportive of this perception is that Rubinstein, s.v. wings, also finds this equation, through the medium of the Latin *penne* (wings), which she believes connects feathers, pens, and any written composition or poem, with *penis,* in illustration of which she cites Sonnet 78, which contains a sequence of *verse, pen, feathers* and *wing.* An interesting aspect of Rubinstein's work is that she often finds Greek and Latin words to be the key to a phallic or erotic meaning in Shakespeare's puns; see, e.g., her discussions of *chin, curse, feather, fistula, grace, re, spirit, torch* (which list is limited to phallic words); this suggests either that Shakespeare was familiar with these languages, or that (like one of my nephews), although he didn't really know the languages, he was familiar with their sexual and scatalogical vocabularies.

6.   Nashe, III, 403–416.

7.   *Ibid.*, p. 413, lines 241–242.

8.   Harvey, *The Trimming of Thomas Nashe*, sig. G^v.

9.   Harvey, *Pierce's Supererogation*, p. 45.

10. Nashe, III, 403.
11. DNB, s.v. Stanley, Ferdinando.
12. E.g., Sidney Lee, *A Life of William Shakespeare*, p. 667; Adams, p. 153; Stopes, *The Life of Henry, Third Earl of Southampton*, p. 57; H. McClure Young, p. 70; Rowse, *Shakespeare's Southampton*, p. 95; Akrigg, *Shakespeare and the Earl of Southampton*, p. 199; Waite, pp. 116-117.
13. Chambers, *William Shakespeare*, I, 568.
14. Nicholl, p. 293, note 34.
15. Onions, p. 258. This was translated by Marlowe as

> Let base conceited wits admire vilde things,
> Fair *Phoebus* lead me to the Muses springs!

and by Johnson as:

> Kneele hindes to trash: me let bright *Phoebus* swell,
> With cups full flowing from the *Muses* well.

Both translations are in Marlowe, II, 300, 339.
16. Nashe, III, 415-416.
17. Spenser, p. 482.
18. That Spenser would know of the story of Shakespeare, Nashe and Wriothesley is not surprising, for several reasons: first, Spenser was a friend of Gabriel Harvey, who apparently kept himself abreast of all of Nashe's doings; second, Spenser spent a part of the summer of 1590 in Hampshire, in the village of Alton (Spenser pp. ix, xxix), about 25 miles from Titchfield, and probably heard all the gossip from miles around; and third, as set forth in Chapter VI, Spenser was, and Shakespeare may have been (and in my opinion definitely was), a part of the large network of people connected to each other through their membership in the circle of the Earl of Essex.
19. Nashe, I, 244.
20. See Nashe, IV, 151.
21. Nashe, III, 332 (I have modernised the spelling).
22. Nashe, V (Supplement), p. 69.
23. This, of course, creates a problem, for Shakespeare's *Hamlet* is generally considered to have been written too late to have been referred to by Nashe in 1591. But this is not the only such early allusion by Nashe to a *Hamlet*: in the Preface to Robert Greene's *Menaphon*, published in 1589, Nashe wrote, "yet English *Seneca* read by Candlelight yeelds many good sentences, as *Blood is a begger*, and so forth; and if you intreate him faire in a frostie morning, hee will affoord you whole Hamlets, I should say handfuls of Tragicall speeches." Nashe, III, 315. The usual explanation of these and other early references to a *Hamlet* is that they allude to an earlier, non-Shakespearean version of the play (see Chambers, I, 411-412), but at least one non-Stratfordian writer has invoked this possible evidence that "Shakespeare's" *Hamlet* had already been written by 1589 or 1591 as proof that the plays were written by someone other than the actor

from Stratford — in this case William Stanley, the sixth Earl of Derby. Evans, p. 104. My conclusion that Nashe's preface to *Astrophel and Stella* directs barbs at Shakespeare does not require *Hamlet* to have been written as early as 1591 — but if in fact Shakespeare had written a version of that play at so early a date, then Shakespeare's being the target of Nashe's ridicule would be all the more certain, as would also be Shakespeare's retaliation in the "proud full saile" and "proudest saile" sonnets.

24. Nashe, II, 187.
25. *Ibid.*, 201-202.
26. *Ibid.*, 191-192; IV, 255.

Notes to Chapter VI — Scholars, Statesmen, Soldiers, Spies, Sodomites and Sources

1. Barber, p. 17.
2. Partridge, p. 14; see also Hubler, pp. 151-161.
3. Rowse, *Shakespeare's Sonnets: The Problems Solved*, p. 43.
4. See e.g., Bruce R. Smith, *Homosexual Desire in Shakespeare's England* (University of Chicago Press, 1991); Gregory W. Bredbeck, *Sodomy and Interpretation — Marlowe to Milton* (Cornell University Press, 1991); Joseph Pequigney, *Such is my Love* (University of Chicago Press, 1985); Richard A. Levin, *Love and Society in Shakespearean Comedy* (University of Delaware Press, 1985); Frankie Rubinstein, *A Dictionary of Shakespeare's Sexual Puns and their Significance* (London?: Macmillan, 1984), and my *The Labyrinth of Shakespeare's Sonnets* (London: Skilton, 1974).
5. Clarendon, p. 4.
6. See, e.g., *The Diary of Sir Simonds D'Ewes*, pp. 92–93 (where in 1622 the then 20 year old student wrote of his fear of some horrible punishment which might befall the realm because of the prevalence in London of the "sinne of sodomye, ... especially it being as wee had probable cause to feare, a sinne in the prince as well as the people. . . .") and William Harris, *The Lives and Writings of James I. and Charles I.*, pp. 78 - 87 (where Harris lists the evidence for his conclusion that "from his [King James'] known love of masculine beauty, his excessive favour to such as were possessed of it, and unseemly caresses of them, one would be tempted to think, that he was not wholly free from a vice most unnatural").
7. In Elizabethan times, marriage (at least among the moneyed classes) was "essentially a business proposition" having little to do with "true love" (Esler, pp. 56-57) and thus a condition unrelated to the sexual preferences of the parties. Illustrating the irrelevance of the emotions to the state of marriage is a letter written by Essex's secretary, Henry Cuffe, to Southampton's friend, Sir Charles Danvers. In this letter (CM VIII, pp. 284-285), Cuffe writes that Essex's mother had asked her son to find a husband for her niece and namesake, Lettice Knollys, and Essex had decided that Sir Charles, if he were available and so inclined, would be a good choice. Cuffe continues: "The gentlewoman I think you know; and of her portion [the lands and money her husband might receive upon the wedding] and all other circumstances I doubt not but you have long since

received sufficient information; so that it only remains that you send me your resolution whether you can be contented to have your purgatory in this life, or had rather defer it to another world." As it turned out, Danvers did not marry Lettice Knollys, or anybody else, and both he and Henry Cuffe were in 1601 executed for their participation in the Essex "rebellion," neither having endured their purgatory in this life.

8. Erasmus, I, 235.
9. Colet early in his career opposed the reading of pagan authors. See Colet, *An Exposition of St. Paul's First Epistle to the Corinthians*, pp. xxxii–xl.
10. Marriott, p. 134.
11. *Id.*
12. A practice followed not only in grammar school, but also in college. See the account in Appendix I of Thomas Wriothesley and William Paget, both of whom had attended St. Paul's School, appearing in a Cambridge production of *Miles Gloriosus*. Also, see generally, Motter, *The School Drama in England*.
13. Quoted in Berdan, *Early Tudor Poetry*, p. 318.
14. *Ibid.*, p. 320. Juan Luis Vives was one of the most famous humanists of his day. He was born in 1492 in Valencia, Spain, the son of converted Jews, whose conversions, however, did not meet the high standards of the Inquisition, for his father was burned at the stake in 1522, and in 1528, the remains of his mother, who died in about 1508, were disinterred from the Christian cemetery in which she was buried, and burned. (This family background, however, was not generally known to his contemporaries.) In 1509, at the age of seventeen, Vives left Spain, never to return. He studied in Paris, and in 1519 was appointed professor of humanities at Louvain. He met and became a friend of Erasmus. In 1522 he dedicated to Henry VIII a commentary on Saint Augustine's *De Civitate Dei*, and the following year moved to England, where he enjoyed the friendship of Sir Thomas More and Thomas Linacre, and the patronage of Thomas Wolsey. He lectured at Oxford, supervised the education of Princess Mary, and wrote text books for students, and books on his philosophy of education for professors. Because he opposed Henry's divorce from Catherine of Aragon, he was imprisoned for six weeks in 1528. Upon his release from prison, he went to Bruges, where he lived in the Jewish community and married the daughter of a Jewish merchant from Valencia. He died in Bruges in 1540. See Noreña, generally, and Berdan, pp. 301-304. Yates, in *A Study of Love's Labour's Lost*, at pages 58-59, has convincingly explained one of the seemingly incomprehensible passages which abound in that play as a parody of a colloquy in Vives' Latin textbook, *Linguae Latinae Exercitatio*.
15. Horace for Ligurinus, among others; Catullus for Juventius, and Tibullus for Marathus. Lyne, pp. 170-175, 198-200, 214.
16. PR, Elizabeth, 1558-1560, p. 61.
17. GEC, s.v. Leicester.
18. PR, Elizabeth, 1558-1560, p. 540.
19. GEC, s.v. Leicester.
20. Kingsford, "Essex House, formerly Leicester House and Exeter Inn," p. 6.
21. Stow, II, 92.
22. Hutton, *The Greek Anthology in Italy*, p. 323.

23. Rosenberg, pp. 355-362. Leicester may have played a particularly significant role in Stow's career, for it was upon the presentation by Stow to Leicester of a copy of a treatise written by Leicester's grandfather, Edmund Dudley (which treatise Stow had acquired not because of his interest in history, but because of his interest in literature), that Leicester suggested to Stow that he write on historical subjects. *Ibid.*, pp. 69-70; Stow, I, ix.
24. Rosenberg, pp. 116-151.
25. DNB, s.v. Gentili, Alberico
26. Rosenberg, p. 352; Yates, *John Florio*, pp. 53-58.
27. *Ibid.*, pp. 358-359.
28. *Dizionario Biografico degli Italiani*, s.v. Bruno, Giordano; Yates, pp. 92-97.
29. Hannay, p. 71.
30. Chambers, *The Elizabethan Stage*, II, 85-91. But if "Will, my lord of Lester's jesting plaier" *was* Shakespeare, then Shakespeare's connection with the Leicester/Essex House group was even earlier and closer than I contend.
31. *Aubrey's Brief Lives*, pp. 138-139, 278.
32. DNB s.v. Sidney, Philip; Rebholz, p. 318. "Trophaeum Peccati" appears to mean something like "Monument to Sin."
33. Sargent, pp. 38-39.
34. DNB, s.v., Sidney, Philip and Hakluyt, Richard.
35. James M. Osborn, pp. 24-27.
36. Henry R. Plomer and Tom Peete Cross, pp. 1-3.
37. Deborah Jones, pp. 290-292.
38. Touwaide, figure 4 (genealogical table following text). Surprisingly, Lodovico Guicciardini was one of the many people in Europe who at some time or another was in correspondence with Francis Walsingham. *Ibid.*, pp. 56, 100.
39. James M. Osborn, p. 36.
40. Thomas Smith was "an excellent linguist, and a master in the knowledge of the Latin, Greek, French, Italian, and English tongues." Strype, p. 164. His library consisted of a thousand books of various learning and arts, most of which were in Latin or Greek. *Ibid.*, pp. 165, 274-281. When he was at Cambridge (in the early 1540's, before embarking upon his career as a statesman and diplomat) he and John Cheke stirred up a great controversy by their advocacy of a pronunciation of Greek which more nearly approximated that used in classical times. Eventually Bishop Gardiner, the Chancellor of the University, "being against all innovation," prohibited the teaching of these "rectified sounds." Smith's letter to Gardiner, urging him to change his mind (which he never did) was published by Smith under the name *De Recta et emendata Linguæ Grecæ Pronunciatione*, in 1568, while he was ambassador at Paris, *Ibid.*, pp. 22-25. Also while he was in Paris, Smith became acquainted with Ramus. *Ibid.*, p. 166.
41. DNB, s.v. Walsingham, Sir Francis; Bakeless, I, 159-160.
42. Hotson, *The Death of Christopher Marlowe*, p. 64; Bakeless I, p. 83; Wraight and Sterne, pp. 87-100; Austin K. Gray, pp. 682-700.
43. DNB, s.v. Bacon, Anthony; du Maurier, pp. 31-63.
44. du Maurier, pp. 60-61; Read, III, 277, 288-292.
45. Parks, pp. 99-111.

46. Brooks, pp. 430-431, 448-449, 464-470.
47. Rosenberg, pp. 90, 233-236; Conway, pp. 23-25; McLane, pp. 340-342.
48. Constable, pp. 21-23.
49. Yates, *John Florio*, pp. 84-85. In *Giordano Bruno and the Embassy Affair* John Bossy argues that Giordano Bruno, who lived at the French embassy during the time that Florio was employed there, was also a spy for Walsingham.
50. Bakeless, I, pp. 84, 161-162.
51. Eccles, *Christopher Marlowe in London*, p. 8.
52. *Ibid.*, pp. 9-10; 36, 42, 61-64.
53. Camden, *The Historie of . . . Princesse Elizabeth*, Book Three, pp. 75,76; Boas (1940) pp. 124-126; Hotson, *The Death of Christopher Marlowe*, pp. 51-52; SP Scot., 1586-1587, pp. 274, 595-596.
54. Seaton, pp. 273-287.
55. Kuriyama, pp. 343-358; Seaton, pp. 275-277.
56. Hotson, *The Death of Christopher Marlowe*, pp. 42-49.
57. *Ibid.*, p. 32.
58. Wernham, pp. 344-45.
59. Wraight and Stern, pp. 308-309.
60. *Ibid.*, pp. 354-355.
61. *Journal of Sir Francis Walsingham*, pp. 3, 8, 9, 13; SP For., January-June 1583, pp. 354-356; James M. Osborn, pp. 50-53, 215-217.
62. James M. Osborn, pp. 71-72; Albert W. Osborn, pp. 27-29; Rosenberg, pp. 272-273.
63. DNB, s.v. Wotton, Edward.
64. Buxton, p. 58.
65. Albert W. Osborn, p. 34.
66. James M. Osborn, pp. 323-344.
67. Nichols, I, 418-419.
68. Gascoigne, II, 91-131.
69. Prouty, pp. 64-65, 95-96.
70. Rosenberg, pp. 168-169.
71. Duncan-Jones, pp. 98-99; Goldman, pp. 190-191.
72. A letter from Daniel Rogers to George Buchanan, quoted in Dorsten, p. 49.
73. James M. Osborn, p. 450.
74. So stated by Dorsten, pp. 47-49, but questioned by James M. Osborne, p. 452.
75. Ollard and Cross, s.v. Rogers, John.
76. Dorsten, p. 21.
77. *Ibid.*, p. 10.
78. *Ibid.*, p. 19.
79. *Ibid.*, p. 29, n. 3.
80. In 1580, while on a diplomatic mission to Germany, Rogers was captured by forces then allied with Spain, and held prisoner for four years. Leicester and Walsingham unsuccesfully urged the Queen to arrest the Spanish Ambassador B. De Mendoza and hold him in exchange for Rogers. Rogers was ransomed in 1584, after which he returned to England. He had no money, and he was not helped financially by Walsingham, or, apparently, Sidney, and his contacts with

Leicester House seem then to have lapsed. In 1587, when he was about 45 years old, he married Susan Yetsworth, and at about the same time was made a Clerk of the Privy Council. He died in 1591. Dorsten, pp. 68-75.

81. *Ibid.*, p. 40.
82. Wood, I, Column 570.
83. Dorsten, p. 30, 69, 75, 92.
84. Prescott, pp. 21 and 94.
85. Dorsten, pp. 42, 46-47.
86. Hume Brown, pp. 111, 143, 145, 184, 262-263, 335-336, 342-345.
87. Dorsten, pp. 50, 173-184, 211.
88. McLane, p. 88.
89. Phillips, p. 55.
90. DNB, s.v. Spenser, Edmund.
91. *Ibid.* The composition — and even the existence — of this group is in dispute. See, e.g., Schrickx, p. 98; Dorsten, p. 39.
92. Stern, *Gabriel Harvey*, pp. 46, 68.
93. Ungerer, II, 256-258.
94. Rosenberg, p. 150, n. 61; Blok, pp. 90-91.
95. Kelley, pp. 92-93.
96. *Ibid.*, p. 150.
97. Albert W. Osborn, p. 30.
98. Kelley, pp. 236, 238, 268, 287, 323; SP Dom., January-June 1583, pp. 355-356; *Francisci et Joannis Hotomanorum . . . Epistolae*, pp. 165, 166, 169-170, 185, 198-203, 245-246, 339, 346-347, 349-350, 404-406, 414-442.
99. For Hotman's friendship with these persons, see *Francisci et Joannis Hotomanorum . . . Epistolæ*, pp. 269-271, 273-278, 279-281, 285-288, 296, 298-301. 303-304, 312-314, 318-319, 321-322, 316-328, 384.
100. Blok, pp. 91-93.
101. Buxton, p. 41.
102. These friendships are evidenced by *V. Cl. Gugliemi Camdeni . . . Epistolæ*, pp. ix, 3, 4, 7, 8, 10, 11, 12, 14, 16, 17, 19, 20, 108, 124.
103. James M. Osborn, p. 89; Goldman, p. 74.
104. DNB, s.v. Sidney, Sir Philip.
105. DNB, s.v. Temple, Sir William.
106. *Letters and Memorials of State*, I, 112.
107. By his will, Leicester gave to his child by Lady Douglas Sheffield, Robert Dudley, whom he refers to as his "base son", a number of properties, and, among other things, the Lordship of Chirk. Leicester provided, however, that "if my said base Son Robert should dye without Issue, and that the Mannor of Denbigh and Chirk be redeemed, I do give and bequeath forever the Lordship of Chirk, to my well-beloved Son in Law [i.e., step-son] the Earl of Essex, as also my House in London called Leicester House; if the said Robert, my base Son dye without Issue to whom I give and grant as other the former Lands, *after the Decease of my dear Wife* [emphasis supplied], the said House, and the remainder, if he dye without Issue, to my said Lord the Earl of Essex my Son in Law, and the Heirs of his Body lawfully begotten" (Leader, p. 165). Thus the interests,

such as they might be, either of Robert Dudley or of the Earl of Essex, in Leicester House, could not vest until the death of Leicester's widow. Leicester's widow acted promptly to take possession of the building, which she immediately renamed Essex House, but thereafter she and her new husband, Christopher Blount, lived mostly at Drayton Basset, while Essex House became the London residence of her son, the Earl of Essex (Arthur Gould Lee, p. 51). Since Essex predeceased his mother (who died on Christmas day in 1634, having lived to see the grandchildren of her grandchildren, Nichols II, 623-624), title to Essex House never vested in him. (It was fortunate for all involved that Essex was not the legal owner of Essex House, else title to it would have reverted to the crown upon his conviction for treason; as it was, Essex' mother and his sister Penelope lived there after Essex' execution.) Robert Dudley was still alive upon the death of the dowager Countess of Essex, but he was by then living in Italy, and (perhaps because he may have forefeited his English estates as a consequence of his failure to return to England when ordered to do so by the Government, see Dugdale, *The Baronage*, II, 224) seems never to have acquired any interest in the property. For more about Robert Dudley, see note 286, *infra*. The second Earl of Essex' son, who after the accession of James I to the throne was restored in blood and created the third Earl of Essex, was born in Essex House in 1591, resided there during most of his life, and died there in 1646. Henry Wriothesley's son Thomas, the fourth earl of Southampton, was living there in 1660. Essex House was sold in 1675 or 1676 to Dr. Nicholas Barbon, a real estate developer, who took down most of it, and sold a portion of the grounds to the adjacent Middle Temple. Kent, p. 621; Kingsford, "Essex House," p. 16.

108. G. B. Harrison, *The Life and Death of Robert Devereux*, pp. 49-68.
109. Wood, I, column 244.
110. G. B. Harrison, *The Life and Death of Robert Devereux*, p. 65; CM IV, pp. 165-166.
111. Nichols, III, 144-160.
112. PC, XXIV, 1592-1593, p. 78.
113. Gelly Merrick had been Essex' steward since 1587, Lacey, p. 22; Reynolds was in Essex' service by about 1589. Harrison, *The Life and Death of Robert Devereux*, p. 37.
114. DNB, s.v. Devereux, Robert. See also Strachey, pp. 47-49.
115. CM, III, 435-436.
116. *Ibid.*, pp. 438-439, 441-442; Constable, pp. 27-31.
117. So described by G.B. Harrison, p. 48.
118. Constable, pp. 34-36.
119. CM V, p. 403; CM VI, pp. 519 et seq.; Constable, pp. 36-39.
120. Birch I, 66-68, 108; du Maurier, pp. 60-61. 81-85.
121. CM V, p. 291 (but see also *ibid.*, pp. 188-189); SP Dom., 1595-1597, p. 220.
122. Herford and Simpson, I, 142; XI, 243.
123. DNB, s.v. Savile, Sir Henry.
124. Sargent, pp. 144-145.
125. Rebholz, p. 94; Wood, I, column 248.
126. Rebholz, p. 90.

127. DNB, s.v. Killigrew, Catherine or Katherine; Killigrew, Sir Henry, and Killigrew, Sir Robert; Miller, pp. 223-225.
128. DNB, s.v. Bacon, Francis.
129. In *Jacobean Pageant*, at pp. 287-288, Akrigg writes, "In the face of such obligations [to Essex], Bacon might have been expected to keep clear of any part in the proceedings against Essex. No office held by Bacon required that he appear in court against his former friend, and every decent feeling must have urged refusal of the employment. Bacon, however, was a cold man; and feeling was never his long suit. Not for nothing did John Aubrey later report that he hade the 'Eie of a viper'. Francis Bacon decided to act for the prosecution, and was as effective as any in sending Essex to his death." Daphne du Maurier, however, in *Golden Lads*, suggests, at p. 216, that Francis Bacon was ordered by the Queen "to appear for the Crown and speak against the Earl of Essex,", and that he obeyed this command "because, had he refused, his brother Anthony would have been arrested, put into prison along with Henry Cuffe and other prisoners not considered of high enough rank to be committed to the Tower, there questioned and even tortured so as to extort confession, and, like Cuffe and Gilly Mericke later, hanged, drawn and quartered at Tyburn."
130. Hurstfield, pp. 249-259. The system of wardship is succinctly summarized at p. 18 of his book:

> If a tenant of the crown died, while holding land by a so-called knight-service, then his heir, if under age, became a ward of the crown. He rarely stayed a royal ward except in name. Soon his guardianship would be sold, sometimes to his mother, more often to a complete stranger. With his guardianship would go his 'marriage' — the right to offer him a bride whom he could rarely afford to refuse, for his refusal meant that he must pay a crushing fine to his guardian. Meanwhile his land would also have passed into wardship, either to his guardian or to someone else, for them to snatch a quick profit until the ward was old enough to reclaim his own.

131. SP Dom., pp. 680, 688; Akrigg, *Shakespeare and the Earl of Southampton*, pp. 31-32.
132. Akrigg, *Shakespeare and the Earl of Southampton*, pp. 33-34. There is doubtless a story behind the dedication of this poem to Southampton, but what it is we don't know. Akrigg speculates that Clapham, as "a household jest" which Burleigh might enjoy, wrote this poem about a young man's self-love as a reproach to Southampton for having refused to marry Burleigh's granddaughter. Clapham (ca 1566-after 1613) seems to have been in Burleigh's service until Burleigh's death; afterwards, Clapham was appointed one of the Six Clerks of Chancery. In addition to *Narcissus*, Clapham during his lifetime published a translation (from the French) of Plutarch's *De tranquilitate animi*, and two works on early English history. Manuscript notes entitled "Certain Observations concerning the Life and Reign of Elizabeth," edited by Evelyn Plummer Read and Conyers Read were published in 1951, from which work this biographical information was obtained. Robert Kilburn Root suggests (at p. 88-89) that

Shakespeare's assertions, in *Venus and Adonis* and *Lucrece*, that Narcissus died by drowning, are derived from Clapham's *Narcissus* rather than from Ovid (for in Ovid's poem, Narcissus wasted away from love of the unattainable image in the water, and after his death his body became a yellow flower) but this is not convincing, for as Root himself concedes, Narcissus dies by drowning in various versions of the Narcissus story both in ancient and Elizabethan times.

133. Akrigg, *Shakespeare and the Earl of Southampton*, p. 35.
134. *Manuscripts of . . . the Duke of Rutland*, IV, 392-393.
135. Hurstfield, p. 249.
136. DNB, s.v. Manners, Roger, Fifth Earl of Rutland.
137. *Manuscripts of . . . the Duke of Rutland*, IV, 413.
138. Constable, p. 17.
139. Bedford is generally assumed to have been a ward of Burleigh, chiefly because Burleigh took the trouble on 6 October 1589 to write in his diary the names and ages of Southampton, Rutland and Bedford (see Akrigg, *Shakespeare and the Earl of Southampton*, p. 31) thus suggesting that Bedford occupied the same status as Southampton and Rutland, who definitely were wards of Burleigh. But Hurstfield states (at p. 250) that "In the absence of fuller evidence, however, it is safer to omit Bedford from the noble retinue to whom Burghley stood guardian." I believe that Hurstfield is too cautious: the devotion to Essex and Southampton which induced both Bedford and Rutland to attempt to aid them in the uprising against the Queen suggests to me that the four earls' unusually strong bonds of friendship had been formed in youthful associations which Burleigh's guardianship of all of them would explain.
140. Akrigg, *Shakespeare and the Earl of Southampton*, p. 182.
141. *Ibid.*, pp. 41-46; CM V, pp. 84-90. Or it may be that they *returned* to the service of Henry IV, where at least one report places them as early as 30 May 1594. Birch I, 248.
142. John Sanford, "Apollonis et Musarum Eidylla," pp. 293-294. The relevant portion of the poem is as follows:

> Proximus accuibit reliquis Essexius heros,
> Nobilis & sapiens, superās iuuenilibus annis
> Cognitione senes, canosque ætate magistros.
> Qui doctos homines miratur, doctior ipse;
> Mæcenasque bonos passis amplectitur vlnis.
> In bello pugnax, vir strenuus ὄξος Ἄρηος,
> Cuius in Hyspanos res forti pectore gestas,
> Sensit ab occiduo Lusitania sole tepescens,
> Dum per agros medios ruit acer, & ipse superbæ
> Pulsat Vlyxbonæ ferratâ cuspide portas.
> Cuius & insultus (dum vitæ ardet
> Afflictos Gallos tegere auxilaribus armis)
> Laudibus Armoricæ celebrat gens incola terræ.
> Ille cito subuectus equo qui naribus ignes.
> Spirat, & indocilis rigidum mordere lupatum

Spumeus exultat, sequitur te Regia Virgo
Clarus eques, milesque ferox, Equitūque magister.
    Post hunc insequitur clarâ de stirpe Dynasta,
Iure suo diues quem South-Hamptonia magnum
Vendicat heroem; quo non formosior alter
Affuit, aut docta iuuenis præstantior arte;
Ora licet tenerâ vix dum lanuguine vernent.

143. Nichols, III, 281, 277-279.
144. *Letters and Memorials of State*, I, 112.
145. Seaton, p. 282; Kuriyama, p. 349; SP Dom., 1591-1594, pp. 35, 84, 222; CM IV, 77, 147.
146. Ungerer, I, 187-188, 257. Ungerer's work is a valuable source of information about the persons and politics of England in the 1590's. For other material on Pérez, see the entry under his name in *Biographie Universelle*, the biography by Marañon, and Martin Hume's article "Antonio Perez in Exile."
147. Ungerer, I, 162-163.
148. Hume, *The Great Lord Burghley*, pp. 466-467.
149. Hume, "Antonio Perez in Exile," pp. 85-86.
150. Consult the index to Ungerer for the many letters to and from Pérez and these persons.
151. Hume, *Spanish Influence on English Literature*, p. 62.
152. Ungerer, II, 256-259.
153. *Ibid.*, I, 188.
154. Harrison, *The Life and Death of Robert Devereux Earl of Essex*, pp. 96-100.
155. Ungerer, I, 306.
156. Harrison, *The Life and Death of Robert Devereux Earl of Essex*, p. 108.
157. Ungerer, I, 306-309.
158. CM VI, p. 102.
159. SP Dom., 1595-1597, pp. 203, 205; Akrigg, *Shakespeare and the Earl of Southampton*, p. 57.
160. GEC, s.v. Sussex X. 1593, Robert (Radcliffe or Ratclyffe), Earl of Sussex.
161. *Id.*; G. B. Harrison, *The Life and Death of Robert Devereux Earl of Essex*, pp. 108-130. Essex later gave most of the Bishop's books to the great library established at Oxford by Sir Thomas Bodley.
162. Kingsford, "Essex House," pp. 10-11.
163. G. B. Harrison, *The Life and Death of Robert Devereux Earl of Essex*, pp. 137-167; Akrigg, *Shakespeare and the Earl of Southampton*, pp. 59-66; CM VII, p. 369.
164. Akrigg, *Shakespeare and the Earl of Southampton*, pp. 69-72; *Letters and Memorials of State*, I, 348.
165. SP Dom., 1598-1600, p. 19.
166. *Letters and Memorials of State*, II, 90.
167. Burton, *Anatomy of Melancholy*, ed. Dell and Jordan-Smith, p. 798.

168. CM IV, p. 96, where the letter is assigned to the year 1591, but Akrigg, in his *Shakespeare and the Earl of Southampton*, at p. 34, claims that the letter was probably written in 1598, which seems more reasonable.

169. CM VIII, p. 91. Three nights later, Southampton was one of the members of the English delegation who supped with the King, CM XXIII, p. 48.

170. This was not the Marshal Biron (Armand de Gontaut, ca 1524-1592) who had fought with Essex against the Spanish in France in 1591, and whose head was blown off at the battle of Épernay, but his son, Charles de Gontaut (1562-1602), who succeeded his father as Duc de Biron. He was appointed Marshal by Henry IV in 1594. His constant need for money was either the cause or the consequence of his presence at the gaming tables, and may have led to the intrigues against Henry IV which ultimately resulted in his conviction for treason and decapitation.

171. CM VIII, pp. 358-359.

172. SP Dom., 1598-1600, p. 90; CM VIII, p. 357.

173. SP Dom., 1598-1600, p. 92.

174. Akrigg, *Shakespeare and the Earl of Southampton*, pp. 67-73.

175. *Ibid.*, p. 70.

176. *Aubrey's Brief Lives*, p. 78; Coningsby, p. 71; DNB, s.v. Danvers, Henry, Earl of Danby.

177. Birch II, 42; Ungerer, I, 123, 251, 437; DNB s.v. Danvers, Sir Charles.

178. Camden, *The Historie of . . . Princesse Elizabeth*, Book Four, p. 135.

179. Birch I,157, II,182; Deborah Jones, p. 328; CM IV, pp. 447, 472, 476; CM V, pp. 402, 437-438, 502-503, 506-507, 510; CM VI, pp. 154-156, 459, 518; CM VII, pp. 95, 109-111, 204, 235, 547, 548; CM VIII, 493.

180. The work Alberici dedicated to Walsingham was his *Disputationum Dicas Prima*, published in 1587.

181. Akrigg, *Shakespeare and the Earl of Southampton*, p. 53.

182. *Ibid.*, pp. 75-79; CM IX, p. 133.

183. SP Dom., 1598-1601, p. 169. Rutland apparently as early as 21 January 1597 had under consideration the possibility of marrying Elizabeth Sidney, for in a letter written on that date to Sir Robert Sidney, Rutland is reported to have "waxen more cold, in the matter of marriage with your niece." *Letters and Memorials of State*, II, 83.

184. SP Dom., 1598-1601, pp. 156, 222.

185. DNB, s.v. Manners, Roger, Fifth Earl of Rutland. Rutland feared severe punishment, but was, in fact, gently dealt with. SP Dom. 1598-1601, p. 227; CM IX, pp. 173, 197, 246.

186. SP Ire., 1599-1602, p. 62.

187. Akrigg, *Shakespeare and the Earl of Southampton*, p. 90.

188. Harrison, *The Life and Death of Robert Devereux*, pp. 211-247; Birch, II, 443.

189. *Letters and Memorials of State*, II, 132.

190. Akrigg, *Shakespeare and the Earl of Southampton*, p. 104.

191. *Correspondence of King James VI of Scotland*, pp. 103-104.

192. SP Dom., 1598-1601, p. 445; CM X, p. 291.

193. Akrigg, *Shakespeare and the Earl of Southampton*, pp. 105-106.

194. Harrison, *Life and Death of Robert Devereux*, pp. 269-270.

195. *Correspondence of King James VI of Scotland*, pp. 90, 95, 97.
196. Nichols, *Progresses of Queen Elizabeth*, III, 247.
197. Harington, *Metamorphosis of Ajax*, ed. Donno, p. 174.
198. DNB, s.v. Barnes, Barnabe.
199. In lines 183-198 of the third sestiad, according to Tucker Brook, ed., *Works of Christopher Marlowe*, p. 486.
200. Newdigate, p. 93.
201. Meres, ff. 281-281ᵛ.
202. *Ibid.*, f. 284ᵛ·, where Meres writes, "*James* the 6, nowe King of Scotland is not only a favorer of Poets, but a Poet, as my friend Master *Richard Barnefielde* hath in this Distiche passing well recorded:

> The King of Scots now living is a Poet,
> As his Lepanto, and his furies show it. . . ."

203. Morris, p. 26.
204. DNB, s.v. Munday, Anthony; Stow, I, xx.
205. Munday also wrote plays in collaboration with Dekker, Middleton, Webster and Chettle, DNB, s.v. Munday, Anthony — and perhaps also with Shakespeare, if Shakespeare is indeed one of the co-authors of *The Book of Sir Thomas Moore*. See Chambers, *William Shakespeare*, I, 499-515.
206. Bullen, *Some Longer Elizabethan Poems*, p. 265.
207. Fuller, III, 104; DNB s.v. Daniel, Samuel; Seronsy, pp. 14-15.
208. Yates, *John Florio*, p. 54; Seronsy, p. 14.
209. Michel, pp. 36-51. Samuel Daniel had a brother John (referred to in Samuel's will dated 4 September 1619 as "my faithfull Brother John Danyel whome I here ordaine my sole executor", Grosart, p. xxvi). John was a musician, and may have been the same John Daniel whose access to Essex House is evidenced by The Curious Affair of Lady Essex' Letters. At his trial for treason, Essex referred to this John Daniel as an "arrant Thief, one that broke a Standard of mine, and stole a Casket of my Wife's, and many other things." *Complete Collection of State Trials*, I, 201. The incident alluded to by Essex is recounted by Camden:

> The Countesse his wife misdoubting her husband and her selfe in this trouble-some time, put into a cabbinet certaine love-letters which shee had received from him, and committed them to the trust of a *Dutch*-woman named *Rihove*. This *Dutch*-woman hid them at her house. By chance *John Daniel* her husband lighted upon them, reading them, and observing that there was somewhat in them, which might endanger the Earle, and incense the Queene, caused them to be written out by a cunning Scrivenor, very like the Originall: and then the fearfull woman, being ready to lye in, he told her that he would presently deliver into the Earles enemies hands, unless shee would forthwith give him 3000. pound. She, to avoyd the danger, gave him presently 1170 pound, and yet for so great a summe, she received not the Originall letters, but the copies from the impostor, who purposed to wipe the Earles adversaries also of a great

summe of money for the originals. For this imposture, he was condemned to perpetuall imprisonment, fined at 3000 pound, whereof the Countess should have 2000. and to stand with his eares nayled to pillary, with this inscription, *A wicked forger and Impostor*. [*The Historie of . . . Princesse Elizabeth*, Book Four, pp. 195-196.]

John Daniel was released from prison by virtue of a general pardon proclaimed at the time of James I's accession, SP Dom., 1603-1610, p. 185, but since he had not paid to the Countess the full amount required to be paid to her, continued to be prosecuted by the Countess and her new husband, Richard, Earl of Clanricarde, *ibid.*, pp. 371, 457, from which prosecution Daniel sought relief, claiming "that the Countess of Essex would not have prosecuted him, but for a false report that he was bribed to betray [to the Queen, or to Robert Cecil] the contents of the late Earl of Essex's letters to . . . [Lord Cobham and Sir Walter Raleigh]," *Ibid.*, p. 6, which charge, and others, Daniel denied. *ibid.*, pp. 6 and 586-587. There is doubtless more to this story than can be made out from the official records. On 2 May 1595, the Countess of Essex released "to her servant, Janes Daniell, as well of the sum of 8,000*l.* contained in her books of accounts, as also of all other moneys, actions, debts, duties, and demands whatsoever, to this date," SP Dom, 1580-1625, p. 375: whatever this transaction was, it was a curious one to take place between a countess and her servant. The "cunning Scrivenor" who copied the letters for John Daniel was Peter Bales, whose story was that John Daniell had brought him the letters, which he had copied, but that he had not "imitated" the letters (by this I assume he meant that he had not attempted to write the letters in Essex' hand). He made above a dozen copies of one letter in particular, containing the sentence "The Queen's commandment may break my neck, but my enemies at home shall never break my heart." Daniell told Bales "that the Countess had ordered him to have the frequent copies made that he might better gull somebody." Bales, perplexed, thereafter went to see the Countess, but to what end, and with what result, is not clear. The letter of which Bales made so many copies seems not to have survived; in his statement, Bales identifies it as beginning, "Franke, I send unto you Cuffe, my man, whom you may believe in what he saith," (thus informing us both of the way in which Essex addressed his wife, Frances, and of the personal and confidential nature of Cuffe's service to Essex) and as ending, "When your belly shall be laid [i.e., after you give birth], I will provide for your being here." SP Dom., 1601-1603, pp. 77-78.

210. The shift by the members of the Leicester/Sidney circle from the Countess of Pembroke and Wilton to Essex and Essex House as their patron and centre is evidenced by a comparison of the relative number of works dedicated to or praising the Countess and the Earl during the years 1588 to 1601, as shown by the chart on the next page. Only *published* works are included in the table. The list of works dedicated to the Countess of Pembroke is taken from Frances Berkely Young, pp. 150-204, and the list of works dedicated to Essex is taken from an unpublished dissertation by Ray Heffner, both lists being augmented by such other published works as have come to my attention. In her biography of the Countess of Pembroke, Margaret Hannay states (at pages 68) that although the

Date	Works dedicated to, or praising Countess of Pembroke	Works dedicated to or praising Earl of Essex
1581	Thomas Howell, *Devises*	
1587	Abraham Fraunce, *Lamentations of Amyntas*	John Philip, *Life and Death of Sir Philip Sidney*
1588	Abraham Fraunce, *Arcadian Rhetorike* Babington, *A Profitable Exposition of the Lords Prayer*	Anthony Munday, *Palladino of England*
1590	Spenser, *The Ruine of Time*	Thomas Watson, *Madrigals*
1591	Fraunce, *Countess of Pembrokes Ivychurch* Fraunce, *Countess of Pembroke Emmanuell* Sidney (unauthorized edition, dedication by Nashe), *Astrophel and Stella*	
1592	Nicholas Breton, *Pilgrimage to Paradise* Fraunce, *Third Part of Countess of Pembrokes Ivychurch* Samuel Daniel, *Delia* Thomas Watson, *Aminta Gaudia* William Gager, *Ulysses Redux*	R.D., tr., *Hypnerotomachia* William Gager, *Meleager*
1593	Michael Drayton, *Shepherds Garland* Thomas Morley, *Canzonets*	Richard Harvey, *Philadelphus*
1594	Samuel Daniel, *Cleopatra*	
1595		Vincent Saviolo, *His Practice* Samuel Daniel, First Two Books of *Civile Wars* Barnabe Barnes, *A Divine Centurie of Spirituall Sonnets* Robert Parsons, *A Conference about the Succession to the Crown of England**
1597	Nicholas Breton, *Auspicante Jehovah*	John Stockwood, *Progymnasma Scholasticum* Joshua Sylvester, tr., *DuBartas* John Racaster, *Book of Seven Planets*
1598		Richard Nicols, *Englands Eliza* George Chapman, tr., *Homer* Alberico Gentili, *De Jure Belli Commentationes duae*
1599	Moffitt, *Silkwormes*	Thomas Churchyard, *The Fortunate Farewell* Thomas Churchyard, *A Welcome Home* John Hayward, *History of Henry IV** George Silver, *Paradoxes of Defence*
1601	Nicholas Breton, *A Divine Poem* Charles Fitzgeoffrey, *Assaniae*	*These were dedicated to Essex as embarrassments to him.
	Countess of Pembroke died 25 September 1621.	Earl of Essex beheaded 25 February 1601.

Earl of Essex sought to become Sidney's heir, he "never quite succeeded in replacing Mary Sidney as Philip's Phoenix." Whatever she might mean by that, I think it is clear that, from 1594 until his disgrace in 1599, Essex was the centre of the old Leicester/Sidney group.

211. CM IV, pp. 138, 144.

212. SP Dom., 1591-1594, pp. 35, 37, 47, 204, 320; CM IV, pp. 77, 147.

213. SP Dom., 1595-1597, pp. 54-55, 92, 338, 324.

214. When Skeres was arrested on 13 March 1594/5 for having dealings with a man apparently engaged in the purchase and sale of stolen goods, he was identified as a servant to the Earl of Essex. CM V, p. 139. Skeres was released on the following day. *Ibid.*, pp. 141-142.

215. PC, 1601-1604, p. 130.

216. CM XI, p. 44; CM XIV, p. 171; PC 1600-1601, p. 160.

217. *Ibid.* See also William Reynolds' letter of 13 February 1601, CM XI, p. 46, which describes Orrel's participation in the "rebellion" and characterizes Orrell as "a most desperate rakehell as lives".

218. CM XI, p. 44; CM XIV, p. 171; PC 1600-1601, p. 160. This Richard Cholmley was eventually released upon the payment of £200. CM XI, p. 214; CM XIV, p. 171; PC, 1600-1601, p. 261.

219. I know that Ethel Seaton has written, at p. 276, that the Richard Cholmley who accused Marlowe of atheism

> is not . . . to be confused with the Richard Cholmley who was imprisoned in the Essex conspiracy of 1600-1601, and was let off with a fine of £200. This later Richard was the son of Sir Henry Cholmley of Whitby, and was born only in 1580. It is very probable that the earlier Richard was a younger son of the great Cholmley clan with its branches in Cheshire and Yorkshire, but there is no clear proof where he comes. He might well be the Richard who was the brother of the Sir Hugh (*d.* 1601) of the Cheshire Cholmleys, and who died without issue.

Seaton does not give any reason or authority for her assertion that the Richard Cholmley of Marlowe fame is not the Richard Cholmley of the Essex "rebellion," but I assume that her conclusion is based upon the letter dated 10 February 1600/1 from Sir Thomas Posthumous Hoby to Sir Robert Cecil. The letter, CM XI, pp. 39-40, begins, "Understanding that Richard Cholmly, son and heir apparent of Henry Cholmly, Esq., one of the outrageous defendants to my bill in the Star Chamber [Henry Cholmley was also, along with Hoby, a justice of the peace of the North Riding of Yorkshire, SP Dom., 1598-1601, pp. 188, 363], is apprehended as one of the rebellious Earl's assistants, and hearing that his friends would have it thought that he was there by chance, and that he was a man of no power, I thought it my duty to certify your Honour my knowledge of him." Which Hoby proceeds to do, giving Cholmley a bad character. My suspicion is that Hoby, who probably was not in London at the time of the Essex uprising (which was on Sunday, 8 February 1600/1601), but having heard that a Richard Cholmley was involved, jumped to the conclusion that this was the son of the defendant in his suit, and rushed to write a self-serving letter to his first cousin, Sir Robert Cecil, to help his cause. But Hoby's conclusion, I believe, was incorrect, as may be inferred from the silence in Hoby's subsequent letters relating to the lawsuit about young Cholmley's supposed participation in the Essex affair. See CM XI, 456, SP Dom., 1611-1618, p. 126. That Hoby was confused cannot be surprising, since, as every student of the Tudor period knows, it was common for dozens of contemporaries to bear the same name, and there were quite a few Richard Cholmley's around in the early 1600's, just as there were several John Davies's, John Vaughn's and Richard Martin's. Even when the first names were different, there was confusion: in CM XI, pp. 267-268, is set forth the deposition of a man who got into trouble as a result of being misinformed that the Cuffe involved in the Essex affair was a prominent man in Munster — doubtless Hugh Cuffe — rather than the hapless Henry Cuffe of our story.

Seaton's suggestion that the Cholmley involved with Marlowe was from Yorkshire is probably correct, for many persons of that name lived in Yorkshire at the time (see *Victoria History of Yorkshire, North Riding*, II, pp. 100, 108, 126, 347, 504, 521, and Cliffe, pp. 41-42). Bakeless' suggestion (I, 125-126) that the Marlowe Cholmley was a Richard Cholmley of Ingleton accords with my independent conclusion (although perhaps not the one who inherited an estate from a Sir Richard Cholmley who died in 1583, for this Richard Cholmley seems to have died in 1600, Cliffe, p. 42). But whoever was the Richard Cholmley who accused Marlow of atheism, he was, I am confident, the same person who on 19 March 1592/3 was summoned to appear before Essex and other members of the Privy Council (PC, 1592-1593, p. 130), who on 15 November 1593 was a servant of the Earl of Essex under suspicion of having committed a crime (Fourth Report Comm'n on Hist. Mss., p. 330), and who, along with his confrères Skeres, Tipping and Orrell, was in the service of Essex on 8 March 1600/1601, and was imprisoned for his participation in the Essex conspiracy. (Also on the staff of the Earl of Essex in the late 1590's was a man named *William* Cholmley, CM IX, pp. xiii, xvii, 270; Fifth Report Comm'n on Hist. Mss., p. 362, who arguably could have been the Cholmley in the service of Essex on 15 November 1593, but I rather think that this William Cholmley was the boy who, being in wardship in 1595, CM V, p. 529; Hurstfield, pp. 82-83, was too young to have been so early in the service of the Earl of Essex.)

220. See. e.g., Spenser, p. xiv (E. de Selincourt's Introduction).
221. *Ibid.*, pp. 422-423.
222. *Id.*
223. Hughes, "Virgil and Spenser," p. 290.
224. Webbe, pp. 54–55.
225. Nashe, III, 92.
226. Spenser, p. 455 (E. K.'s gloss to *The Shepheardes Calendar*, "September").
227. Duncan-Jones, p. 240.
228. James M. Osborn, p. 433.
229. *The Correspondence of Sir Philip Sidney and Hubert Languet*, p. 102.
230. *Ibid.*, p. 133.

231. *Ibid.*, p. 144.
232. *Ibid.*, p. 148.
233. Duncan-Jones, p. 240. Duncan-Jones takes the words "tiny handful" from Lawrence Stone's book, *The Crisis of the Aristocracy 1558-1641*, where Stone, writing about the nobility and gentry, states (at p. 654) that "Only a tiny handful did not marry at all, and their cases are sufficiently exceptional to suggest that they were inspired by strong private idiosyncrasies. So far as we know none of them — except possibly Lord Brooke — was homosexual, and one can only speculate about why men like the Earls of Danby and Northampton chose to let their lines and titles die out." Since people of means almost always married for financial and dynastic reasons (see note 7 to this chapter), the fact that most such people were married tells us nothing about their sexual preferences; consider, for example, the fact that Francis Bacon, Roger Manners, Antonio Pérez and King James I *were* married, and Richard Barnfield and William Burton married after leaving London. In the event, more than a "tiny handful" of the men associated with Leicester/Essex House were not married; among them, in addition to Dyer and Greville, were Gabriel Harvey, Charles and Henry Danvers (Henry was created Earl of Danby by Charles I in 1626), George Chapman, Christopher Marlowe, Henry Constable, Michael Drayton, Matthew Gwynne, Anthony Bacon, Henry Wotton, Henry Cuffe and William Camden.
234. Davison, I, 8. Francis Davison (ca 1575-ca 1619) was intimately involved with the Leicester/Essex House group. His father, William Davison (ca 1541-1608), was a close friend and associate both of Leicester and Walsingham, and was in Holland in an official capacity when Leicester was offered the Governorship of the United Provinces, which, after consulting with Davison and Sir Philip Sidney, he accepted. When Leicester was installed in this position on 25 January 1586, Davison was at his side, as were also Sir Philip Sidney and the Earl of Essex. And it was Davison who received the brunt of the Queen's wrath when, upon his return to England, he informed her of Leicester's acceptance of this high position. But Davison not long thereafter regained the Queen's favour, was appointed to the Privy Council, and in 1586 became an assistant to Francis Walsingham, the secretary of state. In the following year, Davison had the misfortune of being the person to whom Elizabeth gave her signed warrant authorizing the death of Mary, Queen of Scots, which warrant Davison caused to be executed, claiming later he understood that to be the Queen's wish. Elizabeth — whether genuinely or not, we shall never know — was furious when she learned of the execution, as a consequence of which Davison himself seemed likely to be executed, but escaped with only a few years' imprisonment. Essex, a loyal friend to Davison, had the poor judgment to incense Elizabeth by urging her to appoint Davison as Secretary of State after the death of Walsingham.

William's son Francis was admitted to Gray's Inn in May 1593, and wrote part of and acted in the famous Gesta Grayorum of 1594 (Davison, II, 43) — which festivities, as we have seen, both Essex and Southampton, and perhaps also Antonio Pérez, attended. Davison, in any event, knew, and evidently was well disposed toward, Pérez (Ungerer, I, 256). Francis Davison received the Queen's licence to travel abroad on 27 May 1595 (Davison, II, 44), during which time he wrote and sent back to Essex House "relations" of the countries he visited (Ungerer, I, 256). Davison was in Venice by January 1596, and in Florence during the autumn of 1596, returning to England late in 1597 (Davison II, 44), and thus his stay in Florence may have overlapped that of Essex' secretary, Henry Cuffe, who was in Florence from the spring or summer of 1597 until the summer of 1598 (see Chapter VIII, p. 201).

Duncan-Jones speculates (at p. 240) that the text of Sidney's poems on his friends could have reached Francis Davison as a consequence of the fact that William Temple, who had been Sidney's secretary, and in whose arms Sidney died, next worked for William Davison, to whom he showed the Sidney papers he had acquired; but Francis Davison's many contacts with the Leicester/Essex House group make it more likely, I think, that he obtained the manuscripts either from Dyer or Greville, without whose consent, we may assume, Davison would not have published the poems.

235. *Ibid.*, I, 11-12.
236. D'Israeli, II, 108.
237. Sidney, *The Countess of Pembroke's Arcadia* (Original Version), p. 24 (spelling modernised). The reader should remember that Isaac D'Israeli (in the preceding note) was referring to the version of *Arcadia* published by William Ponsonbie in 1590, because that was the only version known to 19th century readers, whereas the quotation in the text is from the so-called "Old Arcadia", an earlier draft first published in 1926. It is generally agreed that the "Old Arcadia" is much closer to what Sidney himself wrote than is the 1590 *Arcadia*. Also, the 1590 *Arcadia* is a bit more restrained in its description of the friendship between Musidorus and Pyrocles than is the "Old Arcadia," so the statement by D'Israeli quoted in the text would apply with even greater force to the version I have cited than it does to the version which D'Israeli knew.
238. Sidney, *The Countess of Pembroke's Arcadia* (Original Version), p. 2; see also the 1590 edition, p. 327.
239. Horne, pp. 235-236.
240. Morris, *Richard Barnfield, Colin's Child*, pp. 8-9.
241. *Id.*
242. Watson, p. 142.
243. *Ibid.*, p. 12.
244. Eccles, *Christopher Marlowe in London*, pp. 163-164.
245. Summers, p. 222. Summers also says that "Written in a period during which homosexual practices were invariably denounced as unspeakable and as the source of corruptions that threatened church and state alike, when sodomy was routinely linked with heresy and sorcery and considered a violation of natural order 'against the King Celestial or Terrestial,' and when sodomy was punishable by death and the confiscation of property, *Edward II* is remarkable precisely because it fails to echo such condemnations." At one time I would have agreed with this statement as to the perils of being a "sodomite" in the late Elizabethan period, and, indeed, in *The Labyrinth of Shakespeare's Sonnets*, I concluded that Shakespeare's use of puns to veil his revelations was a consequence of "the urgent necessity for the sodomite to conceal himself" (p. 99); I am now persuaded, from

the material presented in this chapter, and Chapter VII, that Elizabethan officials honoured the laws against sodomy mainly in their breaches — that the attitude, at least among the privileged, was one of great tolerance, and that Shakespeare's use of puns and dark conceits was for artistic, not legal reasons.

246. A similar list makes a surprising appearance in Book IV of the *Faerie Queene*, where on the grounds of the Temple of Venus stroll not only men and women in love with each other, but also

> another sort
> Of louers lincked in true harts consent;
> Which loued not as these, for like intent,
> But on chast vertue grounded their desire,
> Farre from all fraud, or fayned blandishment;
> Which in their spirits kindling zealous fire,
>   Braue thoughts and noble deeds did euermore aspire.
>
> Such were great *Hercules*, and *Hylas* deare;
> Trew *Ionathan*, and *Dauid* trustie tryde;
>   Stout *Theseus*, and *Pirithous* his feare [companion];
> *Pylades* and *Orestes* by his syde;
> Myld *Titus* and *Gesippus* without pryde;
> *Damon* and *Pythias* whom death could not seuer:
> All these and all that euer had bene tyde
> In bands of friendship, there did live for euer,
>   Whose liues although decay'd, yet loues decayed neuer.
>   [Book IV, Canto X, Stanzas 26, 27.]

This is yet another example of Spenser's acceptance of those who, in Venus' domain, were linked to each other by "bands of friendship" rather than bonds of matrimony.

247. Morris, "Richard Barnfield, 'Amyntas,' and the Sidney Circle," p. 324. Michel Poirier, at page 21 of his book *Christopher Marlowe*, suggests that Barnfield, who "shared Marlowe's partiality for handsome youths" probably met Marlowe through their mutual friend Thomas Watson.

248. Bullen, p. 151.

249. *Ibid.*, p. 190.

250. Morris, *Richard Barnfield*, p. 52.

251. Bullen, p. 204.

252. *Ibid.*, p. 266.

253. Meres, ff. 284, 284ᵛ.

254. Morris, *Richard Barnfield*, pp. 13, 189-191; DNB s.v. Barnfield, Richard.

255. Perry, pp. 348-349.

256. B[urton], p. 8. Burton's translation was probably made from a Latin translation of the work by "L. Annibale Cruceo" (Annibale della Croce, a Milanese scholar) published in Cambridge in 1589, and on the Continent some 40 or 50 years earlier. Also, "Italian and French translations existed before Burton's time, and

it is possible that he may have made occasional use of them." B[urton], pp. xix-xx. (See also the table on p. 68.) *Clitophon and Leucippe*, in Latin, Italian or French (or perhaps all three), seems to have been known to Sidney, for the names Clitophon, Leucippe and Clinias appear in his *Arcadia*, as well also as the pairing of cousins, and the causing of confusion as a consequence of the death of one person in the disguise of another. Hill, pp. 8-12. Strangely, no copy of Burton's translation was known to exist until one was discovered in 1905 "in the debris of an old library believed to come from the neighbourhood of Winchester. . . ." Another copy was found in 1923. B[urton], pp. xvii-xix. The book was printed by Thomas Creede, who in subsequent years also printed quarto editions of *Richard III* (1598), *Romeo and Juliet* (1599) and *The chronicle history of Henry the fift* (1600). McKerrow, pp. 80-81.

257. William Burton, *Description of Leicestershire*, p. 92.

258. See notes 28, 29 and 111, *supra*.

259. Yates, *A Study of Love's Labour's Lost*, p. 93, note 2.

260. Bakeless, I, 86.

261. Vaughan, *The Golden Grove*, sig. C4ᵛ.

262. Hotson, *The Death of Christopher Marlowe*, pp. 14-15; Bakeless, I, pp. 231-240.

263. Dugdale, *Baronage*, II, 470.

264. DNB, s.v. Meyrick, Sir Gelly or Gilly; CM XI, pp. 107-108.

265. PC, 1600-1601, p. 208.

266. *Ibid.*, p. 150.

267. *Ibid.*, p. 208.

268. *Ibid.*, p. 289. That our Sir John Vaughan was not in the custody of the government at this time establishes that he is not the John Vaughan who was imprisoned immediately after the Essex uprising, but soon thereafter "discharged upon bond," and not subsequently prosecuted. *Ibid.*, pp. 160, 485. This other John Vaughan was, I suspect, the "Vaughan" who was "servant to Gelley Merricke," *ibid.*, p. 266, and thus probably a relative of Sir John Vaughan.

269. Vaughan, *The Golden Fleece*, p. 23.

270. *Ibid.*, p. 27.

271. Robert Burton, *Anatomy of Melancholy*, ed. Dell and Jordan-Smith, p. 416.

272. Robert Burton, *Philosophaster*, pp. 12-13. Burton's play was written in 1606, and acted at Christ Curch College, Oxford, on 16 February 1617. The play, in Latin, was first published in 1862. *Ibid.*, pp. xii, 16-17.

273. *Ibid.*, pp. 160-161.

274. Robert Burton, *Anatomy of Melancholy*, ed. Dell and Jordan-Smith, pp. 29, 438.

275. *Biographia Britannia*, s.v. Burton, William.

276. This is not to say that they necessarily liked each other's friends, or tastes — for, if their writings and dedications are any indication, Robert and William Burton seem to have had different approaches to sexual matters. Robert Burton was, of course (like all other educated people of his time), keenly aware of the prevalence among the Greek and Romans of sexual love between men, but when he dealt with the subject in his great book, he was able to do so only in Latin, calling it *foeditatem* and *spurcitiem* — "nastiness" and "filth" — at the same time recognizing (to quote from a translation of Burton's Latin) that "we have not to this

day, in the matter of men with men or women with women, so many sorts of vile actions as among your memorable and famous heroes [of antiquity]," examples of whom are Socrates, who "used to frequent the Gymnasium because of the beauty of the youngsters" ("*Socrates pulchrorum Adolescentum causa frequens Gymnasium adibat*" and "Hercules following beardless comrades, mad for his friends, &c. . . ." ("*Hercules imberbem sectans socium, amicos deseruit &c.*") Robert Burton, (English, ed. Dell and Jordan-Smith) pp. 651-653; (Latin, ed. Shilleto) III, pp. 55-57. William Burton, on the other hand, if we may judge from the fact that he translated *Clitiphon and Leucippe* (which work, according to his brother, was invoked by Italians to justify a sin than which among whom nothing was more familiar) and dedicated it to Southampton, and then dedicated another work to George Villiers (both dedicatees being of ambiguous libidinal leanings), seems at the very least to have found the vice, and those who practiced it, tolerable: in any event, William translated from Latin into plain English that which Robert, in an otherwise English book, felt constrained to write in Latin.

277. Robert Burton, *Anatomy of Melancholy*, ed. Dell and Jordan-Smith, p. xi.
278. A contributor to the April 17, 1852 issue of *Notes and Queries* (London) reports (at Volume V, pp. 365-366) that he has a copy of Weever's *Ancient Funerall Monuments* which once belonged to William Burton, the historian of Leicestershire, and that at the end of the volume, under the heading "Antiquarii temp. Eliz. Reg." is a list in Burton's own handwriting of forty-five persons. Included in the list (in the form they are there designated), are Mr. Atey, Arthur Goulding, Willm̃ Camden, Daniell Rogers, Tho. Saville, and Henry Saville. All the persons on the list, to the extent they are identifiable, seem to have been contemporaries of William Burton, and it is tempting to think that the names on the list were not merely of antiquarians, but of antiquarians who were friends of his. If that is true, then the close connection with the Leicester/Essex House group of the persons whose names I have selected from the list would support my conclusion that William Burton had numerous and close contacts with that group.
279. W[illiam] B[urton], p. 8.
280. But Plutarch reports scepticism in some quarters over the claim frequently made, and such as this appears to be, that men's love for boys was a chaste one: "If as Protogenes saith this Paederastium aimed not at carnall conjunction, how then can it be love, if Venus be not there?" Plutarch, *The Philosophie*, tr. Philemon Holland, p. 1135. Holland's translation was dedicated to James I, whose arms are on the cover of the copy at the Folger Shakespeare Library.
281. W[illiam] B[urton], p. 46.
282. The English climate was to change in a few years. In 1638, another translation of *The Loves of Clitiphon and Leucippe* was published. The new translator, A.H. (Anthony Hodges), deleted the shipboard discussion over whether the love of women or boys is to be preferred, and in his introduction explained that "by the exection of the two testicles of an unchaste dispute, and one immodest expression, I have so refined the author, that the modest matron may looke in his face and not blush."
283. Who is this William Reynolds, who knows so much that is of interest to us? Mrs. Stopes, in *The Life of Henry, Third Earl of Southampton*, at p. 199, thinks that

he may be a brother of Edward Reynolds, the Secretary to the Earl of Essex, but this is highly improbable. Nor is it even remotely likely that he is the William Reynolds to whom Shakespeare in his will left money for a ring. However, it is quite possible that our William Reynolds was related to either of these other Reynolds'. Eccles states, in *Shakespeare in Warwickshire*, at p. 123, that there was a "Willyam Raynoules of Stretfard" in prison at Warwick in 1613, and this sounds like a promising lead.

284. CM XI, pp. 93–94.
285. Hotson, *Shakespeare's Sonnets Dated*, pp. 142, 147.
286. Camden states that Essex had four children: by his wife, Frances Walsingham, he "begate *Robert* his sonne, and two daughter [sic] *Frances* and *Dorothy*; and on Mistresse *Southwell*, his paramore, *Walter.*" *The Historie of . . . Princesse Elizabeth*, Book Four, p. 190. A nineteenth century Walter Devereux writes that

> It appears by a law paper in the State Paper Office, containing an abstract of the remainders of the Earl of Essex' estates, that Essex House was in remainder to "Walter Devereux, the base reputed son of Robert Earl of Essex, begotten on the body of Elizabeth Southwell." Whether this frail Lady was Elizabeth, daughter of the Lord High Admiral [Charles Howard, second Baron Howard of Effingham and first Earl of Nottingham (1536-1624)], and wife of Sir Robert Southwell, or whether she was the Mrs Southwell [the daughter of Sir Robert Southwell and Elizabeth Howard], who in 1599 was appointed maid of honour to the Queen, is not quite clear. Elizabeth Howard married Sir Robert Southwell in 1583; she must, therefore, in all probability, have been the Earl's senior. [Devereux, I, 475, note 1.]

Robert W. Kenny, in *Elizabeth's Admiral* (at p. 93, note 11), interprets the foregoing as a surmise that the Elizabeth Southwell who bore Essex a son was the *daughter* of Sir Robert Southwell, and suggests that it is more likely that the Elizabeth who was the mother of Essex' child was the *wife* of Sir Robert Southwell (or rather his widow, for Sir Robert died in 1598), she being, according to Kenny, only about two years older than Essex. Possibly supporting Kenny's contention is the report of 12 July 1600 (*Letters and Memorials of State*, II, 206) that the "Queen went to see Lady Southwell, who is in *Westminster*, very weak," for this seems to be an allusion to the widow of Sir Robert, and her "weakness" could have been related to her pregnancy or delivery.

In aid of the younger Elizabeth Southwell's claim to being the mother of Essex' child is that she was one of the Queen's Maids of Honour (she was officially made a member of this group on 5 January 1599/1600, *Ibid.*, II, 156; see also *Ibid.*, II, 141, 152, 159 and 201), becoming thus a member of a group of young women particularly susceptible to being impregnated by Earls: Elizabeth Vernon had been a Maid of Honour when she was impregnated by Henry Wriothesley, as had been Mary Fitton when she was impregnated by William Herbert. (I refrain from here mentioning another impregnated maid of honour, Elizabeth Throckmorton, because her seducer, Sir Walter Raleigh, was not an earl.) That the same fate had befallen this maid of honour *might* be what is hinted at in a letter written on 22 December 1599 describing the people in attendance at the christening of Robert Sidney's daughter Barabara: the letter refers to "My Lady *Mollins*, she that was Mrs *Southwell*, the Mayde of Honour, [who] came with my Lady Effingham [i.e., her maternal grandmother]." *Ibid.*, II, 152. Is it possible that the Lord High Admiral of England had conveniently arranged a marriage for his "frail" granddaughter? If this Elizabeth Southwell was "My Lady *Mollins*," it was not for long. In 1605, disguised as a page (how many of Shakespeare's plays might she have seen?), she accompanied Sir Robert Dudley to France, and thence to Italy, where they married, and had twelve children. She died in 1631; her husband died in 1649. Leader, pp. 48-49, 101, 108, 127.

The Sir Robert Dudley whom she married was Leicester's son by Douglass Sheffield, and thus the step-brother to the Earl of Essex (see note 107, *supra*). From the age of 17 Robert Dudley devoted his life to maritime and navigational activities. On a voyage to the West Indies in 1594 he made various geographical discoveries, and seized and sank a number of Spanish ships. In 1597 he "was admiral of the English vanguard in the battle of Cadiz in Spain, when they burnt the fleet from the Indies, and took the city. Then he besieged Faro in Algarna (Algarve) in Portugal, and next took command of the English galleons sent to the rescue when Calais in France was taken . . . [by the Spanish]." Leader, pp. 33-34. This, of course, is the expedition on which Essex made his reputation, and that Essex and his step-brother had a harmonious relationship may be inferred not only from their working with each other during the Cadiz expedition, but also from the fact that Dudley participated in Essex' uprising on 8 February 1600/1601, and was at that time taken prisoner, but shortly after released, Leader, p. 43 (although, strangely, Dudley is not on any of the lists of prisoners.

After Essex' execution, Robert Dudley initiated legal procedings to establish himself as the legitimate son of the Earl of Leicester. His claim was opposed by Essex' mother, and the issue was decided against him in 1605. Leader, pp. 44-46. Not long after this, Dudley, accompanied by his "page," left England never to return.

Elizabeth Southwell's marrying Sir Robert Dudley does not necessarily mean that she was not already married, for just as Dudley left behind him in England a wife and four children, so may she have left behind her a husband Mollins and a son Walter; why she might wish to leave both is not hard to imagine.

We cannot be certain, however, that either this Elizabeth Southwell or her mother was the lady favoured by Essex, for, so far as I can discover, the only thing we know about that woman is her name, and there were other Elizabeth Southwell's around. One Elizabeth Southwell, the daughter of Richard Southwell (a cousin of the Robert Southwell who married the daughter of the Lord High Admiral), and the sister of Robert Southwell, the martyred Jesuit, married Michael Lister, a first cousin of the Earl of Southampton (see Tables IV and VI). In view of the fact that the Elizabeth Vernon by whom Southampton had fathered a child was the first cousin (by blood) of the Earl of Essex, would not our yearnings for symmetry be satisfied could it be established that the Elizabeth Southwell by whom Essex fathered a child was, had been, or later became, the first cousin (albeit by marriage) of the Earl of Southampton?

347

Little has been made in the literature on Essex of this out-of-wedlock child, whose fate is unknown to history, but whose existence probably is the real reason for the Queen's harsh treatment of Essex after his return from Ireland.

287. du Maurier, pp. 49-53.

288. Halliwell, ed., *The Autobiography and Correspondence of Sir Simonds D'Ewes, Bart.*, I, p. 192. Times change; D'Ewes' "gross" text is as follows:

Had he followed the just and vertuous steps of Sir Nicholas Bacon, knight, his father, that continued lord keeper of the great seal some 18 years under queen Elizabeth of ever blessed memory, his life might have been as glorious, as by his vices it proved infamous. For although he were an eminent scholar, and a reasonable good lawyer, both which he much adorned with his elegant expression of himself and his graceful delivery; yet his vices were so stupendous and great as they utterly obscured and outpoized his vertues. For he was immoderately ambitious, and excessively proud; to maintain which he was necessitated to injustice and bribery, taking sometimes most basely on both sides. To this latter wickedness the favour he had with the beloved marquis of Buckingham emboldened him, as I learned in a discourse from a gentleman of his bedchamber, who told me he was sure his lord should never fall as long as the said marquis continued in favour. His most abominable and darling sin I should rather bury in silence than mention it, were it not a most admirable instance how men are enslaved by wickedness, and held captive by the devil: for whereas presently upon his censure at this time his ambition was moderated, his pride humbled, and the means of his former injustice and corruption removed, yet would he not relinquish the practice of his most horrible and secret sin of sodomy, keeping still one Godrick, a very effeminated youth, to be his catamite and bedfellow, although he had discharged the most of his other houshold servants; which was the more to be admired, because men generally after his fall began to discourse of that his unnatural crime, which he had practiced many years, deserting the bed of his lady, which he accounted, as the Italians and Turks do, a poor and mean pleasure, in respect of the other: and it was thought by some that he should have been tried at the bar of justice for it, and have satisfied the law most severe against that horrible villany, with the price of his blood; which caused some bold and ward man to write these verses following, in a whole sheet of paper, and to cast it down in some part of York-house in the Strand, where viscount St. Alban yet lay:

Within this sty a hog* doth ly,
That must be hang'd for sodomy.

But he never came to any public trial for this crime; nor did he ever, that I could hear, forbear his old custom of making his servants his bedfellows, so to avoid the scandal that was raised of him; though he lived many years after his fall in his lodgings in Grays Inne in Holbourne, in great want and penury.

---

*Alluding to his surname of Bacon, and to that swinish abominable sin. [*Extracts from the MS Journals of Sir Simonds D'Ewes*, pp. 25-27.]

Bacon's "lady" was Alice Barnham, whom Bacon married in 1606, when he was 45 years old, and she about 14. Their union, which lasted until Bacon's death in 1626, produced no issue. Citing "just and great causes," Bacon in his will left to his wife only what would otherwise have passed to her as a matter of law, perhaps because he knew that his wife was having an affair with one John Underhill, whom she married eleven days after Bacon's death. Epstein, pp. 176-176. Her new husband, Aubrey writes (at page 11), "she made deafe and blinde with too much of Venus."

289. [Begley], p. 255. This book, written in support of the contention that Bacon was the true author of the works attributed to Shakespeare, marshals (at pages 32-52) the then available evidence to show "that in the recorded life of Bacon there was a hidden scandal which was more akin to the veiled scandal of the Sonnets than anything we know or could infer from what has been handed down to us about Shakespeare, their reputed author."

290. Marañon, *Antonio Pérez*, pp. 151-155.

291. Ungerer, I, 192-195.

292. *Ibid.*, I, 142. According to this account, the Englishmen go on to say that because of this, "la reina lo aborrece y no hace caso de él," I, 142, (i.e, "the Queen abhors him and pays no attention to him"), which may have been a true statement about the Queen's attitude toward Pérez, but does not correctly reflect the attitude toward Pérez of Essex and his friends: for such sins as Pérez may have committed in England and known to Essex, Blount and Standen at the time of the sack of Cadiz in June or July of 1596, must have been committed and become generally known during his *first* visit there, yet, as we have seen (on page 123) when Pérez left England in August, 1595, he was feted by the Essex House group, and treated by Essex with deference and respect.

293. *Letters and Memorials of State*, I, 193.

294. *Ibid.*, I, 219 (spelling modernised).

295. *Ibid.*, I, 220; Birch I, 66-68, 107; [Begley], pp. 49-50.

296. Birch, I, 278, 315.

297. CM XI, pp. 107-108. That Edmonds was indeed "of . . . [Essex'] charges maintained" is confirmed by the existence of "a great number of receipts in 1599 and 1600 of sums of money paid by Sir Gilly Merrick to various persons," including "Capt. P. Edmonde." *Fifth Report of the Royal Commission on Historical Manuscripts*, p. 363.

298. DNB, s.v. Lopez, Roderigo.

299. Godfrey Goodman, pp. 152-153.

300. Marañon, p. 308 (English); I, 638 (Spanish).

301. *The Manuscripts of . . . the Duke of Rutland*, p. 439.

302. Herford and Simpson, I, 54; VIII, 224; XI, 88.

303. *Ibid.*, VIII, 224.

304. Beaumont and Fletcher, XI, 508.

305. Herford and Simpson, VIII, 10.

306. *Ibid.*, I, 138.

307. *Correspondence of King James VI of Scotland*, p. 90.

308. *Ibid.*, pp. 82-83.

309. *Ibid.*, pp. xxvii-xxviii, 80-81.
310. Willson, *King James VI and I*, p. 153.
311. Greek Anthology, Book V, epigram 65 (Loeb Classical Library, I, 161). This epigram appears on pp. 281^v -282 of the 1550-1 Aldine edition of the Greek Anthology, and on p. 483 of Estienne's 1556 edition of the Anthology. It also appears in a Latin translation on page 686 of Fausto Sabeo's *Epigrammata* (1556). Hutton records a Latin translation in Natale Conti's *Mythologia* (1568) and a French verse translation by Jean de Montlyard in a 1597 French edition of Conti's *Mythologia*. An English translation by Simon Raven is printed in *Eros*, pp. 58-59. I shall take advantage of the conscientious reader (i.e., the reader of endnotes) by here foisting upon him or her my own version of this epigram:

> Swooping down as an eagle, Zeus Ganymede plucked;
> In the shape of a swan, he fair Leda - - - - - -:
> Why then may not mortals, like Jupiter Rex,
> Love whom they find lovely, regardless of sex?

Essex House is not an unusual phenomenon, but only one example — perhaps the first that is documentable — of the pansexual coteries, groups or salons which from time to time have existed in England. It is only of the relatively recent groups that we have any detailed knowledge, but what we do know about, say, the Bloomsbury group, illuminates our understanding of Essex House: for in Lytton Strachey, E. M. Forster, John Maynard Keynes, Roger Fry, Duncan Grant, Virginia and Leonard Woolf, Clive and Vanessa Bell and Bertrand Russell, to name only a few Bloomsberries, we have ability and accomplishment such as we saw (on an undeniably larger scale) in the Essex House group and, also as in Essex House disregard for gender in choosing sexual partners.

312. Hotson, *Shakespeare's Sonnets Dated*, p. 154.
313. Devlin, *Hamlet's Divinity*, p. 117.
314. Eccles, *Shakespeare in Warwickshire*, p. 119; Chambers, *William Shakespeare*, II, 127-141]
315. Chambers, *William Shakespeare*, II, 324-325; SP Dom., 1598-1601, p. 575.
316. Chambers, *William Shakespeare*, II, 325; SP Dom., 1598-1601, p. 578.
317. Chambers, *William Shakespeare*, II, 324; SP Dom., 1598-1601, pp. 573, 575.
318. Chambers, *William Shakespeare*, II, 326.
319. Ill-will existed between Anthony Bacon and Merrick, CM IX, p. 158. See also Abbott, pp. 207-234, setting forth a number of instances where the testimony of the participants in the Essex uprising when offered as evidence against the defendants (not by the witnesses in person, but only through the government-obtained depositions) was suppressed or distorted, and quoting Clarendon's characterization of Bacon's *A Declaration of the Practises and Treasons . . . by Robert Late Earl of Essex* as a "pestilent libel."
320. *Letters and Memorials of State*, II, 90. Evidently it was not unusual for acting companies to perform at the homes of those rich enough to engage their services. A particulary pertinent example of this is the subject of Sir Walter Cope's letter,

written probably in 1604, to Robert Cecil, then Viscount Cranborne, relating his efforts to find on Cecil's behalf a suitable entertainment for Anne of Denmark:

> Burbage ys come, & Sayes ther ys no new playe that the quene hath not seene, but they have Revyved an olde one, Cawled *Loves Labore lost*, which for wytt & mirthe he sayes will please her excedingly. And Thys ys apointed to be playd to Morowe night at my Lord of Sowthamptons, unless yow send a wrytt to Remove the Corpus Cum Causa to your howse in Strande. Burbage ys my messenger Ready attendyng your pleasure. [Chambers, *William Shakespeare*, II, 332.]

I take this to mean that *Love's Labours Lost* had already been scheduled for performance on the following evening at Southampton's house, but that, should Cecil so desire, the performance could be staged instead at his House on the Strand, for the entertainment of the Queen. The custom of staging plays in the homes of noblemen inevitably invited the introduction into the plays of allusions and jokes which would be understood by the select few attending the play, but which would be lost upon others. "Everyone is agreed," writes Frances Yates in *A Study of Love's Labour's Lost*, at p. 2, "that *Love's Labour's Lost* is one of the most topical of all Shakespeare's plays, that it bristles throughout with allusions to contemporary events and to living persons. . . ." Thus Holofernes in the play is thought by Yates to be a representation of John Florio, Moth is Thomas Nashe, etc. Widely accepted is the suggestion first made by Martin Hume, *Spanish Influence on English Literature*, pp. 268-274, that the model for Armado was Antonio Pérez. Obviously, for Shakespeare to have been able to depict these persons in his plays, he must have been in a position to observe them — and since these persons are presented with notable and doubtless distinctive personal mannerisms, quirks and eccentricities, Shakespeare must have been in a position to observe them as private individuals: thus revealing, to the extent that Essex House characters appear in the plays, that Shakespeare must in fact have had the access to Essex House which Yates and Hume, and others, take for granted, but which this chapter is devoted to proving, because of the hitherto unappreciated implications and consequences of this access.

321. Chambers, *William Shakespeare*, II, 250.
322. Joseph, p. 18 (of the facsimile edition of John Hall's book, *Select Observations on English Bodies*).
323. Chambers, *William Shakespeare*, II, 102.
324. Hotson, *I, William Shakespeare*, pp. 145-171.
325. *Ibid.*, p. 143.
326. Eccles, *Shakespeare in Warwickshire*, pp. 93-94. In 1595, Thomas Bushell senior held jointly with Lord Burleigh the wardship of one William Cholmley (CM V, p. 529), who is probably the same William Cholmley whose sister had married a Bushell (CM XIII, 601) and who was a secretary to Essex in 1599 and 1600 (CM IX, pp. 270-271; Fifth Report of the Royal Commission on Historical Manuscripts, 1876, pp. 362-363), and perhaps a relative of the Richard Cholmley who was in Essex' service at the same time. Probably having something to do

with the Cholmley wardship is the presence among Burleigh's papers in 1595 of a pedigree of "Sir Rich. Cholmley" (SP Dom., 1595-1597, p. 158). I have not seen this document, the contents of which might be helpful in sorting out all of the Cholmley's with whom we must deal.

327. Jardine, I, 348.
328. CM IX, pp. 213, 290, 298, 341; CM XI, 33, 44, 46.
329. Chambers, *William Shakespeare*, II, 324; SP Dom., 1598-1601, p. 573.
330. SP Dom., 1598-1601, p. 572.
331. Adams, p. 138; Lee, *A Life of William Shakespeare*, p. 115; Greene, I, p. 49.
332. Chambers, *William Shakespeare*, II, 188.
333. Adams, p. 139; Lee, *A Life of William Shakespeare*, p. 116; Schoenbaum, *Shakespeare's Lives*, p. 50.
334. Herford and Simpson, Vol. VIII, pp. 44-45. "Poet-ape" is a term used by Sidney in *The Defence of Poesie* (at signature Kᵛ): "So that since the euer-praise woorthie *Poesie* is full of vertue breeding delightfulnesse, and voyd of no gift that ought to be in the noble name of learning, since the blames layd against it, are either false or feeble, since the cause why it is not esteemed in England, is the fault of Poet-apes, not *Poets*."
335. Although not published until 1616, Jonson's *Epigrams* (of which the Poet-Ape Sonnet is number LVI) was entered in the Stationer's Register by John Stepneth on 15 May 1612.

Notes to Chapter VII — *Chiaroscuro*

1. Martin Green, pp. 1-3.
2. Bradbrook, p. 80.
3. Martin Green, p. 10.
4. *Shakespeare's Ovid*, p. iii.
5. *Ibid.*, p. 17.
6. *Wilson's Arte of Rhetorique*, p. 195.
7. Sidney, *Defence of Poesy*, last page (of 1595 edition).
8. There is uncertainty as to the identity of the author of the *Arte of English Poesie*. I use Puttenham's name only because it has for so long been associated with the work.
9. Puttenham, p. 186.
10. Shakespeare's Sonnet 99, for example, so convincingly appears on its face to be about flowers having stolen their beauty from a person that the *other* story it relates (see pages 56-59) has long gone unnoticed.
11. Puttenham, p. 188.
12. Spenser, p. 418.
13. *Ibid.*, pp. 443, 448, 451, 456.
14. *Ibid.*, pp. 436, 439.
15. *Ibid.*, p. 422.
16. *Id.*
17. *Ibid.*, p. 423.
18. *Ibid.*, pp. 422.

19. Sidney, *Arcadia* (Original Version), p. 52.
20. In his *Arte of English Poesie*, Puttenham, who had probably read the *Arcadia* in manuscript, echoed and somewhat expanded Sidney's statement, which expansion (italicized below) *seems* anticipatorily to disagree with my statement. Puttenham wrote:

> The Poet devised the Eglogue . . . *not of purpose to counterfait or represent the rusticall manner of loves and comunications*: but under the vaile of homely persons, and in rude speeches to insinuate and glaunce at greater matters, and such as perchance had not bene safe to have disclosed in any other sort, which may be perceived in the Eglogues of *Virgill*, in which are treated by figure *matters of greater importance then the loves of Titirus and Corydon.* [Puttenham, pp. 38-39.]

But Puttenham's expansion of Sidney's statement is not inconsistent with my own observation, for Puttenham does not deny that the Eglogues relate details of the loves of the shepherds, but only insists that the Eglogues deal *also* with *other* matters of greater importance. What these matters of greater importance are, is often difficult to figure out, and students of Virgil and Spenser have yet to identify all of them; this does not mean that matters of less cosmic importance, such as who is pursuing whom, are not treated, albeit darkly.

21. An interesting exposition of one possible item of gossip in *The Shepheards Calendar* is provided by Charles E. Mounts, in "Spenser and the Countess of Leicester." Mounts finds in the March eclogue allusions to Leicester's affair with Lettice Knollys, the wife of Walter Devereux, first Earl of Essex and the mother of Robert Devereux, the second Earl of Essex. The affair is generally supposed to have antedated the demise of the first Earl of Essex, and indeed it is often suggested that the affair precipitated that demise (by poison). After the death of Walter Devereux, Leicester secretly married Lettice. Mounts suggests that lines such as

> Tho shall we sporten in delight,
> And learne with Lettice to wexe light,
>   That scornfully looks askance . . .

refer to Lettice and Leicester, and that Leicester's anger over this "sneering personal allusion by a dependent" cost Spenser his position in Leicester House. Mounts suggests also that this is the mysterious matter apologetically referred to by Spenser in the sonnet preceding his *Virgils Gnat*, published in 1591 and dedicated to the Earl of Leicester, "late deceased."

22. Spenser, p. 407.
23. Saunders, pp. 29, 34.
24. The consensus today seems to be that the Stella of Sidney's sonnets is the second Earl of Essex' sister, Penelope Devereux, who in 1581 married Robert Lord Rich. This identification is based upon the puns on "rich" in Sonnets 9 (see item 5 in

Appendix III), 24, 35 and 37 of *Astrophel and Stella*. The pun appears most clearly in Sonnet 37:

> My mouth doth water, and my breast doth swell,
> My tongue doth itch, my thoughts in labour be:
> Listen then Lordings with good ear to me!
> For of my life I must a riddle tell.
> Toward Aurora's Court, a nymph doth dwell
> Rich in all beauties which man's eye can see:
> Beauties so far from reach of words, that we
> Abuse her praise saying she doth excel.
> Rich in the treasures of deserved reknown.
> Rich in the riches of a royal heart.
> Rich in those gifts, which give th'eternal crown:
> Who, though most rich in these and every part,
> Which makes the patents of true worldy bliss;
> Hath no misfortune, but that Rich she is.

In addition to the evidence offered by the puns in these sonnets, a sonnet by Mathew Gwynne which follows the dedication of John Florio's translation of Montaigne's *Essays* to Lady Rich (published in 1603) is interpreted by some as a statement that Lady Rich was the Stella of Sidney's poems. Essex and his sister were friends (at least until 8 February 1601) rather than rivals, and she was often at Essex House; consequently, if Essex' sister was in fact the person to whom Sidney wrote his poems of praise and love, then we have yet another link between Sidney and Essex to add to those mentioned in Chapter VI, and more evidence in support of my conclusion that Essex House was the continuation of the personnel and spirit of Leicester House.

My failure to mention Sidney's Stella as being, along with Sidney's wife and Sidney's sword, accoutrements of Essex, reflects the difficulty I have in accepting the identification of Stella as Penelope. The case against Essex's sister being Stella, or Sidney's love for Stella being genuine, has been set forth by James M. Purcell in *Sidney's Stella*, Walter George Friedrich in *The Stella of Astrophel*, and Thomas P. Roche in "Autobiographical Elements in Sidney's *Astrophil and Stella*." A point which I find persuasive is that the elegies for Sir Philip Sidney written by Spenser and others, and published in 1595, were dedicated "To the most beautifull and vertuous Ladie, the Countesse of Essex" — that is, Sidney's widow. Spenser's poem, entitled *Astrophel*, states of the "Gentle Shepheard borne in *Arcady*" that:

> For one alone he cared, for one he sight,
> His lifes desire, and his deare loues delight.
> *Stella* the faire, the fairest star in skie,
> As faire as *Venus* or the fairest faire:
> A fairer star saw neuer liuing eie,
> Shot her sharp pointed beames through purest aire.

Her he did loue, her he alone did honor,
His thoughts, his rimes, his songe were all upon her.
To her he vowd the seruive of his daies,
On her he spent the riches of his wit:
For her he made hymnes of immortal praise,
Of onely her he sung, he thought, he writ.
Her, and but her, of loue he worthie deemed,
For all the rest but litle he esteemed.

[Spenser, p. 547, lines 53-66.]

Surely by Elizabethan times conventions had advanced to the point where a man of Spenser's station could not possibly be so insensitive and tactless as to dedicate to Sidney's widow a poem stating that some *other* woman (even though she was by then the widow's sister-in-law) was the only person that Sidney had ever loved! Spenser knew Sidney, and Sidney's circle, and the gossip and secrets of that circle, and it is unlikely that he would have dedicated a poem praising Stella to the wife of the person from whom he still sought patronage, had Stella, the love of Sidney's life, been someone other than Sidney's own wife (and now the wife of Essex). Sir Sidney Lee wrote, "The dedication of *Astrophel* to Sidney's wife deprives of serious autobiographical significance his description in the sonnets of his pursuit of Stella's affections," Lee, *Elizabethan Sonnets*, I, xliii, and with this conclusion, premised upon Spenser's being an honourable man, I agree.

However, in my less charitable moments, I think it not inconceivable (the Elizabethans having been a devious lot) that Spenser, acquainted with all the gossip of his time, knew that Stella was Penelope Rich, a fact which could not but reflect unfavourably both on the virtue of Essex' sister and the dignity of Essex' wife, and purposely attempted to salvage their honour and dignity by the untruthful assertion that Stella was Lady Essex — perhaps thereby, in his own mind, atoning for the disservice he may at one time have done Leicester (see note 21 above).

Also, Sonnet 37 of *Astrophel and Stella*, whose puns on the word "rich" seem so conclusively to reveal Stella's true identity, was not published until 1598 (three years after the publication of Spenser's *Astrophel*), in an edition of Sidney's works prepared by Sidney's sister and entitled *The Countess of Pembrokes Arcadia*. This was published at a time when the Pembrokes and Essex were not on the best of terms, and it may have been the Countess of Pembroke's intention, by the publication in 1598 of Sonnet 37, to refute Spenser's assevertion, in his *Astrophel* of 1595, that Stella was Sidney's wife, and thus to expose Essex' wife (unloved by Sidney) and Essex' sister (loved too well by Sidney) to opprobrium.

Further undermining Spenser's seemingly dispositive identification of Lady Essex as Stella are Thomas Watson's elegies published in 1590 on the death of Sir Francis Walsingham. These consist of a poem in Latin entitled *Meliboeus*, and an English translation thereof entitled "An Eglogue Vpon the death of the Right Honorable Sir *Francis Walsingham*. . . . " The Latin version of the elegy was dedicated by Watson to his friend Thomas Walsingham, who, as we have seen in Chapter VI, was a close friend of Watson, and a friend also of Christopher

Marlowe. The English version of the elegy was dedicated by Watson to Francis Walsingham's daughter, "the most vertuous Lady, Lady Frances Sydney." From this designation of her, we may assume that the poem was written prior to Lady Sidney's marriage to Essex.

In a prefatory note "To the courteous Reader," Watson apprehends that a fault in his poem may be "that my pastorall discourse to the vnlearned may seeme obscure" — "which to preuent," he goes on, "I have thought good, here to aduertise you, that I figure England in *Arcadia*; Her Maiestie in *Diana*; Sir Francis Walsingham in *Meliboeus,* and his Ladie in *Dryas*; Sir Phillippe Sidney in *Astrophill*, and his Ladie in *Hyale*, Master Thomas Walsingham in *Tyterus*, and my selfe in *Corydon*." Watson, p. 147. Obviously, since Philip Sidney is here represented as Astrophil (thereby revealing Watson's knowledge of Sidney's *Astrophil and Stella*), one would expect that Francis Sidney, if she were indeed the person to whom Sidney wrote his sonnets, would be represented by Watson as Stella; that she is not so represented (and this by a person who knew the Walsinghams well), renders Spenser's evidence suspect. (Of course, Watson's clarification for the "unlearned," while casting doubts upon Frances Sidney's being Stella, does not establish that Lady Rich is Stella.)

Another of the *Astrophel and Stella* poems in which some have seen an allusion to Lady Rich is Sonnet 13, in the line and a half italicised below:

> Phoebus was judge between Jove, Mars and Love;
> Of those three gods, whose arms the fairest were.
> Jove's golden shield did eagle sables bear,
> Whose talons held young Ganymede above.
> But in vert field, Mars bare a golden spear,
> Which through a bleeding heart his point did shove.
> Each had his crest. Mars carried Venus' glove;
> Jove on his helm, the thunderbolt did rear.
> Cupid then smiles. For on his crest there lies
> Stella's fair hair. *Her face, he makes his shield;*
> *Where roses gule are borne in silver field.*
> Phoebus drew wide the curtain of the skies
> To blaze these last: and sware devoutly then,
> The first, thus matched, were scantly gentlemen.

Here the allusion is not in a pun but in the heraldry. It has been suggested that the arms which Cupid appropriates from Stella's face, *roses gule in silver field,* are based upon the arms of the Devereux family, *argent, a fesse, gules, in chief three torteaux* (torteaux being represented heraldically as red circles, roundels or discs). Ringler, p. 465; R. B. Young, pp. 21-22. While this suggestion cannot be rejected out of hand, it seems to me that an Elizabethan versed in heraldry, knowing that a *torteau* was a round cake or flat piece of bread, would not think he was blazoning the Essex arms when he spoke of *roses*, nor indeed would the three pancakes on the Essex arms readily suggest roses. Consequently, Cupid's arms, in this instance, are derived, I believe, only from the red and white beauty of Stella's face, and not the tinctures or charges of the Essex arms.

Henry Constable, in "Sonet 7" expressly addressed to Lady Rich, blazoned a similar coat of arms:

> Heralds at armes do three perfections quote
> To wit most fayre, most rich, most glittering:
> Now when these three concurre within one thing,
> Needs must that thing of honoure be of note.
>
> Lately I did behold a rich fayre coat,
> Which wished fortune to myne eyes did bring:
> A lordlye coate, but worthye of a king,
> Wherein all these perfections one might note.
>
> A field of lilies roses proper bare,
> Two stars in chiefe, the crest was waues of gold:
> How glittering was the coate the starrs declare
> The lilies made it fayre for to behold.
>
> > And rich it was, as by the gold apeares,
> > So hapie he which in his armes it beares.
>
> > > Constable, p. 151.

This sonnet, published in 1594, was obviously inspired by Sidney's sonnet. Now, one can argue on the one hand that Constable's attribution to Lady Rich of a coat of arms similar to the one derived by Cupid from Stella's face reflects his knowledge that Stella and Lady Rich are the same person, or one can on the other hand argue (a) that the coats of arms are in fact different, Constable's bearing stars (for eyes), as well as roses on a field of lilies (which, to give the benefit of the doubt to the Stella = Penelope equation, I take to mean a white field, and not a field charged with lilies), thus clearly indicating that his blazon for Lady Rich, like Sidney's for Stella, is derived solely from the lady's beautiful features, and not from her family's heraldry, and (b) that Constable would not have addressed to Lady Rich as an example of his ingenuity an imitation of Sidney's poem, had the Sidney poem itself also been addressed to Lady Rich.

This is a convenient place to mention the similarity (noted by Bradbrook, at pp. 110-111) of Cupid's arms in Sidney's Sonnet 13 to the "Herauldry in LUCRECE face" in *The Rape of Lucrece*. Shakespeare's probable indebtedness to Sidney for this image, far from undermining my contention that the face of Lucrece, like the person of Adonis, blazons the badge of Wriothesley, provides yet another example, augmenting those already cited in Chapter IV, of Shakespeare's extraordinarily apposite application to Henry Wriothesley of seemingly conventional poetical images: for while Stella in Sidney's poem bears red roses on a field of white, allusive, so far as can be found, to nothing other than her beauty, Lucrece in Shakespeare's poem has a face which is not only white (from doves) and red (from roses), but also a face whose red and white colours strove with each other which should underprop her fame,

> The soveraignty of either being so great,
> That oft they interchange ech others seat,

thus utilizing Sidney's image in a way which while praising Wriothesley (as it might anyone) for his red and white beauty, also identifies him (as it could only he) by the reference to a feature peculiar to the Southampton coat of arms - the alternation of its colours between red and white.

Having in this note cited good reasons for being on all sides of the question, I come finally to my real, and purely visceral reason for being unable to accept the identification of Stella as Lady Rich; and this is a reason having much to do with the theme of this chapter. In Sonnet 37, quoted at the beginning of this note, Sidney states "I must a riddle tell," and then he describes a Nymph whose identity is no mystery at all, for it is stated in every line but one of the concluding sestet. Now this, to paraphrase Captain Fluellen, is not according to the disciplines of the riddle. Puttenham in his discussion of *Allegoria* tells us that

We dissemble againe vnder couert and darke speaches, when we speake by way of riddle (*Enigma*) of which the sence can hardly be picked out, but by the parties owne assoile, as he that said:

> It is my mother well I wot,
> And yet the daughter that I begot.

Meaning it by the ise which is made of frozen water, the same being molten by the sunne or fire, makes water againe.

My mother had an old womã in her nurserie, who in the winter nights would put us forth many pretie ridles, whereof this is one:

> I have a thing and rough it is
> And in the midst a hole I wis:
> There came a yong man with his ginne,
> And he put it a hanfull in.

The good old Gentlewoman would tell vs that were children how it was meant by a furd glooue. Some other naughtie body would peradventure haue construed it not halfe so mannerly. . . . [Puttenham, p. 188.]

By Puttenham's standard, Sidney's "riddle" is patently *not* a riddle, for it points so clearly to its apparent answer. Too attuned, perhaps, to the not-so-obvious word-play of Shakespeare's Sonnets to be willing to recognize anything less subtle (at least in the works of one of the finest of all Elizabethan poets) as a genuine dark conceit, I suspect that Sidney, who knew as much about dissembling under covert and dark speeches as anyone of his period, was planting false clues to throw us off the scent, and that the riddle in Sonnet 37 has yet to be given its true "assoile."

In the final analysis, the identification of Stella is either very difficult, or altogether too easy. Because I think it appears to be altogether too easy, I find it suspicious, and therefore have not in Chapter VI preferred as an example of the close connections between Essex and Sidney the possibility of Essex' sister being Sidney's Stella; in which opinion, if I am wrong, then my contentions in Chapter VI are strengthened.

25. Martin Green, p. 1.

26. *Ibid.*, pp. 12-41.

27. John Nichols writes "The greatest wound, which music ever received in England, was (as I think Mr. Ant. Wood somewhere observes) from the suppression of Monasteries; after which the Puritans often made it their business to run it down as a relique of popery. For both these reasons, very few Englishmen regarded it in Queen Elizabeth's time. (Her own band of musicians were many of them foreigners (Venecians). . . .)" Nichols, III, 153, note 3. It was as a consequence of this lack of knowledge of music among Englishmen, Nichols in the same note observes, that Matthew Gwin (the friend of Florio, Savile, Greville, Burton, etc.) "was chosen Music Professor of this University of Oxford in 1582 . . . though he understood not a tittle either of the therory or practice of that science (as he himself most frankly owns in his inauguration Speech); but he made good amends for his deficiencies in that science by the elegancies of his Latin Oration in praise of it."

28. Rowse in *Shakespeare's Sonnets: The Problems Solved*, at p. xxxv, states that Emilia had a son named Henry, "who was evidently named after the Lord Chamberlain," and this probably is so; an intriguing, and perhaps not so remote possibility, however, is that the boy was named after some other Henry.

29. *Ibid.*, pp.xxxiv-xliii; Rowse, *The Poems of Shakespeare's Dark Lady*, pp. 9-16. Forman's contemporary, Sir Anthony Weldon, wrote (at pp. 34-35) that

> this *Forman* was a fellow dwelt in *Lambeth*, a very silly fellow, yet had wit enough to cheat Ladies, and other women, by pretending skill in telling their Fortunes, as whether they should bury their husbands, and what second husband they should have, and whether they should enjoy their Loves, or whether Maids should get husbands, or enjoy their servants to themselves without corrivals — but before he would tell anything, they must write their names in his Alphabetical book, with their own hand-writing; by this trick he kept them in awe, if they should complain of his abusing them, as in truth he did nothing else. . . .

30. Schoenbaum, *Shakespeare, A Documentary Life*, p. 127.

31. Rowse, *The Poems of Shakespeare's Dark Lady*, p. 13.

32. *Id*.

33. Giroux, p. 179.

34. CM XVI, p. 274; Rowse, *The Poems of Shakespeare's Dark Lady*, p. 19.

35. Rowse, *The Poems of Shakespeare's Dark Lady*, p. 19.

36. *Fifth Report of the Royal Commission on Historical Manuscripts*, p. 363.
37. Martin Green, p. 14.
38. *Ibid.*, p. 25.
39. *Ibid.*, pp. 16-25.
40. *Ibid.*, pp. 31-35.
41. Seymour-Smith, p. 187. See Also Rollins, I, p. 371.
42. *Grande Dizionario della Lingua Italiana*, s.v. basso (13).
43. See, e.g., Rollins, I, 248; Rowse, *Shakespeare's Sonnets: The problems Solved*, p. 207; Seymour-Smith, p. 161.
44. I was surprised to notice, some time after writing this chapter, that the name *Luce (or Lucy) Negro* is an exact equivalent, in Latin or Spanish, of the Italian word which is the title of this chapter. But *chiaroscuro* is my word, not Shakespeare's; *his* word is *base*, and, in my opinion, the basis for *base* is *Bassano*.
45. Martin Green, p. 11.

Notes to Chapter VIII — A Bunch of Keys

1. Roger Williams, p. 18.
2. Fairchild, p. 74.
3. See Furness, pp. 284-285, and Pafford, p. 150.
4. Elze, pp. 286-287.
5. Romano, in typical Renaissance fashion, was a sculptor and architect as well as painter, and in all fields excelled; the high esteem in which he was held by his contemporaries for his painting ability is evidenced by one of the *decreti* bestowing Mantuan citizenship and property upon Giulio Romano upon his removal to Mantua from Rome:

   Among the various outstanding arts of mankind painting has always seemed to us the most famous one. It is given to us by that most apt imitator of nature to look at our own images and likenesses and those of all other things. We have learned that Alexander of Macedon attributed to it so much dignity that he wanted to be painted only by Apelles, because he alone knew how to embrace with most excellent colors all the majesty, grace and ornament through as many indications of the most perfect art in him as could be expected. We too have always admired such outstanding achievements of art, and we have gladly received the artists themselves and we accorded them our graces and favors increasingly from day to day, and we found out that among them our dear Giulio Pippi Romano has to be considered most outstanding. [Verheyen, pp. 43-44.]

6. Saslow, pp. 97-141.
7. Antonio Pérez, for example, at one time was the owner of two famous paintings of this *genre*: Correggio's *Rape of Ganymede* (reproduced in Saslow, at p. 64) and Parmigianino's *Amor* or *Cupid Shaping his Bow* (reproduced in Saslow, at p. 130). Saslow, p. 226, notes 68 and 1. It is only fair to add, however, that these

were but two of almost 100 fine paintings owned by Pérez, among which were Titian's *Adam and Eve* and *The Adoration of the Magi*. Ungerer, I, 193, note 1.

8. The catalogue is reprinted in Hope, *Cowdray and Easebourne Priory*, pp. 59-63.

9. *Ibid.*, p. 61.

10. Warton, p. 42.

11. Hope, *Cowdray and Easebourne Priory*, p. 37.

12. *Ibid.*, p. 46. Among the paintings *saved* were a portrait of the Earl of Southampton (William Fitzwilliam) "walking by the sea-side, in a fur gown and cape, with a staff like a high constable's," which is now in the FitzWilliam Museum in Cambridge, and the painting described by Richard Gough as being "the famous picture, by [Isaac] Oliver, of three brothers of the family who accidentally met abroad, and their page, whole lengths," which is now in the Burghley House Collection. These three brothers are the grandsons of Anthony Browne, 1st Viscount Montagu. Their parents were the Anthony Browne and Mary Dormer for whose marriage Gascoigne wrote the mask associating the Montagus of England with those of Italy (see Chapter III, pp. 46-51). The mask was played by persons wearing Venetian clothes, and it seems quite possible that the young men in this painting wear clothes worn at their parents' wedding mask.

13. Roger Jones and Nicholas Penny, pp. 183-190.

14. Verheyen, pp. 116-117.

15. Hope, *Cowdray and Easebourne Priory*, pp. 39-46 and 48-57.

16. Lees-Milne, p. 66.

17. The true explanation of this seeming anachronism may have been hit upon by Joseph Jacobs, who noting (at p. xxx) that Angel Day includes in his translation of *Daphnis and Chloe* a passage where "Lesbian swains of the fifth century shout the praise of Queen Elizabeth," wrote that "Time itself stands still in Arcady."

18. Honneyman, pp. 27-47.

19. See, e.g., French, charts facing pages 448 and 466; Lee, *A Life of William Shakespeare*, p. 7; Adams, p. 16; Stopes, *Shakespeare's Family*, pp. 27–28, and, for interesting conjectures about Shakespeare's family, Honneyman. Chambers, however, thinks that the Ardens of Wilmcote must have split off from the Ardens of Park Hall earlier than French supposes. *William Shakespeare*, II, 32.

20. *The Ven. Philip Howard, Earl of Arundel*, p. 45.

21. Chambers, *William Shakespeare*, II, 149. See also, Rupert Taylor, pp. 81–94.

22. Beal, "A Brief Account of . . . Green's Norton," pp. ix-x.

23. For John Arden, see *Visitation of Warwickshire*, p. 73; for Thomas Greene, see *Visitation of Worcestershire*, p. 71.

24. Devlin, *Life of Robert Southwell*, p. 15.

25. *Ibid.*, p. 264.

26. *Ibid.*, pp. 257–273; see also, Milward, pp. 54-60. Southwell's book of poems, *Saint Peter's Complaint*, was first published in 1595, after his execution earlier that year. In this edition, the dedication read merely, "The author to his loving cousin"; the dedication as quoted in the text, containing the initials "W.S.," first appeared in an edition of the work published in 1616 by the Jesuits at the College of St. Omer, in France. Devlin, after stating these facts, concludes (at p. 355) that the dedication as published in 1616 "was the original form — unless we are to accuse the Jesuits of an utterly pointless forgery."

27. Murray, II, p. 45.
28. *Ibid*, II, p. 46.
29. *Ibid*, II, p. 47.
30. GEC, s.v. Sussex (Thomas Radcliffe, third Earl).
31. Murray, I, pp. 305–308.
32. GEC, s.v. Sussex (Thomas Radcliffe, third Earl; Henry Radcliffe, fourth Earl).
33. Murray, II, 307–308.
34. GEC, s.v. Sussex (Henry Radcliffe, fourth Earl).
35. GEC, s.v. Sussex (Robert Radcliffe, first Earl); Southampton (Henry Wriothesley, second Earl).
36. Schoenbaum, *William Shakespeare, A Documentary Life*, p. 136.
37. See, e.g., Honigmann, pp. 59–76; Metz, pp. 112–117.
38. Honigmann, pp. 60–62. In Chapter IV, note is taken of the fact that an image in a poem by Matthew Grove published in 1587 (excerpt 61 in Appendix III) is similar to images in *Titus Andronicus*. The possibility that one might be derived from the other (regardless of whether the poem or the play is deemed the earlier) is consistent with an early date for the play. I would therefore assume that the image in a poem by Barnfield (excerpt 62), also similar to an image in the play, and published in the same year as the play (1594), would be derived from — or at least later than — the play.
39. Chambers, *William Shakespeare*, I, 312.
40. See, e.g., Chambers, *ibid*, I, 318–321; Honigmann, pp. 60–62.
41. Stopes, *Shakespeare's Warwickshire Contemporaries*, pp. 32-33. See also Adams, pp. 80–89. The traditional legend linking Thomas Lucy with William Shakespeare is that the young Shakespeare was caught poaching deer on Sir Thomas' estate, for which Sir Thomas had him whipped and imprisoned, finally causing Shakespeare to flee to London; Justice Shallow in *II Henry IV* is supposedly a satirical depiction of Thomas Lucy. As Stopes shows, *ibid.*, pp. 33-41 (see also Adams, at pages 83-86), this story is unsubstantiated, and on its face improbable. Adam's point that Sir Thomas Lucy's ancestor, Sir William Lucy, is respectfully portrayed in *I Henry VI* seems to me to be especially damaging to the legend. On the other hand, Heinrich Mutschmann and Karl Wentersdorf suggest (at pages 96–99 of *Shakespeare and Catholicism*) that while the poaching story is improbable, hostility between Shakespeare and Lucy may have existed because Lucy was a staunch Protestant who (allegedly) was a persecutor of Catholics in the Stratford area, among whom, presumably, was Shakespeare.
42. DNB, s.v. Henslowe, Philip.
43. Chambers, *William Shakespeare*, II, 166; Berry, p. 195.
44. Hotson, *I, William Shakespeare*, pp. 172-202.
45. In 1594, Henry Wriothesley leased a substantial portion of his London home to one John Bellingham, Akrigg, *Shakespeare and the Earl of Southampton*, p. 47, and for the next ten years, when in London (and not in prison), lived elsewhere, frequently at Essex House, resuming his residence at Southampton House in about 1604. *Ibid.*, p. 143, note 3. This does not affect my suggestion that the garden of Southampton House was the site of the "Temple Garden" scene in *Henry VI, Part 1*, since the play was written prior to 1594, and thus at a time when Henry

Wriothesley (and thus, as I suppose, Shakespeare, too) had ready access to South-ampton House when in London.

46. Williamson, *The History of the Temple*, pp. 8-9; Williams, *Early Holborn*, II, §1234.
47. Stow, II, 47, 87; Williamson, *The History of the Temple*, p. 8.
48. Williams, *Staple Inn*, p. 28.
49. *Valor Ecclesiasticus*, IV, 6; Williams, *Staple Inn*, p. 29.
50. PR, Edward VI, I, 183, 184; *Chapter Acts of the Cathedral Church of St. Mary of Lincoln*, pp. 4-5; Williams, *Early Holborn*, II, §1236.
51. Williams, *Early Holborn*, I, §§359, 360, II, §1230; Stow, II, 87. In his will, Thomas Wriothesley refers to "my howse in London called Southampton howse, lately the Busshop of Lincolnes, and after my lordes of Warwick." *Trevelyan Papers*, p. 212.
52. Williams, *Early Holborn*, II, § 1225. Southampton House in Holborn continued to be the London residence of the Earls of Southampton until the mid-1600's, when the fourth Earl of Southampton built a new Southampton House on the family's property in Bloomsbury. Some sources state that Southampton House in Holborn was pulled down in 1638 (e.g., Williams, *Early Holborn*, II, §1230); others state that it was demolished in about 1652 (e.g., *London Topographical Record*, p. 59).
53. Saccio, p. 112.
54. Holinshed, III, 247, 249.
55. Neilsen and Hill, p. 747; Chambers, *William Shakespeare*, I, 293.
56. Johnson, IV, 526.
57. E.g., Neilsen and Hill, p. 760; Samuel Johnson and George Steevens, XIII, 70.
58. *Master Worsley's Book*, p. 14.
59. *Ibid.*, pp. 23-24.
60. Stow, II, 87.
61. See Rollins, I, 395.
62. Baedeker, 1879, p. 130; 1883, p. 134; 1885, p. 134; 1889, p. 142; 1898, p. 178.
63. Sunderland, pp. 38-40.
64. Merrifield, p. 139. Merrifield's statement that the "Roman bath" is on the site of a building once appertaining to Arundel House is questionable, and probably incorrect. This idea seems to have originated in an exchange of letters in *Notes and Queries*. A letter from one A.W.M. printed on 29 November 1862 (3rd Ser., II, p. 429) notes that Pinkerton in *Essay on Medals*, 1719 (Vol. I, p. 10), in alluding to Thomas Howard, Earl of Arundel and Surrey, "well known by the Arundelian Tables, and other monuments of antiquity which he imported into the island from Greece and Italy," states that "In the cellar of a house on Norfolk Street, in the Strand, is a fine antique bath, formerly belonging to this Earl of Arundel, whose house and gardens were adjacent" and asks "Is anything known of this bath?" A response from Edward F. Rimbault, printed on 27 December 1862 (3rd Ser., II, pp. 518-519), replies that

> this is undoubtedly "the old Roman Spring Bath," situated between Surrey Street and Strand Lane. . . . The bath itself is Roman; the walls being layers

of brick and thin layers of stucco; and the pavement of similar brick covered with stucco, and resting upon a mass of stucco and rubble. The bricks are 9½ inches long, 4½ inches broad, and 1¾ inches thick, and resemble the bricks in the old city wall. It is stated in Timb's *Curiosities of London*, that the property can be traced to the D'Anvers family, of Swithland Hall, Leicestershire, whose mansion stood upon the spot. The entrance to the bath is now in Strand Lane, between Nos. 162 and 163, but the bath itself lies immediately behind the east side of Surrey Street, and must have been in close proximity to the Earl of Arundel's mansion.

The information contained in these letters is, so far as I can find, the entire basis for all subsequent conjecture that the so-called "Collector" Earl of Arundel, Thomas Howard (1585-1646, the son of the canonised Philip Howard), either built or installed the "Roman bath" now in the Strand. If this conjecture is correct, then, of course, the bath would not have been in existence during the lifetime of the Earl of Essex, and my various speculations concerning it could not be correct. But the conjecture, unsupported by any facts, that Arundel built the bath is not inherently more worthy of credence than the tradition, also unsupported by any facts, that the bath was established in 1588 by the Earl of Essex.

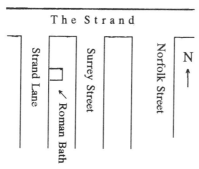

Figure 14. Diagram
of Strand Lane area.

Moreover, the exchange of letters in *Notes and Queries* presents on its face a problem. In A.W.M.'s letter, the antique bath is in the cellar of a house in Norfolk Street; the Strand bath, as Edward F. Rimbault points out, is between Surrey Street and Strand Lane. (Surrey Street and Norfolk Street, as well as Arundel Street, were established in the 1670's, on land which had formerly been the site of Arundel House, which was torn down in about 1676.) Even if we assume that the house in Norfolk Street was on the west side of the street, we immediately perceive, from the adjoining diagram, that only in the unlikely (but not impossible) event that the celler of the house in Norfolk Street extended a full block westward, and *under Surrey Street* further westward yet another block, would it be possible for the bath in Strand Lane to have been in the celler of a house on Norfolk Street. Now, it is possible, as suggested by E. Beresford Chancellor, at page 135, that the "antique bath" in the House in Norfolk Street "was a portable marble or stone one removed from Arundel House and forming, in fact, a portion of the famous Arundel marbles," but it is unlikely that the rather substantial bath in Strand Lane, situated over a spring, could at any time have been moved there from another location.

If we put to one side the "antique bath" in the celler of the House on Norfolk Street, and look for other ways to connect Arundel House with the "Roman bath" in Strand Lane, we find one seemingly promising lead. In 1589, the "Collector" Earl's father, Philip Howard, was found guilty of treason. As a consequence of the attainder automatically attendant upon such a conviction, Arundel House, together with all of the rest of the Earl's property, reverted to the Crown. As usual in such situations, a Commission was appointed to survey and assess the property thus acquired by the Crown. The Commission examined the property on 4 April 1590; one feature of Arundel House described in its report was "One Vault in the Cellor [which] conteyneth in length xxx foote and in breadth vj foote: there is a square Court paved over the same vault: the decayes of which pavement doth lett the water sewe through the vault, which Court conteyneth in length xxv foote and in breadth xx foot and will take in stone, besydes that which remayneth there allredy, CCCl fote of new stone: and requyreth of necessyty to be amended with new stone; new laying the same and repayring the ould will cost by estimacion, xiij*li*." Kingsford, "Bath inn or Arundel House," p. 269. A question to consider is whether the underground vault described in this report is the same underground vault now housing the "Roman bath." My examination of the maps and plats accompanying Kingsford's article on "Bath Inn or Arundel House" persuades me that the Arundel House vault could not have occupied the site where the "Roman bath" in Strand Lane now is, for the entrance to the Strand Lane bath is some 60 feet south of the Strand, whereas the maps and plans in Kingsford's article show that no portion of the buildings or gardens of Arundel House were nearer than 100 feet to the Strand. In the remote event that my conclusion based on these maps and plats is incorrect, my contention that Essex established the bath is not necessarily invalidated, for if the Strand Lane bath is in the vaulted structure described in the 1590 survey of Arundel House, then that structure, if it was not in fact already a bath when the Commissioners saw it, could yet have been converted into a bath in the early 1590's by the Earl of Essex, whose own house was immediately to the east of Arundel House: which event could have been, as I suggest, the occasion for the composition of Shakespeare's Sonnets 153 and 154.

65. *Calendar of the Inner Temple Records*, p. 354.
66. Even in the nineteenth and twentieth centuries, there is almost no evidence of anybody ever using the baths. David Copperfield states, in chapters 34 and 35 of his eponymous story, that he had many a cold plunge in the Roman bath near the Strand, but this may reflect the fantasies, rather than the experiences, of Charles Dickens, who as a boy loved to wander through the areas adjacent to the Strand. James Bone, in *London Echoing*, published in 1948, writes (at p. 168) that a draper in Oxford Street who at one time owned the bath offered to open it to subscribers for two guineas a year. Two men subscribed: "Out of the millions of Londoners only those two went down that obscure little lane to the dingy house with its rusty little front railing and opened the door with their keys and entered the dim, arched room. . . . Nobody bathes there now and its ownership — even its Roman origin — is in dispute!" The bath is now owned by the London County Council, and is not open to the public.
67. Robert Burton, *Anatomy of Melancholy*, ed. Dell and Jordan-Smith, p. 404.
68. *Id.*

69. *Aubrey's Brief Lives*, pp. 12-13.
70. See Cleugh, pp. 154-172.
71. OED, s.v. stew (4) and stufe.
72. Robert Burton, *Anatomy of Melancholy*, ed. Floyd Dell and Paul Jordan-Smith, p. 652. In its original Latin, this reads,

> Hæc si apud votarios, monachos, sanctos, scilicet homunciones, quid in foro, quid in aulâ, factum suspiceris? quid apud nobiles, quid inter fornices, quam non fœditatem, quam non spurcitiem! [Shilleto, III, 56.]

73. Hutton, *The Greek Anthology in France*, pp. 7-13. Hutton states that "there are roughly 3750 epigrams in the Palatine Anthology against about 2650 in the Anthology of Planudes, which lacks some 1500 epigrams that are found in *Pal.*, but preserves some 400 there omitted." *Ibid.*, p. 7, note 20. Paul Schede, or Melissus, after spending the winter of 1585-1586 in England (where he must have seen many of his English friends during his visits to Oxford and Cambridge, and was received in London by Queen Elizabeth, to whom he gave a copy of his works) returned to Germany, where for the rest of his life (he died on 3 February 1602) he held the position of Conservator or Librarian of the Palatine Library. Joseph Scaliger complained that "Melissus, who was the librarian of the Palatine Library, permitted no one to enter" (*Biographie Universelle*, s.v. Melissus (Paul)), and this, if true, might explain why the Palatine Manuscript of the Greek Anthology was so long in being discovered.

74. I am specific about the location of the text of the Marianus poem because, contrary to what is commonly written (see, e.g., Hutton, "Analogues of Shakespeare's Sonnets 153 and 154," p. 150 and Rollins, I, 392) this poem is *not* to be found in the edition of the Greek Anthology published by Lascaris in 1494. On the page marked with the signature BBIII, the Lascaris edition does include a poem by Marianus entitled "On another Bath called Love", but this is the poem printed in the Loeb and other modern editions of the Greek Anthology as epigram number 626 of Book IX (Loeb, III, 347-349), while the epigram translated by Shakespeare is number 627 of Book IX. The Marianus epigram translated by Shakespeare *is* in the Stephanus edition of 1566 (the edition which one supposes would be best known to the Leicester/ Essex House circle, Stephanus being their contemporary and personally known to many of them), as well as in the 1550-51 Aldine edition of the Greek Anthology and the 1600 Wechel edition (and may be in others, but these are the only editions which I have been able to examine).

75. See John Churton Collins, p. 15.
76. DNB, s.v. Cuff or Cuffe, Henry; *Francisci et Joannis Hotomanorum . . . Epistolae*, pp. 270-301; *V. Cl. Gulielmi Camdeni . . . Epistolae*, pp. 3-24, 99, 174, 187, 195, 201, 202, 264.
77. "Dr. Bathurst told me, that our Cuffe was of Trinity College, and expelled from thence upon this account: the Founder, Sir Thomas Pope, would, wheresoever he went a visiting his friend, steal one thing or another that he could lay his hands on, put it in his pocket, or under his gown. This was supposed rather an humour than of dishonesty. Now Cuffe upon a time, with his fellows being merry, said,

a pox this is a poor beggarly College indeed, the plate that our Founder stole would build such another. Which coming to the President's ears, was thereupon ejected, though afterwards elected into Merton College." Anthony Wood, quoted in *Biographia Britannica*, IV, p. 550, note A. The note continues: "How dear he was to Sir Henry Savile, at that time Warden of Merton College, appears not only from his procuring him to be elected upon the very first occasion that offered after his own preferment, but also from a letter of his to the learned Camden, in which, in a very few words, he gives him the highest character, and stiles him his own and Camden's intimate friend."

78. *Biographia Britannia*, IV, 549.
79. CM VII, pp. 234-235, 423-424, 524-525; CM VIII, pp. 76, 353.
80. CM VII, p. 424; CM VIII, pp. 76.
81. A good guess, however, would be that Cuffe's presence in Italy had something to do with Essex' program for gathering intelligence in Italy. A Dr Henry Hawkins was despatched by Essex to Venice in November 1595, and from the time of his arrival there in December 1595 until the beginning of 1598, engaged in espionage activities and transmitted intelligence to Essex. Ungerer, II, 168 ff. Cuffe may have been sent to Florence either to do as much from there in coordination with Dr Hawkins, or to provide some kind of check on Dr Hawkins.
82. CM VII, pp. 423-424.
83. Zannoni, pp. 1-9.
84. I must confess I find it difficult to believe that Cuffe's meeting with Adriani was accidental, for surely any Greek scholar from England, finding himself in this great centre of Renaissance learning, would eagerly have sought out the company of fellow Greek scholars.
85. *Longi Pastoralium, de Daphnidae & Chloë*, p. 94.
86. *Ibid.*, pp. 83, 86, 88, 93, 95.
87. DNB, s.v. Cuff or Cuffe, Henry; *Biographia Britannia*, IV, 557, note I.
88. SP Ire., 1598, January—1599, March, pp. 505-507.
89. J. Payne Collier, I, CLIII.
90. SP Ire., 1600, March-October, pp. 136-137, 140-141, 149-153.
91. Dowland, sig. K2^v-L. The poem has also been attributed to John Lyly (Lyly, III, 445-447; 494-497) but A. H. Bullen, who includes the poem on pp. 128-129 of *Shorter Elizabethan Poems*, questions the attribution (at pp. xiii and xvii).
92. May, pp. 266-269.
93. *Sixth Report of Royal Commission on Historical Manuscripts*, Part I, p. 459.
94. DNB, s.v. Cuff or Cuffe, Henry.
95. R. M. is, I think, Richard Montagu (1577-1641), elected Bishop of Chichester in 1628 and Bishop of Norwich in 1638. The clues to this identification are R.M.'s statements, in the dedication of Cuffe's book to Lord Willoughby, (a), that he, R. M., is "of that right-woorthy house, into which by marriage your Honor is inserted," (b), that R. M. "did never, de facie, know" the author of the work, although he was aware of his reputation for being "as skillfull a Master in this trade, as our shoppes have brought fourth anie," and (c) that the work was a "transcript from the first originall, which I am informed was his own." The Robert Bertie, Lord Willoughby (1582-1642) to whom the book was dedicated

(and who in 1626 was created Earl of Lindsey by Charles II) was the son of Peregrine Bertie, Lord Willoughby de Eresby (1555-1601) and the great-grandson of the Thomas Bertie who is the subject of note 26 to Appendix II. Since his wife was Elizabeth Montagu, daughter of Edward Lord Montagu of Boughton (Dugdale, *Baronage of England*, II, 410), I assume that the last name of the R.M. of the same right-worthy house is Montagu. A check of the R. Montagu's in the DNB immediately uncovers Richard Montagu, the bishop. I have not established whether this Montagu really is related to the Montagu's of Boughton, but, as it turns out, he was in his early years associated with Henry Savile at Eton, assisting him in editing Greek texts for publication. Montagu's association with Henry Savile readily explains both the good report R. M. had of Cuffe, and the means by which Cuffe's own draft of his book could have come into R.M.'s hands. Nor need we suppose that because R. M. was a bishop, he could not have written the light and chatty dedication, for Richard Montagu's letters to John Cosin, Bishop of Durham (often signed merely R.M.) disclose a light and amusing writing style. *Correspondence of John Cosin, D.D.*

Both Robert Bertie and his father Peregrine Bertie were friends to Essex. Robert Bertie was one of the persons, including Gelly Merrick and the Earl of Sussex, knighted by Essex in Cadiz on 27 June 1597, and Essex, in a letter to Peregrine Bertie, called him "another myself." CM IX, p. 11; see also pp. ix-x. Cuffe certainly knew Peregrine who, perhaps unknowingly, played some slight role in the Essex uprising, for it was he, according to Henry Cuffe, who gave John Norton, the bookseller (see note 127, *infra*), a letter from Essex to be delivered to James VI. SP Dom., 1601-1603, pp. 2-3; *Correspondence of King James VI of Scotland*, pp. xxvi, 90. R. M.'s dedication of Cuffe's book to Robert Bertie implies R. M.'s knowledge, doubtless through Savile, that Cuffe and Robert Bertie knew each other, and that the dedication would be well received.

96. *Biographia Britannica*, IV, p. 557, note I.
97. Samuel C. Chew, p. 15.
98. Whitaker, pp. 8-9.
99. William Vaughan, p. 112.
100. Bullen, ed., *Some Longer Elizabethan Poems*, pp. 123-146.
101. Rosenberg, pp. 138, 295-300.
102. Bullen, ed., *Some Longer Elizabethan Poems*, pp. xiii-xiv. The dedication consists of the initials E.D. followed by the lines "Libenter hic, et omnis exantlabitur/ Labor, in tuae spem gratiae," meaning "This and all labors shall be gladly undertaken in the hope of pleasing you," modeled after lines in Horace's *Epodes* (i, 23-24) stating that "This war and every war shall be gladly undertaken in hope to win thy favor."
103. The Idyl entitled "The Thirty-First Idillion" in *Six Idillia* is actually Theocritus' Thirtieth Idyl.
104. Baldwin, pp. 42-43;
105. *Piers Plainnes seauen yeres Prentiship*, p. 37. An instructive illustration of how wrong and long a person can be in attempting to explain a sentence which he has not seen in context can be found in Klawitter, at pp. 21-22.
106. Jenkins, pp. 44-48.

107. *Piers Plainnes seauen yeres Prentiship*, p. 2.
108. *England's Helicon*, pp. 85, 98, 167, 176.
109. Jenkins, pp. 45-48.
110. Quoted in Pooler, *Shakespeare's Poems*, p. xxviii.
111. For Cuffe in Paris, see CM VII, pp. 235 (assigned to June 1597, but its contents reveal that it must have been written in June 1598); CM VIII, p. 353; CM XIV, pp. 63-64. One of the ways in which Cuffe tried to distract Southampton is revealed in a letter written a few days after the Essex uprising by Southampton's brother-in-law, Thomas Arundell, to Robert Cecil. In this letter, the grasping Arundell asked to be granted such lands as Southampton might forfeit as a consequence of his anticipated attainder, and, hoping perhaps thereby to ingratiate himself with Cecil, passed on information which he thought might be helpful:

> There is one Cuff, a certain Puritan scholar, one of the hottest-headed of my Lord of Essex his followers. This Cuff was sent by my Lord of Essex to read to my Lord of Southampton in Paris, where he read Aristotle's *Politics* to him, with such expositions as, I doubt [i. e., think] did him but little good. Afterwards he read to my Lord of Rutland. I protest I owe him no malice, but if he should be faulty herein, which I greatly doubt [think], I cannot but wish his punishment, *verbum sapienti*. [Quoted in Akrigg, *Shakespeare and the Earl of Southampton*, p. 130.]

Now, it is possible and even probable (see CM VII, pp. 524-525), that Cuffe while in Italy met the author of a treatise on the three first books of Aristotle's *Politics*, acquired a copy of this treatise, and had it with him in Paris, but it seems to me extremely improbable that Cuffe's reading with Southampton either Aristotle's *Politics* (which I think unlikely) or a treatise on Aristotle's *Politics* (which seems more likely) was at the express direction of Essex. Nor is it likely that Southampton, deeply in debt and apprehensive over his impending punishment for his marriage to Elizabeth Vernon, absorbed much of what he and Cuffe read together.

112. CM VIII, p. 353.
113. *Reliquiæ Wottonianæ*, p. 32
114. *Ibid.*, p. 33.
115. *Ibid.*, pp. 31-32.
116. William Camden, *The Historie of . . . Princesse Elizabeth*, Fourth Book, p. 194. The *Biographie Universelle* observes that "Ce jugement sévère était celui d'un homme qui avait vécu avec Cuff dans la plus grande intimité," and subsequent writers repeat the harsh assessments of Wotton and Camden: Naunton writes that Cuffe was "a vile man and of a perverse nature," "Fragmenta Regalia," p. 277; Hotson calls him Essex' Machiavelli, *I, William Shakespeare*, p. 159; Robert Lacey writes, at p. 109, that Cuffe was a Mephistopheles to Essex' Faust, and G. B. Harrison writes that Cuffe was Essex' evil genius, *Robert Devereux, Earl of Essex*, p. 259.
117. Lacey Baldwin Smith shows (at pp. 243-254) that Cuffe, depicted by the government and by Essex' friends as a person of low birth who corrupted the

noble Earl of Essex, served as a scape-goat to excuse or absolve Essex for ulti-
mate responsibility for his actions. Consistent with this is Professor Akrigg's
discovery of a note written by Charles Stanhope stating that his father John
Stanhope, who held high offices under Elizabeth and James, would have spared
the life of Cuffe, but that Robert Cecil (who in addition to being a foe of the
Essex party was one of the Commissioners who sat in judgment on Cuffe,
Complete Collection of State Trials, VIII, column 48) was bent on his destruction.
Akrigg, "The Curious Marginalia of Charles, Second Lord Stanhope," p. 794.

Lacey Baldwin Smith also suggests (at p. 253) that Cuffe was a model for
Shakespeare's Iago, but this, I think, is untenable, the critical difference between
the two being their *intention*: Cuffe's counsel, although unwise, was never
intended to disgrace or undermine his master, nor can anyone doubt Cuffe's love
for Essex, whereas Iago's counsel, born of hate for and jealousy of Othello, *was*
intended to bring about Othello's disgrace and downfall. The ill-intending Iago
was successful in his scheme, and ruined his master; the well-meaning Cuffe
ruined his master, too, but that was never his intention.

118. SP Dom., 1598-1601, p. 588.
119. *Biographia Britannia*, IV, 556.
120. Godfrey Goodman, II, 17, where Essex is reported to have said, "I must accuse
     one who is most nearest to me, my sister, who did continually urge me on with
     telling me how all my friends and followers thought me a coward, and that I had
     lost all my valour. . . ."
121. *Complete Collection of State Trials*, VII, column 59.
122. *Ibid.*, columns 57-61.
123. *Ibid.*, column 61.
124. John Stow, *Annales*, quoted in Akrigg, *Shakespeare and the Earl of Southampton*,
     p. 128.
125. *Complete Collection of State Trials*, VII, column 62.
126. Camden, *The Historie of . . . Princesse Elizabeth*, Book Four, p. 193.
127. *Biographia Britannia*, IV, 556. A few days before his execution, Cuffe prepared
     a will which, while not expressly designating "my honorable and trew freind M^r
     William Killigrew" as executor, imposed upon him duties clearly evidencing
     Cuffe's intention that the distribution of the bequests was to be made by Killigrew
     (who, ironically, was the uncle of Robert Cecil). Among the persons mentioned
     in the will are Cuffe's friend Henry Saville, to whom Cuffe left a bequest of one
     hundred pounds (with a request "to contynue the memorye of his unfortunate
     freind, and ever to thinke charitably of him, howsoever some endeavor to ruyne
     and deface as well his name as his estate"), Saville's deceased brother Thomas
     ("with whom I doe assuredly trust to meet shortly in heaven") in remembrance
     of whom Cuffe gives £250 to Merton College, Cuffe's nephews, John and Adam,
     of whose education Cuffe beseeches Saville to have a care, Cuffe's "poore aged
     mother"; Essex's daughters Francis and Dorothy, and "Lastly, . . . my honest
     freind Jhon Norton the bookseller, . . . to give him some recompence for the
     trouble which this great tempest (I feare) is like to bring vppon him." *Corre-
     spondence of King James VI of Scotland*, pp. 91-92. As a matter of law, Cuffe's
     will was inoperative, because the property of all persons convicted of treason

automatically escheated to the crown. However, shortly after Cuffe's death, the crown granted to William Killigrew "the money and goods forfeited by the attainder of Henry Cuffe." SP Dom., 1601-1603, p. 23. Since the grant was absolute, and Cuffe's will invalid, Killigrew undoubtedly had the legal right to retain for himself all of Cuffe's money and goods; let us hope, however (a hope which experience teaches is likely to be disappointed), that he was the "honorable and trew freind" Cuffe thought he was, and that he made the distribution contemplated by Cuffe.

128. SP Dom., 1601-1603, p. 14. Even Sir Gelly Merrick, "with a minde al-together undaunted, who, as it were weary of his life, interrupted *Cuffe* once or twice, wishing him to let passe his unseasonable wisedome now that he was to dye." Camden, *The Historie of . . . Princesse Elizabeth*, Book Four, p. 194.

129. SP Dom., 1601-1603, pp. 17, 88. (This latter document gives the wrong date for the execution.

130. Camden, *The Historie of . . . Princesse Elizabeth*, Book Four, p. 194.

131. Lacey Baldwin Smith, p. 255.

132. *Correspondence of King James VI of Scotland*, p. 101.

133. SP Dom., 1601-1603, p. 7.

134. SP Dom., 1598-1601, pp. 551, 553.

135. *Ibid.*, pp. 547, 551, 558.

136. *Ibid.*, p. 550.

137. *Ibid.*, pp. 555, 584, 599.

138. Nichols, III, 552.

139. Chambers, *William Shakespeare*, I, 375-376.

140. Hotson, *Shakespeare's Sonnets Dated*, pp. 153-154; Chambers, *William Shakespeare*, II, 198.

141. Jardine, I, 313.

142. *A Complete Collection of State Trials*, I, column 207.

143. *Chamberlain's Letters*, p. 106.

144. *A Complete Collection of State Trials*, I, column 208.

145. Akrigg, *Shakespeare and the Earl of Southampton*, p. 127.

146. *Sixth Report of the Royal Commission on Historical Manuscripts*, Part I, p. 459.

147. Robert Cecil's sympathy for Southampton is evident in a letter to Sir George Carew written on 26 February 1601, where after recounting the events which led to the executions of Essex, Merrick and Cuffe, he continues:

> It remayneth now that I lett you know what is lyke to become of the poore yong Erle of Southampton, who meerely for the loue of the Erle [of Essex] hath ben drawen into this action, who, in respect that most of the conspirascies were at Drury Howse, where he was alwaies cheef, and where Sr Charles Davers laye, those that would deale for him (of which number I protest to God I am one as farre as I dare) are much disadvantaged of arguments to saue him; and yet when I consider how penitent he is, and how mercifull the Queen is, and neuer in thought or deed but in this conspiracy he offended, as I can not write in despaire, so I dare not flatter myself with hope. [*Letters from Sir Robert Cecil to George Carew*, p. 74; SP Dom., 1598-1601, p. 598.]

371

After the commutation of Southampton's death sentence, Southampton's mother wrote to Robert Cecil that she would never forget "my bond to you for me and mine, who, under God, breathe by your means." The endorsement on the letter describes it as "Giving my Lord [Robert Cecil] thanks for her son's life." CM XII, p. 562.

148. SP Dom., 1601-1603, pp. 88, 89, 91. Lawrence Stone, in *Family and Fortune*, at pages 182-183, states that Rutland was never actually required to pay the fine.
149. WP 1001.
150. Halliwell, *The Life of William Shakespeare*, pp. 203-204. The letters patent issued pursuant to the King's order of 17 May 1603 were dated 19 May 1603, and are printed in Chambers, *The Elizabethan Stage*, II, 208-209.
151. GEC, s.v. Southampton (Henry Wriothesley).
152. Wilson, *The History of Great Britain*, p. 284.
153. Mrs Ann Matthews, the archivist at Beaulieu, has brought to my attention a macabre story from *Hogs at the Honeypot*, by Frank Vernon, p. 21. This tale

concerns the fine monuments to the Earls of Southampton, the Wriothesleys, intombed in the family vault under their superb monuments in the church of St.Peter at Titchfield. Lead sarcophagi hold the remains of the first four Earls. The story had been current that these worthies had been "buried in honey" [honey is a substance used from the earliest times as a preservative for corpses; see Crane, pp. 455, 456; Eckels and Callaway, p. 31; *Oxford Latin Dictionary*, s.v. *mel* (b)]. In the early years of the present century, when some subsidence had slightly crushed one of the lead coffins, a thin trickle was seen by one of the workmen to be issuing from a damaged seam. Undaunted, one of those engaged in the repairs, anxious to prove or disprove the legend, ran his finger up the trickle and then, putting it to his mouth, was able to confirm that it was indeed honey.

And so, in a curious fashion, one of the ways in which Shakespeare said that his friend was like Roses — that "Of their sweet deathes, are sweetest odours made" (Sonnet 54) — came to be, *mutatis mutandis*, literally true.

154. WP 262.
155. Hare, "The Documentary Evidence for the Southampton Monument in Titchfield Church," Book V, Vol. ii.
156. Lee, *A Life of William Shakespeare*, p. 496; *Manuscripts of . . . the Duke of Rutland*, IV, 397.
157. *Manuscripts of . . . the Duke of Rutland*, pp. 397-399.
158. Hare, "The Documentary Evidence for the Southampton Monument in Titchfield Church," Book V, Vol ii.
159. See pages 276-277.
160. Lee, *A Life of William Shakespeare*, p. 497; *Manuscripts of . . . the Duke of Rutland*, p. 517.
161. Quoted in Chambers, *William Shakespeare*, II, 183.
162. Lee, *A Life of William Shakespeare*, p. 496.
163. Adams, p. 478.

164. John Combe's will, printed in Halliwell's *Life of William Shakespeare*, at pp. 234-240, directs that "a convenient tomb of the value of three score pounds shall be by my executors hereafter named, out of my goods and chattels first raised, within one year after my decease, be sett over me." Comb also bequeathed "To Mr. William Shackspere five pounds. . . . "

165. This was the year of the publication of the First Folio of Shakespeare's Plays. The monument at Stratford must by then have been in place, for one of the prefatory poems in the volume (by Leonard Digges) refers to it:

> *Shake-speare*, at length thy pious fellowes giue
> The world thy Workes: thy Workes, by which, out-liue
> Thy Tombe, thy name must: when that stone is rent,
> And Time dissolues thy *Stratford* Moniment,
> Here we aliue shall view thee still.

166. On the tablet underneath the bust is this inscription:

> Judicio Pylium, genio Socratem, arte Maronem:
> Terra Tegit. populis maeret, Olympus habet.
>
> Stay Passenger, why goest thou by so fast?
> Read if thou canst, whom envious Death hath plast,
> With in this monument Shakespeare: with whome,
> Quick nature dide: whose name doth deck y^s tombe,
> Far more than cost: Sieh all, y^t He hath writt,
> Leaves living art, but page, to serve his witt.
> > Obiit ano do^i 1616
> > Aetatis 53 die 23 Ap^r.

The author of this inscription is unknown. Stopes, at pp. 381-383 of her *Life of Henry Wriothesley, Third Earl of Southampton*, and Hugh Ross Williamson, at pp. 62-65, suggest that it was written by the third Earl of Southampton. Southampton in 1623 may have been in a reflective mood, for in that year the Chapel at Lincoln's Inn, to the construction of which Southampton undoubtedly contributed (for in it were installed stained glass windows, which still exist, bearing his coat of arms), was dedicated, and a sermon preached by John Donne, who long ago had been with Southampton on the Islands voyage. Perhaps the memories thus aroused, and the knowledge that he had spent a substantial sum of money for a cause which might not have been too close to his heart, impelled him to spend additional money for a cause which was.

Note to Conclusion — No Rose but One

1. "Pelleas and Ettarre," *Idylls of the King*, line 398.

Notes to Appendix I — Thomas Wriothesley

1. Stow, I, 302–303.
2. Fuller, II, 363.
3. Gammon, p. 16.
4. GEC, s.v. Southampton (Thomas Wriothesley); Godfrey, Wagner and London, pp. 43 and 184.
5. Campbell, p. 640.
6. GEC, s.v. Southampton (Henry Wriothesley) and Paget of Beaudesert; DNB, s.v. Leland or Leyland, John. See also L & P Addenda, Part 1, No. 357, p. 110, which shows that Thomas' cousin Charles was also a student at Cambridge at the same time.
7. Muller, p. 11.
8. *Ibid.*, p. 9.
9. *Ibid.*, pp. 10-11; Bradner, pp. 400-403.
10. *Ibid.*, p. 11.
11. Stopes, *The Life of Henry, Third Earl of Southampton*, p. 487.
12. Muller, p. 10.
13. *Ibid.*, p. 341, note 34.
14. In a letter dated 8 July 1535, Peckham addresses Wriothesley as "heartily beloved cousin." L & P IX, Appendix, No. 3, p. 403. The sixth quartering of the arms on Wriothesley's tomb (Plate VIII-A) bears "Sable, a chevron or, between three crosses-croslet fitchy, argent," the arms of the Peckham family: as is shown on Table VI, Wriothesley's maternal grandmother was Sir Edmund Peckham's sister (a striking illustration of the fact that women married young in that era). It is likely that Peckham's wife, Ann, daughter of John Cheyne of Chesham-Bois, was a close relative of Thomas Wriothesley's wife, Jane, daughter of William Cheney of Chesham Bois. DNB, s.v. Peckham, Sir Edmund; GEC, s.v. Southampton (Thomas Wriothesley). Stopes, *Life of Henry, Third Earl of Southampton*, pp. 501–502, states that Wriothesley's wife and Peckham's wife were sisters. Sir Edmund survived Thomas, and was one of the executors of his will.
15. Ridley, pp. 168–169.
16. See, for example, L & P IV, Part 1, No. 650, p. 284; No. 1499 (26), p. 673; No. 1688, p. 752; No. 1833 (3), p. 815; No. 1834, p. 816; No. 3141, p. 1429; etc.
17. L & P IV, Part 3, No. 5772, p. 2573; L & P Addenda, No. 1468, p. 503.
18. L & P XIV, Part 1, No. 434, p. 175.
19. L & P IV, Part 1, No. 650, p. 284; Part 2, No. 2445, p. 1092; No. 2457, p. 1096; No. 2605, p. 1156; No. 2725, p. 1214; No. 4131, p. 1826; etc.
20. L & P IV, Part 3(1), No. 5729, p. 2537.
21. Muller, p. 19.
22. *Ibid.*, pp. 20–21.
23. *Ibid.*, pp. 22–27.
24. L & P IV, Part 3, No. 6489, p. 2916.
25. Cavendish (ed. Lockyer), p. 180(n).

26. Cavendish (ed. Singer), p. 322.
27. Muller, p. 31.
28. *Ibid.*, p. 36.
29. Ridley, p. 232-233. The College in 1546 became Christ Church College, by which name it is known today. Headlam, p. 308.
30. SP Sp., 1529-1530, IV, Part 1, No. 211, p. 326.
31. Ridley, pp. 235-237.
32. Scarisbrick, pp. 228-240.
33. L & P IV, Part 3, No. 5945, p. 2653.
34. L & P IV, Part 3(1), No. 5979, p. 2664.
35. See L & P IV, Part 3(1), No. 6600 (11), p. 2976.
36. L & P IV, Part 3, No. 6600(11), p. 2976; PR, 1547-1548, p. 252.
37. Gammon, p. 31; L & P V, No. 559 (9), p. 254.
38. Gammon, pp. 19-21.
39. See L & P XII, Part 1, No. 1209, p. 557; Part 2, No. 47, p. 16; L & P XIII, Part 1, No. 266, p. 92; L & P Addenda, Part 1, No. 1021, p. 356; DNB, s.v. Wriothesley, Sir Thomas.
40. Scarisbrick, p. 236; Ridley, pp. 245, 251.
41. Ridley, pp. 249-253.
42. See, for example, L & P V, No. 202, p. 96; No. 328, p. 185; No. 548, p. 250; No. 742, p. 353; etc.
43. Scarisbrick, p. 255.
44. L & P V, No. 5 (5), p. 2; Sp. Cal. 1529-1530 IV, Part 1; No. 455, p. 753.
45. Muller, p. 42.
46. *Ibid.*, pp. 43-44.
47. *Ibid.*, pp. 46-47.
48. The original document has upon it the endorsement in Wriothesley's hand, "The submission of the clergy to the king's highness." L & P V, No. 1023, p. 470.
49. Scarisbrick, p. 309.
50. *Ibid.*, p. 310.
51. *Ibid*, pp. 311-312.
52. L & P VI, No. 525, p. 230; No. 529, p. 231; No. 661, p. 299.
53. Muller, p. 51.
54. L & P VI, No. 584, p. 264; No. 585, p. 266; No. 661, p. 299.
55. L & P VI, No. 807, p. 357.
56. Muller, p. 51.
57. L & P V, No. 1602, p. 671; VI, No. 1306, p. 527. In the letter from Marseilles (No. 1306), Wriothesley complains that "apparel, and play sometimes, whereat he is unhappy, have cost him above 50 crowns." Sixty-six years later, his grandson, when in Paris, in only a few days lost 3,000 crowns to one person, and possibly more to others.
58. Muller, p. 55
59. *Ibid.*, p. 57.
60. *Ibid.*
61. L & P VII, No. 1378, p. 523.
62. Hughes, I, 278-279.

63. Ridley, pp. 277–283. Two weeks earlier, on 22 June 1535, John Fisher, Bishop of Rochester, had been executed for the same reason. John Fisher and Thomas More were canonized on 19 May 1935. Macklem, pp. 202–207, 252.
64. Muller, p. 57.
65. *Ibid.*, pp. 60–65.
66. *Ibid.*, pp. 66–78.
67. *Ibid.*, p. 79.
68. L & P VIII, No. 121, p. 38.
69. Muller, p. 79.
70. GEC, s.v. Cromwell.
71. Wriothesley, I, 55.
72. GEC, s.v. Southampton (Thomas Wriothesley).
73. L & P X, No. 12, p. 3; No. 226(2), p. 79.
74. WP 141; L & P X, No. 870, p. 358.
75. WP 141.
76. "The wealth of the many statesmen who made their fortunes under the Tudors never consisted solely of land purchased from or granted by the crown, or of their 'profits of office' of legitimate fees and (to modern thinking) less legal pourboires. These sources did provide the majority of their incomes, but a surprisingly large portion was derived from the steady trickle of petty sinecures which dripped from the crown into the perennially parched palms of favoured suitors." Gammon, p. 34.
77. Scarisbrick, p. 348
78. Wriothesley, I, 189–198; *Lisle Letters*, III, 233; Scarisbrick, 349.
79. This was probably the purpose of the group assembled on 9 May 1536. L & P X, No. 834, p. 348.
80. Scarisbrick, 349.
81. L & P X, No. 876, p. 362.
82. *Lisle Letters*, III, 240.
83. L & P X, No. 876, pp. 361–363.
84. *Ibid.*
85. L & P X, p. 381 (note). Brereton and Smeaton were also disembowelled and quartered. *Ibid.*, No. 911, pp. 381–382.
86. L & P X, xxvii.
87. L & P X, No. 915, p. 384.
88. L & P X, No. 1000, p. 413.
89. *Lisle Letters*, III, 232-243.
90. *Ibid.*, 234.
91. Dietz, pp. 34–50. Empson and Dudley were detested because, on behalf of Henry VII, they had squeezed the realm for money. Dietz writes, at pp. 48–49, that their executions were ordered "not on the charge of extortion, for which there could have been no real evidence which did not compromise the late king [Henry VII] and his whole policy, but on a trumped-up charge of constructive treason. . . . [L]ike the true Machiavellian that he and all the Tudors were, Henry VIII broke the tools by whom in large part the supremacy of the law had been established."

92. *Lisle Letters*, III, 241.
93. Scarisbrick, pp. 337-338; Dietz, p. 128 (an excellent account of the suppression of the monasteries).
94. 27 Henry VIII c. 28. Another statute, authorizing the suppression of the remaining monasteries, was enacted in 1539. 31 Henry VIII c. 13.
95. L & P X, No. 364, pp. 137-144. See also, Gasquet, I, 289, 291, 325-378.
96. L & P XII, No. 401, p. 155. The artistic and cultural loss resulting from this appalls us today, but we must remember that Erasmus and other humanists were, in their day, and before the Reformation, appalled by the veneration of material objects and relics (many of which were laughably spurious). Erasmus' views had their consequences, hence the 16th century observation that "Erasmus laid the eggs and Luther hat[c]hed them." Gardiner, p. 403.
97. *Lisle Letters*, V, 224-226.
98. Ridley, p. 2.
99. Hughes, I, 296-320.
100. During the legal proceedings before the executions, one of the accused spoke prophetically to Cromwell:

> Cromwell, it is thou that art the very original and chief causer of all this rebellion and mischief, and are likewise causer of the apprehension to us that be noble men, and dost daily earnestly travail to bring us to our end and to strike off our heads, and I trust that or [ere] thou die, though thou wouldst procure all the noblemen's heads within the realm to be stricken off, yet shall there one head remain that shall strike off thy head. [L & P XII, Part 1, No. 976, p. 441.]

101. Although he had assisted the King by presiding at the proceedings which led to the execution of his niece and nephew, Norfolk had not thereafter been in the King's good graces, and had retired to his manor; the King's need for his martial services to suppress the uprising brought him back on center stage. *Lisle Letters*, III, 249; Hughes, I, 303.
102. See, for example, SP I, No LX, p. 488; No. LXI, p. 490; No. LXII. p. 491; No. LXX, p. 511; No. LXXII, p. 519; No. LXXIII, No. 521; etc. Byrne writes (*Lisle Letters*, III, 586):

> [Cromwell's] (literal) place at the King's side was mostly supplied during the critical weeks of November and December, ably and discreetly, by his own man, Mr. Wriothesley, whom the King found a wholly admirable secretary, and who incidentally happened to have the bold, handsome appearance that he appreciated in the men he liked to have about him. It seems probable, therefore, that at this very time when the King interposed his own royal person between the hatred of the commons for his upstart minister, he may have realized — whether subjectively or objectively — that useful as he had been and was to continue to be over the acquisition and management of the royal revenues, Cromwell himself might not be irreplaceable.

103. L & P XIII, Part 2, No. 1, p. 1. See also, *ibid.*, No. 1204, p. 506.
104. Dietz, pp. 148–149.
105. L & P VI, No. 1067, p. 451; Kennedy, p. 81.
106. Kennedy, p. 81.
107. DNB, s.v. Wriothesley, Sir Thomas.
108. L & P IX, Appendix, No. 14, p. 407.
109. L & P XI, No. 580(1), p. 232.
110. *The Third Book of Remembrance of Southampton*, no. 156, p. 61.
111. Kennedy, p. 68. Kennedy explains that the chief steward of a monastery was

> normally a man of rank and substance, influential in the neighbourhood where the monastery was situated. His precise duties would not always have been easy to define, but, in general, he was intended to represent the house in its more important relationships with secular bodies. As a man of the world he might be thought competent and influential to serve the interests of the monastery in ways which be less open, say, to the head of the monastic community. For his value to the institution, the chief steward was paid an annual fee and received a number of perquisites.

> It appears, however, that Wriothesley never saw the inside of Titchfield Abbey until after it became his property. See Appendix II, p. 271.

112. *Ibid.*, p. 67.
113. *Id.*
114. *Id.*
115. *Ibid.*, p. 75.
116. *Id*; *Lisle Letters*, I, 4-5.
117. Scarisbrick, p. 342.
118. Kennedy, p. 81.
119. *Id.*
120. See Appendix II, p. 271.
121. Kennedy, p, 81. The present Lord Montagu of Beaulieu writes that Wriothesley paid £1,350 6s 8d for Beaulieu. Montagu, p. 39.
122. Kennedy, p. 81.
123. L & P XII, Part 2, No. 1265, p. 444; Nott, II, 421 - 429.
124. Edgerton, p. 116, n. 10.
125. *Lisle Letters*, I, 379; WP 119.
126. Kennedy, p. 81.
127. Scarisbrick, p. 353.
128. DNB, s.v. Leland, John. He and his friend Nicolas Udall had also written poems and ditties which were recited and sung at Anne Boleyn's coronation. *Ballads from Manuscripts*, pp. 378-401.
129. L & P XII, No. 1004, p. 345; see SP VIII, p. 1, note 1.
130. SP VIII, p. 143, note 1.
131. Scarisbrick, p. 357.
132. SP, VIII, 51 (spelling modernised).
133. Muller, p. 78.

134. L & P XIII, Part 2, No. 881, p. 368.
135. Emmison, p. 55.
136. *Lisle Letters*, VI, 241, note 5; IV, 208. See also, Byrne, 235-236.
137. This alleged statement is reported, without documentation, in Constant, p. 274, Emmison, p. 43 and Bowle, p. 225. A source near the actual event writes that the Duchess of Milan said to Thomas Knight, Wriothesley's brother-in-law (see note 151, *infra*), that "I like not to be wife to such a husband that either putteth away or killeth his wives" (Harpsfield, p. 278), and it may be that the young Duchess' statement was no more trenchant than this.
138. SP, VIII, p. 143 (spelling modernised).
139. *Ibid.*, p. 144.
140. *Ibid.*, p. 146.
141. *Id.*
142. L & P XIV, Part 1, No. 321, pp. 125-126; Cartwright, p. 199, 201. A document among the Wriothesley Papers at the Public Record Office in London (SP7, fol. 70Aʸ) has a staff with some notes of music on it. If this was written out by Wriothesley, it may reflect more than a mere passive love of music.
143. L & P XIV, Part 1, No. 247, p. 98.
144. Dr. Edward Carne, "proctor for the King of England" (L & P IV, Part 3, No. 6605, p. 2977), "a learned lawyer whom Henry had sent [to Brussels] to assist [Wriothesley] in drawing up the marriage treaty" (Cartwright, p. 182) writes to Cromwell, "Mr. wriothesley takes his [Phillips'] escape so heavily that unless your lordship comfort him I fear a return of his ague." L & P XIV, Part 1, No. 248, p. 99.
145. L & P XIV, Part 1, No. 264, p. 103.
146. *Lisle Letters*, VI, 241-242; see also Byrne, pp. 235-236.
147. SP Sp., 1538-1542 VI, Part 1, No. 33, p. 97.
148. L & P XIV, Part 1, No. 433, p. 174.
149. Scarisbrick, p. 364.
150. L & P XIII, No. 1124, p. 470.
151. Thomas Knight was the first husband of Wriothesley's sister Anne. He appears on the scene as a household servant to Cromwell, L & P XII, Part 1, No. 607, p. 277, and subsequently becomes a servant to Thomas Wriothesley. L & P XIII, Part 1, No. 324, p. 108. Against Wriothesley's advice, he becomes a Proctor of the University of Oxford. L & P XII, Part 1, No. 926, p. 422; Part 2, No. 429, p. 173. He helps Wriothesley with the conversion of Titchfield Abbey into a residence, at which time he has not yet married Wriothesley's sister. L & P XII, Part 1, No. 749, p. 282. He is a messenger between Cromwell and Wriothesley while Wriothesley is in Brussels. L & P XIV, Part 1, No. 308, p. 121; No. 321, pp. 125-127; No. 335, p. 130; No. 365, pp. 139-140; No. 434, pp. 174-175; Part 2, No. 781, f. 59, p. 304, f. 63b, p. 306. In April, 1540, when Wriothesley becomes one of the King's two principal secretaries, Knight succeeds him as a clerk of the signet. L & P XV, No. 611 (17), p. 286. He receives from the Crown grants of portions of the lands formerly belonging to Southwick Monastery. L & P XVIII, Part 2, No. 107 (44), p. 57. On 1 May 1545 he becomes Under Treasurer of the Mint, L & P XX, Part 1, No. 631, p. 331, and

works on the debasement of the Irish coinage. L & P XX, Part 2, No. 231, pp.100–101. He receives a grant of a coat of arms on 8 April 1546 (*Visitation of Hampshire*, p. 219), and is dead some time prior to 20 June 1549, on which date his widow enters into a marriage agreement with Oliver Laurence.

Knight's coat of arms, like those of other men who became armigerous after marrying into Wriothesley's family, echo the Wriothesley arms or crest: Thomas Knight's arms include the birds of the Wriothesley arms and the bugle's head, ringed, of the Wriothesley crest (*Visitation of Hampshire*, p. 219); John White's arms duplicate the Wriothesley cross and four birds ("Brasses of the White Family at Southwick," p. 86; *Visitation of Hampshire*, pp. 138 and 229); and Richard Lister's shield depicts the cross and birds (*ibid.*, p. 45).

152. L & P XIII, No. 1140, p. 475.
153. DNB, s.v. Wriothesley, Sir Thomas.
154. L & P XIV, Part 1, No. 520, p. 201; No. 573, p. 224; No. 662, p. 331. As the candidate of the King, Wriothesley was assured of victory. "In the time of Henry VIII. the House of Commons was not really an elective body at all. The members represented the king rather than the people, and were in fact nominated by the crown. Together with the writ ordering the election, the sheriff received a letter mentioning the name of the candidate the king wished to be chosen. The 'free' electors, or as many as the sheriff in his discretion thought good to call, were summoned together and informed of the royal will and pleasure, and as no opposition was of any use the royal nominee was declared chosen to represent the burgesses in parliament." Gasquet, I, 291–292.
155. Muller, p. 79.
156. *Ibid.*, p. 80.
157. *Ibid.*, pp. 80–81.
158. Emmison, p. 43.
159. L & P XIV, Part 2, pp. xx–xxiii.
160. L & P XIV, Part 2, No. 697, p. 257.
161. L & P XV, No. 823, p. 391.
162. GEC, s.v. Cromwell.
163. L & P XV, No. 541, p. 243.
164. GEC, s.v. Paget of Beaudesert.
165. L & P XV, No. 850(11), p. 423.
166. Muller, p. 91; Scarisbrick, p. 378.
167. Campbell, I, 647–648.
168. L & P XV, No. 429, p. 164. Wriothesley and Gardiner appear to have remained on good terms for the rest of their lives. On 1 October 1542 a grant by Gardiner recites that "for the good love and singular affection which he bears toward Sir Thomas, the bishop [i.e., Gardiner] further grants to him and to Lady Jane his wife that they shall come with as many servants or other persons as they please, to hawk, hunt and chase within the said warrens [i.e.,Fareham and Havant]." WP 132.
169. *Lisle Letters*, VI, 118. Viscount Lisle remained in the Tower for two more years, and died there. Byrne, *ibid.*, VI, 183–184, quotes Holinshed's account of Lisle's end:

After that by due trial it was known that he was guilty of nothing to the matter, the King appointed Sir Thomas Wriothesley, His Majesty's secretary, to go unto him, and to deliver to him a ring, with a rich diamond, for a token from him, and to tell him to be of good cheer, for although in that so weighty a matter he would not have done less to him if he had been his own son, yet now upon thorough trial had, sith it was manifestly proved that he was void of all offence, he was sorry that he had been occasioned so far to try his truth, and therefore willed him to be of good cheer and comfort, for he should find that he would make account of him as of his most true and faithful kinsman, and not only restore him to his former liberty but otherwise further be ready to pleasure him in what way he could. Master Secretary set forth this message with such effectual words, as he was an eloquent and well-spoken man, that Lord Lisle took such immoderate joy thereof, that, his heart being oppressed therewith, he died the following night through too much rejoicing.

Which occasioned the comment by another chronicler, also quoted by Byrne, that "this King's Mercy was as fatal as his Judgements." Byrne, who admires Wriothesley for his masterful writing abilities, suggests that Wriothesley wrote this account, which was subsequently obtained and utilised by Holinshed, thereby (for Byrne sees Wriothesley's account as commissioned by the King and "the nearest thing to an apology that Henry VIII ever made in his life") making amends to posterity for the wrongs done to Arthur Lisle during his life. *Ibid.*, 252–253.

170. L & P XV, No. 737, p. 351.
171. Wilding, pp. 298–299.
172. Scarisbrick, p. 376; L & P XV, No. 804, p. 377.
173. L & P XV, No. 821, p. 387.
174. L & P XV, No. 722, pp. 388–389. Valuable insights into the incredible paranoia of the Tudor Court are provided by Lacey Baldwin Smith's book, *Treason in Tudor England*. One of the philosophical bases for this paranoia, according to Professor Smith, and a basis which might explain the fall of Cromwell, as well as most of the other persons who lost their heads during the reign of Henry VIII, is the "evil minister" theory: the king is good, and if bad things happen, it is because his ministers are evil; when the bad ministers are removed, the King's goodness shines forth again. Smith, pp. 171–177. So here, the fact that King Henry VIII got involved in a bad marriage, thus putting him in bad spirits, and preventing him from attending wholeheartedly to his royal duties may, in light of the evil minister theory, be justification enough for the liquidation of the minister who urged the marriage so detrimental to the King's happiness and his subjects' well being. The "evil minister" theory was clearly the premise of Essex' attempt, in 1601, to remove Robert Cecil as an advisor to the Queen.
175. The concept that a "pre-contract" or promise to marry is in effect a marriage is invoked by the Duke in *Measure for Measure* to assure Mariana that it was not improper for her to be substituted for Isabella in the bed of Angelo: "He is your husband on a pre-contract." IV,i,72.
176. L & P XV, No. 821(5), p. 387.

381

177. L & P XV, No. 823, p. 391.
178. GEC, s.v. Cromwell.
179. L & P XV, No. 860, p. 429; No. 861, p. 430.
180. Scarisbrick, pp. 429-430.
181. L & P XVI, No. 503(12), p. 239.
182. L & P XV, No. 813, p. 385; DNB, s.v. Wriothesley, Sir Thomas. This incident may be related to Walter Chandler's charge that Thomas Wriothesley was keeping from Chandler certain lands to which he (Chandler) was entitled. The matter was heard by the Privy Council in December 1540, and Wriothesley exonerated of the charge. Chandler was required to apologize, which he did. *Lisle Letters*, I, 379-380.
183. L & P XVI, No. 1328, p. 611.
184. See L & P XVI, No. 1317, p. 607; No. 1321, pp. 608-609; No. 1334, p. 616; No. 1337, p. 617; No. 1339, pp. 618-619; No. 1414, pp. 660-661; No. 1415, pp. 661-663; No. 1440, p. 672.
185. L & P XVI, No. 1328, p. 611.
186. Wriothesley, I, 130-131.
187. L & P, XVII, No. 28, p. 13; Scarisbrick, p. 432.
188. L & P XVII, No. 100, p. 44.
189. L & P XVI, No. 1395, p. 649; No. 1433, p. 670.
190. SP Sp., 1542-1543, No. 74, p. 167.
191. L & P XVII, No. 714(24), p. 400; WP 150.
192. GEC, s.v. Southampton (Thomas Wriothesley).
193. GEC, s.v. Southampton (William Fitzwilliam).
194. Stopes, p. 494.
195. L & P XVII, No. 1154(7), pp. 631-632.
196. *Lisle Letters*, V, 481.
197. L & P XVII, No. 1154 (2) and (6), pp. 630-631.
198. L & P XVII, No. 949, p. 538; L & P XVIII, Part 2, No. 526, p. 277.
199. L & P XVIII, Part 1, No. 100(35), p. 69.
200. L & P XVIII, Part 1, No. 873, p. 483; No. 894, p. 490.
201. See L & P XVIII, Part 1, No. 918, p. 498; No. 919, p. 498; No. 935, p. 504.
202. L & P XVIII, Part 2. No. 293, pp. 164, 165; No. 438, p. 232; No. 458, p. 250.
203. See L & P XVIII, No. 516, p. 272.
204. L & P XIX, Part 1, No. 1, p. 1.
205. L & P XIX, Part 1, No. 368, ff. 58, 59.
206. L & P XIX. Part 1, No. 459, p. 292. That Audley had been ill for some time, and that Wriothesley had early on been selected as his successor, may be inferred from the grant to Wriothesley, on 22 January 1544, of an "annuity of 100 *l* until he shall be advanced to any office the yearly fee of which amounts to 100 *l*." L & P XIX, Part 1, No. 1036, II 33b, p. 644.
207. L & P XIX, Part 1, No. 459, p. 293; Campbell, p. 643.
208. Muller, p. 108.
209. Muller, p. 109; L & P XVIII, Part 2, No. 327 (9), p. 184.
210. Bolwell, p. 36.
211. Muller, p. 112.

212. Others sent to prison at the same time are probably the persons described, in the pardon eventually given to John More, as "detestable traitors"; in addition to John Heywood and Germain Gardiner, these persons were John Eldryington, John Bekynsale, Wm. Daunce, John Larke, clk., and John Ireland, clk. L & P XIX, Part 1, No. 444 (6), p. 285.
213. Bolwell, p. 38; Muller, pp. 113, 361, n. 7.
214. L & P XIX, Part 1, No. 459, p. 292. His salary in this position was 300 pounds per year. WP 242.
215. L & P XIX, Part 1, No. 812 (109), p. 504.
216. Harington, p. 102. The "six-stringed whip" was the name by which the Six Articles were known, but it was the Act of Supremacy, and not the Six Articles, which Heywood was accused of having violated. Bolwell, p. 40.
217. Harington could have known this from his father, also John Harington, who had served in the Court of Henry VIII and whose first wife, Ethelreda Malte, is said to have been the illegitimate daughter of Henry VIII (Harington, p. 1), or from his friends, the third Earl of Southampton and the Earl's sister, Mary, in whose company he conceived the notion of writing *The Metamorphosis of Ajax*. Harington, pp. 18 and 174.
218. David Lloyd, pp. 78–79.
219. *Ibid.*, p. 79.
220. Campbell, p. 645; L & P XIX, Part 2, No. 527(24), p. 316.
221. L & P XIX, Part 1, No. 864, p. 537.
222. Cited by Dietz, p. 147.
223. L & P XIX, Part 1, No. 513 (5), p. 319.
224. Dietz, p. 175.
225. L & P XX, Part 1, No. 631, p. 331.
226. Dietz, p. 155.
227. L & P XIX, Part 1, No. 513 (5), p. 319; Dietz, p. 154.
228. Dietz, p. 177.
229. De Roover, p. 51, n. 59.
230. And Challis argues, at pp. 84–85, that although Wriothesley may have administered, he did not originate, Henry's program of currency debasement.
231. Gammon, pp. 73–75.
232. Dietz, p. 153.
233. Dietz, pp. 164–165.
234. Dietz, pp. 150–151.
235. SP I, ccxxxvi, p. 831; L & P XX, Part 2, No. 366, pp. 163-164.
236. L & P XX, Part 2, No. 746, pp. 354–355.
237. SP I, ccxl, p. 838.
238. L & P XX, Part 1, No. 566, pp. 275–276.
239. L & P XX, Part 1, No. 806, p. 398; SP, X, No. MCLVI, p. 441 (note 1).
240. Wheatley, p. 282.
241. L & P XX, Part 1, No. 846(91), p. 426.
242. WP 996.
243. Martienssen, p. 40.
244. Campbell, I, 646.

245. Foxe, V, 547.
246. *Id.*
247. *Ibid.*, 548.
248. *Ibid.*, 564.
249. Campbell, p. 648.
250. *Id.*
251. *Ibid.*, p. 650. This event is depicted in Samuel Rowley's play, *When You See Me You Know Me*, published in 1605, sigs. I2ᵛ–K2, with the curious alteration (out of deference to, or at the insistence of, Henry Wriothesley?) that Bishop Gardiner (accompanied by Edmond Bonner, Bishop of London), rather than Thomas Wriothesley, is depicted as the person who comes to arrest the queen, and is berated by Henry VIII.
252. L & P XXI, Part 2, No. 756, p. 387.
253. Muller, p. 205.
254. Campbell, I, p. 652.
255. Foxe, V, 691; Scarisbrick, p. 489.
256. L & P XXI, Part 2, No. 697, p. 365.
257. L & P XXI, Part 2, No. 753, p. 385.
258. L & P XXI, Part 2. No. 620, p. 316.
259. L & P XXI, No. 555(8), p. 287.
260. Casady, pp. 205-206; L & P XXI, Part 2, No. 696, p. 364.
261. *Ibid.* (Both preceding citations.)
262. Casady, p. 216.
263. L & P XXI, Part 2, No. 647, p. 366; xlvii.
264. L & P XXI, Part 2, No. 753, p. 385; No. 759, p. 389; L & P XXI, Part 1, p. xlviii; Campbell, I, 654.
265. L & P XXI, Part 1, p. xlviii.
266. Campbell, I, 656-657.
267. *Ibid.*, p. 654. The first act of Queen Mary upon coming to the throne in 1553 was to release Norfolk from prison. He died a year later, at about 81 years of age.
268. Campbell, p. 654.
269. L & P XXI, Part 2, No. 634, pp. 320 - 322. The fifteen other Executors and Councillors were Thomas Cranmer, Archbishop of Canterbury; William Paulet, Lord St. John of Basing; Edward Seymour, Earl of Hertford; Sir John Russell; John Dudley, Viscount Lisle; Cuthbert Tunstall, Bishop of Durham; Sir Anthony Browne; Sir Edward Montague; Sir Thomas Bromley; Sir Edward North; Sir William Paget; Sir Anthony Denny; Sir William Herbert; Sir Edward Wotton and Dr. Nicholas Wotton. *Id.* See also Jordan, p. 80.
270. L & P XXI, Part 2, No. 634, p. 321.
271. Campbell, I, 656–657.
272. Muller, p. 142.
273. PC, 1547-1550, pp. 15–22.
274. *Ibid.*, p. 35.
275. Campbell, I, 659.
276. L & P XIV, Part 2, Appendix, No. 54, p. 372.

277. Gammon, p. 134.
278. Hoak, p. 346, note 18.
279. Campbell, I, 658–661; APC pp. 48–59; Sp. Cal., 1547–1549, pp. 91–92, 100–101. Professor Arthur J. Slavin suggests, at pp. 49–69 of *Tudor Men and Institutions*, that Wriothesley's opposition to the broadening of the jurisdiction of the Court of Augmentations at the expense of the jurisdiction of the Court of Chancery may have contributed to Wriothesley's fall.
280. Campbell, I, 660
281. *Ibid.*, p. 661.
282. Muller, p. 181.
283. Hoak, pp. 49–50. One explanation may be, however, that Wriothesley finally assented to changes in the State religion sought to be effected by the Council, and for this reason was reinstated. See SP Sp., 1547–1549, p. 345.
284. Pollard, p. 38.
285. *Id.*
286. *Ibid.*, p. 39.
287. *Ibid.*, p. 41.
288. The likely cause of this confusion is that both men in 1549 lived in what had been the other's house, for they had exchanged houses in 1547. E. Williams, I, (359). Wriothesley in his will refers to "my house in London called Southampton House, lately the Bishop of Lincolnes, and after my lordes of Warwick." *Trevelyan Papers*, p. 212. See Chapter VIII, p. 190.
289. Campbell, I, 662.
290. *Id.*
291. Pollard, p. 42.
292. Ponet, I, iii-iiiᵛ.
293. Hoak, p. 255.
294. *Ibid.*, p. 256.
295. PC, 1547-1550, pp. 330 et seq.
296. SP Sp., 1547–1549, p. 477; Pollard, p. 45.
297. GEC, s.v. Paget of Beaudesert.
298. Pollard, p. 45.
299. SP Sp., 1550-1552, p. 44.
300. *Ibid.*, p. 47.
301. GEC, s.v. Southampton (Thomas Wriothesley).
302. See Hoak, p. 257.
303. Nott, I, xcvii. The poem was first published in 1815. The text has been more recently reprinted in *The Arundel Harington Manuscript of Tudor Poetry*, I, 344, and commented upon at II, 442-443.
304. *Trevelyan Papers*, pp. 206-216.
305. *Ibid.*, p. 209.
306. According to the DNB, Wriothesley had four sisters: Elizabeth and Anne, born in 1507 and 1508 respectively, and two additional sisters mentioned in his will. However, the will in fact mentions three sisters, one of whom, "Laurence," is the Anne mentioned in the DNB, and the other of whom, "Breton," is probably Elizabeth. The third sister, "Pounde," is Ellen, or Eleanor. The DNB also states

that Thomas had a brother, Edward, born in 1509. Edward probably died young, for nothing about his life can be found.

307. L & P XXI, Part 1, No. 302 (64), p. 149.

308. *The Herald & Genealogist*, II, p. 141. The settlement for the marriage of Anne Knight to Oliver Lawrence was dated 20 June 1549; Anne is said to have been living as late as 1608. "By Anne Wrythe or Wriothesley he [Oliver Lawrence] had issue three sons, and his descendants remained at Creech Grange in worshipful estate for five subsequent generations." *Ibid.* In the *Visitation of Lancashire* of 1567, Harleian Manuscript 891, appears a badge showing the arms of Lawrence (argent, a cross raguly gules) quartered with those of Washington (argent, two bars and in chief three mullets gules — i.e., red stripes and stars on a white background), which suggests an ancient connection betwen these two families, Nichols, pp. 142-143; 346-348, but when and by whom is unknown. Wriothesley's daughter Katherine, married one Thomas Cornwallis — a consequence of which is that the two generals who opposed each other at Yorktown were most probably of families distantly — very distantly — allied to each other through the sister and daughter of Thomas Wriothesley.

309. "Diocesan Returns of Recusants for England and Wales, 1577," p. 40. Ellen is sometimes said to have been the wife of John Ponde, Somerset Herald, but John Ponde, who was the second son of John Ponde of Drayton (see Godfrey, Wagner and London, p. 153), was probably a cousin of Ellen's husband.

310. *Lisle Letters*, 329.

311. "Diocesan Returns of Recusants for England and Wales, 1577," p. 40. Of Henry Pounde, little is known.

312. Chambers, *The Elizabethan Stage*, III, 468–469.

313. *Ibid.*, I, 162.

314. Stopes, *The Life of Henry Wriothesley, Third Earl of Southampton*, p. 501.

315. Chambers, *The Elizabethan Stage*, III, 468.

316. GEC, s.v. Sussex, Thomas Radcliffe (third Earl).

317. Chambers, *The Elizabethan Stage*, III, 468.

318. *Id.*

319. "Diocesan Returns of Recusants for England and Wales, 1577," p. 40; Chambers, *The Elizabethan Stage*, III, 468–469. See also, Foley, III, 568–657.

320. Berry, pp. 194–195; *Lisle Letters*, III, 329; "Brasses of the White Family at Southwick," pp. 86–87.

321. VCH, II, 168.

322. L & P XIII, Part 1, No. 748, pp. 281–282.

323. *Lisle Letters*, III, 331.

324. Berry, pp. 194–195; "Brasses of the White Family at Southwick," pp. 86–87.

325. This, and all the following information about the Breton family, including their connection with William Capon, comes from the will of William Breton, as printed in Grosart's edition of Breton's *Works*, I, xii–xvii.

326. Pinto, p. 238.

327. Breton, I, xi.

328. *Trevelyan Papers*, p. 214.

329. Breton, I, xi.

330. Flournoy, p. 267.
331. Chambers, *The Elizabethan Stage*, III, 320.
332. See Prouty, pp. 293-304.
333. Prouty, p. 62, suggests that Gascoigne's election was a reward for writing the Montagu-Dormer mask. But Gascoigne may never have served in Parliament: see SP Dom., 1547-1580, No. 59, p. 444, where reasons are given for opposing his being seated.
334. *Notes and Queries*, 10th Series, Vol. IV, Sept. 30, 1905, p. 271.
335. Breton, I, xi.
336. DNB, s.v. Capon, William.
337. *Id.*
338. See *supra*, p. 231 and also DNB, s.v. Capon, William.
339. *Trevelyan Papers*, pp. 207-208.
340. WP 281; GEC, s.v. Sussex, Thomas Radcliffe (third Earl).
341. WP 932; Greenfield, p. 70.
342. WP 933; Greenfield, p. 74. Lady Katherine Cornwallis, a recusant, was still alive in August 1604. CM XVI, p. 288.
343. WP 935; Greenfield, p. 74.
344. Goulding, p. 23.
345. See Rowse, *Shakespeare's Southampton*, p. 24.
346. Wriothesley had two other male children: William, who died in 1537, and Anthony, who died in about 1542. GEC, s.v. Southampton (Thomas Wriothesley).
347. See Appendix II.
348. Muller, pp. 218, 291
349. GEC, s.v. Paget of Beaudesert; Kingsford, "Essex House," pp. 6-8; Gammon, p. 168.
350. L & P XXI, Part 1, No. 1, p. 1.
351. DNB, s.v. Leland or Leyland, John.
352. *Id.*
353. SP VII, 485; also L & P VI, No. 806, p. 357.
354. Marriott, pp. 82, 131. Erasmus, in his biography of Colet, as printed in *Ecclesiastical Biography*, I, 44, states that the number of students in the school was limited to 153 because, as related in John XXI, ii, this was the number of fish caught by Simon Peter in the Sea of Tiberius when he cast his net where directed by Jesus after his resurrection.
355. Lancashire, p. 192.
356. Shapiro, p. 4.
357. Wilson, *English Drama*, p. 103; Marriott, p. 129.
358. Although the relationship of the St. Paul's grammar school with the St. Paul's Cathedral choir school is far from clear (see Marriott, pp. 132 and 202 on the one hand, and Bolwell, p. 49, on the other, as well as Motter, pp. 126-131), it is conceivable that Wriothesley, whose love of music we have had occasion to observe, not only acted with the St. Paul's grammar school boys but also sang with the St. Paul's Cathedral choir boys.

359. Lancashire, pp. 193–206. See also the list of Pageants, Masks and other Revels during the reign of Henry VIII in Bolwell, pp. 169–174.
360. Boas, *University Drama in the Tudor Age*, p. 14.
361. L & P XII, Part 1, No. 230, p. 112. Bales in 1549 wrote the Preface for the printed edition of Leland's *New Year's Gift* presented to Henry VIII in 1546. Dorsch, pp. 20, 23.
362. Jesse W. Harris, *Bale*, pp. 15–28.
363. See Chambers, *The Medieval Stage*, II, 443–452.
364. Bolwell, p. 80.
365. Edgerton, p. 116, note 10.
366. DNB, s.v. Udall or Uvedale, Nicholas.
367. Lee, *A Life of William Shakespeare*, p. 91.
368. Edgerton, pp. 37–38.
369. *Ibid.*, pp. 41–45; L & P XVIII, Part 2, No. 545, p. 290.
370. Edgerton, p. 39.
371. Bolwell, pp. 19, 33.
372. *Ibid.*, pp. 62–63.
373. Chambers, *The Medieval Stage*, II, 444.
374. Jesse W. Harris, pp. 27, 28.
375. Chambers, *The Medieval Stage*, II, 448–449; Bullough, IV, 3–4.
376. Such letters as survive from Wriothesley to Wyatt (printed in Nott, II, 421–429), consist primarily of instructions to Wyatt in his capacity as the King's ambassador in Spain, but they also touch upon personal matters, such as Wriothesley's purchase from Wyatt of land in Hampshire (Nott, II, 425; apparently what Wriothesley bought was the reversion), and are all written in an intimate and friendly manner reflecting a personal, as well as a professional, relationship. On 17 January 1541, Wyatt was arrested for treason. The charge against him was that on an occasion when Wyatt was ambassador to the Emperor, he plotted with Cardinal Pole against the King. L &P XVI, Nos. 640 and 641, pp. 304–310. Wriothesley, for once, seems not to have participated in preparing a case against the accused. Wyatt was pardoned on 21 March 1541, before any trial. L & P XVI, No. 641, fn., p. 306. (Muir, who states at page 214 of his *Life and Letters of Sir Thomas Wyatt* that Wriothesley was one of his judges in a 1541 trial, is in error.) Wyatt died in 1542, while again serving as ambassador for the king. His friend, John Leland, wrote in Latin a number of Elegies (Nott, II, ciii–cx; Muir, pp. 261–269), which he addressed to Wyatt's friend, Henry Howard, the Earl of Surrey.
377. Akrigg, *Shakespeare and the Earl of Southampton*, p. 223.
378. L & P Addenda, I, Part 2, No. 1304, pp. 445–446.
379. As, for example, Thomas Audley (who preceded Wriothesley as Lord Chancellor), Sir Richard Rich (who succeeded him), Thomas Cromwell, Lord Lisle, the Earl of Arundel, the Duke of Somerset, Sir Ralph Sadler, etc. Murray, I, 297; II, 20, 36, 51, 68, 77, 94; see also Chambers, *The Elizabethan Stage*, Volume II.
380. He may be the John Hemings of London who in a grant of arms made in 1629 is described as "Sonne and Heire of George Hemings of Draytwiche in the

Countye of Worcester Gent." Chambers, *Elizabethan Stage*, II, p. 321. Droitwich is a town near Worcester. Of George Hemings, I have been able to find no record.

381. Tyson, p. 13.
382. *Collectanea Topographica*, VII, pp. 394–400.
383. Sidney Lee, *Great Englishmen*, p. 274.
384. DNB, s.v. Pope, Sir Thomas.
385. Sidney Lee, *Great Englishmen*, p. 274; Adams, pp. 247–248.
386. CM XIII, p. 27.
387. DNB, s.v. Herbert, Sir William, first Earl of Pembroke of the second creation, and Herbert, William, third Earl of Pembroke.

Notes to Appendix II — Titchfield House

1. *Titchfield, A History*, p. 6.
2. *Ibid.*, p. 7.
3. *Ibid.*, p. 12.
4. Hare, *The Parish Church of St. Peter, Titchfield, Fareham*, p. 7.
5. *Titchfield, A History*, pp. 13–14.
6. Minns, "Titchfield Abbey and Place House," pp. 318–319.
7. VCH, II, 181.
8. *Ibid.*, 222.
9. *Ibid.*, 181, 182.
10. Graham and Rigold, p. 6. The legend on the engraving of Titchfield Abbey reproduced as Figure 8 recites that "the marriage of K. H. 6th with Margaret of Anjou was here solemnized," but other sources state that this event occurred at Southwick Priory. See VCH, II, 161; Minns, "Titchfield Abbey and Place House," p. 323. Yet another source reports that Margaret and Henry VI were married at the Parish Church at Titchfield. G. H. Green, *Southwick Priory*, p. 324.
11. VCH, II, 185.
12. Indicative of a keen interest in acquiring Titchfield Abbey, regardless of its not falling within the letter of the statute, are L & P XII, Part 1, No.1108, p. 517 and L & P XII, Part 2, No. 1159, p. 412.
13. L & P XII, Part 2, No. 1274, p. 446.
14. L & P XII, Part 2, No. 1238, pp. 434–435.
15. This appearance of the word "quondam," used as a noun, to designate a former member of a monastic order — of whom there must have been thousands in England after 1539 — may provide the solution to the mystery of the origin of the word "condom." In *The Labyrinth of Shakespeare's Sonnets*, pp. 22–24, I showed that "quondam," in Shakespeare's time, was pronounced "condom," and I suggested that a number of Shakespearean lines, such as

Your *quondam* wife swears still by *Venus* Glove,
[*Troilus and Cressida*, IV, v, 179, following typography in First Folio]

389

have a mordant wit about them, if the word "quondam" is understood to be a punning reference to "condom." This observation was made in aid of an interpretation of Sonnet 34 to the effect that the "cloak" therein referred to was a protective device like a condom; I pointed out that *any* article of clothing is an apt metaphor for "condom," and noted that common French terms for that device are articles of clothing: "la redingote anglaise" (English coat or cloak) — and "la capote anglaise" (English cloak). But I was unable to offer any explanation for the origin of the word. (Nor has anyone else explained the word; see William E. Kruck's *Looking for Dr. Condom* (University of Alabama Press, 1981).) Now, however, I venture to suggest that the quondams of England, going about the countryside in their monastic garb, often wearing hoods or cowls, were the inspiration for the term. The quondams persisted in wearing their habits, out of habit: DNB, s. v. Cromwell, Thomas, relates that Cromwell, "happening to meet one Friar Bartley near St. Paul's still wearing his cowl after the suppression, 'Yea,' said Cromwell, 'will not that cowl of yours be left off yet? And if I hear by one o'clock that this apparel be not changed, thou shalt be hanged immediately, for example to all others.'" Cromwell could not police all of England, however, and we may suppose that many cowl-wearing quondams in the provinces escaped his notice, and were a striking enough part of the landscape to give their name to the then newly-devised disease prevention sheathe, which physically and functionally resembled their cowls, hoods and capes. (The use of the word "quondam" in the quoted letter as a noun is not unique; other examples in the L & P are VII, No. 1658, p. 613; XII, Part 2, No. 822, p. 289; XIII, Part 1, No. 19, p. 6 and No. 847, p. 314.)

I also speculated that Shakespeare had a special connection with condoms, and that his father, who was a glover, may have been in the business of making them (for they were then made of soft animal skins). It has since occurred to me that Robert Greene's famous attack upon "*those Gentlemen of his Quondam acquaintance, that spend their wits in making plaies,*" (see Chapter VI, p. 161) may be an allusion to that connection; if we remember the old meaning of "spend" (to ejaculate), and are aware of Herbert A. Ellis' discovery that "wit" to Elizabethans meant the sexual organs of either sex (Ellis, pp. 103–110), then Greene's line becomes especially apposite and sarcastic.

16. L & P XII, Part 2, No. 1245, pp. 436–437.
17. L & P, XII, Part 2, No. 1311(40), p. 473.
18. Hope, "The Making of Place House," pp. 233–235.
19. L & P XII, Part 2, No. 1270, pp. 444–445.
20. L & P XIII, No. 20, p. 7.
21. Prior to entering into Wriothesley's service, Anthony Roke had been a servant to Catherine of Aragon. See L & P XI, No. 1082, p. 435; No. 1436, p. 573, and XIV, No. 190, p. 71.
22. Hope, "The Making of Place House," p. 236.
23. L & P Addenda, Part 1, No. 1304, p. 445.
24. L & P, XII, Part 2, No. 642, p. 287. Although this is printed in the L & P as though dated 12 March 1536/7, it actually must have been written on 12 March 1537/8. On 25 March 1538 (L & P XIII, No. 594, p. 220), Richard Lee writes

to Wriothesley that "my ship has come thither with your stuff," and the letter of Crayford to Wriothesley dated 12 April 1538, quoted in the text at endnote marker 27, refers to the "stone & freight which now ys comed from Cane."

25. VCH, II, 168.
26. Mr. Bertie is the founder of one of the most upwardly mobile families in all of Tudor history. The man we here encounter is Thomas, a mason working upon the renovation of Titchfield Abbey; his son Richard, who was born in 1516 or 1517, was admitted to Oxford on 17 February 1533/4, subsequently joined the household of Sir Thomas Wriothesley, and thereafter became a member of the household of the dowager Duchess of Suffolk, who was the daughter of William, the Lord Willoughby de Eresby and Maria de Salines (or Saluces), a Spanish lady who had come to England as a maid of honour to Queen Catherine. This girl was only 15 when she was married to Charles Brandon, Duke of Suffolk, and 26 when he died in 1545. In spite of her background, the Duchess was of the reform party in the matter of religion. Richard Bertie and the Duchess were married in 1552. In 1554, Stephen Gardiner, after first inquiring of master sergeant Stampford about Richard Bertie, "because master sergeant was towards the lord Wriothesley, late earl of Southampton and chancellor of England, with whom the said master Berty was brought up" (Foxe, VIII, 570; *quaere*, whether this master sergeant Stampford was the William Samford mentioned in Wriothesley's will?), summoned Richard Bertie, to discuss his wife's religious views, and to exhort him to change those views. Not long after, Bertie and his wife left England for the continent, where their son Peregrine was born, on 12 October 1555. After Elizabeth came to the throne, they returned to England, where Peregrine was accorded the title of Lord Willoughby de Eresby. Peregrine, who lived in Cripplegate in Barbican House, married Mary, daughter of John Vere, the 16th Earl of Oxford. His eldest son, Robert, born in 1582 (created Earl of Lindsey in 1626) married Elizabeth, daughter of Edward, Lord Montague. Round, *Peerage and Pedigree*, I, 34–54; DNB, s.v. Bertie, Richard, and Bertie, Robert, first Earl of Lindsey; *A Memoir of Peregrine Bertie*, p. 91.
27. Hope, "The Making of Place House," p. 237.
28. *Ibid.*, p. 240.
29. Leland, I, 281.
30. Graham and Rigold, p. 6.
31. Graham and Rigold, plan inside back cover.
32. *Ibid.*, p. 16.
33. Woodward, p. 386. See footnote 38 for a slightly different blazon.
34. Rothery, p. 328; see also, Franklyn, pp. 17-18; *The Manual of Heraldry*, p. 17, and almost any book on heraldry. Some authorities, e.g., Fox-Davies, *A Complete Guide to Heraldry*, p. 132, state that although a chief is theoretically the uppermost third of the area of the field, it is usually drawn to contain about one-fifth of the area of the field.
35. Berners, the fourth page following the signature b iii.
36. Bossewell, p. ci^v. This excerpt, together with the one from *The Book of St. Albans*, indicates that W. H. St. John Hope was not correct in stating (in *A*

Grammar of English Heraldry, p. 11), that "in early heraldry there was practically no difference between a chief and party fessewise."

37. The fess point is the exact centre of an escutcheon, and a shield "party per fess" is parted in the centre by a horizontal line through the fess point. *The Manual of Heraldry*, pp. 77 and 104.

38. Randle Holme, in that part of *The Academy of Armory* which was not published in his lifetime, gives as the arms for Southwick Priory "A[rgent] on a cheif [sic], S[able] 2 roses, A[rgent] buttoned or Leaved, V[ert]." Exactly what this means is not clear. "Buttoned" could be a mistransliteration of "Barbed," which means "with little green leaves around the rose," and thus the words "or leaved" could be merely an alternate description of the same little green leaves. Again, "leaved" could be intended to mean "slipped," that is, showing a stalk and a leaf. Or (and this seems to me most likely) "buttoned" could mean "seeded" — that is, with little round seeds or buttons showing; "leaved" could mean "barbed"; and the "or," instead of being a conjunction, could be the heraldic colour, Or, so that the blazon is intended to be the very frequently encountered "seeded Or barbed." All of which would further negate the likelihood that the chief on the Southwick arms would be charged with Tudor roses. The blazon here discussed is found on page 291 of the Roxburghe Club's 1905 edition of the "second volume" of Holme's *Academy of Armory*. The first volume was published in 1688, but Holme was unable to raise the money to publish the rest of his work.

39. Hope, *Cowdray and Easebourne Priory*, pp. 109-110.
40. Minns, "Titchfield Abbey and Place House," p. 335, note 2.
41. Hope, *Cowdray and Easebourne Priory*, p. 71.
42. DNB, s.v. Wriothesley, Sir Thomas.
43. Akrigg, *Shakespeare and the Earl of Southampton*, p. 11.
44. DNB, s.v. Wriothesley, Sir Thomas.
45. DNB, s.v. Wriothesley, Henry.
46. Hare, "Documentary Evidence for the Southampton Monument in Titchfield Church."
47. *Ibid.*
48. Akrigg, *Shakespeare and the Earl of Southampton*, p. 131.
49. DNB, s.v. Wriothesley, Sir Thomas (fourth Earl of Southampton).
50. *Ibid.*
51. Ibid. See also, Godwin, pp. 263-268.
52. DNB, s.v. Wriothesley, Sir Thomas (fourth Earl of Southampton). This Cromwell, of course, is Oliver Cromwell, the Protector. He was the grandson of "a certain Richard Williams, who rose to fortune by the protection of Thomas Cromwell, Earl of Essex, and adopted the name of his patron." DNB, s.v. Cromwell, Oliver.
53. During the years 1903 to 1905, Louis Ambler, who had been commissioned by Lord Montagu of Beaulieu to restore the Wriothesley Tomb, interested himself in the Wriothesley family genealogy, and, apparently thinking that they might wish to contribute toward the cost of restoring the Monument, prepared a list of then-living peers descended from the Wriothesleys. The list compiled by Ambler, the original of which is in the Muniment Room at Beaulieu, is here set forth:

Duke of Abercorn;
" " Argyl;
" " Atholl;
" " Beaufort;
" " Bedford;
" " Buccleuch;
" " Devonshire;
" " Leinster;
" " Marlborough;
" " Newcastle;
" " Norfolk
" " Northumberland;
" " Portland;
" " Roxburghe;
" " Rutland;
" " Sutherland;
" " Westminster;
Marquess of Bath;
" " Bristol;
" " Camden;
" " Lothian;
" " Waterford;
Earl of Amherst;
" " Ashburnham;
" " Aylesford;
" " Bessborough;
" " Bradford;
" " Carlisle;
" " Clancarty;
" " Courtown;
" " Crewe;
Countess of Cromartie;
Earl of Dartmouth;
" " Devon;
" " Drogheda;
" " Durham;
" " Ellesmere;
" " Essex;
" " Fitzwilliam;
" " Galloway

Earl of Granville;
" " Harewood;
" " Harrowby;
" " Home;
" " Ilchester;
" " Kinnoull;
" " Lichfield;
" " Londesborough;
" " Macclesfield;
" " Mexborough;
" " Oxford;
" " Portsmouth;
" " Romney;
" " Russell;
" " St. Germans;
" " Shaftesbury;
" " Shannon;
" " Wharncliffe;
" " Wilton;
Viscount Churchill;
Baron Ampthill;
" Arundell of Wardour;
" Ashburton;
" Calthorp;
" Clonbrook;
" De Clifford;
" De Mauley;
" Digby;
" Foley;
" Forester;
" Fortescue;
" Hatherton;
" Hillington;
" Howard de Walden;
" Howard of Glossop;
" Lamington;
" Montagu of Beaulieu;
" Redesdale;
" Stalbridge;
" Wenlock.

Ambler's list of 80 peers seems to include only persons whose ancestry was traced back to the three daughters of the fourth Earl, thus excluding many persons whose ancestry might be traced back to the daughters of the first, second and third Earls or a sister of the first Earl. The list does not do as much credit to the fecundity of the Wriothesleys as may at first appear to be the case, for all of these peers, if they are descended from the Earls of Southampton, are equally the descendants of hundreds of other Tudor persons, famous and unknown, high born and low. Indeed, as a pure matter of mathematics and genetics, there are probably few people in England today of whatever level of society who could not trace their ancestry back to a Tudor Wriothesley.

54. WP, Introduction and Index, pp. v-vi.
55. Trent, p. 167. See also, Russell, p. 90.
56. WP, Introduction and Index, p. vi. See also, Montagu of Beaulieu, pp. 40, 54–70.
57. *WP, Introduction and Index*, p. vi.
58. *Bucks' Antiquities*, I, Plate 111.
59. These rooms are listed in the various inventories among the Wriothesley Papers. There were inventories in 1699 (WP 1444), 1710 (WP 1446), 1717 (WP 1445), 1719 (WP 1447), 1723 (WP 1448 and 1449), and 1741 (WP 1451). The 1699 inventory lists the following rooms: King's Room, Little Room in King's Room, King's Drawing Room, Closet Adjoining, Queen's Room, Queen's Drawing Room, Gatehouse Chamber, Gallery (with "25 large old pictures"), Gallery closet, Drawing Room, Great Dining Room, Little Dining Room, Lord's Dressing Room and Footman's Room, Ladies' Passage, Anne Speershot's Room, Mrs. Rosse's Roome, Mrs. Knottsford's Chamber, Laundry Maids' Room, Virgins' Hall, The Room next Mrs. Sparke's, the Walcott's Room, Richard Lewis' Room, Cooke's Room, Thomas Nelson's Room, Br. Bruie's Room, John the Shooter's Room, First Matted Room, Mr. Griffith's Chamber, Giles' Room, Ann Green's Room, Thomas Bradfield's room, Auditt Room, Mr. Newsham's Chamber, Mr.Newsham's Closet, Mrs. Sparke's Room, Further Matted Room, Lodge, Steward's room, Gardner's room, Kitchen, Linen, Coachman's Room, Solamen's room, The Gentlemen of the Horses' Rooms, Hall, Glass Room, Servants' Hall, Dairy, Laundry, Wash House, Still House and Small Roome, Sellers and Brewhouse, Ward Robe, Long Gallery, and Evidence Room.
60. WP 1558.
61. WP 450.
62. WP 1560.
63. Scott-Giles, *Shakespeare's Heraldry*, p. 190.
64. Barrington, p. 200.
65. Scott-Giles, *Shakespeare's Heraldry*, p. 190.
66. Barrington, p. 199.
67. Rothery, p. 186.
68. *Ibid.*, p. 227.
69. The windows in the Victoria and Albert Museum bear the acquisition numbers C-452-1919, C-453-1919, C-454-1919 and C-455-1919; the windows in the Burrell Collection, in Glasgow, bear the acquisition numbers 45/180, 45/181, 45/182/,45/183, 45/184, 45/185, 45/186 and 45/187. These windows were purchased by both museums from the collection of one A. L. Radford, who wrote that "some years since, near Guildford, I obtained a great treasure trove of ancient art, which once adorned some regal palace of the time of Henry the Eighth. This conclusion I come at, from the circumstance that the glass is chiefly

of that period; and that it is regal, the badges of Henry VII. and VIII., Jane Seymour, Katherine Parr, and upwards of 20 different crowns, denote. When I obtained this treasure, it was in newspapers 60 years old, and I think had never seen the light during that time." Radford's surmise was that these windows came ultimately from Nonsuch, which was pulled down by the Duchess of Portsmouth, and its glass and art objects used for a house built by the Duchess near Guildford, which house in turn was pulled down at about the date of the papers in which the windows were wrapped when Radford acquired them. Of course, as Achard's sketches demonstrate, the regal heraldry of the windows does not necessarily indicate their origin in a royal residence, but even if Radford is correct in his surmise, the windows in the Victoria and Albert and Glasgow Museums must resemble closely the windows at Titchfield. For the information in this footnote, I am indebted to D.M. Archer, of the Department of Ceramics, Victoria and Albert Museum, London, and Linda Fraser, Stained Glass Conservation, the Burrell Collection, Glasgow.

70. Rothery, p. 187.
71. Greenfield, p. 77.
72. Minns, "Titchfield Abbey and Place House," p. 331.
73. [Boswell], XX, 434.
74. Graham and Rigold, p. 8.

BIBLIOGRAPHY

Of Books and Articles cited in the text and footnotes.

(Editions of Shakespeare's poems and plays are listed alphabetically by editor.)

Abbot, Edwin A., *Bacon and Essex* (London: Seeley, Jackson, & Halliday, 1877).

Acheson, Arthur, *Shakespeare's Sonnet Story* (New York: Edmond Byrne Hackett, 1933).

Acts of the Privy Council of England, 32 vols., ed. John Roche Dasent (London: HMSO, 1890-1907).

Adams, Joseph Quincy, *A Life of William Shakespeare* (Boston: Houghton Mifflin, 1923).

Akrigg, C.P.V., "The Curious Marginalia of Charles, Second Lord Stanhope," *Joseph Quincy Adams Memorial Studies* (Washington: Folger Shakespeare Library, 1948).

————, *Jacobean Pageant* (London: Hamish Hamilton, 1962).

————, *Shakespeare and the Earl of Southampton* (London: Hamish Hamilton, 1968).

[Anstis, John,] *The Register of the Most Noble Order of the Garter* (London: Barker, 1724).

Arundel Harington Manuscript of Tudor Poetry, ed. Ruth B. Hughey, 2 vols. (Ohio State University Press, 1960).

Astronomici Veteres, Iulii firmici libri octo, Marci Manili libre quinque . . . Procli Sphaera Thoma Linacro britanno interprete (Venice: Aldus Manutius, 1499).

Aubrey's Brief Lives, ed. Oliver Lawson Dick (University of Michigan Press, 1957).

Bacon, Francis, "The Use of the Law," *Works*, ed. James Spedding, Robert Leslie Ellis, Douglas Denon Heath, Vol. XIV (Boston: Brown and Taggard, 1861).

Baedeker, Karl, *London and its Environs* (Leipzig: Karl Baedeker, various years, as cited in text).

Bakeless, John, *The Tragicall History of Christopher Marlowe*, 2 vols. (Harvard University Press, 1942).

Baldick, Julian, *Mystical Islam* (New York University Press, 1989).

Baldwin, T. W., *On the Literary Genetics of Shakespeare's Poems and Sonnets* (Urbana: University of Illinois Press, 1950).

Ballads from Manuscripts, ed. Frederick J. Furnivall (London: Taylor and Co., 1868–1872).

Banks, Thomas C., *The Dormant and Extinct Baronage of England* (London, 1809).

Barber, C.L., "An Essay on Shakespeare's Sonnets," in *Shakespeare's Sonnets*, ed. Harold Bloom (Philadelphia: Chelsea House, 1987).

Barnes, Barnabe, *Parthenophil and Parthenophe*, ed. Victor A. Doyno (Southern Illinois University Press, 1971).

Barnfield, Richard, *The Complete Poems*, ed. The Rev. Alexander B. Grosart (The Roxburghe Club. London: J.B. Nichols & Sons, 1876).

Barrington, Archibald, *A Familiar Introduction to Heraldry* (London: H. G. Bohn, 1848).

Bartlett, Alan, *Beaulieu in Tudor and Stuart Times* (Hampshire Record Office, 1973) (typewritten manuscript).

Bates, Steven L. and Sidney D. Orr, *A Concordance to the Poems of Ben Jonson* (Ohio University Press, 1978).

BIBLIOGRAPHY

Beal, Samuel, "A Brief Account of the Manor and Parish Church of Green's Norton, Alias Norton Davey," printed in (partial) facsimile edition of *Succinct Genealogical Proofs of the House of Greene, that were Lords of Drayton* by Robert Halstead, 1685 (New York: Francis Vinton Greene, 1896).

Beaumont and Fletcher, *Works*, 11 vols., ed. Alexander Dyce (London, E. Moxon, 1843-1846; facsimile edition by Books for Libraries Press, Freport, New York, 1970).

[Begley, Walter], *Is it Shakespeare?* (London, John Murray, 1903).

Benner, Allen Rogers, and Francis H. Fobes, *The Letters of Alciphron, Aelian and Philostratus*, Loeb Classical Library No. 383 (Harvard University Press, 1979).

Benson, John, ed., *Poems Written by Wil. Shakespeare, Gent.* (London: Tho. Cotes, 1640; reprinted by Smith, London, 1885).

Berdan, John M., *Early Tudor Poetry* (New York: The Macmillan Company, 1920).

Berners, Dame Juliana, *Book Containing the Treatises of Hawking, Hunting, Coat-Armour, Fishing, and Blasing of Arms* [generally called *The Book of Saint Albans*] *As printed at Westminster by Wynkyn de Worde, the Year of the Incarnation of our Lord MCCCCLxxxxvi*, ed. Joseph Haslewood (London: White and Cochrane, 1810; reprinted by Abercrombie & Fitch, New York, 1966).

Berry, William, *Pedigrees of the Families in the County of Hants* (London: Sherwood Gilbert and Piper, 1833).

Birch, Thomas, *Memoirs of the Reign of Queen Elizabeth*, 2 vols. (London: A. Millar, 1754).

Black's Guide to Hampshire (Edinburgh: Adam and Charles Black, 1875).

Blok, P. J., ed., "Correspondance inédite de Robert Dudley . . . et de Francois et Jean Hotman," *Archives du Musée Teyler*, Serie II, Vol. XII, Deuxième partie (Haarlem: Les Héritiers Loosjes, 1911).

Blore, Edward, *Remains of Noble and Eminent Persons* (London: Harding, Lepard & Co., 1826).

Blum, Rudolf, *La Biblioteca della Badia Fiorentina, e i codici di Antonio Corbinelli* (Città del Vaticano: Biblioteca Apostolica Vaticana, 1951).

Boas, Frederick S., *Christopher Marlowe* (Oxford: Clarendon Press, 1940).

———, *University Drama in the Tudor Age* (Oxford, 1914).

Bolwell, Robert W., *The Life and Works of John Heywood* (New York: Columbia University Press, 1921).

Bone, James, *London Echoing* (London: Jonathan Cape, 1948).

Booth, Stephen, ed., *Shakespeare's Sonnets* (New Haven: Yale University Press, 1977).

Bossewell, John, *Works of Armorie* (London: Richard Tottell, 1572; facsimile edition by Theatrum Orbis Terrarum Ltd., Amsterdam and Da Capo Press, New York, 1969).

Bossy, John, *Giordano Bruno and the Embassy Affair* (Yale University Press, 1991).

[Boswell, John, ed.], *The Plays and Poems of William Shakespeare*, 21 vols., (London: F.C. and J. Rivington, et al., 1821).

Boutell, Charles, *English Heraldry* (London: Reeves & Turner, 1883).

Boutell's Heraldry, ed. J. P. Brooke-Little (London: Frederick Warne & Co., 1970).

Bowle, John, *Henry VIII* (London: Allen and Unwin, 1965).

398

Bradbrook, M. C., *Shakespeare and Elizabethan Poetry* (London: Chatto and Windus, 1951).

Bradner, Leicester, "The First Cambridge Production of Miles Gloriosus," *Modern Language Notes*, LXX, No. 6, June, 1955.

"Brasses of the White Family at Southwick," *Papers and Proceedings of the Hampshire Field Club, 1894-1897* (Southampton, 1898).

Bredbeck, Gregory W., *Sodomy and Interpretation — Marlowe to Milton* (Cornell University Press, 1991).

Breton, Nicholas, *Works*, ed. Alexander B. Grosart, 2 vols. (Edinburgh: T. and A. Constable, 1879).

Bright, Timothy, *A Treatise of Melancholie* (London: Thomas Vautrollier, 1586; facsimile edition by Da Capo Press, Amsterdam, New York, 1969).

Brittons Bowre of Delights 1591, ed. Hyder Edward Rollins (New York: Russell & Russell, 1968.)

Brooke, Ralph, *A Discoverie of Certaine Errors Published in Print in the Much Commended Britannia* (London, 1595).

Brooke, Tucker, ed., *Shakespeare's Sonnets* (Oxford University Press, 1936).

————, ed., *The Works of Christopher Marlowe* (Oxford: Clarendon Press, 1910).

Brooks, Alden, *Will Shakspere and the Dyer's Hand* (New York: Charles Scribner's Sons, 1943).

Brown, A.D. Fitton, "Drink to me, Celia," *Modern Language Review*, Vol. LIV (Cambridge University Press, 1959).

Brown, Charles Armitage, *Shakespeare's Autobiographical Poems* (London: James Bohn, 1838).

Brown, Ivor, *Shakespeare* (London: The Reprint Society, 1951).

Brown, P. Hume, *George Buchanan, Humanist and Reformer* (Edinburgh: David Douglas, 1890).

Buck's Antiquities (London: Robert Sayer, 1774).

Bullen, A. H., ed., *Shorter Elizabethan Poems* (Westminster: Archibald Constable and Co., Ltd., 1903).

————, *Some Longer Elizabethan Poems* (Westminster: Archibald Constable and Co., Ltd., 1903).

Bullough, Geoffrey, *Narrative and Dramatic Sources of Shakespeare*, 8 vols (London: Routledge and Kegan Paul, 1966-1975).

Burke, John Bernard, *The General Armory* (London, 1884; reprinted by Genealogical Publishing Co., Baltimore, 1969).

————, *A General Heraldic Dictionary of the Peerage and Baronetage of the British Empire* (London: Colborn and Bentley, 1832).

Burnet, Gilbert, *The History of the Reformation of the Church of England*, 4 vols. (London: J. F. Dove. 1830).

Burton, Robert, *Anatomy of Melancholy*, ed. Floyd Dell and Paul Jordan-Smith (New York: Tudor Publishing Company, 1948).

————, *Anatomy of Melancholy*, ed. The Rev. A. D. Shilleto, 3 vols. (London: George Bell & Sons, 1893).

399

BIBLIOGRAPHY

Burton, Robert, *Philophaster*, ed. Paul Jordan Smith (Stanford University Press, 1931).

Burton, William, *Description of Leicestershire* (London: John White, 1622).

B[urton], W[illiam], tr. *The Most Delectable and Pleasaunt History of Clitiphon and Leucippe*, by Achilles Statius [i.e., Tatius], eds. Stephen Gaselee and H.F.B. Brett-Smith (Oxford: Basil Blackwell, 1923).

Bush, Douglas, and Harbage, Alfred, eds., *Shakespeare's Sonnets* (Baltimore: Penguin Books, 1961).

Butler, Samuel, ed., *Shakespeare's Sonnets* (London: A.C. Fifield, 1899(?)).

Buxton, John, *Sir Philip Sidney and the English Renaissance* (London: Macmillan & Co., 1954).

Byrne, Muriel St. Clare, "The Foundations of Elizabethan Language," *Shakespeare Survey*, No. 17 (Cambridge University Press, 1965).

Calendar of the Inner Temple Records, ed. F. A. Inderwick (London: Masters of the Bench, 1896).

Calendar of the Manuscripts of the Marquis of Salisbury, Preserved at Hatfield House, Herfordshire, 24 vols., London: HMSO, 1883-1976).

Calendar of the Patent Rolls, Edward VI, 5 vols., *Philip and Mary*, 4 vols., *Elizabeth*, 2 vols. [volumes identified in text by years covered], (London: HMSO, 1924-1929, 1936-1939, 1939-1948).

Calendar of State Papers, Domestic Series, of the reigns of Edward VI, Mary, Elizabeth, James I and *Charles I*, ed. Robert Lemon, Mary A. E. Green, John Bruce [volumes identified in text by years covered], (London: Longman, Brown, Green, Longmans and Roberts, 1856-1872).

Calendar of State Papers, Foreign Series, of the reigns of Edward VI, Mary and Elizabeth, William B. Turnbull, Joseph Stevenson, *et al.* [volumes identified in text by years covered], (London: Longman, Green, Longman & Roberts, 1861-1950).

Calendar of State Papers, Ireland, Vol. IX, 1600, March-October, ed. Ernest George Atkinson (London, HMSO, 1903).

Calendar of State Papers, Scotland, Vol. VIII, 1585-1586, ed. William K. Boyd (Edinburgh, HMSO, 1914).

Calendar of State Papers Relating to Spain, ed. G. A. Bergenroth, Pascual de Gayangos, Garrett Mattingly, M. A. S. Hume and Royall Tyler, 13 volumes and 2 supplements (London, 1862-1954).

Calendar of State Papers, Venice, VI, Part 1, 1555-1556, ed. Rawdon Brown (London: Longman & Co., 1877).

Camden, William, *Britannia* [Latin] (London: Georgii Bishop, 1607).

———, *Britannia. Newly Translated into English* (London, Edward Gibson, 1698).

———, *The Historie of the Most Renowned and Victorious Princesse Elizabeth, Late Queen of England* (London: Benjamin Fisher, 1630).

———, *Remains Concerning Britain* (London: John Russell Smith, 1870).

Campbell, John, *The Lives of the Lord Chancellors and Keepers of the Great Seal of England*, 10 vols., (London: John Murray, 1846 (2nd ed.)).

Campion, Thomas, *Works*, ed. Percival Vivian (Oxford: Clarendon Press, 1909).

Cartwright, Julia, *Christina of Denmark, Duchess of Milan and Lorraine* (New York: E. P. Dutton, 1913).

Casady, Edwin, *Henry Howard, Earl of Surrey* (New York: Modern Language Association of America, 1938).

Cavendish, George, *Thomas Wolsey*, ed. Roger Lockyer (London: Folio Press, 1973).

———, *The Life of Cardinal Wolsey*, ed. Samuel Weller Singer (London: Harding & Leopard, 1827).

Challis, C.E., *The Tudor Coinage* (Manchester University Press, 1978).

Chamberlain's Letters During the Reign of Queen Elizabeth, ed. Sarah Williams (London, Camden Society (No. 79), 1861).

Chambers, E.K., *The Elizabethan Stage*, 4 vols. (Oxford, 1923).

———, *The Medieval Stage*, 2 vols. (Oxford, 1903).

———, *William Shakespeare: A Study of Facts and Problems*, 2 vols. (Oxford: Clarendon Press, 1930).

Chambrun, Clara (Longworth), Countess de, *The Sonnets of William Shakespeare* (New York: G. P. Putnam's Sons, 1913).

Chancellor, E. Beresford, *The Annals of the Strand* (London: Chapman & Hall, LImited, 1912).

Chapman, George, *The Poems*, ed. Phyllis Brooks Bartlett (New York: Modern Language Association of America, 1941).

Chapter Acts of the Cathedral Church of St. Mary of Lincoln, ed. E. E. G. Cole (Horncastle: Lincoln Record Society, 1920).

The Charters of the Borough of Southampton, ed. H. W. Gidden (Southampton: Cox & Sharland, 1909).

Chew, Samuel C., "This Strange Eventful History," *Joseph Quincy Adams Memorial Studies* (Washington: Folger Shakespeare Library, 1948).

Child, Heather, *Heraldic Design* (London: G. Bell, 1965).

Clapham, John, *Elizabeth of England: Certain Observations Concerning the Life and Reign of Queen Elizabeth*, ed. Evelyn Plummer Read and John Conyers Read (University of Pennsylvania Press, 1951).

Clarendon, Edward, Earl of, *The History of the Rebellion and Civil Wars in England* (Oxford University Press, 1843).

Cleugh, James, *Love Locked Out* (New York: Crown Publishers, 1964).

Cliffe, J.T., *The Yorkshire Gentry* (University of London, 1969).

Cokayne, G.E., *Complete Peerage of England, Scotland, Ireland, etc.*, 14 vols. (London: St. Catherine Press, 1910-1959).

Collectanea Topographica, 8 vols. (London: J. B. Nichols, 1834-1843).

Colet, John, *An Exposition of St. Paul's First Epistle to the Corinthians*, ed. J. H. Lupton (London: George Bell and Sons, 1874).

Collier, J. Payne, ed., *The Works of Edmund Spenser*, 5 vols. (London, Bickers and Son, 1873).

Collins, John Churton, *Studies in Shakespeare* (Westminster: Archibald Constable & Co. Ltd., 1904).

401

BIBLIOGRAPHY

A Complete Collection of State Trials and Proceedings for High Treason and other Crimes and Misdemeanors, 4th ed., 11 vols. in 6 (London: T. Wright, 1776-1781).

Coningsby, Sir Thomas, "Journal of the Siege of Rouen, 1591" (London: Camden Society (No. 39), 1847).

Constable, Henry, *The Poems*, ed. Joan Grundy (Liverpool University Press, 1960).

Constant, G., *The Reformation in England: The English Schism (1509 - 1547)*, trans., The Rev. R. E. Scantlebury (New York: Sheed & Ward, n.d.).

Conway, Eustace, *Anthony Munday and Other Essays* (New York, 1927).

Cooke's Baronage, British Museum, Harley 216.

Correspondence of John Cosin, D.D., ed. George Ornsby, Surtees Society, Vol. LII (London, 1869).

Correspondence of King James I with Robert Cecil and Others, ed. John Bruce (London: Camden Society (No. 78), 1861).

Correspondence of Sir Philip Sidney and Hubert Languet, tr. and ed., Steuart A. Pears (London: William Pickering, 1845).

Court Leet Records, ed. F.J.C. and D.M. Hearnshaw (Southampton: M. Gilbert & Son, 1906).

Crane, Eva, *Honey, A Comprehensive Survey* (New York: Crane, Russak, 1975).

Cuffe, Henry, *The Difference of the Ages of Mans Life* (London: Arnold Hatfield for Martin Clearke, 1607).

Davison, Francis, *A Poetical Rhapsody*, 2 vols., ed. Hyder Edward Rollins (Harvard University Press, 1931).

De Roover, Raymond, *Gresham on Foreign Exchange* (Harvard University Press, 1949).

Devereux, Walter Bourchier, *Lives and Letters of the Devereux, Earls of Essex*, 2 vols. (London: John Murray, 1853).

Devlin, Christopher, *Hamlet's Divinity* (New York: Books for Libraries Press, 1970).

————, *The Life of Robert Southwell, Poet and Martyr* (London: Sidgwick & Jackson, 1967).

The Diary of Sir Simonds D'Ewes, ed. Elisabeth Bourcier (Paris: Didier, n. d.).

Dickenson, John, *Prose and Verse*, ed. the Rev. Alexander B. Grosart ([London?], 1878.)

Dietz, Frederick C., *English Government Finance*, University of Illinois Studies in the Social Sciences, Volume IX, No. 3, September, 1920 (Urbana, Illinois).

"Diocesan Returns of Recusants for England and Wales, 1577," *Miscellanea*, vol. XII, (London: Catholic Record Society, 1921).

D'Israeli, Isaac, *Amenities of Literature* (New York, 1841).

Dizionario Biografico degli Italiani (Rome: Instituto delli Enciclopedia Italiana, 1972).

Donne, John, *The Complete Poetry*, ed. John T. Shawcross (New York University Press, 1968).

Dorsch, T. S., "Two English Antiquarians: John Leland and John Stow," *Essays and Studies*, XII (London: John Murray, 1959).

Dorsten, J. A. van, *Poets, Patrons and Professors* (Leiden: University Press, 1962).

Douce, Francis, *Illustrations of Shakespeare and of Ancient Manners*, 2 vols. (London: Longman, Hurst, Rees and Orme, 1807).

Dowden, Edward, ed., *Romeo and Juliet* (London: Methuen & Co., Ltd., 3rd ed., 1927).

Dowland, John, *The Third and Last Booke of Songs or Aires* (London, Thomas Adams, 1603; reprinted in *English Lute Songs, 1597-1632* (Menston, England: The Scolar Press, Limited, 1970).

Drake, Nathan, *Shakespeare and His Times*, 2 vols. (London: T. Cadell and W. Davies, 1817).

Dugdale, William, *The Baronage of England*, 2 vols. (London: Tho. Newcomb, et al., 1675, 1676).

————, *Origines Judiciales* (London: Thomas Newcombe, 1671).

du Maurier, Daphne, *Golden Lads* (New York: Doubleday & Company, Inc., 1975).

Duncan-Jones, Katherine, *Sir Philip Sidney, Courtier Poet* (Yale University Press, 1991).

Early Poems of Daniel and Drayton, ed. J. Payne Collier (London: Privately printed, 1869-1870).

Eccles, Mark, *Christopher Marlowe in London* (Harvard University Press, 1934).

————, *Shakespeare in Warwickshire* (University of Wisconsin Press, 1961).

Ecclesiastical Biography, ed. Christopher Wordsworth, 4 vols. (London: J.G. & F. Rivington, 1839).

Eckels, John H. and C. F. Callaway, *Modern Mortuary Science* (Philadelphia: Westbrook Publishing Company, 1946).

Edgerton, William L., *Nicholas Udall* (New York: Twayne Publishers, 1965).

Edmondson, Joseph, *Complete Body of Heraldry* (London, 1780).

Edwards, A.S.G., *Stephen Hawes* (Boston: Twayne Publishers, 1983).

Elizabethan Lyrics, ed. Norman Ault (New York: Capricorn Books, 1960).

Elizabethan Sonnets, ed. Sidney Lee, 2 vols. (Westminster: Constable, 1904).

Ellis, Herbert A., *Shakespeare's Lusty Punning in Love's Labour's Lost* (The Hague: Mouton, 1973).

Elze, Karl, *Essays on Shakespeare*, tr. L. Dora Schmitz (London, Macmillan and Co., 1874).

Emmison, Frederick George, *Tudor Secretary: Sir William Petre at Court and Home* (Harvard University Press, 1961).

Englands Helicon (London: John Flasket, 1600; reprint by Frederick Etchells and Hugh Macdonald, London, 1925).

Englefield, Henry C., *A Walk Through Southampton* (Southampton: Baker and Fletcher, 1801 (1st ed.) and 1805 (2nd ed.)).

Epistolæ diversorum philosophorum, oratorium, rhetorum sex et viginti (Venice: Aldus Manutius, 1499).

Epstein, Joel J., *Francis Bacon: A Political Biography* (Ohio University Press, 1977).

Erasmus, *Collected Works*, tr. R.A.B. Mynors and D.F.S. Thomson (University of Toronto Press, 1974).

Eros, An Anthology of Male Friendship, ed. Alistair Sutherland and Patrick Anderson (New York: Citadel Press, 1963).

Esler, Anthony, *The aspiring mind of the Elizabethan younger generation* (Duke University Press, 1966).

403

BIBLIOGRAPHY

Essays on the Life and Work of Thomas Linacre, ed. Francis Maddison, Margaret Pelling and Charles Webster (Oxford: Clarendon Press, 1977).

Evans, A.J., *Shakespeare's Magic Circle* (London: Arthur Barker, 1956).

Extracts from the MS Journals of Sir Simonds D'Ewes (London: J. Nichols, 1783).

Fairchild, Arthur H. R., *Shakespeare and the Arts of Design* (Columbia, Missori: Artcraft Press, 1937).

Fifth Report of the Royal Commission on Historical Manuscripts (London: Her Majesty's Stationery Office, 1876).

Fitzgerald, Edward, *Rubaiyat of Omar Khayyám, and the Saláman and Absál of Jámí* (New York: A. L. Burt, n.d.).

Flournoy, Fitzgerald, "William Breton, Nicholas Breton and George Gascoigne," *Review of English Studies*, Vol. XVI, No. 63, July, 1940

Foley, Henry, ed., *Records of the English Provinces of the Society of Jesus*, 8 vols. (London: Burks and Oates, 1877 - 1883).

Fourth Report of the Royal Comission on Historical Manuscripts (London, HMSO, 1874).

Fox-Davies, Arthur Charles, *The Art of Heraldry* (London: T.C. & E.C. Jacks, 1904; reprinted by Benjamin Blom, New York and London, 1968).

————, *The Book of Public Arms* (London: T. C. & E. Jack, 1915).

————, *A Complete Guide to Heraldry* (London and Edinburgh: T.C. & E. Jack, revised edition, 1925).

————, *Heraldry* (New York: Hitchcock, 1926).

————, *Heraldry Explained* (London and Edinburgh: T.C. & E. Jack, n.d.).

————, *The Right to Bear Arms* (London: Elliott Stock, 1900).

Foxe, John, *Acts and Monuments*, ed. George Townsend (London: R. B. Seeley and W. Burnside, 1837-1841).

Francisci et Joannis Hotmanorum, Patris ac Fillii et Clarorum Virorum ad Eos Epistolai (Hague: Georgium Gallet, 1700).

Franklin, Charles A.H., *The Bearing of Coat-Armour by Ladies* (London, 1923; reprinted by Genealogical Publishing Co., Baltimore, 1973).

Franklyn, Julian, *Shield and Crest* (New York: Sterling Pub. Co., 1960).

French, George Russell, *Shakespeareana Genealogica* (London and Cambridge: Macmillan, 1869).

Friedrich, Walter George, "The Stella of Astrophel," *ELH, A Journal of English Literary History*, Vol. 3, No. 2, June, 1936.

Fuller, Thomas, *Worthies of England*, 3 vols., ed. P. Austin Nuttall (London: Thomas Tegg, 1840).

Furness, Horace Howard, ed., *The Winter's Tale* (Philadelphia: J.B. Lippincott, 1898).

[Galen] Galeni Pergamensis, *De Temperamentis, et de Inaequali Intemperis*, Libri Tres, Thoma Linacro Anglo Interprete, with an Introduction by Joseph Frank Payne (Cambridge: Alexander MacMillan and Robert Bowes, 1881).

Gammon, Samuel Rhea, *Statesman and Schemer: William, First Lord Paget* (Newton Abbot: David & Charles, 1973).

The Garden Book of Sir Thomas Hanmer, ed. Eleanour Sinclair Rohde (London: Gerald Howe, 1933).

Gardiner, Stephen, *Letters*, ed. James Arthur Muller (Cambridge: University Press, 1935).

Gascoigne, George, *Complete Works*, ed. John W. Cunliffe, 2 vols. (Cambridge University Press, 1907).

Gaselee, Stephen, "Appendix on the Greek Novel," *The Love Romances of Parthenius and other Fragments* (Loeb Classical Library No. 69; London, William Heinemann Ltd.).

Gasquet, Francis Aidan, *Henry VIII and the English Monasteries*, 2 vols. (London: John Hodges, 1902).

Gaw, Allison, *The Origin and Development of 1 Henry VI* (Los Angeles: University of Southern California, 1926).

Gesner, Carol, *Shakespeare and the Greek Romance* (University Press of Kentucky, 1970).

Giroux, Robert, *The Book Known as Q* (New York: Atheneum, 1982).

Godfrey, Walter H., Wagner, Anthony and London, H. Stanford, *The College of Arms* (London: HMSO, 1963).

Godwin, The Rev. G.N., "Charles I at Place House and Hurst Castle," in *Memorials of Old Hampshire*, ed. G. E. Jeans (London: Bemrose and Sons, 1906).

Goldman, Marcus Selden, "Sir Philip Sidney and the Arcadia," *Illinois Studies in Language and Literature*, Volume XVII, Numbers 1-2, 1934.

Goodman, Anthony, *The Wars of the Roses* (London: Routledge & Kegan Paul, 1981).

Goodman, Godfrey, *The Court of King James the First* (London: Richard Bentley, 1839).

Googe, Barnabe, *Eglogs, Epytaphes & Sonettes 1563*, ed. Edward Arbor (London, 1871).

A Gorgeous Gallery of Gallant Inventions (1578), ed. Hyder E. Rollins (Harvard University Press, 1926).

Goulding, Richard W., "Wriothesley Portraits," *The Eighth Volume of the Walpole Society* (Oxford: Frederick Hall, 1920).

Graham, Rose, and Rigold, S. E., *Official Handbook, Titchfield Abbey* (London: HMSO, 1969).

Grande Dizionario della Lingua Italiana (Torino [Turin], Unione tipografco editrice torinese, 1961-).

Grange, John, *The Golden Aphroditis* (London, 1577; facsimile edition by Scholars' Favsimiles & Reprints, New York, 1936).

Gray, Austin K., "Some Observations on Christopher Marlowe, Government Agent," *Publications of the Modern Language Association* [PMLA], Vol. 43, 1928.

Greek Anthology, tr. W. R. Paton (Loeb Classical Library Nos. 67-68, 84-86; Harvard University Press).

Green, A. Wigfall, *The Inns of Court and Early English Drama* (Yale University Press, 1931).

Green, G. H., "Southwick Priory," *Papers and Proceedings of the Hampshire Field Club* (1898).

BIBLIOGRAPHY

Green, Martin, *The Labyrinth of Shakespeare's Sonnets* (London: Charles Skilton, Ltd., 1974).

Greene, Robert, *The Plays and Poems of Robert Greene*, ed. J. Churton Collins, 2 vols. (Oxford: Clarendon Press, 1905).

Greenfield, Benjamin W., "The Wriothesley Tomb in Titchfield Church: Its Effigial Statues and Heraldry," *Papers and Proceedings of the Hampshire Field Club* (Vol. 1, 1885-1889).

Greville, Fulke, Lord Brooke, *Caelica*, ed. Martha Foote Crow (London: Kegan Paul, Trench, Trubner and Co., 1898).

Grosart, Alexander B., ed., *The Complete Works in Verse and Prose of Samuel Daniel* (London: Privately printed, 1885).

Grove, Matthew, *The Poems*, (1587), ed. Alexander B. Grosart ([London?], 1878).

Guttman, Selma, *The Foreign Sources of Shakespeare's Works* (New York: King Crown's Press, 1947).

Hall, Winifred, *Canting and Allusive Arms of England and Wales* (Canterbury: Achievements, 1966).

Halliwell, James Orchard, *The Autobiography and Correspondence of Sir Simonds D'Ewes, Bart.* (London: R. Bentley, 1845).

———, *The Life of William Shakespeare* (London: John Russell Smith, 1848).

Hamilton, Charles, *In Search of Shakespeare* (San Diego: Harcourt Brace Jovanovich, 1985).

Hampshire County Handbook and Industrial Review (Cheltenham: Burrow, 1970).

Hannay, Margaret P., *Philip's Phoenix* (Oxford University Press, 1990).

Hare, Michael, "The Documentary Evidence for the Southampton Monument in Titchfield Church," *Fareham Past and Present*, Book V, Vol. II.

———, *The Parish Church of St. Peter, Titchfield, Fareham* (Ramsgate: Church Publishers, 1984).

Harington, Sir John, *A New Discourse of a Stale Subject, Called the Metamorphosis of Ajax*, ed. Elizabeth Story Donno (Columbia University Press, 1962).

Harpsfield, Nicholas, *Treatise Touching the Pretended Divorce of Henry the Eighth*, ed. Nicholas Pocock (London: Camden Society, Vol. 21, n.s., 1878).

Harris, Jesse W., *John Bale* (University of Illinois Press, 1940).

Harris, William, *The Lives and Writings of James I. and Charles I.* (London: F.C. and J. Rivington, 1814).

Harrison, G.B., *The Life and Death of Robert Devereux, Earl of Essex* (New York: Henry Holt, 1937).

———, *Shakespeare under Elizabeth* (New York: Henry Holt, 1933).

Hart, H.C., ed., *The First Part of King Henry the Sixth* (Indianapolis: Bobbs Merrill, n.d.).

Harvey, Gabriel, *Pierce's Supererogation* (London: John Wolfe, 1593; facsimile edition by Scolar Press, Menston (Yorkshire), 1970).

Harvey, Gabriel, *The Trimming of Thomas Nashe* (London: Philip Scarlet, 1597; facsimile edition by Scolar Press, Menston (Yorkshire), 1973).

Headlam, Cecil, *The Story of Oxford* (London: Dent, 1907).

Heffner, Ray, *The Earl of Essex in Elizabethan Literature* (Unpublished Dissertation, Johns Hopkins University, 1928).

The Herald and Genealogist, ed. John Gouge Nichols, 8 vols. (London: J.C. Nichols and R. C. Nichols, 1862-1874).

Herbert, George, *The Works*, ed. F. E. Hutchinson (Oxford: Clarendon Press, 1941).

Herford, C. H., and Percy and Evelyn Simpson, *Ben Jonson*, 11 vols. (Oxford: Clarendon Press, 1925-1952).

Hill, Herbert Wynford, "Sidney's Arcadia and the Elizabethan Drama," University of Nevada Studies, Vol. 1, No. 1 (1908).

Hoak, D. E., *The King's Council in the Reign of Edward VI* (Cambridge University Press, 1976).

H[odges], A[nthony], tr., *The Loves of Clitiphon and Leucippe* (Oxford: W. Turner for John Allam, 1638).

Holinshed, Raphael, *Chronicles of England, Scotland and Ireland*, 6 vols. (London: J. Johnson, 1808).

Holme, Randle, *The Academy of Armory*, Vol. II, ed. I. H. Jeayes (London: Roxburghe Club, 1905).

Honigmann, E. A. J., *Shakespeare: the "lost years"* (Manchester University Press, 1985).

Honneyman, David, *Closer to Shakespeare* (Braunton, Devon: Merlin Books Ltd., 1990).

Hope, W. H. St. John, *Cowdray and Easebourne Priory in the County of Sussex* (London: Country Life, 1919).

———, "English Municipal Heraldry," *Archaelogical Journal*, LII (1895).

———, *A Grammar of English Heraldry* (Cambridge University Press, 1913).

———, "The Making of Place House at Titchfield, Near Southampton, in 1538," *Archaeological Journal*, Vol. 53 (1906).

Horne, David H., ed., *The Life and Minor Works of George Peele* (Yale University Press, 1952).

Hotson, Leslie, *The Death of Christopher Marlowe* (London: Nonesuch Press, 1925).

———, *I, William Shakespeare* (London: Jonathan Cape, 1937).

———, *Mr W.H.* (New York: Alfred A. Knopf, 1965).

———, *Shakespeare's Sonnets Dated* (New York: Oxford University Press, 1949).

Howell, Thomas, *The Poems*, 1568 - 1571, ed. the Rev. Alexander B. Grosart (London?, 1879).

Hubler, Edward, *The Sense of Shakespeare's Sonnets* (Princeton University Press, 1952).

Hughes, Merritt Y., "Virgil and Spenser," *University of California Publications in English*, Vol. 2, No. 3 (1929).

Hughes, Philip, *The Reformation in England*, 2 vols. (London: Hollis & Carter, 1952).

Hulse, S. Clark, "'A piece of Skilful Painting' in Shakespeare's 'Lucrece'," 31 *Shakespeare Survey* (Cambridge University Press, 1978).

Hume, Martin, "Antonio Perez in Exile," *Transactions of the Royal Historical Society*, New Series, Volume VIII (London: Longmans. Gren, and Co., 1894).

———, *The Great Lord Burghley* (London: Eveleigh Nash, 1906).

———, *Spanish Influence on English Literature* (London: Eveleigh Nash, 1905).

407

BIBLIOGRAPHY

Hurstfield, Joel, *The Queen's Wards* (Harvard University Press, 1958).

Hutton, James, "Analogues of Shakespeare's Sonnets," *Essays on Renaissance Poetry* (Cornell University Press, 1980).

————, *The Greek Anthology in France* (Cornell University Press, 1946).

————, *The Greek Anthology in Italy to the Year 1800* (Cornell University Press, 1935).

The Itinerary of John Leland, ed. Lucy Toulmin Smith (London: Bell, 1907).

Jacobs, Joseph, ed., *Daphnis and Chloe — The Elizabethan Version from Amyot's Translation by Angel Day* (London: David Nutt, 1890).

Jardine, David, *Criminal Trials*, 2 vols. (London: M. A. Nattali, 1847).

Jenkins, Harold, *The Life and Work of Henry Chettle* (London: Sidgwick & Jackson, Ltd., 1934).

John, Lisle Cecil, *The Elizabethan Sonnet Sequences* (Columbia University Press, 1938).

Johnson, Samuel, ed., *Plays of William Shakespeare*, 8 vols. (London: J and R Tonson, 1765).

Johnson, Samuel and George Steevens, ed., revised and augmented by Isaac Reed, *Plays of William Shakespeare*, 21 vols. (London: J. Johnson et al., 1803).

Jones, Deborah, "Lodowick Bryskett and his Family," *Thomas Lodge and Other Elizabethans*, ed. Charles J. Sisson (Harvard University Press, 1933).

Jones, Roger and Nicholas Penny, *Raphael* (Yale University Press, 1983).

Jordan, W.K., *Edward VI: The Young King* (Harvard University Press, 1968).

Joseph, Harriet, *Shakespeare's Son-in-law: John Hall, Man and Physician* (Hamden, Connecticut: Archon Books, 1964).

Journal of Sir Francis Walsingham, ed. Charles Trice Martin (London: Camden Society No. 104, 1871).

Kelley, Donald R., *François Hotman* (Princeton University Press, 1973).

Kendall, Paul Murray, *The Yorkist Age* (New York: W. W. Norton & Co., 1962).

Kennedy, Joseph, "Laymen and Monasteries in Hampshire, 1530 - 1558," *Proceedings of the Hampshire Field Club and Archaeological Society*, XXVII.

Kenny, Robert W., *Elizabeth's Admiral* (Johns Hopkins Press, 1970).

Kent, William, ed., *An Encyclopaedia of London* (New York: E. P, Dutton & Co., 1937).

Kerrigan, John, ed., *The Sonnets and A Lover's Complaint* (Harmondsworth, England: Penguin Books, 1986).

Kingsford, Charles Lethbridge, "Bath Inn or Arundel House," *Archaeologia*, Vol. 72, 1922.

————, "Essex House, formerly Leicester House and Exeter Inn," *Archaeologia*, Vol. 73, 1923.

Klawitter, George, *Richard Barnfield — The Complete Poems* (Susquehanna University Press, 1990).

Kruck, William E., *Looking for Dr. Condom* (University of Alabama Press, 1981).

Kuriyama, Constance Brown, "Marlowe's Nemesis: The Identity of Richard Baines," *"A Poet and a filthy Play-maker" — New Essays on Christopher Marlowe*, ed. Kenneth Friedenreich, Roma Gill, and Constance B. Kuriyama (New York: AMS Press, Inc., 1988).

408

Lacey, Robert, *Robert Earl of Essex, An Elizabethan Icarus* (London: Weidenfeld and Nicolson, 1971).

Lancashire, Ian, *Dramatic Texts and Records of Britain: A Chronological Topography to 1558* (University of Toronto Press, 1984).

Lathrop, Henry Burrowes, *Translations from the Classics into English from Caxton to Chapman* (University of Wisconsin Press, 1932, facsimile edition by Octagon Books, New York, 1967).

Leader, John Temple, *Life of Sir Robert Dudley* (Florence: 1875).

Lee, Arthur Gould, *The Son of Leicester* (London: Victor Golancz, Ltd., 1961).

Lee, Sidney, *Elizabethan Sonnets*, 2 vols. (Westminster: Archibald Constable and Co., Ltd., 1904).

————, *Great Englishmen of the Sixteenth Century* (New York: Charles Scribner's Sons, 1904).

————, *A Life of William Shakespeare*, new and revised edition (New York: Macmil-lan, 1909).

Lees-Milne, James, *Tudor Renaissance* (London: B. T. Batsford, 1951).

Legh, Gerard, *The Accedence of Armorie* (London: Richard Tottell, 1591).

Leishman, J. B., *Themes and Variations in Shakespeare's Sonnets* (London: Hutchinson, 1961).

Letters and Memorials of State, ed. Arthur Collins, 2 vols. (London: T. Osborne, 1746).

Letters and Papers, Foreign and Domestic, of the Reign of Henry VIII, ed. J. S. Brewer, J. Gairdner and R.H. Brodie, 21 vols. (London, 1862-1910), plus *Addenda*, vol. i (London, 1929-1932).

Letters from Sir Robert Cecil to Sir George Carew, ed. John MacLean (London: Camden Society (No. 88), 1864).

Levin, Richard A., *Love and Society in Shakespearean Comedy* (University of Delaware Press, 1985).

The Lisle Letters, ed. Muriel St. Clare Byrne, 6 vols. (The University of Chicago Press, 1981).

Lloyd, A.T., "Place Names of Hampshire," *A Survey of Southampton and its Region*, ed. F. J. Monkhouse (Southampton, 1964).

Lloyd, David, *The Statesmen and Favourites of England* (London, 1665).

Lodge, Thomas, *Complete Works*, 4 vols. (London (?): Hunterian Club, 1883).

Looney, J. Thomas, *"Shakespeare" Identified* (London: Cecil Palmer, 1920).

London Topographical Record, ed. T. Fairman Ordish (London: London Topgraphical Society, 1903).

Longi Pastoralium, de Daphnidae & Chloë, Libri Quatuor, ed. Raphael Columbanius (Florence: Philippum Iunctam, 1598).

Lord Burghley's Papers in the British Library in London, Microfilm Edition (London: The Harvester Press, 1976).

Lyly, John, *The Complete Works*, ed. R. Warwick Bond, 3 vols. (Oxford: Clarendon Press, 1902).

Lynch-Robinson, Sir Christopher and Lynch-Robinson, Adrian, *Intelligible Heraldry* (Baltimore: Heraldic Book Co., 1967).

BIBLIOGRAPHY

Lyne, R.O.A.M., *The Latin Love Poets* (Oxford: Clarendon Press, 1980).

Machyn, Henry, *Diary*, ed. John Gough Nichol (Camden Society, No. 42, 1848).

Macklem, Michael, *God Have Mercy* (Ottawa: Oberon Press, 1967).

Malone, Edmond, *Supplement to the Edition of Shakespeare's Plays Published in 1778 by Samuel Johnson and George Steevens*, 2 vols. (London: C. Bathurst, et al., 1780).

The Manual of Heraldry (London: Arthur Hall, Virtue & Co., 5th ed., n.d.).

The Manuscripts of His Grace the Duke of Rutland, 4 vols. (London: HMSO, 1905).

Marañon, Gregorio, *Antonio Pérez (El Hombre, El Drama, La Época)*, 2 vols. (Madrid: Espasa-Calpe, S.A., 1952).

——, *Antonio Pérez, "Spanish Traitor"*, tr. Charles David Ley (London: Holis and Carter, 1954).

Marks, Richard, *British Heraldry from its Origins to 1820* (London: British Museum, 1978).

Marlowe, Christopher, *Complete Works*, 2 vols., ed. Fredson Bowers (Cambridge University Press, 1973).

Marriott, Sir J.A.R., *The Life of John Colet* (London: Methuen and Co., 1933).

Marston, John, *The Poems, 1598 - 1601*, ed. the Rev. Alexander B. Grosart ([London?], 1879).

Martienssen, Anthony, *Queen Katherine Parr* (London: Secker & Warburg, 1973).

Martin, Robert Bernard, *With Friends Possessed* (New York: Atheneum, 1985).

Marvell, Andrew, *Poems and Letters*, 2 vols., ed. H. M. Margoliouth (Oxford: Clarendon Press, 1927).

Massey, Gerald, *The Secret Drama of Shakespeare's Sonnets* (London: Kegan Paul, Trench & Co., 1888).

Master Worsley's Book on the History and Constitution of the Honorable Society of the Inner Temple, ed. Arthur Robert Ingpen (London: Masters of the Bench, 1910).

McLane, Paul E., *Spenser's Shepheardes Calendar: A Study in Elizabetha Allegory* (University of Notre Dame Press, 1961).

McLean, Teresa, *Medieval English Gardens* (New York: Viking Press, 1981).

McKerrow, R.B., *A Dictionary of Printers and Booksellers 1557-1640* (London: Bibliographical Society, 1910).

A Memoir of Peregrine Bertie, Eleventh Lord Willoughby de Eresby (London: John Murray, 1838).

Meres, Francis, *Palladis Tamia* (London: Cuthbert Burbie, 1598; facsimile edition by Scholars' Facsimiles & Reprints, New York, 1938).

Merrifield, Ralph, *Roman London* (New York: Frederick A. Praeger, 1969).

Metcalfe, Walter C., *A Book of Knights Banneret, Knights of the Bath, and Knights Bachelor* (London: Mitchell Hughes, 1885).

Metz, G. Harold, "The Date of Composition of Titus Andronicus," *Notes and Queries*, Vol. 25 (new series) (Oxford University Press, 1978).

Michel, Laurence, ed., *The Tragedy of Philotas*, by Samuel Daniel (Yale University Press, 1949).

Miller, Amos C., *Sir Henry Killigrew, Elizabethan Soldier and Diplomat* (Leicester University Press, 1963).

Milles, Thomas, *The Catalogue of Honor* (London: William Jaggard, 1610).

Milward, Peter, *Shakespeare's Religious Background* (Indiana University Press, 1973).

Minns, G. W., "On the New Device or Seal of the Hants Field Club and Archaeological Society," *Papers and Proceedings of the Hampshire Field Club* (1898).

——, "Titchfield Abbey and Place House," *Papers and Proceedings of the Hampshire Field Club* (1898).

Minto, William, *Characteristics of the English Poets from Chaucer to Shirley*, 2nd ed. (Edinburgh: W. Blackwood and Sons, 1885).

Mirrour of Maiestie, ed. Henry Green and James Croston (Manchester: Holbein Society, 1870).

Montagu of Beaulieu, Edward John Barrington Douglas-Scott-Montagu, Baron, *The Gilt and the Gingerbread* (London: Michael Joseph, 1967).

Morris, Harry, 'Richard Barnfield, 'Amyntas,' and the Sidney Circle," PMLA LXXIV (1959).

——, *Richard Barnfield, Colin's Child* (Florida State University, 1963).

Motter, T. H. Vail, *The School Drama in England* (London: Longmans, Green and Co., 1929).

Mounts, Charles E., "Spenser and the Countess of Leicester," *That Soveraine Light* (Baltimore: Johns Hopkins Press, 1952).

Mowat, Barbara A., *The Dramaturgy of Shakespeare's Romances* (University of Georgia Press, 1970).

Muir, Kenneth, *Life and Letters of Thomas Wyatt* (Liverpool University Press, 1963).

Muir, Kenneth, ed., *Shakespeare's Sonnets* (London: George Allen and Unwin, 1979).

Muller, James Arthur, *Stephen Gardiner and the Tudor Reaction* (New York: Macmillan, 1926).

Murray, John Tucker, *English Dramatic Companies*, 2 vols. (London: Constable and Company, Ltd., 1910).

Mutschmann, Heinrich and Karl Wentersdorf, *Shakespeare and Catholicism* (New York: Sheed and Ward, 1952).

Nashe, Thomas, *Works*, ed. Ronald B. McKerrow, 5 vols. (Oxford: Basil Blackwell, 1958).

Naunton, Robert, "Fragmenta Regalia," *A Collection of Scarce and Valuable Tracts ... from . . . Libraries, particularly that of the Late Lord Somers*, 2d ed., ed. Walter Scott, Vol. 1 (London, T. Cadell and W. Davies, *et al.*, 1809).

Neilson, William Allan and Charles Jarvis Hill (eds.), *The Complete Plays and Poems of William Shakespeare* (Boston: Houghton Mifflin, 1942).

Ness, Frederic W., *The Use of Rhyme in Shakespeare's Plays* (Yale University Press, 1941).

Newdigate, Bernard H., *Michael Drayton and His Circle* (Oxford: Basil Blackwell, 1961).

Newdigate-Newdegate, [Anne Emily], Lady, ed., *Gossip from a Muniment Room* (London: David Nutt, 1897).

411

Nicholl, Charles, *A Cup of News* (London: Routledge & Kegan Paul, 1984).

Nichols, John, *The Progresses and Public Processions of Queen Elizabeth*, 3 vols. (London, 1823; facsimile edition by Burt Franklin, New York, n.d.).

Nisbet, Ulric, *The Onlie Begetter* (London: Longmans, Green, 1936).

Noreña, Carlos G., *Juan Luis Vives* (The Hague: Martinus Nijhoff, 1970).

Nott, Geo. Fred., ed., *The Works of Henry Howard, Earl of Surrey and of Sir Thomas Wyatt*, 2 vols. (London: T Bensley, 1815 (Vol. 1) and 1816 (Vol. 2).

Ogburn, Charlton, *The Mysterious William Shakespeare* (New York: Dodd, Mead & Company, 1984).

Ollard, S.L., and Gordon Crosse, *A Dictionary of English Church History* (London: A. R. Mowbray and Co., Ltd., 1912).

Onions, C.T., *A Shakespeare Glossary* (Oxford: Clarendon Press, 1953).

Osborn, Albert W., *Sir Philip Sidney en France* (Paris: Librairie Ancienne Honoré Champion, 1932).

Osborn, James M., *Young Philip Sidney* (Yale University Press, 1972).

Oxford Latin Dictionary, ed. P. G. W. Glare (Oxford: Clarendon Press, 1973).

Pafford, J.H.P., ed., *The Winter's Tale* (London: Methuen & Co., 1963).

Parks, George Bruner, *Richard Hakluyt and the English Voyages* (New York: Frederick Ungar, 1961).

Partridge, Eric, *Shakespeare's Bawdy* (New York: E. P. Dutton, 1948).

Pequigney, Joseph, *Such Is My Love: A Study of Shakespeare's Sonnets* (University of Chicago Press, 1985).

Perry, Ben Edwin, *The Ancient Romances* (University of California Press, 1967).

Phillips, James E., "George Buchanan and the Sidney Circle," *Huntington Library Quarterly*, Volume XII, 1948-1949 (San Marino, California).

Philostrati Lemnii Opera Quae Exstant, ed. Fed. Morellus (Paris: Marcum Orry, 1608).

Philostratus, *Imagines*, tr. Arthur Fairbanks (Loeb Classical Library No. 256; Harvard University Press).

————, *The Life of Apollonius of Tyana*, 2 vols., tr. F. C. Conybeare (Loeb Classical Library Nos. 16 and 17; Harvard University Press).

Piers Plainnes seauen yeres Prentiship, by H.C., 1595, ed. Hermannus Varnhagen (Erlangen, 1900).

Pinto, V. de Sola, *The English Renaissance 1510-1688* (New York: Robert M. McBride, 1938).

Plomer, Henry R., and Tom Peete Cross, *the Life and Correspondence of Lodowick Bryskett* (University of Chicago Press, 1927?)

Plutarch, *Amorous Tales*, tr. James Sandford (London: H. Bynnerman, 1567).

————, *The Philosophie*, tr. Philemon Holland (London: Arnold Hatfield, 1603).

Poems Written by the Honorable William Earl of Pembroke . . . and Sir Benjamin Ruddier (London, Matthew Inman, 1660, facsimile edition by the Augustan Print Society (Publication No. 79), William Andrews Clark Memorial Library, University of California, 1959).

Pohl, Frederick J., *Like to the Lark* (Clarkson N. Potter: New York, 1972).

Poirier, Michel, *Christopher Marlowe* (London: Chatto and Windus, 1951).

Pollard, A.F. *The History of England from the Accession of Edward VI to the Death of Elizabeth (1547-1603)* (London: Longmans Green, 1910; facsimile edition by AMS Press, New York, 1969).

Ponet (or Poynet), John, *A Short Treatise of Politike Power* (Strassburg?, 1556).

Pooler, C. Knox, *Shakespeare's Poems* (London: Methuen and Co., 1911).

Prescott, Anne Lake, *French Poets and the English Renaissance* (Yale University Press, 1978).

Prouty, C. T., *George Gascoigne, Elizabethan Courtier, Soldier and Poet* (Columbia University Press, 1942).

Purcell, James M., *Sidney's Stella* (Oxford University Press, 1934).

Puttenham, George, *The Arte of English Poesie*, ed. Gladys Doidge Willcock and Alice Walker (Cambridge: University Press, 1936).

Rader, Ralph Wilson, *Tennyson's Maud: The Biographical Genesis* (University of California Press, 1963).

Read, Conyers, *Mr Secretary Walsingham and the Policy of Queen Elizabeth*, 3 vols. (Oxford: Clarendon Press, 1925).

Rebholz, Ronald A., *The Life of Fulke Greville* (Oxford: Clarendon Press, 1971).

Reliquiæ Wottonianæ (London: Thomas Maxey, G. Bedel and T. Garthwait, 1651).

Ridley, Jasper, *Statesman and Saint: Cardinal Wolsey, Sir Thomas More, and the Politics of Henry VIII* (New York: Viking Press, 1983).

Ringler, William A., Jr., ed., *The Poems of Sir Philip Sidney* (Oxford: Clarendon Press, 1962).

Robinson, Thomas, *The British Herald*, 3 vols. (Sunderland, 1830).

Roche, Thomas P., "Autobiographical Elements in Sidney's *Astrophel and Stella*," *Spenser Studies*, Vol. 5 (New York: AMS Press, 1985).

Rohde, Eleanour Sinclair, *Shakespeare's Wild Flowers* (London: Medici Society, 1935).

Rollins, Hyder Edward, *The Sonnets* (Variorum Edition), 2 vols. (Philadelphia and London: J. B. Lippincott Company, 1944).

Root, Robert Kilburn, *Classical Mythology in Shakespeare* (New York: Henry Holt and Company, 1903).

Rosenberg, Eleanor, *Leicester, Patron of Letters* (Columbia University Press, 1955).

Ross, Charles, *The Wars of the Roses* (London: Thames and Hudson, 1976).

Rothery, Guy Cadogan, *ABC of Heraldry* (Jacobs: Philadelphia [1915]).

Round, J.Horace, *Geoffrey de Mandeville* (London: Longmans, Green, 1892).

——, *Peerage and Pedigree*, 2 vols. (London: James Nisbet & Co., Ltd., 1910).

——, *Studies in Peerage and Family History* (London: Constable, 1901).

Rowe, Nicholas, ed., *Works of William Shakespeare*, 6 vols. (London: Tonson, 1709).

Rowley, Samuel, *When You See Me, You Know Me* (Oxford: Malone Society Reprints, 1952).

Rowse, A. L., ed., *The Poems of Shakespeare's Dark Lady* (London: Jonathan Cape, 1978).

——, ed., *Shakespeare's Sonnets: The Problems Solved*: (New York: Harper & Row, 2d ed., 1973).

——, *Shakespeare's Southampton* (New York: Harper & Row, 1965).

BIBLIOGRAPHY

Rowse, A. L., *William Shakespeare* (New York: Harper & Row, 1963).

The Roxburghe Ballads, 3 vols. (Hertford: Stephen Austin and Sons, 1875).

Rubinstein, Frankie, *A Dictionary of Shakespeare's Sexual Puns and their Significance* (London?: Macmillan, 1984).

Russell, John, Duke of Bedford, *A Silver-Plated Spoon* (London: Cassell & Co., 1959).

Sabeo, Fausto, *Epigrammata* (Rome: Valerium & Aloysium Doricom, 1556).

Saccio, Peter, *Shakespeare's English Kings* (New York: Oxford University Press, 1979).

Sandell, Elsie M., *Southampton Panorama* (Southampton: Wilson, 1958).

Sanford, John, "Apollonis et Musarum Eidyllia," *Elizabethan Oxford*, ed. Charles Plummer (Oxford: Oxford Historical Society, 1887).

Sargent, Ralph M., *The Life and Lyrics of Sir Edward Dyer* (Oxford: Clarendon Press, 1968).

Saslow, James M., *Ganymede in the Renaissance* (Yale University Press, 1986).

Saunders, J. W., "The Facade of Morality," *That Soveraine Light*, ed. William R. Mueller and Don Cameron Allen (Johns Hopkins Press, 1952).

Savage, Henry L., "Heraldry in Shakespeare," *Shakespeare Quarterly* (1950), Vol. I.

Saviolo, Vincentio, *His Practice* (London: John Wolfe, 1595, reproduced in *Three Elizabethan Fencing Manuals*, Scholars' Facsimiles & Reprints, Delmar, New York 1972).

Scarisbrick, J. J., *Henry VIII* (University of California Press, 1968).

Schaar, Claes, *Elizabethan Sonnet Themes and the Dating of Shakespeare's 'Sonnets'* (Lund: C.W.K. Gleerup, 1962).

Schoenbaum, S., *Shakespeare's Lives* (New York: Oxford University Press, 1970).

———, *William Shakespeare, A Documentary Life* (New York: Oxford University Press, 1975).

Schrickx, W., *Shakespeare's Early Contemporaries* (Antwerp: De Nederlandsche Boekhandel, 1956).

Scott, Janet G., *Les Sonnets Elizabethains* (Paris: Librairie Ancienne Honore Champion, 1929).

Scott-Giles, C. Wilfrid, *Civic Heraldry* (London: Dent, 1953).

———, *Looking at Heraldry* (London: Phoenix House, 1967).

———, *Shakespeare's Heraldry* (London: Heraldry Today, 1971).

Seaton, Ethel, "Marlowe, Robert Poley, and the Tippings," *Review of English Studies* [RES], Vol. 5, 1929.

Selden, John, *Titles of Honor* (London: E. Tyler and R. Holt, 1672).

Seronsy, Cecil, *Samuel Daniel* (New York: Twayne Publishers, Inc., 1967).

Seward, Barbara, *The Symbolic Rose* (Columbia Iniversity Press, 1960).

Seymour-Smith, Martin, ed., *Shakespeare's Sonnets* (London: Heinemann, 1963).

Shackford, Martha Hale, "Rose in Shakespeare's Sonnet," *Modern Language Notes*, 33 (1918).

Shakespeare Newsletter, ed. Louis Marder (Evanston, Illinois)

Shakespeare's Ovid, ed. W. H. D. Rouse (New York: W. W. Norton & Co., Inc., 1966).

Shakespeare's Poems [A facsimile of the earliest editions], (Yale University Press, 1964).

Shapiro, Michael, *Children of the Revels* (Columbia University Press, 1977).

Sidney, Sir Philip, *The Countess of Pembroke's Arcadia* (Original Version), ed. Albert Feuillerat (Cambridge University Press, 1926).

———, *The Countess of Pembroke's Arcadia — 1590*, ed. Albert Feuillerat (Cam-bridge University Press, 1939).

———, *Defence of Poesy* (London: William Ponsonby, 1595, facsimile edition by Noel Douglas, London, 1928.

Silver, George *Paradoxes of Defence* (London: Edward Blount, 1599, facsimile edition included in *Three Elizabethan Fencing Manuals*, by Scholars' Facsimiles & Reprints, Delmar, New York 1972).

Sixth Report of the Royal Commission on Historical Manuscripts (London: Her Majesty's Stationery Office, 1877).

Slavin, Arthur, "Lord Chancellor Wriothesley and Reform of Augmentations: New Light on an Old Court," *Tudor Men and Institutions*, ed. Arthur J. Slavin (Louisiana State University Press, 1972).

Smith, Bruce R., *Homosexual Desire in Shakespeare's England* (University of Chicago Press, 1991).

Smith, Lacey Baldwin, *Treason in Tudor England* (Princeton University Press, 1986).

Southampton City Council, *Coat of Arms of the City of Southampton* (Southampton: City Council, 1978).

Speed, John, M.D., *The History and Antiquity of Southampton*, ed. Elinor R. Aubrey (Southampton: Cox & Sharland, 1909).

Spenser, Edmund, *Poetical Works*, eds. J. C. Smith and E. de Selincourt (Oxford University Press, 1924).

Spurgeon, Caroline F. E., *Shakespeare's Imagery and What it Tells Us* (New York: Macmillan, 1935).

Stapfer, Paul, *Shakespeare and Classical Antiquity* (London: C. Kegan Paul & Co., 1880).

State Papers during the Reign of Henry VIII, 11 vols. (London, 1830-1852).

Stern, Virginia F., *Gabriel Harvey, His Life, Marginalia and Library* (Oxford: Clarendon Press, 1979).

Stone, Lawrence, *The Crisis of the Aristocracy 1558-1648* (Oxford: Clarendon Press, 1965).

———, *Family and Fortune* (Oxford: Clarendon Press, 1973).

Stopes, Charlotte C., *The Life of Henry, Third Earl of Southampton* (Cambridge University Press, 1922).

———, *Shakespeare's Family* (London: Elliot Stock, 1901).

———, ed., *Shakespeare's Sonnets* (London: Alexander Moring Limited, 1904).

———, *Shakespeare's Warwickshire Contemporaries* (Stratford-upon-Avon: Shakespeare Head Press, 1907).

Stow, John, *A Survey of London*, ed. Charles Lethbridge Kingsford, 2 vols. (Oxford: Clarendon Press, 1971).

Strachey, Lytton, *Elizabeth and Essex* (London: Chatto & Windus, 1929).

BIBLIOGRAPHY

Strype, John, *The Life of the Learned Sir Thomas Smith* (Oxford: Clarendon Press, 1820).

Suckling, Sir John, *Works*, 2 vols., ed. Thomas Clayton (Oxford: Clarendon Press, 1971).

Summers, Claude J., "Sex, Politics, and Self-Realization in Edward II," in *"A Poet and a filthy Play-maker" — New Essays on Christopher Marlowe*, eds. Kenneth Friedenrich, Roma Gill, and Constance B. Kuriyama (AMS Press, New York, 1988).

Sunderland, Septimus, *Old London's Spas, Baths and Wells* (London: John Bale Sons & Danielsson, 1915).

Tannenbaum, Samuel Aaron, *The Shakspere Coat of Arms* (New York: Tenny Press, 1908, reprinted by AMS Press, New York, 1974).

Taylor, G. R. Stirling, *An Historical Guide to London* (London: J. M. Dent, 1911).

Taylor, Rupert, "Shakespeare's Cousin, Thomas Greene and his Kin: Possible Light on the Shakespeare Family Background," *PMLA*, Vol. 60 (1945).

Tennyson and his Friends, ed. Hallam, Lord Tennyson (London: Macmillan, 1912).

Tennyson, Emily, *Journal*, ed. James O. Hoge (Charlottesville, Virginia: University Press of Virginia, 1981).

The Third Book of Remembrance of Southampton, ed. A. L. Merson (University of Southampton, 1952).

Thomas Watson's Latin Amyntas (1585), ed. Walter F. Staton, Jr. and *Abraham Fraunce's Translation The Lamentations of Amyntas* (1587), ed. Franklin M. Dickey (University of Chicago Press, 1967).

Thomson, J.A.K., *Shakespeare and the Classics* (London: Allen & Unwin, 1952).

Titchfield, A History (Titchfield: Titchfield Historic Society, 1982).

Tottels Miscellany, ed. Hyder Edward Rollins, 2 vols. (Harvard University Press, 1965 (rev. ed.)).

Touwaide, R.H., *Messire Lodovico Guicciardini, Gentilhomme Florentin* (Nieuwkoop: B. DeGraaf, 1975).

Trent, Christopher, *The Russells* (London: Frederick Muller, 1966).

Trevelyan Papers, ed. J. Payne Collier (London: Camden Society (No. 67), 1857).

Tucker, T.G., ed., *The Sonnets of Shakespeare* (Cambridge University Press, 1924).

Tuve, Rosemond, *Elizabethan and Metaphysical Imagery* (University of Chicago Press, 1947).

Tyler, Thomas, ed., *Shakespeare's Sonnets* (London: David Nutt, 1890).

Tyson, William, "Heming's Players in the reign of Henry VIII," *Shakespeare Society's Papers*, Vol. III (London: Shakespeare Society, 1847).

Ungerer, Gustav, *A Spaniard in Elizabethan England: The Correspondence of Antonio Pérez's Exile*, 2 vols. (London: Tamesis Books Limited, 1974).

V. Cl. Gulielmi Camdeni et Illustrium Virorum ad G Camdenum Epistolæ (London: Richardi Chiswelli, 1691).

Valor Ecclesiasticus Temp. Henr VIII, Autoritate regia Institutus, 6 vols. (London, 1810-1834).

Vaughan, William, *Approved Directions for Health. both Naturall and Artificiall, Devised from the best Physitians as well moderne as auncient* (London: Roger Jackson, 4th edition, 1612).

————, *The Golden Fleece* (London: Francis Williams, 1626).

————, *The Golden Grove* (London: Simon Stafford, 1600).

————, *Poematum Libellus* (London: Georgium Shaw, 1598)

————, *Speculum humane condicionis* (London: Georgium Shaw, 1598).

Velz, John W., *Shakespeare and the Classical Tradition* (University of Minnesota, 1968).

The Venerable Philip Howard, Earl of Arundel, ed. John Hungerford Pollen and William MacMahon (London: Catholic Record Society, 1919).

Verheyen, Egon, *The Palazza del Te in Mantua* (Baltimore: Johns Hopkins University Press, 1977).

Vernon, Frank, *Hogs at the Honeypot* (Bridgewater (Somerset): BBNO, 1981).

Vesey-Fitzgerald, Brian, *Hampshire and the Isle of Wight* (London: Robert Hale, 1949).

Victoria County History, Hampshire and the Isle of Wight, ed. R. B. Pugh, 3 vols. (London: Archibald Constable, 1908).

Victoria History of the County of York, North Riding, ed. William Page, 2 vols. (London: Constable and Company, 1914-1923).

Visitation of County of Buckingham, ed. W. Harry Rylands (London: Harleian Society, Vol. LVIII, 1909).

Visitation of County of Gloucester, ed. Sir John Maclean and W. C. Heane (London: Harleian Society, Vol. XXI, 1885).

Visitation of Hampshire, ed. W. Harry Rylands (London: Harleian Society, Vol. LXIV, 1913).

Visitation of County of Sussex, ed. W. Bruce Bannerman (London: Harleian Society, Vol. LIII, 1905).

Visitation of County of Warwick, ed. John Featherston (London: Harleian Society, Vol. XII, 1877).

Visitation of Worcestershire, 1569, ed. William P. W. Phillimore (London: Harleian Society, Vol. XXVII, 1888).

Vyvyan, John, *Shakespeare and the Rose of Love* (London: Chatto & Windus, 1960).

Wade, W. Cecil, *The Symbolisms of Heraldry* (London: G. Redway, 1898).

Wagner, Anthony R., *English Genealogy* (Oxford: Clarendon Press, 2d edition, 1972).

————, "Heraldry," *Medieval England*, ed. Austin Lane Poole (Oxford, 1958).

————, *Heralds and Heraldry in the Middle Ages* (Oxford University Press, 1956).

————, *Heralds of England* (London, 1967).

————, *Historic Heraldry of Britain* (Oxford University Press, 1939).

Wait, R.J.C., *The Background to Shakespeare's Sonnets* (London: Chatto & Windus, 1972).

Warner(?), Richard, *Collections for the History of Hampshire* (London: [1795]).

Warton, Thomas, *Specimen of a History of Oxfordshire* (London, J . Michels, J. Robson, C. Dills, 1783).

Watson, Thomas, *Poems*, ed. Edward Arber (London, 1870).

BIBLIOGRAPHY

Webbe, William, *A Discourse of English Poetrie* (1586), ed. Edward Arber (London, 1871)

Welch, Edwin, *Southampton City Charters* (City of Southampton, Southampton Papers Number 4, 1966).

Weldon, Anthony, *The Court and Character of King James* (London: G. Smeeton, 1817).

Wentersdorf, Karl P., "Shakespeare and Carding," *Shakespeare Quarterly*, Vol. 36 (1985).

Wernham, R. B., "Christopher Marlowe at Flushing in 1592," *English Historical Review*, Vol. 91, 1976.

Wheatley, Henry B., *London Past and Present* (London, 1891).

Whitaker, Virgil K., *Shakespeare's Use of Learning* (San Marino, California: The Huntington Library, 1969).

Wilde, Oscar, "The Portrait of Mr W.H.," *The Riddle of Shakespeare's Sonnets* (London: Routledge & Kegan Paul, 1962).

Wilding, Peter, *Thomas Cromwell* (London: William Heinemann Ltd., 1935).

Williams, E[lijah], *Early Holborn*, 2 vols. (London: Sweet & Maxwell, 1927).

————, *Staple Inn* (London: Archibald Constable, 1906).

Williams, Roger, *A Key into the Language of America* (London: Gregory Dexter, 1643; reprinted in *Collections of the Rhode Island Historical Society*, Providence: John Miller, 1827).

Williamson, Hugh Ross, *The Day Shakespeare Died* (London: Michael Joseph, 1962).

Williamson, J. Bruce, *The History of the Temple, London* (London: John Murray, 1924).

Willson, David Harris, *King James VI and I* (Oxford University Press, 1956).

Wilson, Arthur, *The History of Great Britain* (London: Richard Lownds, 1653).

Wilson, F.P., *The English Drama 1485-1585* (Oxford University Press, 1969).

Wilson, Katharine M., *Shakespeare's Sugared Sonnets* (London: George Allen & Unwin, 1974).

Wilson's Arte of Rhetorique, 1560, ed. G. H. Mair (Oxford: Clarendon Press, 1909).

Wolff, Samuel Lee, *The Greek Romances in Elizabethan Prose Fiction* (Columbia University Press, 1912).

Wood, Anthony à, *Athenæ Oxoniensis* (London: Thomas Bennett, 1691-1692).

Woodbridge, Linda, "Black and White and Red All Over: The Sonnet Mistres Amongst the Ndembu," *Renaissance Quarterly,* Volume 40 (1987).

Woodward, John, *A Treatise of Ecclesiastical Heraldry* (Edinburgh and London: W. & A.K. Johnston, 1894).

Wraight, A.D., and Virginia F. Stern, *In Search of Christopher Marlowe* (New York: Vanguard Press, 1965).

Wriothesley, Charles, *Chronicles*, ed. W. D. Hamilton, 2 vols. (London: Camden Society, New Series, No. 11, 1875 (Vol. 1) and No. 20 (1877) (Vol. 2)).

Wriothesley Papers, 5M53, Hampshire Record Office, Winchester.

Wyndham, George, ed., *The Poems of Shakespeare* (London: Methuen and Co., 1898).

Yates, Frances A., *John Florio* (Cambridge University Press, 1934).

————, *A Study of Love's Labour's Lost* (Cambridge University Press, 1936).

Young, Frances Berkeley, *Mary Sidney, Countess of Pembroke* (London: David Nutt, 1912).

Young, H. McClure, *The Sonnets of Shakespeare* (Columbia, Missouri: 1937).

Young, R. B., "English Petrarke," *Yale Studies in English*, Vol. 138 (Yale University Press, 1958).

Zannoni, G. Batista, *Storia della Accademia della Crusca* (Firenze: Tipografia del Giglio, 1848).

437